THE NEW AMERICANS

HARVARD
UNIVERSITY
PRESS
REFERENCE
LIBRARY

THE NEW AMERICANS

A GUIDE TO IMMIGRATION SINCE 1965

EDITED BY

Mary C. Waters & Reed Ueda

with Helen B. Marrow

HARVARD UNIVERSITY PRESS

Cambridge, Massachusetts

London, England   2007

Publication of this book has been supported through the generous provisions of the
Maurice and Lula Bradley Smith Memorial Fund

Library of Congress Catalog Card Number 2006048524

ISBN-13: 978-0-674-02357-4
ISBN-10: 0-674-02357-9

Contents

Contents

THE NEW AMERICANS

Introduction

Mary C. Waters and Reed Ueda

Several years ago, a longtime resident of a "streetcar suburb" of Boston remarked, "Somerville is changing . . . You see it in Union Square, where there are Asian, South Asian, Caribbean, Portuguese, and Latin American markets and Cambodian-French, Armenian-Lebanese, Portuguese, country Korean, Brazilian, Chinese, Indian, Greek, and French bistro joints" (Gross, "Welcome to Somerville," *Boston Globe,* July 23, 1994). Somerville typifies numerous American neighborhoods where multiplying food stands, restaurants, stores, markets, and mass-media vendors have been established by the new American immigrants.

In greater "Chicagoland," a scholar touring the area noted that "Suburbia's commercial district is now dominated by the Latino culture. Puerto Rican, Mexican American, and Cuban food stores, restaurants, and jewelry stores are some of the leading business establishments in suburbia" (Moore and Pinderhughes, *In the Barrios,* p. 144). A new nationwide commerce reflects the cultural and lifestyle ingredients of Haitians, Jamaicans, Cubans, Indians, Koreans, Thai, Vietnamese, Brazilians, Colombians, and Lebanese. Latino music CDs, West Indian groceries, videos from India, and magazines from China lay a new international culture over old neighborhoods.

Kay Haugaard, a college writing teacher, described her encounters with the spread of intermarriage in her personal and professional life in terms that are growing more familiar to many other Americans: "One of my cousins married a woman of Chinese descent, and one of my sons married a third-generation American of Japanese descent . . . The son of our white/American Indian . . . friends married a blond woman of Irish extraction. Another of their sons married a Chicana . . . My students are a rich ethnic amalgam with various combinations of parents and partners. One pale blond, Scandinavian-appearing married woman has a Japanese surname . . . Many women who are not Hispanic have names like Lopez, Morales, and

Montez from their husbands. Many students have hyphenated names that are oftentimes quite long and ethnically diverse, such as Nakabayashi-Rodriguez" (Haugaard, "More than Ever, a Melting Pot," *Wall Street Journal*, Dec. 30, 1993).

These quotations describe some of the visible markers of an enormous change in American society that began in the decades following World War II. During this era, the United States adopted a set of policies that would lead to the reception of an unprecedented worldwide flow of immigrants. In 1965, Congress passed the Hart-Celler Immigration Act, which repealed the restrictionist admissions system based on discriminatory nationality quotas that had severely limited immigration to the U.S. since the 1920s. This act installed a new global admissions system under which immigration reached all-time high levels by the end of the 20th century. It also put numerical limits on immigration from the Western Hemisphere for the first time—limits that would lead to growing undocumented or illegal immigration in the coming decades. At the same time, demographic and political changes in the post–World War II period created a number of conditions that encouraged international migration. The rise of the global economy, the huge growth of the population in developing countries through high fertility and lowered mortality, and wars and conflicts in various parts of the world all brought enormous pressures for migration, from developing to developed countries and increasingly across the borders of developing countries as well.

From 1971 to 2000, 19.9 million legal immigrants arrived in the U.S., along with several million more who were undocumented, eclipsing the 18.2 million immigrants who came in the 30-year period from 1891 to 1920 (once remembered as the high-water mark in American immigration). Between 2000 and 2005 an estimated 7.9 million immigrants arrived, the largest number arriving in a five-year period in the nation's history. As a result, the foreign-born population has steadily increased since 1960, rising from 9.7 million in that year to 35.2 million in 2005. The foreign-born of the early 21st century are more numerous than ever before, but at 12.1 percent of the population, they constitute a smaller proportion of the total population than they did a century ago, when they were 14.7 percent.

The movement to the U.S. is part of a global phenomenon. Worldwide, it is estimated that 1 in every 35 people is an international migrant. According to United Nations figures, around 175 million people lived outside the country in which they were born in 2002, including approximately 16 million refugees. Immigrants move about in every part of the globe, with an estimated 56 million living in Europe, 50 million in Asia, and 41 million in North America. International migrants make up 1 in 10 people in developed countries and 1 in 70 in developing countries. As Reed Ueda points out in his essay in this volume, the U.S. has towered over other countries with the largest number of international migrants in the world—35 million—

followed by the Russian federation (13.3 million), Germany (7.3 million), Ukraine (6.9 million), and France (6.3 million).

How has the absorption of so many international migrants from so many different places around the world affected our society? How do the immigrants and their children fare over time? What happens as these immigrants become "new Americans"? What are the reasons people come, and how are they treated once they get here? How are they doing socially and economically? How do they affect the institutions of our society, the everyday lives of Americans, the content of our culture, and the future of our nation? These are some of the questions we explore in this volume.

Of course, the United States is quite experienced at absorbing immigrants. Unlike some European countries, which are receiving large numbers of immigrants with no historical experience of doing so, the U.S. is a nation that has been peopled largely through successive waves of new immigrants. And Americans increasingly look to our past successes at absorbing immigrants to ask how we did it then and whether we will do it the same way now. But these historical comparisons bring up new questions. For the most part, the new immigrants do not come from the same places as the ones who came before. The increasing influx permitted by the 1965 law was accompanied by a shift away from the typical pattern of immigration found earlier in the 20th century. In 1900 the vast majority of newcomers came from European countries such as Italy, Russia, Austria-Hungary, Germany, Ireland, Sweden, and Great Britain, whereas in 2000 most of the new immigrants came from countries in Latin America, the Caribbean, Asia, the Middle East, and Africa. The countries from which most immigrants arrive are now Mexico, the Philippines, the Dominican Republic, Haiti, India, and China.

The arrival of millions of newcomers has affected all of the major institutions of American society, including schools, hospitals, housing, and labor markets. By 2000, 1 of every 9 American residents was an immigrant, but 1 of every 5 children under age 18 was the child of immigrants—a fact with huge implications for schools. The influx of educated professionals and technical workers aided the development of a high-technology economy, and the larger working class supplied the labor needs of new service and mass-manufacturing sectors. By 2000, according to the U.S. Census, Latinos had surpassed African Americans in numbers, and major cities in the U.S. registered record low proportions of native-born whites.

The liberalization of immigration policy created a new social framework of multiethnic and multiracial diversity, which has reconfigured American pluralism and national identity. Up to the 1960s, "immigrant America" in the public mind had formed during the industrial revolution and consisted chiefly of European immigrants and their descendants, who were destined to blend into the melting pot. Race relations consisted of interactions between whites and blacks, and Asians and

Latinos were present only on the margins. Of course, this public notion was always incomplete and reflected an East Coast establishment view of the world, as the late 19th and 20th centuries saw a great deal of immigration from Mexico and Asia, mostly to the West and Southwest.

Since the 1960s, the new immigration has transformed the parameters of pluralism and the dynamics of movement into the mainstream. Latinos and Asians in combination with other immigrant groups have greatly outnumbered European immigrants. Efforts toward assimilation and the "soft" cultural pluralism typical of the ethnic Americanization of the European immigrants have been displaced by initiatives for multiculturalism, bilingualism, and minority empowerment of Latinos, Asians, and black immigrants. The composition of the major ethnic-racial groups in America has also been transformed. One tenth of black Americans are now immigrants or the children of immigrants, as African Americans have been joined by West Indians, Haitians, Cape Verdeans, and Africans. The Hispanic population of the U.S., which had been primarily Mexican and Puerto Rican, is now much more varied, comprising immigrants and their children with origins in the Caribbean and Central and South America. Asians, who had primarily been Chinese and Japanese, are also much more diverse, as South Asians from India, Pakistan, and Bangladesh have arrived along with Filipinos, Vietnamese, Cambodians, Thais, and Laotians. White immigrants come from traditional sending countries in Europe, including England, Italy, Germany, Ireland, and Russia, but also from less recognized sources, including South Africa and Zimbabwe, Australia, and New Zealand, and of course from a major source of "invisible" immigrants, Canada.

This transformation of our society through immigration, as well as the historical changes in the sources of immigrants, have not occurred without conflict in American society. Immigration cuts across the usual left/right or Democratic/Republican divisions in American politics. Free-market Republicans tend to support high levels of immigration, while cultural conservatives worry about the effects of so many immigrants on the American social fabric. Democrats tend to support immigrants and immigrants' rights, but some worry about the effects of large numbers of unskilled newcomers on the wages and living conditions of poor, unskilled native-born Americans, particularly African Americans. Since the terrorist attacks of September 11, 2001, the issue of immigration has often been tied to issues of homeland security and has taken on more ominous connotations. Undocumented or illegal immigration has increasingly become a front-page issue. Americans worry that we have lost control of our borders, that undocumented immigrants pose a security threat to the nation, that they are a fiscal drain on state and local governments, and that the presence of large numbers of people living in the country without permission poses great problems both for the immigrants themselves and for their communities. The question of whether undocumented immigrants should be able to get driver's licenses is an example of the everyday dilemmas Americans face on this issue. Do we condone law-breaking by issuing driver's licenses to undocumented immigrants, and do those licenses serve as identification cards that they can use to extend their stay in the U.S.? But isn't it a good idea to regulate who is driving cars in a state? Does it make sense to have people driving without licenses? What happens when there are accidents?

Public opinion polls find that Americans are very conflicted about immigration. Native-born Americans who live in states with high concentrations of immigrants tend to regard immigration as more of a problem than those in states with fewer immigrants. At the same time, native-born Americans who interact with immigrants frequently tend to have more positive opinions of them than those who do not have much contact with them. A consistent finding in public opinion polls is that exposure to and experience with immigrants leads to greater acceptance of them. In addition, there is a marked class difference in attitudes: people with higher levels of education and income tend to be much more positive about immigration than those with low levels of education, perhaps because the less skilled have greater fears about competition for jobs and housing.

Immigration is also becoming more of a national issue as increasing numbers of newcomers settle in areas of the country that have previously seen little or no immigration. While just six states—California, New York, Florida, New Jersey, Illinois, and Texas—account for 67 percent of the foreign-born population, a number of states in the South, West, and Midwest are seeing unprecedented growth in the numbers of new immigrants settling there, among them North Carolina, Georgia, Nevada, Arkansas, Utah, Tennessee, Nebraska, Colorado, and Arizona. Between 1990 and 2000 the foreign-born populations of North Carolina and Georgia increased by 274 percent and 233 percent, respectively. As immigrants fan out across the country, small-town schools are facing issues of bilingual education for the first time, hospitals are scrambling for translators, and mosques and Buddhist and Hindu temples are growing up next to churches and synagogues.

The New Americans is a comprehensive and scholarly reference guide to the recent wave of immigrants from Latin America, the Caribbean, Asia, Europe, the Middle East, Africa, and the Pacific, who now form the largest foreign-born population in the history of the United States. As an accessible and up-to-date source of general knowledge about these people, their impact on American life, and their adaptation to our society, it constitutes an update to *The Harvard Encyclopedia of American Ethnic Groups* (1980). That encyclopedia surveys the ethnic landscape created by immigration to the U.S. in the preceding centuries and the early part of the 20th century, but it does not include most of the immigrants who have come since the 1960s. We designed *The New Americans* to gather into one volume qualitative and quantitative information that is often scattered in many disparate sources. Social statistics are gleaned from a variety of official government records and presented in a format that permits meaningful comparisons. New insights are offered by experts who are able to use sources from Latino, Asian, African, and Middle Eastern communities. The editors have designed *The New Americans* to serve as a guidebook, not an encyclopedic compendium. As a guidebook, it can help scholars, policymakers, journalists, students, and the informed public to approach and understand the significant features of immigrant life, at the national and community levels, and how these have changed over recent decades.

The editors worked with a board of advisory editors, scholars drawn from the social sciences and history, whose expertise covering the major immigrant groups tapped complementary scholarly networks and brought many fields of knowledge to the table. In consultation with these experts, we determined which groups and themes would be treated and selected the contributors. We also relied on the advisory editors to evaluate and edit essays in their areas of expertise.

The editors, in consultation with the advisory editors, decided that the groups from which the 40 largest flows of immigrants who have arrived since 1965 are drawn should receive primary treatment. We felt that this procedure was a better way of determining the major newcomer groups than utilizing solely U.S. Census population-report figures of the foreign-born—an approach that would inevitably include older and earlier immigrants who were not part of the wave since 1965. The populations identified by flows of immigrants would correspond to ethnic communities that have the largest numbers of first-generation immigrants (foreign-born) and second-generation immigrants (native-born of foreign parentage). The annual statistical reports of the U.S. Immigration and Naturalization Service were used to obtain totals of immigrant arrivals by country of birth from 1970 to 1998. The ranked sizes of these groups confirmed certain impressions about who the new Americans are but also yielded some mild surprises. Immigrants from Latin America, the Caribbean, and Asia occupied most of the top 40 slots, but some sizable groups of foreign-born Europeans appeared. For example, the total number of arrivals from the former USSR, the United Kingdom, Poland, Germany, Italy, and Portugal ranked in the top 25. There are 31 entries on immigrant groups, of which 17 concern single countries of origin and 14 examine several groups together.

For each group, characteristics of immigrants and their households were tabulated from Public Use Microdata Samples (PUMS) from the U.S. Census of 2000, providing a data set that formed a longitudinal sequence with previous tabulations of PUMS from the 1990 and 1980 Censuses. The tabulations included country of birth, age, sex, marital status, race, Hispanic ethnicity, number of children, geographical settlement by state, year of immigration, employment, income, citizenship, ancestry, language, and education.

In general, authors used three major sources of data for the thematic and group entries, and the reader should be aware that different definitions and data sources can lead to different numerical estimates of immigrants and the foreign-born. The decennial census counts everyone present in the United States on census day—including legal immigrants, undocumented immigrants, and people born abroad and present in the United States through different kinds of temporary visas. As a result the census classifies people as American-born or foreign-born and makes no determination of their immigration status, although it does provide information on year of arrival in the U.S. In 2000 the census counted 33 million people who were foreign-born, including 1.9 million people who were born abroad to one or two American parents and thus eligible for citizenship. This latter category is a large proportion (over 15 percent) of the foreign-born for a few source countries in Western Europe, as well as for Bermuda, Japan, Panama, Saudi Arabia, and Australia. Tables based on the census definition of foreign-born in the PUMS include all those who report their birthplace as outside the U.S. unless otherwise noted. The other major source of demographic data on immigrants in the U.S. is the Current Population Survey. It also classifies people by birthplace, but as a sample survey it includes the noninstitutionalized population, excluding those people who live in nursing homes, hospitals, prisons, and other "group quarters." It also has less complete coverage than the census of hard-to-find populations such as undocumented immigrants. In 2000 the Current Population Survey counted 28.4 million foreign-born people in the U.S. Finally, the USCIS (United States Office of Citizenship and Immigration Services of the Department of Homeland Security, formerly the INS, Immigration and Naturalization Services) provides figures on those people legally immigrating to the U.S., on the different types of visas issued to those coming temporarily or permanently, and on the characteristics of these legal immigrants and on refugees. Rubén Rumbaut (2004) has written a thoughtful and nuanced discussion of the implications of using these different statistical sources in the study of immigration and the differences that different definitions of immigrants, the foreign-born, and new arrivals make in analyses of immigration and assimilation, and interested readers should consult that source.

Contents and Organization

A core feature of *The New Americans* is a series of 20 thematic articles—interpretive essays that define the central themes of the new immigration, the evolution of immigrant communities, and the immigrants' incorporation into American society, culture, and government.

   Authors of thematic articles were invited to link their exploration of their subject with the questions and controversies that have made it a vital topic, and to bring to bear personal insights derived from their scholarship. These essays offer an original and fresh examination of the central themes of key subjects relevant to immigration. They supply, according to the expert judgment of the authors, a mix of empirical material and scholarly interpretation that helps elucidate each topic. Collectively, the thematic articles in effect constitute an interpretive platform that sets the table for the essays based on case studies, providing a general framework for under-standing the specific empirical content of articles about specific groups.

The first five essays explore the movement of people across borders to the U.S. and the policies that have been developed to try to control these flows of people. Reed Ueda sets these flows in a global and historical context, describing the central role the U.S. has played as a destination for international migrants and the increas-ing volume and pace of immigration in an increasingly interconnected world. Aristide Zolberg and Peter Schuck review the laws and the policies we have devel-oped to control who gets in and who is a citizen, showing the ways in which policies and laws enacted for one purpose often have unintended consequences. The 1965 immigration law itself is a prime example. When the law was debated, Senator Ed-ward Kennedy, chair of the immigration subcommittee, made a speech in its de-fense: "First, our cities will not be flooded with a million immigrants annually. Un-der the proposed bill, the present level of immigration remains substantially the same . . . Secondly, the ethnic mix of this country will not be upset . . . Contrary to the charges in some quarters, [the bill] will not inundate America with immigrants from any one country or area, or the most populated and deprived nations of Africa and Asia . . . In the final analysis, the ethnic pattern of immigration under the proposed measure is not expected to change as sharply as the critics seem to think" (Senate Subcommittee on Immigration and Naturalization, Feb. 10, 1965, p. 1-3).

In hindsight, these things did come to pass, because of the ways in which the law was structured to allow for family chain migration, as Zolberg points out. But im-migration also grew because of the growth in the number of refugees, who were not subject to numerical quotas, and because of undocumented immigration, the sub-ject of the next two essays, by David Haines and Frank Bean. Before the 1965 law, immigration from the Western Hemisphere was not limited, and there was fairly fluid movement back and forth across the U.S. border with Mexico. Undocu-mented immigration began to be a public issue in the 1970s, as it became apparent that the push from Mexico and other developing countries and the pull of low-wage jobs in agriculture and services were powerful forces bringing people across the bor-der despite laws that prohibited it.

Many of the thematic and group essays discuss the intended and unintended ef-fects of U.S. immigration laws on the flows of immigrants and on their experiences in the U.S. In the appendix we provide a list and description of all the laws govern-ing immigration and naturalization passed between 1790 and 2005, including both the official name of the law and the other names it is known by, if applicable (for in-stance, the Immigration Act of 1965 is also known as the Hart-Celler Act, after the lawmakers who crafted it). In the essays these laws are identified by the year in which they were passed, and we refer the reader to the appendix to learn more about the specifics of the legislation.

The next group of essays explores some of the patterns of integration and social change among immigrants and the host society. John Logan explores immigrants' settlement in the nation's cities. Just 13 metropolitan areas—Los Angeles, New York, Chicago, Miami, Houston, Orange County, Washington, D.C., Riverside–San Bernardino, San Diego, Dallas, Oakland, San Jose, and San Francisco, which together have a quarter of the U.S. population—house more than half of all new-comers. But the old pattern of immigrants settling in central cities and gradually moving to suburban areas over time has been supplanted. Logan shows that immi-grants are increasingly moving directly into the suburbs, bypassing the central cities altogether.

The essays on identity explore the interaction of new immigrants with the racial and ethnic hierarchy. Herbert Gans looks at the ways in which immigrants and their children think about who they are and how their identities are likely to change over time. Joel Perlmann and Mary Waters extend this study of identity to the chal-lenge of intermarriage. How do ethnic identities and the existence of ethnic groups change over time as more group members intermarry?

In their essay on assimilation, Richard Alba and Victor Nee argue that this concept is useful in understanding the dynamics of immigrant integration in the 21st century. They regard assimilation as a two-way street on which immigrants change as they become new Americans but the American mainstream also changes as it absorbs them. Roger Waldinger also explores this issue, but he points to a fun-damental tension between immigrants' new identity as citizens of their new country and their continuing identity as people from their ethnic community. That is, new immigrants become members of the nation-states they settle into, but they are ethnicized, and the tensions between their ties to their ethnic communities in the sending states and the sharp borders of their new nation-state become heightened. This highlights a broader phenomenon, explored by Ewa Morawska: trans-nationalism. With the advent of cheap air travel, phone connections, the Internet, dual citizenship, and similar developments, many have argued that new immigrants are now living transnational lives—going back and forth between sending and re-ceiving countries and taking part in political, social, and economic transactions that cross borders. Morawska takes a historical approach, arguing that we have over-looked much of the transnational activity that existed among European immigrants who came between 1880 and 1920, but also arguing that the shrinking and inte-grated global economy allows for much greater transnational activity today. Finally, Jennifer Hochschild explores how intergroup relations in the U.S. are being affected by immigration. Are traditional pluralist accommodations between ethnic and ra-cial groups getting better or worse because of immigration? Hochshild provides evi-dence for both conclusions.

The next seven essays explore the effects of immigration on major institutions in American life: the economy, politics, the media, religion, language, education, and the family. Many of these essays investigate the two-way changes suggested by Alba and Nee. In his article on politics, Michael Jones-Correa shows how the presence of immigrants of color is changing traditional race-based politics in the U.S. Diana Eck looks at the way the major religions in the U.S. are being changed as they absorb new immigrants and how transplanted religions change and often follow an American Protestant congregational model, even though their content remains different from that of the Protestant churches familiar to native-born Americans. This fusion is evident in many examples; for instance, Roman Catholic parishes increasingly celebrate Spanish masses and events such as the Day of the Dead and the Feast Day of Our Lady of Guadalupe, and the Brooklyn and Queens diocese in New York has added masses in Ashante and Fante, the two main dialects of Ghana.

In their essay on language, David López and Vanesa Estrada examine the possibility of two-way changes in American society in language ability. They turn the usual arguments about this subject on their head by arguing that the U.S. loses a great deal by failing to maintain immigrant languages while teaching immigrants English. Despite the sometimes fevered pitch of public debates about language use by immigrants and their children and the related debate about bilingual education, the fear that English will no longer be the dominant language is unfounded. While the absolute number of people who speak a language other than English in their home is quite high—47 million—documented changes over time in language use all point to high levels of language assimilation, so that by the third generation, virtually all descendants of immigrants are monolingual English-speakers.

The articles on the family, education, the media, and the economy all show how it is impossible to describe fundamental institutions in American society at this time without taking immigration into account. Whether it is the changing media market, the demographics of schoolchildren, changing gender roles, or the shape of low-wage labor, immigrants are transforming American society in far-reaching and subtle ways.

Finally, the last thematic article explores patterns of adaptation and change among the second generation—the children of immigrants who are now entering young adulthood and who make up 10 percent of the U.S. population. These young people grow up as Americans but share their parents' immigrant heritage. Nancy Foner and Philip Kasinitz take a close look at the second generation and reach a generally positive conclusion: that these young people are showing intergenerational mobility vis-à-vis their parents and are not showing a great deal of conflict while reconciling their parents' ethnic origins with their own American destinies.

Because of limited space, the editors decided to employ two kinds of articles for investigating immigrant groups. The largest immigrant populations are treated in essays devoted only to single groups; for example, immigrants from India are treated in one essay, immigrants from Haiti in another, and so on. In order for *The New Americans* to be as comprehensive and inclusive as possible, smaller groups are treated within the framework of a multiple-group essay; for example, in the article on South Asia, groups from Pakistan, Bangladesh, Sri Lanka, and Nepal are examined.

Articles on all the new immigrant groups provide key demographic, sociological, and historical information about them in a framework that enables readers to make comparisons among them and with earlier immigrant groups. In general, these essays look at a number of issues concerning specific immigrant populations:

1. The existence of subgroups defined by socioeconomic factors, ethnicity, religion, and cultural and political factors. For example, in examining immigrants from India, it is important to distinguish people of different religions, castes, ethnicities, and regional cultures.
2. The extent to which immigrants have created new ethnic communities or reshaped the structure and the boundaries of preexisting ethnic communities they have joined.
3. The development of group consciousness and collective identity, and the factors affecting this process.
4. A historical perspective on how group patterns have changed, persisted, and evolved.

In addition, various specific themes pertaining to the workings of group life are investigated, including immigration and settlement patterns, social structure, family and gender, education, assimilation, economic activities, ethnic and racial identity, transnationalism and internationalism, multiple identities, intermarriage, religion, relations with other groups, ethnic media, politics, institutional organization, and language.

Taken together, the group entries show the vast variety of contemporary immigration. Immigrants are enormously diverse—economically, phenotypically, and in terms of age, immigration status, region of origin, and region of settlement. And they enter a society that is also quite diverse and unequal. Many of the authors address the question of whether the experience of new immigrants and especially of their children is best described through the concept of segmented assimilation. This model, developed by Alejandro Portes and Min Zhou and refined by Portes and Rubén Rumbaut, takes seriously the divisions in our society and posits that new immigrants and their children enter different segments of American life. For some, especially those racially defined as nonwhite, downward assimilation into the ranks of poor native minorities in poor urban neighborhoods is a distinct possibility. Others enter the middle-class mainstream and quickly lose their ethnic distinctiveness, while still others experience upward social mobility while maintaining strong ethnic ties, competence in the immigrant language, and other kinds of bicultural skills. This model is used to explore the pattern of outcomes among Southeast Asians, Haitians, Central Americans, and other groups.

One can see the footprints of recent American history in the timing and volume of immigration of specific groups, including the legacy of American colonialism in the Philippines; the impacts of the Korean and Vietnam Wars in Asia and U.S. military interventions in Haiti, the Dominican Republic, and Central and South America; and the cold war creation of refugees from Cuba, Russia, and the countries of central Europe. Many of the essays note the changed circumstances for some ethnic groups following 9/11. South Asians, Middle Easterners, and Iranians all report more discrimination and greater difficulty in conducting transnational activities and sponsoring further immigration in the years since 2001.

The issues explored in the thematic essays are often amplified in the group essays. Thus Neeraj Kaushal, Cordelia Reimers, and David Reimers describe the role of immigrants in the economy and stress the importance of entrepreneurship and ethnic specialization and recruitment in particular industries, whereas group articles give specific figures and explanations for why Koreans own small groceries, liquor stores, and nail salons, why Jamaicans are so often nurses, why Indian doctors work throughout the country, and how important Mexican and Central American immigration is to U.S. agriculture. Morawska describes transnationalism among a number of different groups, but in the essay on Jamaica we learn about the existence in New York City of 12 organizations of alumni from particular Jamaican high schools. In the essay on Dominicans we learn about the significant degree of transnationalism among Dominican immigrants and the role they played in the 2004 Dominican national election.

Diana Eck describes the huge importance of religion in immigrant life and the ways in which immigrants are transforming the American religious scene, but it is in the group profiles that we hear details about, for example, links between Mormonism and immigration from Australia and New Zealand, explaining why Utah is the second most common destination state for newcomers from these countries. In Carl Bankston and Danielle Hidalgo's essay on Southeast Asians, we learn that there are now 6 Cambodian temples in Long Beach, California, and 87 Theravada Buddhist temples in 29 states. We learn in the essay on Middle Easterners that large numbers of Syrian Jews reside in New Jersey and that Lebanese Christians belong to the Maronite, Melkite, Syrian, and Greek Orthodox churches. In other essays we learn that churches play a large role in providing social services to new immigrants such as Romanians, who have established or revitalized Orthodox, Pentecostal, and Seventh-Day Adventist churches.

We have not included an essay on immigrant music, but the group essays abound with information on African musical forms such as juju, dancehall, and highlife, Dominican merengue and bachata, and Indian hip-hop bhangra, as well as the 88 Polynesian dance troupes established by Pacific Islanders in northern California.

The sheer volume and breadth of the voluntary organizations organized by immigrants and their children is staggering. They range from sports organizations, such as the Arlington Bolivian Soccer League in northern Virginia, to cultural organizations, such as the Uruguayan Cultural Association in West Palm Beach, Florida.

Ethnic groups within national-origin groups establish such organizations as the Egbé Omo Yoruba, the National Association of Yoruba Descendants in North America. Some immigrants organize along occupational lines, such as the Polish Teachers' Association. Others form groups that bring together migrants from the same village or city, such as the Krakow Society. Some organizations are panethnic and serve immigrants from many different countries who share an ethnic identity, such as the Arab Community Center for Economic and Social Services, which serves the social, legal, employment, health, cultural, and educational needs of Arab Americans. Indeed, it is possible to find rather obscure groupings of immigrants by region of settlement, such as the South Africa Association of Indiana or the New Zealander associations in New York, Atlanta, San Francisco, and Los Angeles. Recent Italian immigrants, well-educated professionals, have formed a new organization, Italiani all'Estero, which furthers diasporic and transnational ties among new immigrants who would have very little in common with their largely blue-collar, later-generation coethnics who populate the Sons of Italy.

Taken together, the single- and multiple-group entries provide an image of an America that is highly affected in big and small ways by the increasing diversity that immigration brings. The Dominican baseball stars David Ortiz, Manny Ramirez, and Pedro Martinez represented Boston in the World Series. Senegalese immigrants in Atlanta prepare Thanksgiving with West African fufu and palava sauce along with turkey and cranberries. Trinidadian Carnivals take place in Miami, West Hartford, and Baltimore. There is a large festival for Samoan Flag Day in San Francisco, and the Chicago Polish-language phone book contained more than 1,500 pages in 2001. Some of the snowbirds populating Florida and Arizona are Canadian retirees. And Mexican Americans are increasingly transforming small towns throughout the South as grocery stores stock up on tortillas and salsa next to grits and black-eyed peas.

As a reference book, *The New Americans* is a guide to this new world, and it is our hope that it will bring some scholarly research and balanced scientific data to bear on a topic that sometimes generates more heat than light. Like it or not, immigration has changed American society in fundamental ways since the mid-20th century. The new Americans we profile here are in many ways America's destiny. The richness of their experiences is recreating and transforming our society, and it will continue to do so in the years to come.

Bibliography

Rumbaut, Rubén G. 2004. "Ages, Life Stages and Generational Cohorts: Decomposing the Immigrant First and Second Generations in the United States." *International Migration Review* 38, no. 3 (Fall): 1160–1205.

Immigration in Global Historical Perspective

Reed Ueda

With the passage of the Immigration Act of 1965, Congress abolished the restrictionist quota system established in the 1920s and opened up the United States to receive the flows of worldwide migration propelled by globalizing changes in the international polity and economy. In the last decades of the 20th century, the U.S. admitted a multiracial influx of immigrants from all regions of the world. Of the total foreign-born population in the country in 2000, 51 percent came from Latin America, 25 percent from Asia, 15 percent from Europe, and the rest from other areas (see Table 1). The rank order of immigrant groups by country of origin underscores the predominant role of Latin America and Asia as source regions. According to the U.S. Census Bureau, in 2000, 20 of the 25 largest foreign-born populations came from countries outside of Europe, mostly in Latin America and Asia.

The global wave of immigration that rose rapidly after the 1965 change in admissions policies may appear to be sudden and unprecedented, but a historical perspective reveals that it is the product of a long-term process and is marked by patterns of both discontinuity and continuity with the past. While the majority of recent immigrants have not come primarily from Europe, as in previous eras, but from Latin America, the Caribbean, Asia, Africa, the Middle East, and Oceania, and while they have transplanted cultural and social forms from these regions, they still participate in the core immigrant traditions—visible since the nation's founding—of establishing permanent communities, obtaining security, gaining citizenship, and seeking economic, familial, and personal betterment.

The Atlantic-to-Global Shift in American Immigration

If "one were speaking of migrations," explained the global historian Bruce Mazlish, "one would have to go back to the diasporas of the past to understand what is in-

Table 1   Foreign-born population by region of birth: selected years, 1850–2000

Year	Region of origin (Percentage of total foreign-born population)				
	Europe	North America	Latin America	Asia	Other areas
2000	15.3	2.5	51.0	25.5	5.7
1990	22.9	4.0	44.3	26.3	2.5
1980	39.0	6.5	33.1	19.3	2.1
1970	61.7	8.7	19.4	8.9	1.3
1960	75.0	9.8	9.4	5.1	0.7
1930	83.0	9.2	5.6	—	2.2
1900	86.0	11.4	—	—	2.6
1880	86.2	10.7	—	—	3.1
1850	92.2	6.7	—	—	1.0

Source: Diane Schmidley, *Profile of the Foreign-Born Population in the United States, 2000*, U.S. Census Bureau, Current Population Reports Series P23-206 (Washington, D.C.: Government Printing Office, 2001), Figure 2-1 and Figure 2-2, p. 11.

volved in many migrations today." Applying a historical perspective to American immigration in the era of globalization reveals how it is the most recent part in a series of migration contexts linked together chronologically in a developmental and causal pattern. Current immigration trends are an outgrowth of worldwide population movements—rising and falling, shifting and changing over several centuries—that have been generated by the actions of states and economies and by demographic forces. The original context for American immigration sprang from the process of peopling the transatlantic empires created by Portugal, Spain, England, France, and the Netherlands. From the 16th to the 18th century, the coerced migration of the African slave trade and the voluntary immigration of European settlers built new creole societies and reduced the indigenous Amerindian population to minorities in these dominions.

In the 19th century, the industrial revolution and the abolition of slavery in European empires reconfigured the international demand for settlers and laborers in New World societies. The origin points of Atlantic immigration were extended from northern and western Europe to southern and eastern Europe, forming a wider migrant network that would supply labor to the factories and farms of developing economies in the Western Hemisphere. From 1846 to 1932, 52 million European immigrants journeyed to overseas countries, and the U.S. received most of them. The ending of slavery in the British, French, and Spanish empires resulted in India and China becoming international suppliers of indentured labor to peripheral zones of economic development. From 1830 to World War I, between 30 and 40 million Indian laborers and between 10 and 15 million Chinese laborers migrated overseas, primarily to borderland and colonial zones such as southern and eastern

Africa, Malaysia, Hawai'i, and the underdeveloped regions of Canada, the U.S., the Caribbean basin, and Latin America. The triple waves of immigration from Europe, India, and China produced a global total of approximately 100 million migrants from the start of the 19th century to the early 20th century. Migrations from southeastern, central, and northeastern Asia as well as the Middle East, Africa, and Japan may have swelled the global total in this period to roughly 150 million. Many of these migrants were only temporary overseas settlers and eventually returned to their countries of origin. (All these figures are based on estimates of the actual numbers of people compiled from various expert studies, but they provide a gauge of comparative magnitudes.)

In the 20th century, the disintegration of empires created new conditions for mass displacement. After World War I, the fragmentation of the Hapsburg, Romanov, and Ottoman empires forced marginal groups to relocate after political boundaries were redrawn. Similar popular displacements occurred again in Europe and Asia as a result of the devastation of World War II and the spread of communist regimes. The postwar breakup of European empires in Asia, Africa, and the Middle East led to the founding of newly independent and modernizing states and migrations of their new minorities. Forced migration continued to expand in the latter half of the 20th century as intrastate militarized conflict and ethnic cleansing campaigns created waves of displaced people who spilled across international boundaries or were resettled as refugees.

Former colonies and partitioned fragments of colonies evolved into emergent nations that sought to "catch up" in economic and political development. International capital flow increased in the two decades after World War II, but it did little to eliminate material maldistribution in the developing world or inequalities between it and the developed tier of nations. By the 1980s and 1990s, whatever growth capital flow had generated in the postwar decades had subsided and was overtaken by negative economic changes in the developing world, which caused emigration to become an increasingly attractive survival option for the poor and the opportunistic.

The expansion of advanced industrial economies produced capital investments that reconfigured international migration in a new global framework for marketing labor. Industrialized regions that invested in new factories, infrastructure, and services tapped into pools of underemployed laborers spreading in impoverished distant areas where growth was uneven or stagnant. The post–World War II physical and economic rebuilding programs of European countries recruited several million laborers from southern and eastern Europe, North Africa, Turkey, and the Middle East.

Labor migrants from the developing world sought more opportunity and security by moving in the opposite direction from the historic international European migration, "back" toward the old core societies of the North Atlantic region that had once been the chief exporters of immigrants. The new migration pattern involved countries such as the United Kingdom, France, and Germany, which in the modern era had never functioned as large-scale receivers of migrants from outside Europe. The "reverse" flow tended to have a south-to-north direction, with many of the sending countries lying to the south of the receiving countries. The rank order of receiving and sending countries reflected the international movement of populations from developing southern-tier countries to developed northern-tier countries. From 1970 to 1995, the U.S., Russia, Canada, Germany, and France stood at the top of all countries in intake of international migrants, while among the leading countries of emigration were Mexico, Bangladesh, the Philippines, Kazakhstan, Vietnam, Sri Lanka, and Colombia.

The currents of immigration were affected by worldwide demographic transitions. In the past two centuries, natural-increase rates rose in Europe, then in Asia, Latin America, and the Middle East. In 1950 world population reached 2.5 billion; by 2000 it had more than doubled, reaching over 6 billion. The growth of world population enlarged the potential magnitude of moving populations. The concentration of population increase in the less developed countries to the south of industrialized countries put greater pressure on limited economic resources, inducing the underemployed and the poor to seek better conditions by migrating abroad.

Rises in rates of immigration occurred in a world of accelerating geographic mobility and increasing regional interconnectivity. From the onset of the cold war, the global expansion of corporate capital, commerce, mass media, jet air transportation, and foreign military institutions created new networking points that stimulated immigration. Transnational microstructures of informal support networks among migrating individuals functioned within economic macrostructures shaped by interstate economic differentials and world market relations to propel the flow of immigrants. Economic differentials were usually not sufficient in themselves to generate the movement of populations, however. The impulse for self-betterment and the willingness to live and work in another country were based on social communication about immigration opportunities and also on subjective factors shaped by attitudes toward risk and a psychology of future-mindedness.

From the cold war to the start of the 21st century, immigration achieved unprecedented velocity, mass, spatial extension, and complexity. Concurrent with waves of permanent settlement, transient migration and repeat migration developed into commonplace phenomena, and the maintenance by migrants of active connections with their homelands coexisted with their integration into their host nations through acquisition of citizenship, acculturation, and social mobility.

Through international migration, the whole world was in motion as never before. Estimates of the global total of international migrants rose from 75 million in 1965 to 120 million in 1990 and to 175 million in 2000. The number of immigrants grew more in the last decade of the 20th century than it had in the previous

25 years. Furthermore, it is likely that the cumulative worldwide total of immigrants in the last half of the 20th century surpassed the total of immigrants from 1830 to 1930.

Throughout the 500-year evolution of modern world migration, the 13 colonies in British America and the successor United States acted as a destination hub of international migration. The role of the U.S. in the globalization of international migration became paramount because it was produced by powerful long-term historical trends. In the country's colonial beginnings, the search for and recruitment of immigrants was a matter of constant concern. During the industrializing and urbanizing era of the 19th and 20th centuries, as Americans sought settlers for continental expansion and laborers for manufacturing, the U.S. attracted 70 percent of migrants from European countries and began to receive influxes from outside Europe (particularly China, Japan, Korea, the Philippines, India, the West Indies, and Mexico), which were halted only by the adoption of restrictive admissions policies. After a hiatus in immigration lasting from the late 1920s through the Great Depression and World War II, the U.S. transformed itself into an even greater immigration magnet by liberalizing admissions policies so that immigrants from every region of the world could enter and become citizens.

The U.S. moved again to the forefront in receiving immigrants, with newcomers drawn mostly from non-Western and developing countries. From 1951 to 2001, 27 million immigrants were admitted. In addition, an estimated several million more undocumented immigrants arrived, bringing the total in this period to well over 30 million, roughly equivalent to the total number of American immigrants during the industrial revolution. The prominence of mass migration to the U.S. over the past two centuries remained the dominant and constant factor in the international system of migration, even as population movements to the third world and to other parts of the developed world ebbed and flowed.

To gain a global perspective on immigration in the U.S. from the last half of the 20th century, it is helpful to disaggregate the vast numerical totals of international migration. (The discussion that follows is based on methodology and published data from the statistical offices of the International Organization for Migration and the United Nations that provide for the identification of "migration" and "migrants" and "international migration" and "international migrants," and the enumeration of migrants by origin, residency, and status.)

At the turn of the 21st century, the U.S. towered above all other countries in the number of immigrants received, as it had a century before. From 1995 to 2000 the U.S. received a net migration of 6.25 million, followed in order by Germany (924,000), Canada (720,000), Italy (588,000), the United Kingdom (475,000), and Australia (474,000). With the greatest intake of immigrants, the U.S. had by far the largest population of international migrants. According to the International Organization for Migration, of the top 15 countries with international migrant populations in 2000, the U.S. had the largest (35.0 million), followed by the Russian Federation (13.3 million), Germany (7.3 million), Ukraine (6.9 million), France (6.3 million), India (6.3 million), Canada (5.8 million), Saudi Arabia (5.3 million), Australia (4.7 million), Pakistan (4.2 million), United Kingdom (4.0 million), Kazakhstan (3.0 million), Côte d'Ivoire (2.3 million), Iran (2.3 million), and Israel (2.3 million).

Although it had the greatest population of international migrants, the U.S. placed far down in the rank order of countries as measured by the number of international migrants *as a percentage of the total population.* According to the International Organization for Migration, while migrants composed 12 percent of the U.S. population in 2000, they constituted 74 percent of the population in the United Arab Emirates, 58 percent in Kuwait, 40 percent in Jordan, 37 percent in Israel, 34 percent in Singapore, 27 percent in Oman, 26 percent in Estonia, 26 percent in Saudi Arabia, 25 percent in Latvia, Switzerland, and Australia, 23 percent in New Zealand, 20 percent in Gabon, and 19 percent in Canada and Kazakhstan. The U.S. was the foremost destination country of international migrants, but migrants remained a small demographic minority compared to their proportional representation in other countries. Furthermore, this proportional lag was not wholly unprecedented: while the U.S. reached a high point of 14.7 percent foreign-born in its population in 1910, Argentina's percentage of foreign-born was nearly 33 in 1914 and Canada's was 22 in 1911.

The federal government enacted a policy of managed admissions to regulate its intake of immigrants. The major subcategories of American immigrants since the 1960s corresponded to the principal groups of global migrants. From the 1970s to the 1990s, immigrants came increasingly in one of two major socioeconomic groups: human capital migrants (highly educated white-collar and professional employees) and labor migrants (who were low-skilled and undereducated). In these decades, the bimodal distribution of immigrants according to employment and education became a consistent pattern. Reflecting the rise of global female migration as a result of increasing family reunification and labor migration, female immigrants began to outnumber male immigrants in annual admissions totals, from the early 1980s on. In addition, the U.S. responded creatively and sensitively to the global rise in forced migration. In 1980 Congress permanently institutionalized an administrative system for admitting refugees on a regular basis. Admitting 3.5 million refugees and asylum-seekers from the end of World War II to the start of the 21st century, the U.S. was a mainstay in the world for the resettlement of forced migrants.

States and Migrations

Worldwide immigration of the late 20th century increasingly became the byproduct of interstate and intrastate activities: the tightening or relaxation of border controls, schemes for ending labor shortages, partition, population of territories, civil war, ethnic cleansing, and the solution of unemployment and economic underdevelopment problems. In a paradoxical way, states often became victimized by their own efforts to engineer immigration for strategic purposes. For example, guest worker programs led to the creation of transnational social networks facilitating immigration that resisted government efforts to halt flows through restrictive policies and tighter border controls. Once immigration had been started by the state, whether for recruiting guest workers or permanent settlers, it resisted termination through state action.

Conditions of violent conflict and persecution of groups have generated new waves of forced migration. In the aftermath of World War I and World War II, displaced persons uprooted by persecution, civil chaos, and governmental regime changes sought havens in foreign countries. The global flow of refugees, asylum-seekers, and IDPs (internally displaced persons, who share central characteristics with refugees but have not crossed international borders) rose in the last decades of the 20th century with regime failures, civil wars, and ethnic cleansing programs. The World Refugee Survey estimated in 2000 that the world total of IDPs was more than 21 million and the annual average total of refugees and asylum-seekers for the 1990s was 15.3 million people.

The global expansion of forced migration has been an important factor increasing immigration to the U.S., which has played a pivotal role in the international system for refugee resettlement through state programs. According to the UN High Commission on Refugees, for example, 72,500 refugees were resettled in the U.S. in 2000, compared to 13,500 in Canada, 6,600 in Australia, 1,500 in Sweden and Norway, 760 in Finland, 700 in New Zealand, 460 in Denmark, and 140 in Japan (the main countries of refugee resettlement). While nearby countries absorbed most of the refugees from the leading refugee-producing countries—Afghanistan, Palestine, Burundi, Iraq, Sudan, Bosnia-Herzegovina, Somalia, Angola, Sierra Leone, Eritrea, and Vietnam—the U.S. was characterized by the worldwide diversity and distant sources of its refugee population. The top 10 refugee groups by nationality admitted in 1999 were, in rank order, from Bosnia-Herzegovina, Yugoslavia, the former Soviet Union, Vietnam, Cuba, Somalia, Liberia, Iran, Sudan, and Iraq.

The U.S. has also been extraordinarily welcoming to asylum-seekers. In the 1990s it received almost a million asylum applications, about one sixth of the total number of asylum applications filed throughout the world. Only Germany surpassed the U.S. in the total number of asylum applications received. In 1999, 2,700 people who were granted asylum in the U.S. came from Europe, 5,800 from Asia, 7,100 from Africa, and over 2,000 from Latin America and the Caribbean basin.

The U.S., like many countries in Europe, received a growing flow of undocumented aliens that accumulated over the years to several million illegal residents in the 1980s and 1990s. The growth of an illegal alien population reflected the existence of porous borders and the multiplication of state policies to restrict immigration. Illegal immigration became severely problematic everywhere in the world after states established more stringent admissions requirements that excluded more categories of people who wished to enter but were unable to secure their borders against those seeking to cross over illegally.

The general trend since the 1950s toward world political integration has also affected global patterns of migration. The creation of the European Union fostered migration between member states. New relationships between states that permitted immigrants to hold dual nationality also promoted immigration. The growing integration of the international political order required that U.S. immigration control policy become more closely coordinated with diplomatic relations and the structure of foreign relations. A prime example was the strategic utilization of refugee admissions policies to further U.S. alliances with foreign nations and to promote its interests against adversaries, especially during the cold war.

The role of the state in creating and regulating flows of international migration has grown as interstate frameworks for cooperation have taken root. In the Middle East, in Europe, and in Asia, states sought to control and manage human resources through treaties to regulate international migration. The U.S. engaged with Mexico in an agreement called the *bracero* program, which permitted the admission of temporary guest workers from 1942 to 1964. The North American Free Trade Agreement (NAFTA), which also included Mexico, was partly an attempt to control immigration from Mexico to the U.S. indirectly by coordinating economic development in Mexican regions of high cross-border labor migration.

Forced migration assumed greater salience as postcolonial and emergent states grew more active in engineering population movements for the purposes of national and regional domination. The rise of intrastate conflict caused by ethnic hostilities and violence between dominant and minority subgroups accelerated this trend. Regimes used military aggression to relocate or expel marginalized groups in order to consolidate control of their territory or define the nation. The militarization of ethnic conflict escalated all too frequently into civil war, anarchy, or international war and thereby fed the growing numbers of unfortunate people at risk of becoming forced migrants. The UN High Commission on Refugees' statistics on "persons of concern"—those who benefited from the organization's protection and assistance—provided a barometer of the size of this vulnerable population. From 1990 to 1995, the annual worldwide total of UNHCR persons of concern spiraled from 15 million to over 27 million.

The perception that transnational patterns of immigrant life had reached a new level of development through a radically transformed system of mass communication and transportation led to a growing sense that the present and near future might produce the end of assimilation in the nation-state. Nevertheless, focusing on this possibility meant that recent migration patterns were too often regarded as unprecedented and overlooked instructive historical parallels. Transient immigrant populations who were not fully assimilated in one country or another have existed in the past. Among Chinese immigrants in the 19th century, Italian and Slavic immigrants at the turn of the 20th century, and West Indian, Mexican, and Puerto Rican migrants in the first half of the 20th century were cohorts who in their individual and collective lives sustained transnational economic, political, and cultural connections bridging the U.S. and their homelands. Importantly, however, these immigrant groups were actively participating in the core patterns and institutions of American life within two or three generations.

Dual citizenship, which facilitated transnational public life, gained a new level of worldwide recognition and was adopted by an increasing number of countries at the turn of the 21st century. In 1999 no liberal democracy absolutely prevented the acceptance of dual citizenship. France, Canada, Russia, and the United Kingdom allowed their immigrants who naturalized to retain their former citizenship and their emigrants to become naturalized citizens in other countries without having to give up their native citizenship. The U.S., Australia, Germany, Israel, Mexico, and South Africa had policies that de facto permitted their immigrant residents and their emigrants in foreign countries to hold dual citizenship in varying degrees and situations. In Europe, new forms of plural and dual citizenship were developed and accepted by the countries undergoing integration under the umbrella of Euro-community.

Many of the countries that established dual citizenship policies were those that sent primary cohorts of immigrants to the U.S. For example, Michael Jones-Correa shows that by 2001 dual citizenship received recognition from 10 countries in Latin America: Brazil, Colombia, Costa Rica, the Dominican Republic, Ecuador, El Salvador, Mexico, Panama, Peru, and Uruguay. Nine nations of the Caribbean basin also recognized dual citizenship: Antigua, Barbados, Belize, Dominica, Jamaica, St. Kitts, St. Lucia, St. Vincent, and Trinidad and Tobago. Although traditional nationalist leaders worried that dual citizenship undermined loyalty to the nation-state, it also possessed the potential to promote incorporation within the nation-state. Immigrants may be more willing to naturalize and embrace the national identity of their host country if they have the security of not losing the benefits of citizenship in their country of origin. This tendency toward naturalization was reinforced by the powerful capacity of nation-states to serve as providers of adopted national identities among immigrants.

Owing to its global leadership in intake of immigrants and its relatively open naturalization process, the U.S. far surpassed other countries in the numbers of immigrants who naturalized for citizenship. In 1999, for example, 840,000 immigrants were naturalized in the U.S., compared with 248,000 in Germany and 159,000 in Canada (see Table 2). The rate of naturalization in the U.S. rose sharply from 1980 to 2000, even faster than the rate of immigration. In the 1980s nearly 2.5 million

Table 2   Acquisition of citizenship (in thousands), by year, 1995–1999

Country	1995	1996	1997	1998	1999
Australia	114.8	111.6	108.3	112.3	76.5
Canada	227.7	155.6	154.6	134.5	158.8
France	92.4	109.8	116.2	122.3	145.4
Germany	313.6	302.8	278.7	291.3	248.2
Italy	7.4	7.0	9.2	9.8	11.3
Netherlands	71.4	82.7	59.8	59.2	62.1
Norway	11.8	12.2	12.0	9.2	8.0
Sweden	32.0	25.6	28.9	46.5	37.8
United Kingdom	40.5	43.1	37.0	53.9	54.9
United States	488.1	1,044.7	598.2	463.1	839.9

Source: www/migrationinformation.org/GlobalData/charts1.cfm (Migration Policy Institute website, 2002).

naturalizations occurred, while in the 1990s 5 million aliens were naturalized, reflecting not only the accumulation of immigrants who had gained the minimum years of residency required for naturalization but also the popular desire to secure the protections of American citizenship, which intensified when policies were enacted in the 1990s that curbed the rights of immigrants and aliens.

Naturalization, like immigration, reflected a worldwide representation of immigrants in the U.S. Among the 840,000 immigrants naturalized in 1999, 247,300 were from Asia, 244,000 from Mexico and Central America, 97,400 from Europe, 95,700 from the Caribbean basin, 47,400 from South America, and 17,400 from Africa.

The intensive focus on globalization in internationalist policy discourse has at times distracted attention from the continuing importance of regional integration. Regionalization has remained a strong dynamic in the pattern of international migration and has intensified in key geographic arenas. For example, since the 1960s the largest flows of immigration to the U.S. have come from the nearby countries of North America and the Caribbean. Indeed, cross-border immigration from Mexico and Canada alone accounted for a large share of total immigration to the U.S.

The North American pattern of regional immigration had parallels in other parts of the world. In western and central Europe, immigrants came chiefly from nearby countries such as Turkey, countries of the former Soviet bloc, and North African states. In the Russian Federation, a large wave of immigrants arrived from Kazakhstan. In East Asia and the Pacific, major flows of immigrants originated in the subregions of this wide area and nearby parts of South Asia. Middle Eastern oil-producing countries also recruited their labor force almost entirely from nearby areas abroad—Pakistan, Bangladesh, Sri Lanka, and Palestine.

It is also within the spheres of regional migration that the most active forms of transient and repeat migration occurred. Regional migration patterns were offshoots of internal migration within countries. People moved from local areas with intense migration into a regional matrix of countries, where they constituted a network of communities linked across political boundaries by transient and repeat migrations. Frequent repeat migrations accumulated in a circular pattern of flow in transborder areas, such as the southwestern U.S. and northern Mexico.

This circulation of immigrants created a conduit connecting the U.S. with foreign nations for the international flow of social and economic remittances. Social remittances—social assistance provided to pay for received or anticipated social favors and support—were exchanged in the interpersonal networks of migrants and their sponsors to facilitate the process of chain migration. Economic remittances (monetary payments) sent by immigrants to relatives and organizations at home helped sustain local economic activity in communities of origin. Largely as a result of the role that migrant populations in the U.S. played in the flows of economic remittances, the Americas, which in 1988 ranked behind every world region except Africa as a source of remittances, rose above every region except Asia in 1999 (see Table 3). By generating remittance flows, global immigration to the U.S. and other industrialized countries became a key factor sustaining foreign monetary exchange between the advanced economies and the developing economies that received them (see Table 4).

Table 3   Migrant remittances from various world regions, 1988–1999 (in US$ millions)

| Year | Region of origin | | | | |
	Africa	Americas	Middle East	Asia	Europe
1999	5,993	14,589	6,203	17,906	6,520
1998	6,492	13,235	6,154	15,566	7,650
1997	6,389	12,036	6,560	21,066	6,130
1996	5,464	11,239	5,825	15,380	5,609
1995	5,383	11,499	5,590	11,786	5,113
1994	4,884	9,653	5,864	11,097	3,938
1993	4,946	7,470	7,782	7,807	3,534
1992	4,838	7,252	8,005	7,254	3,280
1991	3,423	5,793	5,539	7,317	4,924
1990	3,589	4,751	6,320	6,777	12,722
1989	3,119	3,737	4,828	6,921	9,370
1988	2,998	3,194	5,644	6,365	6,396

Source: International Organization for Migration, *World Migration 2003: Managing Migration, Challenges and Responses for People on the Move,* Vol. 2—IOM World Migration Report Series (Geneva: International Organization for Migration, 2003), Table 17.15, p. 311.

Table 4   Top 20 receiving countries of migrant remittances, 2000

Country	Remittances (in US$ thousands)
India	11,585,699
Mexico	6,572,599
Turkey	4,560,000
Egypt	3,747,000
Spain	3,414,414
Portugal	3,131,162
Morocco	2,160,999
Bangladesh	1,948,999
Jordan	1,845,133
El Salvador	1,750,770
Dominican Republic	1,688,999
Greece	1,613,100
Colombia	1,553,900
Ecuador	1,316,700
Yemen	1,255,206
Indonesia	1,190,000
Sri Lanka	1,142,329
Brazil	1,112,999
Pakistan	982,899
Jamaica	789,299

Source: International Organization for Migration, *World Migration 2003: Managing Migration, Challenges and Responses for People on the Move,* Vol. 2—IOM World Migration Report Series (Geneva: International Organization for Migration, 2003), Table 17.14, p. 311.

The United States as a Global Immigration Country

Immigration to the U.S. has been reconfigured by new global processes that are changing the worldwide distribution of human, economic, and cultural factors. Immigrants have come from a global order shaped by unevenly distributed economic development, explosive demographic imbalances, and dangerous political instabilities. The all-too-frequent collapse of national governments into "failed states" and the related rise of intrastate conflict and violence have generated unprecedented waves of refugees. Newcomers to the U.S. in recent times have been part of a worldwide flow of "people in transit" produced by intrastate conditions and interstate relations developing in the context of a global community undergoing accelerated political, economic, and cultural integration.

American immigration has occurred in a worldwide environment of rapid resource and asset flow that involves international capital, transcultural images and ideas, and technology and human capital transfers. Advanced transportation and communication systems, transnational social networks, and migrant facilitators and traffickers have multiplied the possible pathways for the movement of populations into and out of the country.

Although the U.S. has been a country of immigrant incorporation since its colonial origins, it is increasingly a country of transit, as temporary, circular, and undocumented migration have risen. As a result, the distinction between the U.S. as a host country and foreign sending countries has become less clear-cut. This general trend has been manifested in the growth of dual citizenship, transnational socioeconomic connections, and multiple cultural and national identifications among immigrants. Another aspect of the weakening distinction between the U.S. as a host country and foreign immigrant-sending countries has been the treatment of immigrant populations as diaspora populations by states from which they have emigrated. As a result, the U.S. can be said to share immigrants with their countries of origin. This process is facilitated by dual nationality policies, transnational politics, and transnational capital flows in the form of immigrant remittances. Countries that have recently sent large waves of immigrants have crafted policies to treat emigrant populations as part of a diasporic community that can be tapped as a socioeconomic and geopolitical resource.

Although the pattern of immigration in the U.S. has reflected changing forces that are integrating the world to an unprecedented degree, the accommodation of immigrants still reflects distinctive internal historical patterns that continue to affect America's involvement with the new global immigration. Except for the handful of large European-offshoot creole societies such as the United States, Canada, Australia, Argentina, and New Zealand, countries that achieved integration as ethnic nation-states have resisted giving a prominent place to immigration and immigrants in the shaping of national identity. Germany, for example, was one of the major immigrant-receiving countries of the 20th century, yet it eschews identification as an "immigration country." The historian Dirk Hoerder pointed out in *People in Transit*, a study of German global migration, that "the German people experienced as much—or perhaps more—migration than most other people in the North Atlantic economies." Transfers of people to areas of Germany from France, Austria, Bohemia, Denmark, and Poland occurred from the 17th century to the early 20th century, and after World War II, Germany recruited laborers from southern Europe and Turkey. However, according to Hoerder, the national experience of migration was never accepted by Germans "as a way of life" and "they rarely welcomed those who came to them." He pondered over how "some nations accept ethnic pluralism and multiculturalism as part of their heritage, while other nations—with almost as many shifts in population and with histories of in- as well as out-migration—continue to resist the very idea."

The U.S. stands diametrically opposite Germany in the correlation of its national self-image with mass immigration. Conceptions of the early American nation as an immigration country and an immigrant asylum, and the perception of immigrants as refugees, were built into the popular discourse of the American Revolution and post–Revolutionary era nationalism. In its foundational national ideology, the U.S. was conceived as a global civic sanctuary. In a time of political challenges to the old regimes of Europe, the new American republic was to serve as a haven for individuals seeking freedom from feudal, ancestral, and religious oppression. In the view of public commentators and policymakers, immigrants possessed an essential refugee identity and were shaped by experiences of oppression that made them incipient republican citizens. In 1776, Tom Paine argued in *Common Sense,* "The world is overrun with oppression," and the duty of America was to receive "the fugitive, and prepare in time an asylum for mankind." George Washington announced in 1783 that "the bosom of America is open to receive not only the opulent and respectable stranger but the oppressed and persecuted of all nations and religions." During the congressional debate over a landmark naturalization bill that passed into law in 1795, Representative Thomas Fitzsimons of Pennsylvania stated, "Nature seems to have pointed out this country as an asylum for the people oppressed in other parts of the world." He encouraged his fellow congressmen to adopt a policy of naturalization that would be popular among immigrants. As a Roman Catholic immigrant from Ireland, Fitzsimons empathized with the foreign newcomer and worried that an unduly long residency requirement before aliens could become citizens would "make this class of people enemies to your Government." The *Annals of Congress* recorded, "He was firmly of opinion that emigrants deserved to be encouraged; and to discourage them was an idea which till this day he had never heard either in or out of the House." The U.S. has long recognized and institutionalized in its public policies the concept of refugee immigration, and it has consistently led the world in the multinational diversity of its refugee intake.

Furthermore, a fundamental cosmopolitan citizenship allowed American pluralist traditions to grow and to accommodate voluntary hyphenated identities. This pluralist tradition has distinguished the U.S. from contemporary European states—historically shaped by ethnic nationalism and unitary national identity—which face the challenge of accommodating the unprecedented phenomenon of immigrant-based identities in public life. France, for example, has placed a greater demand on immigrants to eschew hyphenation and to embrace full cultural assimilation. American hyphenated pluralism also has contrasted with the corporate pluralism of multiethnic states such as Lebanon, India, and Russia, where the constitution and laws require the legal identification of all citizens as members of designated official ethnic subgroups for the purposes of economic allocation, political representation, official recognition, and power-sharing. Nevertheless, the U.S. too has sought to empower and provide security to particular groups deemed vulnerable to discrimination, through preferential policies advocated by political leaders, opinion-makers, and critical race scholars concerned that the widening ethnic differences created by global immigration could lead to new patterns of racial hierarchy and group inequality.

The U.S. continues to evolve as a society that maintains its sense of historical destiny as a quintessential immigration country, providing security, rights, and material assets to newcomers in a world where these are not equitably distributed. As it adjusts to the new pressures of a globalizing era, the U.S. functions as an immigration country within a world in which its character as a country of one-way destination and irreversible nationalist incorporation has been blurred, as transnational linkages and an international ethos of global citizenship have intensified. Its continuing role as a central point of immigrant destination reflects the new ambiguities of globalizing processes, worldwide ethnic diversity, and multiracial divisions, but its management of immigration is still affected by its historic institutional traditions of international asylum, assimilating cosmopolitanism, and democratic pluralism.

Bibliography

Aleinikoff, T. Alexander, and Douglas Klusmeyer, eds. *Citizenship Today: Global Perspectives and Practices.* Washington, D.C.: Carnegie Endowment for International Peace, 2001.

Baseler, Marilyn C. *"Asylum for Mankind": America, 1607–1800.* Ithaca, N.Y.: Cornell University Press, 1998.

Castles, Stephen, and Mark J. Miller. *The Age of Migration: International Population Movements in the Modern World.* New York: Guilford, 1998.

Curtin, Philip D. *The World and the West: The European Challenge and the Overseas Response in the Age of Empire.* Cambridge, Eng.: Cambridge University Press, 2000.

Hoerder, Dirk, and Jörg Nagler, eds. *People in Transit: German Migrations in Comparative Perspective, 1820–1930.* Cambridge, Eng.: Cambridge University Press, 1995.

Jones-Correa, Michael. "Under Two Flags: Dual Nationality in Latin America and Its Consequences for Naturalization in the United States." *International Migration Review* 35 (2001): 997–1029.

Massey, Douglas, et al. *Worlds in Motion: Understanding International Migration at the End of the Millennium.* New York: Oxford University Press, 1998.

McKeown, Adam. "Global Migration, 1846–1940." *Journal of World History* 15 (2004): 155–89.

McNeill, J. R., and William H. McNeill. *The Human Web: A Bird's Eye View of World History.* New York: W. W. Norton, 2003.

Weiner, Myron. *The Global Migration Crisis: Challenge to States and to Human Rights.* New York: HarperCollins, 1995.

Weiss, Thomas Lothar, ed. *World Migration 2003: Managing Migration—Challenges and Responses for People on the Move.* Geneva: International Organization for Migration, 2003.

Immigration Control Policy: Law and Implementation

Aristide R. Zolberg

As of the mid-20th century, the United States was no longer a "nation of immigrants" except in collective memory, as the proportion of foreign-born people had fallen to approximately 5 percent. This reflected a deliberate political choice enacted in the 1920s through legislation that drastically reduced annual "main gate" immigration from Europe and established national-origins quotas designed to restore the country's pre–Civil War ethnic profile. The principal targets were eastern and southern Europeans, whose assimilation was considered problematic, as well as Asians, deemed unacceptable. The policy was implemented through "remote control" of the country's sea borders by requiring immigrants to obtain visas from American consulates before embarking. This created a distinction between visitors and immigrants, utilizing shipping lines to enforce the regulations.

Because immigration policy involves distinct economic and identity considerations, its political dynamics straddle the conventional left-right divide and foster unusual coalitions. The restrictionist regime was imposed by a broad alliance of cultural conservatives, consisting mainly of Republicans and southern Democrats, who concurrently imposed Prohibition, promoted an assertively patriotic public culture, and reinforced racial segregation and social discrimination; it was also supported by organized labor. The opposition included the targeted immigrant groups, concentrated in urban constituencies, as well as industrialists and agricultural entrepreneurs concerned with maintaining an ample labor supply.

While the industrialists adjusted to the elimination of their traditional European workers by encouraging the internal migration of African Americans from the Deep South, agriculture managed to retain an open back door by preventing the imposition of restrictions on people from the Western Hemisphere, despite objections from the cultural conservatives that Mexicans posed an even greater threat to national identity than southern and eastern Europeans did. This was legitimized on foreign policy grounds as well. Although immigration from Mexico was potentially limited by the literacy requirement enacted in 1917, in effect movement remained largely unregulated, except for ad hoc deportations in periods of economic downturn, and led to settlement throughout the Southwest and in the Great Lakes region. During World War II the U.S. and Mexico established the *bracero* program, a government-operated temporary worker program, which reinforced ongoing flows and enhanced the dependence of both economies on their continuation. After a brief interruption at the end of the conflict, the program was revived and expanded. Black immigration from the English-speaking Caribbean also grew during this period, as the immigrants had access to the very large British quota by virtue of their British nationality.

Despite the political clout that southern and eastern Europeans achieved within the New Deal coalition and their incorporation into mainstream American society during World War II and its aftermath, discriminatory quotas were reenacted in 1952, albeit with a shift from outright prohibition of Asians to severe restriction of them. However, the ascent of the U.S. to international hegemony prompted the opening of a side entrance for the intake of refugees. Although largely governed by foreign policy considerations, this also allowed the admission of groups restricted by the quota system, notably Jewish Holocaust survivors and Italians and Greeks thought to be vulnerable to mobilization by communist parties, thereby somewhat reducing pressures for reform.

Nevertheless, by the early 1960s many Americans regarded the national-origins system as on a par with deliberate segregation, contrary to the spirit of the Constitution, and few were prepared to defend it explicitly. But in keeping with the rules of the Washington political game, the reformers—notably Senator John F. Kennedy, who made it a key issue in his campaign for the presidency—could be made to pay for achieving their objective. Determined to limit the settlement of Mexicans and West Indian blacks, conservatives imposed an unprecedented numerical limit on immigration from the Western Hemisphere. The ease with which the reformers paid up reflected their ambivalence about the back door. Under pressure from organized labor, the Democratic administration terminated the *bracero* program in 1964, but since Mexican labor was by then vital to U.S. agro-industry, it was evident that the flow was likely to continue in an unregulated mode.

The compromise was reflected in the Immigration Act of 1965, scheduled to go into effect on July 1, 1968. Celebrated in a solemn signing ceremony at the foot of the Statue of Liberty on October 3, 1965, it was hailed as on a par with the previous year's Civil Rights Act. This law established an annual limit of 170,000 entries for the Eastern Hemisphere, with a maximum of 20,000 from any one country; however, it provided for the unlimited admission of children, parents, and spouses of American citizens, thereby allowing for considerable immigration beyond the ceiling. An overwhelming 74 percent of per-country entries was allocated to family reunion, including 24 percent for siblings of citizens. Another 20 percent was distributed on the basis of personal qualifications considered of value to the U.S. (10 percent for professionals, scientists, and artists; another 10 percent for skilled and unskilled workers in short supply), and the remaining 6 percent was set aside for refugees, initially defined as people fleeing from communism or the Middle East, as well as victims of natural calamity. The law imposed a ceiling of 120,000 on immigrants from the Western Hemisphere starting in 1968, unless decided otherwise in the interim; however, there was no schedule of preferences to allocate Western Hemisphere entries if the ceiling came into effect, as it was expected to do.

The law effectively expressed the policymakers' determination to maintain immigration as the marginal feature it had been reduced to. Given the limited number of living relatives of Americans of European origin, its authors did not anticipate a significant increase in annual admissions once the backlog of applications was disposed of. It therefore came as a surprise that legal admissions soon increased by half, from 3.3 million in the 1960s to 4.5 million in the following decade, and that the foreign-born population, which included undocumented entrants, increased by half as well, from 9.7 million in 1960 to 14.1 million in 1980. Although as a proportion of the country's total population the foreign-born remained at less than half the record level of 1890 to 1910, immigration gained considerable importance from a demographic perspective: its contribution to population growth doubled, from about 10 percent in the postwar decades to slightly over 20 percent in the 1970s. Moreover, its visibility was compounded by a dramatic shift in its composition. European immigration began to decline as the family backlog was taken care of and most European countries turned into receivers, while arrivals from the rest of the world climbed from an average of 42.6 percent of the annual total in the final years of the old system to 58.8 percent from 1965 to 1969, stabilizing at approximately 75 percent in the mid-1970s. The admissions allocated to labor procurement provided unprecedented opportunities for Asians in particular, and these newcomers created new family networks. A similar process operated within the Western Hemisphere component as well, further stimulating the growth of Mexican and Caribbean immigration. Moreover, the inclusion of brothers and sisters as well as adult children and their spouses within the family reunion system produced a "chain" effect, as the in-laws initiated the formation of new networks of blood relatives.

As a consequence, the U.S. once again turned into a nation of immigrants, but now one that uniquely mirrored humanity as a whole. As the leading source of both legal and unauthorized immigration, Mexico became a central concern. The basic factor was a demographic explosion, which boosted that country's population from 26.3 million in 1950 to 69.7 million in 1980. When the Mexican government's neoliberal policies in the 1970s removed the traditional protection of guaranteed purchase of corn above the market price, displaced farmers sought opportunities by moving northward, within Mexico and across the border. Although these developments prompted the U.S. to impose a 20,000-per-country limit on the Western Hemisphere in 1976, the deterrent was once again largely nullified by unauthorized immigration.

The refugee situation was becoming unmanageable as well, as cold war foreign policy considerations and constituency pressures prompted Congress to broaden the definition of "refugee" and admit much larger numbers than the 10,200 a year provided for under the 1965 law. The limit was formally raised to 17,400 when the Western Hemisphere was included. Initiated mostly under presidential "parole" authority, which gave the executive considerable leeway, the major new sources included Cuba, in the wake of the Castro revolution; the Soviet Union, which allowed Jews to leave as a condition for détente and access to U.S. trade; Indochina, in the wake of the Vietnam War; Haiti; and, later, Central America. These flows too led to the formation of family networks that fostered an expanding demand for immigration visas, independent of the conditions that prompted the initial refugee movement. Efforts to control the refugee side entrance arose as Congress sought to restrict presidential foreign policy autonomy in the wake of Vietnam. Human rights organizations entered the fray as well, in order to bring American refugee and asylum policy in harmony with international norms.

These developments stimulated an expanding debate over the desirability and consequences of immigration, recalling the confrontations of an earlier era, with social scientists and public intellectuals once again playing a prominent role in the production of ideologies justifying alternative policies. This was reflected in the emergence of such neorestrictionist groups as the Federation for American Immigration Reform (FAIR) and its offshoot, the Center for Immigration Studies (CIS). Such groups charged that immigration negatively altered the nation's cultural identity, as indicated by the emergence of Spanish as a lingua franca; that the emphasis on family reunion imposed an intolerable burden on the welfare system and social services; and that the growth of undocumented settlement constituted a major source of crime. Added to these traditional themes were new considerations regarding population pressure on the environment. On the other side, employers formed informal alliances with civil libertarians and organizations representing the new immigrant groups to keep the door wide open. As globalization fostered the relocation of labor-intensive industries (notably garment manufacturing), U.S. enterprises became increasingly dependent on cheap immigrant labor, legal or undocumented, for their survival; unions too were dependent on the survival of these enterprises, prompting some to do a 180-degree turn toward immigrant defense. This was reflected in the creation of the National Immigration Forum (NIF) by the garment workers' union UNITE in 1981, and was subsequently extended to organized labor as a whole. Thanks to the size of the Hispanic population and its concentration in key states, Hispanics quickly achieved critical weight in the political process and generated a precocious "immigrant feedback" that played a major role in forestalling a replication of the 1920s outcome.

In light of these developments, in 1979 Congress established the Special Commission on Immigration and Refugee Policy (SCIRP) to make recommendations for modifying the law. Meanwhile, in the wake of the Indochina refugee crisis, Senator Edward Kennedy moved refugee policy to the top of the Judiciary Committee's agenda. Under the unusual partnership of Kennedy and Strom Thurmond, a measure establishing a separate policy for refugees and bringing it into accord with international norms gained unanimous approval in the Senate and comfortably cleared the House as well. An annual numerical guideline of 50,000 was set, with presidential authority to admit a higher number if the need arose, but parole authority was to be used for individual cases only, as originally intended. At the time some 8 million people met the international definition of "refugee," most of them in first-asylum countries awaiting resettlement, so admissions had to be selective; accordingly, the law gave preference to people "of special humanitarian concern to the United States." In keeping with international law, it also established a process whereby any alien physically present in the U.S. could file an asylum claim on grounds of meeting the refugee definition. The law placed no limit on the number of asylum grants per year, but the drafters seemed to assume that no more than 5,000 applicants would succeed, because they imposed that ceiling on the number who could become lawful permanent residents (after at least a year as asylees). In fact refugee policy continued to be applied largely on an ad hoc basis: admissions rapidly escalated to over 100,000, and asylum emerged as an especially problematic feature, with a huge backlog and a tug-of-war between immigrants attempting to use asylum to gain admission and U.S. authorities increasingly regarding asylum claims as inherently suspect.

As a solution to the problem of illegal immigration, SCIRP voted unanimously to recommend the legalization of a substantial portion of undocumented aliens, popularly referred to as "amnesty," with eventual access to citizenship, in keeping with the aspirations of Mexican American leaders and the liberal camp; but it astutely combined this with a major innovation designed to appeal to partisans of law and order, the imposition of sanctions on employers of illegal aliens. Such sanctions, long advocated by organized labor, would require employers to check on the immigrant status of their employees and were viewed by many as a dangerous extension of federal regulation. The inclusion of revisions of the H-2 program to provide additional temporary workers in agriculture enhanced the possibility of horse-trading among the various interests concerned. SCIRP also proposed to reorganize the Immigration and Naturalization Service (INS), notorious for its ineffectiveness and vulnerability to corruption.

By the time SCIRP issued its recommendations in February 1981, Ronald Reagan was president. The incoming administration was divided on immigration issues, as were Republicans more generally. On one side were those who adhered to the view set forth by free-market economists connected with the Council of Economic Advisers and the American Enterprise Institute, that immigration was of net economic benefit to the U.S. but could be made even more valuable by shifting priorities from family reunion to the acquisition of human capital. As the former governor of California, Reagan was close to fruit and vegetable growers who relied heavily on an ongoing supply of undocumented immigrant workers. On the other side were the cultural traditionalists, who perceived immigration mainly as a threat to America's identity. Among them was Senator Alan K. Simpson of Wyoming, whose outlook was shaped by the neo-Malthusian demographer Leon Bouvier, close to the new restrictionist lobby FAIR. When the Republicans gained control of the Senate for the first time in a generation, Simpson, who had pressed unsuccessfully within SCIRP for an overall ceiling on immigration, became chair of the Immigration Subcommittee and a key player until his retirement in 1996.

Negotiations over the package deal resulted in the Immigration Reform and Control Act of 1986 (IRCA). The final votes again reflected unusual alignments, with the minority made up of liberal Democrats, who warned of discrimination, and conservative Republicans, who objected to the generous treatment of illegal aliens and to the prospect of future guest workers. Amnesty involved two categories of persons. The first was aliens present in the U.S. before 1982, most of whom had been admitted under one of the ongoing temporary programs and had subsequently overstayed; they had to apply within an 18-month period starting 6 months after the bill became law and upon approval would hold the transitional status of "lawful temporary resident." After a year they would be eligible to apply for permanent residence upon demonstration of "minimal understanding of ordinary English" and a basic knowledge of U.S. history and government—requirements usually imposed on applicants for naturalization. The second category, designated "special agricultural workers" (SAWs), covered aliens who entered legally or illegally and worked in agriculture for at least 90 days in 1985–1986; they too would become eligible for permanent residence after a two-year period as "temporary residents." Both programs were designed to be self-funded by way of application fees. To prevent a sudden swell in the welfare rolls, IRCA denied most applicants access to federal needs-based assistance for five years; however, because this increased the burden on states and localities, it also established a grant system to reimburse them for certain expenses incurred on behalf of eligible legalized aliens during the transition period. Curiously, the law set aside 10,000 immigrant visas for countries disadvantaged by the 1965 law; hailed by its supporters as "affirmative action" on behalf of Europeans, it largely reflected the efforts of Irish organizations to open a door for Irish nationals who had no immediate family members in the U.S. and who failed to qualify on the basis of skills. These came to be known as "diversity visas."

IRCA's most evident achievement was the legalization of nearly 3 million people, mostly of Mexican origin. The big surprise was that there were twice as many applications under the SAWs program as estimated, prompting suspicions that many of the claims were fraudulent. Overall, an estimated 91 percent of the pre-1982 illegal population was legalized, with residents of California well in the lead (59.2 percent of the total). Legalization vastly expanded the Latino community's potential political power and gave it an unprecedented voice in the determination of immigration policy.

However, as a design for closing the back door, IRCA was worse than inadequate, because the elements that made its enactment possible were structurally contradictory. Employer sanctions failed because they went against the interests of all employers. The new regulations entailed a wholesale transformation of business practices, requiring the country's 7 million employers to file for three years forms attesting that they had checked the work eligibility and identification documents of every employee; matters were complicated by the many variants of the alien registration card as well as the wide availability of fraudulent documents, notably Social Security cards. Enforcement entailed a monumental and unprecedented joint undertaking by the Department of Labor and the Department of Justice, which lacked organizational capacity and adequate funding to do so. By 1991 a commissioned report noted that "growth in the enforcement budget has halted due to government-wide stringency" and that Congress was likely to abandon employer sanctions altogether. There was considerable debate over the deterrent effect of sanctions as well, and a comprehensive review concluded that IRCA probably brought about a reduction in illegal Mexican immigration during the three years immediately following enactment but that after 1989 the illegal flow was again on the rise.

While implementation of IRCA got under way, Congress tackled the remainder of the SCIRP agenda. The commission had proposed to reduce chain migration by reducing numbers in the married-brothers-and-sisters preference or limiting the preference to unmarried siblings. Yet despite rising concern over immigration in the country, further stimulated by the onset of a severe economic downturn, the alliance of concerned ethnics and free-market advocates managed to block attempts to limit or even reduce immigration. Senators Kennedy and Simpson introduced a proposal imposing an overall cap on annual immigration, excluding refugees. Immediate relatives of citizens remained unlimited, but the number admitted in a given year would be deducted from the family allocation the following year, so that as the mass of immediate relatives grew, the number available for other family-reunion preference visas would substantially shrink. The cap would thus eventually take on a restrictive function, which would affect the siblings of recent immigrants most severely. The proposal also sought to limit chaining by restricting the fifth preference to unmarried brothers and sisters. It substantially increased independent admissions, to be allocated on the basis of a system inspired by Canadian policy, providing "points" for education, skills, age, working experience, and English-language proficiency. Individuals could also qualify for admission by investing $1 million and creating at least 10 jobs, a provision promptly decried as a fat-cat measure.

After two years of maneuvering, the measure was signed into law by President

George H. W. Bush in November 1990. As Senator Simpson put it, Congress had built a ceiling with a hole in it. The law established an overall cap on annual immigration of 675,000, including immediate relatives of citizens but excluding refugees, beginning in fiscal year 1995, and slightly increased the per-country ceiling to 25,520. Although it retained the provision to deduct the number actually admitted in a given year from the following year's allocation to relatives, it also insured a minimum of 226,000 admissions for the latter, so that if more than 254,000 immediate relatives of citizens were admitted in a given year, the cap would have to be lifted above 675,000 the following year. Visas for siblings were reduced, and employment-based immigration was more than doubled, from 54,000 to 140,000, constituting 21 percent of the total. The law also institutionalized the category "diversity immigrants" from underrepresented countries and enlarged it to 55,000; Ireland was guaranteed 40 percent during the transition period, a demonstration of residual Irish clout within the Democratic party.

Meanwhile, anti-immigration sentiment continued to climb. Even as the law neared enactment, a Roper poll reported that 75 percent of the public thought legal immigration should not be increased and nearly half that it should be reduced; furthermore, a majority believed that legal as well as illegal immigrants displaced American workers, burdened the social welfare system, and threatened American culture. Over the next few years, support for outright reduction climbed to 54 percent, then 61; it reached 66 in 1995, while those who thought policies should be revised rose to 80 percent, with a majority disapproving of President Bill Clinton's handling of the matter. Blatantly neorestrictionist literature gained considerable public attention, and even some economists went on record on behalf of limitation. The cultural struggle was acutely manifest in efforts to eliminate bilingual education and generally protect the public sphere against encroachments by the Spanish language, with dire predictions that if immigration continued at the present rate, "non-Hispanic whites" would fall to below half the population by 2050.

Yet although concern remained largely focused on the flow from Mexico, the U.S. pursued policies that in effect encouraged northward movement, notably the North American Free Trade Agreement (NAFTA), passed in 1992, which required Mexico to relinquish protectionist agricultural policies that enabled subsistence farmers to remain on their land and stimulated the expansion of transborder economic linkages, particularly truck traffic, which facilitated undocumented entry. Asylum policy also turned into a battleground; although the procedures instituted by the Reagan administration initially appeared to be an effective deterrent, a series of court rulings to the effect that Central American claimants had been rejected in a summary fashion imposed additional procedural guarantees and abruptly reversed the trend, so that applications as well as the backlog approximately tripled between 1991 and 1995.

Although immigration policy did not rank high among the incoming Clinton administration's concerns, the subject was abruptly propelled into the headlines in January 1993 when the nominee for attorney general was found to have employed an undocumented Peruvian as a babysitter. In the same month a Pakistani gunman launched an attack on CIA headquarters, and in February a bomb exploded in the basement garage of the World Trade Center, a crime for which six Middle Eastern men were later convicted. On June 6 immigration burst out as a made-for-TV event when the freighter *Golden Venture* ran aground off New York City, with a cargo of over 300 undocumented Chinese, and a similar incident made primetime on the West Coast shortly afterward when the freighter *Pai Chang* dumped its human cargo near the Golden Gate Bridge and then led the Coast Guard on an eight-hour chase in San Francisco Bay.

Under public pressure to adopt a tough stance but obligated to his political allies, who included many of the "new" ethnics, President Clinton adopted a middle course. He appointed as commissioner of the INS an unusually experienced professional, Doris M. Meissner, who had served as a senior manager within the agency in the early 1980s and subsequently conducted research at the Carnegie Endowment. He also established the Commission on Immigration Reform (USCIR), called for by the 1990 law, appointing former Texas representative Barbara Jordan as its chair. Overall, the commission's makeup afforded the prospect of control-minded initiatives. In mid-1993, Operation Hold the Line, the first of a series of Border Patrol efforts to reduce surreptitious crossing within densely populated urban districts along the U.S.-Mexican border, was launched in El Paso, Texas. Asylum regulations were toughened around the same time.

Immigration emerged as an especially hot issue in California, a vital state in Clinton's electoral victory. Seeking to make a political comeback in the wake of the collapse of the defense industry and the Los Angeles riots, Governor Pete Wilson, who throughout his two terms in the Senate had relentlessly advocated an expanded guest worker program, seized upon illegal immigration as the scapegoat for the state's financial difficulties. In early 1994 his allies launched Proposition 187, cleverly dubbed "Save Our State," which would deny social services, nonemergency health care, and primary education to illegal immigrants—the latter in violation of the Supreme Court's 1982 ruling in *Plyler* v. *Doe*. The proposition carried by 59 percent, with a high of 63 percent among white voters and a low of 23 percent among Hispanics, and Wilson was easily reelected. As a political experiment, Prop 187 revealed the strategic value of reinforcing the boundaries of social citizenship. By the same token, it revealed to those targeted the value of political citizenship, prompting more Hispanics to vote than in any previous state election and a nationwide rush to naturalize.

Policy prospects changed abruptly with the 1994 Republican conquest of Congress, for the first time since 1954. Although immigration did not figure prominently in the Republicans' program, in the face of public pressure for reduction the party was expected to move in that direction. The Jordan Commission's report of spring 1995 provided support for this, by recommending the elimination of the family-based admission categories that contributed to chain migration. Nevertheless, the strange-bedfellows syndrome came into play with a vengeance: with the prospect of a significant reduction of immigration, the concerned economic interests entered into an explicit alliance with immigrant advocates and the now Hispanic-oriented AFL-CIO. Welcoming an unusual opportunity to cooperate, the (Protestant) Christian Coalition and the Catholic Bishops Conference joined in.

By mid-1996 a tradeoff between the Democratic president and the Republican Congress neared completion, providing for a reduction of immigrant access to the social welfare system in exchange for maintenance of the family-reunion provisions. A turning point in both social and immigration policy, Title IV of the Personal Responsibility, Work Opportunity, and Medicaid Restructuring Act significantly narrowed the boundaries of social citizenship. To begin with, it confirmed the ineligibility of illegal and nonimmigrant aliens for most welfare benefits; as for legal immigrants, it imposed greater responsibility on the people who sponsored them by making affidavits of support legally enforceable either by the immigrants or by any government agency providing means-tested social services, and allowed states to deny the immigrants access to certain types of assistance, notably Medicaid and Temporary Assistance for Needy Families.

Later that year Congress also passed the Illegal Immigration Reform and Immigrant Responsibility Act (IIRIRA). Signed by President Clinton on September 30, it focused largely on enforcement, doubling the number of border agents, constructing physical barriers in heavily trafficked areas, stiffening civil and criminal penalties for illegal entry and for assisting it, buttressing state and local authority to enforce immigration laws, and creating an "integrated entry and exit data system." The law also imposed limitations on the ability of aliens to challenge INS decisions and deportation rulings in federal court, paralleling those of the same year's Antiterrorism and Effective Death Penalty Act. In addition IIRIRA provided for "expedited removal" of persons arriving with false papers or no documents at all. However, as a result of a hard-fought compromise, if the person claimed asylum, the case would be referred to a trained asylum officer, who would interview the individual to determine whether the claim was plausible and so should receive a full hearing before an immigration judge.

While Proposition 187 helped Pete Wilson secure reelection, it jeopardized the Republican party's future in California, and this was compounded by the policies subsequently enacted by the Republican Congress. The 1998 state and midterm congressional elections were the California Republicans' Waterloo, and the Democratic surge was largely attributable to mobilization of the Mexican American electorate. These realities quickly affected policymaking, leading to the curtailment of Proposition 187, the abandonment of further restrictionist efforts by the Republican leadership in Congress, and eventually the identification of George W. Bush as a promising presidential candidate on the basis of his relative success with Mexican Americans as governor of Texas.

With the Clinton impeachment overshadowing all other activity throughout most of 1998 and the economy escalating to unprecedented heights, immigration disappeared from the headlines and the mood shifted away from restriction. A 1999 Gallup Poll reported that only 44 percent favored reduced immigration, the lowest level since 1977. Immigration largely receded from the congressional agenda, except for attacks on the INS, whose survival became another bone of contention between the Clinton administration and its opponents, as did persistent efforts to enlarge the guest worker program and proposals to provide additional legalization.

While the crystallization of anti-immigration sentiment in response to what restrictionists perceive as a tidal wave of immigration originating beyond the established European-based boundaries of American identity echoed developments in the early decades of the 20th century, the restrictionists' limited success also draws attention to some important differences between the two time periods. One is the structure of the political party system. Whereas the restrictions of the 1920s were enacted by a coalition of conservative Republicans and southern Democrats, leaving the business-minded to find substitute workers, today's business-minded Republicans no longer have access to ample reserves of cheap labor. The contemporary political configuration also affords recent immigrants a greater measure of political power by virtue of their strategic location in swing states. As a consequence of their demographic profile (relative youth and higher fertility), new immigrants and their offspring accounted for half the total growth in the U.S. population between 1990 and 2000 and thereby carried considerable weight in the reapportionment process. While Hispanics tend to vote Democratic, they do so much less than African Americans, and their conservatism on family issues, notably abortion, makes them promising prospects for Republican cultivation.

A final difference arises from the configuration of immigration itself. In the early 20th century the U.S. was in effect an island, whose makeup could be determined by way of remote control; once decided upon, both Asian exclusion and European restriction were easily implemented by ordinary administrative procedures. But today, while remote control still works with regard to most of the world, it is not practicable with respect to the neighboring south. To overcome this handicap, the U.S. would have to venture well beyond immigration policy and undertake a fundamental transformation of the system. In keeping with these facts, George W. Bush repressed anti-Hispanic agitation within his party's ranks at the outset of his campaign and made a point of delivering an occasional speech in Spanish following his election. At the same time he undertook to restructure the uneasy relationship between the U.S. and Mexico by negotiating a guest worker program that includes some possibility of access to permanent residence as well as legalization.

Although border control took on renewed significance in the wake of 9/11, the terrorist attacks revealed that the most severe threat to U.S. security has little to do with immigration but arises from international travel, which poses a staggering challenge, because border inspectors would have to make over 1 billion correct decisions every year to keep terrorists and their weapons out of the country. Leaving aside daily commuters from Canada and Mexico, documented foreign entrants number some 60 million, about half of whom are covered by the Visa Waiver Program, which in 2001 exempted nationals of 29 countries. That year the U.S. issued 7 million visas, of which only some 800,000 were awarded to immigrants, with another 600,000 going to students and the remainder to tourists and business visitors. Approximately 1 of every 500,000 visas awarded in the two-year period preceding 9/11 went to a hijacker or a suspected associate. The task remains staggering even when scrutiny is narrowed down to presumed "dangerous" people: for example, some 120,000 visas were issued to Saudi nationals, of which 15, or 1 per 8,000, went to future hijackers, and the leading detained suspect was a Morocco-born individual who acquired French nationality and hence was admitted without a visa. While control of entries by air is carried out by remote control, investigations in the wake of 9/11 revealed that consular officials have very limited information and that much of the investigative task is delegated to unreliable travel agencies.

While many countries supplement border controls with internal scrutiny of aliens, in this respect the U.S. has been at the extreme liberal end of the continuum. Although concern with terrorism occasioned by the Iranian hostage crisis of 1979 prompted the INS to require educational institutions to report the movements of foreign students, by 1988 forms were piled so high that the agency asked the institutions to stop sending them in. Following the first attack on the World Trade Center, IIRIRA mandated the creation of an "integrated entry and exit data system," but the Clinton administration and Congress caved in to pressure from the education and business lobbies to postpone its development, and the Bush administration followed suit. Moreover, tighter border control was handicapped by protracted turf wars between the State and Justice Departments.

The most significant legislative measure explicitly designed to offset the vulnerability exposed by 9/11 is the Uniting and Strengthening America by Providing Appropriate Tools Required to Intercept and Obstruct Terrorism Act of 2001, an unwieldy title designed to produce the bombastic acronym USA PATRIOT. Although it was broadly supported by both parties, an early version permitting indefinite detention evoked the treatment meted out to Japanese Americans in World War II, and liberals insisted on both tighter limits on the new detention power and the inclusion of a "sunset clause" providing for the law's expiration in 2005 unless explicitly renewed. Among other things, the act imposed a two-year deadline for the implementation of the integrated entry and exit data system. The events also triggered a spate of proposals to make the U.S. more secure by subjecting foreign residents to systematic verification; but given the magnitude of the task (involving 11 percent of the population), despite repeated reassurances by public officials, this was carried out on the basis of ethnic profiling, targeting groups considered dangerous, namely "Arabs" and "Muslims," or, more diffusely, "Middle Easterners," including many South Asians. The early post-9/11 roundups led to the incarceration of numerous Middle Easterners for violations of immigration regulations, mostly by way of over-staying, and a spate of deportations. However, none of those rounded up was charged as a terrorist. It is noteworthy that the 1996 statutes emerged as the Justice Department's preferred control devices. Under a bill passed in November 2002, the INS was dissolved effective March 2003 and its responsibilities were assumed by the newly created Department of Homeland Security.

It is remarkable that despite continuing pressure by dedicated restrictionists, who argue that security considerations require a reduced intake, the U.S. refrained from tightening its immigration policy. In 2002 illegal immigration quickly reached its previous level, and it rose further in 2003, following the elimination of tariffs on Mexican agricultural imports from the U.S. In 2003 the Census Bureau released new figures indicating that the growth of the Hispanic population "continues at a dizzying rate," increasing by nearly 10 percent in the first two years of the new century. After a prolonged hiatus, motivated in part by Mexican opposition to U.S. intervention in Iraq, negotiations on the guest worker program resumed in 2003, and in January 2004, President Bush proposed a sweeping two-part program that would enable undocumented immigrants to apply for temporary worker status, while other plans spoke of "earned legalization." Despite further postponements, movement along these lines continued throughout 2005, suggesting that settlement of the most recent immigration crisis would include the institutionalization of a special relationship with Mexico.

Bibliography

Andreas, Peter. *Border Games: Policing the U.S.-Mexico Divide.* Ithaca, N.Y.: Cornell University Press, 2000.

Fix, Michael, and Jeffrey S. Passell. *Immigration and Immigrants: Setting the Record Straight.* Washington, D.C.: Urban Institute, 1994.

Gimpel, James G., and James R. Edwards, Jr. *The Congressional Politics of Immigration Control.* Boston: Allyn and Bacon, 1999.

Haus, Leah. "Openings in the Wall: Transnational Migrants, Labor Unions, and U.S. Immigration Policy." *International Organization* 49, 2 (Spring 1995): 285–313.

Huber, Gregory A., and Thomas J. Espenshade. "Neo-isolationism, Balanced Budget Conservatism, and the Fiscal Impacts of Immigrants." *International Migration Review* 31, 4 (Winter 1997): 1031–54.

Laham, Nicholas. *Ronald Reagan and the Politics of Immigration Reform.* Westport, Conn.: Praeger, 2000.

LeMay, Michael C. *Anatomy of a Public Policy: The Reform of Contemporary American Immigration Law.* Westport, Conn.: Praeger, 1994.

Loescher, Gil, and John A. Scanlan. *Calculated Kindness: Refugees and America's Half-Open Door, 1945 to the Present.* New York: Free Press, 1986.

Martin, Philip L. *Harvest of Confusion: Migrant Workers in U.S. Agriculture.* Boulder, Colo.: Westview, 1988.

Miller, Harris N. "The Right Thing to Do: A History of Simpson-Mazzoli." *Journal of Contemporary Studies* 7 (Fall 1984).

Miller, Mark. "Continuities and Discontinuities in Immigration Reform in Industrial Democracies: The Case of the Immigration Reform and Control Act of 1986." *International Review of Public Policy* 1 (1989): 131–51.

Reimers, David. *Still the Golden Door?* 2d ed. New York: Columbia University Press, 1992.

Schuck, Peter H. *Citizens, Strangers, and In-Betweens: Essays on Immigration and Citizenship.* Boulder, Colo.: Westview, 1998.

Tichenor, Daniel J. *Dividing Lines: The Politics of Immigration Control in America.* Princeton, N.J.: Princeton University Press, 2002.

Zolberg, Aristide R. *A Nation by Design: Immigration Policy in the Fashioning of America 1750–2000.* Cambridge: Harvard University Press, 2006.

Citizenship and Nationality Policy

Peter H. Schuck

Not since the McCarthy era in the early 1950s, when many Americans aggressively questioned the loyalty of their fellow citizens and when relatively few immigrants were admitted and thus became eligible to become citizens, has the public debate about citizenship been so energetic and morally charged. In Congress, at the bar of public opinion, and even in the courts, citizenship in both its normative and positive dimensions is being closely reexamined. One aspect of the tragedy of September 11, 2001, that has been little remarked upon is the renewed prominence it has given to the status of citizenship.

The significance of citizenship depends on the meanings that attach to it in three analytically distinct domains where its values are conflicting and contested. The first is international law and politics. Here the nation defines the scope of its sovereignty by classifying all individuals as either insiders or outsiders. By insiders, I mean those whom the polity brings into its constitutional community by granting them legal rights within and against it. The American constitutional community includes citizens, noncitizen nationals, legal permanent resident immigrants (LPRs), legal nonresident (temporary) visitors, and in some cases undocumented persons. Outsiders are everybody else in the world. The second domain is national politics, where public law classifies the body of insiders into different categories, defining what the polity owes to each and what they in turn owe to the polity. The third domain is federalism, in which the polity is structurally divided into multiple, overlapping sovereignties. I am primarily concerned with the second of these domains, national politics, and especially with the distinctive character of national citizenship status as it is framed by public law and policy.

First, clarification of the terms "citizen" and "national" is in order. All citizens of the United States are also U.S. nationals, but the reverse is not always true; some nationals are not citizens. Citizens enjoy all of the privileges and responsibilities of full membership in the polity; noncitizen nationals do not. Thus, noncitizen nationals—inhabitants of American possessions that are not states—do not possess full political rights (primarily, the right to vote in national elections), and at times they have not enjoyed full rights to migrate to the mainland. Although this distinction was significant following the Spanish-American War, when the U.S. acquired large colonies, it is no longer of much importance; today, only the inhabitants of American Samoa and Swains Island are noncitizen nationals. Here, then, I look at citizenship, the more important but slightly more limited of these categories.

American citizenship crowns a hierarchy of statuses, each bearing a distinctive set of legal rights and obligations. David Martin has likened this to concentric circles: a community of citizens at the central core is surrounded by a series of those with more peripheral status, having ever more attenuated ties to the polity, weaker claims on it, and more limited rights against it. We can infer the normative meaning of citizenship from, among other things, the magnitude and nature of the gap between the citizens and those in the outer circles with respect to their rights and duties.

American citizenship, as the legal scholar Alexander Bickel famously observed, "is at best a simple idea for a simple government." By this, Bickel meant that the ratification of the Fourteenth Amendment made membership in the American polity widely and easily available, that the legal rights and duties associated with citizenship have long ceased to be an important or divisive public issue, and that this consensus has been highly desirable. In 1989, I found merit in Bickel's point and suggested that it was probably more accurate then than it had been in 1973, when he first asserted it.

Today, however, Bickel's (and my) confident assurances seem themselves simplistic. In a radically altered political environment, the question of citizenship is becoming more salient and potentially divisive. To understand the large significance of what has transpired, we need to consider the basic structure of U.S. citizenship law and the differences between the rights and duties of citizens and those of LPRs and then discuss the reevaluation of citizenship that is now occurring in the shadow of more prominent debates—notably, those concerning the role of immigration in America's future, the legitimacy and shape of the welfare state, and the launching of a war on international terrorism. Some reflections on what has been called "postnational" citizenship serve as a conclusion.

The Legal Structure of U.S. Citizenship

American citizenship can be acquired in three ways. The most common way—citizenship by birth in the U.S.—reflects the Anglo-American tradition of *jus soli*, a right protected by the Fourteenth Amendment's citizenship clause, which provides that "all persons born or naturalized in the United States, and subject to the jurisdiction thereof, are citizens of the United States and of the State wherein they reside." Judicial interpretation of this clause has long been understood as extending this status to native-born children of noncitizens who are in the country, even if they are present illegally or on a temporary visa. This interpretation has never been seriously questioned in the courts, although it has recently come under scrutiny, and some criticism, from politicians, commentators, and scholars.

A second route to citizenship, also mentioned in the citizenship clause, is through naturalization. More than 463,000 individuals naturalized in 2003, well below the historical peak reached in 1996, when more than 1 million naturalized. Approximately 625,000 petitions for naturalization were pending at the end of 2003. In order to naturalize, an LPR must have resided in the U.S. with that status for five years, be of good moral character, demonstrate an ability to speak, read, and write English, and demonstrate a basic knowledge of U.S. government and history. More than 85 percent of all naturalizations occur under these general provisions, although some people are permitted to use less restrictive procedures. Spouses of citizens can naturalize after only three years; children who immigrate with their parents can be naturalized more or less automatically (simply by obtaining a certificate) when their parents naturalize; and adopted children of citizens can also naturalize in this fashion. Certain noncitizens who served with the American military during past wars may naturalize easily, and some individuals or groups are naturalized directly by statute. Significantly, a large number of immigrants who are eligible for citizenship choose not to naturalize or wait a long time to do so.

The third route to citizenship is through descent from one or more American parents. This principle, know as *jus sanguinis,* is codified in the immigration statute. For example, a child of two citizen parents born outside the U.S. is a citizen if one of the parents resided in the U.S. before the child's birth. If one of the parents is a noncitizen but the citizen parent was physically present in the U.S. or a possession for a total of five years, two of which were after the age of 14, the child is a citizen. Over time, Congress has liberalized these eligibility requirements, and the Supreme Court, while sometimes sustaining gender-based distinctions in this area, has made it more difficult to enact such distinctions.

Plural citizenships are quite common in the U.S. owing to the combination of the American *jus soli* rule with the various *jus sanguinis* rules of other countries. Thus, noncitizens who naturalize in the U.S. must renounce their prior allegiance. This renunciation may or may not effectively terminate the individual's foreign citizenship under the foreign state's law, but U.S. naturalization law does not require the renunciation actually to have that legal effect. As a result of this policy, as well as its policy of allowing U.S. citizens to naturalize elsewhere, the U.S. government tolerates and protects plural citizenships, and this receptivity has increased in recent years. Most of the countries from which the largest groups of immigrants come— Mexico, the Dominican Republic, and Canada, for example—recognize children born to their nationals abroad as citizens, and other sending countries, such as India, allow dual citizenship until a certain age, when the individual must choose one or the other. For all of these reasons, plural citizenship among Americans will continue to increase.

Once acquired, American citizenship is virtually impossible to lose without the citizen's express consent. Supreme Court decisions since the 1960s have severely restricted the government's power to denationalize a citizen for disloyalty, divided allegiance, or other reasons. Today the government cannot prevail against a birthright or *jus sanguinis* citizen unless it can prove that the citizen specifically intended to renounce his or her citizenship. This standard is difficult to satisfy—as it should be. Relatively few denationalization proceedings are brought, and the number of successful ones is probably declining. Denaturalization proceedings against people who procured citizenship by misrepresenting their backgrounds or through other illegal means are largely directed against former Nazi and Soviet persecutors, and the standards that the government must satisfy to prevail are quite demanding.

The Rights and Duties of Citizens

Until Congress enacted statutory changes in 1996, the differences between the legal rights enjoyed by citizens and those enjoyed by LPRs were more political than legal or economic, and those differences had narrowed considerably over time. In 1989, I argued that the narrowing of these differences constituted a devaluation of citizenship, one that raised important questions about the evolving political identity of the United States. Today, partly in response to widespread dissatisfaction with this trend, a reevaluation of citizenship is in progress, one in which the differentiation of the rights of citizens and LPRs is a central theme.

The power of Congress to treat citizens and LPRs differently is subject to certain constitutional constraints. U.S. courts have established that the constitutionality of government-imposed discriminations between citizens and LPRs turns in part on whether the discrimination being challenged is imposed by the federal government or by a state. In several decisions during the 1970s, the Supreme Court held that Congress could exclude LPRs from public benefits under Medicare (and presumably under other federal programs as well) but that states could not do so without the federal government's blessing. Since then, the constitutional rationale for decisions restricting the states' power to discriminate may have changed. The Court earlier seemed to view state law discrimination on the basis of alien status as a "suspect classification," like race. This would mean that under the equal protection clause, the state must show that its interest in discriminating against noncitizens was "compelling" and narrowly tailored to achieve its purpose—a very demanding test. In subsequent cases, however, the Court relied on a constitutional theory based on the supremacy clause, not equal protection. This latter theory, known as "federal preemption," is discussed below, along with the recent developments in federalism reflected in the 1996 welfare reform law.

Despite these constitutional constraints on discrimination against noncitizens, some noteworthy differences in legal rights between LPRs and citizens emerged long before the 1996 welfare changes, which significantly increased those differences. Three are political in nature: the right to vote, the right to serve on federal and many state juries, and the right to run for certain high elective offices and to serve in some high (and not-so-high) appointive offices. Each of these restrictions seems to be premised on one or more of the following assumptions: that noncitizens' political socialization is too fragmentary and embryonic to be trusted in matters of public choice; that confining political participation of this kind to citizens carries an important symbolic message about the value and significance of full membership; and that exclusion of nonimmigrants from such participation encourages them to naturalize as soon as possible.

Although various American states during the 19th and early 20th centuries permitted noncitizens to vote in national elections, only citizens may do so today—a rule that applies in virtually all other countries as well. A number of communities allow noncitizens (occasionally including the undocumented) to vote in some or all local elections, and proposals to extend the franchise to noncitizens have been advanced in several large cities, including Washington, D.C., and Los Angeles. In 2004 voters in San Francisco rejected a proposal to permit noncitizens to vote in school board elections. Some academic commentators support such a change, drawing on the historical precedent for noncitizen voting and on liberal, republican, and natural rights theories. Noncitizens can and do participate in politics in other ways, including contributing to electoral campaigns.

Most individual LPRs (as distinct from immigrant rights' advocates) probably do not view the inability to vote as a major disadvantage, although they may well resent the second-class status that it implies. Immigrants' collective political identities have emphasized their ethnicities more than their alien status per se; most empowerment campaigns have been mounted by ethnic organizations and promote naturalization, not legal changes to allow noncitizens to vote. Indeed, in 1996 Congress made it a federal crime for noncitizens to vote in federal elections and made voting in violation of any federal, state, or local law grounds for removal. But now that Congress has imposed legal disadvantages on LPRs as a class, the political salience of alien status and hence the value that noncitizens place on the vote are likely to increase. Little support for such a change exists even among liberal citizen voters.

Citizenship requirements for jury service are less of an issue. In framing the Bill of Rights, which protected the right to trial by jury in both criminal and civil cases, the founders saw jury service as an important political as well as legal institution, protecting the people from the oppression of governmental and private elites. Despite some controversial jury verdicts, Americans still esteem the institution of the jury. Although most serve conscientiously, some view jury participation as a duty rather than a privilege. The notion of extending jury service to noncitizens has not surfaced in the recent public debate about improving the jury system.

The policy of barring immigrants from federal employment, which is similar to the practice of most nations, is likely to be a greater concern to LPRs than the bar to jury service. Few, if any, LPRs are likely to seek high elective or appointive offices before they are naturalized. Many, however, might want to work in the federal, state, and local civil service systems. In two decisions in the mid-1970s, the Supreme Court applied the constitutional principles relating to discrimination against immigrants in the civil service setting. It held that the Constitution permitted Congress and the president to limit federal civil service jobs to citizens (which has been done since the 1880s) but that the states could not impose citizenship requirements for their own civil service systems. The Court emphasized the exclusive federal interest in regulating immigration. It recognized, however, the states' power to exclude LPRs from particular job categories that represented their "political function," such as schoolteachers and police officers. This distinction, between jobs that involve a political function and those that do not, has proved exceedingly difficult to apply but continues to enjoy the Court's support.

Two other advantages of citizens over LPRs are worth mentioning. First, LPRs have a lesser right to sponsor their family members for immigration. Citizens' spouses, minor unmarried children, and most parents receive a preferred immigration status without regard to numerical limits, and citizens' siblings and adult children have a preferred status under the admissions system. In contrast, the spouses and unmarried children of LPRs qualify for a numerically limited preference, and their siblings receive no preference at all. In addition to different sponsorship rights, citizens and LPRs differ in that the latter, but not the former, are subject to removal under certain circumstances. Removal of a long-term resident can wreak enormous suffering on noncitizens and their families and friends. Although the Supreme Court has repeatedly held that removal is not punishment and therefore does not implicate due process and other constitutional guarantees that surround the imposition of criminal sanctions, the fact is that, as Justice Douglas once put it, removal "may deprive a man and his family of all that makes life worthwhile."

Still, it is important to place this risk of removal in realistic context. The actual risk for noncriminal LPRs in the U.S. has been extremely low. Even after the 1996 immigration control legislation, formal removal of LPRs, especially noncriminal ones, remains a costly process for the government. Statutes, regulations, and judicial rulings require the U.S. Citizen and Immigration Services (USCIS) to observe high standards of procedural fairness in adjudicating whether LPRs may remain. Severe administrative difficulties further limit the government's ability to implement even the relatively few formal removal orders and the far more numerous informal departure agreements that it does manage to obtain. Except at the border, where the government can often effect the voluntary departure of noncitizens, the agency has been notoriously ineffective at actually removing those who are determined to remain—even the "aggravated felons" against whom Congress provided special summary enforcement and removal powers. As a legal and practical matter, a long-term, noncriminal LPR's chances of remaining in the U.S. are almost as great as a citizen's. The 1996 law, which was intended to facilitate the removal of noncitizens who were inadmissible at entry, who commit crimes in the U.S., who lack credible asylum claims, or who are otherwise out of status even though they may have had proper documentation when they entered, has not significantly increased this risk. In 2003 the government formally removed 186,000 noncitizens; 79,000 of these were criminals. A far larger number (1.3 million) were removed informally.

Today the most controversial issue concerning the differential treatment of citizens and LPRs concerns LPRs' ineligibility for public benefits. Before the 1996 welfare reform, LPRs and some legal immigrants who would probably gain LPR status in the future (such as family members of amnestied noncitizens, refugees and asylum-seekers, and parolees) were eligible for many cash assistance, medical care, food, education, housing, and other social programs, albeit subject to some restrictions. In addition, LPRs were often eligible for benefit programs, such as low resident tuition in state university systems. The 1996 reform significantly limited LPRs' access to nonemergency federal programs and federally funded state programs.

These discriminations, however, are palliated by several developments. In the late 1990s, Congress restored many of these benefits to pre-1996 immigrants while enacting new amnesties for hundreds of thousands of undocumented immigrants. New York, California, and other states with large immigrant populations have extended benefits to those who do not qualify for federal assistance. Some states and cities (New York City, for example) have been lax and even obstructionist in their enforcement of federal restrictions. Many of those who are ineligible have managed to circumvent restrictions through fraudulent applications. Most important, the vast majority of ineligible LPRs can escape the restrictions by naturalizing within five years, although persistent administrative backlogs have extended this period as a practical matter in many regions.

The Reevaluation of Citizenship

In recent years, public discourse about citizenship has returned to first principles: its nature, sources, and significance. So fundamental are these principles that the new discourse amounts to a reevaluation of American citizenship in both its normative and its positive dimensions. This reevaluation has been prompted by deep concerns about the unity and coherence of the civic culture in the U.S., which flow from a number of developments: the accumulation of multicultural pressures; the loss of a unifying ideology; technological change; the expansion of the welfare state; public backlash against the devaluation of citizenship; and the post-9/11 war on international terrorism.

Multicultural pressures. The 1965 immigration law radically changed the composition of the immigration stream to the United States. Of the top source countries, only the Philippines and India have sent large numbers of native English-speaking immigrants. Bilingual education has thus become a major issue in public education, and teaching in literally dozens of languages has become necessary not just in large urban school systems but in the smaller communities where many immigrants now live. With the growing politicization of ethnicity and new challenges to the traditional ideal of assimilation, anxieties about linguistic and cultural fragmentation have increased. These anxieties have led approximately half the states to establish English as the official language. California and several other states have adopted laws limiting affirmative action and bilingual education.

In the late 1960s, the civil rights movement took a turn toward separatism. Blacks, already severely disadvantaged, were increasingly obliged to cede political and economic influence to more recently arrived Hispanic and Asian voters. Many of the newer groups qualified for affirmative action programs, which exacerbated tensions among the groups and magnified fears that immigration and affirmative action were fragmenting American society. Certain economic sectors came to depend almost entirely on immigrant workers, legal and illegal. Relatively parochial immigrant enclaves grew larger. These developments caused many Americans to feel more and more like strangers in their own country.

Loss of unifying ideology. The end of the cold war deprived the U.S. of an ideology, anticommunism, that had served for many decades as a unifying, coherent force in American political culture and as an obsessive preoccupation and goal in U.S. foreign policy. No alternative ideology has yet emerged to replace it; the war on terrorism, although a unifying crusade, is unlikely to take its place. Only constitutionalism, our civic religion, seems potentially capable of performing the function of binding together a nation of diverse peoples.

Technological change. Rapid changes in transportation and communication technologies have transformed a world of sovereign nations into a global web of multinational enterprises and interdependent societies. Migration and return have become less expensive, making it easier for immigrants to retain emotional and other ties to their countries and cultures of origin. There is also a growing concern that television and other forms of popular culture tend to induct many second-generation immigrant youths into an adversarial underclass culture rather than the American mainstream, thereby assimilating them into a perverse and alienating value system.

Welfare state. In the U.S., the welfare state—especially the creation of entitlements to income support, food stamps, medical care, and subsidized housing—expanded rapidly during a brief period, at least when compared to the more gradual, long-term evolution of European social support systems. With this growth, the behavior, values, and economic progress of immigrants became matters of great fiscal significance and public policy concern. Immigration did not ebb and flow with the business cycle as much as it had historically, in part because of the growth of the social safety net. Immigration has increasingly pitted citizens against noncitizens in a zero-sum competition for scarce public resources, particularly at the local level. This competition sometimes has taken overt political forms—for example, California's passage in 1994 of Proposition 187, a restriction on access to benefits by undocumented immigrants, which a federal court invalidated as an interference with preemptive federal authority over immigration. (Arizona enacted a similar measure in 2004.)

The perennial debate over how the polity should conceive of community, affinity, and mutual obligation has taken on a new significance as the stakes in the competition have increased. Some insist that Americans' obsession with legal rights should be balanced by an equal concern for their social and civic responsibilities. Such demands, which have only succeeded in slowing the growth rate of the welfare state, culminated in the 1996 law severely restricting immigrants' eligibility for federally funded benefits and requiring the states to move welfare recipients, citizens and noncitizens alike, off the dole and into jobs and training.

Devaluation of citizenship. The egalitarian thrust of the welfare state and its promotion of entitlement as an ideal has led to a progressive erosion of citizenship as a distinctive status bearing special privileges and demanding special commitments and obligations. The rights of LPRs have converged with those of citizens until there is little to separate them but citizens' right to vote, greater immigration sponsorship privileges, and eligibility for the federal civil service. Americans have begun to feel that U.S. citizenship has lost much of its value and that it should somehow count for more.

These concerns, which have parallels in other countries, have prompted calls for a revitalization of citizenship. One kind of proposal, which led to the enactment in 1993 of the National Community Service Corps, looks to the creation of a spirit of public service among young people. Another approach, a centerpiece of both 1988 and 1996 welfare reform legislation, seeks to combat the entitlement mentality by insisting that able-bodied citizens work or get training and eventually leave welfare altogether. A third approach, exemplified by the 1996 restrictions on immigrants' access to public benefits, is largely motivated by the desire to save scarce public resources and to favor citizens in the allocation of those resources. Its incidental effect, however, is to increase the value of citizenship by widening the gap between the rights of citizens and those of noncitizens, thereby increasing the incentives for the latter to naturalize. Whether this incentive is the kind of motivation for naturalization that proponents of a more robust citizenship have in mind is a question that is seldom asked.

Two other kinds of reform aim directly at citizenship itself. The Clinton administration sought to enhance the attractiveness of the naturalization process, thereby encouraging more LPRs to acquire citizenship. The "Citizenship USA" initiative, which led to a sharp increase in the number of naturalizations before the 1996 elections, was caught up in a congressional investigation of fraud in and partisan manipulation of the naturalization process. An internal investigation by the Justice Department found that the government had failed to conduct a complete criminal history background check of 18 percent of those who were naturalized under this program, resulting in the naturalization of more than 75,000 people who had arrest records when they applied. A significant number of these had committed crimes that would have rendered them legally ineligible for citizenship. While sharply critical of the program's management, the department found no proof of wrongdoing by the administration, a conclusion disputed by some outsiders.

A more radical reform proposal, not inconsistent with encouraging naturalization, would deny citizenship to some who would otherwise obtain it automatically. This approach would alter, by statute or by constitutional amendment, the traditional American understanding of the *jus soli* rule so that it would exclude the U.S.-born children of temporary residents and undocumented immigrants from automatic citizenship, on the theory that the polity has not consented to their membership—and in the latter case has legally precluded it. Advocates of such a change emphasize the importance of mutual consent—the polity's as well as the immigrant's—in legitimizing American citizenship. They also point to the irrationality of permitting an immigrant woman with no claims on the U.S. to be able to confer American citizenship on her new child simply by crossing the border and giving birth, perhaps at public expense, in an American hospital. Defenders of the existing rule stress the importance of avoiding the creation and perpetuation of an underclass of long-term residents who do not qualify as citizens, a condition similar to that of many guest workers and their descendants who are stranded in countries that reject the *jus soli* principle.

Despite growing criticism of the traditional understanding of the birthright citizenship rule, Congress would never eliminate it. There would be more support for limiting automatic citizenship status for those born in the U.S. to parents in illegal status but still enabling undocumented immigrants who continue to reside in the U.S. for many years the opportunity, or perhaps the right, to naturalize at some point. The trend in Europe is in this direction; in the late 1990s, France and Germany reformed their citizenship laws to expand the naturalization rights of native-born children of noncitizen parents. Another policy option is to reduce the perverse incentive effects of the traditional American *jus soli* rule by denying parents in illegal status any immigration benefits derived through their birthright-citizen children.

War on terrorism. The catastrophic attack of September 11, 2001, unleashed convulsive forces that ramify in many different directions and domains. At this writing, more than four years after the event, the effect on citizenship law and policy can be a matter only of speculation. Any war, particularly one as unprecedented and unstructured as this, is bound to increase the importance of citizenship to both individuals and states. Most of the people whom the U.S. government has taken into custody as alleged terrorists or combatants against the U.S. are noncitizens, but a few are American citizens. Despite a Supreme Court decision in 2004 extending minimal due process rights to those held in the U.S. and on Guantánamo, it is not yet clear how the rules of constitutional, criminal, and military law, as well as the international law of war, will be applied to them. Some of those rules will no doubt apply regardless of the detainees' citizenship, but other procedural rights may depend on whether or not they are Americans.

Concerns about terrorism may generate reformist pressure on several elements of current citizenship law. The wisdom of the uniquely expansive American version of *jus soli* may be called into question by the arrest of terrorism suspects who were born in the U.S. but moved to other countries at an early age. Congress may feel constrained to make the loyalty and good-moral-character requirements for naturalization more demanding or require the USCIS and courts to apply them more strictly in the case of petitioners from states thought to sponsor terrorism. The government's policy toward dual citizenship has grown steadily more permissive since the 1950s, but post-9/11 fears of terrorist acts by U.S. citizens with little or no attachment to American society may generate political pressures to tighten the rules.

Postnational Citizenship

In recent years a number of scholars have pointed to a new development in thinking about citizenship—what Yasemin Soysal and others have called "postnational citizenship." In this conception, transnational diasporic communities of individuals bearing multiple, collective identities make and ideally enforce claims against states. In contrast to a traditional national model of citizenship, individuals, simply by virtue of their personhood, can legitimately assert claims on the basis of their universal human rights, whether or not they are citizens, or even residents, of those states— rights whose existence is not necessarily linked to membership in a particular polity.

Visions of postnational citizenship are undeniably attractive. A just state will respect and vindicate minority groups' claims to cultural diversity and autonomy. Detaching the legitimacy of these claims from their conventional territorial moorings in traditional citizenship law, as such visions seek to do, may sometimes promote their recognition. In general, however, the ostensible goals of postnational citizenship—human rights, cultural autonomy, and full participation in a rich civil society—are tragically elusive, and its achievements are extremely fragile.

The problem is not merely that partisans of exclusion and discrimination will oppose postnational citizenship at every turn and often succeed in establishing illiberal policies in traditional nation-states. More fundamentally, postnational citizenship ultimately depends on its ability to transcend, or at least enlarge, the domains of normal politics and law. Such a transcendence, however, would leave postnational human rights vulnerable, with no firm political and institutional grounding. Without such a grounding, national courts enforcing principles of international law are unlikely to provide durable, reliable protection. The often feckless and politicized international human rights tribunals are even less plausible guarantors of those principles.

One response to this concern is that even episodic protection for postnational citizenship is better than none. But the problem is not simply that courts are institutionally ill-equipped to defend their rulings in the political arena. The greater risk is that the normative foundation of a postnational citizenship may be so thin and shallow that it can easily be swept away by the tides of tribalism or nationalism. In reasonably democratic states—and postnational citizenship is only possible and meaningful in such states—even an imperfect constitution recognizing minority rights, and even a majoritarian politics in which groups must compete for acceptance of their communal aspirations, are likely to provide more certain guarantees of liberal human rights. This is especially true to the extent that the postnational, transnational ideal is institutionally grounded only in politically isolated courts and lends itself, because of its substantive indeterminacy, to repressive applications. A discourse whose success requires overcoming the messy exigencies of normal politics, where expansive conceptions of human rights must contend for legal recognition, seems destined to be either irrelevant or antidemocratic.

On the more positive side, a growing number of international human rights are being recognized by and incorporated into many states' positive law, particularly in Europe. This is true even in the U.S., which often declines to ratify treaties making such rights binding but observes most of them nonetheless. In addition, there is a valuable role for the ideal of postnational citizenship. It should serve as a compelling vision of tolerance, diversity, and integration that people of good will can aspire to and that normal politics in democratic states can sometimes realize, and as a model that states' failures can be fairly judged against. Postnational citizenship has begun to play this role in the United States. But to claim too much for it—to promote it as an alternative to or as a cure for the weaknesses of democratic politics—would ultimately discredit the reformist human rights agenda. If it can succeed in mobilizing normal politics to win that recognition in positive law, however, it will be truly transformative, even as it thereby ceases, in an important sense, to be "postnational."

Bibliography

Aleinikoff, T. Alexander. *Semblances of Sovereignty: The Constitution, the State, and American Citizenship.* Cambridge: Harvard University Press, 2002.

Aleinikoff, T. Alexander, and Douglas Klusmeyer, eds. *From Migrants to Citizens: Membership in a Changing World.* Washington, D.C.: Brookings Institution Press, 2000.

———. *Citizenship Today: Global Perspectives and Practices.* Washington, D.C.: Carnegie Endowment for International Peace, 2001.

Cott, Nancy F. "Marriage and Women's Citizenship in the United States, 1830–1934," *American Historical Review* 103 (1998): 1440–74.

Kettner, James H. *The Development of American Citizenship, 1608–1870.* Chapel Hill: University of North Carolina Press, 1978.

Raskin, Jamin B. "Legal Aliens, Local Citizens: The Historical, Constitutional and Theoretical Meanings of Alien Suffrage," *University of Pennsylvania Law Review* 141 (1993): 1391–1470.

Schuck, Peter H. *Citizens, Strangers, and In-Betweens: Essays on Immigration and Citizenship,* chaps. 7–10. Boulder, Colo.: Westview Press, 1998.

———. "Citizenship After 9/11: Continuity and Change," in Peter H. Schuck, *Meditations of a Militant Moderate: Cool Essays on Hot Issues.* Lanham, Md.: Rowman & Littlefield, 2006.

Smith, Rogers M. *Civic Ideals: Conflicting Visions of Citizenship in U.S. History.* New Haven: Yale University Press, 1997.

Soysal, Yasemin. *Limits of Citizenship: Migrants and Postnational Membership in Europe.* Chicago: University of Chicago Press, 1994.

Spiro, Peter J. *The End of Citizenship.* Forthcoming.

Refugees

David W. Haines

The line that distinguishes refugees from other immigrants is not always easy to draw. Indeed, through most of American history, the distinction was not important as a matter of immigration policy. It has, however, become extraordinarily important since World War II, determining whether particular people have been allowed into the U.S. and how they have been treated after arrival. The story of refugees and America is one that necessarily includes both the experience of the refugees and how Americans, as a people and as a government, have responded to them.

Definitions and Admissions

The idea that refugees exist and deserve special consideration for entry into the U.S. is a simple one, but its incorporation into U.S. law has been a long, slow process. Perhaps the most important initial policy debate involved the failed attempt to gain additional admissions of Jewish refugees both before and during World War II. The failure to aid fleeing Jews, and indeed the creation of what David Wyman has called "paper walls" to keep them out, has been a shadow over American refugee policy ever since.

The first significant refugee legislation passed by the U.S. Congress came only after the end of World War II, and even that in its initial form was somewhat prejudicial against Jews. Nevertheless, the presence of numerous displaced persons (DPs) stranded in refugee camps or otherwise requiring international assistance—an estimated 844,000 in 1946—generated a series of measures to settle those people in different countries. The U.S. concern with displaced persons, in contrast, had more to do with the rapid disintegration in relations between the U.S. and the Soviet Union. Many of the people in the European camps were in danger of being repatriated to countries in eastern Europe that were now under communist control. That possibility spurred the U.S. to admit them despite what was still a very restrictive general immigration policy. Congress thus passed the Displaced Persons Act of 1948, which allowed for the entry of 205,000 people (increased to 415,744 when the act was amended in 1950).

The ideological reaction against communism that underlay assistance to DPs was to be the backbone of the U.S. refugee program for the next three decades. It was at the core of the response to Hungarian refugees after the failed uprising there in 1956, to Cuban refugees after Fidel Castro's rise to power at the end of 1959, to smaller numbers of refugees from a variety of other communist countries (e.g., Czechoslovakia, China), to Jewish refugees from the Soviet Union, and to refugees from Cambodia, Laos, and Vietnam after the collapse of their American-supported governments in the spring of 1975. All of these people had fled what Americans understood to be the intolerable conditions of life under communist governments. The admission of these refugees thus had support among people who viewed them as being of general humanitarian concern and also among those who viewed them as important witnesses to the virtues of democracy and capitalism—and the corresponding evils of totalitarianism and communism. In political terms, this often resulted in an alliance of liberals and conservatives and the infusion of refugee issues into other political debates. For example, the 1974 Jackson-Vanik amendment, largely responding to the plight of Soviet Jews, linked freedom of emigration to the awarding of favorable trading status.

By the end of the 1970s, this refugee program had resulted in the admission of about 1.5 million people. Although those who arrived were considered refugees, they actually came in under a variety of legal statuses authorized by ad hoc legislation and broad use of the attorney general's authority to "parole" people into the U.S. outside of more formal immigration channels. For example, the Cuban Adjustment Act of 1966, under which most Cubans in the U.S. gained permanent legal status, did not even use the word "refugee." Whatever the exact legal status, most of these refugees were resettled in new homes and communities with a mixture of federal funds, voluntary agency support, and family and community networks. After that initial assistance, most research indicated, they did fairly well in economic terms. Indeed, they often did so well that they were lauded as exemplary success stories.

In 1980 all this changed, for three reasons. First, the standard account of refugee economic success—that refugees were not only deserving as refugees but successful as immigrants—came under increasing scrutiny. In the late 1970s, refugee flows from Southeast Asia were outpacing anything the U.S. had ever seen. Although refugees were still only a fraction of overall immigration, they were becoming a noticeable component of it. The 1975 resettlement of about 130,000 people had been followed by arrivals of 20,000 or less in each of the three following years, but the number of arrivals from Southeast Asia rose to around 80,000 in 1979 and more than doubled the next year. These new refugees came from a broad range of ethnic, linguistic, economic, and social backgrounds. Many were relatively uneducated, and some were not literate. For many, exodus was far more traumatic than it had been for earlier arrivals. Escapes by land and sea were extremely hazardous, and many died. Many also spent long periods in refugee camps in Southeast Asia, with inevitable aftereffects such as missed schooling, strained family ties, and enduring uncertainty about the future. By 1980 it was clear that more refugees would be having serious adjustment problems after arrival and, given the larger numbers, that more of them would be "slipping through the cracks."

The second reason for change was the passage of the Refugee Act of 1980. For many years refugee advocates had argued that the U.S. should move beyond its concern with those fleeing communism and accept the standard international definition of the United Nations Convention (1951) and Protocol (1967) on refugees. That definition specified that in legal terms, a refugee was someone who had fled his or her own country because of a well-founded fear of persecution on five specific grounds: nationality, race, religion, political opinion, and membership in a particular social group. Refugee advocates and program personnel had also long argued for administrative improvements to the U.S. refugee program, especially a clearer allocation of responsibilities among federal agencies (particularly between the Department of State and what is now the Department of Health and Human Services), among federal, state, and local levels of government, and between the public and private sectors. These concerns were addressed in the Refugee Act of 1980, which accepted the UN refugee definition, clarified program responsibilities, and legislated a wide range of other program adjustments. One new requirement was an annual consultation process between the president and Congress to set the admissions level for refugees for the following year. The Refugee Act set the base planning estimate at 50,000 admissions per year. That number was less than a third of the number of refugees who were arriving that year from Southeast Asia alone, which suggests that while there was an intent to improve the program, there was also an intent to reduce it.

The Refugee Act of 1980 broadened the definition of "refugee," tightened the administration of the program, and aimed to reduce the number of refugees as well. Whether that mix of goals could have been achieved is unknown, because of the third reason that the situation changed in 1980: the mass arrival of Cubans and Haitians in Florida. On April 1, 1980, a busload of Cubans entered the Peruvian embassy in Havana seeking asylum. When they were granted temporary asylum, Castro allowed another estimated 10,000 asylum-seekers onto the embassy grounds. On April 21, he announced that anyone who wished to leave Cuba could do so from the port of Mariel. Ultimately some 125,000 Cubans arrived in the U.S. that year. They were joined in Florida by some 11,000 Haitians who made the longer boat escape from Haiti. The Refugee Act's stipulations collapsed. Instead, an entirely new legal status was created for these people: "Cuban-Haitian Entrant Status Pending."

This large group, combined with the even larger number of Southeast Asian arrivals that year, helped to create for the first and only time in U.S. history a set of refugees who were not simply a modest segment of immigration but a major and highly visible component of it. Furthermore, these new arrivals had a wide range of problems, including English-language limitations, health concerns, and sharp cultural differences. There were also enough cases of serious problems (criminals among the Cubans, AIDS among the Haitians) to provoke media attention, and sufficiently different treatment of Cubans and Haitians to raise concerns about racism in U.S. refugee policy.

At roughly the same time, unrest and civil war in Central America caused increasing numbers of people, especially from El Salvador and Guatemala, to cross into the U.S. illegally. Unlike the Cubans, they were fleeing not from communist governments but from governments that were U.S. allies. Thus fewer among them were granted refugee status, even though the refugee standard in U.S. law was now no longer formally tied to anticommunism. One result was a burgeoning sanctuary movement. Sanctuary activists argued that it was morally and legally imperative to recognize these people as refugees. By 1984 some 150 churches were actively providing sanctuary to Central American refugees. In the following year the U.S. government brought leaders of this movement to trial, but a broad consortium of refugee advocates initiated a legal case (*American Baptist Churches [ABC] et al.* v. *Richard Thornburgh* et al.) that eventually gave many Central American refugees additional chances to have their cases heard and reviewed.

Many of these problems continued throughout the 1980s and 1990s. Legal status for those who had fled Central America was still in dispute even after the provisions of the 1996 Nicaraguan Adjustment and Central American Relief Act. Concerns that Haitians were not treated as fairly as Cubans lingered even after passage of the 1998 Haitian Refugee Immigration Fairness Act. Despite such problems, by the mid-1990s U.S. refugee admissions had come in many ways to resemble the program envisioned by the 1980 Refugee Act. Flows finally came under 100,000, and the origins of refugees were more evenly balanced around the globe. Somalis and Sudanese, for example, accounted respectively for 5,000 and 6,000 admissions in fiscal year 2001, compared to an entire African contingent of fewer than 3,000 in 1981. During that 20-year period, Africans increased from less than 2 percent to over 25 percent of refugee arrivals. Aggregate data on refugee arrivals since 1990 (see Table 1) underscore diversity not only in terms of region but in terms of specific countries of origin. Increasingly, as well, refugee status was based on individual determinations that people met the UN refugee definition rather than simply being people of particular political interest to the United States.

The relative balance and stability of the refugee program, however, were badly

Table 1   Refugee arrivals by nationality, 1990–2002

Nationality	Number	Percentage of total
Afghan	12,559	1.08
Albanian	3,301	0.28
Angolan	145	0.01
Bosnian	144,430	12.37
Bulgarian	1,085	0.09
Burmese	2,256	0.19
Burundian	614	0.05
Chadian	73	0.01
Chinese	83	0.01
Congolese/Zairean	2,528	0.22
Croatian	6,083	0.52
Cuban	36,421	3.12
Czech	531	0.05
Ethiopian	18,989	1.63
Haitian	6,893	0.59
Hungarian	283	0.02
Indonesian	37	0.00
Iranian	30,071	2.58
Iraqi	32,073	2.75
Khmer	2,397	0.21
Lao: Highland	37,691	3.23
Lao: Lowland	7,822	0.67
Liberian	13,078	1.12
Libyan	354	0.03
Mozambican	24	0.00
Namibian	6	0.00
Nicaraguan	624	0.05
Nigerian	823	0.07
Polish	2,065	0.18
Rumanian	9,933	0.85
Rwandan	1,063	0.09
Salvadoran	31	0.00
Sierra Leonean	4,021	0.34
Somali	40,539	3.47
South African	78	0.01
Soviet/Former Soviet	414,554	35.51
Sudanese	18,415	1.58
Togolese	952	0.08
Ugandan	346	0.03
Vietnamese	297,175	25.46
Yugoslav	15,003	1.29
Other	1,875	0.16
Total	1,167,324	100.00

Source: U.S. Department of State, Office of Refugee Resettlement, *Annual Report to the Congress* (1993), p. 119; *Refugee Reports* 23, 9 (2002): 10–12.

shaken by the 2001 terrorist attacks. For security reasons, the program was in effect shut down for about two months. Those already approved for admission were stranded in refugee camps in other countries. Even after the moratorium was officially lifted, on November 21, 2001, processing remained slow. Only 27,000 refugees were admitted in fiscal year 2002—the lowest number of arrivals since 1978 and less than half of the planned figure of 70,000. Admissions for fiscal year 2003 were again about 27,000. In fiscal year 2004, when the program claimed to be fully operational again, there were only 53,000 arrivals—less than 60 percent of the average annual number of refugee arrivals from 1975 to 2000.

The Experience of the Refugees

Through these programmatic shifts and changes, expansions and contractions, a large number of people have come to America in ways and for reasons that are at least somewhat different from those of other new Americans. Their experience in the U.S. is thus both a part of the overall American immigration experience and in some ways a contrast to it.

For most, the path to the U.S. is lengthier, more dangerous, and more unpredictable than it is for other newcomers. Many refugees never expected to come to the U.S., and although they are almost universally grateful for the opportunity to be here, many would—circumstances permitting—rather be in their countries of origin with the many people they left behind or lost during exodus. Furthermore, after arriving, they are distributed very widely across the country (see Table 2). Although they often subsequently move (so-called secondary migration), at least in their initial settlement site they may be with very small numbers of compatriots. They must thus function in an alien environment without the full family and community resources that could provide practical and emotional support. Their memories of a lost home, lost kin, and lost community are painful, and the demands of the new country are forbidding because of age, lack of schooling, physical ailments, psychological trauma, and lack of experience in navigating the complex bureaucracies, dangerous streets, and loose community ties of the United States.

However, although the difficulties that refugees face may be unusual, many of the patterns of their adjustment mirror those of other immigrants. Over time, for example, refugees are able to join the U.S. labor market more effectively, obtaining jobs with greater success and at least sometimes with better wages. Many refugees have been adept at mixing employment and education to increase their future income potential. They may initially be limited in that effort by their lack of English-language skills, but a wide range of data indicates that those skills improve over time. The federal government's 2002 survey, for example, showed a strong aggregate increase in the percentage of refugees speaking English well, from only 11 percent at the time of arrival to 57 percent at the time of the survey. In progress toward better

Table 2   Refugee arrivals by state of initial resettlement, 1983–2002

State	Number	Percentage of total
Alabama	4,371	0.24
Alaska	778	0.04
Arizona	31,048	1.67
Arkansas	1,848	0.10
California	415,850	22.39
Colorado	18,774	1.01
Connecticut	19,314	1.04
Delaware	680	0.04
District of Columbia	12,293	0.66
Florida	218,076	11.74
Georgia	45,510	2.45
Hawai'i	4,007	0.22
Idaho	8,064	0.43
Illinois	71,057	3.83
Indiana	7,471	0.40
Iowa	18,245	0.98
Kansas	9,870	0.53
Kentucky	16,106	0.87
Louisiana	12,165	0.65
Maine	4,600	0.25
Maryland	28,270	1.52
Massachusetts	55,049	2.96
Michigan	40,770	2.19
Minnesota	45,827	2.47
Mississippi	1,463	0.08
Missouri	31,824	1.71
Montana	930	0.05
Nebraska	9,574	0.52
Nevada	8,477	0.46
New Hampshire	5,559	0.30
New Jersey	35,693	1.92
New Mexico	6,676	0.36
New York	240,853	12.97
North Carolina	18,027	0.97
North Dakota	6,011	0.32
Ohio	27,744	1.49
Oklahoma	6,848	0.37
Oregon	31,415	1.69
Pennsylvania	53,877	2.90
Rhode Island	6,412	0.35
South Carolina	2,006	0.11
South Dakota	4,662	0.25
Tennessee	18,862	1.02
Texas	93,840	5.05
Utah	15,425	0.83
Vermont	4,192	0.23

Table 2   (continued)

State	Number	Percentage of total
Virginia	34,665	1.87
Washington	81,103	4.37
West Virginia	399	0.02
Wisconsin	19,949	1.07
Wyoming	155	0.01
Unknown	888	0.05
Total	1,857,572	100.00

Source: U.S. Office of Refugee Resettlement, *Annual Report,* FY 2002. The starting date reflects the completion of a new refugee data system in response to the Refugee Act of 1980. Also note that the number of "unknown" in the original table is a typographical error and is corrected here.

education and better jobs, the social support of family and community is essential. Many refugees, like other immigrants, have strong family ties that lay the basis for extended-family households that can mix employment, education, and child-rearing tasks in ways that are not possible in the smaller, more nuclear households of most native-born Americans. When the U.S. economy is strong, as it was at the end of the 1990s, the portrait of refugee economic adaptation can be very positive. The federal government's 2002 survey, for example, indicates significant increases in labor force participation over time, and clear decreases in unemployment as well (see Table 3). Even if the most recent arrivals are included in the analysis, refugee labor force participation at that time was nearly as high as among the general U.S. population. For refugees who had been in the U.S. for at least three years, labor force participation was actually higher than among the general U.S. population.

Such general patterns mask the specific experiences of particular refugee groups. Cubans and Vietnamese, the largest refugee populations, make an interesting comparison. Despite many differences, both sets of refugees come from communist countries with which the U.S. has had particularly bitter relations. Both have developed fairly dense concentrations in certain parts of the country, despite initial government efforts to disperse them widely. Both Cubans and Vietnamese have also prospered in educational and economic terms. The claims of success may be overstated, but a wide range of census and survey data show both populations doing relatively well—certainly better than many other refugee groups. Finally, both populations remain remarkably politicized, reflecting the ideological opposition to communism that originally lay at the core of the U.S. refugee program. Displaying a picture of Fidel Castro in Miami or of Ho Chi Minh in Westminster, California, still elicits a negative and sometimes violent response.

These refugee populations also highlight the extent of diversity in the refugee experience. Cubans, for example, have always exhibited a range of class and racial backgrounds, which was amplified by the Mariel exodus of 1980. Furthermore, de-

Table 3 Employment status of recent refugee arrivals, 2002

Year of arrival	Labor force participation			Unemployment		
	All	Male	Female	All	Male	Female
1997	68.4	74.0	62.9	4.4	5.2	3.6
1998	71.7	73.0	70.0	2.1	1.5	2.8
1999	72.9	77.2	68.5	7.6	7.4	8.0
2000	61.3	70.6	52.4	8.0	10.8	5.3
2001	69.0	78.0	58.5	9.1	8.7	9.9
2002	51.6	50.9	42.5	11.1	10.5	13.9
Average for all years	67.1	72.3	61.3	6.4	6.8	6.1
U.S. rates	67.8	74.8	61.3	5.8	5.9	5.6

Source: U.S. Office of Refugee Resettlement, *Annual Report,* FY 2002.

spite their concentration in Miami, there are Cubans in many other parts of the country. Their experience in places where their presence is less noticeable is often very different from the Miami experience. Likewise, Vietnamese society has great internal diversity, and the experience of Vietnamese in different parts of the U.S. has often varied. In terms of background characteristics, for example, there is strong representation of both Catholics and Buddhists and of minority groups, whether hill tribes from Vietnam's extensive uplands or ethnic Chinese from the cities and towns. Refugees come from the whole country, including many northern Vietnamese who moved south in 1954, following the First Indochina War (against the French), only to flee again in 1975 at the conclusion of the Second Indochina War (against the United States).

Yet there is still more diversity in the refugee experience in America. Refugee groups that have exceeded 10,000 arrivals over the past decade include Afghans, Bosnians and others from the former Yugoslavia, Cubans, Ethiopians, Hmong (the major highland Lao group), Iranians, Iraqis, Liberians, Russians and those from other parts of the former Soviet Union, Somalis, Sudanese, and Vietnamese (see Table 1). Many of these populations are diverse in ethnic and religious affiliation. Thus, any discussion of Iranians immediately yields further distinctions among Iranians who are Baha'i, Christian, Jewish, or Muslim. Discussion of former Soviet refugees requires attention to both Jews and evangelical Christians as well as all the countries that have emerged out of the former Soviet Union. Earlier discussion of Ethiopian refugees now yields to separate discussions of Ethiopians and Eritreans. Consideration of refugees' own conceptions of their identity highlights this diverse mix of backgrounds. A question about ethnicity in the federal government's annual survey of refugees, for example, usually elicits conventional ethnic and national categories (e.g., Iranian, Cambodian, Hmong) but also sometimes identifications based on religious affiliation and race.

As a final example, consider a set of 12,000 Africans who began arriving in 2003. The refugees were originally from Somalia, but they were hardly Somali in any standard national or ethnic sense. Instead they were Bantu people who had in centuries past been trafficked as labor from countries to the south into Somalia. Often originally slaves, they eventually became small-farm holders. They were adversely affected by the collapse of public order in Somalia in the early 1990s and fled to Kenya. After some 10 years in refugee camps there—where they were often victimized by non-Bantu Somali refugees—they were accepted for admission to the U.S. Illiterate and lacking relevant job skills, they will have a difficult experience in the U.S. economically.

The Response to Refugees

The American response to refugees has been as varied as the refugees themselves. Much of it reflects the broader context of immigration, of which refugees are a very small part—roughly a tenth, on average, over the past 30 years, although much smaller since 9/11. Periodic polls suggest that Americans are usually aware of the contributions that immigrants make but also concerned that there may now be too many immigrants from too many places. The reaction to refugees, however, also often reflects strong feelings about the countries from which they come. When most refugees came from communist countries, there was much popular support for them, since they were "voting with their feet" for the American system versus the communist one. In contrast, refugees from Cambodia, Laos, and Vietnam were reminders of failed American efforts, which elicited strong support from those who had fought with them but unpleasant memories about a war many wished to forget.

The American response to refugees has two features that merit more detailed attention. One is the direct involvement of the government in admitting refugees and overseeing their initial adjustment; the other is Americans' extensive personal involvement with refugees and the refugee program.

Although it has often been suggested that the U.S. should be more active—and even more forceful—in the Americanization of immigrants, the government's current role regarding immigrants after arrival is quite limited. By contrast, its role regarding refugees is very detailed. For example, the government, in cooperation with voluntary agencies, decides where refugees will live initially, ensures that their health is monitored, decides what special cash and medical assistance should be available to them, allocates money for language and employment training, and has conducted a wide range of research on what factors hasten or retard their adjustment. The result is a level of social planning that is uncharacteristic of American government and thus a rich source of practical information on what more extensive Americanization programs might be like.

For example, there has been extensive debate on the appropriate mix and timing of education and employment. As the Refugee Act was being developed in the late 1970s, many argued that in the long run it was better to invest in early language, vocational, and even professional training. Such an approach, they believed, would increase refugee earnings and thus even the taxes they would pay. Others argued that refugees should go to work as soon as possible, lessening the immediate costs to the government in providing educational support and other transitional assistance. The early-employment proponents generally won the debate, partly because of their ideological consistency with efforts at so-called welfare reform. Indeed, the period of eligibility for special refugee cash and medical assistance—designed to address predictable needs for transitional assistance—shrank rapidly, from 3 years in 1981, to 18 months in 1982, to 12 months in 1988, to 8 months in 1991. Yet for refugees, the results of this emphasis on early employment have often been negative. Achieving rapid self-sufficiency has often meant that households manage by having several adults working at low-paying jobs. Families with many young children or those headed by a single parent—both of which are common among refugees—face particularly severe problems in adopting such a strategy. One casualty may be the education that would increase their earnings in the future, either for the refugees or for their children.

The American involvement with refugee adjustment is also of interest because of its organizational complexity. Multiple federal agencies, state governments, and an often complicated mix of county and municipal governments play roles. Furthermore, much of the effort is made by voluntary agencies, some faith-based and some secular, some focusing on all refugees and some on particular national or ethnic groups, some composed of the native-born and some of former refugees themselves. The U.S. refugee program is thus an important case study in how the relative roles and responsibilities of the public and private sectors can be synchronized. In the case of refugees, the private sector is the senior partner in terms of program origins, but the government is clearly now the stronger partner in terms of program direction and funding. The net result may be a usefully eclectic involvement of the public and private, the national and local. The system does, however, hold the potential for inconsistency and confusion.

Involvement with refugees goes well beyond the formal organizational level and into the very heart of American communities. Particularly during the Southeast Asian refugee crisis, many citizens directly sponsored refugees as part of religious groups, as part of other kinds of community groups, and sometimes simply as concerned individuals. At times this was a direct manifestation of religious commitment (sometimes with explicit or implicit pressures toward conversion), and at other times it was a more neighborly reaching out to people in need, often with recognition of and remorse for the extent to which the forces that uprooted the refugees were fueled by the U.S. Over time, those open arms have sometimes closed; "compassion fatigue" has set in. Initially supportive attitudes sometimes turn negative as refugees lag in their economic progress or seem to dwell too much on the past.

Problems and Prospects

The American experience with refugees and the refugee experience with Americans have often been good. The relationship, however, has not always been easy. One fundamental problem is that the U.S., like other nation-states, prefers to have orderly procedures for people crossing its borders, whereas the refugee experience is inherently disorderly. By definition, refugees are uprooted and out of their proper place. If they flee, can reach a place of temporary refuge, have access to U.S. or UN officials, and can prove they meet the refugee definition, then much will flow smoothly. They can be processed in an orderly fashion, come to the U.S. with proper documentation, and find the transitional support provided by public and private organizations. But a great deal can go wrong. It is difficult, for example, to prove a fear of persecution if the country from which you have fled denies the charges and has taken from you any documentation that might support your claim.

In many cases, it is not possible for refugees to establish their legal case in a regular fashion overseas. It may not even be possible to contact officials to whom they could present their case. One option, then, is to try to enter the U.S. first and then make a claim for legal asylum. (In U.S. legal terminology, refugees and asylees must meet the same standard, but refugee status is conferred before arrival and asylee status after arrival.) It is possible to make a claim for asylum at a land border or airport, but the chances of being denied entry are high, and there is a risk of being imprisoned—especially given the strictures of the 1996 Illegal Immigration Reform and Immigrant Responsibility Act. To avoid those consequences, an asylum-seeker can enter the country illegally and claim asylum when he or she has better access to legal counsel and the full protections of the U.S. judicial system (even though that too has become more difficult under the asylum-related strictures of the Real ID Act of 2005). Those seeking to enter without documentation often become part of the increasingly lucrative—and sometimes deadly—trafficking of people across U.S. borders. As the U.S. attempts to combat illegal border crossing, it is thus also combating those seeking asylum.

Even those refugees who have been interviewed and recognized as legal refugees encounter problems. Refugee processing was greatly slowed after the 9/11 attacks. People already approved for resettlement were stalled overseas. For those not yet approved, delays may be even greater, since a return to the high entry levels of earlier years seems unlikely. The very fact that refugees are people out of place makes them a focus for increased suspicion in times of heightened national security—especially if they come from areas associated with terrorism. Suspicion of newcomers is rising, and any faltering in the U.S. economy is likely to strongly affect those who are newest to the labor market and who have marginal employment and language skills.

For refugees who have been in the country longer, the prospects are brighter, both for themselves and for their children. For many, the cumulative efforts of two generations have paved the way for relative economic security and some measure of integration into American life. Some, such as Afghans, Cambodians, and even some of the DPs from just after World War II, have the opportunity for renewed participation in their countries of origin, whose borders are now open to former refugees and whose governments may actively desire their involvement in reconstruction. For other refugees, however, relative economic success in the U.S. cannot fully dissipate the pain of loss of home and country. The irrevocability of the decision to flee and the hazards—and sometimes horrors—of flight leave a residue that marks their experience in America as a distinctive intertwining of loss and perseverance, despair and hope, dreams of the past and demands of the future.

Bibliography

Daniel, E. Valentine, and John Chr. Knudsen, eds. *Mistrusting Refugees.* Berkeley: University of California Press, 1995.

Einolf, Christopher J. *The Mercy Factory: Refugees and the American Asylum System.* Chicago: Ivan R. Dee, 2001.

Fadiman, Anne. *The Spirit Catches You and You Fall Down.* New York: Noonday, 1997.

Foner, Nancy, ed. *The New Immigrants.* Boston: Allyn & Bacon.

Haines, David W., ed. *Refugees in America in the 1990s: A Reference Handbook.* Westport, Conn.: Greenwood, 1996.

Haines, David W., and Carol A. Mortland, eds. *Manifest Destinies: Americanizing Immigrants and Internationalizing Americans.* Westport, Conn.: Praeger, 2001.

Helton, Arthur C. *The Price of Indifference: Refugees and Humanitarian Action in the New Century.* New York: Oxford University Press, 2002.

Loescher, Gil. *Beyond Charity: International Cooperation and the Global Refugee Crisis.* New York: Oxford University Press, 1993.

Martin, David. *The United States Refugee Admission Program: Reforms for a New Era of Refugee Resettlement.* Washington, D.C.: Migration Policy Institute, U.S. Department of State, 2004.

Robinson, W. Courtland. *Terms of Refuge: The Indochinese Exodus and the International Response.* New York: Zed Books, 1998.

U.S. Committee for Refugees. *World Refugee Survey.* Washington, D.C. Annual.

U.S. Department of Health and Human Services. *Report to the Congress: Refugee Resettlement Program.* Washington, D.C.: Office of Refugee Resettlement. Annual.

Wyman, David S. *Paper Walls: America and the Refugee Crisis, 1938–1941.* New York: Pantheon, 1968.

Wyman, Mark. *DP: Europe's Displaced Persons, 1945–1951.* Ithaca, N.Y.: Cornell University Press, 1998.

Zucker, Norman L., and Naomi Flink Zucker. *Desperate Crossings: Seeking Refuge in America.* New York: M. E. Sharpe, 1996.

Unauthorized Migration

Frank D. Bean and B. Lindsay Lowell

Understanding unauthorized migration requires clarifying what constitutes immigration. The first point to note in this regard is that the word "immigration" has an official connotation. That is, an immigrant is someone who has been granted legal permanent residence by a national government, or formal permission to live and (usually) work in a given country. An immigrant is thus not identical to an international migrant, because the latter may move from one country to another without being granted a visa. From a legal point of view, tourists, students, temporary workers, and people who either cross borders illegally or stay beyond their legally allotted time limits are not immigrants; rather, they are international migrants. The second point is that individuals may become immigrants through processes of settlement. By this criterion, international migrants who have lived in a country for quite some time, even though they entered or stayed illegally, can also be immigrants. In this essay, immigrants are defined as persons who have established long-term residence in a country, whether or not they have done so on a legal basis.

This consideration of immigration emphasizes a behavioral basis for residence. As many observers have noted, the numbers of so-called illegal immigrants in this sense appear to be increasing in many countries, especially in those with advanced industrial and postindustrial economies, and apparently the largest number of such people live in the United States. But the phrase "illegal immigrant" is arguably inaccurate when applied in the U.S. case. As an alternative, the term "unauthorized migrant" is employed here to refer to persons who reside in the U.S. but whose status is not that of U.S. citizens, permanent residents, or other authorized visitors. Various labels have been applied to unauthorized migrants, including "undocumenteds," "illegals," "illegal aliens," and "illegal immigrants." Each of these has a somewhat different meaning and connotation. The word "undocumented" is not entirely appropriate, because many contemporary unauthorized migrants possess documents, although usually counterfeit ones. The term "illegal" does not exactly fit, because the U.S. expressly made it legal to hire such people before the Immigration Reform and Control Act (IRCA) was passed in 1986. Moreover, the federal government since then has not systematically enforced the provisions of IRCA that make it illegal to hire such workers.

Apart from these characteristics of unauthorized migrants, what are some of the other most important features of this population in the U.S.? The first is the group's large size, estimated at around 11.1 million people in 2005, a figure up from about 2.5 million in 1990. Unauthorized migrants constituted about 30 percent of all immigrants of any kind in the country in 2005. The second is that most of the people in this population enter the country at the U.S.-Mexico border, where they cross undetected as "EWIs," to use official government jargon for those who "enter without inspection." An unknown minority (but probably only about one fourth to one third) enter legally and then overstay a visa. The few data available on visa overstays indicate that such individuals do not come from just a few countries but are spread among many countries of origin. Also, those who overstay visas often do not stay permanently in the U.S. Their effects on the country are thus probably minimal. In any case, because of the lack of data, it is almost impossible to draw conclusions about the characteristics and impacts of those who overstay visas, particularly those from a given country. The third characteristic is that most EWIs are people of very low education whose reason for coming to the U.S. is a strong desire to work. That is, they are overwhelmingly labor migrants, both in number and in motive. Their success in finding employment is due not only to the fact that they are inexpensive (i.e., they constitute low-wage labor) but also to the fact that they do jobs that employers do not want to pay higher wages for and that native Americans are unwilling to do at the low wages paid.

Finally, most (about three fifths) of these unauthorized migrants are Mexicans; the next largest national-origin group, Salvadorans, is barely one tenth as large. Hence, to speak of unauthorized migration in the U.S., the leading destination country in the world in terms of relative numbers and the nation arguably containing the most unauthorized immigrants, is for all practical purposes to refer to Mexican labor migrants. Thus, just as to talk about U.S. immigration without making a distinction between legal and unauthorized migration would risk vastly oversimplifying the reality of the U.S. immigration experience, to focus on unauthorized migration without devoting paramount attention to the Mexican case would fail to acknowledge that Mexicans not only dominate unauthorized migration flows but also drive U.S. policy debates about international migration, whether the specific issue at hand involves legal immigration, unauthorized migration, or temporary guest worker programs. Hence, the rest of this essay concentrates on unauthorized Mexican migration to the United States.

The Mexican Case

The U.S. has long experienced a love-hate relationship with unauthorized migration, particularly unauthorized migration from Mexico. A good example of this ambivalence can be found in the now eliminated contradictions embedded in the so-called Texas proviso, a quirk of U.S. immigration law that made it legal for nearly 30 years to hire unauthorized workers (for example, to employ them to take care of your lawn) but illegal to harbor them (for example, to invite them into your home for a drink of water). Unauthorized migration has also received significant media attention, frequently galvanized public opinion, and attracted the attention of U.S. policymakers. This is illustrated by four special governmental initiatives mounted to address immigration issues directly. First, in 1981 the Select Commission on Immigration and Refugee Policy (SCIRP) released its report, noting that "one issue has emerged as most pressing—the problem of undocumented/illegal migration." Second, in 1986 Congress passed the Immigration Reform and Control Act in an effort to reduce unauthorized migration. Third, in 1994 the U.S. Commission on Immigration Reform issued its first report calling for policies to increase legal but reduce unauthorized migration. Fourth, in 1996 Congress passed welfare reform and immigration legislation partly in an effort to curtail unauthorized migration by limiting the public benefits available to noncitizen immigrants.

The frequent obsession in the U.S. with unauthorized Mexican migration unfortunately distorts views of immigration policy. Many observers ignore a vast research literature on unauthorized migration and focus almost exclusively on how many unauthorized Mexican migrants reside in this country. For example, in a front-page story about the results of the Mexico-U.S. Binational Migration Study, the *New York Times* in 1997 emphasized only the study's research findings about the size of this population. This imbalance is also reflected in the fact that policymakers often focus on immigration in general or on unauthorized Mexican migration in particular but pay little heed to legal Mexican immigration. For instance, the two largest immigration-related studies sponsored by the U.S. Commission on Immigration Reform during the 1990s focused on the demographic and economic effects of immigration in general (in a major 1997 National Research Council study) and on unauthorized Mexican migration (in the Binational Migration Study). In a similar vein, Congress has often focused its attention on "controlling" unauthorized migration, even concentrating recent legislative initiatives on border enforcement rather than on legalization or settlement (integration) issues.

In reflecting on the misperceptions that have often characterized U.S. approaches to unauthorized Mexican migration from a policy point of view over the past 30 years, we should perhaps emphasize that unauthorized migrants differ in how long they stay in the U.S. For observers to avoid misunderstanding evidence about migration flows, it is particularly crucial to recall distinctions based on duration of stay, such as that between temporary and permanent migrants (or sojourners and settlers, to use the more sociological vocabulary). Much of the historical and current debate about unauthorized migration derives from differences in perceptions about whether sojourners or settlers dominate such flows. Insofar as the unauthorized migrant population is made up of sojourners, return migrants represent outflows that may offset inflows. Outflow is a critical component, because in the case of unauthorized Mexican migrants, the majority of entrances have often been offset by exits, at least until recently, as indicated by estimates of repeat entrances and net inflows. During the 1970s many observers mistook substantial numbers of border apprehensions as an indication of large net inflows. By failing to account for outflow, however, such observers greatly exaggerated the rate of growth of the unauthorized migrant population. In effect, the error was to assume that there were more settlers than sojourners, when in fact the opposite was the case. Similarly, during the 1990s and more recently, increased border enforcement policies have failed to anticipate that such policies themselves will increase the size of the unauthorized population living in the country by discouraging return migration.

Historical and Economic Background to Mexican Migration

What historical and economic background factors have led to such a high current public-policy profile for unauthorized Mexican migration? Until recently, Mexican migration, compared with that from other nations, was not particularly large, and in practice, if not always in law, was relatively unrestricted, with exceptions such as the repatriation of large numbers of Mexican migrants in the 1930s and again in 1954. Compared with the huge immigrations from Europe in the last half of the 19th century and the first decades of the 20th century, Mexican immigration contributed only a small part of U.S. population growth until relatively recently. Its pre–World War II peak occurred in the 1920s, when the economic disruptions of the Mexican Revolution (1910–1920) and the civil dislocations that followed led many Mexicans, with the assistance of U.S. labor recruiters, to migrate to the U.S. in search of jobs, often in railroad construction and maintenance. In the 1920s, 459,000 Mexicans were registered as immigrating to the U.S., equivalent to 3.2 percent of the total Mexican population in 1921. Such numbers were not to be surpassed until the 1970s, but they were not viewed as exceptional in their time. Not only was Mexican migration not seen as particularly voluminous, but much of it was temporary in nature. Partly as a result, Mexican immigrants have had one of the lowest naturalization rates of any immigrant group to the U.S.

Until the 1960s, Mexican immigrants were predominantly employed in work that was temporary and seasonal in nature. The rapid expansion of California agriculture depended on a seasonal labor force. Fruit and vegetable production did not offer year-round employment and consequently was attractive only to the newest entrants into the labor force, immigrant or not, who had no other sources of employment. For most workers in California, seasonal work in agriculture was a step toward finding more permanent work either in the rural areas or in the cities. Thus, turnover was high. The difficulties of recruiting workers from California's resident population made Mexican migrant labor an attractive option for farmers. It was also attractive for the migrants themselves, who could earn much higher wages than they could in Mexico and could save enough to maintain their families in their home villages and at times to invest in land or animals. As long as the Mexican migrants wished to return to Mexico, the arrangement suited both sides. Until the 1970s, most Mexican migrants did in fact wish to return, but in the last three decades of the 20th century, Mexican immigration both increased in volume and increasingly involved permanent immigration. A major reason for this shift was and continues to be the gradual erosion of the economic viability of small-scale agriculture in Mexico, a change that has at once promoted migration to large metropolitan areas within Mexico and discouraged those who migrate to the U.S. from returning to and investing in small-town and rural Mexican enterprises.

Other transformations in Mexican economic conditions and policies also took place over this time, especially during the 1980s, when Mexico's approach toward economic development underwent a major revision. Before the 1980s, the postwar model of development adopted and implemented in the country involved what was called import substitution industrialization (ISI). In terms of delivering overall economic growth, in the Mexican case the policy succeeded. Gross domestic product increased by some 5 to 6 percent a year for three decades, from the 1950s through the 1970s. However, the benefits of the growth were not equitably distributed, and Mexico's income distribution became even more skewed in favor of upper-income families. Emigration from Mexico to the U.S. was substantial during all of this high-growth period, presumably in part because poverty persisted, particularly in rural areas, and there were inadequate opportunities for those who shared only marginally in the overall economic growth. The "push-pull" factors that explain much of the migration were evident. Migration networks and patterns that had been established during the *bracero* program, which allowed temporary agricultural workers into the country legally between 1942 and 1964, became institutionalized and consolidated during the ISI period.

The strong economic growth generated by the substitution policy began to stall during the 1970s. Thanks to high oil prices following the 1973–1974 Yom Kippur War and easy loans from foreign lenders, however, Mexico did not encounter major difficulties until 1982, when oil revenues declined and U.S. and world interest rates rose sharply. The old development model no longer appeared to work. Other than oil, which in 1982 accounted for 72 percent of the value of exports, Mexican products were not competitive in export markets. One option would have been to default on external loans, but the country chose instead to reschedule them. Mexico could have deepened the ISI model and even expanded the already substantial role of government enterprises in the economy, as some Mexicans advocated. But this was rejected, probably because it would have had to be accompanied by debt repudiation under difficult circumstances and conditions imposed by foreign creditors.

The third main option, which was selected, was to change the model in the direction of building an export economy. In 1986, Mexico acceded to the General Agreement on Tariffs and Trade (GATT), but improvements in economic performance came slowly. The new export-led recovery model required a reduction in the cost of imported goods, particularly intermediate products making up the bulk of Mexican merchandise imports, in order not to burden exporters unduly. By the time negotiations for Mexican participation in the North American Free Trade Agreement (NAFTA) took place, the trade-weighted Mexican import tariff averaged 11 percent. Even more significantly, import licensing was reduced and then eliminated in the NAFTA agreement, which was signed by the three North American governments in late 1992. The policy of free trade under NAFTA formally went into operation on January 1, 1994. Shortly after December 20, 1994, when Mexico decided to devalue the peso by about 15 percent, investors realized that the amount of outstanding Mexican dollar-indexed, short-term treasury obligations, called *tesobonos,* was several times greater than Mexico's foreign reserves.

The economic consequences were severe, and the Mexican authorities were forced to devote most of their time in 1995 to dealing with the financial and economic fallout. GDP in 1995 fell by 6.9 percent. Real wages declined by about 15 percent and urban unemployment rose by about 2 million people. By early 1996 the financial situation had stabilized: the peso was steady, the stock market was high, and Mexico was able to borrow on world money markets. Led by the export sector, the Mexican economy has continued to perform quite well, with overall growth rates in GDP of around 5 percent per year, in considerable measure because of the strength of the U.S. economy, since the U.S. made up the market for much of Mexico's exports. Thus, after a rocky start, Mexico seems to have made a successful transition to a new economic growth model, although the global economic slowdown that started in 2001 and increasing competition with low-cost manufacturing in China and elsewhere continues to place strains on the country's economy. In any case, the economic difficulties that led to NAFTA can be said to have been followed by a period of fairly strong Mexican economic growth.

Conditions in the United States

The juncture of the economic crisis in Mexico in the early 1980s and the coterminous rising volume of Mexican migration to the U.S. coincided with a shift in U.S. immigration policy in which unauthorized migration became a critical, if not always explicit, issue. Other changes in the flows of immigrants in the 1970s and

1980s, particularly increases in immigration from Asia, played a part in changing immigration policy. The result was the 1986 Immigration Reform and Control Act, which remains the primary U.S. legislation directly targeted at limiting unauthorized migration. IRCA and the policy debates around it were substantially affected by the peculiar challenge posed by unauthorized Mexican immigration. Legislators, confronted with the reality of millions of unauthorized persons residing in the U.S. and the prospects of many more following them, sought in IRCA both to recognize the de facto situation of Mexican migrant settlement (through legalization) and to limit the labor market's demand for further unauthorized migration (through employer sanctions). As various observers have pointed out, NAFTA was, in its political justification and consequences if not its intent, an arm of the strategy embedded in IRCA. Many legislators hoped that increased trade between the two countries might have the effect of reducing unauthorized migration by increasing job growth in Mexico. What has not been previously emphasized is that IRCA's failure to stem unauthorized migration, except for the probably spurious reductions occurring during the first couple of years after it was passed, helped to create political conditions in the U.S. favorable to the passage of NAFTA.

If IRCA failed to curtail unauthorized migration, the same was true of NAFTA. The number of gross apprehensions of Mexicans attempting to enter the U.S. illegally during the first year after the 1994 Mexican peso devaluation rose nearly 40 percent (see Table 1). But factors besides the peso devaluation also contributed to the increase: lower overall U.S. unemployment rates (from 6.6 percent to 5.6 percent over the period); appreciably higher aggregate U.S. employment from the beginning of 1994 to early 1995; and more hours devoted to border enforcement. These factors alone, independent of increases in line-watch hours (net hours spent by border agents watching the border), accounted for as much as two thirds of the increase in apprehensions of Mexican migrants during 1995. Thus, economic conditions in the U.S. affected Mexican emigration fluctuations as much as conditions in Mexico after the peso devaluation. The strength of the U.S. economy also continued to work its influence during the latter half of the 1990s, when substantial increases in the size of the Mexican-born population, including its unauthorized segment, occurred. These increases were consistent with changes in annual apprehension statistics, the levels of which rose steadily during the latter half of the 1990s, reaching new highs by the end of the decade.

Some of this increase in apprehensions undoubtedly resulted from higher levels of border enforcement, since the number of Border Patrol officers was nearly tripled. Interpreting such statistics is difficult, however, because the dynamics of border crossing and apprehension and of duration of stay among migrants changed substantially after 1993, when a new INS enforcement regime was conceived and implemented. The new approach involved saturating sectors of the border with additional Border Patrol agents, a practice that was first carried out in the El Paso sec-

Table 1   Southwest border (line-watch) apprehensions, officer hours, and apprehensions per
           officer hour, 1977–2003

Fiscal year	Apprehensions	Officer hours	Apprehensions per officer hour
1977	441,265	1,740,446	0.254
1978	481,612	1,762,616	0.273
1979	488,941	1,935,926	0.253
1980	428,966	1,815,797	0.236
1981	452,821	1,929,448	0.235
1982	443,437	1,871,173	0.237
1983	646,311	1,976,126	0.327
1984	623,944	1,843,179	0.339
1985	666,402	1,912,895	0.348
1986	946,341	2,401,575	0.394
1987	750,954	2,546,397	0.295
1988	614,653	2,069,498	0.297
1989	521,899	2,436,788	0.214
1990	668,282	2,549,137	0.262
1991	711,808	2,390,500	0.298
1992	814,290	2,386,888	0.341
1993	840,326	2,713,024	0.310
1994	687,163	3,074,060	0.224
1995	958,900	3,397,049	0.282
1996	1,114,089	4,073,542	0.273
1997	1,019,787	4,807,669	0.212
1998	1,185,831	6,650,692	0.178
1999	1,237,623	8,601,055	0.144
2000	1,354,356	8,905,352	0.152
2001	1,020,390	9,544,260	0.107
2002	778,606	9,397,940	0.083
2003	711,203	9,139,501	0.078

Source: Unpublished data provided by the Office of Immigration Statistics, Department of Homeland Security.

tor in 1993, in the San Diego sector in 1994, and then in other high-traffic sectors in Arizona and Texas in 1998 and 1999. Only a few low-traffic areas have never been covered by this strategy. But where such efforts took place, they resulted in a tripling of the number of officer line-watch hours from 1993 to 2000. Note also that this increase was accompanied by a substantial reduction in the average number of apprehensions per officer hour over this time.

Some analysts have claimed that this overall enforcement increase has coincided with a notable rise in inefficiency on the part of the Border Patrol, with more time and money being spent on enforcement and less being achieved in the way of results. However, this argument fails to consider that more officer hours might have deterred attempted crossings and might have resulted in a higher percentage of crossers being apprehended. To the degree that this actually happened, the average number of apprehensions per office hour would in fact have declined, in which case a reduction in the number of apprehensions per hour would represent successful deterrence (at least of attempted border crossings without papers) rather than enforcement inefficiency. This was what happened in the El Paso sector when the first saturation strategy, called Operation Hold-the-Line, was adopted and implemented in 1993. Only long-distance labor migrants appeared to continue to migrate (although only after having been diverted by Hold-the-Line to entry through other sectors), whereas the vast majority of other kinds of crossings at El Paso largely ceased, apparently deterred by the operation.

Table 2   Southwest border (line-watch) apprehensions per officer hour for sectors according to program type, 1977–2003

Fiscal year	Enhanced border program	No border program
1977	0.254	0.254
1978	0.273	0.273
1979	0.253	0.253
1980	0.236	0.236
1981	0.235	0.235
1982	0.237	0.237
1983	0.327	0.327
1984	0.339	0.339
1985	0.348	0.348
1986	0.394	0.394
1987	0.295	0.295
1988	0.297	0.297
1989	0.214	0.214
1990	0.262	0.262
1991	0.298	0.298
1992	0.341	0.341
1993	0.451	0.284
1994	0.268	0.176
1995	0.300	0.261
1996	0.242	0.310
1997	0.136	0.293
1998	0.146	0.234
1999	0.134	0.225
2000	0.142	0.230
2001	0.104	0.128
2002	0.084	0.078
2003	0.080	0.069

Source: Unpublished data provided by the Office of Immigration Statistics, Department of Homeland Security.

Table 3   Southwest border (line-watch) apprehensions by sectors according to program type,
             1992–2003

Fiscal year	Enhanced border program	No border program
1992	0	814,290
1993	189,408	650,918
1994	427,006	260,148
1995	558,139	400,761
1996	534,585	579,504
1997	337,367	682,420
1998	708,457	868,099
1999	1,024,720	212,903
2000	1,117,086	237,270
2001	858,794	161,596
2002	679,635	98,971
2003	603,512	107,691

Source: Unpublished data provided by the Office of Immigration Statistics, Department of Homeland Security.

Thus, a change in the meaning of "effectiveness" as applied to interpreting apprehension statistics at the border may be warranted. Fewer apprehensions could mean more effectiveness. That such a change took place is also suggested by the fact that by the end of the 1990s, the size of the Border Patrol along the southwest border (about 12,000 agents, as compared with approximately 3,000 at the beginning of the period) was approaching the 15,000 agents believed necessary to achieve a Hold-the-Line level of effectiveness along the entire 2,000-mile border. When we look at the apprehension pattern in those sectors with saturation programs, the average number of apprehensions per hour steadily declined as more saturation programs came on line during the 1990s (see Table 2), even as the overall number of apprehensions remained fairly high (see Table 3), implying that a much higher percentage of attempted crossers were initially being apprehended under the new saturation regime than under the old. But with the implementation of the last saturation programs in 1999, apprehensions steadily declined from 2000 to 2003, suggesting that potential crossers may have learned to seek other forms of entry. Of course, numerous other factors could have also contributed to this decline, including the election of President Vicente Fox in Mexico, the events of September 11, 2001, and the subsequent economic recession in the U.S. Time and further research will make clear the degree to which migrants have increasingly switched to ways of entering the U.S. other than attempting to cross the border without papers, possibilities that at the moment are supported more by anecdote than by statistical evidence.

What then accounted for the increases in the size of the unauthorized migrant population during the latter part of the 1990s and the early 2000s? Undoubtedly a substantial part of the increase was the result of some migrants staying in the U.S. for longer periods of time. Some undoubtedly also stemmed from continuing inflows, albeit perhaps from inflows occurring via forms of entry other than walking or wading across the border. The conclusion that seems most warranted is that the number of unauthorized Mexican migrants in the U.S. has increased in recent years for two major reasons. First, some of the growth (perhaps one half to two thirds) is due to longer stays, although factors other than greater border enforcement undoubtedly account for a large part of this. (The strong U.S. economy during the latter half of the 1990s and the continuing construction boom during the early 2000s, because of low interest rates, both encouraged longer stays.) Second, a large fraction (perhaps one third to one half) derives from weakness in the Mexican economy during the early 2000s. Whatever the reasons, growth in the number of unauthorized migrants in recent years seems to have continued almost as rapidly as before.

Looking to the Future

High unauthorized Mexican migration flows to the U.S. during the latter part of the 1990s and early 2000s, especially given that these occurred at a time when border enforcement was reaching its apex, have invited the conclusion that the program of border enforcement has been a failure and perhaps even futile from the beginning. However, this conclusion risks overlooking the fact that it was only around fiscal year 2000 that enough personnel were deployed at the border even to begin to make it possible for enforcement to be effective. Until that time, the number of officers had simply been too small for any effectiveness to be feasible. This is not to endorse border enforcement as the best policy instrument for dealing with unauthorized Mexican migration. Rather, it is simply to note that we cannot really evaluate whether border enforcement policies are working in the ways intended until enough officers have been assigned to give such policies a chance to work. But even when enough officers have been present to give such policies some possibility of effectiveness, unauthorized migrant flows have unquestionably continued, probably because migrants have found other ways to enter, either through legal means (subsequently overstaying their visas) or by using counterfeit documents. The twin results of dramatic declining apprehensions at the border since 2000 combined with the continued growth of the unauthorized Mexican population in the U.S. suggests that this may have occurred.

Some observers advocate continuing border enforcement efforts as stopgap measures until Mexican economic growth rates rise and birth rates decline enough to reduce Mexican migration. An important question for the future concerns the degree to which economic growth and declining fertility in Mexico might lead to reduced migration to the U.S. over the next two or three decades. Mexican birthrates have fallen precipitously over the past couple of decades, from an average of 6.1 children per woman in 1974 to 2.4 children per woman in 2000. These drops have been so steep that each of the past six or seven Mexican birth cohorts has been smaller than the one immediately preceding it, reversing the pattern of steady increases that occurred before. The number of people looking for employment in Mexico each year might thus stop growing and perhaps shrink sometime between 2010 and 2015. Moreover, if economic growth in Mexico were to reach the attainable but not unrealistic level of about 6 percent each year, the number of jobs could roughly equal the size of the workforce by 2010, a circumstance that has not held in the country for as long as anyone can remember. But with the slowdown in the growth of the Mexican manufacturing export sector because of the movement of such jobs to China, optimistic projections about job growth seem unlikely to be realized.

Even if they were, there are other reasons to think that Mexican migration will continue. First, so much migration has already occurred that it will continue to spawn more migration (this is the cumulative causation phenomenon noted by Massey and his colleagues). Second, further economic restructuring in Mexico and continuing relatively higher wages in the U.S. are likely to continue to foster migration, even if the demographic and economic pressures on finding employment in Mexico ease considerably. Thus, while certain kinds of forces inducing migration might lessen, other factors driving migration can be expected to continue to exert their influence.

Bibliography

Bean, Frank D., Jeffrey S. Passel, and Barry Edmonston. 1990. *Undocumented Migration to the United States: IRCA and the Experience of the 1980s.* Washington: Urban Institute Press.

Bean, Frank D., and Gillian Stevens. 2003. *America's Newcomers and the Dynamics of Diversity.* New York: Russell Sage Foundation.

Binational Study. 1997. *Report of the Binational Study on Migration.* Mexico City and Washington, D.C.: Mexican Ministry on Foreign Affairs and U.S. Commission on Immigration Reform.

Cornelius, Wayne, Takeyuki Tsuda, Philip L. Martin, and James F. Hollifield. 2004. *Controlling Immigration: A Global Perspective.* Stanford, Calif.: Stanford University Press.

Freeman, Gary P., and Frank D. Bean. 1997. "Mexico and U.S. Worldwide Immigration Policy." In F. D. Bean, R. O. de la Garza, B. R. Roberts, and S. Weintraub, eds., *At the Crossroads: Mexican Migration and U.S. Policy,* pp. 21–45. Lanham, Md.: Rowman and Littlefield.

Massey, Douglas, Jorge Durand, and Nolan J. Malone. 2002. *Beyond Smoke and Mirrors: Mexican Immigration in an Era of Economic Integration.* New York: Russell Sage Foundation.

Passel, Jeffrey S. 2005. "The Size and Characteristics of the Unauthorized Migrant Popula-

tion in the U.S.: Estimates Based on the March 2005 Current Population Survey."
Washington, D.C.: Pew Hispanic Center.

Reimers, David M. 2005. *Other Immigrants: The Global Origins of the American People.*
New York: New York University Press.

Tichenor, Daniel J. 2002. *Dividing Lines: The Politics of Immigration Control in America.*
Princeton, N.J.: Princeton University Press.

Weintraub, Sidney, ed. 2004. *NAFTA at Ten: Strengthening the North American Community.*
Washington, D.C.: Center for Strategic and International Studies.

Settlement Patterns in Metropolitan America

John R. Logan

The American metropolis is once again being reshaped by immigration. Although some immigrants—about 10 percent—can be found in rural America, the story of contemporary immigration is primarily about the cities and suburbs. The 2000 Census counted nearly 29 million immigrants living in metropolitan regions throughout the United States, up by 10 million since 1990. Nearly half of these (over 13.1 million) are Hispanics, mainly from Mexico but increasingly also from the Dominican Republic and Central and South America. The next largest share (7.9 million) are Asians, the only major racial/ethnic group that is predominantly immigrant (two out of three Asians were born abroad). A surprise to many Americans may be that almost as many non-Hispanic whites as Asians are foreign-born (6.4 million). The remaining 1.4 million immigrants are black, mostly from Haiti, Jamaica, and sub-Saharan Africa.

These counts are provided in Table 1, which shows the number of U.S.-born and foreign-born people in each major racial/ethnic category who lived within a metropolitan region in 1990 and 2000. Whites and blacks include only non-Hispanics, and Hispanics include people of any race. In 2000 the census questionnaire allowed people to list multiple races, so in order to compare with 1990 figures, blacks include those who listed their race as black alone or black and another race; Asians include those who listed Asian alone or Asian and another race except for black; and whites include those who listed white as their only race. A small number of Asians are Hispanic, and they are included in both the Asian and the Hispanic categories.

These four broad racial and ethnic categories are useful, but for many members of these groups, and perhaps especially for first-generation immigrants, their region or country of origin is more meaningful. People of the same broad race or ethnicity but from different origins often live in distinct regions of the U.S., and even within a single metropolitan area they may be found in somewhat different kinds of neighborhoods. (More detailed information about these subgroups can be found

Table 1 Native and immigrant populations in metropolitan areas, by race and Hispanic ethnicity

Population	Total		Native-born		Foreign-born	
	1990	2000	1990	2000	1990	2000
Hispanic	20,467,541	32,170,919	12,835,653 (62.7%)	19,003,663 (59.1%)	7,571,895 (37.0%)	13,167,256 (40.9%)
Asian	6,870,137	11,647,649	2,411,827 (35.1%)	3,769,745 (32.4%)	4,352,711 (63.4%)	7,877,904 (67.6%)
White	145,233,383	149,091,035	139,472,419 (96.0%)	142,682,117 (95.7%)	5,751,303 (4.0%)	6,408,918 (4.3%)
Black	24,930,677	30,379,161	23,691,763 (95.0%)	28,994,746 (95.4%)	1,170,685 (4.7%)	1,384,415 (4.6%)
Total	198,391,586	225,981,711	179,601,145 (90.5%)	196,614,669 (87.0%)	18,790,948 (9.5%)	29,367,042 (13.0%)

Sources: Data in this table and subsequent tables are calculated by the author from U.S. Census Bureau, 1990 Census, Summary Tract File 4A, and 2000 Census, Summary File 3.

Note: In this and subsequent tables, whites and blacks are non-Hispanic. Hispanics include people of all races. Hispanic Asians are included in both Hispanic and Asian categories.

in the data tables and reports of the American Communities Project, http://www.s4.brown.edu/S4/acproject.htm.)

The settlement patterns of immigrants can be compared with those of natives in several ways. First we will look at which metropolitan regions they are most likely to be living in. Second, we will consider the extent to which immigrants are integrated into mainstream neighborhoods, including integration with the white native majority. Finally, we will investigate the quality of their living environments in terms of income and poverty levels.

It is important to emphasize from the outset that immigrants are spread very unevenly around the country, and very large sections of the U.S. are still relatively untouched by this phenomenon. Though foreign-born people now make up 13 percent of the total metropolitan population, there are many metropolitan areas in which immigrants are notably missing. Less than 5 percent of the residents of 175 metropolitan regions, including 9 of the largest 50, are immigrants. The nine largest include six in the Midwest: Cincinnati and Pittsburgh (both only 2.6 percent immigrant), St. Louis, Indianapolis, Kansas City, and Columbus. The other three are in the South: Norfolk, Nashville, and New Orleans.

These seem like exceptional places in the context of the national averages. But they are not alone. Indeed, we might just as well argue that areas with concentrated immigration are the exception, because so much of the country is more like Cincinnati than like Los Angeles. In 262 metropolitan regions (out of 331 in the nation), immigrants make up less than 10 percent of the population. These regions include just over half of the population of metropolitan America but less than 20

Percent Foreign-Born

☐ Less than 5% foreign born

■ More than 10% foreign born

Figure 1. Metropolitan areas where foreign-born residents are over 10 percent or under 5 percent of the population.

percent of its immigrants. That means that of a total metropolitan population of 115.7 million, only 5.7 million were born abroad—actually less than 5 percent.

The map of the continental United States in Figure 1 identifies the location of metropolitan regions where immigrants are plentiful (over 10 percent of the population) or scarce (under 5 percent). The sections with few immigrants cover most of the Midwest and the Mississippi Valley. Sections with many immigrants are concentrated along the East and West Coasts and in the Southeast and Southwest.

These data show that two very different situations exist. In some areas immigration has reached record levels, but in others it is only a trickle. These latter places have not been entirely untouched; for example, Nashville had very few immigrant residents in 1990—only 18,000—but this number tripled during the following decade and grew from 1.8 percent to 4.7 percent of the total population. Still, places like this (and many others with much smaller population changes) have been largely shielded from the influx of newcomers that is so large a factor in social relations, the economy, and politics in the country as a whole.

Major Destinations of Metropolitan Immigrants

Immigrants are found in every part of the country, but just 13 metropolitan areas, which together have a quarter of the U.S. population, house more than half of

Table 2   Foreign-born population in major metropolitan areas, 1990 and 2000

	Foreign-born		Percentage of population	
	1990	2000	1990	2000
1. Los Angeles–Long Beach, CA	2,892,456	3,449,444	32.7	36.2
2. New York, NY	2,285,024	3,139,647	26.8	33.7
3. Chicago, IL	885,081	1,425,978	11.9	17.2
4. Miami, FL	874,569	1,147,765	45.1	50.9
5. Houston, TX	440,321	854,669	13.3	20.5
6. Orange County, CA	575,108	849,899	23.9	29.9
7. Washington, DC	489,641	832,016	11.6	16.9
8. Riverside–San Bernardino, CA	360,643	612,359	13.9	18.8
9. San Diego, CA	428,810	606,254	17.2	21.5
10. Dallas, TX	234,522	591,169	8.8	16.8
11. Oakland, CA	337,435	573,144	16.2	24.0
12. San Jose, CA	347,201	573,130	23.2	34.1
13. San Francisco, CA	441,290	554,819	27.5	32.0

Sources: These data have been aggregated from information for census tracts in U.S. Census Bureau, 1990 Census, Summary Tract File 4A, and 2000 Census, Summary File 3, using the Census Bureau's 2000 definitions of Metropolitan Statistical Areas.

them. Table 2 gives the 1990 and 2000 numbers of immigrants in each one, along with the percentage of the total population that is foreign-born. Reviewing these one at a time, we notice not only the scale of immigration but also the variations across the country in where the newcomers originate.

Los Angeles, by virtue of its size and location near the Mexican border and the Pacific Ocean, claims the largest foreign-born population, with 3.4 million. By far the largest number—more than 2 million—are Latino, especially Mexicans. This is more than double the number of Latino immigrants in any other metropolitan area. Los Angeles also has the largest number of Asian immigrants—nearly 900,000. Many of its 400,000 white immigrants are from Iran rather than Europe. Los Angeles continued to experience massive immigration in the 1990s, but it has nevertheless been losing ground to other areas. In 1990 it was the home of 15.4 percent of the total metropolitan foreign-born population, but by 2000 its share had dropped to 11.7 percent. A trend that had already begun in the 1980s—migration of Hispanic immigrants from Los Angeles to nearby areas, including Orange County, Riverside–San Bernardino, and San Diego—accounts for some of this change. These areas are also among the 10 areas in the nation with the highest number of foreign-born residents. Counting Los Angeles, these four Southern California metropolitan areas are the home of fully 19 percent of America's immigrants.

New York is the other great immigrant metropolis. It has nearly as many immigrants as Los Angeles (3.1 million), but this population is growing faster (up about 40 percent in the past decade) and has more diverse origins. While New York is second to Los Angeles in the number of Hispanic and Asian immigrants, it nearly makes up the difference as the nation's major destination for white immigrants from Europe and the Middle East (nearly 750,000) and black immigrants from the Caribbean and Africa (over 500,000). It draws far fewer Mexicans than is common in the Southwest (though their numbers are now growing quickly). Instead it has a distinctive mix of Dominicans (more than 600,000), Central Americans, and South Americans, groups who generally live in or near New York's large Puerto Rican neighborhoods. And it has over 700,000 Asians, including especially large numbers of people from China and India. Together with Newark and the surrounding suburbs in New York and northern New Jersey, Greater New York accounts for 16 percent of America's immigrants.

Chicago is the only major destination for immigrants in the Midwest. Only about one in six Chicagoans is foreign-born, compared to more than a third of residents of the New York and Los Angeles metropolitan regions. But its nearly 1.5 million immigrant residents place it third in the nation, and it is one of the fastest-growing, up from about 900,000 in 1990. Chicago has an old reputation for immigration from eastern Europe, and over 400,000 of its foreign-born residents are non-Hispanic whites. But the largest number, close to 700,000, are Hispanic, and of these, most are Mexican. Another 300,000 are Asian.

Miami, famous for its Cuban minority, has over 1.2 million immigrants. The vast majority (over 900,000) are Latinos, with growing numbers of Salvadorans and Nicaraguans to augment the Cuban population. Nearly 100,000 of these immigrants are black, about equally from Haiti and the English-speaking Afro-Caribbean nations. These combine with Fort Lauderdale's black immigrants to create a strong Afro-Caribbean presence in south Florida.

Houston (850,000) and Dallas (nearly 600,000) are both among the top 10 in number of immigrants. Neither metropolis has historically had a very large Hispanic minority compared to areas closer to the Mexican border, but both of their Hispanic immigrant populations more than doubled between 1990 and 2000. Houston has also become one of the major destinations for Salvadoran immigrants in the U.S. Additionally, both of these metropolitan areas now have over 100,000 Asian immigrants, a figure that has more than doubled since 1990.

The nation's capital, Washington, D.C., completes the list of top 10 immigrant destinations, with 832,000 immigrants. It is like New York in the racial diversity of those it attracts, including nearly equal shares of Asians and Hispanics along with a significant minority of white and black immigrants.

Three additional metropolitan regions have more than 550,000 immigrants, all in the San Francisco Bay Area—Oakland, San Jose, and San Francisco. Taken together, they have about the same number of immigrants as Chicago, or Miami and

Fort Lauderdale combined. Like the rest of California, the Bay Area has few black immigrants. In contrast to the rest of the state, the largest immigrant group here is Asian, with a total of more than 900,000, compared with over 500,000 Hispanics and close to 300,000 whites.

Including these 13 metropolitan areas, there are 69 metropolises around the country where at least 10 percent of the population is immigrant. These 69 areas are the home of almost 24 million immigrants, four fifths of the metropolitan total. There are many reasons that immigrants are so highly concentrated. Those who come are naturally routed through America's main ports and its busiest international airports, as well as across its porous border with Mexico. It is well known that immigration is organized through social networks of family and friends in both the origin and destination countries; as a result, people's ideas about where to live and how to get there are shaped by the experiences of those who came before them. Further, existing immigrant communities become poles of attraction for new immigrants, because they offer social and cultural institutions and job markets that ease the way for newcomers. Brooklyn, New York, gained a reputation as an Afro-Caribbean destination early in the 20th century, for example. Much of the Southwest was predominantly Mexican at the time it became part of the United States. Florida, by virtue of its proximity to Cuba, was a natural destination for Cuban exiles in the 1960s. Chicago's growth and economic expansion attracted many Mexicans in the mid-20th century, positioning it for an explosion of Hispanic immigration after 1965.

In contrast, much of the country is new territory for immigrants. These places tend to attract minorities in the second generation, or immigrants who initially settled in a more traditional port of entry and then moved on in search of better opportunities. We might expect that within another decade, the footholds established by these pioneers will have primed the areas for sustained growth.

Growth in the Cities and Suburbia

The foreign-born have had a great impact on their core areas of settlement in the past 10 years, especially in terms of population growth. Table 3 shows that total population increase in the 69 major immigrant metropolitan areas was about 16.5 million people, split almost exactly between natives and immigrants. In some major metropolitan regions there would even have been a population loss if not for immigration. In the New York metropolis, for example, the U.S.-born population dropped by about 80,000 between 1990 and 2000, while the number of foreign-born residents jumped by 850,000. The number of white natives dropped even more, by nearly 450,000, and there were few new white immigrants. In this case the region would have lost population if not for growth in the number of black, Hispanic, and Asian immigrants.

Table 3   Urban and suburban population growth in 69 major immigrant metropolitan areas, 1990–2000

	Total growth	Urban growth	Suburban growth
All groups			
Total	16,520,069	4,963,910	11,556,159
Native	8,262,612	1,510,060	6,752,552
Immigrant	8,257,668	3,453,809	4,803,859
White			
Total	210,924	−1,239,196	1,450,120
Native	−265,553	−1,362,654	1,097,101
Immigrant	481,147	127,319	353,828
Black			
Total	2,561,516	455,270	2,106,246
Native	2,496,619	489,147	2,007,472
Immigrant	93,295	−23,559	116,854
Hispanic			
Total	9,219,015	3,945,188	5,273,827
Native	4,705,921	1,944,153	2,761,768
Immigrant	4,523,844	2,007,094	2,516,750
Asian			
Total	3,550,647	1,381,287	2,169,360
Native	975,207	386,409	588,798
Immigrant	2,609,701	1,013,067	1,596,634

Sources: These data have been aggregated from summary data on census tracts, using constant 2000 metropolitan and central city definitions and boundaries.

Table 3 shows that loss in the number of U.S.-born whites was typical during the 1990s, though on the whole it was outweighed by growth in foreign-born whites. The black population of these immigrant-intensive metropolitan areas grew more substantially, primarily because of increases in its U.S.-born component. But the big gainers were Hispanics, up more than 9 million, and Asians, up 3.5 million. Half of the Hispanic growth and about three quarters of the Asian growth was due to immigration.

Historically, immigration—especially immigration by newer minority groups—has been a city-centered process. This partly reflects the location of job opportunities. Although there have always been some jobs in satellite communities outside the central city, immigrants in the early 20th century mostly joined the still expanding manufacturing and service sector labor force in central cities. Here, too, were older and denser neighborhoods with affordable housing. But the character of suburbs has been changing rapidly. Suburbs today are the location not only of agricultural and gardening industries on the periphery, but also of most job development in metropolitan regions. At the same time, the composition of the suburban housing stock has shifted (with apartment development in some places and deteriorated housing in others), and suburbs currently offer a much wider range of housing types and prices than they did before.

In Table 3, the term "suburban" refers to all tracts within the metropolitan region except those within the boundaries of census-designated central cities as defined by the Census Bureau in 2000. This table provides strong evidence that immigrants are now a major contributor to suburbanization in the 69 metropolitan areas included here. Of the 11.5-million-person growth in the number of suburbanites in these areas, 4.8 million were immigrants. Their role varies greatly by race and ethnicity, however. Among whites, there was a substantial drop in the urban population—entirely due to loss of white natives—and a shift to the suburbs, continuing a pattern that began decades earlier.

The black population also shifted toward suburbia, but in this case it was the immigrants who declined in cities but gained in suburbs. Hispanics and Asians experienced much more balanced growth. For both of these groups, and for both their U.S.-born and foreign-born members, there was considerable growth in the cities but even stronger increase in suburbs.

Indeed, the nation's 3 all-suburban metropolises are among the top 30 in number and share of immigrants in 2000: Long Island, New York (the Nassau-Suffolk metropolis, 14.4 percent immigrant); Bergen-Passaic, New Jersey (25.7 percent immigrant); and Middlesex-Somerset-Hunterdon, New Jersey (20.8 percent immigrant). Many new immigrants now move directly to homes in suburban areas, whether traditional dormitory suburbs, declining inner-ring suburbs, or larger and denser satellite towns. To some extent this represents their upward social mobility. In most metropolitan areas there is a high degree of selectivity in who lives in suburbs, favoring those who have better educations, higher incomes, longer residence in the U.S., and greater English-language fluency. Further, compared to immigrants in the central cities, those in suburbs are somewhat less segregated by race and ethnicity. This does not mean that they are fully assimilated, however. As we shall see, the main trend is for immigrants to join growing clusters of newcomers from the same racial or ethnic group in the kinds of ethnic neighborhoods that we used to associate only with cities.

Formation of Immigrant Neighborhoods

Neighborhoods have an important function for new arrivals, especially for people whose customs or language set them apart from the majority population. A long-established line of thought holds that concentrated immigrant settlement areas arise and are maintained because they meet newcomers' needs for affordable housing, family ties, a familiar culture, and help in finding work. Scholars note that immigrants' limited market resources and ethnically bound cultural and social capital are mutually reinforcing; they work in tandem to sustain ethnic neighborhoods. But these are typically viewed as transitional neighborhoods—they represent a practical and temporary phase in the incorporation of new groups into American society. Their residents search for areas with more amenities as soon as their economic situations improve, their outlooks broaden, and they learn to navigate mainstream American life. People with more financial resources and jobs in the larger economy avoid ethnic zones, and these areas are left behind by immigrants with more experience and by the second generation in search of the Promised Land.

Such ethnic settlements are not the only form of immigrant neighborhood. The contemporary immigration stream is quite diverse and includes many well-educated and middle-class people who find professional or other high-status positions in the U.S. As a result, some groups are now able to establish enclaves in desirable locations, often in suburbia. Group members may choose these places even when they have the financial resources to assimilate within the larger community. For some, the ethnic neighborhood is a favored destination, not just a starting point.

It is difficult to discern what immigrant neighborhoods represent to their residents. Some recent research has approached this question by studying whether people who live in ethnic concentrations are more likely to be immigrants, non-English-speaking, and relatively poor, which fits the profile of the traditional immigrant enclave. It is also helpful to look at how the neighborhoods where immigrants live compare with neighborhoods where U.S.-born people of the same ethnic background reside.

Tables 4, 5, and 6 provide information about the neighborhoods (more precisely, the census tracts) where the average group member lives: the average white, the average white native, the average white foreign-born person, etc. These are census tract averages across all 69 immigrant-intensive metropolitan areas, but they have been weighted by the number of specified group members who live in the tract. Therefore, they count more heavily the situation in tracts and metropolitan regions where more members of a particular group live. Table 4 provides information on the immigration-related characteristics of neighborhoods: the percent of inhabitants who are foreign-born and the percent of people over five years old who speak a language other than English in their home. These variables give the answer to several questions about immigrants' residential patterns. First, how is immigration changing the *average* neighborhood in these metropolises? Second, how different are the neighborhoods where natives and immigrants live? This tells us about the degree of integration or separation between these groups. Third, how do differences between natives and immigrants fit into the racial and ethnic boundaries across neighborhoods? Commentators have pointed out that Asians and Hispanics, who have particularly large shares of foreign-born members, may be establishing separate neighborhoods for this reason—but perhaps their U.S.-born members live in areas much more similar to those of white natives.

Table 4   Nativity and language use in neighborhoods

	Total		Native-born		Foreign-born	
	1990	2000	1990	2000	1990	2000
Percentage of foreign-born residents						
White	12.4	15.7	11.9	15.0	20.4	25.4
Black	15.1	20.3	13.8	19.1	28.8	33.1
Hispanic	28.2	32.0	23.3	28.0	35.4	37.2
Asian	25.6	30.1	21.4	26.4	28.0	31.9
Percentage speaking a language other than English at home						
White	18.5	23.1	17.9	22.2	27.8	34.2
Black	21.5	27.6	20.6	27.3	29.4	30.1
Hispanic	49.4	53.6	45.8	50.3	54.8	58.0
Asian	35.5	41.2	31.1	37.3	38.0	43.0

Let's begin with neighborhoods where the average white or black resident lives. The average white lives in census tracts where about 15 percent of neighbors are foreign-born and just under a quarter speak another language at home. To put these figures in perspective, if we count whites in all metropolitan areas, only 9 percent of their neighbors are immigrants and only 14 percent speak another language at home. So we might think of the figures in Table 4 as evidence that in some parts of the country whites have at least a moderate exposure to immigration, and clearly this exposure is growing. Blacks live in neighborhoods with somewhat higher levels of newcomers.

Hispanics' and Asians' neighborhoods are markedly different—nearly a third of the average Hispanic or Asian person's neighbors are immigrants, and around half use a language other than English at home. One reason that Hispanics and Asians have greater exposure to newcomers is that larger shares of these groups are immigrants themselves.

How different are the census tracts where immigrants live from those of natives? Among whites the differences are very large—foreign-born whites live in neighborhoods with a 10 percent larger share of immigrants and a 12 percent larger share of bilingual neighbors than native whites do. To varying degrees the same pattern is found for every group.

But this is not the only reason. Race and ethnicity also make a difference. Whether we look at natives or at immigrants, Hispanics are the most likely to live in immigrant neighborhoods, followed by blacks and Asians, and whites are least likely. Hispanics are also most likely to live among people who speak another language at home, regardless of whether we compare native or immigrant group members. Asians are intermediate on this dimension, and whites and blacks are least likely.

Several factors converge to make Hispanics stand out so strongly from the other groups. They are a very large minority, and they form large Hispanic enclaves in the metropolitan regions where they are most concentrated. For example, in the Los Angeles metropolis, about 45 percent of the population is Hispanic, and the average group member is in a neighborhood that is 63 percent Hispanic. Half of them are immigrants, and even in the second and third generations a large number continue to speak both English and Spanish. The immigrant experience and native language use are very much the norm in their neighborhoods.

Asians have an even higher share of immigrants than Hispanics, and this shows up in the composition of their neighborhoods. But other factors counterbalance this effect to some degree. First, Asians are a smaller group—for example, they are 12 percent of the population in Los Angeles, where they are greatest in absolute number. Second, they tend to separate themselves from the black and Hispanic populations, and in most metropolitan areas—with the exception of a few distinct Chinatowns—they live in neighborhoods where Asians are overrepresented but still far less than half of the residents. Third, Asians come from several different language groups, so they tend to use English as a common language in neighborhoods where people from several different Asian nations reside.

Segregation or Spatial Assimilation of the Second Generation?

Social scientists have long been aware of the formation of immigrant enclaves, based on the experiences of white ethnic groups who entered the U.S. from about 1850 until 1920. Immigrants from Italy and east European Jews were especially likely to live in separate neighborhoods—separate both from one another and from more established whites. The popular view is that this was a temporary phenomenon, and that by the second generation there was a substantial shift to less segregated, more mainstream locations, a process described as spatial assimilation.

Table 5 assesses immigrants' spatial assimilation in terms of exposure to the white majority. Let us focus first on the data for 2000 and compare the percentage of non-Hispanic white residents in the average immigrant's neighborhood and the aver-

Table 5   Percentage of whites in neighborhoods

	Total		Native-born		Foreign-born	
	1990	2000	1990	2000	1990	2000
Percentage of non-Hispanic white residents						
White	78.8	71.9	79.0	72.3	75.1	67.0
Black	27.1	25.7	26.9	26.0	27.8	22.7
Hispanic	37.7	31.6	40.5	34.1	33.6	28.4
Asian	52.2	45.6	51.2	45.3	52.8	45.8

age native-born person's neighborhood. There is only a modest difference among whites, blacks, and Hispanics, with the immigrant generation living in neighborhoods with a 3 to 5 percent lower white share than natives of the same race or ethnicity. There is no difference among Asians.

Exposure to whites seems to be much more a matter of people's race and ethnicity than of their country of birth. Whites, regardless of nativity, live in neighborhoods where whites are a clear majority. This majority is shrinking, to be sure, affected by the growing presence of immigrant minorities throughout metropolitan areas. Whites still make up two thirds of neighbors in the tracts where the average white person lives in these immigrant-intensive metropolises.

Asians have the next highest level of exposure to whites, living in neighborhoods where on average there is a near majority of white residents. This reflects the well-documented fact that Asians are only moderately segregated from whites, while they tend to avoid districts with black or Hispanic majorities. But segregation is part of the Asian experience, as Asians live in zones with much larger Asian populations and fewer white residents than whites do. There is no "assimilation advantage" for Asians born in this country.

Blacks and Hispanics, regardless of where they were born, live in neighborhoods with a minimal white presence, varying around a quarter of the population. The white share has dropped sharply in the past decade in Hispanics' neighborhoods, at the same time that these areas have become more Hispanic. The disparity in racial composition of the neighborhoods of white natives and black natives in 2000 is 46 percent; between white and black immigrants, it is almost the same, 44 percent. The disparity between white and Hispanic natives is a little smaller, and this reveals that Hispanics are less segregated from whites than blacks are. Yet this 38 percent gap is the same if we compare white and Hispanic immigrants.

These results are very consistent. Asian immigrants, to a degree, and black and Hispanic immigrants, to an even greater extent, live separately from the metropolitan white population, and this division is not very much caused by their immigrant status. Segregation falls mainly along racial and ethnic lines.

Social-Class Differences among Neighborhoods

Another way to assess immigrants' access to the mainstream is to look at their class composition. As indicators of social class, we use the census tract's median household income (half of households earn more than this amount, half earn less) and the percentage of residents whose incomes fall below the poverty line. These income data are for households. Income data for 1990 have been adjusted to 2000 dollars; the poverty thresholds are those used by the Census Bureau in each year.

Again we have to take into account very strong racial and ethnic differences. Table 6 shows that the average white in these metropolitan areas lives in a neighbor-

Table 6   Economic standing of neighborhoods

	Total		Native-born		Foreign-born	
	1990	2000	1990	2000	1990	2000
Median household income						
White	$54,702	$60,192	$54,767	$60,402	$53,815	$57,529
Black	$36,605	$40,348	$36,219	$40,211	$39,963	$41,910
Hispanic	$37,239	$39,728	$37,627	$40,644	$36,668	$38,549
Asian	$51,998	$56,560	$54,890	$58,682	$50,471	$55,535
Percentage below the poverty line						
White	8.0	8.2	8.0	8.1	9.1	10.0
Black	21.0	19.1	21.4	19.3	17.6	17.1
Hispanic	20.5	19.5	20.3	18.9	20.7	20.3
Asian	11.4	11.5	10.0	10.9	12.2	11.8

hood where the median income is over $60,000 and only 8.2 percent are below the poverty line. Asians' neighborhoods are somewhat less affluent but still very advantaged compared to blacks' and Hispanics' neighborhoods (both of which have median incomes of around $40,000 and nearly 20 percent poverty rates). Overall racial/ethnic inequality was quite stable between 1990 and 2000.

Other studies have shown that these gaps are not significantly affected by the higher incomes of whites and Asians compared with blacks and Hispanics. For example, the average black household earning over $60,000 lives in a neighborhood that has a higher poverty rate than the neighborhood of a white household earning less than $60,000. When analyses are conducted at the level of individuals, asking who lives in neighborhoods with more resources, race consistently trumps class as a predictor, with disadvantages for both blacks and Hispanics.

Still, it is worth examining whether nativity has an independent effect. First, how much more advantaged in class composition are the neighborhoods where U.S.-born people live, compared with those of immigrants? This is another way to think about spatial assimilation: as advancement in neighborhood quality that is not necessarily linked to living with whites. Second, how much is the overall gap between racial and ethnic groups (seen in the group totals) reduced when we compare natives with natives and immigrants with immigrants?

We can answer the first question using the 2000 values for natives versus immigrants. Among whites, Hispanics, and Asians there is an advantage for natives: they live in neighborhoods that are about $2,000 to $3,000 wealthier and have a poverty rate 1 or 2 percent lower. Among blacks, however, the advantage rests with immigrants.

This reversal of the expected native advantage among blacks is an important clue about race relations in the United States. Other analyses show that Afro-Caribbeans and immigrants from Africa have somewhat higher educational levels and higher income than African Americans. In the labor market, and apparently also in the housing market, they appear to find greater opportunities than other blacks do. However, this will turn out to be a temporary advantage if their children and grandchildren do not manage to avoid falling to the African American average. After all, the assimilation model cuts in two directions: it predicts disadvantage for the immigrant generation but social advancement for the next.

Generational advancement in neighborhood quality for whites, Hispanics, and Asians is very weak in relation to the disparities across groups. For example, consider that immigrant Hispanics live in neighborhoods where residents earn $20,000 less than people in immigrant whites' neighborhoods and where the poverty rate is twice as high. In this context, the immigrant vs. native difference of $2,000 or one percentage point in the poverty rate has little practical effect. Hence, for Hispanics the effect of ethnicity is much more important than status as an immigrant.

For Asians, the overall $3,500 disadvantage between their neighborhoods and whites' neighborhoods (that is, $56,650 vs. $60,192) does recede to a disadvantage of about $1,700 between white and Asian natives, or $2,000 between white and Asian immigrants. Being an immigrant makes a difference, and the large share of immigrants in the Asian population means that Asians live in somewhat less affluent neighborhoods.

But the larger picture is that differences between whites and Asians are small to begin with, and the main message of the figures in Table 6 is the large gap between these two groups and blacks and Hispanics.

As powerful as the current wave of immigration has been, we can see that its influence on metropolitan residential patterns has been very localized. Some parts of the country are relatively untouched, while some neighborhoods in certain areas have been entirely rebuilt and repopulated.

A major factor here is geographic region. The U.S. is split between those zones where immigrants are plentiful, mainly near major ports of entry, and zones where native whites and blacks are the only visible groups. Immigration was perhaps more dispersed in the 19th century, when newcomers played a major role in settling the prairies. There may be some centrifugal forces in play now. For example, secondary migrations are bringing Mexicans and Central Americans to more sections of the Midwest and South. But even now the principal routes of secondary migration are between the old immigrant centers, such as the two-way movements between New York and Los Angeles.

Another decisive factor is the strong boundary created by race and ethnicity. This is seen most clearly at the scale of communities within metropolitan regions, where the location of immigrants' neighborhoods seems to be determined more by whether they are white, black, Hispanic, or Asian than by whether they are foreign-born, or even by their income and education. To be sure, there is evidence of significant clustering of immigrants in certain neighborhoods and limited spatial assimilation of U.S.-born generations of the same racial or ethnic group. But assimilation occurs in the context of enduring boundaries between groups.

Bibliography

Alba, Richard D., John R. Logan, Brian Stults, Gilbert Marzan, and Wenquan Zhang. "Immigrant Groups and Suburbs: A Reexamination of Suburbanization and Spatial Assimilation." *American Sociological Review* 64 (June 1999): 446–60.

Denton, Nancy A., and Douglas S. Massey. "Residential Segregation of Blacks, Hispanics, and Asians by Socioeconomic Status and Generation." *Social Science Quarterly* 69 (Dec. 1988): 797–817.

Fischer, Claude S., Gretchen Stockmayer, Jon Stiles, and Michael Hout. "Distinguishing the Geographic Levels and Social Dimensions of U.S. Metropolitan Segregation, 1960–2000." *Demography* 41 (Feb. 2004): 37–59.

Frey, William H. "Immigration, Domestic Migration, and Demographic Balkanization in America: New Evidence for the 1990s." *Population and Development Review* 22 (Dec. 1996): 741–63.

Logan, John R., Richard D. Alba, and Wenquan Zhang. "Immigrant Enclaves and Ethnic Communities in New York and Los Angeles." *American Sociological Review* 67 (Apr. 2002): 299–322.

Logan, John R., Brian Stults, and Reynolds Farley. "Segregation of Minorities in the Metropolis: Two Decades of Change." *Demography* 41 (Feb. 2004): 1–22.

Newbold, K. Bruce. "Internal Migration of the Foreign-Born: Population Concentration or Dispersion?" *Population and Environment* 20 (Jan. 1999): 259–76.

Waldinger, Roger. "From Ellis Island to LAX: Immigrant Prospects in the American City." *International Migration Review* 30 (Winter 1996): 1078–86.

White, Michael J., and Afaf Omer. "Segregation by Ethnicity and Immigrant Status in New Jersey." In *Keys to Successful Immigration: Implications of the New Jersey Experience,* ed. Thomas J. Espenshade, pp. 375–94. Washington, D.C.: Urban Institute, 1997.

Ethnic and Racial Identity

Herbert J. Gans

Research fields sometimes give rise to, or are taken over by, buzzwords, and in American immigration research, the major buzzword since the beginnings of the post-1965 immigration has been *identity*. In a broad sense, identity is just a new term to cover mainstream research into ethnic and racial structures and cultures, perhaps a replacement for ethnic or racial status. However, here we will consider identity in a narrower, literal sense—as the perceptions that people construct about and for themselves and others. In the narrow sense, research into identity begins with a question such as "How do you identify yourself?" After the simple answers have been supplied, identity becomes a subtler concept that must be construed as a variable for empirical research purposes. Consequently, this essay seeks to lay out some principal meanings and uses of ethnic and racial identities, as well as what social scientists should be looking for in the study of these identities once they proceed beyond the standard ethnic identity questions.

Because most researchers of ethnic and racial identity study samples of individuals, our focus will also be on individual identities, and thus we will not consider the collective identities that ethnic, racial, and other groups try to develop for political and other purposes. However, individual identity is a social phenomenon, for the categories and classifications that people use to create identities are socially constructed and shared. Ultimately, ethnic and racial identities exist in America because Americans label, stereotype, and rank each other in part by behavior patterns, values, and attitudes that they associate with skin color, visible facial and other physical features, and ancestral country or region of origin.

Biologists may agree that race is not a biologically determinable variable, but laypeople still proceed as if it were. Indeed, Americans generally construct it as a palette of five skin colors—black, white, yellow, brown, and red—even though a visitor from another galaxy might observe that most Americans' skins are actually various shades of pink and brown. No palettes exist for ethnicity, although a number of stereotypes have been attached to the immigrant groups that have arrived on these shores over the centuries. For example, almost every immigrant group has at some point been described as "clannish."

Definitions of identity are numerous, and psychologists view the term differently from sociologists. For the purpose of empirical social research, identity can be thought of as a person's self-image of his or her attributes and roles associated with race and ethnicity. The importance that each of these images holds in people's lives varies—and whether, when, in what situations, and why people actually develop ethnic and racial identities is one of the first questions identity researchers must ask.

Actually, the standard ethnic research question "How do you identify yourself?" is loaded, because it assumes that the respondents have already constructed such an identity, whereas the more typical lay question "Where are you [or your ancestors] from originally?" neatly avoids asking whether the respondent identifies with that ancestry. Having Ecuadorian ancestors does not automatically require a person to develop an Ecuadorian identity.

Identity and Identification

As a term, *identity* is one half of a twin concept, the other half being *identification*. People not only identify themselves but are identified by others. As Cornell and Hartman point out, identity is *asserted,* while identification is *assigned.* As a result, racial and ethnic affiliations have to be looked at with both concepts.

Moreover, the relation between identity and identification differs for race and ethnicity. In the case of race, they are usually the same. Once immigrants are identified as black by the white majority, they must also choose a black identity for themselves, or at least that has been the case in the U.S. to the present day. In the case of ethnicity, assignment has less influence on assertion. The children of Russian immigrants may be identified as Russian Americans by others, but they are free to identify as Americans—or, if they do the needed cultural homework, as Hungarian Americans. In Mary Waters's classic phrase, almost all people now have "ethnic options," at least to some degree. Ethnicity is thus on the way to becoming a *chosen* identity, while race remains an *imposed* identification. When two people of different ethnic origin have children, those children can choose between the two parental identities or choose neither and identify as Americans, as many children of intermarriage do.

Intermarriages aside, there are still limits to ethnic options. Most people remain loyal to their parental ethnicity, and eyebrows would most likely be raised if the aforementioned Russian Americans really decided to become Hungarian Americans.

However, there are no racial options. Russian Americans remain whites, just as

Haitian Americans remain blacks. Children of racial intermarriage are assigned the most visible identification, and as long as the children of a black-white intermarriage do not have white skin, they are identified as black. Dominant and recessive genes come into play, however, and some children of Asian-white intermarriages look white enough to adopt that racial identity if they so choose.

Moreover, children of mixed-race marriages can now identify themselves as biracials or multiracials. This racial identity is just emerging, but if the number and varieties of intermarriage increase, several different biracial and multiracial identities may develop. Still, it is safe to predict that even if the children of black-white intermarriages describe themselves as biracials, many whites will continue to identify them as blacks.

Labels and Identities

How people identify themselves or are identified can be looked at in terms of levels of intensity. Labels represent the lowest level of intensity. Indeed, a label should not even be understood as an identity, especially if people choose it as a checkmark on an application or a questionnaire. Labels assigned by others may stick, and racial minorities are rarely allowed to forget how they are being labeled.

Labels can be official or unofficial. When the U.S. Census asks questions about race and ancestry (its current substitute for ethnicity), the result is a set of official labels. Individuals who fill out census questionnaires may forget what ethnic labels they chose, but once all their choices are counted, the census will construct a picture of the country's official ancestral makeup. Because numbers affect political power and census numbers determine the distribution of some federal funds on the basis of race, the government and ethnic and racial organizations often have long and fierce political conflicts over what labels the census should name and count.

People may privately develop unofficial labels to supplement or correct official ones. For example, immigrants who are officially labeled Hispanics may label themselves by their original nationality, although their children are apt to call themselves Hispanics. Likewise, the children of Koreans are labeled and label themselves as Asian Americans.

Perhaps because self-applied labels are attached and detached easily, they can vary according to the individuals' situations. Hyphenated Americans often drop their ethnic labels when they become overseas tourists, becoming unhyphenated Americans. They may even develop greater national pride while they are among foreigners, which recedes once they get home.

Everyone may end up with a label sooner or later, but not everyone develops an identity. Unlike a label, an identity has to be internalized to some extent and felt as well as expressed with a degree of intensity. Some people feel their ethnic or racial identity constantly; others feel it only occasionally and wear it lightly. For example, although white Anglo-Saxon Protestants are now sometimes described as members of just another European-origin ethnic group, they so far show little sign of having a cohesive ethnic identity.

Identities can be as situational as labels—for example, felt only when a person visits an immigrant neighborhood. Racial identities are another matter, for if people are being identified by others as members of a specific race, they are under social pressure to develop the corresponding identity. Black immigrants are reminded of their blackness continually in America; white ones, being the majority race, rarely need to think about their racial identity.

Expressions of Identity

Having an identity and expressing it are different processes. Expressions can take several forms, which scholars have classified in various ways, but for empirical research purposes, when simplicity is a consideration, identity is expressed as thought, feeling, speech, and activity. Each of these can be negative as well as positive; people can feel ethnic or racial pride or self-hatred.

Members of ethnic or racial groups may feel their identity intensely, but it does not really become a social phenomenon until it is expressed in socially visible ways: as discourse or in a group activity. Analyzing the conditions and situations in which people express their identity, as well as those in which they do not, is important for understanding the role of ethnic and racial identity in American life.

Thoughts. Not enough is known yet about whether, when, and how people from various ethnic and racial groups think about their ethnic and racial identities and what they think about. Ethnic and racial intellectuals write publicly about what they think, and so do bloggers, but most people keep their thoughts to their closest relations and friends and are represented publicly only by answers to researchers' questions about their attitudes.

Feelings. However, identities are probably expressed as feelings more often than in thoughts, with pride, solidarity, nostalgia, sadness, and shame among the most frequent emotions. What evokes each of these feelings is a significant clue to the determinants of identity.

Feelings, particularly about others, can be neutral, positive, or negative. Researchers have conducted thousands of studies of the negative feelings we call prejudice and hate. Less is known about neutral and positive feelings toward others, or about self-hatred, ethnic and racial. Even the shame that the children of immigrants often feel about their parents' foreign cultural practices deserves more attention.

Marginality is another kind of feeling associated with identity. During the European immigration of the late 19th and early 20th centuries, all immigrants were thought to suffer from the marginality brought on by trying to live up to both their old immigrant culture and their new American culture. Despite all that has been written about marginality, data on how many people experience feelings of marginality are still scarce. It is quite possible that people feel comfortable with having a foot in two ethnicities or races. Questions about marginality will become relevant again as the increase in intermarriage results in a rising number of multiethnic and multiracial Americans.

Activities. Ethnic and racial identities become most public when they are reflected in activities, especially political and cultural ones that make identities come alive for others. People also express identity by supporting defense and advocacy groups, making charitable donations, joining social clubs, visiting the ancestral country or community, or, less intensively, going to restaurants that feature ethnic or racial cuisines. What kinds of activity people choose and why are of continuing research interest.

For the past quarter-century, probably the most widely discussed activity has been "identity politics"—political activity devoted primarily to expressing and defending activists' ethnic or racial identity. The term *identity* is used loosely here, for identity politics range from fighting deliberate or unintentional insults to people's ethnic or racial identity to struggles for the fair representation of ethnic and racial groups in private firms, public agencies, and other institutions. To what extent ethnic and racial groups become involved in politics to express their identity and to what extent they attempt to obtain the same decision-making influence, jobs, and related resources as other politically active groups is an important question, especially for understanding the politics of cities like New York and Los Angeles, which attract many immigrants.

Identity politics, like the active expression of identity itself, is associated particularly with the post-1965 immigration, but the European immigrants who came to the U.S. between about 1880 and 1920 were no strangers to it. Their political groups may not have flaunted their identity, but they engaged in the same competition for power and resources that contemporary ethnic groups do. Today the competition is fiercer, because there are more such groups, including racial ones of a kind that did not exist among the earlier immigrants. The urban political machines in which the competition then took place are virtually gone, but today's city halls still produce ethnically and racially balanced political tickets, which, as in the past, take account of the groups that participate in party affairs and vote regularly.

Objects of Identity

When people express an identity, they express it as an identity *with* something or someone, be it the accomplishments of an ethnic or racial group, a national hero in the country of origin, or an ethnic or racial symbol. Thus, identity expression is aimed at actual or imagined entities, which can be thought of as objects or targets.

For the most part, the objects seem to be countries, even for racial groups. If identity questions had been asked of the earlier wave of European immigrants, they might have located their identity in their village or province, but most in the second generation lodged their ethnic identity, if any, in the country from which their parents came. Political refugees might have answered the question differently from immigrants seeking economic betterment. Some of the politically oppressed rejected their country of origin, like many of the Armenians who came early in the 20th century; others tried to overthrow the oppressing regime, like many of Miami's Cubans; and many others have developed dual loyalties, like the New Jersey Palestinians. The role of homelands in immigrants' ethnic identity is especially interesting.

Why people lodge their identity in countries or, in the case of Asian Americans, in the eastern part of a continent is intriguing, especially when they are not particularly nationalistic. However, Asian Americans, like Hispanics, take their identity from external identifications made by native-born Americans who are unwilling to make distinctions among the immigrants' various countries of origin. If those speaking for the country's native-born majority decide how to identify the newcomers, it is easier to call them Asian American than Chinese, Korean, or Japanese—and even easier if they look pretty much alike to outsiders. How and why the second generation then adopts the majority label as their identity suggests that sometimes assimilation really takes the form of Americanization.

When immigrants are asked to explain what in their nation of origin affects their identity, they typically describe particular national values, such as the importance of family, respect for the aged, or the belief in hard work—although, ironically enough, most of these values are shared by immigrants from other countries as well as by Americans. Intensive questioning about what being Korean or Asian or Mexican American means to immigrants and the later generations will provide more answers about these identity issues.

Still, some identity objects are concrete. For example, people can feel ethnic or racial pride about specific cultural accomplishments of their country of origin, its military exploits in a war important for world history, or the political leader credited with bringing about the country's independence.

This sampling of identity objects begs a prior question: how much do objects matter, or do they matter at all? Does an immigrant group that associates its identity with a national hero act differently from one that finds its identity among the country's peasantry? Does pride in a country's artistic achievements generate a different identity from memories of its founder? Probably most identity objects are chosen mainly to anchor identity, to maintain affiliation with the ethnic or racial group, and to mark boundaries that differentiate one's own group from others.

Identification and Racial Identity

A continuing question in the study of identity is the relationship between identification and identity, and especially the extent to which the two affect each other. Part of the research problem is logistic, since it is easier to ask ethnic and racial minorities about their identity than to survey members of the majority populations about how they identify each of the minorities. Another part of the problem is substantive: the sponsors of research need to know more about negative identifications that lead to stereotyping and discrimination than about positive and neutral ones.

Obviously, majority identifications put limits on minority identity; immigrants identified as blacks cannot have a white identity. Thus, majority identification of minorities must have effects on minority identity, positive and negative, even if they are not as pervasive as in the example of Asian Americans. Minorities become aware of how the majority views them and during assimilation internalize some or all of this view. Since time immemorial, second and third generations have made fun of later immigrants as greenhorns or FOBs (those "fresh off the boat"), suggesting the extent to which these generations have absorbed majority identifications.

However, Asian Americans point out that outsiders' identification of them as a model minority, and of Asian American young women as "exotic," does not change their identity. Instead, they perceive these identifications as forms of racialization and racial discrimination, even though being praised as a model minority may sometimes aid Asian American upward mobility.

Whatever limits the identification process puts on ethnic and racial identity, minorities are relatively free to choose the frequency and intensity of identity expression as well as the feelings, activities, and objects associated with it. Native-born whites do not care much whether immigrants feel racial or ethnic pride or through what objects they express that pride. They quickly become upset, however, if identity is expressed in ways that threaten the public order or white superiority in that order.

Identity Variables

So far our analysis has dealt mainly with how people express racial and ethnic identities and what they express, assuming that they all do so the same way. However, people vary, as do their roles and positions in the society—and these produce varieties in levels of intensity, forms of expression, and objects of identity. Some of the variation in identity expression stems from differences in gender, age, socioeconomic class, origin, religion, ideology, and all the other "variables" that scientists use to measure American diversity.

For example, men seem to express racial and ethnic identities more vocally than women, although this may merely reflect their continued dominance in public life. Women do more of the emotional work, especially with kin, to keep informal ethnic groups alive and active. Younger people seem to be most involved in identity politics, as they are in social movements around ethnic and racial issues.

Class is particularly important. Sara Lee has found that while upper-middle-class second-generation Korean Americans are proud of their identity and express it in a number of ways, their working-class peers display less interest in their national identity and are more concerned with economic security and class position. Perhaps ethnic identity expression is a luxury of the affluent, better-educated second generation. Conversely, among the descendants of the earlier European immigration, ethnic identity seems to have been stronger among less affluent groups.

Situational variables raise other questions. Ethnic and racial groups feel their identity more intensely when they are threatened, not only by hostility from others but by downward social and economic mobility. For example, Italian American identity feelings are revived whenever the Mafia makes major headlines, in the news or in the entertainment media.

Identity—Cause or Effect?

Research on identity sometimes proceeds on the unstated assumption that holding or expressing an ethnic or racial identity *causes* the discourse and activities, as well as the social structures and cultures, associated with ethnicity and race. The reverse assumption is equally reasonable, however: that identity is an *effect* of ethnic or racial attitudes and behavior—and of the structural and cultural agents and forces that generate them. In addition, the causal arrow can run both ways; some identity expression causes ethnic or racial activity, but ethnic or racial activity can also lead to the expression of identity.

Thus, young people who feel strongly about their identity may marry endogamously, but an endogamous marriage can increase identity feelings as well. So, however, can intermarriage. Although exogamy may stem from or be associated with a weak ethnic or racial identity, the familial and other conflicts that sometimes accompany an exogamous partnership can intensify the ethnic or racial identity of one or both partners.

Similarly, intense feelings of identity may produce identity politics, but so does the coming together of diverse ethnic and racial groups in an institution such as a prison, or in a multiclass one such as a college. Whether identity is cause or effect or both requires us to understand the processes by which and the contexts in which that identity develops.

Ethnic Assimilation and Identity

In the decades before identity became a central concept in ethnic studies, ethnic social structure and culture, together with assimilation and generation, were the dominant concepts. Researchers looked primarily at the erosion of the cultures and social structures the immigrants brought with them, which they called assimilation—a less nationalistic term for Americanization. In assessing the amount and degree of cultural, social, and other kinds of assimilation, they paid—and still pay—particularly close attention to how assimilation processes and outcomes have changed with each new generation.

Many contemporary students of racial and ethnic identity reject this conceptual tradition. These researchers argue that the post-1965 immigrants have come to a different America than earlier immigrants did and are therefore able to resist assimilation. As a result of minimal assimilation, the second and later generations are thought to retain more loyalty to their immigrant origins than earlier immigrants did. In addition, the researchers expect that their communities and therefore their identities will endure for a longer period.

This new view of assimilation is widespread, which is not surprising considering that today's researchers are still mainly studying immigrants, many of whom assimilate slowly. However, now that the second generation of the initial wave of post-1965 immigration has grown to adulthood, researchers are beginning to learn that assimilation has been proceeding much as it did among the second generation of earlier European immigrants. For example, language loyalty is no greater among today's second generation than among past ones.

However, the racial and class diversity of today's immigrants has called attention to the diversity of assimilation processes and outcomes. These were less visible among the uniformly poor European immigrants, although looking back at that immigration with today's concepts suggests that even their assimilation was more diverse, or more segmented, than was once commonly thought. Eastern European Jews and other urban skilled workers moved up America's socioeconomic ladder faster than immigrants who were illiterate peasants or day laborers in the old country.

The assimilation of the post-1965 immigrants will probably have at least two kinds of effects on ethnic identity. One is itself assimilatory: immigrant identities and their expressions will begin to weaken and change as immigrant groups and cultures erode. Conversely, identities might change little among populations who reap considerable economic or political benefit from these identities, as well as among those who are discriminated against and who defend themselves and their dignity in part through expressing their identity.

A second, very different effect is compensatory: as the second generation assimilates, some of its members may compensate for distancing themselves from immigrant groups and cultures by intensifying their ethnic identity. Even some of the people active in identity politics may have been attracted to it by the search for a compensatory identity. Acquiring a compensatory identity is not difficult; it is also entirely compatible with an assimilated way of life. All it really requires is experiencing that identity—feeling Russian, Mexican, or Korean, or for that matter Asian American.

Over half a century ago I discovered that young Jewish people who had newly moved to the suburbs were more concerned with feeling Jewish and instilling that feeling in their children than with maintaining the cultural and religious practices they had known in the city. Since they often used Jewish toys, artifacts, and symbols to produce that feeling in their children, I thought of their Judaism as symbolic.

A quarter-century later, having noticed this phenomenon among other second generations, I broadened the concept to symbolic ethnicity. I observed Italian Americans making an annual visit to a traditional Italian restaurant, or Greek Americans stopping off at the ancestral village during a summer vacation—and in the process feeling and intensifying their ethnicity. If I had been doing the research a decade later, when identity became a central concept in ethnic research, I might have called this phenomenon symbolic identity. In any case, symbolic ethnicity is a form of compensatory identity, for people who seek to feel their ethnicity do so in part to compensate for distancing themselves from the ethnic groups and cultures in which they grew up.

Examples of symbolic ethnicity are now showing up in the second generation of the new wave of immigration—for example, when young Dominican Americans visit the parental village during their vacations. Despite its compensatory qualities, symbolic ethnicity—or a symbolic identity—is also assimilatory. It is normally worn lightly, does not interfere with everyday American ways, and can therefore be given up quickly and easily if people so choose.

Nonetheless, both assimilatory and compensatory identity can persist over many generations. As Richard Alba and others have found, many of the descendants of the European immigrants still report an ethnic identity a century after their ancestors arrived here; and there are Scandinavian and German Americans who identify as such 150 years later. They may do nothing more than label themselves when asked for their ethnic ancestry, and they are numerical minorities. After half a dozen generations in America, most people, some by now the descendants of repeated intermarriages over several generations, will describe their identity as American. Racial identities are not subject to assimilation, because they rest on the identifications that go with skin color. Still, since native-born white Americans once whitened the skins of swarthy European immigrants, future white eyes may see second- or third-generation Asian Americans and mestizo Hispanics as white.

As is so often the case, the rules for blacks are drastically different. White Americans are generally unwilling or unable to distinguish between black immigrants from the Caribbean and East and West Africa and native-born African Americans. Partly as a result, many of the children of black immigrants are identified and identify as African Americans. Being or becoming middle or upper class has not so far changed these identifications, but right now, too few of the descendants of black immigrants are visibly enough middle class for whites to notice.

What racial identities future black Americans will be able to develop therefore depends in part on the future shape of racial prejudice and discrimination. Some observers have predicted that white America may one day divide the country's ethnic and racial minorities into nonblack and black ones. Nonblacks would include, among others, Asians, phenotypically Spanish mestizo Hispanics, and other nonwhites who are not black. Black ones might also include "indigenous" Latinos such as Mayans, Native Americans, and other poor and stigmatized racial minorities, such as the Hmong.

The nonblack groups, especially middle-class segments, might eventually be treated and even perceived like whites—just as the "black Irish" and swarthy southern Europeans "whitened" with time and upward mobility. Those defined as blacks would be the victims of continued discrimination and stigmatization. In effect, ethnic and racial groups would be classified into deserving and undeserving categories.

This dichotomous model is of course only guesswork, and the treatment of many (but not all) middle-class African immigrants suggests an alternative possibility: that even if their skin color is stigmatized, foreigners with the right class position will be exempt from the harassment still experienced by middle-class African Americans. But even that situation could finally change; segregation, discrimination, and prejudice might end if the white majority were finally willing to stop thinking of African Americans as somehow inferior.

In the worst case, African Americans and other blacks may not be allowed to experience racial equality and the freedom to shape their own identities. In that case, the mistreatment of African Americans may continue, if not in the present form, until racial intermarriage has become so widespread that virtually all Americans have become brown-skinned. If their skins are several shades of brown, they will simply make the old distinctions using these shades, but if they all eventually share the same shade of brown, they might stop identifying and ranking each other by skin color—or they might become extremely sophisticated interpreters of minuscule differences of brownness.

The Pros and Cons of Identity

Further empirical research employing identity concepts should add significantly to our understanding of ethnic and racial identities, as well as the role they play among contemporary immigrants and their descendants. The research may show that identity is more useful for understanding America's immigrants than such past conceptual favorites as immigrant social structure and culture, assimilation, and generation.

Even so, the studies may conclude just the opposite: that ethnic and racial identities are not as significant to the immigrants, or to understanding them, as is now often thought. It is even possible that race and ethnicity are above all surrogate determinants of class, power, and other rankings of a hierarchical society—for example, easy ways for dominant populations to decide which groups will receive a smaller share of the scarcest resources. If Americans used other ways of ranking each other or stopped doing so altogether, race and ethnicity might lose most of their significance.

Even assuming that identity is far more than a label, identity research is at best a mixed blessing. It can generate new questions, but it can also become a way of studying old issues with new words. Furthermore, however we define identity, the term basically remains a psychological concept, most suited to the study of individual attitudes and emotions. Some of these are ephemeral and sporadic; studying them may be less productive than focusing on the formal and informal groups in which people act—and feel.

As Rogers Brubaker and others have pointed out, the preoccupation with identity gives short shrift to the institutions and other structures with which people live; the rules, norms, and cultures with which they act and are acted on; and the larger, now even global social, economic, and political forces that affect everyone's existence. Too much emphasis on identity can also draw attention away from struggles over power and resources and from the segregation, discrimination, prejudice, and various other inequalities that minorities must confront regularly. Nevertheless, if these realities can remain in the foreground, the continuing study of identity can help improve the portrait of race and ethnicity in the lives of America's immigrants.

Bibliography

Alba, Richard D. *Ethnic Identity: The Transformation of White America.* New Haven, Conn.: Yale University Press, 1990.

Bakalian, Anny. *Armenian-Americans: From Being to Feeling Armenian.* New Brunswick, N.J.: Transaction, 1993.

Brubaker, Rogers, and Frederick Cooper. "Beyond 'Identity.'" *Theory and Society* 29 (2000): 1–47.

Cornell, Stephen, and Douglas Hartman. *Ethnicity and Race: Making Identities in a Changing World.* Thousand Oaks, Calif.: Pine Forge, 1998.

Gans, Herbert J. "Symbolic Ethnicity: The Future of Ethnic Groups and Cultures in America." In H. Gans, N. Glazer, J. Gusfield, and C. Jencks, eds., *On the Making of Americans: Essays in Honor of David Riesman,* pp. 193–220. Philadelphia: University of Pennsylvania Press, 1979.

Lee, Sara S. "Class Matters: Racial and Ethnic Identities of Working- and Middle-Class Second-Generation Korean Americans in New York City." In Phillip Kasinitz, John H. Mollenkopf, and Mary C. Waters, eds., *Becoming New Yorkers: Ethnographies of the New Second Generation,* pp. 315–38. New York: Russell Sage Foundation, 2005.

Nagel, Joanne. "Constructing Ethnicity: Creating and Recreating Ethnic Identity and Culture." *Social Problems* 41 (1994): 152–76.

Portes, Alejandro, and Rubén C. Rumbaut. *Legacies: The Story of the Immigrant Second Generation.* Berkeley: University of California Press, 2001.

Waters, Mary C. *Ethnic Options: Choosing Identities in America.* Berkeley: University of California Press, 1990.

Woldemikael, Tekle M. *Becoming Black American: Haitian and American Institutions in Evanston, Illinois.* New York: AMS, 1989.

Intermarriage and Multiple Identities

Joel Perlmann and Mary C. Waters

Intermarriage, a process by which group members cross a recognized boundary with increasing frequency and eventually so often that the boundary becomes blurred or disappears, has long been of interest to both the general public and American social scientists because of its connection to assimilation. Since it involves decisions about the most intimate social connections and the creation of new family contexts, it is hard to imagine how to study issues of ethnic group interactions without giving it an important conceptual place. However, it is important to understand that intermarriage is significant to assimilation in two specific ways: first, in measuring a decline in social divisions that has already occurred, and second, as an indication that those social divides will decline still further—as a result of intermarriage itself.

The point that intermarriage is important because it signals a future decline in old social divisions is often only an assumption, because intermarriage studies typically measure this phenomenon at only one point in time. Despite this, however, the substantive importance of intermarriage is that it is part of a social evolution that continues through the decades and generations following the marriage.

Conceptual and Methodological Issues

One insight is critical to all understanding of intermarriage: the contrast between the proportion of a group's *individuals* who marry out and the proportion of mixed *marriages* among all marriages that involve at least one member from the group, which will always be higher. For example, when 38 of every 100 members of a group marry out of the group, they create 38 couples. The other 62 group members in every 100 find a spouse from among their own, forming 31 couples. Thus the proportion of mixed marriages among all marriages that involve at least one member from the group is $38 \div (38+31)$, or 55 percent; yet only 38 percent of individuals married out. This numerical insight is a commonplace in the study of intermarriage rates at any specific time, but it is important to understand its profound implications for the next generation: the prevalence of the mixed-origin children born to the 100 group members is likely to reflect the rate of mixed-origin couples, not the rate of individual out-marriages (assuming roughly equal fertility rates among both groups). Thus, the next generation will include 55 percent who are of mixed origin, even though only 38 percent of their parents out-married.

These dynamics have profound implications for the future of ethnicity, multiculturalism, and assimilation. Even in the moderately long run (a span of three generations, for example), it is very hard for an American ethnic group to retain internal cohesion and distinctiveness, because so many of its descendants are also descendants of other groups—unless, of course, immigration replenishes the relative prevalence of first-generation group members and the ties between the old and new families of arrivals are strong. Ancestral language, interest in country of origin, festivals, and local ethnic issues all command divided attention in a mixed-origin home. Similarly, role models, job contacts, and relatives are drawn from multiple groups.

Among European immigrants of the past, and among Asian and Hispanic immigrants today, intermarriage has played havoc with simple definitions of ethnic origin and generation by the time the grandchildren of the immigrants come of age. Because of intermarriage in the first and second generations, most grandchildren of European immigrants from Italy, for example, were also grandchildren of non-Italians—of Germans, Poles, Swedes, Scotch-Irish, or Mexicans. Also, a great many grandchildren of immigrants are also typically members of some other generation: the granddaughter of Polish immigrants may also be a sixth-generation descendant of a Scotch-Irish immigrant and the fourth-generation descendant of a German immigrant. The concept of generations itself, like the concept of ethnic origin, works moderately well as a classifying category for the first two generations but poorly for later generations; the key is the degree of intermarriage in the preceding generations.

These connections between assimilation and intermarriage may be said to describe how once-distinct peoples become one stock, literally members of one family. At the same time, assimilation also involves social mobility for those groups whose members arrive without the skills provided by extended education. While the immigrants may live "under America" (as a Slavic immigrant once put it to a congressional committee), a majority of their second-, third-, and fourth-generation offspring eventually have a social-class profile more or less like that of the descendants of much earlier immigrants. Thus intermarriage and social mobility must be thought of together. It is not just that the more assimilated members of a group may be more likely to out-marry. By the time the descendants of an immigrant group (such as the Italians) are said to have "made it," great numbers of these descendants are also the descendants of other groups. The challenge is to think of the two group processes working together across generations.

Another implication of mixed-origin and single-origin reproduction is that the mixed-origin population swells the number of descendants with *some* origins in the group. While the ethnic ties of those with mixed origin will generally be weaker than those of people with unmixed origin, they will not be negligible, especially in the first mixed generation. So a group with weaker ties but larger numbers may form as a transitional stage on the way to much weaker (or negligible) ties and still greater numbers.

It is worth noting too that these processes have huge implications for predictions about the future racial (or ethnic) composition of the American people. Projections about the demographic makeup of the American population began to make headlines in the 1990s as the country began to understand how much of an effect new, mostly nonwhite immigration was having. But those projections ignored future-generation intermarriage of Hispanics and Asians as well as of blacks, assuming that all racial and ethnic groups married within themselves and thus grew or declined only through births, deaths, and migration. It is undeniable that the racial and ethnic composition of the American population will evolve as immigration draws in millions from around the world; but it is quite another matter to predict the future ethnoracial divisions of the population as though (for example) all third-generation descendants of Hispanic immigrants will be only Hispanic in origin and will be as involved with their ethnic origin as much as their immigrant forebears are.

If debates about immigration restriction at the beginning of the 20th century had been informed by population projections, headlines would have screamed about how many Italians or Poles would be in our major cities if immigration continued. Such projections could not have foreseen that intermarriage eroded the boundaries between groups, so that the distinctions lost all but their symbolic meanings among white Americans as ethnic identity among the intermarried third and fourth generations became a matter of personal choice.

When the U.S. Census began in 1980 to ask a question about ethnic ancestry—a question also asked in 1990 and 2000—a number of studies began to highlight the contemporary *result* of earlier mixing in the population. The subjective census question "What is your ethnic ancestry?" does not provide information on the generational standing of the respondents or the full scope of their ethnic origins (since respondents list only those they choose to, and only two or three are reported), and it does not record the importance respondents attach to the reported ties. But the question does provide information on what people say about their origins. By the middle of the 20th century, the majority of the descendants of white ethnics in the U.S. were of mixed ancestry. And people with many ethnic options choose among them and often change their minds. The ancestry data have been immensely useful in showing the subjective fluidity of ethnic identities in America, and have stimulated interest in related topics, such as which origins tend to get reported and why. For example, the number of claimants of English, German, or Italian ancestry can rise or fall by a fifth to a third, depending on where a particular ancestry is placed in the list of examples that accompanies the question. In 1980, when English was in the list of examples, it was the largest ancestry group in the U.S. In 1990, when English was removed from the list and German was added, Germans became the largest ancestry group in the U.S. The Irish, a group once seen as severely disadvantaged, became very popular as they moved into the American mainstream, so that whites who have many different ancestors with different European origins are likely to keep an identification with their Irish heritage. Thus Michael Hout and Joshua Goldstein were able to show how 4.5 million Irish immigrants became 40 million Irish Americans, not because they had exceptionally high fertility but because the descendants of those immigrants intermarried and their descendants preferred to keep an ethnic identity that was in part Irish. Using ancestry data to study ethnic socioeconomic change (and intermarriage) is perilous, because we do not know how many and what sort of people are among those failing to claim a particular ethnic origin.

Contemporary Intermarriage

To a very great extent, the traditional field of ethnic intermarriage studies has been stimulated by the long-term social processes related to the European immigration to the U.S. (and related issues, such as religious intermarriage of Protestants, Catholics, and Jews). These studies showed that over time, with more generations of residence in the U.S., the groups had higher out-marriage rates. The question of racial intermarriage had a special place in these studies; it was different from intermarriage among European groups for at least two reasons. First, black-white intermarriage was rare because of extreme social divisions between blacks and whites as a legacy of slavery and because it was illegal in many states until the 1967 Supreme Court decision in *Loving* v. *Virginia* struck down all anti-miscegenation laws. Second, in the big picture, black-white intermarriage was not like immigrant and white-ethnic intermarriage because the very low incidence did not change with the length of time that black families had spent in the U.S.; that is, most black families had experienced forced immigration so many generations back as to make the immigration experience utterly irrelevant by the 20th century.

Thus the current study of intermarriage can draw on two related traditions: one involving racial intermarriage based on two long-resident populations with very low intermarriage rates (blacks and whites), in which researchers ignore the generational status of the populations, and one involving immigrants and their offspring, in which generational status explains a great deal of the behavior. This distinction has begun to break down in contemporary studies. Most immigrants today are classified as nonwhite; most descendants of older European (white) immigrants now cross the old social divides so easily that (to paraphrase Robert Merton's observation) it can hardly be called intermarriage when they do, since such behavior no longer violates any existing norm.

Among native-born blacks and whites, the period since the civil rights movement has shown definite changes in attitudes and behaviors, although attitudes have changed more quickly than behaviors. Daniel Lichter and Zhenchao Qian note that in the 1960s, less than 10 percent of whites expressed approval of interracial marriages. By the 1990s more than two thirds of whites approved. While still relatively rare, intermarriages between blacks and whites increased nearly sixfold, from 65,000 in 1960 to 363,000 in 2000. In 2000 among the native-born, 93 percent of black women married black men, while 84 percent of black men married black women. Endogamy was the norm among whites, with 94 percent of native-born white men married to white women. Yet intermarriage between whites and other racial groups increased even more, from 233,000 marriages in 1970 to over 1 million in 2000.

Five major groupings make up what David Hollinger has described as the ethnoracial pentagon—blacks, whites, Native Americans, Asians, and Hispanics. These categories correspond with how most Americans think about the major racial and ethnic divisions in society and also with the Office of Management and Budget's Directive 15, issued in 1978, which told federal statistical agencies how to report on race and ethnicity. Many studies of intermarriage look at how often couples form across these broad group boundaries; these are summarized in Table 1. In 2000 outmarriage was least prevalent among whites, the largest group. Among whites, 2.7 percent had a spouse from another group. Among blacks, 7 percent had outmarried, among Asians 16 percent, and among American Indians 56.7 percent. Yet even this broad analysis is often more complex than it seems, because of the govern-

Table 1   U.S. interracial marriage rates by Census race categories and gender, 2000 (percentages)

Race	Total	Men	Women
White	2.7	2.9	2.6
Black	7.0	9.7	4.1
American Indian	56.7	55.7	57.6
Asian	16.0	9.5	21.6
Asian native-born		32.0	44.0
Hispanic	14.0		
Hispanic native-born		29.0	31.0

Source: Sharon M. Lee and Barry Edmonston, *New Marriages, New Families: U.S. Racial and Hispanic Intermarriage,* Population Bulletin 60, no. 2 (Washington, D.C.: Population Reference Bureau, 2005), pp. 12, 25.

Table 2   Census race and ethnicity categories by generation, 2000 (percentages)

Generation	Black	Asian	Hispanic	Non-Hispanic white	Total
First	6.3	61.4	39.1	3.6	10.4
Second	3.9	26.6	28.5	7.3	10.0
Third and higher	89.9	12.1	32.4	89.1	79.6
Number (millions)	35.5	10.9	32.8	193.6	

Source: Diane Schmidley, *Profile of the Foreign-Born Population in the United States, 2000,* U.S. Census Bureau, Current Population Reports Series P-23–206 (Washington, D.C.: Government Printing Office, 2001), p. 24.

ment's insistence that Hispanics can be members of any racial group. Thus the census asks a question on race that does not include a Hispanic category and asks a separate question about Hispanic identity. Looking just at Hispanic/non-Hispanic spouses (regardless of race), the 2000 Census found that 14 percent of Hispanics had out-married.

Yet studies of Asian and Hispanic marriage patterns are not meaningful unless they take into account the generational status of the populations. Treating Asian and Hispanic marriage patterns merely as "racial intermarriage," as one might treat black-white intermarriage, can be misleading. Indeed, all of the major "racial" groups are affected by immigration, even whites and blacks. Table 2 gives the breakdown of race and ethnic groups by generation. Asians and Hispanics are most affected by immigration; 61.4 percent of Asians are foreign-born, another quarter are second-generation, and only 13 percent are third-generation or higher. Among Hispanics, a third have been in the U.S. at least three generations, while almost 40 percent are first-generation and another 28 percent are second-generation. Even among blacks immigration is showing large effects, with one out of ten black Americans either first- or second-generation.

Studies that do take generational status into account confirm that generation matters among all racial groups. This is evident in Table 3, which provides estimates of out-marriage rates by racial/ethnic group and generation. These rates, developed by Barry Edmonston, Sharon Lee, and Jeffrey Passel, are based on observed intermarriage rates for foreign-born and native-born Hispanics and Asians and on the maternal and paternal race distribution for U.S. birth data in 1990 (second-generation rates are interpolated as being between those of the first and third generations). Not surprisingly, the native-born routinely intermarry more than the foreign-born. The only exception to this is among blacks. Black immigrants tend to marry across racial lines more than native-born blacks; Frank Bean and Jennifer Lee suggest that this could be because of higher levels of acceptance of foreign-born than native-born blacks by native-born whites. Among Hispanics and Asians, to ignore genera-

Table 3   Estimated intermarriage rates by population group and generation, 2000–2100 (percentages)

Census race or ethnic group	All	Generation		
		First	Second	Third and higher
Asian	20	13	34	54
Black	10	14	12	10
Hispanic	30	8	32	57
White	8	10	9	8
American Indian	40	20	30	50

Source: Barry Edmonston, Sharon Lee, and Jeffrey Passel, "Recent Trends in Intermarriage and Immigration and Their Effects on the Future Racial Composition of the U.S. Population," in Joel Perlmann and Mary C. Waters, eds., *The New Race Question: How the Census Counts Multiracial Individuals* (New York: Russell Sage Foundation, 2002), p. 241.

tional standing is to focus primarily on first-generation members, least likely to intermarry. Many of them arrive in the U.S. already married. To interpret a finding of high in-marriage among a group that is primarily first-generation as evidence of a racial pattern of in-marriage is wrong. As Table 3 shows, among both Hispanics and Asians who have been in the U.S. three generations or more, a majority out-marry racially.

Out-marriage is a function of the timing of migration, the size of the group, and the relative importance of the boundaries separating groups. Sociologists have long noted that smaller groups generally have high out-marriage rates, because the pool of potential in-group mates is small. Thus new immigration can reduce overall out-marriage rates by increasing the proportion of first-generation immigrants, who arrive already married or who have a high propensity to in-marry because they are much less assimilated in terms of language, residence, religion, and other characteristics than later-generation members of the same group. But new immigration also might lower overall out-marriage rates of a group by enlarging the group size and providing possible in-group spouses to later-generation members. So it remains unclear whether the grandchildren of today's Hispanic immigrants will out-marry at the rate of 57 percent, because many members of the current third generation married at a time of relatively low Hispanic immigration, when there were fewer first- and second-generation potential spouses. However, countervailing factors also exist. The currently married third-generation Hispanics came of age at a time of greater discrimination and social distance between Hispanics and Anglos, and descendants of today's immigrants might face fewer social barriers, which would increase intermarriage rates. In general, the strength of "replenishment" effects on the marriage patterns of later-generation descendants of earlier immigrants has not been studied, but this is relevant to the contemporary immigration period, now in its fifth decade.

Of course the situation is much more complicated than these figures suggest. In every one of the five groupings there are great differences in income and education, for example; among Asians and Hispanics, these correspond closely to differences in national origin and generational status—factors related to immigration. Compare affluent and well-educated Cubans and South Americans, for instance, to more disadvantaged groups such as Mexicans and Puerto Ricans; or Japanese and Asian Indians to Cambodians and Laotians. Moreover, while some of these groups first came to the U.S. in appreciable numbers after 1965, others—Mexicans and Chinese in particular—have a much longer history of moderately large immigration. These national group differences within the two corners of the ethnoracial pentagon called Asian and Hispanic mean that any effort to discuss intermarriage among Asians or Hispanics as a whole are bound to be limited in their explanatory power. The census taker has contributed to this; the last three decennial censuses have merely ascertained whether a person is native-born or not, ignoring whether the native-born person is in turn the child of immigrants. Consequently our largest and most authoritative samples have tempted us to ignore generational standing: we know only that a certain native-born person identifies as Chinese in ethnic origin or Asian in racial origin; but the person could be a second- or seventh-generation American.

Nevertheless, national origin matters a great deal. For example, among Hispanic groups in New York City during the 1990s, 66 percent of second-generation Cubans were marrying non-Hispanics, as were 19 percent of second-generation Dominicans; Mexican rates were closer to the Cuban than the Dominican rate. Class background, phenotype, and the size of the national-origin groups probably all help explain these contrasts. In New York, Mexicans have been a very small group until fairly recently, and so their relatively high intermarriage rate may be due to group size. Similarly, in national data from 1990, Japanese and Filipinos were most likely to marry whites, followed by Chinese and Koreans and then by Southeast Asians and Asian Indians, who were the least likely. Also, interracial marriage with whites is more frequent than interethnic marriage with other Asian Americans. The panethnic group "Asian Americans" is an American creation and contains groups with very different languages, religions, and class backgrounds, some with a history of sharp divisions and enmity. Without a concern for Asian national origins, we cannot study the phenomenon of Asian panethnicity, operationally defined as the odds that members of Asian groups will marry members of other Asian national groups more often than non-Asian Americans will. But while panethnicity can hint at a trend toward "racialization" of Asian groups, the finding that out-marriage beyond the boundaries of Asian panethnicity is more prevalent in each of these Asian groups does not support the development of a strong panethnic group called Asians.

Measuring intermarriage and intermixing by ancestry and by generation becomes quite complex very quickly. Take, for example, Mexican Americans, currently the largest immigrant group in the U.S. In an earlier study comparing current Mexican American out-marriage to historical patterns of out-marriage among Italian Americans, we found that the results of previous intermarriage were quite evident in the ancestries of the current children of immigrants. Among Mexicans in the U.S. born between 1966 and 1975, 53 percent were first-generation, having immigrated to the U.S. after the age of 10. Eight percent were 1.5-generation, having immigrated at age 9 or younger. Another 9 percent were second-generation—born in the U.S. to two Mexico-born parents. Six percent were born in the U.S. to one Mexico-born parent and one parent born elsewhere, usually in the U.S. of Mexican parentage or ancestry. Twenty-four percent were third-generation or higher, born in the U.S. to U.S.-born parents. In total, 40 percent of this cohort reported some mixed ethnic origins; while one parent has some Mexican origin, the other parent reports either mixed origin or no Mexican origin.

When we focus only on the "true" second generation, the 9 percent of this group who were born in the U.S. to two Mexican parents, we find that how we define an in- or an out-marriage has a large effect. If we count as out-marriage only those who marry someone with no Mexican origins, then 20 percent of men and 11 percent of women out-married. However, the figures are much higher—45 percent for men and 27 percent for women—when we include the 2.5 generation (i.e., those with one immigrant parent and one native-born parent) and the third and later generations and also when we include spouses of mixed immigrant origins.

But even if we take the strictest definition of intermarriage, the ethnic origins of the next generation result from the rate at which couples form, not the rate at which individuals out-marry. In this cohort, although fewer than one sixth of individuals out-marry, more than one quarter of their offspring will be of mixed origin.

We may still ask how large the rate of "more than one quarter" is. One answer is that the figures cited here are in fact smaller than those often cited for second-generation out-marriage, because we have excluded from the American-born children of Mexican immigrants those who had only one Mexican immigrant parent (a group nearly as large as those whom we include), and among this excluded group out-marriage rates are more than twice as high as for the "true" second-generation members. Another way to gauge this figure is to compare present-day Mexicans to a cohort of second-generation Italian Americans born between 1886 and 1900. Italian American second-generation women, defined in the same way as Mexican Americans above, out-married at the rate of 17 percent. Although this is slightly higher than the second-generation Mexican women (11 percent), Italians were a much smaller group in the population. Hispanics made up 18 percent of the sampled husbands in the young birth cohort we studied, but in 1920 Italians were fewer than 3 percent of the sampled husbands. These numbers imply that, all else being equal, it was some six times as hard to limit one's choice of a spouse to an Italian at that time than it is to limit one's choice of a spouse to a Hispanic today. The fact that the second-generation Italian women nevertheless did limit their choice to their own kind roughly as often as second-generation Mexican women do today strongly suggests that the constraints that operated against out-marriage were actually greater for Italian women living at that time than they are for Mexican women today. At any rate, we should conclude that such constraints are surely not appreciably larger now than they were a century ago.

The Big Changes in Our Time

Recent increases in rates of cohabitation and out-of-wedlock births as well as long-familiar high divorce rates must somehow be incorporated into our conceptualization and measurement of ethnic intermarriage. A study of marriage in 2000 will not capture the same proportion of people that a study of marriage would have captured in 1900, and the differences do not capture all ethnic or racial groups in the same way. One might object that this sort of gradation of relationships—cohabitation vs. marriage—has always been an issue in the study of intermarriage; one need only think of interracial or interfaith dating in comparison with interracial or interfaith marriage. The point is the profundity of the shift: cohabitation is much more intimate and of much longer duration than dating and much more likely to result in offspring.

Lichter and Qiao report that the number of opposite-sex cohabiting couples grew from 440,000 in 1960 to 3.8 million in 2000. We also know that there are large differences in the degree of cross-racial relationships between married couples and cohabiters; 10 percent of cohabiting opposite-sex couples were in interracial relationships, while only 6 percent of married couples were. The 2000 Census also provides information on same-sex couples—individuals who designate themselves as "unmarried partners" of the household head. There were 594,000 same-sex cohabiting couples, although we are unaware of any studies of the degree of racial and ethnic intermixing among them.

The other key challenge is that marriage is not merely less durable but quite simply less universal than it was before, especially for some racial/ethnic groups. For instance, in 1990 only 35 percent of black women under the age of 35 had ever been married. When rates of cohabitation and divorce are both high, the meaning of ethnic intermarriage becomes problematic at both ends of the process. Connections across ethnic lines may be established in premarital or postmarital cohabitation. In this brave new world, can we pay attention only to the "middle stage" of these processes?

The shift to bearing children out of wedlock is just as portentous. At present one third of American children are born to women who are not married. This figure varies dramatically by race and ethnicity. In 2000, according to the National Center for Health Statistics, 22 percent of births among non-Hispanic whites, 69 percent of births among non-Hispanic blacks, and 43 percent of births to Hispanics were to unwed mothers. As the magnitude of the figure suggests, this pattern is not due to particular lifestyles; rather, it is remarkably widespread. Most of the children of out-of-wedlock births do not live with their biological father. While the rates have been increasing rapidly for whites, the figures for blacks deserve special attention in connection with intermarriage because, as noted, black out-marriage has been and remains distinctly low, and at the same time the pattern is shifting somewhat toward greater intermarriage. Black-white intermarriage falls within a context of low levels of black marriage and higher levels of black-white cohabitation than of black-white marriage, which radically complicates the interpretation of the intermarriage rates.

At the same time, the high proportion of blacks born out of wedlock also complicates the interpretation of the multiracial origins of the offspring of black-white unions. Much of a child's ethnic and even racial identity is related to the connection to parents and grandparents. If a child's father is out of the picture, self-identification is more likely to follow the mother's line; still, the father might not be completely absent, and in any case the father's phenotype might make a difference in identity.

In sum, formal marriage and the children born in wedlock provide us with a conservative view of the degree of intermixing—both in terms of interethnic couples and in terms of the production of children of mixed ancestry. How changes in cohabitation, divorce, and child-bearing come to affect interethnic commingling and the resultant ethnic and racial identity in the next generation is a big issue for the future understanding of ethnic blending. In our view, the most important novel features of American ethnic intermarriage are likely to be bound up with these changes. By comparison, differences in formal intermarriage rates between the largest of the immigrant groups of today and the largest immigrant groups of the last great wave of immigration seem minor, even if race plays a somewhat different role in determining contemporary patterns.

Intermixing and Multiple Identities

We have noted that intermarriage bears on how a group is perceived; it is difficult to speak of the descendants of one immigrant group because many, and soon enough most, are also descendants of other groups. A special case involves groups that are today recognized in the federal government's statistical categories as "other" (than white): African Americans, American Indians, Asians, and Hispanics. Even when such groups had very low intermarriage rates or were legally restricted from intermarrying, defining group membership was not always simple because of interracial out-of-wedlock births. Insofar as whites socially defined these offspring as non-white, the problem was solved or reduced (though this was not always the case; consider the American Indian "half-breed" and the descendants of Mexicans in the Southwest). In any case, regarding current intermarriage rates, the conceptual challenge is different, because the offspring may insist on recognizing both their minority racial status and their white origins, and the number of people it covers may be much greater. In this context, the way in which the federal government gathered racial statistics became a subject of debate in the 1990s.

The federal censuses had allowed individuals of European descent to describe their mixed origins; for example, questions about parental birthplaces always turned up millions with parents born in different countries. The ancestry question similarly anticipates multiple ancestries for respondents. Some race data from late 19th- and early 20th-century censuses also recognized race mixture, at least in connection with whites and blacks, by enumerating the number of mulattos, quadroons, and octoroons. But after these classifications were dropped, individuals were listed as members of one race only. And when self-reporting was introduced, the instruction explicitly said to "mark one [race] only." Eventually, a movement of identity politics agitated for change. The upshot was the right to "mark one [race] or more" in federal statistics, and this change to the race question appeared in the 2000 Census. However, how this multiplicity is to be recognized in federal laws that require discrete and nonoverlapping categories to define protected groups is not entirely clear. For the moment, for civil and voting rights legislation and cases, it appears that individuals listing more than one group are counted as members of a protected group and not as whites.

The Hispanic-origin population represents a second variant of the response. Here too the figures may be relevant to civil and voting rights legislation; but the Hispanic-origin question has bypassed the identity struggle in the public domain because it never required one to claim *only* Hispanic origins. The offspring of a Mexican immigrant and an Anglo can routinely answer the Hispanic-origin question in the affirmative without appearing to deny his or her Anglo origins, which can be reported on the race question.

A related set of questions has involved the federal relationship with American Indian tribes. By the early 20th century, many people who said they were Native Americans by race also noted that they were of mixed descent, so the government defined tribal membership in terms of the proportion of an individual's ancestors who had been tribal members and recognition by the tribe as a part of the community—that is, the criteria of membership include both a "blood quantum" and a subjective element of communal recognition.

Similarly, American Jewish intermarriage rates have soared, and for several million people there is no longer a yes-no answer to the question of whether they are Jewish—not because they may be secular in religious outlook but because they are both Jewish (in some respect) and not Jewish. Although in this case the government is not involved, Jewish institutions face the question of how to decide who is Jewish and struggle with the need for clear, nonoverlapping categories in the context of the messiness of large-scale intermarriage.

The new race question that recorded multiple racial identities appeared in the 2000 Census, and 6.8 million people reported more than one race. Among those who reported two or more races, 80 percent reported that they were white and one of the other race categories. Sonya Tafoya, Hans Johnson, and Laura E. Hill report that 2.2 million people, or 35 percent of biracial people, reported that they were white and "some other race"; they were followed by 1 million who reported that they were American Indian and white (17 percent), 868,395 people who were Asian and white (13.6 percent), and 784,764 people who were black and white (12.3 percent). The foreign-born were more likely than the native-born to report more than one race. Six percent of foreign-born people listed multiple races, as opposed to 2 percent of the native-born. This is in great part due to the way the census is organized. Many people answering the race question would like to say that they are Hispanic or a specific group such as Puerto Rican, but the 15 boxes to check on the race question do not include any Hispanic groups. At the bottom is a box for "some other race" and then a blank line where a respondent can write in a race. If someone writes in "Puerto Rican" or "Hispanic," the census codes that individual as "some other race." If someone does this and also checks off "white," he or she is coded as multiple-race. Thus the largest group of multiple-race people are people who are "some other race" and white, and most of them are Latinos—and thus many are foreign-born.

The new ability to report more than one race on the census will no doubt have profound consequences in the coming years. Already the statistical reporting of race is quite complicated. Official tabulations of the census include the broad race categories—white, black, Asian, American Indian, Native Hawai'ian or other Pacific Islander, as well as the residual "some other race." This produces 6 possible monoracial categories, 15 unique biracial combinations, 20 unique three-race combinations, 15 four-race combinations, 6 five-race combinations, and 1 six-race combination, or 63 unique racial identities. If Hispanic or non-Hispanic is added to each of these 63 identities, there are 126 unique racial/Hispanic categories. Many commentators have wondered how long a statistical system with such complexity can survive.

No doubt many of the people who report more than one race are the result of intermarriages among their parents, grandparents, and more distant ancestors. Indeed, half of the people who report more than one race on the census are children, and so the vast majority are being reported on by the person filling out the census, probably a parent. We noted above that as the second and third generations of the post-1965 immigrants come of age, they will probably intermarry at relatively high rates. Thus future censuses will show that an even greater proportion of the children and grandchildren of post-1965 immigrants are of mixed ancestry. It is possible that historians at the end of the 21st century will look back at the population projections of the 1990s with the knowledge that divisions that seemed natural and sharp at the time were already in the process of blurring and perhaps even disappearing. The intermarriage and resulting mixed ancestries of the most recent immigrants to the U.S. are taking on a force of their own, and rigid divisions by race or ethnicity will not remain in place over time.

Bibliography

Bean, Frank D., and Gillian Stevens. 2003. *America's Newcomers and the Dynamics of Diversity.* New York: Russell Sage Foundation.

Edmonston, Barry, Sharon M. Lee, and Jeffrey S. Passel. 2002. "Recent Trends in Intermarriage and Immigration and Their Effects on the Future Racial Composition of the U.S. Population." In Joel Perlmann and Mary C. Waters, eds., *The New Race Question: How the Census Counts Multiracial Individuals,* pp. 227–58. New York: Russell Sage Foundation.

Gilberston, Greta A., Joseph P. Fitzpatrick, and Lijun Yang. 1996. "Hispanic Intermarriage in New York City: New Evidence from 1991." *International Migration Review* 30: 445–59.

Hollinger, David. 1995. *Postethnic America: Beyond Multiculturalism.* New York: Basic Books.

Hout, Michael, and Joshua Goldstein. 1994. "How 4.5 Million Irish Immigrants Became 40 Million Irish Americans: Demographic and Subjective Aspects of the Ethnic Composition of White Americans." *American Sociological Review* 59: 64–82.

Lee, Sharon M., and Barry Edmonston. 2005. "New Marriages, New Families: U.S. Racial and Hispanic Intermarriage." *Population Bulletin* 60.

Lichter, Daniel T., and Zhenchao Qian. 2005. "Marriage and Family in a Multiracial Society." In Reynolds Farley and John Haaga, eds., *The American People Census 2000,* pp. 169–200. New York: Russell Sage Foundation.

Lieberson, Stanley, and Mary C. Waters. 1988. *From Many Strands: Ethnic and Racial Groups in Contemporary America.* New York: Russell Sage Foundation.

Perlmann, Joel, and Mary C. Waters, eds. 2002. *The New Race Question: How the Census Counts Multiracial Individuals.* New York: Russell Sage Foundation.

———. 2004. "Intermarriage Then and Now: Race, Generation, and the Changing Meaning of Marriage." In Nancy Foner and George M. Frederickson, eds. *Not Just Black and White: Historical and Contemporary Perspectives on Immigration, Race, and Ethnicity in the United States,* pp. 262–77. New York: Russell Sage Foundation.

Qian, Zhenchao, Sampson Lee Blair, and Stacey D. Ruf. 2001. "Asian American Interracial and Interethnic Marriages: Differences by Education and Nativity." *International Migration Review* 35: 557–86.

Qian, Zhenchao, and Daniel T. Lichter. 2001. "Measuring Marital Assimilation: Intermarriage among Natives and Immigrants." *Social Science Research* 30: 289–312.

Tafoya, Sonya M., Hans Johnson, and Laura E. Hill. 2005. "Who Chooses to Choose Two?" In Reynolds Farley and John Haaga, eds., *The American People Census 2000,* pp. 332–51. New York: Russell Sage Foundation.

Assimilation

Richard Alba and Victor Nee

The idea of assimilation has undergone a transformation since the middle of the 20th century. Then it was a foundational concept in American thinking about race and ethnicity—not only part of the core of the social science study of these phenomena but accepted by liberal Americans as an ideal toward which their society was inevitably moving, as prejudices were eroded and legal and social handicaps were removed. This dual existence was one source of its subsequent difficulties.

Within a decade of the greatest successes of the civil rights movement in the mid-1960s, the idea of assimilation was under fierce attack. It was now seen on the social science side as the ideology-laden residue of a worn-out functionalism, and on the political and ideological side as an ethnocentric and patronizing imposition on minority peoples struggling to retain their cultural and ethnic integrity. The very word seemed to conjure up a bygone era when the multiracial and multiethnic nature of American society was not comprehended. By 1993, Nathan Glazer could write an essay tellingly entitled "Is Assimilation Dead?"

Yet as social scientists and others struggle to understand the full ramifications of the new era of mass immigration, which began in the U.S. during the 1960s, they are almost inevitably resurrecting the assimilation idea, but now in forms that take into account the critiques of the preceding decades. To be useful as a means of understanding contemporary social realities and their relationship to the past and future, this rehabilitation requires us to strip the concept of assimilation of the normative encumbrances it acquired in its prior existence and provide a theory of assimilation, an account of the mechanisms producing it. At the same time, we must recognize that assimilation is not the only modality of incorporation into American society—that pluralism and racial exclusion are other patterns by which individuals and groups come to be recognized as part of that society.

The Chicago School

Assimilation as a paradigm for the social scientific understanding of the incorporation of immigrants and their descendants is traceable to the Chicago School of Sociology of the early 20th century, and especially to the work of Robert E. Park, W. I. Thomas, and their collaborators and students. At the then newly founded University of Chicago (1890), sociologists took up the challenge of understanding the consequences of the huge migrations flowing into their city. Robert Park and E. W. Burgess defined assimilation as "a process of interpenetration and fusion in which persons and groups acquire the memory, sentiments, and attitudes of other persons and groups and, by sharing their experience and history, are incorporated with them in a common historical life" (p. 735). This definition, which clearly does not require the erasure of all signs of ethnic origins, equates assimilation with changes that bring ethnic minorities into mainstream American life. It expresses an understanding of assimilation with contemporary appeal, leaving ample room for the persistence of ethnic elements set within a common frame.

Nonetheless, Park's legacy is closely identified with a teleological notion of assimilation as the end stage of a "race-relations cycle" of "contact, competition, accommodation, and eventual assimilation," a sequence that, in its most famous statement, was viewed as "apparently progressive and irreversible" (1950, p. 150). Park's analysis referred to the large-scale processes in the modern world economy that are bringing once-separated peoples into closer contact. Competition is the initial, unstable consequence of contact, as the groups struggle to gain advantages over one another, leading to the more stable stage of accommodation, in which a social structure of typically unequal relations among groups and a settled understanding of group positions have emerged. But no matter how stable the social order, ethnic differences would eventually diminish, according to Park, who wrote that "in our estimates of race relations we have not reckoned with the effects of personal intercourse and the friendships that grow up out of them."

Members of the Chicago School were pioneers in the study of city life, and the most enduring empirical studies they produced examine assimilation as a social process embedded in the urban landscape. These studies take as their point of departure Park's axiom that "social relations are . . . inevitably correlated with spatial relations; physical distances . . . are, or seem to be, indexes of social distances" (1926, p. 18). From this it follows that upwardly mobile immigrants and their descendants will leave ethnic enclaves, since "changes of economic and social status . . . tend to be registered in changes of location." In *The Ghetto*, Park's student Louis Wirth analyzed this process for Jewish settlements in Chicago.

The empirical study that had the greatest subsequent impact was W. Lloyd Warner and Leo Srole's *The Social Systems of American Ethnic Groups*, published in

1945. Concentrating on an older industrial city in New England, Warner and Srole observed a series of correlated changes over successive generations of various European ethnic groups. They documented the decline of white ethnic enclaves as the native-born generations shifted out of the working class to higher occupational and class positions and into better residential neighborhoods. In addition, they found behavioral changes in the private spheres of ethnic groups, in the relations between husbands and wives and between parents and children, and in the friendships formed by the children. In interpreting their findings, Warner and Srole posited that assimilation was the direction in which all groups were moving, though they varied greatly in the time required for it to occur.

The Canonical Synthesis

By the middle of the 20th century, the zenith of the melting pot as metaphor, assimilation was integral to American self-understanding and the pivot around which social science investigations of ethnicity and even of race turned. Yet little had been accomplished in the way of developing clear and consistent operational concepts that could be deployed to measure the extent of assimilation. This problem was not solved until Milton Gordon's *Assimilation in American Life* in 1964.

Gordon's singular contribution was to delineate in a lucid way the multiple dimensions of assimilation. Acculturation, he argued, was the dimension that typically came first and was inevitable, to a large degree. He defined acculturation very broadly, as the minority group's adoption of the "cultural patterns" of the host society—patterns extending beyond the acquisition of the host language and such other obvious externals as dress to include aspects normally regarded as part of the inner, or private, self, such as characteristic emotional expression or key life goals. In the U.S., the specific standard that represented the direction and eventual outcome of the acculturation process was the "middle-class cultural patterns of, largely, white Protestant, Anglo-Saxon origins," which Gordon also described as the "core culture." In his view, acculturation was predominantly a one-way process: the minority group adopted the core culture, which remained basically unchanged by acculturation. Only institutional religion was exempt: he did not expect that different immigrant groups would give up their fundamental religious identities—e.g., Catholic or Jewish—as a result of acculturation.

Acculturation could occur in the absence of other types of assimilation, and the stage of "acculturation only" could last indefinitely, according to Gordon. His major hypothesis was that structural assimilation—that is, integration into primary groups—is associated with or stimulates all other kinds of assimilation (*"Once structural assimilation has occurred, . . . all of the other types of assimilation will naturally follow"*; p. 81). In particular, this meant that prejudice and discrimination would decline, if not disappear, that intermarriage would be common, and that the minority's separate identity would wane. All told, Gordon identified seven dimensions of assimilation—cultural, structural, marital, identity, prejudice, discrimination, and civic.

Gordon's legacy also includes codification of alternative conceptions of assimilation in the U.S. Gordon described these as the "theories" of Anglo-conformity and the melting pot, but they are more appropriately viewed as alternative popular beliefs or ideologies about the composition and nature of civil society. The model of Anglo-conformity, which corresponds in spirit with the campaign for rapid, "pressure-cooker" Americanization during World War I, equated assimilation with acculturation in the Anglo-American mold, ignoring its other dimensions. The model of the melting pot has enjoyed several periods of popularity, most recently in the aftermath of World War II. It offers an idealistic vision of American society and identity as arising from the biological and cultural fusion of different peoples; and while its exponents have usually emphasized the contributions of Europeans to the mixture, it allows for recognition of those of non-European groups as well. In terms of Gordon's scheme, the model emphasized cultural and structural assimilation. It forecast widespread intermarriage; a well-known variant, the triple melting pot, defined by Will Herberg, foresaw intermarriage as taking place within population pools defined by religious boundaries. The cultural assimilation portion of the melting pot idea was rather ambiguous, however. Many early exponents spoke in ways that suggested a truly syncretic American culture, blending elements from many different groups, but later commentators were more consistent with Gordon's own conception, that acculturation is a mostly one-directional acceptance of Anglo-American patterns.

Another prominent element of the canonical synthesis is the notion of "straight-line assimilation," popularized by Herbert Gans. This idea envisions a sequence of generational steps: each new generation represents on average a new stage of adjustment to the host society—that is, a further step away from ethnic "ground zero," the community and ethnoculture established by the immigrants, and a step closer to more complete assimilation.

Though Gordon presented a complex multidimensional specification of assimilation, it soon became clear that his account omitted some critical dimensions. One was socioeconomic assimilation, which researchers began to consider in the aftermath of Peter Blau and Otis Dudley Duncan's seminal status-attainment study, *The American Occupational Structure*. The emphasis on socioeconomic position reinforced the preexisting view that assimilation and social mobility are inextricably linked. Socioeconomic assimilation was frequently equated with attainment of average or above-average socioeconomic standing, as measured by indicators such as education, occupation, and income. Since many immigrant groups, especially those coming from agricultural backgrounds, such as the Irish, Italians, and Mexicans, entered the American social structure on its lowest rungs, this meaning of socioeconomic assimilation conflated it with social mobility.

This conception has become problematic in the contemporary era of mass immigration, because immigrant groups no longer inevitably start at the bottom of the labor market; numerous groups today bring financial capital as well as substantial educational credentials, professional training, and other forms of human capital. One way to avoid the historical specificity of the conventional formulation is to define socioeconomic assimilation as minority participation in mainstream institutional structures (e.g., labor market, schools) on a par with ethnic-majority individuals of similar socioeconomic origins. If the emphasis in the first conception falls on equality of attainments or position, the emphasis in the second is on equality of treatment: members of the immigrant minority and similarly positioned others have the same life chances in the pursuit of contested goods, such as desirable occupations. In this sense, the ethnic distinction has lost its relevance for processes of socioeconomic attainment. In this way, one can assimilate into the working class, and many do.

Another addition to the repertoire of assimilation concepts involved residential mobility. Douglas Massey's "spatial assimilation" model formalized the significance of residence for the assimilation paradigm. Its basic tenet holds that as members of minority groups acculturate and establish themselves in American labor markets, they attempt to leave behind less successful members of their groups and convert socioeconomic and assimilation progress into residential gain, by "purchasing" homes in places with greater advantages and amenities. Because good schools, clean streets, and other amenities are more common in communities where the majority is concentrated and these communities have been largely suburban since the 1950s, the search for better surroundings leads ethnic minority families toward suburbanization and greater contact with the majority.

Status attainment and residential segregation research provided assimilation studies with quantitative measures of the extent to which the life chances of immigrants and their descendants were similar or dissimilar to the mainstream experience. The study of ethnic and racial groups was linked to the general interest in understanding social mobility, so that the study of assimilation shifted away from the examination of cultural and interpersonal dimensions to questions of comparative ethnic stratification. Accordingly, ethnic and racial minorities were regarded as moving in the direction of assimilation insofar as their educational, occupational, income, and residential characteristics approached, equaled, or exceeded those of Anglo-Americans or native-born non-Hispanic whites. Numerous findings of persistent inequality in life chances, especially between racially defined groups, were interpreted as evidence of discrimination and restrictions on the opportunity for assimilation.

The Critique of Assimilation

The intellectual blinders of the assimilation literature of the mid-20th century are abundantly illustrated by Warner and Srole's classic study. They concluded that American ethnic groups are destined to be no more than temporary phenomena, doomed by the assimilatory power of the American context. As part of the assimilation process, ethnic groups must, according to these authors, "unlearn" their cultural traits, which are "evaluated by the host society as inferior," in order to "successfully learn the new way of life necessary for full acceptance." Even more disturbing from the current viewpoint, Warner and Srole correlate the potential for speedy assimilation with a hierarchy of racial and cultural acceptability, ranging from English-speaking Protestants at the top to "Negroes and all Negroid mixtures" at the bottom. While the assimilation of fair-skinned Protestants was expected to be unproblematic and therefore of short duration, that of groups deviating from this ethnic prototype in any significant respect would be considerably more prolonged, if not doubtful. Thus, the assimilation of "dark-skinned" Mediterranean Catholics, such as Italians, was expected to demand a "moderate" period (which Warner and Srole equated with six generations or more!). The assimilation of non-European groups was more problematic still and would continue into the indefinite future or even, in the case of African Americans, be delayed until "the present American social order changes gradually or by revolution."

One problem in this formulation is the inevitability of assimilation, which is presented as the natural conclusion of the process of incorporation into American society. Even black Americans, blocked by the racism of U.S. society from full pursuit of the assimilation goal, are presumed to be assimilating, albeit at a glacial pace. Further, by equating assimilation with full or successful incorporation, Warner and Srole viewed racial minorities as in effect incompletely assimilated, rather than as incorporated into the society on some other basis. In relation to black Americans in particular, this conception was consistent with liberal incrementalist strategies for pursuing racial justice, which on the one hand sought to remove legal and institutional barriers to equality and to combat white prejudice and discrimination and on the other urged blacks to seek integration and to become more like middle-class whites.

Another objectionable feature is the ethnocentrism of this formulation, which elevates a particular cultural model, that of middle-class Protestant whites of British ancestry, to the normative standard by which other groups are to be assessed and to which they should aspire. This is bluntly apparent in the ranking of groups by Warner and Srole, which places groups higher on the scale, and thus more rapidly assimilating, the closer they are at the outset to the Anglo-Saxon cultural (and physical) model. Assimilation, then, meant becoming more like middle-class Protestant whites, as Milton Gordon and, more recently, Samuel Huntington also claimed.

From the contemporary standpoint, the view of the predominance of the culture of Anglo-American groups that settled in North America in the colonial era downplays the multiple cultural streams that have fed into American culture, affecting even the English language as spoken by Americans. Not only does this view seem to contradict the riotous cultural bloom of the U.S., but in our rapidly globalizing world it seems quite undesirable to extinguish the distinctive cultural and linguistic knowledge that immigrants could pass on to their children.

The final fatal flaw is the absence of a positive role for the ethnic or racial group. From the assimilation perspective, the ethnic community could provide temporary shelter for immigrants seeking to withstand the intense stresses associated with the early stages of immigration to a new society; according to frequently used images, the ethnic community was a "way station" or a "decompression chamber." But past a certain point, attachment to the ethnic group would hinder minority individuals from taking full advantage of the opportunities offered by American society, which required individual mobility, not ethnic loyalty. What this perspective overlooked is that in some cases the ethnic group could, by dominating some economic niches, be the source of better socioeconomic opportunities than the mainstream. There are also important noneconomic ways in which the ethnic group can contribute to the well-being of its members, such as the solidarity and support provided by coethnics.

Redefining (and Refining) Assimilation

The changing demographic realities of the U.S. and the need for a viable concept of assimilation point to the value of rethinking some of the classical views on assimilation. Some contemporary scholars have taken up the challenge. Rogers Brubaker, for example, describes assimilation as "a process of becoming similar, in some respect, to some reference population." We start from the recognition of assimilation as a form of ethnic change. As the anthropologist Frederick Barth emphasized, ethnicity itself is a social boundary, a distinction that individuals make in their everyday lives and that shapes their actions and mental orientations toward others. This distinction is typically embedded in a variety of social and cultural differences between groups that give an ethnic boundary concrete significance (so that members of one group think, "They are not like us because . . .").

In our own work, assimilation, as a form of ethnic change, can be defined as the decline of an ethnic distinction and its corollary cultural and social differences. "Decline" means in this context that a distinction attenuates in salience—that the occurrences for which it is relevant diminish in number and contract to fewer and fewer domains of social life. As ethnic boundaries become blurred or weakened, individuals' ethnic origins become less and less relevant in relation to the members of another ethnic group (typically, but not necessarily, the ethnic majority group), and individuals from both sides of the boundary perceive themselves with less and less frequency in terms of ethnic categories and increasingly only under specific circumstances. Assimilation, moreover, is not a dichotomous outcome and does not require the disappearance of ethnicity; consequently, the individuals and groups undergoing assimilation may still bear a number of ethnic markers. It can occur on a large scale to members of a group even as the group itself remains as a highly visible point of reference on the social landscape, embodied in an ethnic culture, neighborhoods, and institutional infrastructures.

Our definition calls attention to the importance of boundaries for processes of ethnic stability and change, raising the possibility that features of social boundaries may make assimilation more or less likely and influence the specific forms that it takes. Aristide Zolberg and Long Litt Woon have introduced an extremely useful typology of boundary-related changes that sheds light on different ways that assimilation can occur. Boundary crossing corresponds to the classic version of individual-level assimilation: someone moves from one group to another without any real change to the boundary itself (although if such boundary crossings happen on a large scale and in a consistent direction, then the social structure is being altered). Boundary blurring implies that the social profile of a boundary has become less distinct: the clarity of the social distinction involved has become clouded, and individuals' location with respect to the boundary may appear indeterminate. The final process, boundary shifting, involves the relocation of a boundary so that populations once situated on one side are now included on the other: former outsiders are thereby transformed into insiders.

Boundary crossing could be said to represent assimilation à la Warner and Srole; that is, the boundary is crossed when a minority individual becomes like the majority through wholesale acculturation. But boundary shifting represents a possibility not truly recognized in the older literature but captured recently in the intensive discussion of how various disparaged immigration groups, such as the Irish and eastern European Jews, made themselves acceptable as "whites" in the U.S. racial order: a radical shift in a group's position. Yet boundary blurring may represent the most intriguing and underexplored possibility among the three. Blurring entails the ambiguity of a boundary with respect to some set of individuals. This could mean that they are seen simultaneously as members of the groups on both sides of the boundary or that sometimes they appear to be members of one and at other times members of the other. Under these circumstances, assimilation may be eased, insofar as the individuals undergoing it do not sense a rupture between participation in mainstream institutions and familiar social and cultural practices and identities. Assimilation of this type involves intermediate or hyphenated stages that allow individuals to feel that they are members of an ethnic minority and of the mainstream simultaneously. Boundary blurring could occur when the mainstream culture and identity are relatively porous and allow for the incorporation of cultural elements brought by immigrant groups—i.e., two-sided cultural change.

Another innovation is the concept of segmented assimilation, formulated by Alejandro Portes and Min Zhou. They argue that a critical question concerns the segment of American society into which individuals assimilate and that multiple trajectories are required for the answer. One trajectory leads to entry to the middle-class mainstream. But another leads to incorporation into the racialized population at the bottom of American society. This trajectory may be followed by many of those in the second and third generations of immigrant groups handicapped by their very humble initial locations in American society and barred from entry to the mainstream by their race. On this route of assimilation, they are guided by the cultural models of poor, native-born African Americans and Latinos. Perceiving that they are likely to remain in their parents' status at the bottom of the occupational hierarchy and evaluating this prospect negatively, because unlike their parents they have absorbed the standards of the American mainstream, they succumb to the temptation to drop out of school and join the inner-city underclass.

A New Theory of Assimilation

The successful restoration of the concept of assimilation to its rightful place as an important pattern of incorporation requires a theory, a specification of the causal mechanisms that bring it about. Earlier writings posited that assimilation was an inevitable outcome of human migration to North America. We hold that assimilation should not be assumed but instead must be explained as a variable outcome of the dynamics of intergroup relations. In our theory, the pace and success of assimilation depend principally on three factors. First is the crucial effect of informal and formal institutions—customs, norms, conventions, and rules—which establish the underlying framework of competition and cooperation in a society. Second are the workaday decisions of individual immigrants and their descendants, which often lead to assimilation, not as a stated goal but as an unintended consequence of social behavior oriented to successful accommodation. And third are the network ties embedded in the immigrant community and family, which shape the particular ways in which their members adapt to American life.

Institutional mechanisms. The most dramatic change affecting assimilation in the past half-century took place at the level of law and public policy. Immigrants from southern and eastern Europe did encounter discrimination, but their path to assimilation was never legally blocked, and their constitutional rights provided basic legal safeguards. By contrast, for nonwhite minorities before World War II, the formal rules and their enforcement bolstered the racism that excluded them from civil society. For example, Asian immigrants were ineligible for citizenship until 1952 and faced many discriminatory local and regional laws that restricted their property rights and civil liberties.

But this blockage yielded as a result of the legal changes of the civil rights era, which extended fundamental constitutional rights to racial minorities. These changes have not been merely formal; they have been accompanied by new institutional arrangements, the monitoring and enforcement mechanisms that have increased the cost of discrimination. For instance, Title VII of the Civil Rights Act of 1964 gives the Equal Employment Opportunity Commission the right to intervene in private bias lawsuits when it deems that a case is of "general public importance." Although enforcement of Title VII has been inconsistent under different federal administrations, corporations and nonprofit firms have become more attentive in observing its guidelines, with increasing numbers of firms offering diversity and multicultural training workshops for managers and employees and instituting company rules against racial and gender discrimination. Landmark settlements of federal discrimination lawsuits, such as that against Texaco in 1997, have significantly raised the cost of discrimination.

Institutional changes have gone hand in hand with changes in mainstream values. One of these is the remarkable decline in the power of racist ideologies since the end of World War II. An examination of more than half a century of survey data demonstrates unequivocally that belief in racial separation—endorsed by a majority of white Americans at midcentury, when only a third of whites believed that "white students and black students should go to the same schools"—has steadily eroded. Americans have generally embraced the principle of racial equality, even if they are ambivalent about policies such as affirmative action that are intended to bring about equality as a matter of fact.

Such institutional and ideological shifts have not ended racial prejudice and racist practice, but they have changed their character. Racism is now outlawed and as a consequence has become more covert and subterranean, and it can no longer be advocated publicly without sanction. America's commitment to the rule of law has over the course of the latter half of the 20th century brought about far-reaching institutional change that has removed race as an insurmountable obstacle to assimilation for most of today's immigrants.

Individual action. A satisfactory theory of assimilation must acknowledge that individuals are not merely the passive vectors of abstract social forces and must factor in their purposive action and self-interest by providing an account of the incentives and motivations for assimilation. In adapting to life in the U.S., immigrants and the second generation face choices in which the degrees of risk and benefit are hard to gauge and involve unforeseeable long-term consequences. In contemplating the strategies best suited to improve their lives and those of their children, they weigh the risks and potential benefits of "ethnic" strategies, dependent on opportunities available through ethnic networks, versus "mainstream" ones, which involve the American educational system and the open labor market. Often enough, there may be little choice in these matters. When immigrants have little human and financial capital and/or they are undocumented, they will usually be limited to jobs located through ethnic networks and constrained to residence in ethnic areas. But others may try mixed strategies, built from ethnic and mainstream elements, as when second-generation young adults obtain jobs through family and ethnic networks while continuing their education, thus leaving multiple options open.

Individuals striving for success in American society often do not see themselves as assimilating. Yet unintended consequences of practical strategies taken in pursuit of highly valued goals—a good education, a good job, a nice place to live, interesting friends and acquaintances—often result in specific forms of assimilation. It is not uncommon, for instance, for first- and second-generation Asian parents to raise their children speaking only English in the belief that their chances for success in school will be improved by more complete mastery of the host language. Likewise, the search for a desirable place to live—with good schools and opportunities for children to grow up away from the seductions of deviant models of behavior—often leads immigrant families to ethnically mixed suburbs (if and when socioeconomic success permits this). One consequence, whether intended or not, is greater interaction with families of other backgrounds; such increased contact tends to encourage acculturation, especially for children.

Network mechanisms. Network mechanisms involve social processes that monitor and enforce norms within groups. Norms are the informal rules that provide guidelines for action; they arise from the problem-solving activity of individuals as they strive to improve their chances for success through cooperation with similar others. The role of such mechanisms carries over into the settlement process: newly arrived immigrants turn to relatives and friends for assistance in meeting practical needs, from the first weeks following their arrival to the subsequent sequence of jobs and residences that form the basis of long-term accommodation. Networks lower the risks of international migration and increase the chances of success in making the transition to settled lives in America. Consequently, one can view network ties as a form of social capital, providing an array of tangible forms of assistance, especially timely and accurate information about the availability of start-up jobs and places to live. They become especially critical when discriminatory barriers block an individualistic pattern of social mobility, for then assimilation, when it occurs, depends on collectivist strategies.

Most ethnic groups in America have relied on collectivist strategies to a greater or lesser extent, even though the dominant pattern of assimilation conforms to the individualistic pattern. For instance, Irish Americans, in their effort to shed the stereotype of "shanty Irish," socially distanced themselves from African Americans as a group strategy to gain acceptance from Anglo-Americans, ostracizing those who intermarried with blacks. More recently, South Asians who settled in an agricultural town in northern California evolved norms encouraging selective acculturation while discouraging social contact with local white youths who taunted the Punjabi youths. The Punjabi immigrants' strategy, according to the anthropologist Margaret

Gibson, emphasized academic achievement in the public schools as a means to success, which they defined not locally but in terms of the opportunity structures of the mainstream.

As a form of capital, network ties can become a fungible asset, which, like human capital, can be converted into material gain. Such social capital is accumulated as a byproduct of ongoing social relationships, manifested in the buildup of goodwill and trust between members of a group who have cooperated in the past. For immigrants, it is made up of the webs of network ties that they have accumulated over the course of the migration experience, starting with the strong ties of family, kinship, and friendship and extending to the weak ties of acquaintanceship.

A profound alteration to the social scientific understanding of immigrant group incorporation is that it is no longer exclusively focused on assimilation. Very abstractly, three documented patterns describe today how immigrants and their descendants become "incorporated into"—that is, a recognized part of—American society (or possibly any society). The pattern of assimilation involves a progressive, typically multigenerational process of socioeconomic, cultural, and social integration into the mainstream, that part of American society where racial and ethnic origins have at most minor effects on the life chances of individuals. A second pattern entails racial exclusion and absorption into a racial minority status, which implies persistent and substantial disadvantages vis-à-vis the members of the mainstream. A third pattern is that of pluralism, in which individuals and groups are able to draw social and economic advantages by keeping some aspects of their lives within the confines of an ethnic matrix (e.g., ethnic economic niches, ethnic communities). A huge literature has developed these ideas and applied them to the ethnic and generational groups arising from contemporary immigration.

All three patterns can be found in the American past, and all are likely to figure in the American present and future, though not in ways identical to those of the past. The pattern of assimilation has been the master trend among Americans of European origin. The pattern of racial exclusion has characterized the experiences of non-European immigrant groups, such as the Chinese, who were confined to ghettoes and deprived of basic civil rights because American law defined them as "aliens ineligible for citizenship." The pattern of pluralism is evident in the minority of European Americans whose lives play out primarily in ethnic social worlds, which remain visible in the form of ethnic neighborhoods in such cities as New York and Chicago.

In contemplating contemporary immigration, most observers readily concede the continued relevance of the patterns of racialization and pluralism. The first reappears in the new concept of segmented assimilation, and the second has been elaborated in old and new forms, in the guise of such concepts as "ethnic economic enclaves" and "ethnic niches." It is the pattern of assimilation whose continued significance has been doubted or rejected. But it is increasingly apparent that all three remain relevant. It may be unlikely that the assimilation pattern will achieve the hegemonic status it held for the descendants of the earlier era of mass immigration: in the long term, it applied even to many descendants of Asian immigrants, despite the racial exclusion the immigrants themselves initially suffered. But it is not outmoded, as a great deal of evidence about such matters as linguistic assimilation and intermarriage demonstrates. Any reflection on the American future must take assimilation into account.

Bibliography

Alba, Richard, and Victor Nee. 2003. *Remaking the American Mainstream: Assimilation and Contemporary Immigration.* Cambridge: Harvard University Press.

Brubaker, Rogers. 2001. "The Return of Assimilation? Changing Perspectives on Immigration and Its Sequels in France, Germany, and the United States." *Ethnic and Racial Studies* 24: 531–48.

Gans, Herbert. 1973. "Introduction." In Neil Sandberg, ed., *Ethnic Identity and Assimilation: The Polish Community.* New York: Praeger.

Gibson, Margaret. 1988. *Accommodation without Assimilation: Sikh Immigrants in an American High School.* Ithaca, N.Y.: Cornell University Press.

Glazer, Nathan. 1993. "Is Assimilation Dead?" *The Annals* 530 (Nov.): 122–36.

Gordon, Milton. 1964. *Assimilation in American Life.* New York: Oxford University Press.

Jacobson, Matthew Frye. 1998. *Whiteness of a Different Color: European Immigrants and the Alchemy of Race.* Cambridge: Harvard University Press.

Massey, Douglas. 1985. "Ethnic Residential Segregation: A Theoretical Synthesis and Empirical Review." *Sociology and Social Research* 69 (Apr.): 315–50.

Park, Robert Ezra. 1926. "The Urban Community as a Spatial Pattern and a Moral Order." In E. W. Burgess, ed., *The Urban Community*, pp. 3–18. Chicago: University of Chicago Press.

———. 1950. *Race and Culture.* Glencoe, Ill.: Free Press.

Park, Robert Ezra, and Ernest Burgess. [1921] 1969. *Introduction to the Science of Sociology.* Chicago: University of Chicago Press.

Portes, Alejandro, and Min Zhou. 1993. "The New Second Generation: Segmented Assimilation and Its Variants." *The Annals* 530 (Nov.): 74–96.

Schuman, Howard, Charlotte Steeh, Lawrence Bobo, and Maria Krysan. 1998. *Racial Attitudes in America: Trends and Interpretations.* Cambridge, Mass.: Harvard University Press.

Waldinger, Roger. 1996. *Still the Promised City? African-Americans and New Immigrants in Postindustrial New York.* Cambridge, Mass.: Harvard University Press.

Warner, W. Lloyd, and Leo Srole. 1945. *The Social Systems of American Ethnic Groups.* New Haven, Conn.: Yale University Press.

Waters, Mary. 1999. *Black Identities.* Cambridge, Mass.: Harvard University Press.

Zolberg, Aristide, and Long Litt Woon. 1999. "Why Islam Is Like Spanish: Cultural Incorporation in Europe and the United States." *Politics & Society* 27 (Mar.): 5–38.

Transforming Foreigners into Americans

Roger Waldinger

In popular belief as well as social science wisdom, the bounds of "society" and the "nation-state" normally converge. While society and state generally overlapped during the mid-20th century, conditions at the turns of the 20th and the 21st century took a different form, making it hard for nation-state societies to wall themselves off from the world. Consequently, the long-term view indicates that social relations regularly span state boundaries. For that reason, international migrants, those people from beyond the nation-state's boundaries, persistently reappear.

In the rich, liberal democracies of the old and new worlds, the advent of international migration produces a social dilemma, as it runs into efforts to force society back inside state boundaries. States seek to bound the societies they enclose: they strive to regulate membership in the national collectivity as well as movement across territorial borders, often using illiberal means to fulfill liberal ends. Nationals, believing in the idea of the national community, endeavor to implement it, making sure that membership is available only to some, and signaling to newcomers that acceptance is contingent on conformity.

In large measure the effort is successful, as foreigners get transformed into nationals. Engaging in the necessary adjustments is often acceptable to those who were earlier willing to abandon home in search of the good life; the everyday demands of fitting in, as well as the attenuation of home-country loyalties and ties, make the foreigners and their descendants increasingly similar to the nationals whose community they have joined. But the ex-foreigners also respond to the message conveyed by nationals and state institutions. In this respect, the assimilation literature, emphasizing the decline of an ethnic difference, largely misleads us: the ex-foreigners do not abandon particularism; rather, they replace an old particularism for one that is new. Finding appeal in the idea of a national community, they also think that their new national community should be bounded, agreeing that the gates through which future foreigners enter ought to be controlled.

However, the advent of large-scale migration produces a gap between the people *in* the state and the people *of* the state, to which the nationals respond in ways that galvanize an ethnic reaction. Believing that the people of the state and the people in the state should be one and the same, nationals find divergence disturbing. Questions of belonging become a source of political and social contention, with some nationals inevitably insisting that boundaries *around* the state be tightened and others demanding that the boundaries of the political community *within* the state be narrowed. Thus, as an inherently political phenomenon, migration across state boundaries generates political conflicts that none of the rich, immigrant-receiving democracies can avoid. In the end, those conflicts transform the ex-foreigners into nationals who know that they have yet to be fully accepted, which is why they remain attached to ethnic others of their own kind.

These are the arguments to be elaborated in the pages that follow. The essay seeks to go beyond the usual polarity of assimilation versus ethnic retention. I share the view of the sociologists of assimilation: the demographic dynamism of the rich democracies inexorably pulls the ex-foreigners out of their ethnic enclaves and niches into more diverse settings. But I expand the perspective to include the national boundaries and extend beyond them: the very same factors that produce border blending and shifting within the boundaries of the immigrant-receiving societies also bring foreigners across national lines. Consequently, the cross-state networks of international migrants and the community-building and -maintaining activities of states and national peoples collide, transforming foreigners into nationals but often into nationals of a different, ethnic kind.

The perspective developed here stands at considerable remove from most of the sociological literature on the United States. As that body of work focuses on the remaking of the American mainstream, it highlights the peculiarities of Americans, as opposed to the commonalities shared by the U.S. with the other rich democracies on which international migrants have converged. Americans are surely strange, though not for the reasons emphasized by the usual theories of American exceptionalism. Americans have constructed nationhood in terms that have been both externally and internally contrastive, excluding not just aliens but also the outsiders—most notably, African Americans—found within the territory of the state. While the combination of internal and external contrasts has parallels elsewhere, the American dilemma, as Gunnar Myrdal argued, is of a particular sort. Only in the U.S. does one find so deep a conflict between the fundamentally liberal principles to which the American people have been committed right from the beginning and a contradictory, no less deeply held view that restricts legal or functional membership in the people on the basis of origin and kind. The civil rights revolution notwithstanding, practice still diverges from theory: while Americans publicly proclaim their indifference to ascriptive differences among the peoples of the U.S., they still organize much of national life around distinctions of precisely this kind.

However, the very creed that the ethnic majority has violated—namely, that the U.S. is a nation where membership is available to all who wish to commit—is exactly what the internal outsiders have found attractive. Since the ethnic outsiders have mainly understood themselves as Americans, not as separate nations, the relationship between "majority" and "minority" Americans has been one of contention over the terms of inclusion in the people, not national autonomy or the rights of secession. Consequently, ethnic minorities have had a dual consciousness, attached to a group identity fashioned in contrast to an ethnic majority that has consistently disregarded the liberal, democratic principles it has claimed to profess, and yet as fully American, patriotic, and nationalistic as anyone else. For the same reason, established minorities play a dual role as regards immigrants, serving as instruments of Americanization while providing a counter-community, which proves attractive when the majority is unwilling or reluctant to let individual immigrants make their way upward.

Of course, immigrant assimilation in the U.S. is inevitably affected by the specific conditions on the ground. However, the literature's preoccupation with the divisions particular to this country is a bit like mistaking the forest for the trees. As international migration is an exception to the system by which states bound mutually exclusive populations, the fundamental dilemmas it produces are experienced by the residents of all the rich democracies, not just by Americans. Consequently, the process of taking foreigners and turning them into Americans is a local variation on a common theme, shaped by political factors extending well beyond the frontiers of the United States.

Transforming Foreigners into Nationals

Nationalizing foreigners is a mixture of coercion and consent. People who are prepared to abandon home in search of the good life are often willing to try other novelties as well. The new context also matters: there are few immigrant communities in which the keepers of tradition can fully guard against change; since most migrants are numerical minorities, many have at least some, if not much, exposure to hosts and their ways. While not all are ready or quick to exchange the embrace of one state for another, those who left in order to escape, or for whom "home" offers little promise, have a different view: for them, the price of formal identification with another people and place is not difficult to bear. As for the rest, time does its work, especially where the conditions of membership are relatively open and demands for cultural or ideological conformity are modest, as is true in the U.S. Gradually, ties to the old home attenuate and are replaced with substantive as well as symbolic attachments to a new people and their state.

But a story of foreigners willingly becoming nationals is just too simple. During the last era of mass migration as well as its aftermath, the coercive role of states, not to speak of nationals' racist views, did much to speed the process. While institutionalized, ethnocentric assimilation efforts—such as the Americanization programs offered in U.S. schools and companies earlier in the 20th century—have now largely disappeared, pluralism goes only so far. Understanding the national culture makes for greater competency, which is why immigrants and particularly their children hasten to acquire the appropriate tool kit. Although overtly racist views have disappeared from the political and cultural mainstreams of the rich democracies, newcomers are still expected to shift attachments from the old to the new home. Notwithstanding public institutions and rituals that have been redesigned to accommodate a mixture of national and other identities, expressions of pluralism follow a common template, yielding a homogenizing effect. Consequently, what the sociological dictionary defines as "assimilation"—the voluntaristic shedding of an ethnic difference—turns out to be something else: adhesion to a new national people, in part because strangeness and foreign attachments leave one open to doubt.

In the U.S., however, the continued nationalization of foreigners is largely unseen; the democratization of the American people has transformed the meaning of Americanization. The key lies in the distinction between the internal and external aspects of national identity, the former distinguishing among the various peoples of the U.S., the latter between the Americans at home and the foreigners abroad. Descendants of the founding immigrant groups dominated during the last era of mass migration and its aftermath, when origins, not belief, determined whether or not one belonged. Since, as these dominants saw it, *they* were the Americans, the demands for cultural change were intense; for them, acceptance was to be granted only if the immigrants and their descendants shed all foreign habits, tastes, and attachments. While practical considerations made for greater flexibility, the message was both conveyed and received.

During the current era of mass migration, by contrast, sharply ethnicized conceptions of American identity have been abandoned, and the cultural boundaries of the American "we" have been enlarged to include all the citizens of the state. In postethnic America, as the historian David Hollinger has termed it, ethnicity is respected but not frozen in place. New ethnic groups get formed as part of the normal functioning of a democratic society, and are so accepted. As the sociologists Richard Alba and Victor Nee correctly note, the newest Americans are freer than those in the past to choose strategies of the "mainstream" as well as the "ethnic" type.

But as Hollinger points out, postethnic Americans are not citizens of the world. National identity remains a source of primary affiliation; the political, external component of American identity—the national "us" versus the alien "them" beyond the borders of the U.S.—remains strong, and more so than the sociologists of assimilation are wont to admit. According to the pundits, Americans come from Mars (loving war) and Europeans from Venus (loving love). While that view might be too strong, poll data do indicate that Americans are more nationalistic than members of the other rich democracies are. Moreover, as liberal nationalism embraces the American creed, it is perfectly suited to the normal, multicultural American of the turn of the 21st century. As doctrine, it includes all who want to be full Americans, without ever harassing them for driving while not white or pressing them to sever all attachments to other peoples or places, and yet it does not believe in opening up the club to all newcomers, if only on the grounds that Americans first need to take care of each other. At a macro-sociological level, therefore, what the literature describes as "acculturation" entails the political process of resocializing foreigners, turning them into Americans of a new kind, equipped with new-country instead of old-country solidarities.

Thus, at the turn of the 20th century, founding groups had the view that the state belonged to them; thanks to the Progressive-era transformation of the state, they seized hold of it. As they did elsewhere, schools provided the means by which the state turned the children of peasants into nationals. Of course, that effort entailed other objectives consistent with Americanization—most notably, ensuring that the peasants' children would absorb the dispositions required by good, that is to say, disciplined, factory workers. But as the contemporary records tell us, it also convinced the immigrant children that their ethnic origins made them Americans of a decidedly second class.

From midcentury onward, however, both the American people and the American state were decoupled from the identities of the founding immigrant groups. Involvement in a world war and then a cold war helped turn the despised ethnics from southern and eastern Europe into full-fledged Americans: the salience of an external enemy, as well as the need to mobilize the whole population, helped efface internal differences among Americans of different kinds. The same factors facilitated the advent of the civil rights revolution, which expanded the people of the state so that all of its citizens were included, not just those with origins in Europe. In the post–civil rights era, the cultural differences between Americans of different national or ethnic types also became values to be preserved rather than discarded. Consequently, the public institutions and rituals met by the immigrants and immigrant descendants at the turn of the 21st century have found ways respectfully to incorporate new traditions and practices along with the old.

But the basic rules of the game have not changed: holding on to earlier identities and cultures is perfectly acceptable as long as these are additions to a fundamentally American core. As Alba and Nee note, multiculturalism is profoundly asymmetric. While the new Americans can retain what they wish of the old country, they need to master the native code; moreover, there is no expectation that established Americans will take on foreign ways. Language remains a potent symbol of national unity, which is why established Americans not only expect the newcomers to learn English but want it to remain dominant. Ethnic political organizations are tolerated but are also viewed as possibly undermining national cohesion; the political loyalties of hyphenated Americans are open to suspicion; and there is widespread support for the views that there are too many immigrants and that national borders should be better controlled—evidence that Americans can be more accepting of foreigners who wish to become nationals without ever becoming one-worlders.

In general, the foreigners hear the message. Those who settle down for the long term—a population that excludes likely and perhaps even would-be return migrants—also respond appropriately. Scholars have shown that some groups effectively retain certain ethnic attachments and old-country ways while adding an American tool kit, but there does not seem to be any case in which the foreigners and their children wish to appear as if they are fresh off the boat. Indeed, all the evidence points to the opposite. While Angelenos or New Yorkers may think that their cities have been turned into Towers of Babel, foreign languages quickly lose ground to English. Some groups, especially Spanish-speakers, add English to continued facility in their mother tongue. But the views of such alarmists as Samuel Huntington notwithstanding, the old pattern remains in place: immigrants' children reserve the mother tongue for private places; in public, it is an English-only (or at least English-mainly) world.

Much the same holds for national loyalties. Some foreigners naturalize for purely pragmatic reasons, and the old-country flag or anthem stirs many an immigrant heart; nonetheless, the imprint of adoptive-country nationalization is hard to miss. Though some social scientists contend that immigrants tend toward transnationalism, a possibility that leads others to worry about the specter of "dual loyalty," the political concerns of immigrants are principally focused on the U.S. Those who retain affection for or connections to the old country often find that there is nothing more American than coming together around homeland ties. Accommodations to earlier homeland loyalties ensure that the political system can easily incorporate the old-country attachments of the latest Americans. Having long attended to the importance of the "three I's"—Italy, Israel, and Ireland—New York political figures, for example, have not waited for prompts from social scientists to extend their political antennae to Santo Domingo or Port-au-Prince. Consequently, mobilizing to support the home country usually furthers integration, yielding instruction in that most American of public activities, interest-group politics.

In general, the new Americans consider themselves to be Americans and also think that newcomers should learn (and should be helped to learn) the native tongue. Like the good Americans that they have become, the immigrants also believe that the community of Americans should be bounded, which is why majorities among immigrants of most national origins support immigration restriction, though not with the severity endorsed by Americans of a more established sort. They also rally around the Stars and Stripes. According to a recent survey of the foreign-born population, 49 percent said that it would be "extremely important" for immigrants to serve in the military if drafted; 26 percent either served or had a family member who had served in the U.S. armed forces. And just as in the past, war continues to build an American nation. Recent U.S. chiefs of staff have included a son of Jamaican immigrants (Colin Powell), a Japanese American from Hawai'i (Eric Shinseki), and an immigrant from the former Soviet Union, speaking English with a noticeable accent (John Shalikashvili). A look at the top brass commanding U.S. troops in Iraq makes it clear that fully nationalized Americans can come in just about any ethnic type: the Arabic-speaking descendant of Lebanese immigrants (John Abizaid), heading up Central Command; the Spanish-speaking grandson of Mexican immigrants (Ricardo Sanchez), at one time commanding the U.S. forces on the ground in Iraq; and the Philippines-born son of a Filipino GI (General Antonio Taguba), documenting the supposedly un-American behavior of the American military police. On the battlefields, no small number of soldiers wearing U.S. uniforms are dying for a country that is not yet theirs. The ultimate sacrifice has its rewards, bestowing citizenship on the dead, though not every American is impressed: some insist that military service is for the people *of* the state only, as opposed to the people *in* the state but outside the national community.

Reactions—National and Ethnic

While foreigners get turned into nationals, they are often produced as nationals of a particular kind. The conventional approach assumes that ethnic differences are imported from abroad; the better view understands that differences are produced by the process of migration and the subsequent encounter with hosts whose reactions are rarely welcoming.

To begin with, few international migrants come as lonely adventurers. Rather, they move by making use of the one resource on which they can almost always count—namely, support from one another—which is why social connections between veterans and newcomers lubricate the migration process. Because those ties also provide the means for solving the practical problems of starting a new life— whether securing shelter, getting a job, or just finding one's way around—the networks furnish the foundation out of which a new collectivity gets made. Moreover, new identities arise as the migrants undergo a similar experience: displaced from familiar ground, they get treated as strangers. Consequently, they discover a commonality with people who were seen as different back home but who now, once the context has been transformed, appear as people of the same kind.

By contrast, the hosts see the foreigners as strange, not simply because they are aliens but often just because of the jobs to which they are put by the hosts themselves. The experience of labor migrations furnishes a central case in point. Contrary to the conventional wisdom, labor migrants are wanted precisely because they are different: assessing conditions "here" in light of lower "standards" there, while enjoying fewer entitlements than nationals, they are the ideal candidates for bottom-level jobs that others don't want. In deploying immigrant labor to perform the tasks that natives find dishonoring, nationals generate ethnic inequality in just the way described by Charles Tilly: they durably connect a category exterior to the society—foreigner—with a category interior to the society—low-level, low-prestige work. Consequently, the stigma associated with the jobs ends up sticking to the people who hold them, which is why the same set of stereotypes—"dumb but hardworking," "dependable but unambitious," "hardworking but excessively ambitious"—floats from one group to the next and is found in more or less the same form wherever one goes.

Over time, the impact of initial conditions weakens. Ties to fellow foreigners loosen as the newcomers seek to improve their lot. That search, however, yields greater exposure to the dominants, whose resistance to accepting the newcomers as full members of the club reactivates the very ethnic allegiances that the ex-foreigners would otherwise lose on their own. An ethnic reaction is further galvanized if and when the second generation finds that the linkage between the exterior category of foreigner and the interior category of disreputable work generates a long-lasting effect. Whereas immigrants are preferred as the right workers for the wrong jobs, their offspring are often perceived as too much like everyone else and therefore no longer appropriate for the undesirable tasks on which the foreign-born converge. At the same time, the quest to move ahead frequently occurs under a shadow, as the second generation's effort to trade on ambition and creativity has to overcome the opposing stereotypes associated with the first generation and its jobs.

Beyond these social processes yielding ethnic attachments are reactions bound up with the inherently political nature of migrations that cross state boundaries. Decades of restriction have left an indelible cultural mark, making low immigration the norm, from which departure is seen as a deviant, unsettling event. Thus, while residents of the rich democracies may find individual immigrants acceptable, they nonetheless strongly prefer lower levels of international migration than currently prevail. Though immigration restrictions would seem successful if evaluated in light of the numbers of poor people they deter, boundaries nonetheless prove leaky. Consequently, the rich democracies have all created the "illegal" immigrant, a kind of person whom nationals widely view as undesirable and whose arrival produces ever more stringent exertions aimed at making restrictions stick. People with foreign ways and allegiances to foreign countries also remain open to question, even though popular cultures have become more cosmopolitan and intellectuals often tend toward xenophilia. Suspicions are further heightened when the relevant nation-states coexist on less than friendly terms, as demonstrated during the two world wars and, more recently, in the aftermath of September 11, 2001. Moreover, nationals notice that the advent of foreign people goes hand in hand with the flow of foreign goods. Those disturbed by globalization's steady intrusion—of which the arrival of foreign people is a good deal more visible than the movement of foreign-made things, not to speak of foreign currencies—often want "their" states to fix the problem by keeping boundaries under control. Consequently, adverse political reactions to the influx of foreigners are an endemic condition of the rich democracies. Since the political resocialization of the foreigners is often successful, generating an aspiration to membership as well as a political outlook sharing core values of the nationals, efforts to restrict the national community provide a further catalyst to an ethnic response.

Just how this process works out varies from one context to another. The basic axis of variation distinguishes the liberal democracies of Europe and North America from labor-importing countries elsewhere, whether the autocracies of the Persian Gulf or the ethnocracies of East Asia. Internally, the liberal democracies claim to be universalistic, making increasing efforts to ensure that theory—which prohibits ascriptive distinctions among nationals—conforms with practice. While internal ethnic affiliations in a postethnic society may be of a voluntary sort, membership is a birthright. As for those from beyond the state's boundary, entry into the territory and its people is for the chosen only, not for anyone who just happens to want in. Externally, therefore, the liberal democracies are inherently exclusive, allowing the lucky few to pass on their good fortune to their children and recognizing the common humanity of all people no further than the water's edge.

The advent of international migration turns the tension between these two principles into a social dilemma. On the one hand, the foreign outsiders inside the state seek recognition, contending that liberalism's universalism requires expanding the circle of the "we." On the other hand, since "we" implies "they"—there being no political community without boundaries—some nationals always take a more restrictive view. If the rich democracies were more like their despotic labor-importing counterparts, the foreigners could be easily expelled. If the rich democracies were more ethnocratic, the foreigners' claims could be more easily ignored. As the rich democracies are instead liberal societies, international migration produces conflict over the bounds of community.

Thus, internally liberal societies can't enforce border controls with the ruthlessness that illiberal societies regularly deploy. Liberal humanitarians among the nationals look askance at efforts to turn guns against people whose only offense is crossing a border in search of a better life, and sometimes go so far as to help the border-crossers evade the state's reach. Liberal societies have even greater difficulty with those illegals who successfully traverse the border: if not legal citizens, they do possess some rights, which is why they cannot be deported at will, in contrast to the situation in the first half of the 20th century or in the Persian Gulf today. Illegals also enjoy the support of ethnic and human rights advocates, who provide the practical assistance needed to circumvent or overturn restrictive immigration policies and practices.

While illegal immigration cannot be made to go away, this is not a message that nationals are willing to accept. In the U.S., a public consistently opposed to rising levels of immigration has been particularly insistent on tightened border controls. Social scientists deride the response as symbolic politics. According to the experts, intensified restriction is a matter of "smoke and mirrors" or "border games," to cite two recent widely read books. The social scientists note that stepped-up controls have had largely perverse effects, allowing illegals to cross the border (albeit with much greater loss of life and health than before) while deterring them from going home. Consequently, the number of illegal immigrants in the U.S. doubled during the course of the 1990s.

But making fun of the populace and their politicians misses the point. Designing immigration policies to promote rational ends proves difficult because the policy's fundamental goal rests on a set of inherently illiberal beliefs: namely, that Americans make up an exclusive club, to which membership should be restricted. Those beliefs, however, are implemented only with trouble. As the illegals are often the friends or relatives of legal immigrants and citizens, measures aimed at curbing illegal migration or restricting illegals' options within the national territory inevitably prove contentious, mobilizing a social base beyond the illegals themselves.

The conditions of membership are similarly a source of conflict. A large population of aliens often proves disturbing to nationals believing in the unity of the people *in* the state and *of* the state. However, proposals to bring foreigners into the national fold by reducing the barriers to naturalization, or just disseminating information about naturalization and its procedures, are often opposed. Efforts at restricting membership have the potential for yielding perverse effects: if access to residence or benefits becomes more uncertain, foreigners are likely to respond with increased efforts to gain membership, in turn sparking further initiatives aimed at raising membership bars.

The controversies unleashed by California's Proposition 187 (an amendment to the state constitution passed in 1994) demonstrate the dynamics at play. Proposition 187 banned people not legally resident in the U.S. from receiving public social services, health care, and education; it also required service providers to verify the immigration status of all people seeking public services and to notify state officials about applicants of dubious legal status. The signal sent by the state's voters quickly ramified nationally. In 1996 the U.S. Congress passed a series of bills widening the divide between citizens and legally resident noncitizens: access to a large number of public benefits previously available to the latter was either cut off or cut back. The same legislation also prohibited illegal immigrants from access to federal, state, and local benefits and mandated that state and local agencies verify that immigrants were fully eligible for the benefits for which they applied.

Not surprisingly, threatening benefits previously taken for granted led the targeted people to change their behavior: naturalizations spiked in the late 1990s, as did voter registrations (although neither option was available to illegals). As naturalizations rose, the conditions of citizenship became the next flashpoint. Proponents of a more restrictive view of the national community charged that efforts to naturalize were marked by fraud; Congress began considering legislation that would deny automatic citizenship to the U.S.-born children of foreign parents and also began examining proposals to scrutinize prospective citizens with greater care. By contrast, in the states and localities where immigrants were likely to live, membership expansion moved to the political agenda via new proposals to revive alien voting—once commonplace, but later a casualty of turn-of-the-20th-century restriction. Needless to say, those who held a narrower view of the bounds of the national community mobilized in opposition. As of this writing, the reactive cycle remains in play.

Where mass migrations occur, the question of how the outsiders from abroad will belong inevitably arises. Whether the issue is to be framed in terms of "assimilation" or "integration" varies from one national context to another. However, the underlying approach is essentially the same, as conventional social science and national (that is to say, folk, native, local—call it what you will) understandings of international migration largely overlap. In scholarly and popular views, nation-states normally contain societies (as implied by the concept of "American society"), which is why both the appearance of foreigners and their foreign attachments are seen as anomalies expected to disappear.

However, explaining the decline or disappearance of the immigrants' ethnic difference is a peculiar exercise. The descendants of the people from abroad do gradually lose attachments to the culture and people with roots in the old country. That change, however, transforms them not into rootless cosmopolitans but into nationals, committed to the new place and its people. What the literature calls assimilation or integration is really the political process of nation-building, replacing one particularism for another.

Though usually successful in the long run, the business of turning foreigners into nationals is complicated by the very features that distinguish any one national collectivity from all others. As emphasized by the sociological literature, assimilation entails the search for the good life, pursued at the cost of connections and proximity to kin and friends, and inevitably producing contacts of an ever more diverse kind. But if international migrants are to achieve the good life they seek, they first need to get into some other people's club. The nature of the national people's club—an inherently exclusive, bounded community—makes entry, let alone full acceptance, very hard to secure.

Moreover, the national peoples of the rich, immigrant-receiving democracies want their communities maintained. Keeping membership restricted is of strategic value, especially when the place in question is a rich society that attracts the poor. But the national community is also an ideal: with the exception of the occasional libertarian, nationals believe that maintaining the boundaries delimiting the people is a good thing in and of itself. While restriction, therefore, reflects the people's will, it also sends an unwelcoming message to those foreigners who manage to get through the gates. As nationals further believe that the people of the state and the people in the state should be one and the same, the presence of foreigners on national soil and the questions of whether they should belong and if so, how, inevitably provide grounds for contention.

Consequently, the influx of foreigners produces a *dis*-integrating response among nationals, whose political efforts at *dis*-assimilation impel the ex-foreigners to respond in ways that emphasize their attachments to people of their own kind. Ironically, the decline of an internal ethnic difference between the nationals and the ex-foreigners spurs the reactive cycle: among the latter, those who have most fully learned the national code and internalized its creed are the most likely to experience rejection with the greatest sting. Therefore, the usual dichotomy between assimilation and ethnic retention misleads. The better view, rather, emphasizes the regularity of international migration and its collision with efforts to reproduce the political community that migration disrupts. In the end, foreigners get transformed into nationals, albeit nationals of a different kind.

Bibliography

Alba, Richard, and Victor Nee. *Remaking the American Mainstream: Assimilation and Contemporary Immigration.* Cambridge: Harvard University Press, 2003.

Hollinger, David A. *Postethnic America: Beyond Multiculturalism.* New York: Basic Books, 1995.

Huntington, Samuel. *Who Are We? The Challenges to America's National Identity.* New York: Simon and Schuster, 2004.

Tilly, Charles. *Durable Inequality.* Berkeley: University of California Press, 1998.

Transnationalism

Ewa Morawska

A relatively recent addition to the research agenda in immigration studies, trans-nationalization of immigrant and/or ethnic identities has already become its core element. Regardless of their disciplinary interests and approaches, students of this phenomenon agree that although the numbers of immigrants involved in transnational practices and the intensity of their engagement vary considerably depending on their circumstances, transnational activities constitute an important sociological development as a product of and at the same time a contributor to processes of globalization.

Two different interpretations of the word "transnationalism" can be distinguished in discussions on this subject by immigration scholars. In the first interpretation—in pathbreaking works by scholars such as Yasemin Soysal, David Jacobson, Rainer Baubock, and Stephen Castles and Alistair Davidson—transnationalism is under-stood as a shift beyond or, as it were, vertically past (rather than horizontally across) membership in a territorial state or nation and its accompanying civic and political claims, toward more encompassing definitions such as universal humanism, membership in a suprastate (e.g., the European Union), and panreligious solidarity (e.g., Muslims in western Europe). This approach informs studies concerned with the impact of globalization in general and international migration in particular on the prerogatives of the nation-state. In the second interpretation, more common among students of immigration "from below" (see works by Peggy Levitt, Robert Smith, Michael Smith and Luis Guarnizo, and Nancy Foner), transnationalism refers to some combination of plural civic and political memberships, economic involve-ments, social networks, and cultural identities that reach across and link people and institutions in two or more nation-states in diverse, multilayered patterns. Several studies show that international migrants are the main conveyors of these cross-border connections, and the "new transnational spaces" they create de-territorialize or extrapolate (rather than undermine) the nation-states they link. Here we are concerned with immigrant transnationalism in the second meaning of the term.

The establishment of transnationalism as part of the mainstream research agenda in immigration studies in the 1990s and the resulting proliferation of studies on this subject have been accompanied by lively debates among specialists about the actual novelty of this phenomenon, its different forms and intensities, the relationship between immigrants' assimilation to the host society and their transnational engagements, and the endurance of these practices over time.

Transnationalism of Old and New Immigrants: A Comparison

The debate about the supposed novelty of contemporary immigrants' transnationalism has involved two arguments. One of them concerns similarities and differences between transnational engagements of old and new immigrants, and the other is about the changing conceptual tools with which to identify and assess the phenomena we study. The second issue is easier to resolve. Defenders of the "new transnationalism" thesis, such as Nina Glick-Schiller and Robert Smith, claim that we see this phenomenon as present in the past because we have new conceptual lenses and vocabulary that help bring it to light. This argument is correct. Immigration historians have long been aware of and have extensively documented the enduring binational identities and home-country involvements of nearly all American immigrant groups in the 19th and early 20th centuries, but until recently they did not call it transnationalism. A gradual change of nomenclature from biculturalism and overseas connections to transnationalism in historical studies of immigration has been largely a reaction to the announcement and rapid career of "new transnationalism" in the 1990s.

The question of how different the transnational engagements of contemporary immigrants are from those of their predecessors a century ago requires more elaboration. Although it was not termed transnationalism until recently, the phenomenon of immigrants' loyalties to and engagement with their home country is not new. Millions of southern and eastern Europeans who came to the U.S. during the great wave of immigration from the 1880s to 1914 were involved in transnational activities that they sustained for several decades following their arrival. The majority of Slavic and Italian immigrants intended their transatlantic sojourns to be temporary (Jews, who came to America fleeing religious and political persecution in eastern Europe, were the exception). A significant proportion—between 30 and 40 percent—actually went back to their home countries, and between 15 and 30 percent, according to contemporary studies, made repeated visits there, which were facilitated by advances in transportation technology. The sojourner mentalities of these people, combined with the prejudice and social exclusion they encountered from members of the dominant groups in America, naturally sustained their focus on affairs in their home countries.

In Europe, migrants remained part of their home communities long after their sojourns had lasted significantly longer than they had expected. The back-and-forth flow of migrants and letters created an effective transnational system of communication, social control and household management, and travel and employment assistance (between 1900 and 1906 alone, 5 million letters from migrants in America arrived in Russia and Austria-Hungary). Letters and migrants returning from America to European villages spread information about living and working conditions, wages, and the possibility of saving. They also helped to make travel arrangements for those willing to leave. From across the ocean, immigrants supervised family affairs and managed their farms. Such long-distance management required continuous attention and, above all, the financial means to provide the support expected— and demanded—by the families at home. The enormous sums of money that flowed into southern and eastern Europe during the peak years of overseas migration provide empirical evidence that immigrants in the U.S. continued to fulfill their social obligations as managers of family farms and members of their village communities. In *Round-Trip to America*, for example, Mark Wyman shows that between 1900 and 1906, U.S. immigrant colonies sent a staggering $90 million in money orders to Italy, Russia, and Austria-Hungary.

"Old" immigrants' civic and political involvements in their home countries were also significant. The overwhelming majority of turn-of-the-20th-century Slavic and Italian arrivals in the U.S., more than 90 percent of whom were from rural backgrounds, arrived with a group identity and a sense of belonging that extended no further than the *okolica* (local countryside). Paradoxically, it was only after they came to America and began to create organized immigrant networks for assistance and self-expression, and to establish group boundaries as they encountered an ethnically pluralistic and often hostile environment, that they developed translocal national identities with their fatherlands, as Italians, Poles, Ukrainians, Slovaks, Lithuanians, and so on. (Jews, who brought their "mobile" spiritual community of klal-Yisroel, the community of Jews, which stretched back 25 centuries, were again the exception.) Among the variety of sociocultural agencies created by immigrants, the foreign-language press played an important role in defining group boundaries and fostering solidarity by propagating identification with and ongoing interest in the affairs of the old country.

The cultural and political elites of southern and eastern European sender societies were not indifferent to this nation-building process in immigrant communities across the ocean and actually repeatedly intervened, either by trying to mobilize "their" emigrants' national loyalty and engage them for home-country political purposes or to squash political activities that were deemed subversive. For example, several organized groups in Italy, such as the Istituto di San Raffaele and the Istituto Coloniale, concerned with "keep[ing] alive in the hearts of Italians [in the United States] . . . the sentiment of nationality and affection for the mother country," sought (and obtained) government aid for Italian schools in America and supervised their programs by participating in committees composed of representatives from both sides of the ocean. The Hungarian political elite, worried about growing national consciousness and separatist aspirations among émigrés from non-Hungarian (especially Slovak and Rusyn) groups in the multiethnic Hungarian monarchy, launched a systematic propaganda action in immigrant communities to ensure that their members remained "good Hungarian citizens" and did not fall under the influence of "bad-intentioned leaders" who "corrupt [them] from the national point of view" (Wyman, 1993).

The increasing length of time immigrants spent in America, an upsurge of American nativism hostile to immigrants' "alien loyalties," and a vigorous Americanization campaign launched after the end of World War I by U.S. government institutions and the media effectively undercut such home-bound enthusiasms among immigrants and redirected their attention to domestic issues and engagements. Similarly, the immigration restrictions of the 1920s undercut the previously intense circulation of people and news across the Atlantic. Transnational concerns and attachments of Hungarian, Italian, Polish, and Lithuanian Americans did not wane, however, but took on new configurations as American experiences and opportunities became increasingly important as the framework for activities and plans for the future and American loyalties and involvements grew in significance. Letters continued to cross the Atlantic and financial assistance continued to be sent by immigrants to their dependents in Europe.

Although the transnationalism of that group of immigrants and of the contemporary wave share several features, they are by no means identical. Several new developments shape the situation of present-day immigrants, including their opportunities for transnational engagements. At the macro level, the economic and political variety of home countries or regions of contemporary immigrants and the restructuring of the postindustrial American economy have diversified channels of advancement and integration into the mainstream society. The rapid internationalization of economic markets and labor, the globalization of the media, and the "compression of time and space" resulting from the transportation and communication revolution have made back-and-forth travel and communication much quicker, easier, and more readily available. At the same time, however, the politicization of international migration by the receiver states (i.e., control of entry, duration of sojourn, and permissible pursuits of immigrants) has created a growing army of marginalized "illegal" migrants.

As a counterinfluence on these measures, American public discourse has experienced a renaissance of the ideology of cultural pluralism, along with its practical implementation in the juridical system and public institutions, since the 1960s. Civic and political movements and organizations of laws and declarations upholding universal human rights, civic entitlements of groups and individuals, social justice, and democratic representation and pluralism have simultaneously proliferated around the globe and trickled down to the national level. As a consequence, whereas earlier immigrants and their children, unprotected by legal, institutional, and civic tolerance for the practice of diversity, were forced to be "closet transnationalists," their contemporary successors have legitimate options in terms of identities and participation, ranging from global to transnational, national, and local and different combinations thereof. Although the idea of a "just pluralism" does not equally embrace all communities, especially those of nonwhites (who constitute a large proportion of contemporary immigrants), these laws and public discourse create institutional channels and a juridical/political climate in which groups and individuals can be involved in the civic and political affairs of both their home and their host country without fear of opprobrium and accusations of disloyalty.

At the micro level, the new circumstances include a much greater diversification of contemporary immigrants than their predecessors in terms of regional origin, racial identification, gender, economic and social resources, civic/political culture, and form of assimilation to American society. As a result, present-day immigrants' transnationalism is much more diverse in form and content. Depending on the specific constellation of factors, it can involve single or multiple cross-border activities, which may be regular (in a spectrum of low to high frequency) or prompted by specific situations; it can be carried by individuals, immigrant families, or ethnic groups through informal or institutional channels; and it can be confined to private lives of people on both sides of the border or involve the public sphere.

Diversity of Transnational Involvements of Contemporary Immigrants

The common finding in studies of immigrant transnationalism has been the diversity in scope and intensity of these engagements, depending on different constellations of circumstances in immigrants' lives. We can identify more than 30 factors that shape the forms and contents of immigrants' transnational involvements. In Table 1, they are grouped according to the level—international/national, local, and individual—of their operation.

The diversity of transnational involvements produced by different constellations of these factors can be illustrated by the examples of three immigrant groups: Hong Kong Chinese in Los Angeles and Dominicans and Jamaicans in New York.

Successful global financiers, transnational company executives, and export-import traders have constituted between 40 and 50 percent of immigrants from Hong Kong arriving in Los Angeles since the 1980s. The arrival of these transnational businessmen and managers has coincided with developments conducive to such immigration on both sides of the Pacific. The emergence of East Asian countries as important players in the global economy as exporters of capital and labor and the increased political uncertainty in Hong Kong related to its inclusion in communist China have been the "push" forces for this movement. The "pull" forces have in-

Table 1 Factors influencing immigrants' transnationalism

SENDING COUNTRY
Geographic proximity to receiving country
Transportation and communication
  technology
Dynamics of economic development
Penetration by global (American) culture
Civic/political culture, especially exclusive vs.
  inclusive national membership and loyalty
Government interest in cooperation
  (economic, political) with receiving
  country
Government's attitudes/behavior toward
  émigrés
Economic stability/growth
Political-legal stability

RECEIVING COUNTRY
Transportation and communication
  technology
State-national model of civic/political
  integration
Civic culture/practice of inclusion or
  exclusion of "others," in particular racial
  "others"
State policy toward immigrants
  (undocumented status, dual
  citizenship, and other transnational
  activities)
State policy toward/relations with sending
  country
Structure and dynamics of the economy

LOCAL CONDITIONS IN IMMIGRANTS' PLACE OF SETTLEMENT IN RECEIVING COUNTRY
External
Structure and dynamics of the economy
Degree and institutional embeddedness of
  ethnic/racial segregation or concentration
Civic/political culture and practice regarding
  immigrants, particularly of different race
Degree of intergroup social exclusion/
  inclusion

Intragroup
Group size and residential concentration/
  segregation from native-born Americans
Proportions of foreign- and American-born
Group socioeconomic characteristics
Immigrant/ethnic community's institutional
  completeness
Group sense of civic entitlement in host
  society

CHARACTERISTICS OF INDIVIDUAL IMMIGRANTS
Economic and cultural resources (education, occupational skills, advance acculturation; life
  goals and values)
Race
Gender
Socioeconomic position and prospects of mobility
Residential/work isolation or contact with native-born Americans
Number of years spent in receiving country
Sojourn or permanent immigration
Presence and number of economically dependent family members in home country and/or real
  estate/other possessions
Intensity of ideological and/or emotional attachment to home country
Respect immigrants receive in their hometown/village

cluded the accelerating internationalization of the American and in particular the Los Angeles economy, and the related creation (in 1992) of an "investor" category in the U.S. immigration system, which guarantees permanent residence to 10,000 immigrants annually in exchange for a $1 million investment that results in the creation of at least 10 jobs in the U.S.

While economic and political circumstances have provided the facilitating context for transnational entrepreneurship among Hong Kong immigrants, their personal resources have furnished the necessary tools for their undertaking. Financial capital has been, of course, the necessary base for their operations. Enriched by the rapid growth of their home-country economy, since the late 1970s would-be immigrants have been transferring their monies abroad, including to Los Angeles, so that when they arrive they already have considerable investments in the city. Their business backgrounds, especially their know-how and capitalist mentality and their knowledge of English (many of them were educated in Western, British, or American schools), combined with a strong work ethic and drive for achievement as shared normative values, have made successful management of their fortunes in this country possible.

These immigrants have made their resources still more effective by using traditional Chinese *guanxi,* or networks of informal connections. Working through connections based on trust and mutual obligations within "bamboo networks" of family members strategically placed in different cities and countries, immigrant entrepreneurs are able to maintain a high degree of flexibility and, importantly, significantly lower the operating costs of business. Reliance on *guanxi* and insider dealings with officials has also been the accepted way of conducting business with Chinese institutions, so those who know how to use this process have an additional strength in transnational operations. To the extent that flexible informal networks rather than long-term contractual obligations have become the basis of postindustrial global capitalism, Chinese transnational entrepreneurs are indeed very well equipped to meet its challenges.

Leaders of American capitalism, American politicians, and the national media all see these immigrants as bridge-builders between the United States and Asia, people who have been instrumental in the creation of the Pacific century in the global economy. In order to facilitate American trade with and investment in China, the National Committee on U.S.-China Relations recommended using Americans of Chinese origin, especially those from Hong Kong, as effective messengers between the two countries. These global entrepreneurs either live in Los Angeles permanently or, often, shuttle back and forth between their American and Asian residences (which has gained them the nickname *taikongren,* or astronauts, constantly in orbit in the Chinese immigrant community). Studies of their identities and civic commitments refer to them as "pragmatic cosmopolitans."

The very different situation of Dominican immigrants in New York City makes for a quite different kind of transnationalism. In 1990 the proportion of what Luis Guarnizo calls immigrant "Dominicanyorks" over 25 who did not complete high school was 55 percent; 45 percent were employed in manual occupations, primarily in secondary and informal sectors of the New York economy; and 30 percent lived on incomes at or below the poverty level. More than 50 percent of Dominican immigrants did not speak English at all or spoke very little at the time of the census. A constellation of circumstances makes the lives of a great many Dominican immigrants intensely transnational in a physical sense. An unusually high proportion of the population of the Dominican Republic—12 percent—resides in the U.S., resulting in the economic dependence of a very large number of Dominican households on the earnings of their kin in America. A sojourner mentality in the majority of immigrants, who see their futures in their home country, and the Dominican Republic's geographical proximity, which allows them to travel back and forth and to manage households in both countries at the same time, are also factors.

Dominican immigrants increasingly invest their American savings in small-scale enterprises in their hometowns and villages, often as joint ventures with family members or acquaintances, and personally supervise these enterprises through frequent visits. Financial contributions to public projects (church renovations, new school buildings, road repairs) and frequent visits also sustain their ongoing involvement with their local communities. Dominicans' home-country orientation has been fostered by their limited opportunities for advancement in New York, constrained as they are by lack of English-language skills, low educational attainment and occupational skills, and racial discrimination. Back home, their American savings represent upward mobility in terms of material standard of living and social status.

Because of the dependence of a large proportion of households in the Dominican Republic on immigrants' savings and the significant role of immigrants' investments for the national economy, the Dominican government has vigorously solicited the loyalty of its "temporarily absent citizens." In addition, immigrants living in the U.S. are in an excellent position to lobby for the economic and political interests of the Dominican government in its efforts to gain U.S. aid in the republic's development. An amendment to the Dominican constitution implemented in 1996 allowed immigrants to hold dual citizenship, including the right to vote in national elections. Since this constitutional change, political contenders have regularly come to New York to win votes and raise funds, and major Dominican parties hold political rallies and public forums there to espouse their causes. Because of their intense interest in home-country affairs, fostered by the Dominican government, large numbers of immigrants have indeed participated in Dominican politics and organized to lobby on behalf of the Dominican Republic in the U.S.

In comparison, home-country involvements of Jamaicans in New York City represent still another kind of transnationalism. Unlike the all-encompassing transnationalism of Dominicans, transnational activities of Jamaican immigrant entrepreneurs—about 10 percent of this group's employed foreign-born population—have concentrated in two areas: social, involving frequent visits and sponsorship of family members and acquaintances migrating to the U.S., and economic, involving cross-border household management and regular remittances sent home and import of merchandise from the Caribbean for ethnic specialty shops.

Most of these entrepreneurs are employed in small-scale ethnic businesses in immigrant neighborhoods. This modest but vibrant entrepreneurship has been the result of several circumstances. The entrepreneurial spirit of self-made independence is embedded in Jamaican popular culture and combines with a tradition of small-business activities by black Jamaican peasants going back to the time of slavery. Immigrants' socioeconomic backgrounds and their limited capital resources channel their activities toward such entrepreneurial ventures.

The transnational orientation of Jamaican immigrants' business activities has been a product of five factors. First, advances in communication and transportation technologies allow for the ready movement of people and merchandise across state and national borders. Second, the presence of a large community of fellow immigrants, concentrated in the Flatbush neighborhood of Brooklyn and parts of Queens and the Bronx, and an accompanying vigorous cultural life have provided the clientele for ethnic goods and entertainment, newspapers and magazines, and other material (from food to electronics) imported from Jamaica. Third, as part of New York's thriving global culture business, Jamaican restaurants, bakeries, patty shops, bars, and record shops have also attracted customers from other groups: young African Americans, white middle-class New Yorkers seeking consumer exotica, and international tourists. Fourth, Jamaicans' native knowledge of English eases trading with these outsiders. Finally, involvement in ethnic entrepreneurship has helped Jamaican immigrants escape from or at least reduce the experience of racial discrimination encountered by their fellow nationals employed in the mainstream New York economy.

Jamaican immigrants' engagement in home-country politics has been significantly less intense than that of Dominicans. Although the Jamaican government also recognizes dual citizenship, it has not solicited immigrants' loyalties in the same way as its Dominican counterpart, probably because the Jamaican émigré group in America is smaller relative to the home population and its direct impact on the national economy is less pronounced. Since the political turmoil that rocked Jamaica in the 1970s quieted in the 1980s, Jamaican immigrants, too, have been less preoccupied than Dominicans with their home-country politics. Rather than remaining on "permanent alert," their attention to and involvement in Jamaica's political affairs have fluctuated in response to specific events.

Simultaneity of Transnationalism and Assimilation

Studies of the transnational engagements of immigrants and of their assimilation to the host society have developed parallel to rather than in a dialogue with each other. In the prevailing view, the development of "transnational spaces" as the habitat of contemporary immigrants either detaches them from both sender and receiver societies or produces "bifocal" identities and commitments—a fashionable but vague concept in need of empirical testing. More recent studies, however, conceive of home-country engagements of immigrants and assimilation to the host society not as opposing phenomena but as concurrent ones.

The same three immigrant groups we have already considered illustrate very well the coexistence of transnationalism and assimilation, and, interestingly, different relations between these two processes, contingent on different constellations of circumstances in which they occur. Assimilation is understood here as a multipath, context-dependent process involving the incorporation of immigrants and their offspring in the economic, political, and social institutions and culture of different segments of the host society: mainstream middle and rising lower class (so-called upward assimilation), struggling lower and underclass (downward assimilation), or immigrant/ethnic enclave (called "adhesive assimilation" by Won Moo Hurh and Kwang Chung Kim), which can also follow the middle- or lower-class pattern.

For example, the transnational lives of Chinese global capitalists in Los Angeles do not prevent their integration (primarily economic but also political) into mainstream American life, with the city as its forerunner. In fact, the same characteristics that make Hong Kong Chinese immigrants' transnational activities possible—global business skills and connections and the support of American economic and political leaders—contribute to their successful integration into the avant-garde of American postindustrial society. Interestingly, the recognition by leaders of American capitalism of the necessity of learning Chinese ways of conducting transnational business can be interpreted as a reverse form of this group's cultural integration into the host society's economic elite. Along with Chinese immigrant entrepreneurs' adaptation to different aspects of the American culture comes the integration of their group's cultural traditions in an important segment of the mainstream cultural system.

In contrast, the all-encompassing, "physical" transnationalism of Dominican-yorks—poorly educated, employed in the lowest tiers of the New York labor market, and largely unable to speak English—has slowed their assimilation into American society, though assimilation has nevertheless been progressing on several fronts. Two indicators in particular have been reported: a gradual shift out of manual occupations into self-employment and public-sector employment and the related increase in earnings over time. For the most part, however, in contrast to the mainstream trajectory of Hong Kong Los Angelenos, the assimilation of Dominican immigrants in New York has evolved in the ethnic-adhesive pattern: within the ethnic group and through ethnic channels.

A high concentration of Dominicans in Washington Heights, a multitude of immigrant associations and clubs, and the continuous influx of food, films, and music from the home country have sustained there a vibrant social and cultural life and immigrants' Dominican identity. The integration of Dominican immigrants into political structures in New York City during the 1990s has so far been the most extensively documented ethnic path of their assimilation. The creation of a Dominican-dominated electoral district in Washington Heights as the result of reapportionment of the city's electoral districts facilitated the election in 1991 of Dominican-born Guillermo Linares to the city council as the first non–Puerto Rican representative of the Hispanic population. A shared sense of ethnic assertiveness, pragmatic considerations dictated by anti-immigrant legislation restricting the social services available to nonnaturalized residents, and the possibility of holding dual citizenship and the encouragement to do so by the Dominican government prompted a gradual increase in naturalization among immigrant Dominicanyorks during the 1990s (slightly over 20 percent in 1990).

The intense, multifaceted transnationalism and the ethnic path of the assimilation of Dominican immigrants have been fostered by the racial discrimination they experience in the U.S., where their mulatto identification is not recognized and where they are seen as black, with the accompanying socioeconomic and psychological costs of this label. Home-country orientation and preference for their own ethnic path of assimilation have been not only expressions of Dominican immigrants' natural need for familiarity and togetherness but also defense strategies against racial barriers to mainstream integration into the American society and threats to their individual and collective self-esteem.

Like Dominicans, Jamaican immigrants combine transnational engagements with the process of assimilation. But whereas the intense, all-encompassing transnationalism and socioeconomic disadvantages of lower-class Dominicans have slowed down their assimilation, the transnational activities and ethnic-path assimilation of Jamaican immigrant entrepreneurs have reinforced each other. The success of Jamaican ethnic businesses depends on continued economic activities in the home country and in the Caribbean, and these activities, as well as cross-border social engagements, sustain the ethnic path of Jamaicans' assimilation. Although the experience of racism in America has also hindered Jamaican immigrant entrepreneurs' assimilation into the mainstream society, their higher socioeconomic position and competence in the English language, along with the demand for their services by native-born (white) Americans, make their assimilation middle-class in character.

Jamaicans' civic and political assimilation has also progressed more quickly than that of Dominicans. Besides the factors already mentioned, Jamaicans' much less intense political transnationalism has probably contributed to this difference. Thus, Jamaican immigrants' naturalization rate was more than double that of Dominicans in the 1990s, and Jamaican involvement in New York politics has been more visible and more effective in terms of numbers of elected officials than that of Dominicans.

Transnationalism of the Second Generation

Generally, assimilation has been much more central in the lives of the second generation than in those of their immigrant parents, and probably not even a majority of native-born children of immigrants have maintained active transnational involvements. But significant numbers do engage in different forms of transnationalism parallel to their progressive incorporation into American society.

These forms can be classified according to four assimilation trajectories in the lives of native-born American children of immigrants, as identified in studies by Levitt and Waters and by Morawska: the mainstream (1) middle-class/upwardly mobile and (2) lower-class/underclass, and the ethnic-adhesive (within the ethnic community) (3) middle-class/upwardly mobile and (4) lower-class/underclass. Besides the national (host society), local, and individual circumstances we have already considered (see Table 1), four factors influence second-generation transnational involvements, namely, socioeconomic status of the parents, parental pressure toward assimilation or/and transnational attachments, intergenerational conflicts (at home and in the ethnic community), and position in the life cycle.

The mainstream middle-class integration pattern of second-generation transnationalism involves bicultural identities and practices, such as fluency in and preference for English combined with a fair ability to communicate in the language of national origin, a hyphenated identity, participation in American and (pan)ethnic-group activities and popular culture, and values about educational (and later professional) achievement that are "fused" from those of both the sending country and the U.S. In this category, the most common form of transnational involvement has been cultural: imported entertainment (music, videos), and occasional visits to their parents' country of origin, usually for vacations or to participate in cultural or educational programs. Studies also report that immigrants' native-born American offspring maintain transnational relations with their kin and peers and sometimes participate in transnational politics on behalf of their national-origin countries (particularly among children of political refugees).

The major factors contributing to this combination of assimilation and transnationalism patterns include permanent and legal (documented) resettlement of the parents; residence in mixed (rather than ethnically homogeneous) neighborhoods, facilitating contacts with native-born Americans; middle-class or upwardly mobile status of parents and the pressure exerted by them (and accepted by children) for high performance in school; and retention of national-origin cultural traditions.

Very important, too, has been a relatively hospitable reception or at least absence of exclusion by the mainstream American society.

Whether American society defines immigrants as "different" or "excluded" determines whether a mainstream assimilation trajectory or an ethnic-adhesive pattern develops. The link between being excluded and developing an ethnic-adhesive pattern is represented most distinctly among American-born children of upwardly mobile minority immigrants, particularly blacks, whose skin color puts them on the "wrong" side of the American racial dichotomy and threatens their integration into middle-class American society. The intensified national-origin identities and cultural frameworks that weaken American identities and the sustained social and cultural contacts with the country of origin reported in these second-generation groups serve (as in the case of their immigrant parents) as an escape or a means of preserving self-esteem and social status. That is, they reflect an oppositional transnationalism rather than the optional transnationalism of the first group.

The location of children of poorly educated, low-skilled immigrants in the lower class or inner-city underclass appears to have a greater influence on their transnational activities than on their assimilation trajectories. Thus, lower-class members of the second generation whose integration into American society evolves in a mainstream or ethnic-adhesive pattern are usually proficient in the native languages used in their homes and equally fluent in the American popular culture of their age groups. Transnational participation of immigrants' children in both assimilation groups has involved both formal (organized) and informal activities, both of which have usually been more regular and more encompassing than similar involvements among their middle-class counterparts. Besides frequent visits to national-origin communities for vacations, family occasions, and local religious and cultural rituals and celebrations, this participation involves sustained transnational friendships and, among young adults, management of (often inherited) parental houses in the immigrants' hometowns or villages.

Such regular, sustained involvement in their parents' native communities makes transnational attachments of lower-class second-generation Americans more localized and "natural" in the experiential sense, in comparison with their middle-class counterparts' optional and primarily symbolic identification with the national high culture and history of their parents' homelands. The situations of mainstream and ethnic-adhesive assimilation groups have not been identical, however. Whereas immigrants' children in the former category are usually fluent in English and use their national-origin language primarily at home and socially with friends, their peers who live in large, isolated ethnic communities are immersed in the foreign language in everyday life, in public education, workplaces, shopping malls, banks, professional services, and the media. Such young people's identities have also differed from those of their counterparts in the mainstream lower-class assimilation group, in that they tend to perceive themselves in monoethnic (their parents' home country) or panethnic terms rather than as binationals. Transnational attachments of both lower-class groups provide an important space into which they can escape from the class and racial frustrations of their American experience and display their American status and achievements in their parents' native communities, where they are perceived as genuine. It is probable that this factor is more important for lower-class immigrants' children who live in mainstream American society and whose encounters with class or racial prejudice are more frequent and direct than for their peers residing in more encapsulated ethnic communities.

Transnational engagements of second-generation Americans trapped in the inner-city underclass have been contingent on their assimilation trajectories. Those whose integration follows the mainstream path—primarily young people who associate themselves with the American (usually African American) residents of inner-city ghettos and who identify with their counterculture—have by and large deliberately abandoned ethnic connections and do not forge transnational ones. They may, however, form transnational youth gangs in response to their marginality vis-à-vis the mainstream American society and the dominant culture of their ethnic communities. These gangs are an ethnicized, or "choloized" (from the Mexican American term *cholo,* for the oppositional subculture), version of mainstream American street gangs. The second-generation members of these gangs transplant them to the communities of their national origin during their frequent visits there, either with their parents or on their own, teaching their peers how to paint graffiti on public buildings and how to adorn themselves with "fade" haircuts (with gang initials sculpted into the cut), baggy jeans, and gang-style clothing.

This overview of transnational involvements has demonstrated how these attachments depend on context, particularly on different constellations of economic, political, and cultural features of sender and receiver societies, of local communities, and of the immigrants and second-generation Americans themselves. By the same token, it has suggested a two-step approach to examining these transnational activities: first, by identifying the relevant factors that shape their scope and directions in a particular instance, and second, by comparing these circumstances and their outcomes across several cases.

Bibliography

Basch, Linda, Nina Glick-Schiller, and Cristina Szanton Blanc, eds. 1994. *Nations Unbound: Transnational Projects, Postcolonial Predicaments, and Deterritorialized Nation-States.* Amsterdam: Gordeon & Breach.

Faist, Thomas. 2000. "Transnationalization in International Migration: Implications for the Study of Citizenship and Culture." *Ethnic and Racial Studies* 23, 2: 189–222.

Foner, Nancy. 2000. *From Ellis Island to JFK: New York's Two Great Waves of Immigration.* New York: Russell Sage Foundation.

Glick Schiller, Nina. 1999. "Transmigrants and Nation-States: Something Old and Something New in the U.S. Immigrant Experience," in Charles Hirschman, Philip Kasinitz, and Josh DeWind, eds., *The Handbook of International Migration: The American Experience,* pp. 94–119. New York: Russell Sage Foundation.

Gomez, Edmund Terence, and Hsin-Huang Michael Hsiao, eds. 2004. *Chinese Enterprise, Transnationalism, and Identity.* New York: Routledge.

Hurh, Won Moo, and Kwang Chung Kim. 1984. *Korean Immigrants in North America: A Structural Analysis of Ethnic Confinement and Adhesive Adaptation.* Madison, N.J.: Fairleigh Dickinson University Press.

Levitt, Peggy. 2003. "Keeping Feet in Both Worlds: Transnational Practices and Immigrant Incorporation in the United States," in Christian Joppke and Ewa Morawska, eds., *Toward Assimilation and Citizenship: Immigrants in Liberal Nation-States,* pp. 177–94. London: Macmillan/Palgrave.

———. 2001. *The Transnational Villagers.* Berkeley: University of California Press.

Levitt, Peggy, and Mary Waters, eds. 2002. *The Changing Face of Home: The Transnational Lives of the Second Generation.* New York: Russell Sage Foundation.

Morawska, Ewa. 2003. "Immigrant Transnationalism and Assimilation: A Variety of Combinations and a Theoretical Model They Suggest," in Christian Joppke and Ewa Morawska, eds., *Toward Assimilation and Citizenship: Immigrants in Liberal Nation-States,* pp. 133–74. London: Macmillan/Palgrave.

———. 2001. "Immigrants, Transnationalism, and Ethnicization: A Comparison of this Great Wave and the Last," in Gary Gerstle and John Mollenkopf, eds., *E Pluribus Unum? Contemporary and Historical Perspectives on Immigrant Political Incorporation,* pp. 175–212. New York: Russell Sage Foundation.

Portes, Alejandro, and Min Zhou. 1993. "The New Second Generation: Segmented Assimilation and Its Variants." *Annals of the American Academy of Political and Social Sciences* 530: 74–96.

Smith, Michael, and Luis Guarnizo, eds. 1998. *Transnationalism from Below.* New Brunswick, N.J.: Transaction.

Smith, Robert. 2000. "How Durable and New Is Transnational Life? Historical Retrieval through Local Comparison." *Diaspora* 9, 2: 203–35.

Wyman, Mark. 1993. *Round-Trip to America: The Immigrants' Return to Europe, 1880–1930.* Ithaca, N.Y.: Cornell University Press.

Pluralism and Group Relations

Jennifer L. Hochschild

What is most apparent about intergroup relations in the United States is how enormously complex, even contradictory, they are. One can find reams of evidence showing that connections among American racial and ethnic groups are strong, constructive, and growing; one can find equivalent reams showing connections to be weak, hostile, and stagnant. It is equally easy to find competing conceptualizations of both groups and relations. Groups can be thought of as small and distinct nationalities or as large, panethnic races; political coalitions can be understood as pragmatic alliances to accomplish discrete goals or as broad movements based on deep identities pursuing fundamental transformation of society. Intergroup relations can best be explained in terms of psychological affect or economic interests or cultural ties or political calculations.

Here we will look at some of the clashing empirical findings and some of the most important conceptual disagreements involved in the idea of intergroup relations. I seek to make sense of this mixture by organizing it into two sets of patterns: a typology of intergroup relations, particularly political coalitions, and an outline of the structure within which members of racial and ethnic groups interact. We can use this material to speculate briefly about how intergroup relations might change as more new Americans are incorporated into the society and polity of the U.S.

Intergroup Relations Are Good and Getting Better

Survey data show a dramatic improvement in the late 20th century in how members of various American racial and ethnic groups understand and engage with one another. In the 1950s, barely 4 percent of Americans endorsed intermarriage; now three quarters do, according to the Gallup Poll. By the beginning of the 21st century, among married couples, seven in ten Native Americans and three in ten Latinos and Asian Americans had chosen a spouse of a different race or ethnicity. African Americans are less likely to marry at all, and many fewer marry outside their race—in 2000, about 13 percent of black marriages were to a nonblack. Still, that is a huge rise over the past several decades, and some demographers predict that black intermarriage is in the early stages of the same sort of rapid rise that we have witnessed among other racial and ethnic groups.

Intergroup relations are also improving if we look at trends in naming. According to the *New York Times,* the most preferred five names for Hispanic boys born in Texas in 2002 included Jonathan; the parallel list for girls included Ashley, Jennifer, and Samantha. The list is similar for New York City.

In another Gallup Poll in 2004, almost three quarters of Americans agreed that relations between whites and blacks and between whites and Hispanics are "very" or "somewhat" good. They judged white-Asian relations to be a little better and black-Hispanic relations to be a little worse, but at least 60 percent of each racial or ethnic group thought all pairs of interactions were good.

Evidence of the success of intergroup relations is not limited to surveys of interracial marriages and naming. Census data reveal that levels of residential segregation have been declining, slowly but surely, over the past few decades, especially in the West and in relatively new communities. Corporations and major institutions seek employees with language skills and cultural backgrounds that will appeal to customers and clients who have newly immigrated from Latin America or Asia. Top military officers, university presidents, and executives of major corporations all endorsed affirmative action to the Supreme Court in the early 2000s on the grounds that it was an essential tool for developing effective intergroup relations, which are themselves essential. A cover of *Newsweek* featured "The New Black Power: Ability, Opportunity, & the Rise of Three of the Most Important CEOs in America"; other cover stories have lauded the appeal of Asian men and the vigor and power of young Latinos. These articles may be patronizing, but they would not appear if editors judged other Americans to be uninterested in or unsympathetic to new Americans as well as to blacks. In a few districts and cities, majority-white constituencies have elected African Americans or Asians to Congress or a mayoralty. The proportion of blacks registered to vote is close to that of the proportion of whites, and the gaps between white voter registration rates and those of Latinos and Asians are slowly but consistently declining. In the U.S. Army, despite its roots in the conservative southern male environment, a large share of officers are black and, increasingly, Latino; this is the one institution in American society where people of color of both genders routinely exercise authority over white men. Proponents of gay marriage urge courts to follow the model of the judicial system when it abolished anti-miscegenation laws several decades ago, and politicians in many states are slowly moving to ensure homosexual rights. For these and other reasons, one can plausibly argue that racial and ethnic groups in the U.S. are learning to respect, work with, and accept the authority of each other—and even enjoy each other's company.

Intergroup Relations Are Bad and Possibly Getting Worse

However, we can also read surveys, laws, residential patterns, and data on employment and elections to come to just the opposite conclusion: racial and ethnic groups are locked into a system of mutual mistrust, white domination, and racialization or exclusion of both African Americans and new Americans who are neither black nor white. The same Gallup Poll that found that a majority of Americans see intergroup relations as good showed that Americans are about evenly split between those who expect black-white relations to be "always a problem for the United States" and those who believe that "a solution will eventually be worked out." The split is virtually identical to the division in 1963, when the question was first asked. African Americans are especially pessimistic, in some surveys more now than several decades ago. In a survey conducted by Michael Dawson and Rovana Popoff, virtually all white Americans agreed that slavery was wrong. But only 30 percent, compared with 79 percent of blacks, further agreed that the federal government should apologize for it; two thirds of blacks but only a meager 4 percent of whites believed that the federal government should "pay monetary compensation to African Americans whose ancestors were slaves."

Survey items inviting respondents to endorse negative stereotypes of members of other groups invariably find many willing to do so. In every survey, members of nonwhite groups, especially blacks and (to a lesser degree) Hispanics, perceive high levels of discrimination against themselves and others in their group in employment, education, the criminal justice system, health care, and daily interactions. In most surveys, native-born Americans agree that rates of immigration should be slowed or even halted, and in many a plurality or majority agree that immigration in recent decades has harmed their community or the nation.

Here, too, surveys are mainly a window on broader patterns of behavior. Residential racial separation may be declining from its height of a few decades ago, but it remains the case that almost two thirds of either black or white Americans would need to move in order for neighborhoods not to be racially identifiable. In 2001 only 30 percent of black students in the South attended majority-white schools—down from a high of 43 percent in the late 1980s and a little lower than the level of racial integration in 1970. At the same time, Gary Orfield and Chungmei Lee show that "the percent of Latino students in predominantly minority schools in the West has almost doubled, from 42 percent in 1968 to 80 percent in 2001." That is partly because of rapid immigration into western states, but it also reflects the difficulty that disproportionately poor immigrant families encounter in moving out of gateway cities into predominantly white communities. Several studies show that banks and real estate agents still consistently discriminate against African American and Hispanic families seeking loans for small businesses, mortgages, rentals, or homes to buy. Others show that black Americans receive poorer medical care for heart attacks than whites do, pay more for a new car, and receive longer sentences for committing the same crimes. White voters still usually decline to elect nonwhite politicians, and corporations are in no danger of appointing a disproportionate share of executives who are not native-born whites. Perhaps the starkest evidence of persistent white racial domination is the fact that the more nonwhites there are in a state (or, in some studies, in a prison system), the harsher the criminal justice laws are and the greater the likelihood is that felons will remain disfranchised for life.

In short, we can paint almost any portrait of current intergroup relations in the U.S., and of their trajectory over the past few decades, with solid evidence of a variety of kinds. The complexities do not stop here, however; the analytic categories used to explicate and evaluate intergroup relations are almost as multiple and contradictory.

How Should We Understand Groups and Explain Intergroup Relations?

Some scholars, as represented by the data cited above, focus on large, panethnic groups, as implied by the terms "black," "white," "Asian," and "Latino." They endeavor to answer the question of how these large aggregates relate to one another. These scholars, like activists in the communities themselves, often combine this analytic choice with a normative value or political calculation; that is, they seek evidence of a strong sense of unity or linked fate across nationalities because they perceive racial identity to be a core value, or they judge that in the American political system, groups have more political and policy influence if their numbers are larger and they are spread across a wider geographic area.

Other scholars or advocates, however, argue that this level of aggregation obscures more than it illuminates and disadvantages small groups. For example, relations between African Americans and the increasing numbers of black immigrants may be at least as tense as those between "blacks" and "whites," as demonstrated by fierce political battles over representation and status in New York City. Nicaraguans and Cubans in Miami similarly perceive little in common; Nicaraguans resent Cuban political, cultural, and economic dominance, which is hidden by the category "Hispanic" or "Latino." The popular image of Asian Americans as a model minority obscures the fact that some immigrants (such as Hmong, Laotians, and Cambodians) suffer from higher rates of poverty and unemployment than any other nationality group in the U.S.

Disaggregation can obscure overall patterns of intergroup relations as well as illuminate nuances and critical pockets of inequality and alienation from other groups. Aggregation highlights crucial trajectories but leaves variation around the central tendency murky. There is no intrinsically correct choice appropriate for all analyses of intergroup relations; nevertheless, the different choices can themselves become politically and normatively fraught.

A deeper source of analytic confusion and political contestation in the study of intergroup relations is the question of what is a race or an ethnicity and whether (if they are different) a given group should be understood in racial or ethnic terms. Some argue that race and ethnicity are conceptually distinct. In this view, race is commonly defined, correctly or not, to have a biological component. The members of a race can be differentiated visually from those of other races, the race is usually a large group encompassing a variety of more specific ethnicities, and it is stable over a long period of time. An ethnicity, in contrast, is defined in this construction as smaller, usually less sharply bounded and more fluid, and constructed more by a shared culture, language, religion, history, and geographical homeland. Others, however, argue that the analytic distinction between race and ethnicity is a conceptual or political obfuscation. Both terms delineate separation among groups; both can have roughly the same political and social connotations or effects; both groups can have more or less porous boundaries depending on context and history; both are socially constructed categories with shifting boundaries whose linguistic evolution can be traced over time.

Depending on how one conceives of race and ethnicity, one is likely to emphasize different features of intergroup relations among old and new Americans. If Latinos are understood mainly as an ethnicity or a loosely bounded set of ethnicities, it is not hard to find evidence of positive connections. Argentines and Cubans in the U.S. are disproportionately white in appearance and arguably face few group-based barriers in relating to non-Hispanic whites once they overcome language differences. More generally, scholars such as Richard Alba and Victor Nee, Michael Barone, and Joel Perlmann, who argue that new American immigrants are assimilating into the social, economic, and political mainstream roughly as immigrants did a century ago, tend to think in terms of porous ethnicities that may eventually be as malleable as "Polish" and "Irish" are today.

Conversely, if Latinos are perceived mainly as a distinct race, or if one understands intergroup relations in terms of racialization rather than assimilation of new immigrants, it is equally easy to find evidence of hostile or harmful intergroup relations. Mexicans, Dominicans, and Panamanians are disproportionately nonwhite in appearance and arguably face individual and systemic discrimination and prejudice. More generally in this view, scholars such as Ian Haney López and Eduardo Bonilla-Silva argue that Hispanics are best understood (despite some exceptions) as a single group whose status lies slightly above that of blacks but well below that of native-born whites in the American racial order. Similarly, even though Asian immigrants speak different languages and come from distinct religious and cultural backgrounds, Claire Kim, Mai Ngai, and other scholars argue that native-born

Americans perceive them to be a single race distinguished mainly by their ineluctable foreignness. As permanent foreigners, in this view, they are all to be mistrusted, kept at arm's length, and denied political power and economic authority despite "minor" internal variations.

The relationship between race and ethnicity and the question of which term best describes new immigrant groups are linked to another conceptual choice essential for studying intergroup relations. Should groups be understood solely in terms of race or ethnicity? Perhaps not; gender, religious faith, economic standing, immigrant status, sexuality, or political ideology may do more to define what group a person is "in" than race or ethnicity. If class differentiation is growing within racial or ethnic groups, as William Julius Wilson argued several decades ago, people might develop relationships based more on their material interests than on their cultural ties. Or if divisions deepen between those who seek a purely secular government and those who want public life to reflect Christian values, then people's allegiance may no longer be predominantly racial or ethnic. Or perhaps groups are best understood in geographic terms. For example, Mark Warren shows how the Industrial Areas Foundation seeks to get urban residents of all racial and ethnic groups to work together to improve their local neighborhoods and schools. Organizers hope that eventually a unified sense of community (and often religiosity) will override divisions of race, ethnicity, and anything else. At a higher level of abstraction, the intergroup dynamics in the American Southwest, where Hispanics, like whites, have been living for centuries and are now a majority in many communities, will be very different from those of the Northeast, where the two oldest groups are African Americans and whites and where many different populations are now converging.

How one understands the connections between racial or ethnic identities and other allegiances will affect what one expects to happen in intergroup relations in the foreseeable future. If the central dynamic appears to be the substitution of a new intense identity (say, religious faith or political ideology) for racial or ethnic solidarity, one would expect connections across groups to remain difficult but less hierarchical, more amenable to entry and exit, and perhaps open to cross-cutting loyalties. Alternatively, if one judges the trajectory to be movement toward an array of less intense identities, or toward commitments with more room for compromise and negotiation than racial ones typically have—if, for example, new Americans increasingly focus on their economic well-being or improvements in their local community—then intergroup relations could become more negotiable and cumulative. If one expects new Americans to be socialized into the American racial hierarchy (whether by assimilating and becoming honorary whites, through segmented assimilation, or by some other means), then high levels of immigration will be expected to reinforce rather than undermine the traditional American racial order.

A final conceptual complication lies in the arena of motivation, which is in turn linked to the disciplinary background used to evaluate intergroup relations. Sociologists focus on social change and assimilation or lack thereof, and examine the relative sizes of immigrant groups, their residential and occupational concentration or dispersion, the patterns of interactions between groups and how they affect beliefs and attitudes, and the changing social definitions of group boundaries and how they are shaped by history and legal definitions. Economists expect calculations about material interests to be central in shaping a person's actions, so economists search for evidence of whether the black or Latino middle class is growing and acquiring capital, moving to communities with better returns on housing investments, or seeking jobs in mainstream firms with higher payoffs to educational investments. They might then anticipate improved intergroup relations, at least within the affluent segment of the population, on the grounds that negotiation promotes acquisition more than hostility does. Psychologists, however, work from the premise that intergroup relations stem from psychological dynamics of perception, categorization, attraction, or fear. They search for evidence of whether, as African Americans or immigrants move into a community, current residents feel threatened individually or for their group, judge that the newcomers did not really earn their status, or include them in a new conception of the neighborhood. Anthropologists focus on cultural practices and consider how much newcomers seek to retain their traditional values, maintain links with the home country, or assimilate into mainstream or countercultural American behaviors. Which direction they and their children choose to move in and how their practices are received by native-born Americans will strongly affect whether intergroup relations become clashes among values or enlightening approaches to another way to view the world (or both). Finally, political scientists analyze the drive for power within a given structure, so they attend particularly to structural and institutional factors, such as whether voting is districted or at large, whether political parties have incentives to mobilize or exclude new immigrants, and whether there are electoral or policy advantages to organization along ethnic or racial lines or some other cleavage.

In short, what people bring to the study of intergroup relations—their political ideology, disciplinary lens and methods, definitional arsenal, and substantive goals—will affect what they see. And given that intergroup relations are genuinely confusing, if not contradictory, the complexities multiply rapidly.

Types of Intergroup Relations

I propose to overlay this complexity with two organizing patterns. The first focuses on how we evaluate the nature and quality of intergroup relations by providing several plausible templates for "good" interactions. Here we will concentrate on political or, more broadly, public coalitions or alliances.

One understanding of good intergroup relations in the public arena accords with the old cliché that "politics makes strange bedfellows." In the ideal type of this coalition, participants identify particular shared interests and seek a pragmatic interracial or interethnic alliance. The underlying logic is that small groups must ally to have any hope of victory in a political system that rewards voting majorities and extensive resources; their motto might be Benjamin Franklin's "We must indeed all hang together, or, most assuredly, we shall all hang separately." Log-rolling coalition leaders do not expect given racial and ethnic groups always to ally with one another. The coalition's longevity depends on whether interests consistently coincide and whether the groups develop successful working relationships; it may dissolve after a single law is passed or be reborn to pursue the next piece of legislation. Examples include black inner-city ministers who provided staunch support for President George W. Bush's initiative to expand faith-based social services, and Latino activists who allied with Republicans and conservatives in California to abolish what they perceived to be a failed and stigmatizing program of bilingual education in public schools.

In the ideal interest-based coalition, participants work around most of the conceptual issues we have raised. They do not care if their current allies are best understood as a race or an ethnicity, if their primary allegiance is racial or religious or something else, if they are motivated more by hope of economic gain or anxiety about a threatening Other. Participants also work around many of the empirical contradictions we have examined. They are fairly indifferent to individuals' level of stereotyping or tolerance, so long as negative feelings do not interrupt the workings of the group. They also do not concern themselves with issues of intermarriage or other emotional and personal ties; they may even ignore instances of discrimination, so long as such behavior does not keep coalition members from accomplishing their tasks. The coalition succeeds—and therefore group relations are "good"—if it accomplishes its clearly defined goal.

The ideal type of opposite relationship in the public arena is an alliance organized around deeply meaningful identities. Such a relationship is not only a means to win a political victory or pursue economic interests but an arena for carrying out moral commitments and attaining personal and collective fulfillment, even transformation. The group expands by seeking allies with the same commitments and identity-based self-understandings, and it is expected to last for years, if not decades, in quest of a powerful vision. Lani Guinier and Gerald Torres, for example, argue that "racialized identities may be put to service to achieve social change through democratic renewal" by "build[ing] a progressive democratic movement led by people of color but joined by others." Labor unions have begun to woo new Americans by focusing on immigrants' rights and amnesty for illegal immigrant workers while trying to teach immigrants to think of themselves as workers whose primary loyalty is to their fellow unionists. Feminist activists wrestle intensely with the question of how to develop a sense of linked fate among women in the face of continued racial and class division and cultural divergences. Muslims from many countries seek to discover what elements of their faith they have in common despite differences in nationality, interpretation of the Quran, and daily practices.

In an identity-based alliance, the conceptual issues we have raised have deep importance. Those who see a few racialized groups will seek different allies, perceive different opponents, and pursue different goals from those who see many ethnic groups or who expect people to align along dimensions such as economic class, religious faith, or political ideology. Identity-based alliances give less credence to economic motives—whether as an explanation for action or as a goal to be pursued— than to psychological, political, or cultural ones. They attend carefully to evidence of discrimination and stereotyping. They perceive interracial marriages and other close personal ties as evidence of either betrayal or allegiance to the group rather than as a personal and idiosyncratic choice among individuals. The most prominent identity-based groups focus on aggregate central tendencies of a panethnic community such as "blacks" or "Latinos," but many such groups form around particular nationalities or even subnationalities.

Overall, pragmatic coalitions tend to emphasize the more successful features of intergroup relations and try to ignore or work around the most intractable elements. Identity-based alliances are more attentive to evidence of an underlying pernicious racial order and are usually less persuaded by indications of positive intergroup interactions or receptivity by the state.

These are, of course, ideal types; actual coalitions are unlikely to conform to all of these elements. Interest-based groups can on occasion be adamant about not negotiating away parts of their program; identity-based groups can demonstrate pragmatic skill in a given situation. Furthermore, intermediate forms of intergroup relations may combine features of both types. Two in particular suggest opposite trajectories over time.

Interracial or interethnic associations may be a transitional step from identity-based alliances toward pragmatic coalitions. This is the political version of the classic sociological theory of straight-line assimilation, which occurs in three stages. First, a recent immigrant is relatively poor, and "ethnic identification color[s] his life, his relations with others, his attitudes toward himself and the world," as Robert Dahl puts it. Immigrants demonstrate a "high degree of political homogeneity" and generally ally with similar others. Intergroup relations will be distant, if not hostile. Later, group members move toward greater heterogeneity, but "even the middling segments retain a high sensitivity to their ethnic origins." Intergroup relations will be touchy but negotiable. This is the era of candidate slates containing both an Irishman and an Italian, voting districts balanced so that blacks, whites, and Hispanics all have a good chance to elect a representative of their own group to a citywide school board, or agreements among civic elites to let African Americans and immigrants run the schools while native-born whites retain control of the downtown business district. Eventually, in the third stage, descendants of immigrants are very heterogeneous socially and economically, and "ethnic politics is often embarrassing or meaningless." Individuals now engage in pragmatic coalitions or identity-based politics along some cleavage other than race or ethnicity. Intergroup relations simply matter less to them.

A final theory, of segmented assimilation or racialization, suggests the opposite trajectory. The logic here is movement away from initial, exploratory pragmatic coalitions based on fluid intergroup relations toward intense, even hostile encounters organized around identities fixed by the racial order of the United States. When immigrants first come, they think of themselves in terms of their nationality or their local community. They are prepared to engage in pragmatic coalitions with members of other groups as needed to attain jobs, legal status, English-language ability, and other necessities. Over time, however, according to this model, many immigrants and their children come to see themselves in terms of aggregated American racial categories, either because they change their own preferred identity or because race is forced on them by native-born Americans and the social, economic, and political orders. Once they are racialized, new Americans are more available for identity-based alliances.

Thus ideal types of intergroup relations and theories of how groups move from one to another of these models give us some purchase on understanding the empirical and conceptual complexities of contemporary American ethnic and race relations. A final pattern completes the picture.

Fluid Identities and an Enduring Racial Structure

Intergroup relations can seem strong, constructive, and growing because many individuals, especially new Americans, believe that they have a great deal of flexibility in defining who they are or will be and how they want to relate to others. The high and growing rate of intermarriage is both an indicator and a cause of this autonomy, as is the almost universal commitment of universities and public schools to a curriculum of multiculturalism. Popular culture, especially in cities, celebrates eclectic mixtures of food, fashion, music, and media. Fewer than 3 percent of respondents to the 2000 Census identified with more than one race, but much higher proportions of the young and well-educated did so; they may be a harbinger of the future. The sober scholarly publication *Migration News,* a quarterly compendium of information about migration around the world, matter-of-factly suggests, "It is possible that, by 2050, today's racial and ethnic categories will no longer be in use." Americans have always redefined themselves, so the stereotype goes, by shucking the past, moving to a new place to start a new life, and being "self-made"; new Americans may be doing just as occupants of covered wagons did a century and a half ago.

But this vigorous exercise of fluid self-definition by individuals and even groups may rest on a deep and apparently immobile racial structure—the existence of which provides the evidence for weak, hostile, and stagnant intergroup relations. Blacks or dark-skinned Latinos remain poorest, least well educated, most likely to be unemployed or exploited, least well represented in the political arena, and most likely to be arrested. Affluent African Americans are almost as racially segregated as their poorer counterparts; the racial achievement gap in education persists for middle-class as well as poor children. In an earlier work (*Facing Up to the American Dream: Race, Class, and the Soul of the Nation*), I showed that many blacks, especially the well-off, continue to believe that other Americans are deeply and irremediably prejudiced against their race and that the racial order will not change. Some new Americans, especially those who are dark-skinned, are unwillingly joining African Americans at the bottom of the historically rooted status hierarchy. Individuals are mixing and allying with people in different racial/ethnic groups, but racial hierarchies themselves remain quite firm, at least to those caught up in them.

The Future(s) of Intergroup Relations

We cannot tell at this point how the conflicting evidence on intergroup relations will evolve over the next few decades. Possibly the U.S. is in transition from a rigid racial structure to a fluid system of Madisonian democracy, in which for the first time in history, almost all adult citizens can participate in the social, economic, and political systems and develop alliances as they wish. That situation is surprisingly new. African Americans and Latinos have formally been full members of the polity for barely a generation, about 15 percent of the time that the U.S. has been a constitutional republic. Asian immigrants have been allowed citizenship for barely two generations. The new Americans are coming into a society that is very different from the one that the last great wave of immigrants joined at the turn of the 20th century—and the new Americans are themselves changing the society even more. If in fact the U.S. is currently in the middle of a transition from a racial order to full Madisonian factional democracy, that would explain the contradictions in the evidence on intergroup relations and the complexity of the concepts we must use to explain them.

Unfortunately, however, another, less optimistic prediction can also make sense of the extant evidence. Possibly most of the new Americans are altogether too much like the old immigrants, in that they are on the way to becoming "white"—or at least not black—and are simply moving up the ranks of the traditional, unchanging racial hierarchy. A few new Americans are simultaneously moving down the ranks, into blackness or at least the low status and dismal prospects that most African Americans have experienced for most of the country's history. Transformation of the status of individuals and groups but not of the structure within which they are ranked would also explain why intergroup relations look strong and positive from one vantage point (the top down) but weak and hostile from another (the bottom up).

At this time in American history, we cannot tell whether the optimistic or pessimistic trajectory of intergroup relations is the most plausible. The evidence is too mixed; the concepts with which people approach the evidence are too fixed; regions, states, and localities have too many particular dynamics to permit many generalizations. Most importantly, how new Americans become incorporated in American society is a matter of politics not yet engaged in, with new leaders, different ideas, changed party dynamics, unstable immigrant streams, and unsettled electoral outcomes. There is genuine contingency in the intersection between politics and the American racial order—which will shape and be shaped by new Americans.

Bibliography

Alba, R., and V. Nee. 2003. *Remaking the American Mainstream: Assimilation and Contemporary Immigration.* Cambridge, Mass.: Harvard University Press.

Bonilla-Silva, E. 2003. *Racism without Racists: Color-Blind Racism and the Persistence of Racial Inequality in the United States.* Lanham, Md.: Rowman & Littlefield.

"Census, Welfare, California, New York City." 2004. *Migration News* 11, 2 (Apr.).

Guinier, L., and G. Torres. 2002. *The Miner's Canary: Enlisting Race, Resisting Power, Transforming Democracy.* Cambridge, Mass.: Harvard University Press.

Haney López, I. 1997. "Race, Ethnicity, Erasure: The Salience of Race to LatCrit Theory." *California Law Review* 85: 1143–1211.

Lien, P.-t., M. M. Conway, et al. 2004. *The Politics of Asian Americans: Diversity and Community.* New York: Routledge.

Orfield, G., and C. Lee. 2004. *Brown at 50: King's Dream or Plessy's Nightmare?* Cambridge, Mass.: Harvard University, Civil Rights Project.

Padilla, F. 1985. *Latino Ethnic Consciousness: The Case of Mexican Americans and Puerto Ricans in Chicago.* Notre Dame, Ind.: University of Notre Dame Press.

Portes, A., and M. Zhou. 1993. "The New Second Generation: Segmented Assimilation and Its Variants." *Annals of the American Academy of Political and Social Science* 530: 74–96.

Rogers, R. 2004. "Race-Based Coalitions among Minority Groups: Afro-Caribbean Immigrants and African-Americans in New York City." *Urban Affairs Review* 39, 3: 283–317.

Warren, M. 2001. *Dry Bones Rattling: Community Building to Revitalize American Democracy.* Princeton, N.J.: Princeton University Press.

Waters, M. 1999. *Black Identities: West Indian Immigrant Dreams and American Realities.* Cambridge, Mass.: Harvard University Press.

Immigrants and the Economy

Neeraj Kaushal, Cordelia W. Reimers, and David M. Reimers

In the last two decades of the 20th century, the United States experienced a dramatic surge in immigration. The new wave of immigrants has been dominated by Hispanics and Asians, while immigrants from the traditional major sending nations of Europe have declined not only in numbers but also as a share of the total. The recent wave also exhibits significant geographic dispersion within the U.S. At the beginning of the 21st century, new immigrant communities are appearing in regions that did not have large foreign-born populations even two decades ago.

The latest newcomers, like earlier ones, have different skills and educational levels, as shown in Table 1. The size, diversity, and dispersion of these people have brought the perennial debates about the impacts of immigration on the American economy, and the effect of the economy on the immigrants, to the center of policymaking.

The Changing Economy

This wave of immigration has coincided with four major transformations in the U.S. economy. First, the share of the U.S. workforce engaged in manufacturing and agriculture has fallen dramatically since 1970, as shown in Table 2. Those jobs have been replaced by jobs in the service sector. In 2000 farmers made up only about 2 percent of the workforce. Manufacturing had shrunk from employing a little over a fourth of all workers in 1970 to employing 15 percent by 2000. Meanwhile, the service sector, broadly defined, grew from 62 to 75 percent of the workforce. Many of the jobs in this sector—including those of doctors, engineers, educators, and computer systems analysts—require advanced degrees, and highly skilled immigrants have often filled them. Many others—such as those of nurse aides, busboys, maids, child-care workers, and gardeners—require very little education or command of English, so they are suitable for low-skilled immigrants.

Table 1   Education of the population aged 25 and over by nativity and decade of entry, 2000

| | Percentage of nativity group with each level of education | | | | | |
| | Foreign-born | | | | | |
Level of education	All	Asia	Europe	Latin America and Caribbean	1990s entrants	U.S.-born
Less than 5th grade	7.2	4.0	3.1	11.2	7.3	0.7
5th to 8th grade	15.0	5.9	9.6	23.4	14.2	4.0
9th to 12th grade (no diploma)	10.8	6.2	5.9	15.8	11.5	8.7
High school graduate (includes equivalency)	25.0	21.8	28.7	24.9	24.0	34.3
Some college, less than bachelor's degree	16.2	17.1	19.7	13.5	14.0	26.7
Bachelor's degree	16.1	28.0	18.7	7.7	19.1	17.2
Graduate degree	9.7	16.9	14.2	3.5	9.9	8.4
Total	100.0	100.0	100.0	100.0	100.0	100.0

Source: Profile of the Foreign-Born Population in the United States, 2000, Tables 14-1A, 14-1B, and 14-1D, www.census.gov/population/www/socdemo/foreign/pp1-145.html.
  Note: Africa, Oceania, and Canada are not shown separately but are included in the "All" and "1990s entrants" columns.

Second, the Sunbelt states have experienced spectacular population growth as people (including immigrants) and economic activity have moved south and west. In 1960 the foreign-born population in Texas and Florida combined was merely 0.6 million. By 2000 the number had risen to 5.2 million. The settlement of immigrants in southern states that attracted few in the past is part of the dispersal of newcomers in the past 20 years and has made these states more demographically diverse. Nevertheless, traditional immigrant-receiving states, such as California and New York, have continued to attract the lion's share of immigrants.

The exodus from manufacturing and the growth of the Sunbelt have contributed to a third major change—the decline of labor unions. At the unions' peak, in the 1950s, nearly one third of workers belonged to them. Half a century later, only 13 percent of the nonagricultural workforce did so. In 1993 the AFL-CIO, which had a history of ambivalence toward newcomers—particularly unauthorized ones—began a new campaign to organize immigrants, and a few years later it called for reaching out to unauthorized immigrants, but with little success. Twenty thousand garment-shop workers in New York City, mostly women from China, joined the International Ladies' Garment Workers Union and won union contracts after a successful strike in 1982. However, the garment business had been shrinking steadily since the 1970s, and in most new garment shops, where the workforce was dominated by both undocumented and authorized immigrants, union leaders had little success in organizing workers. Nor was the situation different for farmworkers. In California, the center for American farm produce, the United Farm Workers and

Table 2   Industry of the total employed population aged 16 and over, 2000

	Percentage of total work force in each industry	
Sector	1970	2000
Agriculture	4.4	2.5
Goods-producing[a]	33.1	22.0
Manufacturing	26.4	15.1
Service[b]	62.5	75.5
Business, professional, recreation, and personal services	25.9	36.8
Total	100.0	100.0

Sources: *Statistical Abstract of the United States: 1990*, Table 650; *Profile of the Foreign-Born Population in the United States, 2000*, Table 16-2, www.census.gov/population/www/socdemo/foreign/pp1-145.html.
   a. Manufacturing, mining, construction.
   b. Transport, public utilities, trade, financial/insurance/real estate, and public administration.

several other unions organized thousands of agricultural laborers in the 1960s and 1970s but suffered huge reversals when trying to unionize unauthorized immigrant farmworkers, estimated to make up over half of the state's agricultural workforce in 2004.

A fourth important development in the past three decades has been the growing inequality of wages. Average wages (adjusted for inflation) of men with a high school education or less fell from 1973 to 1995, while those of college graduates, especially people with advanced degrees, rose dramatically. Most studies have found that the spread of high-tech production methods that place a premium on skill is the main reason for the increase in inequality. However, expanding imports, the decline of unions, and the influx of unskilled immigrants have also contributed to the erosion of wages of workers with few skills. The increase in wage inequality has made it difficult for these workers, including immigrants with less education, to improve their earnings over time. At the same time, rising wages for those with higher education have presented college-educated immigrants with good job opportunities.

Although the American economy changed after 1970, it still needed labor to expand, including immigrant labor. Half of the new jobs created in the 1990s, for instance, went to foreign-born workers. The U.S. economy provides economic opportunities that most immigrants are denied in their home countries. They come, either legally or illegally, to seek higher wages and better career opportunities. Low-paid jobs with poor working conditions, which most native-born Americans disdain, find a ready supply of low-skilled immigrants, who regard these "bad" jobs as quite good when compared to opportunities in their home country. In 2004 immigrants made up roughly 12 percent of the U.S. population, 15 percent of all U.S. workers, and 20 percent of low-wage workers.

Immigrants continue to be a source of labor in traditional sectors such as farming, meat processing, the garment industry, and construction. Although technology has replaced many farmworkers, hands are nonetheless required in agriculture, especially in the fruit and vegetable fields, and Mexican immigrants have proved to be a ready source of labor. About half of American farmworkers are Hispanics, largely unauthorized Mexican immigrants. Major changes in the meatpacking and chicken-processing industries created a huge demand for immigrant labor, which has been met by Central Americans and Mexicans, mostly in small towns in the South and Midwest that had virtually no immigrant presence before 1990. In 1980, 8 percent of workers in the meat-processing industry were Hispanics. By 2000 the number had risen to 35 percent. The positions these workers fill are usually poorly paid, and firms experience high rates of labor turnover. The garment industry, which historically depended on immigrant labor, continues to do so in New York City, Los Angeles, and other centers, though at a much reduced rate, as the manufacture of textiles has moved overseas. The remaining jobs are usually filled by Hispanic or Chinese immigrants. Construction work has also lured Hispanic immigrants away from the Southwest to cities such as Atlanta and New York.

Immigrants, especially Hispanics, do maintenance work in the nation's hotels, office buildings, restaurants, and motels. As increasing demand has outpaced the number of U.S.-born university graduates entering certain fields—particularly health care, engineering, science, and computer science—immigrants have come to represent a sizable share of those professions. While low-wage positions are mostly filled by immigrants with little education, highly educated people from Asia and the Middle East are working in the high-tech industries as engineers and computer experts.

Major changes in immigration law occurred at the same time that the Medicare bill was passed, in 1965, thus creating a large demand for health professionals such as physicians, nurses, and lab technicians and for low-wage employees to maintain hospitals and other medical facilities. The health industry attracted Asians, especially Filipinos and Indians, and people from the Caribbean. As seen in Table 3, foreign-born workers were much more likely than U.S. natives to be in lower-paid blue-collar and service jobs in 2000, and less likely to be in managerial, sales, and clerical work. On average they were about as likely as natives to be professionals, but this masks a dramatic difference between Asian and European immigrants, on the one hand, and Latin Americans, on the other. This disparity reflects the educational differences noted in Table 1.

While immigrants are attracted by employment opportunities in the U.S., immigration is not solely determined by the demand for labor. American immigration policy plays a key role, and it is not guided entirely by the needs of the labor mar-

Table 3   Occupation of the employed population aged 16 and over by nativity and decade of entry, 2000

| | Percentage of nativity group in each occupation | | | | | |
| | Foreign-born | | | | | |
Occupation	All	Asia	Europe	Latin America and Caribbean	1990s entrants	U.S.-born
Executives and managers	10.6	15.7	15.8	5.8	6.8	15.3
Professionals	14.1	23.0	22.3	6.2	13.4	15.6
Technicians	3.0	5.5	3.7	1.5	3.6	3.3
Sales and administrative support	17.8	22.1	20.2	15.0	14.2	27.4
Private household workers	1.9	0.8	1.5	2.7	2.1	0.5
Other service workers	17.3	14.2	13.5	20.2	19.6	12.7
Precision production, craft, and repair	12.1	5.9	12.2	15.9	11.7	10.5
Operators, fabricators, and laborers	18.7	12.0	10.2	24.8	22.7	12.7
Farming, forestry, and fishing	4.5	0.8	0.6	7.8	5.9	2.1
Total	100.0	100.0	100.0	100.0	100.0	100.0

Source: Profile of the Foreign-Born Population in the United States, 2000, Tables 16-1A, 16-1B, and 16-1D,
www.census.gov/population/www/socdemo/foreign/ppl-145.html.
Note: Africa, Oceania, and Canada are not shown separately but are included in the "All" and "1990s entrants" columns.

ket. The inflow of foreigners in a given year is determined by the number of visas issued and the enforcement of border controls. For example, legal immigration dropped by 34 percent between 2002 and 2003, not because of the sluggish labor market but because the terrorist attacks on September 11, 2001, prompted tighter government control of entry to the U.S. During recessions immigrants may have a harder time finding work and may have to take poorer jobs at lower pay, but that does not stop them from coming to the U.S. when they can. Even the flows of unauthorized immigrants are surprisingly insensitive to the state of the U.S. economy. The prospect of a bad job in the U.S. may be better than what is available at home. Although the overall inflows are largely insensitive to fluctuations in the U.S. economy, however, recessions do affect public attitudes toward immigrants. Pressure for more restrictive immigration policies tends to increase during recessions and relax when the economy is expanding.

How Immigration Affects the U.S. Economy

Immigrants—workers and entrepreneurs, skilled and unskilled, legal and undocumented—contribute to the nation's income. A recent report of the International Monetary Fund (IMF) has estimated that the foreign-born population living in the

U.S. contributes 13 percent of the nation's gross domestic product, a proportion slightly higher than their population share.

The IMF estimate does not include the indirect effects of immigration, which are negative as well as positive. When measuring immigration's impact on the economy, social scientists generally refer to these indirect effects—that is, whether immigration has helped or hurt the native-born by enhancing or reducing their economic opportunities; whether immigrants impose a fiscal burden on the economy; and whether immigrants fill specific skill requirements, thus facilitating the functioning of the labor market.

Labor market effects. Diversity of skills and education among natives and immigrants results in a complex economic relationship between the two groups. In 2000 a third of immigrants had not completed high school, compared with only an eighth of native-born people aged 25 or older. A quarter of both the native-born and foreign-born populations had a college degree, but among immigrants 9.7 percent held graduate degrees, compared with 8.4 percent of natives. Again, the differences by region of origin are large. Forty-five percent of all Asian immigrants but only 11 percent of Latin Americans are college graduates.

Do immigrants, skilled or unskilled, displace native-born workers? Does immigration lower native wages and thus contribute to wage inequality? Does an influx of foreign workers push natives to move to occupations with less immigrant competition or to migrate to regions with low immigrant population? The answers to all these questions lie in the economic relationship between immigrants and natives—that is, whether they are "complements" or "substitutes" in the job market. Economic theory suggests that if the two groups are complements, an immigrant influx will increase job opportunities for natives, in turn raising their rate of employment and wages, and may even attract natives from other regions. If, in contrast, the two are substitutes, the opposite may happen—native employment and wages will decline, and some natives may be forced to look for other occupations or migrate to areas with a low immigrant presence. Immigrants and natives with the same occupation and similar skills are most likely to be substitutes, but immigrants and natives with different skills, even within the same occupation, may cooperate with or complement each other. For instance, an influx of Indian doctors may lower opportunities for native doctors but create additional opportunities for U.S.-born paramedics. Similarly, low-skilled immigrants may compete with low-skilled natives but have a complementary relationship with highly skilled natives.

Most research on the effects of immigration on native wages has been based on the hypothesis that immigrants and natives compete for the same jobs and that an influx of immigrants therefore reduces economic opportunities for natives. After a careful examination of previous research, however, a 1997 National Research Council report concluded that "the weight of the empirical evidence suggests that the impact of immigration on the wages of competing workers is small."

A number of economists have inferred from theoretical models of labor demand and supply that immigrant inflows have had a large adverse effect on the wages of low-skilled native workers. However, these studies do not account for the complex ways in which immigrants can affect natives' wages—as substitute or complementary workers, as entrepreneurs, and as consumers.

Others have used what is called the "area approach," in which the uneven geographic distribution of immigrants is used to estimate the impact of immigration on wages in local labor markets. Researchers using this approach have concluded that immigrant influx has a modest effect on the wages of natives.

The area approach can be criticized on three conceptual grounds. First, it assumes that immigrants' destination decisions are largely independent of ups and downs in the local economy, which are called "demand shocks." In reality, immigrants may be attracted to areas of high wage growth. The challenging task for a researcher is to purge the effect of local economic conditions that may pull immigrants to certain areas from the effect of immigration on local wages.

Second, an influx of immigrants to an area may trigger out-migration of the native population affected by immigration. As a result, it is difficult to measure the true effect of immigration on the employment and earnings of competing natives. Empirical research on the effect of immigration on the internal migration of natives has yielded mixed results. While the 1997 National Research Council study suggests that an immigrant influx triggers native out-migration, others have found that immigration inflows result in net native in-migration.

Finally, the area approach ignores interregional trade. Regions that receive more immigrants with certain skills may increase exports of the goods and services produced by these immigrants, thus expanding the demand for workers and absorbing at least some of the increase in supply due to immigration. In short, local "demand shocks," migration, and interregional trade make it difficult to measure the true effect of immigration on native earnings, which gets diffused throughout the economy.

Immigrant entrepreneurs. Immigrants influence the labor market not just as workers but also as entrepreneurs, creating jobs mostly for fellow immigrants but sometimes also for the native-born. Entrepreneurs make up roughly 10 percent of the employed immigrant population—the same proportion as the number of native-born Americans who own small businesses. The 1990 Immigration Act created 10,000 new slots for persons willing to invest $1 million and create new jobs for Americans, but that provision has not been fully utilized. Some newcomers arrive with a visa allotted to those with particular skills and utilize their skills to open businesses. Many who come under the family-unification visa category also open small enterprises.

These small businesses, mom-and-pop firms that families own and manage, vary by immigrant group. Asian newcomers—especially Koreans, South Asians, Middle

Easterners, and Chinese—and older Greek immigrants are more apt to own small businesses than Latin Americans are. Yet Dominicans, a relatively poor group, dominate New York City's bodegas (grocery stores). Particular groups are known for their association with small businesses. In Washington, D.C., taxicab owners and drivers are often African; in New York, they are mostly South Asian and Haitian. As Jews and Italians moved on from owning fruit and vegetable stores, Koreans began to purchase and operate many of these businesses, including some in predominantly black neighborhoods. After riots ruined many Korean-owned stores in Los Angeles in 1992, Koreans looked to different enterprises and opened or purchased dry cleaners and nail salons. Asian Indians and Pakistanis are especially prominent in running motels, newspaper stands, convenience stores, and restaurants. Chinese restaurants are found throughout the United States. At the turn of the 21st century, in California's Silicon Valley, immigrant Taiwanese and Indians owned roughly 30 percent of the high-tech businesses. Immigrant entrepreneurs often employ both husband and wife as well as other family members, so the actual percentage of immigrants in small family-run firms is higher than the official figures indicate. Some scholars estimate that nearly half of all Korean men and women are employed in family-run enterprises.

It is not clear to what extent ethnic businesses help immigrants adjust to their adopted country. The larger and more successful firms aid immigrants because they are in a position to expand and to employ people from the same background or provide capital to them. However, some studies reveal that small ethnic businesses require long working days, and many fail to sustain their operations. For example, the number of immigrant-owned greengrocers declined in both New York City and Los Angeles in the 1990s.

While providing employment for many family members and fellow immigrants, immigrant-run firms also employ others. In Silicon Valley, for example, Indian and Chinese enterprises provided nearly 73,000 jobs in 2000. Some were for highly skilled engineers and computer experts, but Latinos held janitorial positions and other low-skilled jobs. Overall, the Commerce Department reported in 1997 that the 900,000 Asian-owned firms employed over 2 million people and generated $161 billion in receipts.

Whether employing fellow immigrants or others, immigrant firms have helped cities economically. Miami owes much of its economic fortunes to Cubans. In New York City, Chinese and West Indian immigrants have revitalized low-income neighborhoods. In Los Angeles and elsewhere, Koreans manage thousands of stores, many in poor neighborhoods. Chicago, San Francisco, and Boston have also been aided by the newcomers' businesses. Immigrants have also contributed to the growth and economic health of Sunbelt states such as California and Florida in the past 25 years.

Immigrants as consumers. Immigrants are consumers as well as workers, investors, and store owners. They do not limit their shopping to ethnic stores; they also buy goods in shopping malls, large chain stores, and smaller businesses that are not ethnically oriented. Their stimulation of the housing boom has been especially important in recent years. The newest immigrants, like those in the past, become homeowners as soon as they are financially able to. In recent years immigrants have settled and purchased homes in suburbs as well as older cities. In 2000 approximately two thirds of houses were owned by their inhabitants; for immigrants the figure was 48 percent. The longer immigrants reside in America, the more likely they are to purchase homes.

Part of the money earned by immigrants travels back to their countries of origin. Each year immigrants send billions of dollars to their homelands to help families and friends build houses, start businesses, plant crops, purchase goods, or go to school. Because immigrants are diverse in their occupational status and earnings, it might seem that the more successful ones are more apt to send money home. Although highly educated Indians, Koreans, and Filipinos do remit funds, the nations receiving the most remittances from people in the U.S. are in Latin America and the Caribbean and poor nations such as Bangladesh. The Pew Hispanic Center reported in 2002 that 42 percent of Latino immigrants (some 6 million people) sent money home, even though many of these people were undocumented and had low earnings. Many immigrants who visited home frequently took cash or goods rather than utilizing American banks or Western Union. The total amount sent by Latinos from the U.S. was estimated to be $30 billion in 2003.

Fiscal effects. Like natives, immigrants pay taxes and use public services. The net fiscal impact of immigration is computed by deducting the cost of the public services they consume from the taxes they pay. The resulting figure, like most of immigration's effects on the economy, is unevenly distributed across the country. In 1997 the National Research Council computed the fiscal effect of immigration in California and New Jersey, two states with large immigrant populations, and found that the "fiscal burden" of immigration was $229 per native-born New Jersey household and $1,174 per native-born California household. However, after a thorough analysis of the current fiscal impact of immigrants and their descendants, the council concluded, "Immigrants are a net taxpayer benefit to native-born households. This net benefit takes place exclusively at the federal level, and not at the state level. Consequently, residents of some immigrant-intensive states (such as California) experience higher taxes due to immigration."

Despite evidence to the contrary, during the early 1990s there was considerable concern among policymakers, economists, and other social scientists about the fiscal effects of immigration. These concerns were based on two factors. First, immigrant dependence on welfare programs had steadily increased from 1970 to 1995. In 1970 households headed by immigrants were slightly less likely to receive welfare payments than natives were. By 1990 immigrant dependence on cash welfare surpassed that of native households. Second, there was a concern that the U.S. welfare state attracted low-skilled immigrants who were likely to become a fiscal burden.

Public perceptions of growing immigrant dependence on means-tested programs and public services created anti-immigrant sentiment in several key states. In 1994 voters in California passed Proposition 187, banning all public services to illegal immigrants. Although the proposition was later declared unconstitutional by a California court, sentiment toward immigrants remained mixed.

In 1996 the federal government enacted welfare reform legislation that denied post-1996 arrivals access to four means-tested programs (Temporary Aid to Needy Families, Medicaid, Supplemental Security Income, and Food Stamps) in the first five years of their stay in the U.S. Interestingly, several states, including California, created substitute programs for immigrants for the period they were denied benefits under the federal law. As a result, only a small proportion of immigrants were actually denied benefits. However, since 1996 immigrant use of the four programs has declined sharply. This has led many observers to believe that the 1996 welfare law created an atmosphere of fear and confusion among immigrants, a "chilling effect" that discouraged even the eligible pre-1996 immigrants from using benefits to which they were entitled. The 1996 welfare reform has spawned a large literature on immigrants' response to welfare policies. This research challenges the perception that the U.S. welfare state attracts low-skilled immigrants who are likely to become a state liability.

A discussion of the long-term fiscal impact of immigration needs to include the role that immigration plays in supporting Social Security and Medicare programs for the elderly. Because these programs are financed primarily on a pay-as-you-go basis, the "dependency ratio" of workers, including immigrants, to the elderly population is a key factor in balancing current revenues and expenditures. Since 1965 the fertility rate of native-born Americans has declined; at the same time, immigration has been increasing. As mentioned, in the 1990s half the new jobs were filled by immigrants. Moreover, most immigrants arrive when they are relatively young and contribute to the Social Security system for many years before they begin to receive benefits. Half of the immigrants who came to the U.S. from 1995 to 2000, for example, were between ages 18 and 34. Consequently the ratio of workers to the elderly was 23 to 1 within this entry cohort. As immigrants age, most of them eventually become recipients of Social Security, so for the foreign-born overall this ratio was 5.6 to 1, compared with 4.2 to 1 for natives. Thus, some of the payroll taxes currently received from immigrants can help to support native-born elderly people. Whether this will continue to be so in the future depends on trends in immigration. Official Social Security projections assume that the annual number of immigrants will remain constant after 2005 while the U.S. population will continue to grow, so that immigrants will make up a diminishing share of the population in the future. Other assumptions, such as that the number of immigrants will grow in tandem with the population, yield more optimistic projections for Social Security and Medicare revenues.

Economic Progress of Immigrants

Table 4 shows the widely varying incomes reported in the 2000 Census of immigrants from Asia, Europe, and Latin America. Asians have by far the highest household incomes—24 percent higher than U.S. natives at the median—whereas Latin Americans have 29 percent less income than natives. The income distribution of immigrants from Europe is very similar to that of the U.S.-born. Income is largely determined by earnings, and most of the differences in earnings among immigrants are due to differences in educational levels, age, English fluency, time in the U.S., legal status, and possibly discrimination.

A number of researchers have tried to determine how long it takes for the earnings of immigrants to converge with those of natives with comparable skills and education. One challenge they face is not knowing what would have happened to immigrants who returned to their country of origin after a few years versus what would have happened if they remained in the U.S. Another challenge is not knowing whether economic progress, or lack of it, is caused by changes in the immigrants' U.S. labor market skills, by changes in labor market conditions, or, possibly, by changes in discrimination against certain immigrant groups.

Education and experience in the U.S. have strong influences on earnings, which handicaps immigrants who may be deficient in both. The gap in years of schooling

Table 4   Household income by nativity, 1999

	Percent of nativity group in each income bracket					
	Foreign-born, by region of origin					
Household income	All	Asia	Europe	Latin America and Caribbean	1990s entrants	U.S.-born
Less than $15,000	18.9	16.1	16.9	21.8	23.4	16.3
$15,000–$74,999	60.4	50.5	57.9	66.5	61.6	61.1
$75,000 or more	20.7	33.3	25.2	11.6	15.0	22.8
Total	100.0	100.0	100.0	100.0	100.0	100.0
Median income (dollars)	$36,048	$51,363	$41,733	$29,388	$30,604	$41,383

Source: Profile of the Foreign-Born Population in the United States, 2000, Tables 18-1A, 18-1B, and 18-1D, www.census.gov/population/www/socdemo/foreign/ppl-145.html.

Note: Africa, Oceania, and Canada are not shown separately but are included in the "All" and "1990s entrants" columns.

shown in Table 1 explains a large part, though not all, of the gap in earnings between Latin Americans and other groups. In addition, groups with large numbers of recent immigrants have lower earnings because the typical immigrant comes when he or she is young. In 2004, for example, 52 percent of those who had arrived since 2000 were aged 18 to 34, compared with 22 percent of U.S. natives. The fact that the U.S. labor market rewards U.S. schooling and work experience better than foreign schooling and work experience also means that adults who come after acquiring their education and some work experience abroad tend to earn less than those who come as children and acquire the same amount of education and work experience in the U.S.

When they first arrive, immigrants typically earn less than U.S. natives of similar age and educational level. However, as they learn English and become familiar with the U.S. labor market, their earnings rise with time in the U.S. Research suggests that the process of catching up with natives is faster among European immigrants than among Asian and Latin American immigrants, even after controlling for the differences in education and other observed characteristics of these groups. Indeed, white immigrants surpass white natives soon after arriving in the U.S. However, Asian and Latin American immigrants' wages remain below those of U.S.-born Asians and Hispanics. Immigrants with low levels of education have been held back by the decline in wages for less-skilled workers in recent decades. Many, including about half of all Mexican immigrants, lack legal authorization to be in the U.S. and can therefore work only at marginal jobs in small firms. The unexplained gap could also be due to unmeasured personal characteristics such as quality of schooling. Moreover, some nonwhite immigrants may face racial discrimination in the U.S. labor market.

Although nonwhite immigrants may not attain the same earnings as native-born Americans, there is still progress across generations. Today the U.S.-born children of earlier Mexican immigrants average 12.2 years of schooling, 3.5 years more than current Mexican immigrants but still over a year behind white non-Hispanics. The wages of Mexican men are 44 percent lower than those of whites, but more than half of the difference can be explained by gaps in educational attainment and age. U.S.-born Mexican American women earn the same as white women of the same age and education. There is almost no cross-sectional difference in education between the second generation and the third and higher generations of Mexicans in the U.S. today, but third- and higher-generation Mexican men earn 6 percent more than second-generation men of the same age, and today's third and higher generations have more education than their parents' generation, which is 25 years older.

The earnings gap between U.S. natives and immigrants is larger for more recently arrived cohorts than for those who came earlier. This is partly because the more recent entrants have lower levels of education relative to natives than the earlier ones, but the gap has widened even within the same education and age group.

The widening inequality discussed above is partly responsible. Recent immigrants, particularly those without a college education, have confronted an increasingly unfavorable wage structure, as wages of less-skilled workers have fallen further behind those of better-skilled workers.

Bibliography

Bean, Frank D., and Gillian Stevens. *America's Newcomers and the Dynamics of Diversity.* New York: Russell Sage Foundation, 2004.

Borjas, George J. *Heaven's Door: Immigration Policy and the American Economy.* Princeton, N.J.: Princeton University Press, 1999.

Card, David. "Immigrant Inflows, Native Outflows, and the Local Labor Market Impacts of Higher Immigration." *Journal of Labor Economics* 19, 1 (Jan. 2001): 22–64.

Chiswick, Barry R. *The Economics of Immigration.* Northampton, Mass.: Edward Elgar, 2005.

Clark, William. *Immigrants and the American Dream: Remaking the Middle Class.* New York: Guilford, 2003.

Espenshade, Thomas J., ed. *Keys to Successful Immigration: Implications of the New Jersey Experience.* Washington, D.C.: Urban Institute, 1997.

McCarthy, Kevin F., and George Vernez. *Immigration in a Changing Economy: California's Experience.* Santa Monica: Rand, 1997.

Millman, Joel. *The Other Americans: How Immigrants Renew Our Country, Our Economy, and Our Values.* New York: Viking, 1997.

Portes, Alejandro, and Rubén G. Rumbaut. *Immigrant America: A Portrait.* 3d ed. Berkeley: University of California Press, forthcoming.

Smith, James P., and Barry Edmonston, eds. *The New Americans: Economic, Demographic, and Fiscal Effects of Immigration.* Washington, D.C.: National Academy Press, 1997.

Waldinger, Roger, and Michael I. Lichter. *How the Other Half Works: Immigration and the Social Organization of Labor.* Berkeley: University of California Press, 2003.

Ethnic Politics

Michael Jones-Correa

The term "ethnic politics" conjures up images of immigrants arriving in the melting-pot metropolises of the U.S. and being transformed into citizens, albeit citizens whose first loyalties are to their coethnics and whose votes go to politicians who will reward them. The term implies that immigrants and their children can be counted on to mobilize politically as a bloc, and that competing political parties can court and appeal to the support of this bloc. As such, the term is part and parcel of one of the central narratives used to make sense of ethnic and racial diversity in the U.S.—the immigrant story.

This narrative is reflected in the notion that America is a "nation of immigrants." The plot line is familiar—it is a story of individuals choosing to come to the U.S., of their incorporation as Americans, and of their gradual success. In this narrative the focus is on individual striving rather than structural barriers, and on voluntary rather than forced migration or colonization. As a part of this story, "ethnic politics" is seen as a largely transitory phenomenon, one containing the seeds of its own demise. In an unfamiliar and sometimes hostile environment, immigrants may rally at first in support of their own, but with their social, economic, and political incorporation over time, this support becomes more symbolic than real—an endorsement of politicians who march in annual parades or have their pictures taken in the "home" country. The increasingly symbolic role of ethnicity in American politics is considered to be a sign of the incorporation of ethnic groups.

The primary competitor to this immigrant narrative is the race narrative, which is centered on the story of African Americans and slavery but can be expanded to include other "others" and hinges on the difference between whites and others. Both categories, "white" and "other," may change over time, but the differences between them are largely decided and imposed by whites for their own benefit, are structural in nature, and are expressed in almost every aspect of American social life.

That is, these differences are reflected not just in law (formal segregation) but in informal social relations (residence, marriage patterns), culture (music, literature, etc.), and economics (occupations, employment, income, and wealth). The race narrative, then, is a story of persistent, if not permanent, racial difference and inequality.

During the great wave of immigration in the 19th and early 20th centuries, the race and immigrant narratives were seen as largely separate. Immigrants then were overwhelmingly from Europe, and the "race problem" in the U.S. concerned African Americans. The prejudice suffered by blacks and the hardship undergone by immigrants had their similarities but also their own trajectories: African Americans were caught in a web of institutionalized racism, while immigrants, even if initially seen as distinct races, "became white," which allowed them to incorporate into the larger American society (and in so doing to participate in the oppression of black Americans).

Nonetheless, even in the midst of that wave of European immigration, these narratives were already blurring. The immigration of "nonwhites" complicated the stories of both immigration and race. The Supreme Court ruling clarifying the Fourteenth Amendment's birthright citizenship clause dealt not with African Americans but with Asian Americans (*United States* v. *Wong Kim Ark* [1898]), and many of the cases that traced the line between potential citizens and permanent aliens were brought to the court by Asian immigrants who claimed that they were "white" and so should be allowed to naturalize as U.S. citizens (*Ozawa* v. *United States* [1922] and *United States* v. *Bhagat Singh Thind* [1923]). Mexican Americans were incorporated as foot soldiers in local political machines in southwestern states but simultaneously treated as second-class citizens, or at times not as citizens at all, being deported when the economy turned sour.

By the turn of the 21st century, the immigrant and race narratives were inextricably linked. In the political arena this was due in no small part to the impact of two pieces of legislation in 1965, the Voting Rights Act and the Immigration Act. The Voting Rights Act was the culmination of a half-century of carefully calibrated challenges by African American activists to segregationist policies across the country, but primarily in the South, that marginalized blacks in all public arenas. Coming on the heels of the Civil Rights Act of 1964, which ended federally sanctioned segregation, it was designed to rid states of obviously onerous and arbitrary formal barriers to registration and voting and was initially aimed largely at the practices in seven southern states. When the act was renewed in 1975, however, its focus was expanded to include "linguistic minorities"—at the time, mostly native-born Hispanic and Asian Americans. If a locality met the criteria for inclusion under the expanded Voting Rights Act, then not only did it have to provide dual-language ballots for those citizens who requested them, but its electoral laws fell under the scrutiny of the Justice Department. Because the criterion for coverage was language, areas receiving immigrants were more likely to be covered under the act.

Immigration to the U.S. was already on the upswing when Congress passed the Immigration Act of 1965. This act abolished the national-origins quota system that had been in place since the 1920s (which had dramatically favored immigrants of European origin) and placed a new emphasis on family reunification for allocating residency visas. These two provisions together radically (if unintentionally) changed immigration flows. The abolition of national quotas allowed immigration from Asia and together with the new emphasis on family reunification abetted continued immigration from Latin America and elsewhere. By 2003 there were 33.5 million immigrants in the U.S.—11.7 percent of the total population. Whereas previously most immigrants had come from Europe, 80 percent of immigrants arriving between 1970 and 2000 were from Latin America and Asia, with only 15 percent hailing from Europe. This most recent wave of immigration has transformed the Latin American and Asian-origin populations in the U.S. By 2000 the Asian American population had shifted from being largely native-born to being overwhelmingly foreign-born. While the shift was not as dramatic among Hispanics, by 2000, 41 percent of Latinos in the country were foreign-born, and two thirds were either immigrants or the children of immigrants. Immigration also had an effect on the black population, with almost 10 percent being first or second generation by 2000, and up to 30–50 percent in gateway cities like New York and Miami.

Hispanic and Asian Americans were covered under the nation's civil rights statutes after 1964, and after 1975 by the voting rights provisions for linguistic minorities. Under civil rights and voting rights legislation, the 27 million immigrants of Asian and Latin American origin who had entered the U.S. as legal residents through 2003 were also considered to be racial and linguistic minorities, illustrating how the immigrant and race narratives are linked for them. For the 85 percent of immigrants now meeting the definition of racial or linguistic minorities, incorporation into American life is no longer seen simply as a tale of instrumental ethnic solidarity and individual striving. Instead, their experience is compared to that of native-born whites, and their segregation, whether residential, occupational, or institutional, is seen against the backdrop of a history of racial exclusion. The question, then, is how the contemporary immigrant experience plays out against the difficult history of race relations in the U.S. As the narratives of race and immigration intersect, how does this in turn shape contemporary ethnic politics?

The answer to these questions may in part depend on the various characteristics of immigrants themselves. Immigrants may share the sense of being strangers in a strange land, but they obviously do not have identical characteristics, histories, or experiences. Their prior socialization, their education, their occupations, and their English-language skills all influence the formation of "ethnic" politics and their incorporation into American politics. Differences in these areas translate into different political incorporation. As among the broader population, the more educated immigrants are, the higher their income is, and the greater their command of English is, the more likely they are to be active in formal electoral politics. This is also likely to be the case with informal politics, if findings for the population as a whole hold true for immigrants as well. Immigrants with more resources are more likely to be involved in a wider range of ethnic, religious, civic, and other organizations than those with fewer resources. Political incorporation and participation in "ethnic" politics also likely differ by gender, with women likely to be more engaged, or at least engaged differently, than men. For instance, there are indications that because women tend to act as go-betweens for their families and society in education, housing, and social services, and because politically active women are often shut out of leadership roles in immigrant organizations, women are more likely to naturalize and participate in American politics (rather than immigrant or transnational politics) than men.

If individual characteristics shape forms of political incorporation and participation, probably so do those of groups. Some immigrants arrive in the U.S. with a set of organizational resources waiting for them: for example, in the 1980s, Dominicans arriving in New York City and Nicaraguans in Miami came to cities that already had strong linguistic and/or economic enclaves—Puerto Ricans in New York and Cubans in Miami—which enabled them to take advantage of the resources offered by these coethnics. Soviet Jews who immigrated in the 1970s were taken in by a strong network of existing Jewish organizations that eased their transition.

These examples point to a key difference between political refugees and economic migrants, not least because refugees receive additional aid upon arrival, but also because the reasons for migration shape views of politics and its uses in the U.S. Political migrants are more likely to see politics as central to their predicament and thus to focus their resources on avenues of political mobilization. There is some evidence that political migrants become naturalized more quickly than economic ones, and presumably this would lead them to focus as well on U.S. politics. This is an old story—the effects of political exile can be seen in the mobilization of immigrant groups as disparate as Germans after 1848 (many of whom became active in the nascent labor movement) and Cubans after 1958 (who mobilized first as exiles, then as a foreign policy interest group).

The difference between political and economic migrants suggests that immigrants' ties (or lack of ties) to their home countries may affect their political choices in this country. Sociologists and anthropologists have written extensively about the roles of economic remittances, circular migration, and constant communication in the creation of a single social sphere for immigrants, encompassing both sending and receiving countries. If true, this transnational circuit probably has effects on immigrant political incorporation in the U.S. Some scholars suggest that the rise of expatriate politics, or, more precisely, the extension of sending states' polities to include citizens abroad, may affect immigrants' attachment to American citizenship and participation in electoral politics. Others have argued that these forms of transnational politics, while playing an important role for the first generation, will fade with succeeding generations in the U.S. In any case, immigrant experiences of transnationalism are likely to vary, both across groups and across time, and these differences may well play out in different political pathways.

It is also the case that different groups of immigrants are received differently in the U.S. The native-born population evaluates immigrants from different countries of origin differently: Latino immigrants are regarded less highly than Asians, for instance, though both are often regarded more highly (by employers, at least) than native-born blacks. Political contexts for arrival differ as well: the events of 9/11 have complicated any mobilization on the part of Muslim immigrants, or in fact that of many immigrants from the Middle East and South Asia. Similarly, World War I served to demobilize the highly organized German American community, and World War II placed Japanese, German, and Italian Americans under suspicion, with Japanese Americans on the West Coast being placed in concentration camps. This experience had long-term negative effects on their political participation, just as service in the military during the war had mobilizing effects for many immigrants and their children. If these episodes serve as any guide, the climate after 9/11 will have similar long-term effects on Muslim American politics, though what these might be are as yet poorly understood.

Finally, as noted earlier, some immigrants are seen as "minorities" upon entering the U.S. (immigrants from Latin American, Africa, Asia), while others are not (immigrants from Europe). Coverage under statutes aimed at minorities may have a substantial effect on immigrant incorporation—on chances for education, business ownership, and access to public benefits, for instance. But inclusion as a minority has direct political consequences as well, including coverage under the Voting Rights Act and the creation of "majority-minority" districts to facilitate the election of coethnic representatives. Though there has been little research on the matter, presumably immigrants covered under the act find it easier (and perhaps have more incentives) to participate in electoral politics in the U.S. than those who are not.

The political pathways followed by immigrants depend not only on their individual and group characteristics but also on the institutional setting they encounter. Unlike some other nations, the U.S. has never had a national policy or program for the social or political incorporation of immigrants. The decisions to naturalize, to register, to vote, and to join associations have always been seen as individual decisions, and immigrant incorporation is left largely in the hands of each person. If there are organized efforts at political incorporation, these have been generated largely in the private sector—for example, during the "Americanization" campaigns of the early 1900s. Both historically and contemporaneously, private associations such as political parties, labor unions, churches, and civic groups have been the primary actors in political mobilization.

Historically, political parties have been seen as the major engine of political incorporation. But there is a debate about how effective parties ever were in incorporating immigrants. A generation of social scientists, including Robert Dahl, Robert Merton, and Raymond Wolfinger, generally portrayed the recruitment of immigrants by political parties in a positive light. Their writing was deeply influenced by instrumentalist explanations for party politics like those of Joseph Schumpeter and Anthony Downs, who argued that given an environment with open elections and at least two political parties, parties will compete to represent voters and issues so as to acquire and retain power. If possible, rivals and alternative programs are coopted, so they will not form the basis for subsequent challenges.

In this view, because parties compete for votes, they will eventually mobilize potential or marginal political actors. Immigrants do not need to take the initiative, because politicians will do so instead, making it easy for immigrants to become citizens, encouraging them to register, placing them on the party rolls, and addressing their material and symbolic needs. In the past, immigrants did not even have to be citizens to be politically incorporated, because politicians guided them through the court system as fast as (or faster than) the law allowed, making them citizens and leading them to the polling booths. This made sense in the economy of machine politics, which traded in particular benefits—cash, votes, jobs—for all parties involved. If a group wasn't included in the distribution of these benefits, it could always threaten—as Jews and Italians did—to join the opposition. These threats could result in selective incorporation (as it did for Jews) or the creation of a new majority (the inclusion of Italians in Republican-led urban coalitions in the Northeast).

However, this model of incorporation works only if political parties are in fact competitive. The political scientist Steven Erie argues that on the contrary, the goal of local parties historically was to become local hegemonies. As long as local political machines were embryonic, they were mobilizers, facing competitive pressures to increase the number of partisan voters. Entrenched machines, however, were only selective mobilizers; as they nursed their limited resources, it was in their interests to turn out only minimal winning coalitions, so they had little incentive to mobilize newer ethnic arrivals. In this view, the differential incorporation of immigrants into politics can be explained by the timing and context of their arrival: earlier immigrants like the Irish arrived to nascent urban political machines and were incorporated, whereas later immigrants like the Italians and Jews arrived in cities with mature machines and (at least initially) were largely marginalized. In competitive environments immigrants were mobilized; in noncompetitive environments they were not. Though parties and other institutions have changed significantly in the intervening decades, the dynamics of party incorporation may not much differ today.

Contemporary parties are quite different from those of a hundred years ago. It is unclear whether, even if they wished, parties could play the role that proponents argue they did during the earlier wave of immigration. Parties today function as loose networks for recruiting candidates and coordinating fundraising. Grassroots party organization has largely withered away, replaced by professionalized interest-group politics, which targets its audiences with constant focus groups, polling, and mass mailings. Since naturalization procedures were transferred from party-dominated local and state courts to specialized federal courts and since the federal immigration agency was established in the 1890s, local-level parties are likely unable to play the same role in incorporating immigrants into the political system that they once did. In addition, contemporary party politics at the state and local level is often not competitive; one of the two major parties often dominates. Because party organizations understandably make choices about where to place scarce resources on the basis of where they believe their candidates might win, resources go to areas of existing strength. Parties tend to leave their competitors' core areas of strength alone. As a result, relatively few elections are won in close races, and incumbents often go unchallenged.

However, national elections are a different story. Here the major parties continue to be competitive, and it is in national elections that parties are likely to have the greatest impact on mobilizing new ethnic voters. In the 2000 presidential election campaign, for example, both parties reached out to new Latino voters, running Spanish-language ads in media markets across the country and having their candidates make symbolic attempts (speaking Spanish, attending Catholic mass) to reach out to these voters. During the campaign, both Republicans and Democrats targeted Hispanic voters and donors with steering committees, youth organizations, and materials and websites in English and Spanish. At the national level, both parties saw Latinos as a potentially critical voting bloc and appealed to them along ethnic lines, much as parties seem to have appealed to immigrant voters historically.

The case of Latinos in the 2000 and 2004 elections indicates that in competitive situations, parties may in fact reach out to what they perceive to be new swing constituencies. This implies, however, that the role of political parties in immigrant incorporation is likely to be quite uneven, with immigrants in competitive areas being contacted and mobilized and those in noncompetitive areas being left to their own devices. In addition, in these elections Latinos were a large enough population potentially to decide key state elections, and their voting patterns were indeterminate enough to make them appealing to both national parties. This is not true of every immigrant or ethnic group. Some groups, because of their smaller size or because they are too closely identified with one party, may not be the target of competitive mobilization. Asian immigrants, for instance, who are more fragmented along lines of national origin and language and more scattered residentially than Latinos, are less likely to be targeted for mobilization by national political parties.

Of course, parties are not the only mobilizing organizations; unions, religious and civic organizations, and ethnic groups all play a role in the political incorporation of immigrants. Some scholars have gone so far as to argue that in the past, unions and churches did more to incorporate immigrants politically than parties did. Given the weakness of local party organizations, this should be even truer today. Union activism would seem to be an obvious alternative to party mobilization, but the percentage of the American workforce belonging to unions has been declining steadily for decades. There are some indications, however, that although unions are shrinking, they still play a significant role in those areas of the economy where immigrants are concentrated. Among the most visible and active unions over the past decade have been those, like the SEIU, involved in unionizing largely immigrant workers in the service sector. These unions were the only area of significant union expansion in the 1980s and 1990s. As a result, in a radical break from previous policy, in 2001 the AFL-CIO officially advocated the legalization of undocumented immigrants in the U.S. In certain locales—Los Angeles, and perhaps New York City—union mobilization has had a significant impact on local politics. However, for the most part, given their overall decline, unions are unlikely to be the principal agent of incorporation for most immigrants.

Immigrants are more likely to come into contact with nonprofit organizations—churches, neighborhood groups, ethnic organizations, etc.—in their own neighborhoods. Local nonprofits, including immigrant advocacy groups funded by foundations and government, are arguably more numerous and better organized than their counterparts during the earlier wave of immigration. However, the political incorporation of immigrants through nonprofits may have its own limitations. It may be constrained, for instance, by clientalist relations between nonprofits and those they serve. It may also be driven by the goals of those who fund these organizations, such as private foundations or state and local governments, which have their own priorities. In this case the path of immigrant ethnic politics and political incorporation may ebb and flow with the shifting interests and fortunes of its financial backers.

Finally, the proliferation of organizations with transnational ties and agendas provides immigrants with an institutional context that is not wholly determined by the receiving country. As noted, indications of widespread transnational ties among first-generation immigrants in the U.S. have sparked a lively debate on the ramifications of transnationalism, not least for their involvement as citizens and political actors. Clearly immigrants continue to stay in contact with family members in their countries of origin, remitting money, traveling for visits or longer stays, and retaining familiarity with their home country's language (and encouraging their children to do so). At the same time, sending countries are playing a greater role than ever before in seeking to maintain and strengthen ties with emigrants, through dual nationality provisions, which allow their nationals to take U.S. citizenship without losing their original citizenship; through a strong consular presence in the U.S. (as Mexico has); and through matching programs for immigrant remittances. At times these ties are explicitly political; for example, candidates from sending countries campaign and raise funds among immigrant communities in the U.S. It is unclear, however, what impact these transnational ties have had on ethnic politics. One might think that greater ties to immigrants' countries of origin would result in less involvement in American politics and society, but research on immigrants' attitudes, language retention, and dual nationality suggests otherwise: those retaining active ties to their countries of origin may be more engaged in the politics of their home countries but are apparently no less likely to be involved in politics focused on issues in the U.S.

How different is ethnic politics now from what it was at the turn of the 20th century? The absence of any governmental role and the role of private actors in Americanization and political incorporation are striking, in both the past and the present. In both instances, incorporation was left to the private sphere—to immigrants themselves and to those organizations that, for one reason or another, found it in their interests to mobilize these new immigrants politically. But as noted, political incorporation seems to have shifted sites, or at least the emphasis among the sites of incorporation has shifted. The difference this may make to immigrants is unclear. Do different sites of incorporation mobilize immigrants differently, or mobilize different kinds of immigrants? For instance, those immigrants who are politically active through their churches might be engaged in quite different kinds of politics from those who are contacted and mobilized by political parties. Different sites of mobilization might also lead to different avenues of participation. Seen this way, "ethnic politics" might actually describe quite varied forms of political participation. It might also be, however, that political mobilization at one site—labor activism, for instance—gives immigrants the skills and incentives to become politically incorporated in other ways—say, to naturalize or to vote. In this case, ethnic mobilization might be readily transferable from one setting to another.

The discussion thus far suggests that there is substantial variation in immigrant politics, depending on individual and group characteristics and the institutional pathways immigrants follow. This variance may help explain the paradoxical state of immigrant political participation: immigrants in the U.S. seem both more likely and less likely to participate in American politics than ever before. On the one hand, mobilizing institutions seem to be in decline, and large numbers of immigrants remain outside the formal political system. Certainly two of the primary engines of mobilization in the past, political parties and unions, are playing a diminished role in the organization of new immigrants nationally. And nearly half of all immigrants have yet to naturalize almost twenty years after their arrival, with many maintaining transnational ties. Yet by some measures immigrants today seem to be incorporating into electoral politics as quickly as, if not more quickly than, their counterparts in the past.

Take the case of Latinos: in the 20 years before the 1996 election, the number of votes they cast jumped 135 percent, compared with 21 percent of other voters, yet even in 1996 Latinos made up only 5 percent of the national electorate. In the 2000 elections, only four years later, they accounted for more than 7 percent of the electorate, a 40 percent increase. In California, the state with the largest number of electoral votes, 16 percent of registered voters in 2000—about 2.35 million people—were Latino, compared with only 10 percent in 1990. These increases were largely attributable to the naturalization of immigrants. From 1991 to 2000, 5.6 million immigrants were naturalized as citizens; between 1994 and 1996, naturalization rates increased threefold across all immigrant groups in the U.S., to 1.05 million per year. In California alone a record 879,000 immigrant adults were naturalized from 1994 to 1997, and another 623,000 had applications pending at the end of 1997. While the number of naturalizations in the U.S. has declined from its high point in the 1990s, the average number naturalizing each year from 2001 to 2004 was still two times the average number during the 1980s. Almost half of these new citizens were born in Latin America.

While no doubt many naturalized to escape the effects of the anti-immigrant climate of the 1990s, once naturalized, many became active participants in the political system. Forty-five percent of registered Latino voters likely to vote in the 2000 election were foreign-born, compared with 20 percent in 1990. Among Asian Americans, the percentage of foreign-born voters in the 2000 elections was even greater—64 percent of the total. The mobilization of immigrant voters has meant that they are increasingly able to elect coethnics to office. Latinos have made significant inroads at every level, particularly in California. Haitians have been elected to office in North Miami, there are Dominican and West Indian city council members and state assemblymen in New York City, and Asian Americans have been elected to school boards and city councils in Silicon Valley and the cluster of cities between Los Angeles and Pomona. This is not to say that there has been a tidal wave of immigrants elected to office, but their numbers and impact have been steadily increasing. Even more striking, much of this success has been the product of efforts by first-generation immigrants, not those of their children. At least in this respect, immigrants seem to be taking part in American electoral politics more quickly than immigrants in the past did: among earlier immigrant groups, not even the Irish were electing many coethnic political representatives within their first generation of arrival. Yet among current immigrants, some political representation, at some level of government, is not unusual.

How can we account for the disparity between the perspective of immigrants as politically marginalized and that of immigrants as mobilized? The two seem at odds, but in fact both may be true. On the plus side, most immigrants are likely to encounter less overt discrimination in politics (and society) than previous migrants to the U.S. did. There is little de jure exclusion and a great deal more institutional openness than in the past, thanks to the great social movements of the 19th and

20th centuries: the push for abolition, women's suffrage, civil rights, etc. There is plenty of room for anti-immigration and anti-immigrant feeling to surface, but on the whole, at least in the public realm of politics, this is only occasionally directed directly at immigrants themselves. More often than not, in the public realm immigrants are ignored rather than deprecated. This is not to suggest that they do not face considerable hurdles to political incorporation, not least from subtle and not-so-subtle forms of harassment and discrimination. But the passage of the Voting Rights Act and its implementation have opened opportunities for political representation that did not exist for previous immigrants.

There has been remarkably little evaluation of the Voting Rights Act and its effects on minority representation (apart from blacks'), and still less on its implications for immigrants. It seems from the scattered evidence that exists that both immigrant and native-born minorities have benefited from the implementation of the act, particularly when concentrated in sufficient numbers to warrant the creation of majority-minority districts for political representation (at times grouping Latinos, Asians, and blacks in the same district, leading to interesting interracial dynamics). The effects of redistricting to allow immigrant representation have been more evident at the local level than at the federal level, and the fragmentation of local politics makes it more amenable to representation of new groups, offering multiple avenues for incorporation, through school boards, city councils, county commissions, and so on. All in all, the concentration of recent immigrants, the inclusion of many of them under the Voting Rights Act, and the multiplicity of local governments have enabled many immigrant groups to exercise a greater influence on politics than their historical counterparts at a comparable stage in their migration.

This achievement should not overshadow the fact that the election of immigrant representatives often occurs in the context of a broader alienation from political participation of all kinds. Although more immigrants are naturalizing and voting and more are being elected to office, the rates of increase of participation and representation in electoral politics are not keeping up with the rate of increase in immigration itself, so though more immigrants are participating in electoral politics, many more remain outside it. It is also significant that the political representation of immigrants has occurred mostly at the local level. Political turnout in local elections (which are often nonpartisan and at different times from national elections) is often quite low. In districts with a preponderance of immigrants, turnout is even lower. Under these circumstances, small, organized groups can successfully elect their representatives to office. While immigrants and other newcomers to the political system are trying to enter the political arena, the fact that minimal winning coalitions can capture and hold local offices is often problematic: many "immigrant" districts are represented by non-immigrants. Once mobilized, however, immigrants may find that lower participation in local politics works to their advantage, at least in the sense of getting coethnic candidates placed. The fact is that the Voting Rights

Act facilitates political representation but does not necessarily increase political mobilization.

Rodney Hero suggests that minorities as a whole may suffer from a system of "two-tiered" pluralism in American politics. Minorities are able to participate, vote, and elect representatives, but only up to a point: once political districts are no longer majority-minority (as for most congressional seats held by ethnic and racial representatives), or once they become de facto at-large districts (as for most statewide offices and Senate seats), then minorities are rarely elected to these offices. If this is true, then the Voting Rights Act and the opening of electoral politics to ethnic and racial minorities may lead only to the *limited* incorporation of immigrants in American politics. The success of certain immigrant groups in electing representatives at the local level will consequently plateau, with increasing numbers of representatives elected where immigrants are concentrated but little beyond that. Election of candidates in at-large districts may take much longer, depending on the racial and ethnic politics of the group in question. The result could be the political equivalent of what some sociologists call the "segmented assimilation" of immigrants, with groups being trapped into electoral culs-de-sac from which they cannot move.

The most pessimistic interpretation of the intersection of the race and immigrant narratives in the U.S. leads to the conclusion that today's immigrants may learn English, raise their children, and settle down in the U.S., but no matter how "assimilated" they become, if they are seen as racially different, then they will always be set apart, and discriminated against, by the larger society. In this view, race trumps the immigrant experience, implying that ethnic politics will quickly become indistinguishable from "minority politics." The most optimistic rendering of the confluence of the race and immigrant narratives suggests that immigrants today encounter fewer barriers to political participation than ever before in American history, and that ethnic politics will flourish as immigrants essentially mobilize as interest groups in local and national politics.

Both of these interpretations may have some truth to them—for some groups, at least some of the time. The factors outlined above indicate that there will be considerable variance in the experience of ethnic politics across immigrant groups. No single form is likely to be pursued by all immigrants. There is no guarantee, for instance, that even if immigrants as a whole put their energies into electoral politics and the pursuit of ethnic representation, they will all succeed. The success of an electoral strategy depends in part on the characteristics of the immigrant group—its resources, its size and geographic concentration, and perceptions of its importance as a potential political actor—and institutional factors—whether the group is defined as a minority or not, or whether it is concentrated in areas that are contested between the two major parties. The different characteristics of immigrants and immigrant groups will probably result in quite different strategies, ranging from trans-national activism to labor organizing and from mobilization at the neighborhood level to playing a role in national politics. What is clear is that ethnic politics will re-main central to the immigrant experience in the U.S., even as it is reconfigured to reflect shifts in the broader American polity and the process of immigration itself.

Bibliography

Bloemraad, Irene. 2006. *Becoming a Citizen: Incorporating Immigrants and Refugees in the United States and Canada.* Berkeley: University of California Press.

Erie, Stephen. 1988. *Rainbow's End: Irish Americans and the Dilemmas of the Urban Political Machine, 1840–1985.* Berkeley: University of California Press.

Gerstle, Gary, and John Mollenkopf, eds. 2001. *E Pluribus Unum? Contemporary and His-torical Perspectives on Immigrant Political Incorporation.* New York: Russell Sage Founda-tion.

Haney-Lopez, Ian. 1996. *White By Law: The Legal Construction of Race.* New York: New York University Press.

Hero, Rodney. 1992. *Latinos and the U.S. Political System: Two-Tiered Pluralism.* Philadel-phia: Temple University Press.

Jones-Correa, Michael. 1998. *Between Two Nations: The Political Predicament of Latin American Immigrants in New York City.* Ithaca: Cornell University Press.

Lien, Pei-Te. 2001. *The Making of Asian America through Political Participation.* Philadel-phia: Temple University Press.

Ramakrishnan, Karthick. 2005. *Democracy in Immigrant America: Changing Demographics and Political Participation.* Palo Alto, Calif.: Stanford University Press.

Thernstrom, Abigail M. 1987. *Whose Votes Count? Affirmative Action and Minority Voting Rights.* Cambridge: Harvard University Press.

Waters, Mary C. 1999. *Black Identities: West Indian Immigrant Dreams and American Real-ities.* Cambridge: Harvard University Press.

Wong, Janelle. 2006. *Democracy's Promise: Immigrants and American Civic Institutions.* Ann Arbor: University of Michigan Press.

Ethnic Media

K. Viswanath and Karen Ka-man Lee

The truism that the United States is a nation of immigrants took on a profoundly heightened meaning with the reform in American immigration law in 1965. This and subsequent legal reforms in 1985 and 1990 resulted in a historic shift in immigration patterns, resulting in an influx of millions of immigrants from Asia and Latin America. Globalization and the increasing interpenetration of global economies have also resulted in an increase in the number of people with diverse ethnic identities, leading to what Portes and Rumbaut have characterized as a "permanently unfinished" American society. Increasing ethnic diversity is affecting all aspects of American society—culture, economy, and polity. Among the institutions that ethnic groups have established to sustain their ethnicity and ease their transition into mainstream society, the ethnic mass media plays a significant role. Here we will focus on how the ethnic media in the U.S. has contributed to assimilation and reinforcement of ethnic identity among the new immigrants.

History of the Immigrant Press and Other Media

The history of the immigrant press in the U.S. is primarily a history of struggle for recognition and civil rights, though these media have also been used to meet immigrants' nationalist aspirations.

African and African American media. African American print media emerged in the early 1800s, predominantly as a means of protesting against slavery and countering the racist commentary that was rampant in the mainstream media. For this reason, Samuel E. Cornish and a group of free black men in New York began publishing *Freedom's Journal* in 1827. The monthly journal *African Observer* emerged at the same time, providing insight into the history of the African slave trade and viable solutions for ending slavery. Although such journals played a strong advocacy role, they also served many of the other general functions of ethnic media, providing news from home countries, expanding readers' knowledge of the world, highlighting achievements of renowned black figures, and printing birth, death, and wedding announcements.

The African American press began because African Americans needed alternative venues for expressing their views, specifically for molding self-esteem and public opinion and for setting the public agenda. Prominent early black newspapers included the *New York Age,* the *Boston Guardian,* and the *Chicago Defender,* among others.

However, after the late 1800s, magazines took over these functions, because of the declining quality of reporting and commentary in black newspapers and competition from the mainstream media. The black press was perceived as partisan, with views representing either conservative or liberal ideologies rather than a range of political opinion. Janette Dates attributes the decline of black newspapers since the 1960s to desegregation and increasing competition for readers and advertisers from the electronic media. Also, African American journalists were in demand among white publishers and mainstream media. Such factors led the black press to cover more entertainment, social, and crime news, which in turn led to a drop in circulation and waning relevance and credibility.

The growth of immigration from the Caribbean led to a number of new publications. Currently about thirty-three Caribbean/West Indian media outlets distributing in the U.S. are listed in *National Ethnic Media Directory.* These media outlets are predominantly weekly newspapers serving communities in New York, Boston, Atlanta, and Miami. They include several publications targeted toward specific subgroups of Haitian, Guyanian, and Jamaican immigrants. In 1989, Radio Tropical Internationale LLC, based in New York, became the first station to broadcast 24-hour programming in French and Creole. Several of these Caribbean/West Indian publications take advantage of a sense of journalistic freedom that did not or does not exist for journalists in their native countries. Niche trade publications, such as the *Caribbean American and Hispanic Business Journal,* published in New Jersey, are beginning to emerge to serve growing immigrant populations.

Little research has tracked the influence of African American media as an ethnic media for new immigrants from Africa, probably because some of the needs and concerns of immigrants are different from those covered by the American black press. Language is also beginning to become a line of division, as immigration from Francophone countries like Senegal, Guinea, Ivory Coast, and Burkina Faso increases. Contemporary publications like the *Ethiopian Review* and *Tadias,* both published in Washington, D.C., have arisen to serve immigrants from Ethiopia, keeping readers informed about events abroad and offering advice on living in America. New York's *African Abroad* and the *African Sun Times* perform similar functions for African immigrants with a broader perspective.

Meanwhile, the African American media have expanded to include radio, predominantly in California and on the East Coast. News programming is available in English, Amharic, Tigrinya, and Woluf, catering to a variety of cultures and communities. Since July 2002, African American cable television has been available; the African TV Network broadcasts news and programming targeted to African immigrants 24 hours a day.

Asian American media. It is difficult to capture the 150-year history of Asian American media easily, given the vast range of trajectories, languages, dialects, and cultures in this category. Asian American media serve many different ethnic groups—Chinese, Japanese, Koreans, South Asians, Filipinos, Vietnamese, Cambodians and Laotians, and Pacific Islanders, in addition to some groups from the Middle East, among others. Like their counterparts, these media also began as sources for news from home and local communities and a way to promote cultural ideals.

It is reported that the first Asian American newspapers were started to meet the needs of Chinese immigrants in the Bay Area in the mid-19th century. The first Asian American newspaper, *Kim Shan Jit San Luk* (*Golden Hills News*), was published in San Francisco in 1854. The Japanese press also has its roots in San Francisco, initiated by the newspaper *Nineteenth Century* and the magazine *Ensei* (*Explorer*), which were both begun in 1892. Newspapers of other groups have a more recent history. The first Korean newspaper, the *Korean Times,* started in Honolulu in 1905, and the first Asian Indian newspaper was probably *Free Hindustan,* started in Seattle in 1908 to reflect the nationalist aspirations of Indian immigrants. The oldest Asian Indian publication still in existence is *India Abroad,* first published in New York in 1970. The Filipino, Vietnamese, Cambodian, and Laotian papers have much shorter histories, having been established only in the past decade or so.

Early Asian American newspapers catered to the needs of the newly arrived immigrants by providing news from their homelands; by writing about their struggles for recognition and fair wages and against discrimination; and, in the case of the Korean, Asian Indian, and Chinese press, by expressing nationalist aspirations.

After World War II, political and social changes refocused the perspective of these media. The repeal of discriminatory laws such as the Chinese Exclusion Act in 1943, along with an influx of middle-class immigrants, led the ethnic media to broaden their focus to include perspectives on life as new American citizens. The Asian American press experienced a rebirth of sorts. After the war, readership declined, because younger generations could not read their ancestral languages. As demonstrated by the Chinese press, however, interest from abroad fueled a resurgence. Established conglomerates like Taiwan's *World Journal,* backed by a wealth of resources, created a highly competitive environment, forcing community papers to adopt new technology, print more frequently, and send reporters to cover events.

In the late 1960s and 1970s, the Asian panethnicity movement began to bridge Asian American identities, and many new publications, such as *Gidra, Bridge,* and

Amerasia Journal, grew out of student movements. Like many other ethnic media, many of these had short lifespans, and of these three, only *Amerasia Journal* survives today. Additionally, to bridge generational gaps, bilingual media began to appear; an example is San Francisco's *East/West,* first published in 1967.

Hispanic media. The earliest form of Latino news media was *corridos,* or the "musical press," which continued an oral tradition of reporting news through storytelling. In 1848, California subsidized the first newspaper created for and by Mexican Americans. Full-scale newspapers or Spanish sections in newspapers in Texas, New Mexico, and Arizona followed. These publications maintained cultural identity among Mexican Americans and in some cases, like Los Angeles' *El Clamor Público,* represented political activism against mainstream culture. With the onset of the Mexican Revolution, this activist focus changed, and coverage centered on news from Mexico and preventing the exploitation of Mexican immigrants. While working-class publications like *Regeneración,* out of Los Angeles, focused on the impact of the war on Mexican immigrants, *La Prensa,* in San Antonio, was aimed at a small group of middle-class, educated immigrants and served as a cultural forum for exiled literary and political writers.

Beginning with the publication of *El Espectador,* newspapers addressed the Mexican American population less as immigrants and more as permanent residents. They promoted biculturalism and civil rights for Mexican Americans and instigated public campaigns regarding such issues as the desegregation of public housing. The longest-running Spanish-language daily newspaper is California's *La Opinión,* first published in 1926. Its success was supported by the migration of Latinos to urban centers like Los Angeles.

Hispanic media branched into electronic media with the arrival of radio. In the early days, Spanish programs ran during off hours and largely focused on entertainment. However, in the 1930s Pedro González, a prominent radio personality, began integrating community announcements and political commentary into his musical broadcasts, finding sponsorship from mainstream businesses such as Folger's coffee, which had previously ignored the Hispanic community. When World War I and the Great Depression led to mass deportations and government attempts to ban Spanish-language radio programming, some media moved their operations across the border to evade U.S. government control. In the 1930s, Emilio Azcárraga, the owner of a large radio empire in Mexico, including five stations along the border, began broadcasting through a radio station in Los Angeles. Stations in New York, Arizona, Texas, and California also began broadcasting Spanish-language programs, and in 1947, KCOR in San Antonio emerged as the first Latino-owned U.S. Spanish-language station. Outside the Southwest, Spanish-language programming began to increase in the 1950s, as European immigrants assimilated into mainstream culture and programming in other European languages was no longer needed. Maintenance of the Spanish language, strong cultural ties (biculturalism rather than assimilation), and the tradition of oral culture are seen as reasons that Spanish radio has not declined, as other foreign-language programming has.

From 1961 to 1986, U.S. Spanish-language TV was owned, financed, and operated by Televisa—Azcárraga's television company based in Mexico. Azcárraga attempted to sell Spanish-language soap operas and movies to U.S. networks but was turned down. In 1961 he created the Spanish International Network (SIN) by buying KMEX in Los Angeles and KWEX in San Antonio. SIN eventually grew to nine U.S. TV stations, predominantly broadcasting Televisa programming. SIN's monopoly ended in the 1980s, when Reliance Capital established Telemundo.

Arabic media. The Arabic-language press began in 1892, with *Kawkab Amrika* (*The American Star*), providing interpretations of American life and guidance through the many new experiences Syrian immigrants were encountering. Early newspapers were divided along religious lines, maintaining small circulations and reporting social news, highlighting individual achievements, and dealing with the challenges of maintaining cultural values in the midst of economic survival. The Arabic-language press promoted biculturalism, educating immigrants not only about American customs and the English language but also about their own ethnic heritage. A group of Syrian intellectuals in New York developed the Arabic press, providing a way to showcase literary work from such authors as Kahlil Gibran. Aside from New York, Detroit, Michigan, and Lawrence, Massachusetts, served as homes for Arabic-language newspapers. The longest-running were *Al Hoda* and *Al-Bayan,* each published for 60 years.

By the 1920s, a decline in Arabic journalism paralleled increasing apathy toward the Arabic language and cultural heritage. Second- and third-generation Arabs placed more emphasis on learning English than Arabic, and the press adapted by publishing at least partly in English. Newspapers like *The Syrian World* in New York instilled a sense of community and cultural pride among non-Arabic-speakers. By the 1940s, weak ties to the language and the failure to create a publication bridging cultural, religious, political, and geographic boundaries led to serious questions about the survival of the Arabic-language press.

Beginning in 1950, however, Arabic-language publications found new life because of changes in the political environment and U.S. foreign policy in the Middle East. New California Media lists 27 Arabic-language media sources based in the U.S., and the Arab Gateway highlights 3 weeklies and 1 magazine. Their content has focused on the political and economic state of the Arab world, and editorials have spoken out against American involvement in the Middle East.

The Community Press: Some Theoretical Propositions

In his well-known essay, "Structure and Function of Communication in Society," Harold Lasswell wrote that the typical functions of media include environmental surveillance, transmission of cultural heritage, correlation of different segments, mobilization, and entertainment. The extent to which media perform these functions has been a subject of considerable scholarly scrutiny and debate. The most relevant body of work that might explain the functions of ethnic media is research on the local community press, represented in the work of Tichenor, Dohonue, and Olien and summarized in *Community Conflict and the Press.* The local community press, and by extension the local mass media, primarily perform a social-control function by reinforcing community norms and values and underemphasizing community conflict in the interest of stability. This function is carried out through two kinds of information control processes, *feedback* and *distributive control.*

Feedback control information is aimed at drawing attention to potential problems and may result in audience and community reaction either to mobilize in protest or to take action to resolve the problem. In this sense, community media are forums for community groups and institutions in setting the public agenda for discussion, but they may also play an active role in defining issues for the public. For example, both African Americans in the early 1800s and Asian Americans in the mid-1900s used newsletters and newspapers as a means of advocating for social change. As Frederick Douglass noted, media such as the *Baltimore American* newspaper provided contextual meaning for the term "abolition" by making it synonymous with ending slavery.

The distributive function is served when media casually report routine events, distributing information. A news story on a community celebration or the achievements of an immigrant child is an example. News coverage that serves a distributive function depends on the social structure of the community, so that the press in more complex communities is generally more sensitive to the different power groups in the system than that in less heterogeneous communities.

The ethnic press faces seemingly contradictory expectations that might affect its performance. These media operate for a relatively small group of immigrants who are striving to make a living in a system that is complex and heterogeneous. Although the group itself is small—an indicator of relative homogeneity—that fact stands in sharp contrast to the complexity of ethnic backgrounds it may contain. For example, immigrants from India come from one geographical part of the world but may speak many different languages; in the broad group of Chinese-speaking immigrants, people may come from mainland China, Taiwan, Singapore, Hong Kong, and elsewhere. Similarly, most Hispanics may speak Spanish or Arabs speak Arabic, but there is enormous variation in their backgrounds, religions, national histories, and cultures. Even though these groups share a common language, they represent distinct nationalities, cultures, subcultures, and ethnicities.

This complexity leaves the ethnic media in a peculiar position, which Viswanath and Arora have termed "ambiguous pluralism." That is, the small numbers, tight-knit communities, and emphasis on survival and success of immigrant groups may allow them to share the characteristics of a small-town community, yet their varied national, class, linguistic, and cultural differences, and the complex larger environment of the United States, lend them the characteristics of heterogeneous communities. This ambiguity is likely to influence the way in which ethnic media operate and reflect their communities.

For example, the ethnic community may well be reluctant to wash its dirty laundry in the ethnic mass media, in the interest of community stability, yet may not hesitate to report on struggles and conflicts in the homeland. Immigrants may want to maintain their image as hardworking people who are trying to succeed in the new world and see any negative portrayal of themselves as harmful to the long-term interests and stability of the community. At the same time, ethnic communities are pluralistic, and the media's role may be analogous to that of a medium in a more heterogeneous system. In sum, the ethnic media are in a unique position where they have to perform both feedback and distributive functions.

The Functions of Ethnic Media

With this review in mind, let us consider the typical functions of ethnic media.

Cultural transmission. Typical examples of ethnic media serving the distributive function of cultural transmission include the dissemination of information about community events, programs, schedules, and calendars—information that does not primarily question established community institutions and powerful groups. Most such content reports on festivals, community celebrations, local government, and ethnic association meetings. Other examples include information on cultural and religious celebrations, cultural programs, and visits by artists. Whether this has the unintended consequence of reviving or strengthening the ethnic identity of the community and inhibiting its assimilation is an empirical question that warrants more research. Continued celebratory coverage probably also maintains and strengthens ethnic identity among the second generation.

Community-boosting. Ethnic media may strive to present the ethnic community in a positive light, projecting an image of wholesomeness, success, and achievement. A typical ethnic medium may focus on human-interest features and profiles, success stories of immigrants, and their contributions to both the host society and their native lands.

Further, as with local community media, ethnic media rely on merchants and businesses such as groceries, banks, travel agencies, and insurance companies to reach their intended audience. This may result in the muting of radical or dissenting voices. At the same time, relatively less attention is likely to be paid to stories that portray the ethnic community and its members in a negative light. Ethnic media may not report crimes committed by members of the community or any behavior that could be considered "deviant" from the dominant norms and values of the host culture.

Surveillance. An ethnic group is potentially vulnerable to discrimination from other groups, particularly if it is "different" from the mainstream and perceived as a threat to the mainstream culture. Given recent negative reactions in the U.S. toward certain immigrant groups, it is most likely that the role of watchdog may become an important function for the immigrant media. To perform their role as a community sentinel against external threat, the media may provide information about issues that affect the legal rights of the ethnic community, including civil rights violations, changes in immigration laws, and crimes against immigrants. This is also part of the mobilizing function of the community media, which is most frequently witnessed when disasters strike the immigrants' native countries. It is not unusual to see the media volunteering to collect donations to be sent to the country of origin to help those in need, as happened after the 2004 tsunami that affected South and Southeast Asia.

Assimilation. Ethnic media in this country began with concern over two major issues: protection of the rights of immigrants and facilitation of their assimilation to the mainstream. Immigrants strive to assimilate at least superficially, by learning English (especially the American idiom) and adopting American dress, food, and behaviors. Their overall success in the host country partly depends on how well they assimilate and learn the ropes of the system. Similarly, the success of the group as a whole and the way it is received depends on how much it is perceived by the host culture as having assimilated and become a part of the mainstream. Ethnic media may facilitate assimilation by fostering the ethnic community's involvement in local politics, positive feelings between the immigrants' homeland and their adopted country, and demonstrations of patriotism.

Dissemination of information. Last, ethnic media provide information about events occurring not only within the community but also in their homelands. Given the limited coverage of international news in mainstream American news media and the potential language barriers to using these sources, immigrants are likely to rely on ethnic media for this kind of information. Additionally, ethnic media provide a vehicle for them to engage in a dialogue with mainstream culture by expressing their perspective on or feelings about American life. Ethnic media serve as a prism through which ethnic communities sometimes experience the U.S. and share in its culture.

Ethnic Media Today

Ethnic media are likely to be driven by audience size, media and general consumption expenditures, and socioeconomic status. These factors all appear to favor greater growth in media oriented toward different ethnic groups in the U.S.

The numbers are telling. According to the U.S. Census, as of March 2002, about 11.5 percent of the American population (32.5 million people) is foreign-born. Roughly one out of two of these is from Latin America, and one in four is from

Asia. The Census Bureau projects that between 2000 and 2050, the U.S. population will increase from 282 million to roughly 419 million. Yet the growth is unlikely to be uniform across all population subgroups. In fact, the proportion of Hispanics is estimated to grow from 12.6 percent of the total U.S. population in 2000 to about 24 percent in 2050. Increases are also projected for other ethnic groups, though not at the same rate. The number of Asian Americans is projected to more than double, from 3.8 percent to 8 percent, and that of "other races" to increase from 2.5 percent to 5.3 percent. A slight increase also is projected for blacks, from 12.7 percent to 14.6 percent. If these projections hold up, one in two people living in the U.S. in 2050 is likely to be from a nonwhite racial or ethnic group.

There is great variation in schooling and income among different ethnic groups, which may also influence the growth of electronic or print media. While almost 87 percent of Asian and European immigrants have graduated from high school, only 50 percent of immigrants from Latin America have done so. Income levels show similar variation. Latin American immigrants have the highest poverty rates, as revealed in the 2000 Census, compared with European and Asian groups, which have the lowest poverty rates. Asian Americans enjoy one of the highest median household annual incomes ($61,229), followed by Europeans ($59,906) and Latin Americans ($33,706).

Given these demographic trends, it is not surprising that ethnic group members are heavy consumers of media. In their *State of News Media 2004,* the Project for Excellence in Journalism (PEJ) suggests that Spanish-speakers are more likely to rely on native-language electronic media such as TV and radio than other groups; ethnic groups other than Hispanics are more likely to read both native-language and English-language newspapers; and most Asian groups watch TV in both languages.

The same report also discusses the state of media for different ethnic groups. It suggests that Spanish media are experiencing high growth rates in circulation and advertising revenues as a result of growth rates in the Spanish-speaking population, an advantage they enjoy over Asian American media, which operate in multiple languages. The circulation of Spanish-language newspapers went up from 140,000 in 1970 to about 1.7 million in 2002. The number of Spanish-language daily newspapers (not including weeklies or magazines) increased from 8 in 1970 to 35 in 2002. One interesting trend is the attention paid by mainstream American media companies, which have either started Spanish-language segments and sections or acquired media companies catering to the Spanish-speaking audience. The Spanish-language media also enjoy a heavy TV presence, with two networks, Telemundo and Univision, owning roughly 65 TV stations and affiliated with another 74 stations.

The Asian American media landscape is much more varied and difficult to characterize because of its diversity in languages and the socioeconomic status of the individual groups. In general, according to Kang & Lee Advertising, Asian Americans

Table 1   Selected ethnic media

Ethnic group	Population	Median income	Newspapers	Magazines	Radio stations	TV stations
African American[a]	34,658,190	$29,177	5	7	0	1
Arab	1,189,731	$55,673	19	7	0	5
Chinese	2,858,291	$51,444	68	20	25	17
Filipino	2,385,216	$60,570	37	11	24	8
Hispanic	35,305,818	$33,103	550	352	630	157
Asian Indian	1,855,590	$63,669	20	13	26	17
Japanese	1,152,324	$70,849	20	18	23	5
Korean	1,226,825	$40,037	46	16	16	13
Vietnamese	1,212,465	$45,085	34	45	12	11

Sources: U.S. Bureau of the Census, 2000 Census. New California Media, *NCM Directory;* Kang & Lee Advertising, *Asian American Market "101";* Allied Media Corp.; TIYM Publishing Company Inc., *Anuario Hispano–Hispanic Yearbook.*
   a. Census estimate of the population with African ancestry is 1,779,462. The figures for African American media could be an underestimate, as the reports do not usually clearly distinguish clearly between African American media and media of groups that have immigrated from Africa more recently.

are served by a total of 545 media outlets, including newspapers, magazines, TV stations, and radio stations. Chinese-language groups enjoy the largest number of outlets, with 68 newspapers and almost 25 TV stations. The annual buying power of Asian Americans is estimated to increase from $363 billion in 2004 to $528 billion in 2009, creating a market for advertising to these consumers that will undoubtedly support a flourishing ethnic media.

In sum, the contemporary ethnic media landscape in the U.S. is a complex one (see Table 1). Population projections suggest a future that is bright and likely to draw increasing attention. As the population becomes increasingly diverse, as ethnic group membership increases, and as ethnic community members seek to organize, it is likely that the variety and number of ethnic media will also increase.

Globalization and the Information Society

A singular characteristic in the 1990s is the so-called information revolution, which has had a noticeable impact on the ethnic media in the U.S. Three related forces have also profoundly altered the landscape. First is the increasing migration of workers at two ends of the socioeconomic spectrum, catering to the needs of corporate America as well as the domestic needs of American households. This has resulted in a population that is diverse both economically and culturally, with a concomitant impact on ethnic media. The second force is the liberalization in the flow of cultural goods across the globe and the establishment of global media empires. Media companies in both the industrialized world and the so-called developing world have taken a more expansive view of their audience, attempting to cater to people beyond national borders. The third force is the development of information technology that allows easier electronic transmission of cultural goods across national borders and increases the carrying capacity of cable and satellite channels, thus overcoming the limitations of the conventional radio spectrum. The result is a seeming cacophony of cultural and information programs in multiple languages for different ethnic groups, sometimes leaving little in common among them. These changes have both theoretical and practical consequences.

With the emergence of the World Wide Web and other new communication technologies, immigrants now have an array of ways to gather information about their homelands. Internet news services in the U.S., in the home country, or in a third country are increasingly offering immigrants news about developments in their home countries and in the diaspora. Interestingly, such offerings include both established press from the homelands and an alternative press, products of efforts by a small group of people. Further, webzines are published by those in both the developing and the developed world. A question for future research is whether the part of the informational function performed by ethnic media that covers immigrants' native countries is likely to change with competition from websites in those countries.

In addition, it is difficult to distinguish between global and local media companies as new communication technologies and economic liberalization allow companies to form across national borders. For example, Spanish-speaking media in the U.S. have complex ownership and management patterns, which allows cultural material and news to flow back and forth between the U.S. and Latin America, replacing a flow of programs that had gone only from Latin America to the U.S. Such patterns are also beginning to be seen in the Chinese, Arabic, and South Asian media. These developments raise a number of questions for future research:

- As the Internet, the World Wide Web, and communication technologies such as satellite and cable TV breach the geographic and temporal barriers between ethnic immigrants, what are the implications of "virtual ethnic communities" on American society, culture, and politics? For example, the ethnic media may be playing a significant role in reestablishing ties with immigrants' native lands. The communications revolution, with greater penetration of the Internet and satellite TV, has made it possible for some immigrants to move back and forth between the U.S. and their native lands, strengthening economic ties. The degree to which this is occurring and the role played by ethnic media is a subject of further empirical inquiry.
- What are the implications of fragmentation of ethnic and mainstream audiences on social integration and political participation among immigrants?
- What is the impact of the growth of immigrant populations on local ethnic media organizations, which are generally small-budget operations? Will they be able to adapt and survive?

• What is the extent to which new media technologies may bridge or exacerbate the differences between existing social class and cultural divides?

Given the large number and diverse range of ethnic groups and the media, it is surprising that there are few systematic, institutional sources that provide descriptive information on the ethnic media. Scholarly literature, too, is brief and sketchy. It is clear that the range, size, number, and reach of ethnic media will continue to increase in the U.S. They will remain a way to provide the cultural continuity that ethnic communities appear to seek while working to protect their interests in the mainstream American society. Ethnic media will also remain as sources of entertainment and media of socialization. Little is understood about the implications of this triple role—reinforcing ethnic identity, transmitting culture, and facilitating advocacy and political participation. Understanding ethnic media is essential for understanding the role of ethnicity in contemporary America.

Bibliography

Danky, J. P., and W. A. Wiegand. *Print Culture in a Diverse America.* Urbana: University of Illinois Press, 1998.

Dates, J., and W. Barlow, eds. *Split Image: African-Americans in the Mass Media.* Washington, D.C.: Howard University Press, 1990.

Glazer, N., and D. P. Moynihan. *Beyond the Melting Pot.* 2nd ed. Cambridge, Mass.: MIT Press, 1970.

Lasswell, H. "The Structure and Function of Communication in Society." In L. Bryson, ed., *The Communication of Ideas.* New York: Harper, 1948.

Mansfield-Richardson, V. *Asian Americans and the Mass Media: A Content Analysis of Twenty United States Newspapers and a Survey of Asian American Journalists.* New York: Garland, 2000.

Miller, S., ed. *The Ethnic Press in the United States: A Historical Analysis and Handbook.* Westport, Conn.: Greenwood, 1987.

Park, R. E. *The Immigrant Press and Its Control.* St. Clair Shores, Mich.: Scholarly Press, 1922/1970.

Rodriguez, A. *Making Latino News: Race, Language, Class.* Thousand Oaks, Calif.: Sage Publications, 1999.

Tichenor, P. J., G. A. Donohue, and C. N. Olien. *Community Conflict and the Press.* Beverly Hills, Calif.: Sage Publications, 1980.

Veciana-Suarez, A. *Hispanic Media: Impact and Influence.* Washington, D.C.: The Media Institute, 1990.

Viswanath, K., and P. Arora. "Ethnic Media in the United States: An Essay on Integration, Assimilation and Social Control." *Mass Communication & Society* 3:1 (2000): 39–56.

Religion

Diana L. Eck

The new post-1965 immigrants who have come to the United States from all over the world have brought not only their economic and political aspirations but also their Qurans and Ramayanas, their images of the Bodhisattva Guan Yin and the Virgin of Guadalupe. They have brought Thai and South Indian traditional dance forms, Hindu holidays and Muslim prayers, Buddhist ordinations, Baha'i feasts, and Sikh rites of passage. The range of religious centers and practice in the U.S. today is more varied and complex than ever before, a fact that has created new challenges for virtually every public institution. This diversity also poses new challenges to America's Christian majority, revealing the ways in which a presumptively "Christian America" may be in conflict with the ethos of pluralism embedded in the constitutional guarantee of religious freedom.

Immigrants to the U.S. have found that religion is a salient and indeed powerful and protected category of identity. The distinctive voluntary religious energy that Tocqueville described in the early 19th century has not diminished, and the constitutional principles of the free exercise of religion and the prohibition of religious establishment have produced a multitude of denominations, sectarian movements, and religious movements. Over the years religious freedom has been a recipe for religious diversity. Recent immigrants have benefited from that freedom and amplified that diversity. Some cherish the freedom *not* to be religious in a nation with no established religion.

The U.S. Census cannot by law ask questions about religious affiliation, so statistics are imprecise and often contested, especially regarding the number of American Muslims. Some religious communities have undertaken demographic studies. For example, the Mosque Study Project of the Council on American Islamic Relations in cooperation with the Hartford Institute for Religious Research, released in 2000, estimated that there are about 1,400 American mosques, with a combined active membership of at least 2 million. Adjusting for Muslims not affiliated with a mosque, the study estimated the Muslim population at between 6 and 7 million, including African Americans (about 30 percent) and Muslim immigrants from South and Southeast Asia, the Middle East, and Africa. In 2000 the *Encyclopedia Britannica* put its estimate at 4.1 million Muslims. According to the 2001 American Religious Identification Survey of the City University of New York, based on 50,000 telephone calls, a more accurate estimate would be between 1.1 and 2.2 million adults, or about 2.8 million Muslims, including children. The lowest estimate is that of the widely respected General Social Survey of the National Opinion Research Center in Chicago, which estimated the figure at 1.9 million. (Critics say this estimate may well be low because of the many non-English-speaking people among first-generation immigrants who may not have been included in the survey.)

Estimates of other religious communities also vary but now include about 1.3 million Hindus, largely from India but also from East Africa and the Caribbean, especially Trinidad. Also coming from India are Sikhs (approximately 250,000), Jains (approximately 20,000), and a smaller number of Parsis, the Indian branch of the Zoroastrian tradition. From East and Southeast Asia come Buddhists, who, along with Euro-American and African American Buddhists, are estimated to number 3 to 4 million. There are no estimates for those who have brought the traditions of West Africa to the U.S. via the Caribbean or South America, yet it is clear that there are Santeria, voodoo, and Candomble practitioners among Haitian, Cuban, Dominican, and Brazilian immigrants in most major cities. Finally, across the board, Christian immigrants from Asia and the Middle East have disproportionately outnumbered non-Christians.

The largest immigrant Christian groups are from Mexico and Central and South America, which account for roughly half the 32.5 million foreign-born residents in the U.S. Between 1990 and 2003 the Latino population grew from 22.4 million to 37 million, making this America's largest minority. Of these, 93 percent are Christian, of whom 70 percent are Catholic and 23 percent are Protestant. According to the Center for the Study of Latino Religion at Notre Dame, 26 percent of the Catholics testify to being "born again," as do 85 percent of the Protestants, indicating a growing influence of evangelical, Pentecostal, and charismatic forms of Christianity among this large and potentially influential sector of immigrants.

For new immigrants of all traditions, as for those of earlier generations, religious communities have provided important sites for affirming and reformulating their identities in a new context. While ethnic and Asian American studies have tended to ignore the significance of religion, it is increasingly clear that religious communities are often a critical part of the experience of new Americans. Because religion is a recognized and meaningful social category in the U.S., religious affiliation enables immigrants to secure their sense of identity and also gain acceptance in the wider society. For many immigrants, religion and culture are indistinguishable, and religious centers become bridging communities where the comfort zone of language, custom, food, and festival is maintained.

Religious communities may well be even more important to immigrants than they were in the country of origin. People who may have had scant involvement with religious life in India or Brazil have found the temple, the mosque, or the church to be an anchor here. In practical terms, religious centers often provide help with housing, documentation, economic transition, and English-language classes. Just as Swedish immigrants sought out the Swedish Lutheran Church as an important home base at the turn of the 20th century, Korean Christians have often found their church essential in establishing a new life in America. So advantageous is the energetic Korean Presbyterian Church in providing a sense of community and access to American society that many immigrants who were nominally Buddhist in Korea have become members of a church in America.

Some immigrants are drawn into an unaccustomed level of religious participation by the responsibility of creating a religious center in a new environment. For example, Tamils who would never have been active in temple-building in India take the lead in organizing, fundraising, planning, and constructing multimillion-dollar Hindu temples in America. Indeed, the creation of major cultural and religious institutions is a marker of having arrived and become established in a new place.

Encountering One's Own

In encountering America, immigrants have also encountered the diversity of their own communities of faith. They have found earlier immigrants already assimilated in a variety of ways into American society. In addition, they have met people who can be described as "converts," whether African American Muslims, Krishna devotees, Zen practitioners, or Sikh yogis. Both these unfamiliar coreligionists and the diversity of new immigrants of their own faith have shaped the dynamics of settlement for new Americans.

Post-1965 Muslim immigrants, for example, found coreligionists whose parents and grandparents came from the Middle East in the great migrations of the late 19th and early 20th centuries and established mosques in places like Quincy, Massachusetts, Dearborn, Michigan, and Cedar Rapids, Iowa. They also found African American Muslims who had embraced Islam first through the black nationalist Nation of Islam and later through communities that followed Malcolm X and W. D. Mohammed toward a more internationally orthodox form of Islam.

The complexity of this intergenerational and intercultural encounter was compounded by the great diversity of the new Muslim immigrants themselves. While the largest groups were South Asian (Bangladeshi, Indian, and Pakistani) and Arab (from across the Middle East), the sheer diversity of Muslim peoples and forms of practice has meant that Friday prayers in many mosques in the U.S. constitute a weekly awakening to the scope and breadth of Islam, which previous generations experienced only on the hajj, the pilgrimage to Mecca. Muslims attest to the panracial, universal vision of Islam, and in America this has become a lived reality, with all its attendant challenges. As Muslim communities grow, many continue to embrace this diversity. Yet in larger cities, South Asians may gravitate toward mosques where Urdu is spoken, while Middle Eastern immigrants may gravitate toward mosques where Arabic is the conversational language. Still other mosques gather a largely Bosnian or Somali community.

Two Hindu movements of note had already taken root in the U.S. by the 1960s: the Ramakrishna Vedanta Society, launched by Swami Vivekananda in the 1890s, and the Self-Realization Fellowship, started by Yogananda in the 1940s. Both had a presence in a number of cities when the new period of immigration began in the late 1960s. The arrival of gurus from India, who were among the first to take advantage of the new opportunities for immigration, and the "turning east" of the American counterculture converged. Dozens of Hindu-based movements began. Among the most long-lived was that of Swami Bhaktivedanta, who arrived in New York in 1965 and started the Western version of a Bengali tradition of devotion to Krishna, the International Society for Krishna Consciousness (ISKCON), popularly known as the Hare Krishna movement.

For Hindus who came to the U.S. in the 1960s and 1970s, the temples of the Hare Krishnas were often the only places where they could celebrate festivals and engage in *pujas*. In some cases Hindu immigrants attended these temples only until they were able to raise funds to establish temples of their own. In other cases—in Boston, Dallas, Chicago, and Philadelphia, for example—the ISKCON temple continues to attract both Indian-born and American-born Krishna devotees.

By 2000 new Hindu immigrants had created more than 700 temples, as varied as the traditions of Hinduism. Some have a strong regional or sectarian character. For example, the Sri Venkateswara Temple in Pittsburgh maintains a distinctively Tamil and Telugu idiom of South Indian Vaishnava worship. The large Swaminarayan temples in Edison, New Jersey; Chicago; and rural Pennsylvania gather Gujarati-speaking devotees of this sectarian movement. The Chinmaya Mission has temples, retreats, and study centers in many cities, following the line of teaching established by the late Swami Chinmayanada. For most American Hindus, however, the process of creating temples involves the cooperation of people who come from different regions of India and different traditions of Hindu practice. Their temples reflect a pan-Indian Hindu identity, with multiple divine images and forms of observance, such as those at the Bharatiya Temple in Troy, Michigan, the Ganesha Temple in Nashville, and the Hindu Temple of Atlanta. Ironically, the scattering of Hindus in the diaspora has led to a more intense encounter with their coreligionists.

Sikhs who arrived in the 1960s also found a few older Sikh communities, such as the one in Stockton, California, where early Punjabi immigrants had built a *gurdwara* in 1914. As new Sikh immigrants from India settled, new questions arose. Was it right for the older communities to adopt the use of chairs in the *gurdwara* instead of sitting on the floor, as is traditionally the case? Is it essential to maintain distinctive Sikh identity by wearing a turban? As new immigrants met the American-born followers of a Sikh guru, Yogi Bhajan, they asked whether the practice of yoga is an authentic part of Sikhism at all. Thus, even a relatively small tradition encounters internal diversity in the American context. By the 1980s, American Sikhs disputed whether their communities should be oriented toward the political turbulence of the Punjab or toward the social, political, and religious life of Sikhs in the U.S.

Buddhists have come to the U.S. as refugees from Vietnam, Cambodia, and Laos and as immigrants from Thailand, Sri Lanka, Taiwan, Hong Kong, Japan, and Korea. In America they have encountered Chinese and Japanese Buddhist communities dating from the late 19th century as well as American-born Buddhists who have studied with teachers in Asia and established practice centers in the Vipassana, Tibetan, and Zen traditions, with both male and female teachers. These American Buddhists are often lay practitioners with little interest in developing a monastic order or perpetuating distinctively Asian cultural traditions. The encounter of Buddhists from across Asia with the growing numbers of American Buddhist practitioners has been one of the most fascinating stories of contemporary religious life. It is in part the story of new immigrants who seek to find a place in American society as Buddhists and new Buddhists who step outside and even critique American society as Buddhists.

Immigrant Asian Buddhists have also met one another in American cities. Thai Buddhists may never have known Korean Zen Buddhists, Chinese Pure Land Buddhists, or Japanese Jodo Shin Shu Buddhists, let alone Euro-American Zen practitioners or serious American meditators in the Thai forest monk tradition. Buddhists' encounter with their own diversity has led to the beginnings of an American ecumenism, with the rise of groups like the Buddhist Sangha Council of Southern California and the Midwest Buddhist Association. Somewhat formal in structure, these councils began to host joint ceremonial occasions, such as the observance of the Buddha's birthday. While Buddhist life continues in its specific Thai and Vietnamese temples, Cambodian and Taiwanese monastic institutions, and many Euro-American meditation and retreat centers, the American context constantly defines its periphery.

Recent Jewish immigrants have come primarily from the former Soviet Union. In America they have found an influential and well-established Jewish community and a multitude of Jewish institutions and organizations. Unlike their Russian Jewish predecessors a century ago, who brought a vibrant Yiddish culture with distinctive Jewish traditions and values, the new Russian Jews are highly secular and know relatively little of Jewish practice, since they come from a context of 70 years of reli-

gious repression under communist rule. They are on the whole urban and highly
educated; 60 percent have five or more years of higher education. Americans often
see them simply as "Russian." Of course, because many were hosted by Jewish social
service agencies, they have been embraced as Jews and strongly encouraged to participate in Jewish life. Here they encountered a bewildering range of options, from
Orthodox to Reform Judaism.

In many ways the most striking changes in the religious landscape are those
within Christianity. While non-Christian religious communities have more directly challenged the presumptively normative Christian cultures of America, the
diversity of recent Christian immigrants has radically reshaped and essentially de-
Europeanized American Christianity. American Christians now include members of
the Mar Thoma Syrian Christian church from India, Haitian and Vietnamese
Catholics, Korean Presbyterians, Nigerian Anglicans, and Ghanaian Methodists.
Filipinos, among the largest immigrant groups, are predominately Roman Catholics. Immigrants from Korea include Buddhists but are disproportionately Protestant Christians, while refugees from Vietnam are disproportionately Catholics.

As we have seen, the greatest numbers of new Christian immigrants have come
from Mexico and Latin America. This is especially significant for the Roman Catholic Church, as parishes increasingly have Spanish masses and incorporate into the
liturgical calendar such major festivals as the Day of the Dead (November 2), the
Feast Day of Our Lady of Guadalupe (December 12), and *posada* processions during Advent. The National Conference of Catholic Bishops estimates that by 2050
more than half of all American Catholics will be Latino, and the need for Spanish-
speaking priests who understand the devotional vibrancy of Hispanic Catholicism
is urgent.

Evangelical and Pentecostal churches have also begun to flourish among Latino
Christians. Studies indicate that the ratio of Protestant to Catholic Latinos rises
with each succeeding generation in the U.S. Latinos account for more than 60 percent of the growth in the Assemblies of God in America, for example. While evangelical and Pentecostal churches claim most of the Latino immigrants, major Protestant denominations, such as the United Methodist Church and the Presbyterian
Church USA, have developed active Hispanic/Latino caucuses that bring the new
perspectives of immigrants' cultures to the issues and arguments of the denomina-
tion.

In all these cases, the encounter with America has given immigrants an opportunity to choose from a spectrum of religious communities and identify anew as a
Hindu, a Buddhist, a Muslim, a Christian, or a Jew. These are often individual
choices, for individual "religious preference" is an important feature of American religious life. Here the diversity of each tradition has become clearer in the practical
course of living and working together. Gujaratis and Bengalis, Hindi- and Tamil-
speakers, who would never have worked together to create a temple in India, do so

in Nashville. Buddhists in Chicago who never knew one another in Asia come together to observe the Buddha's birthday. Catholics from Mexico, Central and South America, Haiti, and Belize transform an African American parish church in south-central Los Angeles into a bursting multiethnic church with a Latin beat.

Becoming American

Creating visible landmarks of one's presence in the U.S. is part of the process of becoming American. Religious life in the U.S., while separate from the sphere of government, has one important governmental component: the establishing of tax-exempt nonprofit status with the Internal Revenue Service. One of the requirements is having a "membership," although being a "member" of a particular "congregation" is alien to many immigrant traditions. In India, Hindus do not think of themselves as "members" of a particular temple and go to different temples at different times. In Lebanon, a Muslim might attend Friday prayers in many different mosques. As a nonprofit corporation in America, however, the community needs to have members. In addition, because there is no government funding of religious establishments, the community must raise money, necessitating mailing lists, e-mail solicitations, and fundraisers. Temples, mosques, and churches generate newsletters, produce websites, and create volunteer networks. Indeed, the shape of "religion" in the U.S. has been molded by the exigencies of becoming a nonprofit voluntary organization and the necessity of competing as such for adherents and support.

Incorporating also means electing trustees and board members and involving community members in elections. While Thai and Vietnamese monks have traditional authority, they are often ill-equipped to lead the community in an encounter with the IRS or local planning or zoning boards. Elections have sometimes been difficult and painful for the lay pioneers and founders of religious centers, too, as they are challenged by new community members and begin to cede power to a larger group. Running for the governing body of a religious center might well be the first taste of electoral politics for many new Americans, as it was for earlier immigrants from Europe. It is little wonder that these elections are often hotly contested.

Focusing religious life on the temple or mosque is another shift for many immigrants, who come from contexts in which religious life is both embedded in the culture and practiced primarily in the home. Typically, new immigrants first gather in one another's homes to celebrate holy days and festivals. Many intend eventually to return to their country of origin, but as they become more settled and their children start school, their plans to return home recede. If their children are to know the cultural and religious traditions of their homeland, they themselves have to plan for it. The 1970s and 1980s saw the creation of hundreds of new religious groups organized as tax-exempt nonprofit corporations and beginning to rent, renovate, or build religious centers.

At first the Hindu temple society or the Kerala Christian fellowship might meet in a rented hall, a community center, or part of a church. In suburban Boston, the nascent Hindu community rented a Knights of Columbus Hall; a growing Muslim community in Northridge, California, found a home in a former mattress showroom; the Shia community in Queens bought a former watch factory and in Hartford a former bowling alley. If zoning issues are likely to be a problem, purchasing an existing religious institution is a safer bet. The Sikh community in New York purchased a former Methodist church in Queens, while the Hindu community in Minneapolis purchased a former church at the corner of Polk and Pine. Over the course of four decades, new communities have also purchased land and laid plans for the new landmarks of America's religious landscape. At the corner of 96th Street and 3rd Avenue in New York City, Skidmore, Owings, and Merrill designed a new Islamic Center placed at an angle to the intersection, so it is oriented to Mecca. In Houston, Boston, Los Angeles, and dozens of other cities, traditional Hindu temple architects laid out temples as embodiments of the Divine and designed sanctuaries with multiple subshrines, fellowship halls, and skylights, adapting traditional architecture to the American context. Buddhist communities have built large temples with monastic complexes, such as the Taiwanese Hsi Lai Temple in Hacienda Heights, California, and the Cambodian monastery in Silver Spring, Maryland.

By 2000 there were about 1,400 mosques in the U.S., 700 Hindu temples, over 2,000 Buddhist temples and meditation centers, some 250 Sikh *gurdwaras,* and smaller numbers of Jain, Zoroastrian, and Afro-Caribbean places of worship. Along with the expansion of these traditions came the growth of new forms of Christianity and the phenomenon of multicongregational churches. Small ethnic churches moved in with larger but sometimes waning mainline urban churches. A single downtown urban church, like Tremont Temple Baptist Church in Boston, today hosts a mixed-race congregation plus a number of "nesting" congregations such as a Korean Presbyterian church, an Ethiopian evangelical church, and a Spanish-speaking Baptist church.

Creating religious institutions, especially buildings, often involves another range of encounters: dealing with planning commissions, county commissioners, zoning boards, and skeptical neighbors. Interaction, negotiation, and even litigation has often revealed fault lines of fear and prejudice. Controversies over building an Islamic school in Sterling, Virginia, and purchasing a former church for an Islamic center in Palos Heights, Illinois, reveal civic anxiety over the presence of new neighbors, especially Muslims. Regulations requiring a Hindu temple to look more "Spanish" in Norwalk, California, county commissioners' restrictions on the height of a minaret in Sarasota, Florida, the township council's concerns about the traffic that might be generated by a new Hindu temple in Edison, New Jersey, and the city council's discussion of the gold domes of a *gurdwara* in San Diego are part of the immigrant encounter with new neighbors and the structures of civic life.

The Next Generation

As with earlier generations of immigrants, religious institutions have provided anchors of cultural identity for first-generation Americans. In them, immigrants can speak their native language and preserve their religious and cultural traditions. With the steady influx of immigrants, religious institutions will continue to play this bridging role.

In addition to providing a home for immigrants, however, religious institutions are often created with the express intention of passing on traditions of culture and faith to the next generation, those who are American-born. How significant will these institutions be for the second generation? In what ways will they be transformed at the hands of succeeding generations?

Many Chinese and Korean Christian churches have shown how multiple services in native languages and English, in traditional and modern idioms, can serve both grandparents and teenagers at once. At an evangelical church in Boston's Chinatown, for example, older worshippers sing hymns in Cantonese while a younger congregation worships in English with Christian praise music and instrumentation. Evangelical Christian groups, whether Korean, Chinese, or Hispanic, have proven themselves especially successful in maintaining the interest of the second generation. In part this mirrors the evangelical turn in American Christianity more generally, placing the younger generation within the strong currents of evangelical youth culture.

Other religious groups have also focused on the needs of the next generation. The Muslim Students Association (MSA), for example, is one of the oldest Muslim organizations in the country, created when the first generation of immigrants were students in the 1960s. Now the MSA includes their college-age children and continues to tackle questions of Muslim American identity by supporting programs such as Islam Awareness Week on dozens of college campuses. On a smaller scale, the Hindu Students Council has developed a series of organizations, conferences, service projects, and summer camps designed to enable Hindu students to understand and express Hindu identity. The Jain Youth of America provides a forum for Jain young people to meet and network. Groups such as United Sikhs of America and Sikhs Serving America tap into the service-based ethos of young Sikhs. An American adaptation of the Vietnamese Buddhist Youth Association provides for the extensive involvement of young people in the lives of major temples, such as Chua Viet Nam in Garden Grove, California, through a program that resembles scouting. Indeed, groups in virtually every religious tradition have adopted the model of summer camps, popularized by Jewish and Christian groups, as a critical part of identity formation.

Establishing educational programs and institutions is also significant for strengthening religious knowledge. Muslims have given priority to creating weekend and full-time Islamic schools. "If you lose your children, no number of mosques will help you," said one national community leader. Like Catholic schools and Jewish day schools, Muslim schools are designed to incorporate religious education in an accredited academic curriculum. By 2000 there were more than 200 full-time Islamic schools in the U.S. Other new immigrant groups have not focused on educational institutions with such intensity. There are, however, three Buddhist universities (two in California and one in Colorado) and a Hindu university in Florida.

Organization and Participation

The 1980s and 1990s saw the growth not only of religious centers and institutions but also of religious organizations and networks. Connecting with one another through conferences, projects, magazines, and the Internet has helped to secure religious and cultural identities even amid the strong assimilative currents of American popular culture. JAINA, the Federation of Jain Associations in North America, has a large annual conference, has established both youth and young professionals' organizations, and maintains a database of American Jain families. FEZANA, the Federation of Zoroastrian Associations in North America, convenes Zoroastrians who have settled in the U.S. from Iran and India. Buddhists do not tend to organize nationally in ways that span the tradition, although there are pan-Buddhist associations in several regions and urban areas. There are also strong sectarian organizations, like the Buddha's Light International Association, which brings Chinese Fo Kuang laity together across the country, and the Soka Gakkai International, which gathers a racially diverse body of American Buddhists. Among South Asian immigrants, professional, cultural, and regional organizations abound, although they are not explicitly Hindu or even religious. Groups like the Telugu Association of North America, the Kerala Association of Greater Washington, and the Gujarati Samaj of Tampa Bay provide links to the cultures, festivals, and language of the regional homeland and enable young people to meet, share the cultural milieu of their parents, and hear speakers and artists from India. More explicitly Hindu is the Federation of Hindu Associations, based in Southern California, which sees its mission as largely political, providing support for Hindu interests in both India and the U.S.

The range of religious organizations is certainly best developed among American Muslims. The Islamic Society of North America (ISNA), formed in the early 1990s, has become the premier national Muslim organization, with annual Labor Day conferences in Chicago drawing 30,000 to 40,000 attendees. It publishes a magazine (*Islamic Horizons*) and organizes smaller conferences on Islamic schools, Islam in the prisons, and Islamic banking. A somewhat more regionally focused group is the Islamic Circle of North America (ICNA), which gathers Urdu-speaking Muslims from South Asia for its annual meetings. Both groups issue public statements on national and international events, such as the terror attacks in New York, Spain, and London, and both groups coordinate international humanitarian relief programs.

Advocacy groups are also important for religious and cultural minorities. Following the lead of such organizations as the Jewish Anti-Defamation League, the Arab American Anti-Discrimination League, the Arab American Institute, and the Japanese Citizens League, new immigrant religious communities have developed advocacy organizations to bring their voices to political and social issues and to maintain their civil rights. While many of these groups were formed in the 1990s, the national crisis of 9/11 brought a new urgency to speaking out, weighing in on political issues, and being heard in the public square.

Over the years Muslims have formed a variety of advocacy groups, such as the Muslim Public Affairs Council (MPAC), the American Muslim Alliance (AMA), the Council on American Islamic Relations (CAIR), the Muslim Women's League, and Muslim Wake-Up. During election years, some of these groups have joined in loose coalitions to promote voter registration drives, candidates' nights, and town hall meetings at the local and state levels. In 2002, for example, the AMA sponsored a Ballot Box Barbecue in a Dallas stadium that attracted some 7,000 Muslims. The Sikh Coalition and the Sikh American Legal Defense and Education Fund (SALDEF) advocate for Sikh civil rights; for example, they have worked with the Equal Employment Opportunity Commission and the National Transportation Safety Board on disputes involving wearing the turban. The Hindu American Foundation was formed to present Hindu voices on public issues. In 2004 the foundation led in filing an *amicus* brief on behalf of American Hindus, Jains, and Buddhists in the Ten Commandments case before the Supreme Court.

The participation of new religious communities has generated increasingly visible public acknowledgement of their presence. In 1991, for the first time in American history, an imam was invited to open a session of the U.S. House of Representatives with the invocation of the day; in 2000 a Hindu priest from Cleveland offered the first-ever Hindu invocation. During the 1990s the governor of Kansas issued a proclamation for the month of Ramadan, the governor of Arizona took ceremonial note of the Buddha's birthday, and the governor of Ohio proclaimed Sikh Khalsa Day. Prominent African American Muslims, South Asian American Hindus, and Baha'is became regular guests at White House prayer breakfasts. The cumulative effect of countless declarations, invocations, and instances of public recognition has given official notice to the new religious landscape.

Encountering Discrimination

These new Americans have also had firsthand experience of discrimination and prejudice. In the 1980s the dot on the forehead of Hindu women became a symbol of unwelcome difference in the eyes of young Jersey City ruffians who called themselves the "Dot-busters." Their harassing attacks had nothing to do with Hinduism as a religion but were directed at all South Asian immigrants. In 1987 harassment turned to violence, as a 30-year-old Indian immigrant was beaten to death by a gang chanting, "Hindu, Hindu!" Here race, religion, and culture were conflated in one angry cry.

The media tend to illustrate "difference" with images of religious difference, and these visual references become the flashpoints for discrimination. The Hindu woman with a red dot on her forehead, the Sikh man in a turban, and the Muslim woman wearing a *hijab* all bear markers of differences that are threatening in the eyes of some. It is not surprising, therefore, that harassment at the mall or discrimination in the workplace is often aimed at people who bear those markers. In the 1990s the Equal Employment Opportunities Commission saw a sharp rise in the number of cases of religious discrimination in the workplace, many of them brought on behalf of Sikh men and Muslim women.

America's Muslims may face discrimination as South Asians, Arabs, Africans, or African Americans, but they are also targeted solely on the basis of their religion. Muslims have worked to dispel the stereotypes associating them with violence, but that stereotype was put into play almost immediately when the Murrah Federal Building in Oklahoma City was bombed on April 19, 1995. Muslim families all over America felt the backlash of harassment because of the mistaken assumption, broadcast for only a few minutes, that the bombing was linked to "Middle Eastern–looking" men seen in the vicinity. The aftermath of the Oklahoma City bombing brought to prominence the Council on American-Islamic Relations (CAIR), then a newly formed watchdog group. In May 1995 the group released a report detailing more than 200 incidents of anti-Muslim threats, harassment, and property damage in the wake of the bombing. Since then CAIR's annual reports have documented ongoing violence, harassment, and discrimination. Following 9/11, each year's reports have provided specific accounts of the rising incidence of discrimination and intolerance, including ethnically and religiously based interrogations, detentions, and closures of charities.

Bias and racial and religious discrimination have been recurrent through the past four decades, often targeting the most visible marker of religious minorities—their places of worship. The climate of fear and paranoia following 9/11 emboldened the perpetrators, who attacked mosques in Cleveland, Columbus, and Toledo, in Denver and Chicago, in Sterling, Virginia, and Dallas, to mention a few. The rash of incidents included attacks on Hindu temples in Illinois and New Jersey and on a Sikh center in upstate New York. Sikhs, whose turbans conjured images of Osama bin Laden, were especially vulnerable, and one of the first casualties of the 9/11 backlash was a Sikh who was murdered in Mesa, Arizona.

New Boundary Crossings, New Networks

The new Americans have brought the traditions, the religious practices, and above all the faces of the world's religions to America. In the process, new forms of religious networking and even "religious *mestizaje*" are coming into existence. One source of change is interfaith marriage, which has made the issue of religious blending a reality for Muslim-Christian, Jewish-Buddhist, and Christian-Hindu couples. Although first-generation immigrants yearn for the continuity of their religious and cultural values, love and marriage across religious traditions is increasing among the second generation. Along with interfaith marriages is the growing phenomenon of dual religious belonging: people who may be Episcopalians or Jews but are also serious practitioners of Buddhist meditation or Hindu forms of yoga. Robert Wuthnow found in a 2004 survey that 20 percent of all respondents thought it was possible to be a good Buddhist and a good Christian at the same time. Despite the influence of conservative forms of Christianity that seem to establish clear religious boundaries, Christianity, along with other religious traditions, is more fluid today than in the past. Some religious communities, like the Baha'i and the Unitarian Universalists, embrace the diversity of religious paths as part of their central ethos, and both groups are growing.

In the past few decades new instruments of interreligious relationship have developed. Churches, synagogues, mosques, and temples have joined to create interfaith councils, interfaith initiatives, and Abrahamic dialogues—all intentional efforts to bring religious communities together around civic issues or the basic issue of mutual understanding. By 2005 there were about 600 officially recognized interreligious bodies, including the Arizona Interfaith Movement, the Interfaith Association of Central Ohio, and the Interfaith Conference of Metropolitan Washington. Groups like Interfaith Hospitality Network (Family Promise) focus on homelessness, while the Greater Boston Interfaith Organization focuses on low-income housing. All these groups and many more loosely organized networks reveal a significant amount of bridge-building between and among religious communities.

Bibliography

Avalos, Hector, ed. *Introduction to the U.S. Latina and Latino Religious Experience.* Leiden: Brill, 2004.

Ebaugh, Helen Rose, and Janet S. Chafetz. *Religion and the New Immigrants: Continuities and Adaptations in Immigrant Congregations.* Walnut Creek, Calif.: AltaMira, 2000.

Eck, Diana L. *A New Religious America: How a "Christian" Country Has Become the World's Most Religiously Diverse Nation.* San Francisco: Harper San Francisco, 2001.

Glazer, Nathan. *American Judaism.* Chicago: University of Chicago Press, 1989.

Herberg, Will. *Protestant, Catholic, Jew.* Chicago: University of Chicago Press, 1983.

Moore, R. Laurence. *Religious Outsiders and the Making of Americans.* New York: Oxford University Press, 1986.

Numrich, Paul. *Old Wisdom in the New World: Americanization in Two Immigrant Theravada Buddhist Temples.* Knoxville: University of Tennessee Press, 1996.

Prebish, Charles, and Kenneth K. Tanaka, eds. *The Faces of Buddhism in America.* Berkeley: University of California Press, 1998.

Richardson, E. Allen. *Strangers in This Land: Pluralism and the Response to Diversity in the United States.* New York: Pilgrim, 1988.

Seager, Richard. *Buddhism in America.* New York: Columbia University Press, 1999.

Smith, Jane. *Islam in America.* New York: Columbia University Press, 1999.

Smith, Tom W. "Religious Diversity in America: The Emergence of Muslims, Buddhists, Hindus, and Others." *Journal for the Scientific Study of Religion* 41, 3 (Sept. 2002): 577–85.

Williams, Raymond. *Religions of Immigrants from India and Pakistan: New Threads in the American Tapestry.* Cambridge: Cambridge University Press, 1988.

Wuthnow, Robert. *America and the Challenges of Religious Diversity.* Princeton: Princeton University Press, 2005.

Language

David López and Vanesa Estrada

Imagine that a truly multiethnic America had been able to maintain its vast immigrant linguistic heritage. Over the span of a century, huddled masses came to the U.S. in large numbers, speaking virtually every major and minor European language as well as a host of Asian and Middle Eastern tongues. If this dream of Horace Kallen's had come true, we would now be a nation of bilinguals, doing business with each other in English but also chatting with friends and relatives, as well as our international business contacts, in German, Italian, and Polish. Like so much of the rest of the world, we would be passing on our ethnic mother tongues to our children, alongside the lingua franca (English in our case) that binds us together, or at least allows us to communicate across ethnic lines.

However, the actual story is quite the opposite. Today's often muddled notions of "multiculturalism" may be just as impractical as Kallen's idealized "cultural pluralism," but many academics and ethnic activists lament what we have lost, believing that we might have had an infinitely richer culture and be more politically effective and economically adept internationally. But it was not to be. The United States is famous for being among the least linguistically diverse of all nations. Americans' competence in the European languages of the great migration is notoriously low, increasingly reliant on struggling "foreign language" programs that are a minor appendage of college humanities divisions and even more marginal in secondary schools. Americans' competence in French, Italian, and German has never been lower, and the actual use of these languages in or outside American homes is lower still. Whatever the value—economic, political, or cultural—of these "heritage languages" for individuals, groups, or the nation as a whole, it has been lost forever. The trend continues to be rapid language assimilation to English competency. The question we ask here is whether in an increasingly globalized world and in a nation more attuned to multiculturalism and respect for ethnicity, we might expect greater bilingualism in the future. This hinges on the question of whether the children and grandchildren of today's immigrants are maintaining competency in their immigrant languages in addition to being fluent in English.

Concerns about English

The dominance of English is perhaps most often portrayed in the U.S. as a positive development. Many commentators who have wondered how America can accommodate so many immigrants from so many different places into one coherent polity and society have pointed to the shared language of English as a necessary condition for our functioning democracy. Indeed, the specter of division and even threats of secession are evident in the troubled relationship of the Francophone Quebecois with Anglophone Canada. But it is important to note that while none would hope for ethnic conflict rooted in separate language communities, the celebration of our common language does not often recognize the price we have paid in the loss of language competency described above.

Currently language is one of the most controversial issues surrounding immigration. The ability of immigrants and their offspring to speak English is a potent political issue and has long roots in American history. Benjamin Franklin worried about the Germans in colonial America overcoming the English. Theodore Roosevelt declared in 1907 that "we have room for but one language here, and that is the English language." The "refusal" of immigrants to learn English is often used by restrictionists to argue that today's immigrants are inferior to those who came earlier. In a 1996 General Social Survey (GSS) question, 63 percent of Americans supported passage of "a law making English the official language of the United States, meaning government business would be conducted in English only." In a 2000 GSS question, 75 percent of Americans agreed with the statement that "speaking English as the common national language is what unites all Americans." Twenty-seven states have responded to the perceived threat by passing laws requiring that all government activity be conducted in English, and a federal version has been introduced in Congress a number of times but has not yet passed. This concern with language has also fueled a political movement against bilingual education. In 1998, California passed Proposition 227, which ended bilingual education in the state and mandated one-year English-language immersion for children who could not speak English. Arizona passed a similar law in 2000 and Massachusetts in 2002, although in that same year Colorado voters defeated a similar measure.

Despite the sometimes fevered pitch of public debates about language use by immigrants and their children and the related debate about bilingual education, the evidence shows that fear that immigrants will not learn English is unfounded. While the number of people who speak a language other than English in their homes is quite high—47 million—the changes in language use that are documented over time all point to high levels of English-language assimilation. The sociologists Frank Bean and Gillian Stevens, using data from the 2000 Census, point out that among immigrants from non-English-speaking countries, only 10 percent do not speak English at all and 40 percent arrived in the U.S. already able to speak English "very well." They find a strong positive association between the length of time a foreign-born person has been in the U.S. and the ability to speak English well. Among children born in the U.S. to immigrant parents, all but a tiny fraction speak English well. In a large longitudinal study of children of immigrants in Miami and San Diego, Alejandro Portes and Rubén Rumbaut found that 98 percent of those born in the U.S. spoke and understood English well, and by high school graduation, 88 percent of those who grew up in a home where a language other than English was spoken preferred to speak English themselves. Most of the children had lost ability in their parents' languages over time, and by graduation only 28 percent could be classified as fully bilingual.

The U.S. has always been very efficient at stamping out other languages and quickly assimilating the children of immigrants linguistically. The consensus among researchers is that the standard three-generation model of linguistic assimilation still holds here: the immigrant generation makes some progress but predominately speaks its native tongue, the second generation is bilingual, and the third generation is monolingual in English.

Yet social scientists' knowledge of this issue frequently contradicts public concerns. One example is the recent social science speculation that some linguistic assimilation can happen too quickly. Portes and Rumbaut argue that when children rapidly abandon their parents' language, the parents lose authority over their children. This dissonant acculturation leads to poor communication—parents cannot understand English well, and children cannot understand the immigrant language well. Portes and Rumbaut also find that fluent bilingual children do best academically (although it is not clear whether bilingualism contributes to their academic success or they are better able to maintain bilingual ability because they are academically talented). In a study of Asian and Latino youth using 1990 Census data, the sociologist Cynthia Feliciano found that bilingual students are less likely to drop out than English monolinguals, students in bilingual households are less likely to drop out than those in English-dominant or English-limited households, and students in immigrant households are less likely to drop out than those in non-immigrant households.

Whether or not it could have been otherwise, American monolingualism stands in sharp contrast to multilingualism in much of the rest of the world. In most northern European countries, competence in English is widespread and knowledge of a neighboring country's language is common. In France most schoolchildren study English, and some popular university programs are taught entirely in English, giving students an edge in international business. Ironically, it is Europe that increasingly resembles Kallen's linguistic dream, with each nation maintaining its mother tongue and communicating with the others in English, the de facto lingua franca of the 21st century. Furthermore, throughout the postcolonial world the languages of the colonizing powers linger on, as de facto and sometimes de jure tongues of business and politics. It is not uncommon to find people of modest means in Africa and Asia who speak their mother tongue, the language of their colonizers, and at least one other tongue—perhaps a regional lingua franca like Swahili or the language of a neighboring tribe or nation. Even where colonizers' languages were not English, English is increasingly added to the mix. Throughout Latin America, Spanish and Portuguese are the national languages, but indigenous languages survive and even thrive in some places; meanwhile, would-be waiters and bankers all study English in school. Multilingualism and bilingualism, at least of the rough-and-ready sort, are the rule rather than the exception. Americans are the ones who are out of step.

But if the linguistic resources of the U.S. compare poorly to those of the nations we came from, one could argue that the comparison is inappropriate. Contemporary European and Asian states are the products of hundreds of years of struggles between nationalities, not to mention waves of conquest and reconquest. Linguistic diversity is just one dimension of the complex ethnic overlaps and boundary struggles that continue to roil much of the world. In contrast, in the New World, particularly in "settler societies" such as the U.S. where preexisting societies were effectively decimated, there were many reasons to rally around the dominant colonial language and few forces pushing for linguistic diversity. When we compare linguistic patterns in the U.S. with those in other settler societies like Canada, Argentina, and Australia, the similarities far outweigh the differences. Even in Australia, where substantial non-English-speaking immigration is a comparatively recent phenomenon, the shift to English among the second and third generations is clear.

Why is bilingualism among migrants so enduring in many parts of the world yet so fleeting in the U.S. and other settler societies, particularly those whose dominant language is English? Common sense and rational-choice theory would argue that bilingualism is developed or maintained in situations where it is rewarding. The simplest way to think about this is in economic terms: an international migrant or her children and grandchildren will continue to speak their mother tongue when there is a monetary or other reward for doing so. Usually this means that the ethnic language continues to be used in business or employment. Ethnic languages can also be useful cloaks of secrecy, which can give them more economic value. Though difficult to measure, there is undeniable economic value in the use of mother tongues as a symbol of solidarity, particularly in precarious settings. Chinese or Gujarati shopkeepers in southern Africa could probably have dispensed with the use of their mother tongues strictly for the sake of economic exchange, but they had other reasons to maintain them—one being the possibility of expulsion by unfriendly regimes, in which case they would need their mother tongues to get along elsewhere.

Indeed, "middleman minorities," such as the Chinese and Gujarati traders wandering the world, rely on active international ethnic networks for capital, goods, and reliable low-cost labor. Working within networks of trust reinforced by kinship—often through marriages within the ethnic group—substantially reduces transaction costs (for example, it provides access to revolving credit and reduces the need for lawyers, contracts, and compliance with labor laws). In other words, ethnic solidarity pays. In such networks, members' continued facility in the national or tribal mother tongue is essential for doing business; competence in the mother tongue can be "cultural capital" essential for accessing the benefits of the "social capital" found in ethnic networks. To the extent that ethnic networks lead to jobs, this same argument would seem to apply to labor migrants. But the children and grandchildren of these migrants have access to other sources of employment, and thus many of them are not rewarded for maintaining their ethnic language.

Of course, most explanations of language maintenance and other forms of bilingualism do not need to be so elaborate. This is not to say that they can be reduced to economic motivations alone. But the contrast between linguistically self-sustaining middleman minorities, on the one hand, and the typical experience of labor migrants to the U.S. and elsewhere, on the other, does underline the importance of economic and other interests for the individuals and families involved. For the vast majority of the American-born children and grandchildren of European immigrants, there was little reason to continue using their mother tongue and even less reason to pass it on to their children. Italian and Polish immigrants and their children, for example, found work in factories and foundries, where English was often the lingua franca. In contrast, compelling external forces worked against speaking any language other than English in public. Public schooling at the turn of the 20th century was not only conducted in English, it also actively discouraged anything else. The relative importance of these two forces—lack of positive reasons to maintain an ethnic language and the existence of political pressure to excise them—is difficult to assess. Indeed, some combination of the labor force rewards to immigrants with English-language ability and wider cultural forces discouraging the use of other languages affected earlier immigrants.

Ethnic Language Maintenance: A Second Chance?

Looking back, the 1970s was a confusing decade for research on language maintenance and on immigration more generally. At that time ethnic language loss seemed clear to researchers. All the European languages brought to the U.S. by earlier immigrants were dead or dying. The possible exception was Spanish (which of course was brought to the U.S. and maintained by Mexicans and other Latin Americans, not by *peninsulares* from Spain), but researchers had concluded—even if only reluctantly, as in the case of committed scholars like Joshua Fishman—that even Spanish did not seem to provide any real hope for continuing bilingualism. Other languages that had survived owing to geographical and social isolation, such as variants of French in rural Louisiana and Maine or Navajo and Hopi among reservation traditionalists, were in sharp decline as that isolation was diminishing. Spanish-speaking communities maintained by similar forces of isolation, such as in parts of northern New Mexico and south Texas, were also coming undone. It turned out that the "isolation" affecting these communities was largely due to political exclusion; as Mexican Americans moved throughout the Southwest, Spanish monolingualism and bilingualism declined, too.

When David López concluded in 1978 that "in the absence of substantial continued immigration" the decline of Spanish-English bilingualism seemed inevitable, he did not foresee substantial continued immigration in the near future. How wrong he was. Renewed immigration has revitalized Spanish (and to a lesser degree dozens of other tongues) in the U.S., because immigrants from Mexico, Central America, and other parts of Latin America have demographically overwhelmed the pre-1970 Latino population, which was becoming increasingly English monolingual over time. In the mid-20th century the Latino population was dominated by the third-plus generations, and so the generational shift to English was very clear. As immigration grew the generational composition shifted, so that by 2000, 40 percent of Latinos in the U.S. were immigrants, 28 percent were second-generation, and 32 percent were third-generation or higher. Today, entire medium-sized cities, such as Huntington Park and Santa Ana in Southern California, appear to function entirely in Spanish. Without exception, these places are largely inhabited by immigrants and their young children. They may be striking in their "foreignness" to visitors, but they are no more so than immigrant neighborhoods on New York's Lower East Side were a century ago.

Of course, that first-generation immigrants speak Spanish—or Cantonese—is hardly evidence of stable bilingualism. The question is, what happens among the children and grandchildren of these immigrants? Now, some 40 years into the "new" immigration, the ethnic groups that have been enriched by it contain second- and even third-generation members, allowing us to analyze this question. Research over the past decade has generally affirmed previous conclusions—that "only English" seems to be the condition for the descendants of immigrants over two or three generations, and that while the loss of Spanish takes perhaps a generation longer, it is also in the cards. Yet while English monolingualism is indeed the primary trend among all U.S. ethnic groups, intergenerational bilingualism is a strong secondary trend among some Latinos.

There are many ways to name and define "bilingualism." We use this term instead of the somewhat more accurate "mother tongue maintenance" or even "language maintenance" in part for simplicity, but also because we think it better conveys the essence of the phenomenon in question. Bilingualism also emphasizes what is perhaps already obvious—that virtually all children growing up in the United States learn English. Some do so later or better than others, but most speak English better than they speak their parents' mother tongues. Of course, many adult immigrants never completely learn English, and continued immigration is fundamental to the vitality of ethnic language maintenance at the community level. However, our focus here is on the second and later generations, not on first-generation immigrants.

It is possible to become bilingual through language study and acquisition rather than maintenance, but in practice very few Americans do so, and many who appear to learn their second languages in school are in fact building on an inherited language foundation. Furthermore, we refer here not to knowing a language other than English but to actually speaking it at home (the census asks, "Does this person speak a language other than English at home?"). This distinction is important, because we are probably underestimating the nation's linguistic resources, since we have no information about the linguistic abilities of those who report that they do not use a language other than English at home.

Language Use in the U.S. Today

Table 1 provides an overview of home language use in 2000. Nearly 47 million of the 262 million individuals over the age of five (the starting point for information about language use) speak a language other than English at home. This is 18 percent of the total U.S. population, but of course non-English and bilingual households are concentrated in those states that have been most affected by new immigration. California, New York, Texas, and Florida contain over half of these households. Even among these four states there is wide variation; 40 percent of

Table 1   Language spoken at home in the U.S. and selected states, 2000

	United States	California	New York	Texas	Florida
Total population aged five and older	262,375,000	31,417,000	17,749,000	19,242,000	15,044,000
Only English	215,423,000	19,015,000	12,786,000	13,231,000	11,570,000
Other than English	46,952,000	12,402,000	4,963,000	6,011,000	3,474,000
Spanish	28,101,000	8,106,000	2,416,000	5,195,000	2,477,000
Other Indo-European	10,018,000	1,335,000	1,655,000	358,000	755,000
Asian	6,960,000	2,709,000	671,000	374,000	268,000

Source: U.S. Bureau of the Census, 2000 Census, Summary File 3. Constructed from American Factfinder (http://factfinder.census.gov).

Table 2   Language spoken at home by nativity, 2000

	Total	Native-born	Foreign-born
Total population aged five and older	262,375,000	231,666,000	30,700,000
English only	215,423,000	210,211,000	5,203,000
Other than English	46,952,000	21,455,000	25,497,000
Spanish	28,101,000	14,761,000	13,340,000
Other Indo-European	10,018,000	4,432,000	5,586,000
Asian	6,960,000	1,448,000	5,512,000

Source: U.S. Bureau of the Census, 2000 Census, Summary File 3. Constructed from American Factfinder (http://factfinder.census.gov).

households in California speak a language other than English at home, compared with just 23 percent in Florida.

The number of Spanish-speakers in the U.S. has increased 62 percent since 1990, and the number of people who speak Asian languages has increased at about the same rate; in contrast, use of other major western and central European languages (Italian, German, French, Polish) has declined. The 2000 Census identified 322 different languages spoken in the home. Among adults aged 18 to 64 who speak a language other than English at home, the top 10 languages are Spanish (spoken by 56 percent), French (5.2 percent), German (4.6 percent), Chinese, which is best understood as a family of languages, not a single mutually understood tongue (4.3 percent), Italian (3.3 percent), Tagalog (3.1 percent), Korean (2.2 percent), Vietnamese (1.6 percent), Polish (1.6 percent), and Japanese (1.4 percent). These languages represent a historical snapshot of language assimilation and immigration in the U.S., with the European languages and Japanese mostly reflecting an aging second generation who maintained some of their parents' mother tongue and the newer immigrant languages (Chinese, Tagalog, Korean, and Vietnamese) reflecting first-generation immigrants mostly arriving since 1965.

Table 2 illustrates the importance of recent immigration to these patterns: over half of the people who speak another language at home are immigrants. But by no means does this mean that *only* immigrants are speaking non-English languages at home; 45 percent of these people were born in the U.S. This begins to give us a sense of the magnitude of intergenerational bilingualism. Over 21 million native-born Americans continue to use a language other than English at home. Since the overwhelming majority of these people also speak English, we can reasonably label them as native-born bilinguals. We cannot make the same assumption about English-language use among the foreign-born, although we know from the literature on the subject that a large proportion do speak adequate English, including almost all of those who arrive in the U.S. as children.

Table 3   Language spoken at home and English ability by age group, 2000

	Ages 5–17	Ages 18–64	Age 65 and older
Total population age five and older	53,096,000	174,300,000	34,979,000
English only	43,316,000	141,543,000	30,564,000
Language other than English			
Spanish	6,830,000	19,594,000	1,677,000
English spoken not well/not very well	1,038,000	6,218,000	677,000
Other Indo-European	1,445,000	6,641,000	1,932,000
English spoken not well/not very well	131,000	807,000	361,000
Asian	1,159,000	5,172,000	630,000
English spoken not well/not very well	126,000	1,132,000	309,000

Source: U.S. Bureau of the Census, 2000 Census, Summary File 3. Constructed from American Factfinder (http://factfinder.census.gov).

Unfortunately, because these two tables present only a broad overview of the non-English-speaking population, we can conclude little about the social dynamics underlying the data they contain. We do know, however, that the "other Indo-European" category includes both "old" languages like Italian and Polish and "new" languages like Russian and Hindi, as well as variants of French spoken in Louisiana and Maine. Immigrants predominate among speakers of Asian languages (about 7.8 million of the 11.9 Asian Americans enumerated in the 2000 Census are immigrants). But Table 2 shows that only about 1.5 million of the more than 4 million native-born Asian Americans actually speak their mother tongue at home. The corresponding figure for native-born Hispanics is 14.8 million out of over 19 million. This is our first clear, albeit indirect, evidence of the importance of ethnic differences in patterns of language use. A higher proportion of native-born Hispanics than native-born Asian Americans speak their mother tongue at home.

Table 3 adds the dimensions of age and language ability. Although the U.S. Census's measure of language ability is "self-reported," usually by the one person in the household who fills out the census questionnaire, it has been shown to be relatively valid. Table 3 also shows the numbers of people who speak a non-English language at home but who say they do not speak English "well" or "very well." This is a conservative measure of the population that is probably not functionally bilingual. For example, only about one out of eight children who speak Spanish at home does not speak English well; this is less than half the figure for adults. Presumably many of these children are recent arrivals or young children in their early school years. This is impressive evidence that bilingualism, *not* Spanish monolingualism, is the typical pattern among young Latinos who speak Spanish at home. Finally, it is important to emphasize that among children who speak a non-English language at home, difficulty in speaking English is quite low (less than 10 percent).

Patterns of Intergenerational Bilingualism

The October 1999 Current Population Survey (CPS) makes more detailed analysis possible, because this survey includes a question about parents' place of birth. (The U.S. Census asks only where the respondent was born, not where his or her parents were born.) Table 4 provides an overview of how generation affects patterns of language use and provides solid support for our point that it is *bilingualism,* not English-language ability, that varies across generations. When all children are considered, without regard to ethnicity, the rate of speaking only English at home increases considerably over generations, up from only 13 percent among first-generation immigrant children to 97 percent among the fourth generation. But corresponding variation in English adeptness—defined as either speaking English only or speaking it well or very well—is small (85 to 100 percent). In other words, in each generation, those individuals who are not English monolinguals are primarily bilinguals with good facility in English. This fact is often overlooked by pundits and scholars, such as Samuel Huntington, who fear that Spanish-only enclaves are developing into some new "other America."

Table 4   Percentage of children aged 5 to 18 who are adept English-speakers by generation, October 1999

Generation	Speaks only English	Speaks another language and English well or very well	English-adept
First	13	72	85
Second	25	69	94
2.5	67	31	98
Third	82	17	99
Fourth	97	3	100
Total	83	15	98

Source: Tabulated from the October 1999 Current Population Survey Education Supplement (Bureau of Labor Statistics).

Note: First generation = all children who were born abroad and migrated to the U.S. at age 6 or older; *Second generation* = all children who were born in the U.S. to two foreign-born parents (or one foreign-born parent if only one parent is present in the household) and all children who were born abroad and migrated to the U.S. at age 5 or younger; *2.5 generation* = all children who were born in the U.S. to one parent who was born abroad and one parent who was born in the U.S.; *Third generation* = all children who were born in the U.S. to two parents who were also born in the U.S. but at least one grandparent who was born abroad; *Fourth generation* = all children who were born in the U.S. to two parents who were born in the U.S. and two grandparents who were also born in the U.S.

Before examining patterns of bilingualism by ethnicity and generation, we need to get a sense of the generational composition of the four major racial and ethnic groups in the U.S. Census data from 2000 show that whites and blacks are quite similar: nine out of ten are third generation or higher, and only a few are first or second generation. At the other end of the spectrum, nine out of ten Asian American children are either immigrants or the children of immigrants. Of course, there are some third-generation and higher Asian American youth, but they are far outnumbered by Asian American children in new immigrant households. While we do not focus on the links between social class, culture, community structure, and school performance here, it is worth noting that the vast majority of high-achieving Asian American youth are immigrant children struggling and succeeding in a language quite different from their ethnic tongue. Latinos are also predominantly first and second generation, though not as much so as Asian Americans. Twenty-three percent of Latino youth can trace back their origins for three generations or more, but for the most part, "old-time" Mexican American families have roots in the first period of large-scale migration from Mexico, early in the 20th century. That migration slowed to a halt late in the 1920s, ebbed and flowed according to the whims of U.S. economic and political forces until the early 1960s, and then rose sharply alongside other new immigration streams after 1965. Thus, overall, today's fourth-generation American youth are overwhelmingly white, with a considerable black minority, but over half of the total first and second generation are Latino, another 22 percent are Asian, and only a minority are white or black.

Table 5 provides the most recent information on patterns of language use among American youth, broken down by generation and ethnicity. To be sure, these data do not tell us with any certainty if these youth will continue to be bilingual into adulthood, but it does tell us the rate at which they could be. Remember that what is being reported is "speaking a language other than English at home," behavior that is determined as much by the abilities and preferences of these youth's parents as by their own. Table 5 shows that generational differences are substantial within each U.S. ethnic group, but not equally so. Among whites and Asians, eight out of ten first-generation immigrant children speak a language other than English, but the proportion trails off into insignificance among the fourth generation. Much the same is true among African Americans, although in their case a substantial proportion of immigrants (presumably from the Caribbean) are English monolinguals to begin with.

Latino youth are a different story. And it is these data that have given rise to a debate over "Hispanic exceptionalism." Will Latinos fail to follow the generational model of language shift that characterizes so many other groups? On the one hand, Table 5 shows that bilingualism among Latino youth varies substantially by generation, falling from 95 percent among first-generation immigrant children to just 30 percent among the fourth generation. On the other hand, that 30 percent of

Table 5   Bilingualism rates of children aged 5 to 18 by generation and ethnicity, October 1999 (percentages)

Generation	Latino	Asian American	White	Black	Total
First	95	79	79	59	87
Second	90	72	41	23	75
2.5	73	33	16	7	33
Third	43	17 (27)	5	—	18
Fourth	30	4 (30)	1	2	3
Total	72	62	4	5	17

Source: Tabulated from the October 1999 Current Population Survey Education Supplement (Bureau of Labor Statistics).

Note: Cells with 25–50 sample cases noted; cells with fewer than 25 cases not calculated. "Bilingualism" means individual reported speaking a language other than English at home.

fourth-generation Latinos are bilingual is significant in contrast to the other ethnic groups. Without a doubt, even though the trend toward English monolingualism is strong among all U.S. ethnic groups, intergenerational bilingualism is a strong secondary pattern among Latinos (mostly among Mexicans, who make up an even larger proportion of the fourth generation than they do of the first and second generations).

To get a sense of what happens to these children after they leave home, we also examined these patterns among adults aged 18 to 24, a large proportion of whom are no longer living with their parents. The results are quite similar to those among children aged 5 to 18, who are still living with their parents. We found an even higher rate of bilingualism among third- and later-generation Latinos who are between 18 and 24 (45%) than among their younger counterparts.

Can we use these cross-sectional data to make predictions about the future? That is, can we assume that the parents and grandparents of today's third and fourth generations once resembled today's first- and second-generation immigrants, or that the third and fourth generations who descend from today's first and second generations will resemble the current third and fourth generations? Obviously we cannot make either assumption, and so we cannot make predictions with any certainty. However, we can make some broad projections, or at least informed guesses, about what might happen. For example, one could hypothesize that the future rate of bilingualism might increase to over 30 percent. Today's fourth generation is comparatively small, and their parents grew up during a period of comparatively low immigration. In contrast, the children and grandchildren of today's immigrant youth may well grow up in times and places that are heavily immigrant-oriented.

Much of the research about the educational advantages and disadvantages of being bilingual suggests that this could be a positive development. It is also important to note that knowing and using a second language at home is not necessarily isolating, since today's third- and fourth-generation youth (and their parents) are fluent in English, indeed probably more fluent in English than in their ethnic mother tongues. And bilingualism is only a secondary pattern, affecting approximately a third of second-, third-, and fourth-generation households, to the point that many Latino academics who grew up speaking only English at home look at their more bilingual colleagues with envy.

However, an analysis of regional data suggests that this projection may be over-stated. There are several important regional differences in Latino immigration his-tories. California's 19th-century Mexican population was overwhelmed by Anglo in-migration from other parts of the U.S, while significant Mexican enclaves sur-vived in Texas and New Mexico. Meanwhile, Florida lacks a significant third or fourth Latino generation entirely. Table 6 shows how these historical differences af-fect current patterns of language use in these three Latino-heavy states. Fourth-gen-eration Latino youth in California, which is home to the largest Mexican American population, have a much lower rate of bilingualism (17 percent) than their counter-parts in Texas (41 percent). At the same time, the rates of bilingualism among the first and second Latino generations in these two states are similar. This regional dif-ference makes sense sociologically: throughout Texas and the Southwest, much of the Latino population lives in or hails from small towns and rural places. So it may not be that high numbers of Latinos lead to language maintenance, but rather that the relative isolation of Latinos in rural communities does so. Since future popula-tion growth of Latinos is likely to be concentrated in urban areas, this suggests that over time, the pattern of lower bilingualism exhibited by later-generation Latinos in California could be the dominant one. That is, future Latino generations' bilingual-

Table 6   Bilingualism rates of Latino children aged 5 to 18 by generation and selected states, October 1999 (percentages)

Generation	California	Texas	Florida	All United States
First	94	96	98	95
Second	92	93	89	90
2.5	82	87	—	73
Third	34	46 (28)	—	43
Fourth	17	41	—	30
Total	81	68	88	72
Sample number	763	489	179	2,875
Population estimate from sample	2,375,000	1,592,000	479,000	7,458,000

Source: Tabulated from the October 1999 Current Population Survey Education Supplement (Bureau of Labor Statistics).

Note: Cells with 25–50 sample cases noted; cells with fewer than 25 cases not calculated. "Bilingualism" means individual reported speaking a language other than English at home. 2000 Census counts and revised CPS estimates of the population aged 5–18 are higher.

ism rates may well drop below 30 percent, even if they stay above the rates of other U.S. ethnic groups.

In sum, there is no evidence that today's immigrants are developing ethnic communities that are permanent non-English-speaking enclaves, in which public and private life is carried out totally or predominantly in other languages. To be sure, some places *seem* to be this way. But even Santa Ana and Huntington Park, two overwhelmingly Mexican cities in California, are primarily new points of arrival for new immigrants; not too many years ago, Huntington Park was a white working-class suburb. The future of such new "little Mexicos" is impossible to predict, and they are fascinating places that bear watching. However, they include only a small proportion of second- and later-generation Latinos. If they become home to large multigenerational proportions of Latinos one day, then Samuel Huntington's arguments about Latinos' isolation from mainstream America may prove at least partially correct.

But far more likely is another situation, characteristic of the complex and diverse patterns of partial acculturation and assimilation that have characterized the Mexican American experience thus far—that Latinos will remain less acculturated and less assimilated than the "white ethnics" of European origin but not nearly as stigmatized and isolated as African Americans. The language patterns of Mexican Americans and other Latinos are consistent with this "in-betweenness," as are their rates of intermarriage and economic progress, which are higher than those of blacks but lower than those of whites.

Recent federal legislation has tended to be much more concerned with moving quickly to monolingualism in English than with preserving any other languages. The Bilingual Education Act of 1968 expired in 2002 and was replaced with the English Language Acquisition Act. The Office of Bilingual Education and Minority Language Affairs became the Office of English Language Acquisition, Language Enhancement, and Academic Achievement for Limited-English-Proficient Students. While the 1968 law did not mandate how schools should teach non-English-proficient students, the different emphases of the two laws are evident in their titles. In a speech in support of the 1968 law, Senator Ralph Yarborough of Texas declared, "We have a magnificent opportunity to do a very sensible thing—to enable naturally bilingual children to grow up speaking both good Spanish and good English, and thereby be in a position to go forth confidently to deal with the world, rather than retreat in embarrassment from a world which speaks a language which they can understand only imperfectly" (p. 324).

Yarborough's dream of a bilingual America echoes Kallen's dream. Yet it seems that public policy and American public opinion today are fueled by nightmarish fears of an endangered English language. Other than the unique patterns associated with Spanish, there is very little in the current patterns of language shift across immigrant generations to suggest that either dream reflects the reality. For good or bad, the U.S. seems to excel at stamping out any language other than English in a few short generations. The constant infusion of new immigrants that we have become so accustomed to in the past few decades obscures this, but without this continuing immigration, it is unlikely that even Spanish would survive.

Bibliography

Alba, Richard, John Logan, Amy Lutz, and Brian Stults. 2002. "Only English by the Third Generation? Loss and Preservation of the Mother Tongue among the Grandchildren of Contemporary Immigrants." *Demography* 39, 3 (Aug.): 467–84.

Bean, Frank, and Gillian Stevens. 2003. *America's Newcomers and the Dynamics of Diversity.* New York: Russell Sage Foundation.

Feliciano, Cynthia. 2001. "The Benefits of Biculturalism: Exposure to Immigrant Culture and Dropping Out of School among Asian and Latino Youths." *Social Science Quarterly* 82, 4 (Dec.): 865–80.

Fishman, Joshua. 1980. "Language Maintenance." In Steven Thernstrom, A. Orlov, and Oscar Handlin, eds., *Harvard Encyclopedia of American Ethnic Groups,* p. 629–38. Cambridge, Mass.: Harvard University Press.

Huntington, Samuel. 2004. *Who Are We? The Challenges to America's National Identity.* New York: Simon and Schuster.

Kallen, Horace. 1924. *Culture and Democracy in the United States.* New York: Boni and Liveright.

López, David. 1978. "Chicano Language Loyalty in an Urban Setting." *Sociology and Social Research* 62, 2 (Jan.): 267–78.

———. 1996. "Language: Diversity and Assimilation." In Roger Waldinger and Mehdi Bozorgmehr, eds., *Ethnic Los Angeles,* pp. 139–64. New York: Russell Sage Foundation.

Pearson, David. 2001. *The Politics of Ethnicity in Settler Societies: States of Unease.* New York: Palgrave.

Portes, Alejandro, and Lingxin Hao. 1998. "*E Pluribus Unum:* Bilingualism and Loss of Language in the Second Generation." *Sociology of Education* 71: 269–94.

Portes, Alejandro, and Rubén Rumbaut. 2001. *Legacies: The Story of the Immigrant Second Generation.* Berkeley: University of California Press.

Veltman, Calvin. 1983. *Language Shift in the United States.* Berlin: Mouton.

Yarborough, Ralph. 1992. "Introducing the Bilingual Act." In James Crawford, ed., *Language Loyalties: A Source Book on the Official English Controversy,* pp. 322–25. Chicago: University of Chicago Press.

Education

Carola Suárez-Orozco and Marcelo Suárez-Orozco

Immigrants entering the educational system are extraordinarily diverse, and their experiences resist facile generalizations. New immigrants add new threads of cultural, linguistic, and racial difference to the American tapestry of diversity. Some are the children of highly educated professional parents, while others have parents who are illiterate, low-skilled, and struggling in the lowest-paid sectors of the service economy. Some have received schooling in exemplary educational systems, while others arrive from educational systems that are in shambles. Some families are escaping political, religious, or ethnic persecution; others are motivated by the promise of better jobs and the hope for better educational opportunities. Some are documented migrants, while others are in a documentation limbo. Some come with the intention to settle permanently, while others engage in transnational strategies, living both "here" and "there." Some arrive in well-established immigrant-receiving communities with dense informational and tutoring networks that ease the entry of immigrant youth into the new educational system, while others move from one migrant setting to another, forcing students to change schools frequently. The educational experiences of immigrant youth thus vary substantially, depending on their specific constellation of resources and their context of reception.

How immigrant youth fare academically has long-term implications for their future well-being. While at the start of the 20th century there were occupational avenues that allowed social mobility for migrants who had little formal education, the new economy is largely unforgiving to those who do not achieve postsecondary education and beyond. Immigrants who are poorly schooled or unskilled will encounter daunting odds in today's globalizing economy. Many will be facing a life below the poverty line, on the lower rungs of the service sector of the economy. Today more than ever, schooling processes and outcomes are a powerful barometer of current as well as future psychosocial functioning.

Immigrants defy easy generalizations in terms of educational outcomes. Some outperform their native-born peers. Children of immigrants are often the valedictorians of their high schools, and they tend to be overrepresented among the recipients of prestigious scholarly awards. Others demonstrate persistent school-related problems and high dropout rates. These immigrants tend to be "overlooked and underserved," particularly when they enter U.S. schools at the secondary level (Urban Institute, 2001). Findings from a number of recent studies suggest that while some are successfully navigating the American educational system, large numbers struggle academically, leaving school without acquiring the tools that will enable them to function in the highly competitive knowledge-intensive economy.

In addition to a pattern of variability of performance among diverse immigrant groups, a counterintuitive trend is emerging in data from a variety of disciplines. These studies have shown that newly arrived students from Latin America, the Caribbean, and Asia display highly adaptive attitudes and behaviors to succeed in school, yet the longer immigrant youth are in the U.S., the more negative they become in terms of school attitudes and adaptations. Rumbaut and Portes surveyed more than 5,000 high school students, comparing grade point averages (GPAs) and aspirations of first- and second-generation students. They found that length of residence in the U.S. was associated with declining academic achievement and aspirations. Research by Steinberg, Brown, and Dornbusch based on a national study of over 20,000 adolescents uncovered a similar trend of adverse academic and health trajectories across generations.

Most of the studies suggesting such declines over time have relied on cross-sectional (cross-generational) data. Data from the Longitudinal Immigrant Student Adaptation (LISA) study we codirected (1997–2003) assessed the academic performance and engagement of recently arrived immigrant youth and then examined changes over time. Quite strikingly, the grade point average of students coming from Mexico, Central America, the Dominican Republic, and Haiti all declined in a statistically significant manner (while a similar trend emerged for students of Chinese origin, the decline did not reach significance). The GPA of immigrant boys declined significantly more than that of girls for all groups. For both girls and boys, grades in the first two years were considerably higher than grades in the last three years. During the second year the GPAs of both girls and boys peaked, and from the third year on, both girls and boys experienced a steady decrease in GPA. We found that girls consistently had statistically significant higher GPAs than boys throughout the five-year period.

These data and others suggest that the new immigrant experience may complicate past patterns of unilinear assimilation, which indicate that over time and across generations, immigrants tended to do substantially better, eventually reaching parity with the mainstream population. Exposure to certain aspects of American socioeconomic structure and culture today appear to be negatively associated with academic attitudes as well as with the physical and psychological well-being of immigrant youngsters. How can we account for this?

The verdict is still out, but a number of factors are surely at play. First, the new economy is such that the "shop-floor mobility" of the factory era is no longer an option for most working-class immigrants; our hourglass economy limits opportunity for those with low levels of education and skills. Second, the optimism and resilience of many immigrants may erode over time as they encounter structural obstacles—segregation, poor schools, neighborhood violence, limited opportunities for status mobility—to their dreams. Third, both psychological and sociological evidence suggests that immigrant youth may indeed be assimilating but to somewhat dystopic American adolescent norms, which include negative attitudes toward schools and increased engagement in risky behaviors. Fourth, because the majority of young people of immigrant origin are "racially marked," the option of "passing" over the course of generations is no longer likely. Further, exposure to discrimination, disparagement, and being cast into low-status jobs across generations is corrosive to well-being and drive.

Here we will explore the factors implicated in the variability in educational performance and social adaptation of immigrant children by examining interdisciplinary contributions to this topic of growing importance.

Generational Patterns

It is important to distinguish generational differences in people of immigrant origin, as patterns of educational outcomes vary significantly according to generation and country of origin. Newcomers—often referred to as the first generation—are born abroad, spend their childhoods there, and receive the foundations of their education in their birthplace. The 1.5 generation is born abroad but arrives in the new homeland before age 13, so its members are exposed to U.S. schools and culture during their formative years. The second generation is born in the U.S. of foreign-born parents. All share immigrant parents and the repercussions of immigration within their families. In general, the first generation has the advantage of immigrant optimism and the ability to take a dual frame of reference in comparing their current circumstances with those in their homeland. The second generation has the advantage of full citizenship and a consistent exposure to English, facilitating both unaccented speech and curricular access.

Foreign-born nationals—the first generation who arrive as adults after their mid-twenties—generally come with their educational attainments in hand. There is considerable variation in educational attainment by country of origin; some arrive with backgrounds similar to those of the average U.S. citizen, others far exceed U.S. norms, and still others trail significantly behind (see Table 1). These adults generally come to work and are unlikely to encounter the educational system unless they go on to graduate school or take English as a Second Language courses.

Immigrants arriving before adulthood present quite a different challenge. Many enter the educational system at various points in their development, with an array

Table 1 Educational attainment of principal foreign nationalities in 2000

Country of birth	Total population	Percentage college graduates[a]	Percentage high school graduates[a]	Percentage immigrate 1990–2000
Total native-born[b]	250,288,425	24.4	83.3	
Total foreign-born[b]	31,133,481	24.1	61.8	42.4
Above U.S. average				
India	1,027,144	69.1	88.2	54.9
Iran	285,176	50.6	86.4	26.6
Former Soviet Union	618,302	47.3	84.0	69.7
Philippines	1,374,213	45.7	86.8	35.4
Korea	870,542	42.9	86.1	37.4
China	997,301	41.6	68.4	48.8
Near U.S. average				
United Kingdom	567,240	36.6	90.2	27.8
Canada	820,713	33.6	82.5	29.9
Poland	472,544	22.1	73.1	36.7
Colombia	515,206	21.8	72.0	45.1
Vietnam	991,995	19.2	61.6	44.7
Cuba	870,203	18.7	59.0	26.6
Jamaica	554,897	17.8	72.1	31.4
Below U.S. average				
Haiti	422,841	13.7	62.3	39.7
Dominican Republic	685,952	9.5	48.1	42.7
El Salvador	815,570	5.0	34.7	40.4
Mexico	9,163,463	4.2	29.7	48.6

Source: Adapted from Alejandro Portes and Rubén Rumbaut, *Immigrant America: A Portrait,* 3d ed. (Berkeley: University of California Press, 2006), chap. 4. Original data comes from the U.S. Census Bureau, 2000 Census, authors' own 5% Public Use Microdata Sample, weighted data.

a. Persons aged 25 and older.

b. In this table, children born abroad to American parents are counted as native-born, not foreign-born.

of educational backgrounds. Some arrive with strong educational foundations (often stronger than those of their U.S.-born peers with similar levels of academic attainment) from their native land; as they enter American schools, their primary challenge is to acquire English skills concurrently with the academic credits required for graduation and college preparation. Others have repeated grades or have had interrupted schooling and are hence over-aged for their grade level; these youth not only need to play catch-up academically but also need to acquire academic English-language proficiency. This process is often a slow and frustrating one and all too often leads to barely gaining the necessary credits for high school graduation or to dropping out. Yet another group of young people—particularly those who migrate in adolescence with limited educational skills—arrive in the U.S. largely with the intention of working; while they may halfheartedly intend to pursue an educa-

Table 2   College graduates and high school dropouts among young adults aged 25–39, by immigrant generation and national origin, 1998–2002 (percentages)

	College graduate[a]			Not high school graduate[a]		
	First generation (foreign-born) age at arrival		Second generation	First generation (foreign-born) age at arrival		Second generation
National origin	13 or older	12 or younger	(U.S.-born)[b]	13 or older	12 or younger	(U.S.-born)[b]
Total U.S. immigrant origin[c]	26	29	34	34	18	9
Above U.S. average						
India	80	78	79	4	2	3
Iran	61	62	83	2	<1	2
China[d]	61	67	76	9	<1	2
Korea	51	59	66	2	1	5
Great Britain, Canada	54	43	36	7	8	5
Philippines	46	37	33	6	3	3
Near U.S. average						
Cuba	17	26	43	18	7	5
Jamaica, other West Indies	21	37	42	15	7	4
Colombia, Ecuador, Peru	23	29	33	19	13	5
Vietnam	16	39	55	25	8	7
Haiti	15	30	48	31	8	<1
Below U.S. average						
Puerto Rico[e]	20	11	13	30	29	22
Dominican Republic	11	11	25	41	24	8
El Salvador, Guatemala	4	10	21	61	33	12
Mexico	4	7	13	66	42	20
All other national origins	41	35	44	14	8	4

Source: Merged Current Population Survey (CPS) annual demographic files (March), 1998 through 2002. Adapted from Rubén G. Rumbaut, Min Zhou, Charlie V. Morgan, and Golnaz Komaie, "A Tale of Two Immigrant Metropolises: Ethnicity, Generation, and Social Mobility in Los Angeles and New York," in Susan K. Brown, Frank D. Bean, and Rubén G. Rumbaut, eds., *The Immigrant Metropolis: The Dynamics of Intergenerational Mobility in Los Angeles and New York* (New York: Russell Sage Foundation, forthcoming).

a. Educational attainment for persons 25–39 years old.

b. Second-generation estimates are calculated from CPS parental nativity data, adjusting for 2000 Census population counts.

c. Includes all foreign-born persons (first generation) and all U.S.-born persons with at least one foreign-born parent (second generation).

d. Including Hong Kong and Taiwan.

e. Island-born Puerto Ricans, who are U.S. citizens by birth and not immigrants, are classified as "foreign-born" for purposes of this table; mainland-born Puerto Ricans with island-born parents are classified as "second generation (U.S.-born)."

tion concurrently, they often quickly drop out after "dropping in" to school and finding the settings unprepared to meet the educational challenges they present. (We see this pattern clearly when examining the performance of Mexican youth attending New York City public schools. Of those who arrive before elementary school, 47 percent graduate, while 30 percent who arrive before ninth grade graduate and an abysmal 17 percent who arrive after ninth grade graduate.)

It is interesting to compare the academic outcomes of young adults by country of origin and generation of arrival (see Table 2). In Table 1 we see the academic patterns of immigrants educated abroad who arrived as adults, and in Table 2 we see the patterns for youth from the first, 1.5, and second generations who were exposed to U.S. schools. It is interesting to note the close country-of-origin parallels in the two charts. Parents with more education are better equipped to teach their children how to study, access data and information, develop arguments, and structure essays, and can provide necessary resources, including additional books, a home computer, and tutors. In contrast, youngsters whose parents have little or no formal educational experience are often unable to manage these academic tasks.

When we compare the first, 1.5, and second generations for the countries of origin with levels of educational attainment similar to the U.S. average, we find that the second generation tends to do better than the 1.5 generation (arriving before age 13), which in turn tends to do better than the first (arriving after age 13). These differences probably reflect the linguistic advantage of consistent exposure to English, which provides an academic edge. We see a similar advantage among the groups above the U.S. average, with the exception of those arriving from Great Britain, Canada, and the Philippines—all countries with English-language educational systems. In these cases, the first generation reached the highest levels of attainment (reflecting, perhaps, a linguistic advantage combined with immigrant optimism and drive). For the groups who academically underperform when compared to their U.S.-born peers, the disadvantage of arriving after age 13 is clear, as they are far less likely to complete high school or go on to college than the second generation.

Structuring Opportunity

These tables indicate the range of educational backgrounds and trajectories that immigrants tend to experience. While parental education and newcomer students' educational experiences in the home country clearly contribute to patterns of academic performance in the U.S., other factors also influence academic performance.

Poverty. Although some young immigrants come from privileged backgrounds, large numbers of immigrant youth today, especially those originating in Latin America and the Caribbean, must face the challenges associated with poverty. Immigrant children are more than four times as likely as native-born children to live in crowded housing conditions and three times as likely to be uninsured. Poverty has long been recognized as a significant risk factor for educational access. Poverty tends to limit opportunities, and it frequently coexists with a variety of other factors that augment risks, such as single parenthood, residence in violent neighborhoods saturated with gang activity and drug trade, and schools that are segregated, overcrowded, and understaffed. Children raised in circumstances of poverty are also more vulnerable to an array of psychological distresses, including difficulties concentrating and sleeping, anxiety, and depression, as well as a heightened exposure to delinquency and violence—all of which have implications for educational outcomes.

Segregated neighborhoods and schools. Where immigrant families settle strongly shapes the immigrant journey and the experiences and adaptations of children. Latino immigrants in particular tend to settle in deeply segregated and impoverished urban settings—indeed, Latino youth are now the most segregated students in American schools. In such neighborhoods, which offer few opportunities in the formal economy, informal and underground activities tend to flourish. Immigrants of color who settle in predominantly minority neighborhoods will have virtually no direct, systematic, and intimate contact with middle-class white Americans, which in turn affects a host of experiences, including cultural and linguistic isolation from the mainstream.

Segregated and poor neighborhoods are more likely to have dysfunctional schools characterized by an ever-present fear of violence, distrust, low expectations, and institutional anomie. These schools typically have limited and outdated resources and offer an inferior education. Buildings are poorly maintained, and as a rule classrooms are overcrowded. Textbooks and curricula are outdated; computers are few and obsolete. Many of the teachers may not have credentials in the subjects they teach. Clearly defined tracks sentence immigrant students to noncollege destinations. Lacking English skills, many immigrant students are enrolled in the least demanding and competitive classes, which eventually exclude them from courses needed for college. Such settings undermine students' ability to sustain motivation and academic engagement.

Undocumented status. LISA data suggest that undocumented students often arrive in the U.S. after multiple family separations and traumatic border crossings. Once settled, they may continue to experience fear and anxiety about being apprehended, being separated from their parents again, and being deported. Such psychological and emotional duress can take their toll on the academic experiences of undocumented youth. Undocumented students with dreams of graduating from high school and going on to college will find that their legal status stands in the way of their access to postsecondary education.

Seasonal migration. Data suggest that approximately 600,000 children travel with their migrant parents in the U.S. each year. Young people in seasonal migrant families face particular challenges. They experience multiple moves, frequent interruptions in schooling, and harsh working and living conditions. Migrant children are the least likely to be enrolled in school. The lack of continuity in schooling (because of interruptions during the school year, the difficulty of transferring school records, health problems, and lack of English-language skills) contributes to their low attendance and to their high dropout rate (the dropout rate after sixth grade among these children is twice the national average, and typically these students reach only the eighth grade).

English-language acquisition. Most immigrant youth are second-language learners. English-language difficulties present particular challenges for optimal performance in the current context of high-stakes tests. Performance on tests such as the TAAS in Texas, the Regents Exam in New York, and the MCAS in Massachusetts has implications for college access. SATs are also a challenge and serve to limit entry into the more competitive colleges. Second-language acquisition issues can mask actual skills and knowledge, particularly around vocabulary and on subtle "trick" questions using double negatives in multiple-choice tests. Even when immigrant students are able to enter college while they are still refining their language skills, they may miss subtleties in lectures and discussions. They may read more slowly than native speakers and have difficulty expressing more complex thoughts on written assignments. This is likely to bring down their grades, in turn affecting access to graduate or professional schools.

Access to higher education. Many immigrants who complete high school graduate without the necessary credentials to be accepted into college. They are less likely than their native-born counterparts to have taken advanced science and mathematics courses. Among those who perform well academically, immigrants of Latino origin are least likely to have taken the SAT or to receive high scores on the test; they are also least likely to apply to college. Even when students of immigrant origin have the necessary academic credentials to enter college, many encounter strong socioeconomic and structural barriers that jeopardize their college attendance. They tend to be awarded less financial aid and are more likely to attend community college than four-year college, to study part-time rather than full-time, and to work rather than to take out student loans. These factors limit their ability to earn a bachelor's degree, and many of them leave college before completing their degree. Although college enrollment rates for high school graduates in the past decades have risen for both white and black students, there has been no consistent growth for Latino students, two thirds of whom are of immigrant origin. They are also less represented in graduate school than all other racial and/or ethnic groups and are less likely to receive financial aid to support their graduate studies.

Academic Engagement

While some immigrant youth thrive in American schools, many others face a myriad of structural obstacles that truncate their academic trajectories. There is no doubt that such obstacles play a critical role in academic outcomes. Focusing exclusively on such structural issues, however, overlooks the crucial role of agency in the schooling experience.

In order to perform optimally on the educational journey, a student must be engaged in learning. When a student is engaged, she is both intellectually and behaviorally involved in her schooling. She ponders the materials presented, participates in discussions, completes assignments with attention and effort, and applies newfound knowledge to different contexts. Conversely, when academically disengaged, a student is bored, learns suboptimally, and tends to receive lower grades than he is capable of. In its most extreme form, academic disengagement leads to a pattern of multiple failures. In such cases, the student has stopped engaging in his schooling—he is habitually truant, rarely completes assignments, and shows little or no interest in the materials presented.

We claim that academic engagement has three discrete dimensions—cognitive, behavioral, and relational. Cognitive engagement refers to the student's intellectual or cognitive involvement with schoolwork. This dimension includes both intellectual curiosity about new ideas and domains of learning and the pleasure that is derived from the process of mastering new materials. Behavioral engagement refers to the degree to which the student actually exhibits the behaviors necessary to do well in school—attending classes, participating in class, and completing assignments. Relational engagement is the degree to which the student reports meaningful and supportive relationships in school, with adults as well as peers. These relationships can serve both emotional and tangible functions. Cognitive and behavioral engagements are viewed as the manifestations of engagement, while relational engagement is viewed as the mediator of these engagements. Relational supports can serve to mediate the effects of family and contextual risks on individual attributes.

LISA data suggest that patterns of academic engagement have implications for academic outcomes among immigrant youth, with relational engagement playing an important role in their academic trajectories. Academic engagement is a particularly important dimension of schooling, as it would appear to be malleable and hence a promising level for intervention.

Social Disparagement, Identity, and Academic Outcomes

Young immigrants who are subject to negative expectations will suffer in their academic performance. Cross-cultural data on a variety of socially disparaged immigrant minorities in a number of contexts suggest that social disparagement adversely affects academic engagement. The evidence indicates that the social context of reception plays an important role in immigrant adaptation. The work of George De Vos on immigrant minorities in various settings—Europe, Japan, and the U.S.—and the work of John Ogbu among native and immigrant minorities in the U.S. and elsewhere suggest that long-term, cross-generational patterns of structural inequality and social disparagement may generate cultural models, social practices, and psychological responses that keep some individuals from minority backgrounds from investing in schooling as a strategy for status mobility.

In cases where racial and ethnic inequalities are highly structured, such as for Algerians in France, Moroccans in Belgium, Koreans in Japan, and Mexicans in California, social disparagement often permeates the experience of many minority youth. Members of these groups are not only effectively locked out of the opportunity structure (through segregated and inferior schools and work opportunities in the least desirable sectors of the economy) but also commonly become the objects of stereotypes of inferiority, sloth, and inclinations toward violence, gang activities, and, in Europe, terrorism (the second-generation children of Muslim immigrants in Europe experience intense prejudice in the aftermath of the "homegrown" terrorist attacks in London and the earlier attacks in Madrid and Holland). Facing such charged attitudes, socially disparaged youth may come to experience the institutions of the dominant society—and specifically its schools—as alien terrain that reproduces an order of inequality. While nearly all immigrant and racial minority groups face structural obstacles, not all groups elicit and experience the same attitudes of social disparagement across generations. Furthermore, some immigrant groups elicit more negative attitudes—encountering a more negative social mirror—than others do. In U.S. public opinion polls, for example, Asians are seen more favorably and Afro-Caribbeans and Latinos more negatively.

Race and color continue to matter in American society. Mary Waters's data reveal that West Indian immigrants are shocked by the level of racism against blacks in the U.S. Though they arrive expecting structural obstacles such as discrimination in housing and job promotions, they find the intensity of both overt and covert racial prejudice and discrimination particularly distressing. Yet these black immigrants tend to share a number of characteristics that are protective and that contribute to their relative success in the new setting. Their children, however, after encountering sustained experiences of social disparagement, racism, and limited economic opportunity, begin to respond in cultural ways similar to those of African Americans, who have faced generations of exclusion and discrimination.

While cross-sectional data have been used to identify this transgenerational pattern, data from the LISA study suggest that a process of racialization that further excludes many immigrant youth from academic pursuits is unfolding at a rapid pace within a few years of migration. How is identity implicated in these rapid shifts?

Immigrant identities. Some youth develop and maintain a coethnic immigrant identity. They do so because they have limited opportunity to make meaningful contact with other groups in the new society, or in response to an understanding that other groups, such as native minorities, are even more socially disparaged than they are as immigrants. Caribbean immigrants may distinguish themselves from African Americans in an attempt to ward off social disparagement and symbolic violence and to seek better opportunities.

Other young immigrants may develop an adversarial stance, constructing identities around rejecting—after having been rejected by—the institutions of the dominant culture. These children of immigrants are responding in similar ways to those of other marginalized youth, such as many inner-city, poor African Americans and Puerto Ricans, Koreans in Japan, Algerians in France, and Moroccans in Belgium and the Netherlands. If we look back to previous waves of immigration, many disparaged and disenfranchised second-generation Italian American, Irish American, and Polish American adolescents demonstrated a similar dynamic, including the development of elaborate delinquency-oriented gangs.

Like other disenfranchised youth, children of immigrants who develop adversarial identities tend to encounter problems in school, drop out, and consequently face unemployment in the formal economy. Among those engaged in adversarial styles, speaking the mainstream language of the culture and doing well in school may be interpreted as a show of hauteur and a wish to "act white." When immigrant adolescents acquire cultural models and social practices that view doing well in school as an act of ethnic betrayal, it becomes problematic for them to develop the behavioral and attitudinal repertoire necessary to succeed in school.

The children of immigrants who are not able to embrace their own culture and who have formulated their identities around rejecting aspects of the mainstream society may be drawn to gangs. In the absence of productive academic engagement and meaningful economic opportunities, gang membership can provide a sense of identity and cohesion for marginal youth during a turbulent stage of development. When combined with gang orientation, adversarial identities severely compromise the future opportunities of youth of immigrant origin, who are already at risk of school failure because of poverty, segregation, and discrimination. Such young people face increased odds of imprisonment: roughly half of all youth under the supervision of the California Youth Authority (for homicide, robbery, assault, burglary, theft, rape, drugs, arson, kidnapping, and extortion) come from immigrant-origin Latino homes; the delinquency rate among the youth of Korean origin in Japan is four times the rate among the majority Japanese; and approximately half of the French and Dutch prison populations are of immigrant origin.

Ethnic flight. The children of immigrant origin who shed their cultures structure their identities most strongly by identifying with the dominant mainstream culture. These youth may feel most comfortable spending time with friends from the mainstream culture rather than with their less acculturated peers. For them, learning to speak standard English not only serves an instrumental function of communicating; it also becomes an important symbolic act of identifying with the majority culture. Among these young people, success in school may be seen not only as a route for individual self-advancement but also as a way to move away from the world of the family and the ethnic group, symbolically and psychologically. The rapid abandonment of the home culture implied in ethnic flight often results in the collapse of the parental voice of authority. Furthermore, lack of group connectedness can result in feelings of anomie and alienation.

Identification with the mainstream culture may result in weakening of ties to coethnics. These young people may be alienated from their less acculturated peers; they may have little in common with them or even feel that they are somewhat superior. While they may gain entry into privileged positions within mainstream culture, they will still have to deal with issues of marginalization and exclusion. They may find their peer group unforgiving of any behaviors that could be interpreted as ethnic betrayal. It is not necessary for the child of an immigrant to consciously decide to distance himself from his culture.

While there are gains for the immigrant youth who manage to "disappear" into the mainstream culture, there are also hidden costs—primarily in terms of unresolved shame, doubt, and even self-hatred. In earlier waves of European immigration, "passing" was a common style of adaptation among those who phenotypically resembled the mainstream. Passing is not easily available to today's immigrants of color, who mostly come from Latin America, the Caribbean, and Asia and who look visibly like "the Other."

Transcultural identities. In between the coethnic and ethnic-flight gravitational fields we find the large majority of children of immigrants. The task of immigration for these children is the crafting of a transcultural identity. These youth creatively fuse aspects of two or more cultures—the parental tradition and the new culture or cultures. In so doing, they synthesize an identity that does not require them to choose between cultures; rather, they are able to develop an identity that incorporates traits of both cultures while fusing new elements.

Among these young people, the culturally constructed social strictures and patterns of social control of their immigrant parents and elders maintain a degree of legitimacy. Learning standard English and doing well in school are viewed as competencies that do not compromise but enhance their sense of who they are. These people network with similar ease among members of their own ethnic group and with students, teachers, employers, colleagues, and friends of other backgrounds. A number of studies suggest that immigrant youth who manage to forge transcultural identities tend to be more successful in school.

Many who "make it" perceive and appreciate the sacrifices loved ones have made to enable them to thrive in a new country. Rather than wishing to distance themselves from their group, these youth come to experience success as a way to give back to their parents, siblings, peers, and less fortunate members of the community. Transcultural identities adaptively blend the preservation of the affective ties of the home culture with the instrumental skills required to cope successfully in the mainstream culture. They are most adaptive in this era of globalism and multiculturalism, serving both the individual and society at large. By acquiring competencies that enable them to operate within more than one cultural code, these young people are often effective cultural interpreters and bridge-builders between disparate groups.

Social Contexts of Learning

Companionship, a basic human need, serves to maintain and enhance self-esteem and provides acceptance, approval, and a sense of belonging. Instrumental social supports provide individuals and their families with tangible aid (such as baby-sitting, running an errand, or making a loan) as well as guidance and advice (including information and job and housing leads). These supports are particularly critical for disoriented immigrant newcomers. Indeed, LISA data suggest that relational engagement plays a critical role in moderating negative influences such as school violence and low self-esteem.

Affiliative motivations. For many immigrants, social relations are extremely important in initiating and sustaining motivations. While for mainstream white American students achievement is often motivated by an attempt to gain independence from the family, immigrant students are typically highly motivated to achieve *for* their families. Further, we have found that Latino students (more than Asian and Caribbean students) perceive that receiving the help of others is critical to their success.

The family. Family cohesion and the maintenance of a well-functioning system of supervision, authority, and mutuality are perhaps the most powerful factors in shaping the well-being and future outcomes of all children. For immigrant families, extended family members—grandparents, godparents, aunts, uncles, and cousins—are critical sources of tangible instrumental and emotional support. Immigrant parents (particularly those who work long hours and have limited schooling), however, are often unable to support their children tangibly in ways that are congruent with American cultural models and expectations. Further, in sharp contrast to U.S. expectations of parental involvement, many come from traditions that revere school authorities and expect parents not to advocate or meddle.

Communities and community organizations. Family cohesion and functioning are enhanced when the family is part of a larger community displaying effective forms of what Felton Earls has termed "community agency." Culturally constituted patterns of community cohesion and supervision can immunize immigrant youth from the more toxic elements of their new settings. Children who live in cohesive communities where adults can monitor their activities are less likely to be involved with gangs and delinquency and are more focused on their academic pursuits.

Youth-serving organizations, much like ethnic-owned businesses and family networks, can enrich immigrant communities and foster healthy development among their young people by providing support to parents and families. Such urban sanctuaries, often affiliated with neighborhood churches or schools, provide youth with supervised out-of-school safe havens or "second home" settings. Staff can serve as culture brokers, bridging the disparate norms in place in children's homes and in school.

Mentoring relationships. In nearly every story of an immigrant youth's success there is a caring adult who took an interest in the child and became actively engaged in her life. Protective relationships with nonparent adults can provide these young people with compensatory attachments, safe contexts for learning new cultural norms and practices, and information that is vital to success in schools. Mentoring relationships may have special relevance for immigrant youth who have been separated from loved ones during the course of migration, with the attendant ruptures in significant attachments. Since immigrant parents and other adult relatives may be unavailable owing to long work hours or emotional distress, a mentor can engender new significant attachments, filling the void created by parental absence. Transcultural mentors of the same ethnic background can model the ways in which elements of ethnic identity can be preserved and celebrated as features of the receiving culture are incorporated into the young people's lives.

Peer relationships. Peers can also provide important emotional support that aids the development of significant psychosocial competencies in youth. By valuing (or devaluing) certain academic outcomes and by modeling specific academic behaviors, peers establish the norms of academic engagement. They may further support academic engagement by helping each other with coursework, exchanging ideas, and sharing college preparatory information. Because large numbers of young immigrants attend highly segregated poor schools, they may have limited access to school-savvy networks of peers.

Taken together, these networks of relationships can make a significant difference in educational outcomes. They can serve to help immigrant youth develop healthy identities and become motivated, and they can provide specific information about how to navigate schooling successfully.

Young people of immigrant origin are the fastest-growing sector of the student population in many advanced postindustrial democracies. The preponderance of evidence suggests that they arrive sharing an optimism and hope in the future that must be cultivated and treasured; almost universally they recognize that schooling is the key to a better tomorrow. Tragically, over time, however, many immigrant youth, especially those enrolling in impoverished and deeply segregated schools, face negative odds and uncertain prospects. Too many leave our schools without developing and mastering the kinds of higher-order cognitive skills and cultural sensibilities needed in today's global economy and society. The future of our country will in no small measure be tied to the constructive harnessing of the energies of these new young Americans.

Bibliography

Bailey, B. H. 2001. "Dominican-American Ethnic/Racial Identities and United States Social Categories." *International Migration Review* 35, 3: 677–708.

Fuligini, A. 1997. "The Academic Achievement of Adolescents from Immigrant Families: The Roles of Family Background, Attitudes, and Behavior." *Child Development* 69, 2: 351–63.

Harvard Educational Review 71, 3 (2001). Special Volume: *Immigration and Education.*

Hernández, D., and E. Charney, eds. 1998. *From Generation to Generation: The Health and Well-Being of Children of Immigrant Families.* Washington, D.C.: National Academy Press.

Kao, G., and M. Tienda. 1995. "Optimism and Achievement: The Educational Performance of Immigrant Youth." *Social Science Quarterly* 76, 1: 1–19.

Olsen, L. 1997. *Made in America: Immigrant Students in Our Public Schools.* New York: New Press.

Ruiz-de-Velasco, J., M. Fix, and W. B. C. Clewell. 2000. *Overlooked and Underserved: Immigrant Students in U.S. Secondary Schools.* Washington, D.C.: Urban Institute.

Rumbaut, R. 2004. "Ages, Life Stages, and Generational Cohorts: Decomposing the Immigrant First and Second Generations in the United States." *International Migration Review* 38, 3: 1160–1205.

Suárez-Orozco, C., and M. Suárez-Orozco. 1995. *Transformations: Immigration, Family Life, and Achievement Motivation among Latino Adolescents.* Stanford, Calif.: Stanford University Press.

———. 2001. *Children of Immigration.* Cambridge, Mass.: Harvard University Press.

Suárez-Orozco, M., C. Suárez-Orozco, and D. Qin-Hilliard, eds. 2001. *The New Immigrant and American Schools.* Interdisciplinary Perspectives on the New Immigration, Vol. 5. New York: Routledge.

Gender and Family

Patricia R. Pessar

There is a danger in composing a piece on gender and families within the migration process. In pairing these two entities, we risk repeating the fallacy that gender is somehow contained within the "private" spheres of kinship and household units. This is certainly not my intention. Rather, this article examines migration as a gendered process. It is true that some of the earliest and finest work on gender and migration did focus on kinship and domestic groups. More recent scholarship, however, has built upon this pioneering work while turning to the gendered aspects of the global economy, labor recruitments, war and refugee displacement, and nation-building, among other important topics.

The decision to include the analytical units of gender, households, and families in migration studies emerged out of a growing consensus about the inadequacy of theories and research methods that privileged either individual migrants (usually understood to be male or genderless) or global structures and forces, such as the world system and capital accumulation. The inclusion of such mediating units as gender and families helped researchers better account for the causes, consequences, and processes of international migration.

Conceptual Grounding: Gender, Households, and Families

Gender is a human invention that organizes our behavior and thought. Far greater than a set of status structures or roles, it is an ongoing process that is experienced through an array of social institutions, from the family to the state and global economy. People do "gender work," using practices and discourses to negotiate relationships, notions of "masculinity" and "femininity," and conflicting interests. Thinking of gender as a process gives us a praxis-oriented perspective wherein gender identities, relations, and ideologies are fluid, not fixed. Nonetheless, by recognizing that gender becomes embedded in institutions, we must also analyze the structural factors that condition gender relations and practices. People are socialized to view gendered distinctions, such as "women's" and "men's" work, as natural, inevitable, and immutable. Thinking of gender as a process, as one of several ways in which humans create and perpetuate social differences, helps to deconstruct the myth of gender as a product of nature while underscoring its power dimension. Major aspects of life—including sexuality, family, education, economy, migration, and the state—are organized according to gender principles and embody conflicting interests and hierarchies of power and privilege. Of course, gender is not the only axis that power and privilege revolve around. Differentiation based on race, ethnicity, class, nationality, and sexual preference also assumes a role, often in conjunction with gender.

Households are small-scale forms of social organization supporting the survival of their members through socialization, labor allocation, income generation, and budgeting. These household activities occur across time, and in the case of immigrants and migrants, range across countries and continents. The actions of household members may be guided as often by norms of solidarity as by hierarchies of power along gender and generational lines. Although households are microeconomic enterprises, they are linked to other domestic units and are always conditioned by larger economic, political, and cultural forces. For our purposes, family is understood to be that broader social network in which households are embedded. Membership is governed by ideologies of descent and belonging wherein people related by blood and marriage as well as "fictive" members (e.g., *compadres*) are assembled. Both households and families are key units in the organization and management of migration. They also confront and channel its diverse impacts.

From Male-Centered to Gendered Scholarship

For most of the 20th century, scholars assumed that immigrants were somehow genderless or that men's experiences could be generalized to women as well. The epistemological roots of this stance are varied yet mutually reinforcing. First, many migration scholars were influenced by modernization theory, which held that those individuals with the ability to assume the role of "Western man" headed off to cities where the benefits of modern life could be attained. Males were allegedly more apt to be risk-takers and achievers, while women were viewed as guardians of community tradition and stability. Second, migration research suffered from a more general tendency to disregard women's contributions to economic, political, and social life. Not surprisingly, then, much work in the social sciences and history either assumed that only male immigrants' lives were worthy of official documentation and scrutiny or that the experiences of male migrants were gender-neutral, thus making it unnecessary to treat women at all, except perhaps in a few pages on the family.

Third, migration studies contributed to the larger analysis of U.S. state formation. This function is reflected in the title of Oscar Handlin's famous study of U.S. immigration history, *The Uprooted: The Epic Story of the Great Migrations That Made the American People.* Within the larger universe in which migration scholarship operated, males once again were featured, this time as political actors who would soon become U.S. citizens.

It was not until the 1970s that feminist theory began to affect migration studies. This scholarship progressed through a series of stages common to the broader engagement between feminism and the social sciences. Initially researchers sought to fill in major gaps resulting from decades of research based almost exclusively on male immigrants. In their rush to fill this breach, the more empirically-minded scholars tended to treat gender as a mere variable rather than as a central theoretical concept. Thus, studies of the impact of wages on emigration controlled for gender, among other relevant variables, on the erroneous assumption that the way in which human capital is translated into wages is the same for women and men. This stance also begged larger issues, such as the way in which local and external markets utilize gender to segment the workforce, thus creating different incentives for the relocation of men and women. It also overlooked the existence of patriarchal kinship and gender ideologies that constrain women from migrating regardless of the expected financial gains from relocation.

Once feminist theory gained a firmer foothold in migration studies, its proponents sought to correct such inaccuracies and elisions. Initially their work proceeded under the rubric of women and migration, but it soon expanded to address broader matters of gender and migration. Thanks to this pathbreaking scholarship, we now appreciate how gender ideologies and structures constitute the social, economic, and cultural constellations that structure migration and condition its outcomes.

A case in point is economic restructuring and labor-market segmentation. Export-led production in Third World countries carries different implications for female and male workers, although in both instances it induces migration. Offshore production promotes international migration by creating goods that compete with local commodities, by feminizing the workforce without providing equivalent factory-based employment for the large number of under- and unemployed males, and by socializing women for industrial work and modern consumption without providing needed job stability over the course of their working lives. For many decades the U.S. has attracted proportionally more female migrants than other labor-importing countries, and women constitute the majority among U.S. immigrants from Asia, Central and South America, the Caribbean, and Europe. This dominance reflects the growth of female-intensive industries in the U.S., particularly in service, health care, microelectronics, and apparel manufacturing. As feminized and racialized labor, immigrant women are more employable in these labor-intensive industries than their male counterparts. The sociologist Yen Le Espiritu attributes this to patriarchal and racist assumptions, which hold that women can afford to work for less, do not mind dead-end jobs, and are more suited physiologically to certain kinds of detailed and routine work.

While macrostructural transformations are understood to unleash migration pressures, it is households and families that respond to these pressures. To grasp fully who migrates, where, and for how long, we must appreciate how these social units are governed by hierarchical principles of gender and generation. To illustrate, when an unmarried Dominican woman urges her parents to allow her to emigrate alone to the U.S., the parents weigh the threat to the family's reputation posed by the daughter's sexual freedom and possible promiscuity against the very real economic benefits her emigration will bring. Similarly, in assessing the benefits of return migration, many Dominican immigrant women weigh anticipated personal losses against collective household gains. That is, the women measure the personal gains in gender parity that settlement and blue-collar employment in the U.S. have brought them against the expectation of status gains for the family yet probable "forced retirement" for them once they are back on the island.

Migration networks involve not only the provision of assistance to sojourners but also the reproduction of social roles, including those related to gender. Thus, in certain Mexican rural communities, norms of family honor and beliefs that women are inferior and require surveillance mitigate against the mobilization of family networks for women's migration. Yet when household incomes plummet, patriarchal norms must be weighed against the potential earnings of an immigrant wife or daughter. To resolve this dilemma, rural households depend on a limited number of effective network connections for aiding a female migrant, rather than the broader connections they would use for a male one. That is, responsibility for women's migration and settlement is rarely delegated to distant kin, friends, or a *coyote,* as it would be for a father or son, because these individuals cannot be confidently charged with the responsibilities of protection and control. In this way women's mobility is far more restricted than men's, as many women have to depend almost entirely on the existence and willing mobilization of close family migration networks—a migrant father or brother or, less commonly, a network of trusted female compatriots.

Recent work on the gendered boundaries of citizenship and belonging has also enriched migration and refugee studies. Studies of refugee law, for example, point to gross gender inequities in the U.S. and elsewhere in the conferring of refugee status. Rules of international law are purportedly abstract, objective, and gender-neutral. Feminist jurisprudence, however, has documented the ways in which the structures of international law-making and the content of its rules systematically privilege men while marginalizing women. Critics insist that a public/private distinction infuses the law, with the outcome of affording greater significance and privilege to public/"male" domains than to private/"female" ones. This practice has a chilling effect on women's asylum claims, since many assaults on their human rights, such as sexual abuse and forced marriage, occur within household and family settings—sites considered inappropriate for legal intervention.

Gendered research on citizenship and the state also reveals important differences between women and men with respect to modes of political inclusion and participation. As more labor-exporting countries have adopted policies of dual nationality and dual citizenship, men have benefited disproportionately. This is because states and immigrant hometown associations commonly assume that citizenship—including its transnational variant—is a male prerogative. Thus research has shown that while Mexican women's work generates funds for their hometown associations, which are remitted to support projects in communities of origin, these women tend to be excluded from leadership positions, owing in large part to the fact that Mexican state officials will collaborate only with male representatives. Immigrant males are more than willing to accept this proffering of gendered privilege, especially since the feminization of the U.S. welfare state tends to bring women greater opportunities for local-level political participation than men have. Apparently the exclusion of women from key arenas within transnational politics reinforces their resolve to pursue political rights and entitlements within U.S. institutions, since they view this country as more receptive to women's needs and struggles. This in turn has important consequences for men's and women's views about long-term or permanent settlement in the U.S. As research on Mexican immigrants documents, women often favor staying in the U.S., whereas men prefer to return to Mexico, where their status as both males and citizens is usually higher than it is in America.

Migration Studies and Feminist Theory

Scholarship on women, gender, and migration seeks not only to enrich migration studies but also to bring it to the service of women's and gender studies. Pioneering work on women and migration challenged those feminists who advanced essentialized notions of a universal female subject. By refusing to privilege gender over other, equally important structures like race, ethnicity, class, sexuality, and legal status, migration and refugee scholars have contributed to ongoing and lively debates over where and whether broad generalizations about female and male subjects are justified.

One point of contention involves women's well-being within the context of households. In the 1970s and 1980s, leading feminists viewed nuclear families as generally oppressive to women and championed women's wage labor as a means to escape this oppression. Immigration scholars, by contrast, reported that poor immigrant women of color valued their families and viewed their employment as an extension of their primary obligations as wives and mothers. Moreover, when working as domestic laborers in middle-class homes, immigrant women of color usually felt little, if any, sisterhood with their female employers, whose "liberation" was greatly facilitated by the availability of this vulnerable, low-paid, and racialized workforce. Nonetheless, immigrant women's struggles to maintain intact families and their refusal to privilege gender over all other forms of oppression were sometimes interpreted by more mainstream feminists as signs of an underdeveloped female consciousness. Yet when migration scholars brought matters of race, ethnicity, class, and legal status to bear when addressing immigrant women's domestic orientations and behaviors, another, more compelling interpretation of their relationship to families emerged.

Immigrant Households and Families as Bastions of Resistance

Households and families are the contexts in which immigrants live out much of their lives. Their members coordinate the migration process by determining who should emigrate and by mobilizing people and resources to ensure a successful departure and integration into the host society. Indeed, family members often sponsor their kin through the family unification provision of U.S. immigration legislation, and they subsequently provide such needed services as access to housing and employment. Despite the tremendous importance of families, however, many external forces buffet them. Although U.S. immigration policy favors family unification, the definition of "family" in immigration regulations fails to reflect the broader network of cooperating kin who constitute the practical and moral family for many immigrant populations. This lack of fit often forces immigrants to engage in costly and dangerous legal, extralegal (overstaying a tourist visa), and illegal (migration without documentation) strategies aimed at uniting families.

Legislation informed by racist and sexist discourse has in the past (and present) policed women's sexuality and challenged the survival and well-being of immigrant families in the U.S. The 1875 Page Law, for example, severely reduced both the number of Chinese women admitted into the country and the formation of families among this group. Many would-be Chinese female immigrants were forbidden to reunite with their husbands and fathers on the spurious grounds that most Chinese women who emigrated were bound for work as prostitutes, carried virulent strains of venereal disease, promoted opium addiction, and enticed young white boys to a life of sin. On a more contemporary note, immigrant women were targeted by the 1996 Illegal Immigration Reform and Immigrant Responsibility Act, which severely limited their access to crucial social services. Critics maintain that through the passage of this punitive law, politicians sought both to dissuade poor women from immigrating altogether and to coerce already established female immigrants to leave their husbands in the U.S. and return "home" along with their dependent children. These steps effectively transferred the costs of maintaining the women and their children to local communities and labor-exporting states, as was the case, for example, during the *bracero* program.

It is not only immigrant women who face impediments to the successful fulfillment of conventional notions of femininity, marriage, and motherhood. Many immigrant men find themselves frustrated and scapegoated, as they expect and are expected to be the breadwinners yet face structural obstacles that prevent them from performing this role. This failure has sobering implications for the successful fulfillment of masculinity. In Cecilia Menjívar's research with Salvadoran immigrants, an unemployed male interviewee explained, "Believe me, I feel as if my hands are tied, and my head [is] ready to explode from the tension and disappointment. I don't want to be a *mantenido* (supported by another). I don't feel like a man, I feel like a lady, and excuse me, but that's really terrible, insulting for a man who's used to providing for his family." For such men and their female partners, the issue is not so much the presence of the sexual division of labor or the persistence of patriarchal ideologies but the difficulties of sustaining either. The inability of immigrant men to fulfill their side of the conjugal bargain is an important precipitating factor in the disbanding of immigrant households.

The importance of keeping multiple wage-earning families intact is underscored by statistics revealing a far higher incidence of poverty among female-headed immigrant households than among either immigrant conjugal units or households headed by native-born white women. Indeed, the conditions associated with female-headed households among people of color are often different and should be interpreted differently from those characterizing households headed by white women. The latter have higher average incomes than minority families in the same situation. Immigrant female heads typically find themselves and their children at the bottom, with few, if any, financial reserves.

In light of the many assaults on immigrant families, it would be patronizing and inaccurate to interpret women's struggles to maintain intact families as an acquiescence to "traditional" patriarchy. Rather, in many cases these struggles represent acts of resistance against forces within the dominant society that threaten the existence of poor, minority families. This does not mean that immigrant women do not simultaneously experience the family as an instrument of gender subordination, however. Their attempts to use wages as leverage for greater gender parity in certain arenas of domestic life attest to this fact. Successes include parlaying their regular access to wages and their greater contribution to household sustenance into increased control over budgeting and other realms of domestic decision-making. The dilemma confronting many immigrant women, it would seem, is how to defend and hold together the family while attempting to reform the norms and practices that subordinate them.

Immigrant Families as Sites of Generational Conflict

While immigrant families are a nexus of survival and resistance to external forces that threaten to undermine them, families contain their own internal tensions and tyrannies, which are often manifested along generational lines. Although earlier co-lonial and racist ideologies featured sexually promiscuous women of color, contemporary immigrants in the U.S. turn the tables. Indians, Filipinos, and Vietnamese, for example, assert the morality of their communities by denouncing the sexual improprieties of American society and white women and praising the sexual restraints of their own ethnic cultures and women. This assertion may contribute to what Monisha Das Gupta calls, in the context of Indian immigrants, the "museumization of practices." Here first-generation immigrants invent what they understand to be "authentic" homeland customs in order to distance themselves from what is perceived to be American. Such rhetoric and its accompanying discipline can lead to restrictions on the autonomy, mobility, and personal decision-making of second-generation daughters. Moreover, because immigrant and ethnic women are often charged with the responsibility of transmitting and maintaining ethnic traditions, young women who veer from acceptable behaviors may be labeled "nonethnic," "untraditional," and, even worse, betrayers of their cultures and homelands. The move by immigrant communities to resist racism through both an emphasis on their own morality and restrictions on women's sexuality produces its own pain and contradictions.

Yet for young women, the consequences of the strong disciplining of their sexuality and geographic mobility can be paradoxical. The very gender inequalities that root girls in the home and reward female compliance may actually contribute to their academic success. Girls' socialization to be cooperative, compliant, and passive may be rewarded by their teachers in overcrowded and understaffed inner-city schools. Although girls' domestic responsibilities may reduce time spent at home on schoolwork, it does remove them from the unsavory features of street life, which is a more common environment for boys. Reflecting the differences in experiences these gendered social geographies create, the sociologist Mary Waters found that second-generation West Indian boys discussed being black Americans in terms of racial solidarity and rigid racial boundaries. The boys' more adversarial form of African American identity was born out of repeated incidents of social exclusion, harassment, and denigration at the hands of white Americans. Within the school context, this adversarial stance had a chilling effect on academic achievement. For example, second-generation West Indian males were more likely than their female counterparts to suffer social stigma if they spoke standard English among friends, and they were more likely to report that they accused others of "acting white." Although girls also faced exclusion on grounds of race, they discussed being American in terms of the freedom they sought from strict parental control. For girls, education and relatively well-paid jobs were means to acquire this much-coveted freedom. In short, the ways in which second-generation females respond to the constraints placed on their sexuality and physical mobility may position them to acquire the education they need for the social mobility that frequently eludes their parents and brothers.

Many South Asian immigrants in the U.S. also view their older children's re-strained sexuality and acquiescence to arranged marriages as proof of the ethnic group's elevated morality and rightful position as a "model minority." Arranged marriages have become an arena for accommodation as well as creative negotia-tion. Leaders of one South Asian community in New York estimated in 1995 that almost one half of U.S.-born or U.S.-raised people of South Asian ancestry agreed to formally arranged marriages. This practice apparently protects some youth from American dating patterns that they reject as wild and promiscuous. Others, how-ever, have come to demand a greater pool of potential mates and greater involve-ment in the selection of a marital partner. In this pursuit, they are buoyed by the fact that young urban professionals in South Asia, too, are successfully navigating this change. This example illustrates that new immigrants and their offspring are not only influenced in matters of gender and kinship by their exposure to new ide-als and behaviors in the U.S. They also bring cultural constructs with them and re-main informed about changing values and practices in their countries of origin.

Life in the U.S. brings other challenges to the household's generational divide. Because children tend to master English and other aspects of American culture quickly, they are often called upon to act as liaisons between their families and ex-ternal institutions. This not only inverts traditional generational lines of expertise and privileged access to important resources but also creates a situation ripe for ma-nipulation, as children are called upon to interpret the outside world for their el-ders. One Dominican man told me, "I have raised my children to be honorable and respectful. They never deceive us. I know of other children who lie to their parents. Like they tell them a phone bill is for $100 when it really is $70. And then the child pays the bill and pockets the extra $30." While a few other Dominicans I inter-viewed told me of similar suspicions of abuse, the most commonly voiced concern involved a diminution of the fathers' authority; "It's a real pride check [on our par-ents]," as one young man observed.

To some extent the generational tensions found in immigrant households are common to all family units, whether they are immigrant or native-born. Nonethe-less, there are differences in how these strains are perceived and negotiated. Immi-grants and their offspring must balance pre-emigration norms of proper genera-tional conduct (including the museumization of practices) with norms encountered over time in the United States and in their countries of origin. In this process, issues of group morality and the strong disciplining of young women come into play. Moreover, in emigrating, parents may have sacrificed their own class standing, and men may have sacrificed certain gender privileges as well. The first generation's hopes for economic and social advancement lie with its children. The second gener-ation usually acknowledges these struggles and holds the same aspirations. Conse-quently, its members walk a delicate tightrope as they challenge certain features of "traditional" family systems while struggling to retain others.

Modernization and Assimilation

Gender, households, and families have long been privileged sites in migration studies. They have proven especially amenable to explorations of two related theories of social change: modernization and assimilation. Beginning in the 1970s, most scholars predicted that with increased access to wages, immigrant women would enjoy increased autonomy and power within domestic settings. This empowerment and the subsequent transition to more companionate unions, it was argued, would place immigrant families more on par with native-born families—an outcome consistent with both modernization and assimilation theories.

There was far less consensus on whether and how immigrant households and families factored into the broader projects of modernity and assimilation. Such practices as child marriage, female circumcision, and folk medicine were deemed retrograde and injurious to the well-being and adjustment of family members in the U.S. However, the purported stability, cultural continuity, and internal consensus within such immigrant families as the Chinese, Vietnamese, and Korean were touted as the source of their economic success in this country.

Narratives of fully emancipated immigrant women or of immigrant families destined for failure or success based on their cultural repertoires have not proved adequate to capture the complexity of new immigrants' engagements with the U.S. Migration and wage employment do seem to bring many immigrant women modest gains within households, families, and ethnic communities, and refrains like "The United States is a place for women, my country is a place for men" are voiced by many members of new immigrant groups. Nonetheless, gains for women are unevenly distributed both among the various spheres that women and men inhabit and within and across immigrant groups. Pre-emigration cultural notions about gender and spousal relations (which are always multiple and dynamic in form) are an important element. So, too, are the kind and range of employment available to a given population of immigrant men and women before and after migration. For example, in California, where employment options are more readily available for women than for men, indigenous Central American men, whose traditions endorse greater gender parity, are generally more welcoming and supportive of their wives' financial contributions than are mestizo males, who feel diminished when their wives' earnings supplant their own.

Research has also shown that we must be careful to distinguish among levels of analysis when determining continuities and changes in gender and kinship relations. Two examples featuring Indian and Haitian immigrants, respectively, illustrate this point. In the face of relative spatial isolation from ethnic peers in Southern California and in the absence of servants, professional Indian immigrant couples have tended to solidify their conjugal bonds, and men are now more willing to help their working wives with housework. Moreover, in their role as the maintainers of ethnic culture, these women have assumed authority in local religious and cultural associations. Here women are given the opportunity to present Hinduism and Indian culture to children in a variant that features women as strong and independent. These forward strides for women are confounded, however, at the more formal and powerful level of panethnic associations. There, males predominate, and they champion a very different gender ideology and regime. According to this construction, it is Indian women's unconditional faithfulness, homemaking and child-rearing talents, and uncomplaining and self-sacrificing nature that have permitted their hardworking immigrant husbands to have successful careers in the workplace and larger community. Haitian immigrant women also experience uneven gains. Remittances bring them power and prestige among migrant and nonmigrant family and friends. Nonetheless, these very same transfers help to bolster the Haitian state, which systematically limits women's access to political power and secure employment.

As immigration research on gender, households, and families has progressed, once-popular narratives of modernity, women's emancipation, and assimilation have proven grossly inadequate. We find instances of continuity and change in gender ideologies, relations, and practices. These outcomes are determined by many factors, including the varied gender constructs brought from countries of origin, the ways in which these are isolated from or recombined with notions of gendered subjects available in the U.S., access to transnational and global flows of information and images regarding masculinities and femininities, opportunities for employment for immigrant men and women, and settlement within ethnic enclaves or predominantly native-born communities. Immigrant households and families also defy facile characterization. Over time and within differing contexts, they can be nurturing havens, bastions of resistance against poverty, nativism, and racism, and sites for women's and youth's advancement and oppression.

Bibliography

Das Gupta, Monisha. 1997. "'What is Indian About You?': A Gendered Transnational Approach to Ethnicity." *Gender and Society* 11: 572–96.

Espiritu, Yen Le. 1997. *Asian American Women and Men.* Thousand Oaks, Calif.: Sage.

Foner, Nancy. 1999. "The Immigrant Family: Cultural Legacies and Cultural Changes." In Charles Hirschman, Philip Kasinitz, and Josh DeWind, eds., *The Handbook of International Migration*, pp. 257–64. New York: Russell Sage Foundation.

Gabaccia, Donna. 1994. *From the Other Side: Women, Gender, and Immigrant Life in the United States, 1820–1990.* Bloomington: Indiana University Press.

Hondagneu-Sotelo, Pierrette. 1994. *Gendered Transitions: Mexican Experiences of Immigration.* Berkeley: University of California Press.

———, ed. 1999. "Gender and Contemporary U.S. Immigration." *American Behavioral Scientist* 42, 4.

Kibria, Nazli. 1993. *Family Tightrope: The Changing Lives of Vietnamese Americans.* Princeton, N.J.: Princeton University Press.

Mahler, Sarah, and Patricia Pessar, eds. 2001. "Gender in Transnational Contexts." *Identities: Global Studies of Culture and Power* 7, 4: special issue.

Pessar, Patricia. 1999. "The Role of Gender, Households, and Social Networks in the Migration Process: A Review and Appraisal." In Charles Hirschman, Philip Kasinitz, and Josh De Wind, eds., *The Handbook of International Migration,* pp. 53–70. New York: Russell Sage Foundation.

Waters, Mary. 2001. "Growing Up West Indian and African American: Gender and Class Differences in the Second Generation." In Nancy Foner, ed., *Islands in the City: West Indian Migration to New York,* pp. 193–215. Berkeley: University of California Press.

The Second Generation

Nancy Foner and Philip Kasinitz

The term "generation" is used in at least three distinct, albeit interrelated, ways in the social scientific literature. The first is in the sense of an age cohort—that is, people of approximately the same age who experience the same historical events at roughly the same points in their individual development. It is this sense we use when we speak of the "Woodstock generation" or the "baby boom generation," which the late demographer William Alonso said has been passing through institutional structures of U.S. society like a "pig through a python."

A second meaning of "generation," one favored by anthropologists, refers to genealogical rank in a kinship system—for example, the relationship of individuals to parents in the generation before or children in the generation after. Finally, in studies of immigration, "generation" is used as a measure of distance from the "old country." Thus we usually speak of people who move to the U.S. from another society as adults as being "first-generation" immigrants, their American-born children as the "second generation," and their children in turn as the "third generation." This numbering system is not without controversy and has ideological implications. Until the mid-20th century social scientists, social workers, and journalists often referred to people born in the U.S. to immigrant parents as "first-generation *Americans*" rather than "second-generation" *immigrants*. Although this usage has generally fallen out of favor among social scientists, it remains common in everyday speech. In recent years the numbering scheme has also grown more complex, with the widespread adoption of Rubén Rumbaut's term the "1.5 generation" for people born abroad who emigrate as children and are largely raised in the U.S. Further refinements—the "1.25 generation," the "1.75 generation," soon followed.

For the large wave of southern and eastern European immigrants that began around 1880 and ended in the mid-1920s, these three meanings of "generation" were closely intertwined. By the 1930s, even in the most "ethnic" of American communities and neighborhoods, the overwhelming majority of children were born in the U.S. Many (in some cases most) of their parents were immigrants. As this second generation aged together, they experienced a confluence of the historical cohort, kinship, and distance-from-the-old-country meanings of "generation" that often blurred the distinction among the three. Being the children of immigrants (and the parents of the third generation) and experiencing the historical events of the mid-20th century in young adulthood were so commonly linked as to create a distinct second-generation identity, both in the minds of the children of immigrants and in American popular culture.

As early as 1938, Marcus Lee Hansen observed distinct differences in attitudes toward ethnic identity between the second generation and their third-generation children, with the second generation anxious to assimilate and the third generation sentimentally invested in ethnicity. However, as Vladimir Nahirny and Joshua Fishman would later point out, Hansen attributed these differences to largely ahistorical social-psychological processes, ignoring the specific historical context that also shaped the experiences of the two cohorts.

For contemporary immigrants and their children, the situation is different. With continuing immigrant inflows, new first-generation immigrants in many communities today are often younger than third-generation adults. Second- and third-generation young people share neighborhoods, classrooms, and workplaces with recent immigrants their own age. "Old country" ways and identities are thus less associated with chronological age than in the past. Further, new immigrants may bring more up-to-date versions of the sending society's culture to ethnic communities. The situation is also complicated by the greater degree of transnationalism and circular migration among contemporary immigrants. Some second-generation members, although born in the U.S., spend considerable time in their parents' homelands while growing up, and many recent immigrants come from communities where large numbers of returned migrants have already challenged traditional ways.

Contemporary immigrant communities vary in the degree to which they emphasize distance from the old country versus chronological age when thinking about generational divides. Among Japanese and Korean Americans there are clear linguistic designations for people born abroad, those born in the U.S. of immigrant parents, and those whose parents were born in the U.S.: Issei, Nissei, and Sansei in Japanese; Ilsae, Yisae, and Sansae in Korean. Within their communities, these groups are thought of as having different attributes and different relationships to the sending and host societies. Korean Americans also use the term "iljeom osae," which is literally translated as the "1.5 generation." Within the Korean community this generation is often seen as having the greatest difficulty in adjustment, a fact that is a cause for concern among community leaders.

Among other contemporary immigrant groups, generational distinctions seem less precise and less clear. Cuban Americans are very conscious of generational and historical differences between the "exile generation" and those born in the U.S., and they anticipate what it will mean for the community when the former passes from the scene. Mexican Americans make distinctions between those born in the U.S. and in Mexico and distinguish both from the descendants of populations who lived in the Southwest when it was still part of Mexico. Indeed, the terms used for people of Mexican descent of different political stripes and in different parts of the country ("Hispano," "Chicano," "Mexican American," "La Raza," etc.) have implications for the importance of U.S. birth in shaping identity. Moreover, the long and complex history of Mexican immigration makes it difficult to disentangle chronological age from number of generations in the U.S. in shaping generational identity. Dominicans and Puerto Ricans have also developed terms to refer to members of the community born on the U.S. mainland (usually in New York)—"Dominicanyorks" and "Nuyoricans." Yet the high level of back-and-forth migration, changes in home communities, and the importance of a distinctive youth culture mean that these terms are often as much about age cohort as actual birthplace.

One area in which there clearly are strong generational differences among almost all contemporary immigrant groups is language use. As in the past, America remains "the graveyard of languages." Studies have consistently shown that the large majority of second-generation immigrants have made the transition to English, that they are much more likely to speak English fluently than their parents, and that they are far less likely than their parents to speak with a strong accent. This is true even in parts of the country where another language (usually Spanish) is widely spoken and even when media in the parents' original language are widely available. Second-generation groups do differ in the degree to which they maintain fluency in the parental language in addition to English. Not surprisingly, commonly spoken languages in the U.S. and those written in the Latin alphabet, such as Spanish, are maintained more often than those that are rarely spoken in the U.S. or that are extremely different from English. Fluency in written Chinese, for example, is unusual among second-generation Chinese Americans, despite a well-developed infrastructure of Chinese schools dedicated to the maintenance of the language. Further, there is little evidence that maintenance of the parental language comes at the expense of English fluency, even among those groups in which second-generation bilingualism is common.

Immigrant Generations and Social Mobility

By 2000, approximately 10 percent of the U.S. population was "second generation" in the sense that they were born in the U.S. and have at least one foreign-born parent. (About the same proportion are first-generation immigrants.) Although this second-generation group includes many older adults whose parents came to this country before 1965 (and even before 1924), the majority are children and young adults whose parents arrived after 1965. As Table 1 indicates, the Mexican second generation dwarfs all others. More than a quarter of native-born Americans with at least one foreign-born parent are of Mexican origin, as are almost a third of those with two foreign-born parents. Altogether, nearly two out of five second-generation individuals have a parent (or parents) born in Latin America and the Caribbean. As Rumbaut notes, the sizable Canadian and European second generations are largely the surviving offspring of immigrants who arrived before World War II, with a median age in the late fifties, compared to a much younger average of 12 to 13 years for the U.S.-born offspring of immigrants from Latin America, the Caribbean, and Asia.

The second generation now makes up more than a quarter of the nation's Hispanic and Asian populations. By contrast, almost 90 percent of black and non-Hispanic white Americans trace their roots in the U.S. back three generations or longer. The fact that so much of the second generation is of non-European origin and considered "nonwhite" stands in sharp contrast to earlier periods and raises questions about the future of race relations and social mobility in the U.S.

In the academic literature and popular imagery of the incorporation into American society of the overwhelmingly European immigrants of the late 19th and early 20th centuries, the idea of generation was closely associated with ideas of assimilation. The general assumption in the standard accounts of "straight-line" assimilation theory is that each generation (in the distance-from-the-old-country sense of the term) becomes progressively more "American." Whatever cultural and psychological costs this Americanization process may entail, it is generally seen as enabling upward mobility within U.S. society. In popular discussions, the term "assimila-

Table 1   The second-generation population of the U.S. by parental nativity and national origin, 1998–2002 (percentages)

Region and national origin	Total (2.0 and 2.5 generations)	Both parents foreign-born (2.0 generation)	One parent foreign-born, one parent U.S.-born (2.5 generation)
Mexico	26.1	31.5	19.6
Other Latin America and Caribbean	12.5	14.7	9.6
Asia and Middle East	14.4	17.4	10.5
Europe and Canada	43.9	33.4	57.6
Sub-Saharan Africa	0.1	0.1	0.1
All others	2.4	2.2	2.6
Total number	26,990,359	15,297,057	11,693,302

Source: Rumbaut (2004), p. 1184. Based on merged Current Population Survey annual demographic files (March), 1998 through 2002.

tion" came to be used almost synonymously with upward mobility. What these accounts rarely acknowledged was the role of the specific historical conditions—American economic ascendancy, postwar prosperity, suburbanization, the growth of the mass media, and the rise of organized labor—that facilitated both the acculturation and the upward mobility of the children of European immigrants who came of age and carved out work and family careers in the 1940s and 1950s.

In speculating about the possible future of the largely "nonwhite" children of post-1965 immigrants, many social scientists have been less optimistic about second- and third-generation upward mobility. In 1992 Herbert Gans turned the assumptions of traditional assimilation theory on their head, warning that many of the contemporary children of "nonwhite" immigrants were in danger of "second-generation decline" relative to their immigrant parents. Like traditional observers of assimilation, Gans assumes that substantial second-generation acculturation is taking place and that the children of immigrants are coming to share the values and outlooks of their American peers. This, Gans suggests, may lead them to reject the low-status "immigrant jobs" held by their parents. Yet those who face racial discrimination, poor-quality education, and declining real wages may lack opportunities in the mainstream economy and thus be downwardly mobile. The other possibility is that the children of immigrants who are well placed within the American labor market will be less anxious to "become American" and stay tied to their parents' ethnic community. This might lead to better economic outcomes but less cultural assimilation.

Alejandro Portes and Min Zhou make a similar argument in their often-cited 1993 article on segmented assimilation, a model that Portes and Rumbaut expanded in their 2001 book, *Legacies.* The most influential of the "revisionist" perspectives, segmented assimilation describes the various outcomes of different groups of second-generation youth and argues that the mode of incorporation for the first generation gives the second generation access to different kinds of opportunities and social networks. Those who are socially closest to lower-class and particularly to minority Americans may adopt an oppositional, "reactive" ethnicity. In general, the second generation may acquire a host of American bad habits, from low rates of saving to eating high-fat foods to watching too much television, which may actually hinder upward mobility.

By contrast, those groups that maintain strong intergenerational ethnic networks and fewer ties to U.S. minorities, it is argued, experience a "linear" ethnicity which creates networks of social ties and may provide access to job opportunities while reinforcing parental authority and values and forestalling acculturation. Zhou and Bankston's work on Vietnamese youth in New Orleans makes perhaps the clearest case for the benefits of preserving ties to the ethnic community, even at the expense of acquiring connections with the dominant society. They see home-country language retention as an advantage for the second generation, as it facilitates participation in the ethnic economy, where opportunities may exceed those in the main-stream economy.

Of course, the idea that second-generation assimilation has costs is hardly new. Early 20th-century immigrants and those who wrote about them often expressed concern about intergenerational conflict and the heartache it produced. Nor is there anything new about the complaint that the second generation is becoming the "wrong kind" of Americans or the idea that a dense "ethnic enclave" can provide a bulwark against the worst effects of the American streets. Yet in earlier times voices skeptical of the promise of assimilation for the children of European immigrants were in the minority among intellectuals, social scientists, and in the immigrant communities themselves. Today, against a background of such factors as rising income inequality and continuing racial divisions, belief in both the possibility and the value of assimilation seems less pervasive. In fact, since the early 1990s many have speculated that contemporary American culture will actually undermine the ability of the second generation—particularly those seen as nonwhite—to make it in American society.

However, as more of the contemporary second generation has come of age and joined the labor force, the data have generally not supported the dire predictions of second-generation downward mobility. Alba and Nee's review of national data and studies by Kasinitz, Mollenkopf, Waters, and Holdaway in New York, and even Portes and Rumbaut's longitudinal data from Miami and San Diego, all show that on most indicators of social and economic achievement, Asian and European second-generation immigrants often outperform the children of native whites. Black and many Latino second-generation members, while trailing behind native whites, are doing significantly better than members of native minority groups.

The Mexican American second generation is of special concern, because of its enormous size and the low educational and occupational status of a high proportion of the parents. Not only do the children of Mexican immigrants lag behind native whites in educational and occupational attainment, but as Joel Perlmann's analysis of recent census data brings out, they drop out of high school at very high rates. However, young second-generation Mexican male dropouts are likely to be working, the majority of them full-time. Overall, the U.S.-born offspring of Mexican immigrants do better than their parents in education and earnings. They are also more likely than their immigrant parents to work at white-collar jobs. Although Perlmann shows that graduation rates from four-year colleges are much lower among the Mexican second generation (ages 25–34) than native whites, about the same proportion—about a third—had some college education, a figure that implies that a substantial minority of the Mexican second generation is prepared for white-collar positions.

It is also worth noting that second-generation success rarely seems tied to connections with the ethnic enclaves of the parents. If anything, such enclaves can serve as safety nets for the least successful members of the second generation, but they are rarely springboards to upward mobility. Among the most economically successful immigrant groups, such as Dae Young Kim shows among Korean Americans, the second generation is usually anxious to avoid both economic and geographic ethnic enclaves. Of course, the bulk of the contemporary second generation is still young. As Deborah Woo reminds us, we cannot yet say what glass ceilings even relatively successful groups may face in the future. Still, according to most early indicators, today's second generation seems to be assimilating into American society more rapidly than immigrants of the past. While this has not led to universal upward mobility, there is little evidence that a significant portion of the second generation is becoming part of a permanent urban underclass, as some early observers feared.

Relations between the Generations

First-generation immigrants and their American-born children have distinctive experiences and frames of reference, and this affects the relations between them. This is an old immigrant story, and many of the tensions between the generations today are much like those reported in earlier eras. As before, the stress is typically on intergenerational conflict—or the generation gap—between immigrant parents steeped in old-country traditions and values and second-generation children who have grown up in the American social and cultural world.

Of course it is possible to exaggerate the extent to which intergenerational conflict is an immigrant phenomenon. It is important to ask whether the immigrant experience is largely to blame for tensions and conflicts between the first and second generations or if they are attributable, at least in part, to life-stage differences between parents and adolescent children that affect most Americans.

Adolescents in American society typically seek greater independence and autonomy while parents seek to assert their authority. Young people adopt styles of dress, decoration, music, and dance that their parents do not understand—and often cannot stand. Yet the strains resulting from "normal" teenage rebelliousness or lifestyles often become magnified and intensified when parents come from another country and culture and are unfamiliar with or disapproving of mainstream American values and practices. And while many young people bemoan the fact that their parents "just don't understand how things are today," for the children of immigrants, who are literally coming of age in a different society from the one in which their parents did, the complaint may be particularly apt. Whereas rebelliousness among American adolescents represents a conflict between an adolescent world and an adult world, the second generation, as Zhou notes, also has to struggle to make sense of the inconsistencies between *two* adult worlds: that of the immigrant community or family and that of the larger society.

Intergenerational conflicts may be particularly acute in groups whose cultural patterns and practices differ radically from those in the broader American culture. In this regard, it is important to note that immigrant parents often hold up an idealized version of traditional values and customs as a model for their children, even though these values and customs have often undergone considerable change since immigrants left the home country. Indeed, as Foner has noted, immigrant parents in the U.S. may construct a version of old-country traditions as a way to make sense of their current experience or to buttress and legitimate their familial authority.

One source of intergenerational conflict is discipline. In some cultures of origin, such as Vietnamese and Chinese, talking back to parents is a heinous offense. In the West Indies, corporal punishment is widely practiced. West Indian parents often fear that if they discipline children in the way they think best, they risk being reported to state agencies for child abuse. Just how common such reports actually are is unclear, yet even the theoretical possibility that children might appeal to U.S. legal authorities can be a flashpoint for tensions between the generations, giving children added leverage in relations with their parents and laying bare the conflict between U.S. and home-country behavioral norms.

For their part, members of the second generation, reared in an American culture that encourages early independence for children, often view their parents as authoritarian and domineering. The parents, with their often romanticized old-world standards, may think their children rude and disrespectful. A vicious cycle may ensue. As parents feel frustrated and threatened by the new values and behaviors their children are exposed to, they may attempt to tighten the reins, which heightens children's resentment and desire to flout parental controls.

Sexual relations are a particular source of tension. Immigrants from cultures where dating is frowned upon or forbidden can be frightened and appalled by their teenagers'—especially daughters'—desire to go on dates, to say nothing of the issues faced by gay and lesbian young people caught between the norms of their parents' communities and the relative openness of American youth culture. Immigrant parents are often much stricter with daughters than with sons, and seek to keep girls close to home or to control their social activities. In many groups daughters are also given household responsibilities, such as caring for younger siblings, at an age when their brothers are encouraged to be independent. This double standard can lead immigrant families to cut short daughters' educational pursuits or force them to attend less prestigious institutions closer to home. Still, among all but the most highly educated of contemporary immigrant groups, girls outperform boys academically. The work of Nancy Lopez on Haitians, West Indians, and Dominicans and of Robert C. Smith on Mexicans suggest that second-generation girls' more highly structured and monitored lives can have positive effects on educational attainment. Of course, for better or for worse, many second-generation girls experience these restrictions as unfair and are torn between the pursuit of independence, autonomy, and romantic love and the desire to be dutiful daughters.

A further source of conflict is parental pressure to marry within the ethnic group. In the New York Second Generation Study, Kasinitz, Mollenkopf, Waters, and Holdaway report that among the children of immigrants, in almost every group a majority—usually a large majority—reject the notion that it is important to marry within the group, a view they acknowledge is often not shared by their parents. When it comes to actual rates of out-marriage, not only do ethnic groups vary, but there is also considerable variation by gender. Out-marriage among second- and third-generation East Asian women has become common—far more common than among second- and third-generation East Asian men (the gender gap in out-marriage is also true for Latinos, though to a lesser extent). The effect of this gender gap on ethnic identity and family life across the generations has yet to be fully studied. Ethnic groups also vary markedly in age at marriage. Among Chinese and Korean Americans, the typical age of first marriage is now relatively high, partly because large numbers pursue postgraduate education. Yet we suspect that some young people among these groups are forestalling conflicts with parents over acceptable marriage partners by simply postponing marriage altogether.

An extreme case where immigrant norms are out of sync with those of the dominant American culture is arranged marriage, a common practice in many South Asian and Middle Eastern sending societies. Arranged marriages, needless to say, conflict sharply with the emphasis on romantic love and fulfilling one's own destiny so conspicuous in American youth culture. Of course, conflicts over arranged marriages are increasingly common in many of the immigrants' countries of origin as well. Yet in the U.S., children may be encouraged to reject traditional arranged marriages by the mainstream society's culture and in some cases by its legal institutions as well. In response, gradual changes in arranged marriage norms are taking place in U.S. ethnic communities. "Semi-arranged" marriages, in which young people have some elements of choice, are increasingly common. Young people may be given an informal veto power over parental choices or are introduced to acceptable partners and then allowed a brief courtship in which they decide whether or not they wish to marry. Even with these changes, many second-generation youth bristle at parental pressure.

Another point of contention across the generations has to do with intense, and often high, parental expectations for their children. Immigrant parents feel they have made sacrifices so their children will get ahead in America, and when the children do not succeed or make educational or occupational choices at odds with parental expectations, conflicts can result. As Annelise Orleck puts it in her study of Soviet Jews, children can hear the voices of their stressed and tired parents whispering, "We did this for you," and Dae Young Kim reports that among second-generation Korean Americans, the pressure to "repay" the sacrifices of immigrant parents in the form of educational attainment can be intense.

The pattern of pushing children to do well in school or to pursue a course of study that will lead to a high-paying profession can have unintended negative consequences. According to Diane Wolf's analysis, many second-generation Filipinos feel alienated from their parents as a result of these pressures. Filipino family ideology compounds the situation by requiring people to keep problems within the family. Thus members of the second generation feel caught in a lonely bind: they can't turn to their parents, who are causing the problems, nor can they turn to others, for fear of further sanctions. Vivian Louie's study of Chinese American college students also highlights the pressure parents put on their children to pursue "practical" fields of study; while mentors and advisers urge talented young people to follow their dreams, parents urge them to seek out lucrative and secure careers. Yet for all of these concerns, it must be noted that the disproportionate number of second-generation immigrants among the nation's leading young writers, artists, and musicians (and indeed, social scientists) suggests that at least some second-generation young people are being encouraged to pursue their dreams, lack of pecuniary rewards notwithstanding.

Finally, there are the tensions related to children's role as translators, mediators, and interpreters for non-English-speaking parents. This reversal of roles, with children acting as mentors and experts and parents as dependents, can create a host of problems. The young people may be embarrassed by their parents' inability to fill out forms, make appointments, and conduct business on their own and be annoyed by the imposition on their time. They may also feel uncomfortable learning about family secrets—or about intervening and mediating—in the process of translating in medical, legal, and other social settings. Whether boys find the role reversals more difficult than girls is an open question, although evidence suggests that girls tend to take on more translating responsibilities, especially when it comes to home-related matters.

Translating and interpreting can also give children power over their parents, which may exacerbate conflicts and accentuate the gulfs between them. Indeed, children may deliberately use knowledge of English as a tool against their parents and as a way to keep their lives separate. Understandably, this creates resentment among parents, who dislike their dependence on their children for translating government documents and other material and for communicating with English-speaking officials, professionals, and merchants. Parents may worry, in fact, that their children are not translating correctly—and a number of studies report instances where children deliberately mistranslate reports from teachers, saying that a grade of *F* means "fine," for example.

Intergenerational strains and conflicts are most prominent in the family arena, yet they occur in other domains as well—politics, workplaces, and ethnic associations, to name three. Studies of religious congregations indicate that members of the second generation may segregate themselves from the immigrant generation in these settings because they feel estranged from the ethnic ambiance, and in some religious institutions, members of the second generation resent being denied access to meaningful authority roles. In political organizations and community groups, the second generation, particularly those with a U.S. college education, may have a different perspective on ethnic group identity as well as a different style of political expression from those whose early political experience was in another society. Nicole Marwell's work on Dominican activists indicates a far greater influence of the American civil rights movement on both the style and the substance of political expression among the second, as compared with the first, generation, as well as a greater willingness to work closely with other Latinos and African Americans. Similarly, Yen Le Espiritu's study of panethnicity among Asian Americans notes a greater panethnic consciousness of "Asian" (as opposed to "Chinese," "Korean" or "Vietnamese") identity among the second generation. This "Asian American" identity, which often emerges on American college campuses, appears to represent a form of assimilation in which members of the second generation have come to think of themselves in American racial terms.

For all of the potential for intergenerational conflict, it is important to note that strains and conflicts are only one part of the story. Families create emotional ties that bond and bind, and even when members of the second generation chafe under parental constraints and obligations, the vast majority feel deep affection for and loyalty to their parents and recognize the importance of family. These contradictory pulls may be especially strong for daughters, who are subject to strict parental controls yet at the same time are heavily involved in household activities. Portes and Rumbaut argue that when parents and children both acculturate at the same rate ("consonant acculturation")—or when "selective acculturation" occurs in the context of a dense coethnic community that promotes partial retention of the parents' home language and norms—children are less prone to feel embarrassed by their parents and more willing to accept parental guidance, thereby reducing the likelihood of intergenerational conflict.

It should also be noted that multigenerational households are more common among immigrant groups than among natives in the U.S. today. Indeed, for most middle-class Americans it has become normative to leave the parental home before age 20, to pursue higher education, join the armed forces, or simply strike out on one's own. Young adults who return to their parents' home in their twenties are labeled "boomerang kids" or "ILYAS" ("incompletely launched young adults"). They are seen as somehow unsuccessful, and their rising numbers are considered a social problem. By contrast, in many immigrant families young people are seen as making the transition to adulthood not by leaving the parental household but rather by beginning to make financial contributions to it. As Holdaway observes, this propensity to live in multigenerational households, whatever its emotional costs, is a considerable financial advantage, particularly in high-cost housing markets such as New York and Los Angeles, where many immigrants are concentrated. It may partially explain why working-class immigrants in those metropolitan areas are more likely to own homes than natives of the same age and income level.

In general, parents and children often work out accommodations and compromises as a way to get along. Far from being inflexible traditionalists, most immigrant parents adapt and change in the new context. This can mean giving children more say in marriage arrangements, to give an example from South Asian groups, or, as a study of the Haitian second generation reports, extending the evening curfew hour or permitting dating earlier than parents would like. Some West Indian parents, according to Waters, are learning new techniques from their children, who explain how American or Americanized friends are disciplined. Evidence suggests that parents with higher levels of education and economic status are more likely to work out these accommodating strategies to ensure peace and harmony, perhaps because they are more exposed to American coworkers and colleagues than those with less education or lower-wage jobs.

As for the second generation, they are not inevitably rebels, nor do they necessarily reject or entirely abandon their parents' ways. Many West Indian teenagers in Waters's study, for example, defended their parents' disciplinary practices and said that when they grew up and had children, they would try to combine West Indian strictness with American freedom and openness. In general, whatever members of the second generation think about their parents' standards, they often try to conceal their behavior from parents in order to avoid clashes, and they may simply go along with parental expectations to keep the peace, especially when the surrounding community—neighbors and other social contacts—back up parental authority. Relations between the two generations, in sum, are filled with inconsistencies and contradictions, and shift in different contexts and over time. In many (perhaps most) cases, conflict is mixed with cooperation and caring, and rejection of some parental standards and practices is coupled with acceptance of others.

The same can probably be said about relations between the contemporary second generation and their children (the third generation), although it is too early to say much about the nature of these relations. At this point, we know little about the emerging third generation, most of whom are still very young. Among the many important questions is how this third generation—the U.S.-born children of the U.S.-born second generation—will fare educationally and occupationally, and how they will relate to their immigrant heritage and to their grandparents' countries of origin. As only a tiny number of the grandchildren of post-1965 immigrants have reached adulthood, these topics must await further study.

Bibliography

Alba, Richard, and Victor Nee. 2003. *Remaking the Mainstream: Assimilation and Contemporary Immigration.* Cambridge, Mass.: Harvard University Press.

Foner, Nancy. 1997. "The Immigrant Family: Cultural Legacies and Cultural Changes." *International Migration Review* 31: 961–74.

Gans, Herbert J. 1992. "Second Generation Decline: Scenarios for the Economic and Ethnic Futures of the Post-1965 American Immigrants." *Ethnic and Racial Studies* 15 (2): 173–93.

Kasinitz, Philip, Mary C. Waters, and John H. Mollenkopf. 2002. "Becoming American/ Becoming New Yorkers: Immigrant Incorporation in a Majority Minority City." *International Migration Review* 36 (4): 1020–36.

Kasinitz, Philip, John H. Mollenkopf, and Mary C. Waters, eds. 2004. *Becoming New Yorkers: Ethnographies of the New Second Generation.* New York: Russell Sage Foundation.

Kasinitz, Philip, John H. Mollenkopf, Mary C. Waters, and Jennifer Holdaway. Forthcoming. *Inheriting the City: Immigrant Origins and American Destinies.* New York: Russell Sage Foundation.

Lopez, Nancy C. 2003. *Hopeful Girls, Troubled Boys.* New York: Routledge.

Louie, Vivian S. 2004. *Compelled to Excel: Immigration Education and Opportunity among Chinese Americans.* Stanford: Stanford University Press.

Min, Pyong Gap, ed. 2002. *Second Generation: Ethnic Identity among Asian Americans.* Walnut Creek, Calif.: Altamira.

Orelick, Annelise. 1987. "The Soviet Jews: Life in Brighton Beach, Brooklyn." In Nancy Foner, ed., *New Immigrants in New York.* New York: Columbia University Press.

Perlmann, Joel. 2005. *Italians Then, Mexicans Now: Immigrant Origins and Second-Generation Progress, 1890 to 2000.* New York: Russell Sage Foundation.

Portes, Alejandro, and Min Zhou. 1993. "The New Second Generation: Segmented Assimilation and Its Variants." *Annals of the American Academy of Political and Social Science* 530: 73–96.

Portes, Alejandro, and Rubén Rumbaut. 2001. *Legacies: The Story of the New Second Generation.* Berkeley: University of California Press.

Rumbaut, Rubén. 1999. "Assimilation and Its Discontents: Ironies and Paradoxes." In Charles Hirschman, Philip Kasinitz, and Josh DeWind, eds., *The Handbook of International Migration: The American Experience.* New York: Russell Sage Foundation.

———— 2004. "Ages, Life Stages, and Generational Cohorts: Decomposing the Immigrant First and Second Generations in the United States." *International Migration Review* 38 (3): 1160–1205.

Rumbaut, Rubén, and Alejandro Portes, eds. 2001. *Ethnicities.* Berkeley: Russell Sage Foundation and the University of California Press.

Smith, Robert C. 2005. *Mexican New York: Transnational Lives of New Immigrants.* Berkeley: University of California Press.

Suarez-Orozco, Carola, and Marcelo Suarez-Orozco. 2001. *Children of Immigrants.* Cambridge, Mass.: Harvard University Press.

Waters, Mary C. 1999. *Black Identities: West Indian Dreams and American Realities.* New York: Russell Sage Foundation.

Woo, Deborah. 2002. *Glass Ceilings and Asian Americans: The New Face of Workplace Barriers.* Walnut Creek, Calif.: Altamira.

Zephir, Flore. 2001. *Trends in Ethnic Identification among Second-Generation Haitian Immigrants in New York City.* Westport, Conn.: Bergin and Garvey.

Zhou, Min, and Carl L. Bankston III. 1998. *Growing Up American: The Adaptation of Vietnamese Adolescents in the United States.* New York: Russell Sage Foundation.

Africa: West

Marilyn Halter

The U.S. Cer᠁ defines West Africa as a subdivision of the continent that includes the countries ᠁nin, Burkina Faso, Cape Verde, Côte d'Ivoire, Gambia, Ghana, Guinea, Guinea᠁ ᠁u, Liberia, Mali, Mauritania, Niger, Nigeria, Saint Helena, Senegal, Sierra Le᠁ ᠁nd Togo. Of the over 1 million foreign-born people from Africa in the U.S. tod᠁ approximately 36 percent are from this region. Those from Nigeria (140,929) make up the largest population of West Africans currently living in the U.S., followed by people from Ghana (68,122), Liberia (42,754), Cape Verde (27,059), and Sierra Leone (21,944). It should be noted, however, that West African community leaders from each of these groups concur that these figures represent severe undercounts; most report that the totals may be as much as twice the official counts.

With very few exceptions, the new Americans arriving from West Africa are black. Not since the era of the forced migration of half a million Africans in the slave trade have so many newcomers from the region settled in the U.S. This time, rather than being coerced, they are migrating of their own volition. Indeed, while West Africans of the first diaspora were captured and brought to American shores in chains, today a considerable number are entering as refugees seeking a path to freedom.

Beginning in the late 19th century, initially pulled by the labor needs of the American whaling industry, immigrants from the Cape Verde Islands left their drought-stricken archipelago off the coast of Senegal, which had long been colonized by Portugal, to make southeastern New England their new home. These Afro-Portuguese settlers are particularly noteworthy as they represent the first voluntary mass migration from Africa to the U.S. Cape Verdeans are still making the transatlantic journey, but especially over the past three decades they have been accompanied by a broad range of newcomers of diverse ethnic origins from the other major

West African sending countries—Nigeria, Ghana, Liberia, Sierra Leone, and Senegal—as well as smaller numbers from the other countries of the region. Taken together, this kaleidoscopic variety of ethnic, linguistic, and religious groups is transforming the ethnoracial landscape of American society.

During the span of the 20th century, the flow of West African migration shifted course from a pattern of relocation to western European destinations, based on long-standing associations with the former colonial powers of Britain and France, to the United States. Immigration policy in Europe became increasingly restrictive, in part to discourage migration from former colonies in Africa, and this coincided with more liberalized policy on this side of the Atlantic, especially in the areas of family reunification and the criteria to claim refugee status. Two specific pieces of legislation especially contributed to the increased flow. The 1986 Immigration Reform and Control Act made it possible for undocumented migrants to gain legal status, and under its provisions amnesty was granted to approximately 30,000 Africans. The 1986 measure also introduced the lottery system that became part of the 1990 Immigration Act, the other significant recent legislative "pull" factor. The 1990 policy included the Diversity Immigrant Visa Program, meant to broaden the nations of origin of new immigrants to incorporate underrepresented regions of the world. An estimated 20,000 Africans, many of them from West Africa, were able to take advantage of this initiative by lottery. Moreover, in recent years Africans have increasingly been granted refugee and asylee status. Finally, a crucial factor in redirecting the African diaspora was the prolonged recession in Europe during this period, while the U.S. was experiencing growth in the economy.

Since the 1930s, but especially after 1960 and the overthrow of colonial rule, West Africans have been voluntarily migrating to the U.S. primarily to obtain higher education. Many have returned to their home countries once their schooling is complete. In recent years, however, the unrelenting cycles of political conflict resulting in toppled governments and repressive military dictatorships have pushed many West Africans to relocate on a more permanent basis. Often endemic poverty and economic collapse have accompanied the political unrest to create crisis conditions that further impel the migrants to uproot. They come to the U.S. seeking better economic and educational opportunities as well as reunification with families. Among those migrating as refugees, the earliest group was Nigerians escaping the Biafran war of the 1960s. More recently, Liberians and Sierra Leoneans have gained refugee status, fleeing escalating levels of political oppression and persecution. Of the 19,070 refugee arrivals from Africa in 2001, 18 percent were from Liberia and 11 percent from Sierra Leone. Before moving to the U.S., many new immigrants and refugees had been involved in transborder migrations within West Africa, and in some cases to other regions of the continent. The journey to the U.S. can often be the last step in an experience of multiple dispersals.

The term "West African" connotes a panethnic conglomerate, with color as well as some aspects of shared regional and historical experience in common. The nations included under this rubric represent the legacy of colonial intervention, which coerced peoples of a wide variety of traditions, cultures, languages, religions, and worldviews into national groups when otherwise they would not necessarily have grouped themselves in this way. Nonetheless, since this was the part of Africa where much of the transatlantic slave trade was conducted, the region culturally represents continuity between African Americans who are the descendants of slaves and the newest arrivals from the continent. The bulk of West African newcomers, having migrated from the former colonies of Britain, are English-speaking. Smaller numbers hail from Francophone Africa, while those from the Republic of Cape Verde speak Portuguese. Having English-language skills has been a significant advantage to making a successful adjustment to the U.S.

Ethnic identities among West Africans are well formulated before emigration. By the time of arrival, immigrants from Nigeria have a strong sense of their identities as Yoruba, Igbo, or Hausa. Among the Nigerian influx, Yoruba and Igbo are the top ethnic groups and constitute populations that have a long migratory history. Not surprisingly, as the most mobile of African ethnic groups and people accustomed to living in diaspora, today they still represent the largest ethnic concentrations among the immigrants. Migrants from Ghana are primarily Ga, Ewe, Asante, and Fante; those from Liberia are Bassa, Kru, Vai, Hran, and Americo Liberian; Sierra Leoneans are Creoles, Temne, Mende, and Limba; and migrants from Senegal are Wolof, Mandingo, Tukolor, and Jolla. The pattern of multiethnic identification does not extend to the Cape Verdean immigrants, who hold a singular ethnicity. In the case of Cape Verdeans, however, distinct island affiliations may form part of the identity structure that they bring to the U.S. Despite these complex identities, however, officially the immigrants are recognized only by their national origin, since U.S. immigration and census records do not specify ethnic composition.

Multiple belonging is central to the immigrant experience in general, and the case of West African identity very much follows that pattern. While ethnic identification may be most salient at the time of migration, usually the new arrivals begin to develop a stronger, parallel sense of national identity as they settle in the U.S., largely because that is how they are categorized by the host society. For the most part nationality trumps ethnic or island identifications in the perceptions of those outside the West African community. Thus, Yorubas are considered Nigerian, Ewes labeled Ghanaian, Creoles called Sierra Leonean, Fogo islanders classified as Cape Verdeans, and so forth. Even though the national-origin designations imposed by outsiders do not capture the significant cultural distinctions within each population, confronted with the realities of the social dynamics in their new surroundings, eventually most of the immigrants adopt these labels as self-descriptive terms.

Still, ethnicity and ethnic belonging are potent bases for group organization among the immigrants. Many of their associations are formed along ethnic lines and may be extensions of well-established organizations in their home countries, such as the Egbé Omo Yoruba (National Association of Yoruba Descendants in North America), the Asante Descendants of Chicago, the Tegloma Federation, an association of Mende from Sierra Leone, and the Igbo Union of America. Other organizations, such as the Liberian Association of Atlanta and the Organization for the Advancement of Nigerians, reflect a heightened sense of national belonging. Like other immigrant groups, West Africans have established hometown associations to raise money and promote projects in their native towns or region. Immigrant remittances are critical to the economies of their countries of origin, while charitable groups provide relief for those most in need both in the U.S. and in West Africa. Another axis of collective life among West African newcomers is shared educational histories. From student associations to college and even hometown high school networks, alumni gather in their new surroundings to reconstitute these formative connections. A hierarchy of what was considered to be the best schools back at home has been transplanted, and thus membership in the alumni clubs stands as a marker of social status. It is quite common for West Africans to be active in a range of immigrant associations; thus, memberships in ethnic, national-origin, and hometown-based organizations are not mutually exclusive. Because of the strength of the extended family system and ties based on ethnicity, immigrant networks function extremely well in assisting the newest arrivals. The newcomers can count on coethnics already living in the U.S. to provide shelter and sustenance until they become more permanently settled.

Mainly through the activities of the various associations, homeland forms of cultural expression are projected and celebrated in the U.S., underlining the cooperation of the diverse ethnic groups and regions. The social events carried out by these immigrants are in many ways "performing ethnicity." They serve as conduits for continued affirmation of premigration ethnic identification and belonging. Traditional ethnic customs and rituals are observed, modified, and transformed in their new settings. In terms of life-cycle events, almost all West African immigrants conduct naming ceremonies, a tradition that revolves around the official naming of infants seven days (for girls) or eight days (for boys) after birth, but the celebration is particularly elaborate among the Yorubas of Nigeria, the Creoles of Sierra Leone, and the Wolofs of Senegal and Gambia. As for engagements and weddings, although the customs may be somewhat altered in the U.S., the notion that the union is not simply between individuals but between two extended families is still emphasized among both the first and the second generations. Frequently, if members of the extended biological family have not migrated as well, others in the diaspora community are designated to take their place. Thus, West African young people may grow up having "cousins" and "aunties" who are not actually related but whose familial roles mirror those of true kin.

A variety of traditional rites to send off and remember the dead are distinctive to the West African groups. For instance, Ghanaian populations like the Ga and the Ewe are known for their elaborate commemorations honoring those who have passed away. In Ghana, funeral rites are well established and fully embedded in the social and cultural tapestry of the community. The rituals of mourning are protracted, lasting for months after death. Marking the annual anniversaries of deaths also can last for several days. In the U.S., these funeral customs are central to the social fabric of many Ghanaian communities. However, because of their new circumstances, especially the demands of the American workplace, in which many of the migrants hold multiple jobs, Ghanaians have had to modify these transplanted customs by drastically curtailing the length of time devoted to observances in honor of the deceased.

The Creoles of Sierra Leone have also made adjustments to traditional mourning rituals so they can meet the demands of their adopted society. Typically, in Sierra Leonean communities throughout the U.S., on any given weekend an *awujoh,* the commemoration of the fortieth day after death or the annual anniversary, is being performed. In this country these ceremonies, as well as actual burials, are as likely to be scheduled on a Saturday as on a Sunday, yet in Sierra Leone a Saturday funeral or *awujoh* is viewed as completely taboo. Once again the migrants are finding ways to accommodate customary ethnic rituals to the societal expectations of their new living situation.

Although changing rites of remembrance demonstrates West African adaptation practices, in some instances entirely new traditions are being made in the U.S. Although baby showers are unheard of in Sierra Leone and giving gifts for an infant before the child is actually born is frowned upon, the immigrant community has wholeheartedly embraced the ritual of throwing elaborate baby showers, and that of holding bridal showers as well.

Despite all the intragroup diversity, some shared cultural features do span the range of ethnicities and nationalities that constitute the West African population. Ethnic foods are one marker of a collective West African identity that has persisted in the U.S. The extensive use of palm oil in cooking is distinctively West African, as are variations of the signature dishes of jollof rice, fufu, pepper soup, groundnut soup, and palava sauce (a stew). Common ingredients include yams, plantains, cassava, okra, spinach, garri, peanuts, corn, and samp. Different groups might vary in their preparation of certain foods—for example, plantain fufu is Ghanaian, while Sierra Leoneans make their fufu with cassava—but the likelihood of having the opportunity to sample and potentially revise each other's recipes is much greater in the diaspora than at home, because of the increased social interaction among the subgroups in their new communities and greater exposure to an assortment of ingredients on the shelves of West African grocery stores. Thus, in the kitchens of these new Americans, West African cuisine continues to evolve and be reinvented.

Music represents another arena of commonality among West Africans. Although still tied to particular ethnic identities, musical forms such as juju, the music of the Yoruba, and especially highlife, which is Ghanaian, have not only crossed the intergroup boundaries of West African culture but have become transnational in scope. Afrobeat, one of the core elements of world music, also has roots in West Africa. Interestingly, soukous music represents an adaptation that occurred before overseas migration, since it was transplanted from the Congo, in Central Africa, to West Africa, and now the West African diaspora has embraced this genre as well. One of the most striking examples of this type of global hybridization has been the influence of American hip-hop on West African musical forms such as juju, highlife, and dancehall. The contribution of Africans in the U.S. to traditional West African music results in such variations as the formation of musical groups that rap in pidgin English.

The most public displays of the political culture of the West African newcomers are Independence Day festivities marking the overthrow of colonialism in their respective home countries. The occasion typically includes speeches by dignitaries and community leaders as well as cultural performances by both children and adults. Some groups, notably Nigerians and Ghanaians, are beginning to take these celebrations beyond their ethnic communities. For example, in 2003 an amalgam of Nigerian groups and sponsors organized an Independence Day parade in New York with the idea of modeling the festivities after the city's West Indian Carnival or the Saint Patrick's Day parade, as much to showcase and legitimize Nigerian culture to the broader community as to acknowledge the historic significance of the October 1 event. For the Cape Verdean diaspora, that wider recognition has already been accomplished. Since the independence of the Republic of Cape Verde falls on July 5, the annual Independence Day parade in New Bedford, Massachusetts, the historic hub of the Cape Verdean American community, is designed to celebrate both the American independence day and the Cape Verdean one. Cape Verdean community leaders, youth groups, and entertainers wave from floats or march alongside city officials, high school bands, and representatives of other civic associations, and the parade route is mapped to finish in the south end neighborhood that is the heart of the Cape Verdean enclave.

In addition to the Fourth of July, the American holiday that the new West African settlers have enthusiastically embraced is Thanksgiving. Groups of immigrant families join together, taking turns to host the meal each year. The feast typically combines traditional West African dishes such as fufu and palava sauce with the customary turkey, cranberry sauce, and fixings, a gesture to the immigrant children. Thanksgiving has become so intrinsic to the diaspora population that in some instances West African associations take the initiative to organize turkey dinners and even church services for the community. It is not unusual for the celebration to begin the evening before the holiday, with parties, music, and dancing.

Among African immigrants, religious participation is extensive, whether the affiliation is Christian, Muslim, indigenous African, or some combination of these faiths; there are simply very few nonbelievers among this population. While African services in the American setting may be associated with mainline religious denominations such as Methodism and Roman Catholicism, the most rapid expansion has come from evangelical Christianity, which has experienced an ongoing and unprecedented surge in Africa and other parts of the developing world. Thus the African immigrants are following the trajectories of their Latino and African American counterparts in fueling a vibrant evangelical movement. West Africans, especially from Nigeria and Ghana, are at the forefront of the new African church movement in the U.S. Many of the founders were brought up in the Anglican, Methodist, and Orthodox churches but have branched out to Pentecostal, storefront congregations. Paradoxically, for decades the U.S. dispatched missionaries to West Africa to establish start-up churches, but today the reverse is taking place. Many of the independent and indigenous churches of West Africa are routinely sending missionaries to America to minister to new immigrant communities and to recruit additional members for their congregations. This phenomenon illustrates well the complexity of the transcontinental interpenetration and cross-fertilization of culture. African congregations in the U.S. typically maintain close links to churches in their countries of origin, sending pastors for training and exchanging clergy, hymnals, and prayer books.

Meanwhile, denominations have been multiplying at an explosive rate. For example, the Redeemed Christian Church of God, a global Pentecostal movement based in Nigeria, came to New York in 1995 and currently has 14 branches in the city. While many of the leaders of the new African church movement were active in their homeland congregations, "American-made" pastors have increasingly emerged. Retaining their day jobs, as it were, the new men and women of the cloth are ministers on Sundays and designated weekday Bible study days and accountants, nurses, or professors during the rest of the week. Their congregations are primarily West African. Often the dominant group in the membership reflects the national or even ethnic affiliation of the pastor and the leaders. Yet the rapid expansion of venues for worship has not been confined to the Protestant sects. For example, in response to the arrival of growing numbers of Ghanaian Catholics, the Diocese of Brooklyn and Queens recently added an apostolate in which mass is conducted in Ashante and Fante, the two main dialects of Ghana. Furthermore, like the Pentecostal Christians, West African Muslim migrants, most of whom come from French-speaking countries, have developed their own storefront mosques, while others regularly worship together in the homes of the imams. They have also organized their own religious hubs, like the Senegalese Islamic Center in New York.

The vast majority of West African immigrants reside in urban locales. Even refugees who, with the help of their sponsor organizations, are settled initially in rural areas eventually relocate to the cities, especially those with sizable coethnic populations. New York is the largest single destination for those born in West African countries; other metropolitan areas with high numbers of newcomers from the region include Washington, D.C., Atlanta, Boston, Chicago, Philadelphia, Houston, and Dallas. With the exception of "Little Senegal" in New York City and particular neighborhoods where Cape Verdean immigrants are aggregated in selected cities of southeastern New England, such as Brockton, Massachusetts, and Pawtucket, Rhode Island, West Africans do not inhabit visible ethnic enclaves. Although there is some residential clustering in major urban areas, for the most part the newcomers are more dispersed, living in districts where other recent immigrant groups, including other African, Caribbean, and Latino populations, are located.

Increasingly, like many other new Americans, West Africans are acquiring the resources to move to suburban neighborhoods as well. One facet of this residential pattern is the role of the new West African realtors in the American market. Not only do they broker the purchase of new houses for their coethnic clientele, they increasingly represent compatriots eager to procure real estate in their original hometowns. The Ghanaian real estate business is particularly well developed, as more and more immigrants have come to view ownership of a big "dream" home back in Ghana as the preeminent marker of success, even if the buyers may never actually return there to live.

The question of how to make a living is central to the immigrant experience. From the 1960s through the 1980s, a significant proportion of West African newcomers were highly skilled professionals, students, and exchange visitors who never went back. By the 1990s, however, the majority of West African immigrants and refugees no longer represented this cohort, although recent census data show that African immigrants overall are the most educated group in the country, outperforming other immigrant populations as well as native-born whites and blacks. The findings also confirm, however, that high levels of education for African immigrants have not produced comparable levels of income. Indeed, most of the contemporary influx is employed in the service economy—in transportation-related jobs such as taxi drivers and airport porters or in the health-care industry, where they work as nurses, nursing assistants, orderlies, and respiratory and lab assistants. Since the early 1980s, black immigrants have filled the lower-level positions of the health-care industry especially in the cities of the Northeast, such as Boston and New York. Initially migrants of African descent hailing from the West Indies took these jobs, but more recently West African immigrants have become more visible in this occupational sphere, challenging the dominance of those from the Caribbean.

West Africans' high levels of participation in the health-care sector reflect another common occupational trend. Confronted with structural barriers and other practical considerations, many West African men and women, both immigrants and refugees, take jobs that are in many ways radically different from what they did back home. For example, women with degrees, teacher certifications, and teaching jobs in elementary and secondary schools in their countries of origin find themselves having to take an occupational detour when they come to the U.S. First they retrain to become nursing assistants, and then, while working at that lower-level job, many continue to study to gain the credentials to become LPNs and RNs. Moreover, some West African women have begun to establish their own nursing assistant schools and health-care employment agencies, sometimes offering training in English as part of their outreach to newer immigrants. Others have used their experience as nursing home assistants to become proprietors of their own adult-care centers. The owners utilize the economic and social networks of the coethnic community to help advertise these initiatives, bringing their business cards and fliers to immigrant social functions as well as publicizing their ventures throughout the West African business sector.

As has been the case for many immigrant groups before them, some West Africans have gone into business for themselves rather than joining the secondary labor force in order to make it in America. In his ethnographic study of the influx of West African merchants in New York City in the 1990s, *Money Has No Smell,* Paul Stoller found that the primarily Hausa and Wolof street vendors, known for their skill at commerce, had transplanted to the U.S. trading patterns that had been practiced by their forebears for centuries in West Africa. Furthermore, most of those salespeople were Muslim, and their commercial transactions were largely informed by long-established Islamic economic principles that emphasize the centrality of capitalism and entrepreneurship. The Senegalese peddlers bartering trinkets on the sidewalks of New York today are making a living just as their fathers did a generation ago in the open-air markets of Dakar. Indeed, they are replicating the migratory commercial role that itinerant traders played even before the formation of the nation-state of Senegal. In New York many of the immigrant vendors set up their wares at busy Harlem intersections, and in addition to selling West African imports such as masks, leather handbags, and wood carvings, they try to cater to consumer demand for Afrocentric merchandise with a supplement of goods inspired by African American marketing, such as Malcolm X paraphernalia and T-shirts inscribed with the logos of the major black colleges in the U.S. Sometimes the products genuinely come from Africa, while other merchandise are imitations manufactured in Korea and elsewhere. Occasionally the desire to target black customers results in the creation of fanciful hybrid items such as baseball caps made of Mali mud cloth.

In recent years these mainly single and peripatetic New York Senegalese entrepreneurs have moved their ventures off the sidewalks and begun to settle more permanently in central Harlem. Because of the extent of Senegalese residential concentration in the area, along with the establishment of a range of enterprises owned by these Francophone Africans, the neighborhood is now known as "Little Senegal." Not only has the Senegalese community become intertwined with commerce in New York City over the past two decades, its trading networks have led these and other West African merchants to start up small businesses in a variety of cities across the country, selling a range of goods and services. Nigerians predominate in tax preparation services, while some Nigerian and Ghanaian men who worked as cab drivers have been able to become their own bosses by purchasing the taxis themselves. West Africans are renovating dilapidated buildings and breathing new life into once empty storefronts in blighted downtown areas, opening grocery stores in which they sell African foods and spices to primarily coethnic customers. For instance, the tropical food markets that dot many of Atlanta's neighborhoods are designed to cater to the immigrant community, carrying items like garri, various types of fufu, and palm oil. These shops provide continuity in diet and nutrition for the newcomers, but they typically go beyond making familiar foods available. Most also carry newspapers and magazines from the homeland and diaspora communities. Furthermore, many of these local markets have begun to serve as video outlets, where customers can rent movies produced in the budding Nigerian film industry. The sale of special phone cards and CDs of West African and other African and Caribbean musicians is also an important function of the stores. In this way West African businesses not only provide merchandise but also operate as gathering places for the maintenance of compatriot community life. This is also the case for the numerous clubs and entertainment spots owned and operated by West Africans.

Another transplanted cultural strategy that assists in the formation of small business ventures is the tradition of West African rotating credit associations. But not all of the burgeoning ethnic enterprises are geared to a solely West African clientele. For example, the numerous West African restaurants opening up in Houston are frequented by non-African diners as well, and in Pittsburgh, Blemahdoo's African Market Place offers a wide range of imported clothing, fabrics, batik art, and hand-carved items that attract shoppers from a variety of ethnoracial backgrounds. Another niche business that draws particularly on the transplanted cultural skills of female French-speaking Africans but that crosses over to the larger black community in its customer appeal is beauty salons specializing in braiding hair. The proprietors of these shops are also indicative of the process of retooling that occurs so frequently in the West African immigrant experience. Many of these women held professional positions in Senegal but arrived without the language skills to enter into the occupations for which they were trained or even to compete for jobs in the general labor force. Initially they set up braiding businesses in their homes as part of the hidden economy while taking English classes in the evening. Once they have gained proficiency in their new language, they move their enterprise out of the house to a storefront location and establish a bona fide beauty parlor. Similarly, West African women have become self-employed by opening nail salons.

West Africans, like other black immigrants, have adapted and assimilated in three main domains—within the reconfigured African ethnicities, within the milieu of African Americans, and within mainstream America. In spite of the well-documented ethnic conflicts in the region, West Africans, coming from societies with diverse populations, already possess certain multicultural competencies. The question is whether these are the right skills for the distinct complexities of American pluralism. Since race and color hold little relevance at home, many of the newcomers, even the most educated, arrive without a clear grasp of the dynamics of racism and the black experience in the U.S.

The history of the relationship between native and foreign-born blacks in the U.S. has often been an uneasy one, filled with ambivalence on both sides. At times the realities of race have drawn these populations together, particularly when outside discrimination has triggered a reactive solidarity. For example, the turning point in the public's awareness of a growing West African presence was actually an incident of police brutality, when Amadou Diallo, an unarmed Guinean immigrant, was killed by four New York City police officers in 1999. The response to his death led to the consolidation of a West African community in New York that had previously been split by political and ethnic rivalries. The episode further shattered the prevalent misconception among the immigrants of immunity to American racism, jolting many into the realities of racial profiling. This recognition spurred the African and African American leadership to join together in their efforts to demand justice. More often, however, cultural differences have superseded alliances based on color. Immigrants typically attempt to assert their cultural distinctiveness, foster ethnic solidarity, and resist identification with what has been the most subordinated sector of American society, while African Americans may exhibit resentment at the perceived preferential treatment accorded the foreigners, regarding them as a competitive threat in an economy where resources available to racial minorities are scarce. Usually these dynamics get even more complicated as the second generation of black immigrants begins to assimilate and to reshape their identities within the larger American and black American context.

Thus, West African newcomers, like their Caribbean counterparts, tend initially to feel detached from the black community, and very few forge close relationships with African Americans. For instance, West African Muslims find it difficult to interact with African Americans of the same faith. The former consider the latter's brand of Islam watered down and excessively tailored to their long experience of inequality in America. In addition, some West Africans resist the label "black" because, among other things, they see it as eclipsing their unique cultural identities. Furthermore, they arrive with preconceived pejorative stereotypes of this population. In general, however, the longer the West African settlers live in the U.S., the more they realize and accept that in this country they are identified more by the color of their skin than by their nationality. A common pattern has been to self-identify most broadly as "African" or "West African" upon arrival in the U.S., then to redefine oneself in terms of a distinctive ethnic or nationality group, and later, after making a more permanent adjustment to the urban neighborhood in which one lives, gradually to align oneself with the larger black community; some may even identify as "African American." The rate of intermarriage between second-generation West Africans and African Americans is increasing as well and is another factor that minimizes the wedge. In the course of the adaptation process, the new immigrants eventually do become ethnics, often representing integral threads in the fabric of African America.

Bibliography

Arthur, John A. 2000. *Invisible Sojourners: African Immigrant Diaspora in the United States.* Westport, Conn.: Praeger.

D'Alisera, JoAnn. 2004. *An Imagined Geography: Sierra Leonean Muslims in America.* Philadelphia: University of Pennsylvania Press.

Dodson, Howard, and Sylviane Diouf, eds. 2004. *In Motion: The African American Migration Experience.* Washington, D.C.: Schomburg Center for Research in Black Culture and National Geographic Society.

Gordon, April. 1998. "The New Diaspora—African Immigration to the United States." *Journal of Third World Studies* 15, 1: 79–103.

Halter, Marilyn. 1993. *Between Race and Ethnicity: Cape Verdean American Immigrants, 1860–1965.* Urbana: University of Illinois Press.

Logan, John, and Glenn Deane. 2003. "Black Diversity in Metropolitan America." State University of New York at Albany, Lewis Mumford Center for Comparative Urban and Regional Research. mumford1.dyndns.org/cen2000/report.html.

Obiakor, Festus E., and Patrick A Grant, eds. 2002. *Foreign-Born African Americans: Silenced Voices in the Discourse on Race.* New York: Nova Science.

Ogbaa, Kalu. 2003. *The Nigerian Americans.* Westport, Conn.: Greenwood.

Stoller, Paul. 2002. *Money Has No Smell: The Africanization of New York City.* Chicago: University of Chicago Press.

Wilson, Jill. 2003. "African-born Residents of the United States." Migration Policy Institute. www.migrationinformation.org/USfocus/display.cfm?id=147.

Africa: East

Abdi Kusow

The East African region extending from Sudan in the north to Mozambique in the south has a population of more than 200 million. It is home to one of the longest traces of human habitation and an ancient civilization, including a literary tradition dating back several thousand years, a form of Christianity coinciding with the time of the Roman empire, and an Islamic tradition dating back to the early years of Islam. Consequently, the region represents an area of great cultural and human diversity and displays a mixture of African, Asian, Middle Eastern, and European cultural and religious heritages.

Broadly speaking, the region can be divided into two subregions, the northeast and the southeast. The northeastern region includes Djibouti, Ethiopia, Eritrea, Somalia, and Sudan, while the southeast includes Kenya, Tanzania, Uganda, and Mozambique. The most populated country in the entire region is Ethiopia, one of the oldest independent nations in the world. It has cultures and religious foundations that date back several thousand years. Demographically, it has the third largest population (about 67 million) on the continent, after Egypt and Nigeria. Sudan, in contrast, is geographically the largest country on the continent, with an area roughly one quarter the size of the United States. Both Ethiopia and Sudan have tremendous human and natural resources, but their development efforts have been frustrated by civil wars and severe political instability.

Somalia is smaller in both size and population and is religiously and culturally more relatively homogeneous than most countries on the continent. Despite this relative homogeneity, however, it has had its share of political violence. Since the outbreak of civil war in 1991, and despite significant efforts by the international community, particularly the U.S., Somalia remains the only country without a recognized central government in the world today. Widespread human rights violations are the order of the day. The country's social, political, economic, and physical infrastructures have been destroyed as a result of the now 15-year-old civil war. There are no organized educational or health institutions in the country, and the people, particularly the rural masses, live in extreme poverty and malnutrition. Hundreds of thousands live in refugee camps in neighboring countries such as Ethiopia, Kenya, and Yemen. The most fortunate ones are those who have been able to secure resettlement in Europe and North America.

The southeastern region, particularly the coastal cities of Kenya and Tanzania, has a long history of social and cultural interaction between Arab, Indian, and Persian traders and Bantu-speaking communities, who collectively produced what is known today as the Swahili language and culture, shared by Kenya, Tanzania, and Uganda. Despite this Islamic and Middle Eastern influence, however, the majority of the population in the southeastern region is Christian, although a significant number of people follow traditional African religions. The largest country in size, population, and economic output in this region is Kenya. In fact, Kenya has one of the most vibrant economies in Africa. Tanzania has one of the most stable political institutions on the continent, while Uganda is rich with natural and human resources.

Migration and Settlement Patterns

Despite the presence of a small number of East African immigrants in New York City in the first three decades of the 20th century, the history of the East African community in the U.S. is recent. Before 1970 the U.S. Census recorded about 4,000 individuals. The majority of these early-wave immigrants were young male students sent by their governments to study in the U.S. and then return and help lead the social and economic institutions of their newly independent countries. Many of the students did in fact return, but those who stayed behind laid the foundation for development and growth of the East African immigrant community, particularly in the Washington, D.C., metropolitan area.

Table 1   Decade of arrival of foreign-born East Africans (in thousands)

National origin	Total	1990–2000	1980–1989	1970–1979	1960–1969	Before 1960
Ethiopia	71,254	44,139	19,452	6,162	1,162	339
Kenya	43,779	28,420	9,245	4,994	932	188
Somalia	36,595	33,269	2,667	348	200	111
Sudan	18,567	13,958	3,393	611	414	191
Tanzania	11,764	5,222	3,746	2,135	500	161
Uganda	12,214	5,989	3,143	2,549	479	54

Source: U.S. Bureau of the Census, 2000 Census, 5% Public Use Microdata Sample, weighted data.

Since then the number and composition of East African immigrants in the U.S. have changed. From 1970 to 1980, nearly 17,000 immigrants were admitted; that number increased to almost 42,000 from 1980 to 1990, and more than 130,000 were admitted in the last decade of the 20th century. Consequently, East African immigrants are starting to mark their presence in many cities and metropolitan areas around the country. Their communities are concentrated in Washington, D.C., Maryland, Virginia, New York, Seattle, Portland (Oregon), Minneapolis–St. Paul, and Columbus, Ohio. More than 50 percent of Ethiopians are found in the South Atlantic and Pacific Northwest regions. Somalis are primarily concentrated in the midwestern states.

Of the estimated 1 million African immigrants, those from East Africa represent 26 percent, or roughly 263,000 people, the largest group after those from West Africa. Within the East African immigrant population, those from Ethiopia (71,254) make up the largest group, followed by Kenyans (43,779), Somalis (36,595), Sudanese (18,256), Tanzanians (11,747), and Ugandans (12,214). It must be noted, however, that census data, particularly with respect to recent refugees, may not be reliable, and the size of the East African immigrant population, particularly Ethiopians, Somalis, and Sudanese, may be larger than census estimates show. Estimates of Somali immigrants, for example, range from as low as 36,000 to as high as 150,000, depending on whether one uses information from community leaders and local officials or data from the 2000 Census. This problem may result from the fact that East African immigration is a very recent phenomenon, so that many Somalis, Sudanese, and Ethiopians may not have filled out the 2000 Census questionnaire. Another factor may be that a substantial number of immigrants from the region have entered the U.S. illegally.

Structural and political factors in the home and host countries account for the sudden influx of East African immigrants. The combined effects of the cold war, during which the U.S. and the Soviet Union supported autocratic dictators financially and militarily, lack of sustainable economic development, and deep ethnic and internal cultural divisions left permanent political and economic instabilities across the region. The British empire's incorporation of regions claimed by Somalis into Ethiopia, the Ethiopian empire's annexation of Eritrea, and the incorporation of several culturally and racially distinct groups with different political ambitions into the nation of Sudan led to some of the longest and most brutal wars and civil conflicts on the continent. In Uganda, the human rights abuses that followed Idi Amin's overthrow of Milton Obote in 1971, and the subsequent overthrow of Idi Amin by Tanzanian government–supported groups and the return of Obote in 1979, produced ethnic unrest in the 1980s. Ethnic and cultural divisions within Kenya and Tanzania pose formidable challenges to sustainable economic development as well.

The political and economic instabilities that forced many East African immigrants to seek a better life in the U.S. were concurrent with several immigration and refugee policies that made it easier for those with the necessary means to immigrate to the U.S. One of these policies was the Refugee Act of 1980, which amended the definition of refugee to include people fleeing civil conflict and increased immigration per-country limits, which allowed Ethiopian, Eritrean, Somali, and Sudanese refugees to seek admission. The 1986 Immigration Reform and Control Act legalized the status of more than 31,000 Africans and enabled them to bring in their immediate families. Moreover, the 1990 Immigration Act, which introduced the Diversity Visa Lottery, designed to admit more immigrants from countries underrepresented in the overall flow of immigrants, enabled more Africans to immigrate to the U.S. in the 1990s.

An important observation about the differences between the two subregions is that the southeastern region has been and remains relatively more politically stable than the northeast. Consequently, immigrants from the former region have generally immigrated for economic reasons, while those from the northeast have been pushed by political instabilities. Given these differences, it is safe to say that the majority of immigrants from the southeastern region are economic immigrants while those from the northeast are refugees and political immigrants. Those from the southeastern region are more educated and bring with them skills that can be transferred more easily to the U.S. economy. Immigrants from the northeastern region are less well educated and, as we will see, usually face difficulties in adjusting to the American economy.

Another important observation is that English is a semi-official language in the countries of the southeast, and therefore the majority of immigrants from Kenya, Tanzania, and Uganda, particularly the educated, speak fluent English before they come to the U.S., while the majority of immigrants from the northeast come with no prior knowledge of English. The two groups also have different religious backgrounds. Immigrants from the southeastern region come from predominantly Christian countries, while a significant number of those from the northeast come from Islamic countries. One exception is Ethiopia, where Christianity is embraced by a slight majority, although the Muslim population is significant. These cultural, political, and contextual differences are important variables for understanding differences in the degree of economic and cultural assimilation between immigrants from the two regions.

Secondary Structural Assimilation

Overall, African immigrants exhibit significant achievements according to almost all measures of socioeconomic status. The educational attainment of Africans is the highest among any immigrant group in the U.S.

However, to speak of East African immigrants as a homogeneous economic class is to ignore obvious variations. Although Kenyan, Tanzanian, and Ugandan immi-

Table 2 Educational and socioeconomic achievement among African immigrants and major
U.S. racial and ethnic groups, 1990–2000

	Years of education[a]	Median household income[b]	Percentage unemployed[c]	Percentage living in poverty[d]
1990				
African American	11.7	$29,251	12.5	32.8
Afro-Caribbean	12.1	$42,927	9.4	17.8
African	14.3	$35,041	8.5	24.7
Non-Hispanic white	12.9	$47,481	4.7	11.3
Hispanic	10.2	$35,041	9.9	27.0
Asian	13.1	$54,508	5.0	15.9
2000				
African American	12.4	$33,790	11.2	30.4
Afro-Caribbean	12.6	$43,650	8.7	18.8
African	14.0	$42,900	7.3	22.1
Non-Hispanic white	13.5	$53,000	4.0	11.2
Hispanic	10.5	$38,500	8.8	26.0
Asian	13.9	$62,000	4.6	13.9

Source: John Logan and Glenn Dean, "Black Diversity in Metropolitan America" (Albany, N.Y.: Lewis Mumford Center for Comparative Urban and Regional Research, SUNY Albany, 2003), table 4.

Note: Does fish not include children born abroad to American parents.

a. Persons aged 25 and older.

b. All households; in 1989 and 1999 dollars.

c. Persons aged 18 and older who are in the labor force.

d. Persons aged 25–64 in the labor force: in 1989 and 1999 dollars.

grants consistently rank as high as or higher than the national average on most indicators of economic success, the figures for Somali and Sudanese immigrants have been and remain the lowest in the nation. According to the 2000 Census, unemployment rates for immigrants from the region ranged from one of the lowest (2.6 percent, the rate for Ugandan immigrants) to one of the highest (8.5 percent, that for Somali immigrants). Data for poverty rates show a similar trend, with Ugandan immigrants exhibiting one of the lowest rates and Somalis and Sudanese the highest among any immigrant group in the U.S. Poverty rates for Somali and Sudanese immigrants are as high as those of African Americans and Native Americans, the two groups with the highest poverty rates in the nation, both historically and today.

It is also clear from the data that immigrants from Kenya, Tanzania, and Uganda are significantly better educated than those from Ethiopia, Sudan, and Somalia. Moreover, socioeconomic achievement patterns among Kenyan, Tanzanian, and Ugandan immigrants have been consistent across time. The number of college graduates among Kenyan immigrants, for example, has dropped very slightly over the past three decades, from 55 percent in 1980 to 53 percent and 51 percent in 1990 and 2000, respectively. The percentages for Tanzanian and Ugandan immi-

Table 3   Patterns of secondary structural assimilation among foreign-born East Africans, 1980-2000

	Percentage college graduates[a]	Median household income[b]	Percentage unemployed[c]	Percentage below the poverty line[d]
1980				
Ethiopia	42.9	$14,620	4.5	18.1
Kenya	55.2	$22,495	5.4	9.6
Somalia	23.8	$19,195	4.7	23.0
Sudan	51.1	$7,420	7.7	23.2
Tanzania	54.4	$23,365	4.4	9.1
Uganda	52.3	$23,010	3.6	12.0
1990				
Ethiopia	33.4	$26,203	5.4	12.2
Kenya	53.8	$41,291	3.3	7.9
Somalia	35.0	$16,000	11.4	29.4
Sudan	53.1	$28,000	5.5	11.0
Tanzania	50.7	$42,000	3.0	1.6
Uganda	49.3	$38,297	2.8	8.1
2000				
Ethiopia	30.0	$38,400	3.7	10.1
Kenya	51.4	$43,600	2.8	9.0
Somalia	15.3	$19,700	8.5	29.5
Sudan	41.6	$27,600	6.9	26.6
Tanzania	53.5	$60,800	3.9	7.9
Uganda	51.8	$56,200	2.6	4.0

Source: U.S. Bureau of the Census, 1980, 1990, and 2000 Censuses, 5% Public Use Microdata Sample, weighted data.

a. Persons aged 25–64.

b. All households; in 1979, 1989, and 1999 dollars.

c. Persons aged 25–64 in the labor force.

d. Persons aged 25–64 in the labor force; in 1979, 1989, and 1999 dollars.

grants also experienced minor fluctuations over the past three census periods. In contrast, the data for Ethiopian, Sudanese, and Somali immigrants over the same time frame indicate a considerable decrease in the number of college-educated immigrants. In the case of Somalis, the number of college graduates increased from 24 percent in 1980 to 35 percent in 1990 but dropped to almost 15 percent in 2000. Comparable figures for Ethiopian immigrants were 43 percent in 1980, 33 percent in 1990, and 30 percent in 2000.

Similar trends are observable for unemployment rates, poverty rates, and particularly household income. For example, income levels for Kenyan, Tanzanian, and Ugandan immigrants have consistently stayed at or above the national average. The 2000 unemployment rate for Ugandan immigrants is lower than that of any group, including native-born whites, while that of Somalis is among the highest in the nation. Based on these data, it is clear that country of origin is an important factor for the observed socioeconomic differences between different East African immigrant groups. The data specifically show that immigrants from the southeastern subregion consistently score higher on all indicators of socioeconomic status than those from the northeast.

Individual as well as contextual variables account for the observed socioeconomic achievement differences between Kenyan, Tanzanian, and Ugandan immigrants on the one hand and Ethiopian, Somali, and Sudanese immigrants on the other. One factor that may explain the gap between the two groups is the degree of cultural, linguistic, and political assimilation. The 2000 Census data indicate that the rate of cultural and political assimilation among East African immigrants differs from subregion to subregion or country to country. Immigrants from the northeastern region, particularly Somalis and Sudanese, are far more linguistically isolated and have lower percentages of naturalized citizens than those from Kenya, Tanzania, and Uganda.

Linguistic isolation, according to the census, refers to situations in which all members of a household 14 years old and over speak a language other than English and have difficulty speaking English. As shown in Table 4, more than 20 percent of Ethiopian, 30 percent of Sudanese, and 45 percent of Somali immigrant households fall into this category. In contrast, fewer than 9 percent of the Kenyan, Tanzanian, and Ugandan immigrant households are linguistically isolated. The data on naturalization patterns also indicate differences from country to country. Again, Somali and Sudanese immigrants have the highest percentages of noncitizens in their populations, as opposed to Kenyan, Tanzanian, and Ugandan immigrants and, to a certain degree, Ethiopian immigrants.

Another factor that may explain why immigrants from the southeastern region are more academically and economically successful than those from the northeast is

Table 4   Cultural and identity assimilation among foreign-born East Africans (percentages)

	Ethiopians	Kenyans	Somalis	Sudanese	Tanzanians	Ugandans
Linguistic isolation						
Linguistically isolated households	20.8	7.8	45.0	30.8	8.3	6.9
Not linguistically isolated households	79.2	92.2	55.0	69.2	91.7	93.1
Citizenship						
Born abroad of U.S parents	3.9	6.2	1.2	2.3	6.3	3.4
Naturalized citizen	31.6	25.7	11.8	22.3	37.3	36.0
Not U.S. citizen	64.5	68.1	86.9	75.4	56.4	60.6

Source: U.S. Bureau of the Census, 2000 Census, 5% Public Use Microdata Sample, weighted data.

differences in the political economy of the two regions. The northeastern region has been characterized by permanent and acute political instability. Over the past 40 years, Ethiopia, Somalia, and Sudan have been involved in either civil wars or conflict with one neighbor or another. After 30 years of civil war, Eritrea seceded from Ethiopia and became independent in 1993. Just five years later, Ethiopia and Eritrea started a border war that resulted in the death and displacement of thousands of innocent civilians. In fact, as this book goes to print, Ethiopia is on the brink of a widespread civil war because of disagreements over the most recent national election results. Ethiopia and Somalia have fought each other at least three times, officially, since the 1960s.

Since 1991 the Somali civil war has produced one of the worst human tragedies in Africa. Nearly 500,000 individuals, mostly women and children, died of human-induced starvation in the first three years of the conflict alone. Another several hundred thousand were forced into exile in neighboring countries and in several European countries, Canada, Australia, and the U.S. Almost 15 years later, Somalia has no central government and is ruled by warlords who have turned the country into a patchwork of fiefdoms.

For more than 40 years Sudan has been characterized by a combination of racial, ethnic, and religious conflict, the most important being what is generally known as the dichotomy between the Arab Muslim north and the African Christian or animist south. The 2003 Darfur crisis between government-sponsored militia groups and western Sudanese ethnic militias led to the displacement of over 2 million people and the death of nearly 70,000 civilians.

Moreover, political instabilities in the northeastern region have led to environmental problems and several major famines, including the 1984–1985 famine in Ethiopia, the 1986–1988 famine in Sudan, and the 1992 famine in Somalia. The countries in the southeastern region have been and remain relatively more politically stable and therefore have not experienced similar human tragedies. Generally speaking, Kenya, Tanzania, and Uganda have also been more economically stable than Ethiopia, Somalia, and Sudan.

Still another factor that may contribute to socioeconomic differences between immigrants from the two subregions is the fact that a significant percentage of the immigrants from Kenya (20.3), Tanzania (42.2), and Uganda (31.4) are South Asian (mostly Indian) East Africans whose families settled in Africa during British rule, when they functioned as middlemen between African natives and colonial officers and settlers. After the East African countries achieved independence, the South Asians remained as small business owners, and they later controlled much of the private business in the region and were better educated than the native African populations.

The lower achievement levels of northeastern immigrants challenge the commonly asserted statement that sub-Saharan or African-born black immigrants are among the best-educated immigrant groups in the U.S. Indeed, if one looks at the aggregate census data, it is clear that African immigrants have one of the highest percentages of college-educated individuals in the country. However, generalized statements about the socioeconomic success of African immigrants must be looked at with some caution. In reality, the East African immigrant population comes from diverse socioeconomic and class backgrounds.

Cultural Assimilation

One of the most important sociological concerns about immigrants has been and remains the nature and the dynamics of assimilation patterns among nonwhites. The central question is whether immigrants to the U.S. assimilate into culturally and ethnically similar ethnic groups and maintain their homeland identities or assimilate into the mainstream society. Understanding the assimilation patterns of African-born black immigrants is one of the keys to unlocking the binary black-white categories that have been the basis for understanding the nature of racial identities in the U.S. for many centuries.

The increase in the number of African-born immigrants, particularly East Africans, in the U.S. has intensified media and public discussions about whether African immigrants will assimilate into African American identities or create some sort of a black ethnic enclave where identities are articulated more in terms of culture

Table 5   Top five ancestry selections among foreign-born East Africans, 2000 (percentages)

Rank	Country of Birth		
	Ethiopia	Kenya	Somalia
1	Ethiopian (69.3)	Kenyan (31.9)	Somalian (74.7)
2	African (9.2)	Asian Indian (20.3)	Not reported (9.7)
3	Not reported (7.0)	African (20.2)	African (7.5)
4	African American (4.0)	Not reported (6.4)	African American (2.0)
5	Eritrean (2.6)	African American (5.3)	Uncodable/Uncoded[a] (2.0)
	Sudan	Tanzania	Uganda
1	Sudanese (43.6)	Asian Indian (42.4)	Asian Indian (31.2)
2	African (18.3)	Uncodable/Uncoded[a] (18.6)	Uncodable/Uncoded[a] (26.2)
3	Not reported (9.8)	African (14.8)	African (22.4)
4	Arab (3.8)	Not reported (5.3)	Not reported (8.5)
5	Not reported (3.6)	African American (2.0)	African American (2.4)

Source: U.S. Bureau of the Census, 2000 Census, 5% Public Use Microdata Sample, weighted data.

a. Due to confidentiality constraints in the construction of the 5% IPUMS samples, any category representing fewer than 10,000 people was combined with a larger, more generalized category. One such category is "Uncodable" and another is "Uncoded," which includes various reported ancestries, such as Angolan, Burundian, Djibouti, Gambian, Ivory Coast, Senegalese, Afrikaner, Nuer, etc.

and/or nationality than skin color. The 2000 Census ancestry question is quite revealing. It is clear that East African immigrants are not necessarily embracing African American identities. The number of those who identified themselves as "African American" reached a high of 5.3 percent only in the case of Kenyans and Tanzanians to zero in the case of Sudanese immigrants. East African immigrants do not even embrace a pan-African identity. They primarily identify themselves in terms of their homeland national identities—Somali, Ethiopian, or Kenyan—as opposed to African or African American. Although a significant proportion of the East African population, particularly those from Kenya, Tanzania, and Uganda, are of South Asian descent, it is also interesting that they still identify as Africans and not South Asians.

The kinds of identities that East African immigrants seem to employ are in sharp contrast to the way that identities are understood in the U.S. in general and among African Americans in particular. In the U.S., skin color or blackness is one of the most important categories of social understanding. It is applied to any person with stereotypical African characteristics. It is in many ways determined through what is commonly known as the "one-drop rule," meaning that a single drop of black blood makes a person black. Despite recent changes in the racial climate ushered in by the civil rights movement and the increase in the level of racial diversity over the past few decades, the U.S., as Mary Waters has pointed out, "remains a color-conscious society" and skin color as the most important category of social stratification is for the most part collectively shared by blacks and whites.

However, social stratification as well as cultural identities in East Africa are primarily determined through economic and symbolic identities, such as clan or tribal identities or occupational categories. Symbol-based identity is a system of social differentiation where membership is determined through shared ancestors. Although symbolic or clan differentiation is a meaningful category of social understanding and social differentiation, it is not based strictly on skin color. This does not mean, of course, that East Africans fail to understand that skin color is one of the most important categories of social, political, and economic differentiation in the world today; but because it does not provide a meaningful category of social understanding in their own environment, the notion of blackness does not enter their cultural narrative resources until they come to the U.S.

The difference between how blackness is understood by African Americans and by East African immigrants has both everyday and sociological implications. At the everyday level, it informs the way African Americans and African immigrants view each other. No extensive research deals with this issue, but an increasing number of anecdotal and media reports indicate that the two groups lack a collectively shared understanding of what it means to be black in this country, perhaps because they also lack many shared historical and social experiences. One African American interviewed by a local newspaper said that Somali immigrants and African Americans could not relate to each other despite the fact that they were both black, pointing out that "you can look just alike and appear to be on the same team, but we're as different as night and day . . . Just because we are all black or originate from Africa doesn't mean anything." He continued, "We have a separate language, culture, and religion. It is a big thing. This is not an issue of color."

An African American who married a Somali woman clearly articulated the mutual misunderstanding that exists between East African immigrants and African Americans. He talked about how, when he was courting his wife in Nairobi, some of her relatives did not embrace him because he was not Somali. Ironically, though, after the couple moved to Washington, D.C., his friends did not embrace his wife, because she did not look like an African American; they commented that "he has gone and married a white black woman."

Sociologically, such incidents speak to the methodological and conceptual problems that complicate the traditional definition of who is African and who is African American, or, in general, the meaning of blackness in the U.S. Historically, African identity or blackness in this country has been strictly defined in terms of skin color. The presence of the East African immigrant population and African immigrants in general tacitly challenges the black-white dichotomy that underlies our understanding of racial identities. The East African population, both in Africa and in the diaspora, is biologically and culturally diverse and runs the gamut of the human physical spectrum. More important, unlike the African American community, whose collective identity is in many ways informed by the horrors of slavery, the East African immigrant population (despite the existence of certain forms of slavery in Sudan) does not have any meaningful contact with or a true understanding of the implications of institutionalized cultural and economic slavery. One can even make the argument that the majority of East African communities, with the exception of Kenya and Uganda, did not experience colonialism in any significant way. In other words, neither slavery nor colonialism significantly informs the collective memory of the East African population in the U.S.

More importantly, East African immigrants come from societies where blackness is the racial norm and where it is not directly stigmatized historically or currently. Consequently, Africans in general and East African immigrants in particular derive their identities from cultural and ethnic-based categories rather than from skin color. The sociological implications of this include increases in the diversity of the black population and challenges to the meaning of color-based racial categories in the U.S. today.

Bibliography

Arthur, John A. *Invisible Sojourners: African Immigrant Diaspora in the United States.* Westport, Conn.: Praeger, 2000.
Butcher, Kristin, F. "Black Immigrants in the United States: A Comparison with Native Blacks and Other Immigrants." *Industrial and Labor Relations* 47 (1994): 265–84.

Davis, J. *Who Is Black: One Nation's Definition.* University Park, Penn.: Pennsylvania State University Press, 1991.

Diouf, Sylviane. "The New African Diaspora." The Schomburg Center for Research in Black Culture, www.inmotionaame.org/texts.

Eissa, Salih O. "Diversity and Transformations: African Americans and African Immigration to the United States." Immigration Policy Center, www.ailf.org/ipc.

Fears, Darryl. "A Diverse—and Divided—Black Community." *Washington Post,* Feb. 24, 2002.

Global IDP Database, *Profile of Internal Displacement: Sudan.* Compilation of information available in the Global IDP Database of the Norwegian Refugee Council, www.unhcr.org/cgi-bin/texis/vtx/home/opendoc.pdf?tbl=RSDCOI&id=4059b7044.

Holtzman, John D. "Nuer Journeys, Nuer Lives: Sudanese Immigrants in Minnesota." In Nancy Foner, ed., *New Immigrant Series.* Boston: Allyn and Bacon, 2000.

Leigh, Swigart. "Extended Lives: The African Immigrant Experience in Philadelphia." Philadelphia: Balch Institute for Ethnic Studies, 2000.

Logan, John R., and Glenn Deane. "Black Diversity in Metropolitan America." New York: University of Albany, Lewis Mumford Center for Comparative Urban and Regional Research, 2003; mumford.albany.edu/census/report.html.

Waters, M. *Black Identities: West Indian Immigrant Dreams and American Realities.* New York: Russell Sage Foundation, 1999.

———. "Immigration, Intermarriage, and the Challenges of Measuring Racial/Ethnic Identities," *American Journal of Public Health* 90, 11 (2000): 1735–37.

Africa: South Africa and Zimbabwe

Helen B. Marrow

Leaving South Africa

Historically, South Africa is best known as an immigrant-receiving rather than an emigrant-sending country. Originally inhabited by indigenous nomadic tribes, it was settled by Bantu tribes from central and east Africa, Dutch, Huguenot, and British settlers, and East Indian laborers. England occupied the area during the Napoleonic wars, and in the 1830s farmers of Dutch descent (Boers) moved in and established two republics within the country. In the 1870s and 1880s, mineral discoveries in these two republics attracted immigrants from all over the world, including some from the same European countries also sending migrants to the U.S. After the Boer War (1899–1902), Britain annexed the two Boer republics and in 1910 established the Union of South Africa. After joining the British Commonwealth of Nations in 1934, the Republic of South Africa gained independence in 1961. As the country industrialized during the 20th century, white immigrants from Europe, black immigrants from neighboring countries, and white immigrants from Rhodesia (which became Zimbabwe in April 1980) and other neighboring countries all made South Africa their home.

Very few South Africans migrated to the U.S. before 1950 (less than 230 annually, according to the historian Stanley Moss) because of the restrictive immigration policies of the Immigration Act of 1924. However, since World War II there have been five distinct phases of emigration from South Africa. The first four were relatively short-lived, corresponding closely to periods of intense economic, political, and racial strife. In the first phase (1949–1951), South Africans left the country for political reasons; among them were both voluntary immigrants opposed to the new apartheid regime established by the Afrikaner National Party (which came to power in 1948) and political refugees whose lives were threatened by its racial policies. In the second (1960–1961), third (1976–1979), and fourth (1985–1988) phases, emigrants left the country because of new periods of intense political and racial unrest. Since 1994 (the fifth phase), South African figures again show a net population loss due to emigration—that is, more emigrants have left the country than immigrants have entered it. Moreover, while official figures show a net gain of immigration over the past half-century—545,642 emigrants compared to 1,220,863 immigrants between 1945 and 1999—it is only during the post-1994 period that South Africa has witnessed a sustained net loss of immigration for more than six years in a row. This recent emigration from South Africa is polarized; some commentators argue that emigrants are simply seeking lower rates of crime, better working conditions, and better futures for their children, while others connect emigration with white discomfort in post-apartheid South Africa and a belief that their children's futures will be better in majority-white societies.

Today South Africans' top five destination countries are the U.K., Canada, the U.S., Australia, and New Zealand. All are English-speaking countries with high standards of living. South Africans are reported to prefer Australia because of its sunny climate; the U.K., Australia, and New Zealand because of their cultural affinities with South Africa; the U.K. because of its historical ties to South Africa (some 800,000 South Africans currently hold British passports); the U.S. because of its many economic opportunities (especially in the information technology sector during the 1990s); and Canada for its high quality of life and proximity to the U.S. South African Statistics (SSA) show approximately 82,900 South Africans emigrating to these five countries between 1989 and 1997, while the South African Network of Skills Abroad (SANSA) project at the University of Cape Town puts the figure closer to 233,600, based on those countries' records of incoming immigrants. In a 1998 survey by the Southern African Migration Project (SAMP), 24 percent of skilled South Africans indicated that the U.S. would be their preferred destination if they were ever to leave, compared with 22 percent who named Australia, 15 percent who named the United Kingdom, 12 percent who named New Zealand, and 11 percent who named Canada. Thus, while the U.S. was not a major destination for South African emigrants earlier in the 20th century, today it is one of their primary ones.

Leaving Zimbabwe

Zimbabwe shares with South Africa a legacy of British colonialism and minority white rule over a majority nonwhite population. After UDI (unilateral declaration of independence from Britain) in 1965, black nationalist opposition to Ian Smith's white-controlled government in Rhodesia intensified. For 14 years Robert Mugabe's ZANU and Joshua Nkomo's ZAPU organizations waged a bloody guerrilla war on the Smith government (and on that of his surrogate, Abel Muzorewa, after 1979), with violence stemming from both sides. As the security situation steadily deteriorated, emigration (mostly of whites with the financial resources to leave) began to rise in 1972, and a net loss of immigration was recorded beginning in 1976.

In 1980 the Smith-Muzorewa government agreed to a ceasefire and entered into negotiations with the guerrilla opposition (which by that time was an alliance between the ZANU and ZAPU organizations called the Patriotic Front). Although power was transferred peacefully in internationally monitored elections in February of that year, the early 1980s saw a large-scale emigration of white citizens, many of whom were unwilling to live under a new black-majority government committed to establishing a socialist state. The white population of Zimbabwe fell from a peak of 280,000 in 1978 to 100,000 in 1980, and emigration levels stabilized only in 1987, largely because the white population base had been heavily depleted by past emigration. In 2000, Zimbabwe's white population stood at a mere 70,000 (of whom an estimated 20,000 had British passports and another 20,000 could lay claim to one).

As in South Africa, emigrants from Zimbabwe have historically been well educated, highly skilled, and predominantly white, a characteristic Lovemore Zinyama describes as characteristic of migrants from "those African countries where movements are frequently determined by political circumstances and are underpinned by racial or ethnic differences between rulers and the ruled." Most emigrants went either to South Africa (because whites perceived it to be geographically, culturally, and sociopolitically similar to their home country, especially during the apartheid era, and because blacks could find contract work in the mines there) or to the U.K. (Zimbabwe's former colonial power). Others went to Australia, New Zealand, and Canada. According to Stanley Moss, some white Rhodesians migrated to South Africa and then to the U.S. as early as the 1970s.

Southern African Immigrants in the U.S.

Overall, there is remarkably little research on emigration out of South Africa, Zimbabwe, and elsewhere in southern Africa. Moreover, what research there is is more concerned with the impacts of the emigration of skilled workers on those countries than with migrants' experiences in their places of destination. For example, the "brain drain" has disproportionately affected several industries within South Africa and Zimbabwe, including the education and health sectors, business services, banking and finance, computer and information technology services, and the high-tech industrial sector. Researchers and government officials in both countries are concerned about how to manage and compensate for this loss of skills, whether by restricting residents' options for emigration, encouraging emigrants abroad to maintain contact with (and even invest in) their home countries, or recruiting highly skilled immigrants to come to the region to offset the negative effects of emigration.

Table 1   Selected foreign-born Central and South Africans, by country of birth, 1980–2000

Country of birth	Population in U.S. census year (percentage of total U.S. foreign-born population in each year)			
	1980	1990	2000	Percent growth, 1980–2000
5 percent sample				
South Africa	18,180	37,713	67,733	273
	(0.1)	(0.2)	(0.2)	
Zimbabwe	3,920	5,222	12,148	210
	(0.0)	(0.0)	(0.0)	
1 percent sample[a]				
DRC (Zaire)	2,020	4,112	6,995	246
Zambia	1,620	3,448	5,974	269
Congo	—	—	5,613	—
Angola	1,140	2,833	3,317	191
Rwanda	—	—	2,744	—
Mauritius	700	1,449	2,164	209
Malawi	—	—	2,031	—
Mozambique	600	600	1,233	—

Source: U.S. Census Bureau, 1980, 1990, and 2000 Censuses, 5% Public Use Microdata Samples, weighted data.

a. Because of small population sizes, 2000 figures are available only from the 1% Public Use Microdata Sample and have a larger margin for error than figures from the 5% sample. Figures for Botswana, Burundi, Comoros, Lesotho, Madagascar, Namibia, Seychelles, and Swaziland are not available.

They are also concerned with how to ensure adequate provision of social and medical services among their general populations, especially as more teachers and medical personnel are leaving.

Because of the dearth of knowledge about these migrants' experiences after leaving southern Africa, here I paint a portrait of them using data from the Immigration and Naturalization Service (INS) and the 1980–2000 decennial U.S. censuses. Some attention is also paid to immigrants from other southern (and even central) African nations, about whom little is known in the U.S. immigration literature. However, South Africans and Zimbabweans are the only southern and central African immigrant groups with significant numbers in the U.S., although as Table 1 shows, they accounted for no more than 0.2 percent of the total foreign-born U.S. population in 2000. Immigrant groups from other southern and central African nations are so small that 5 percent sample data from the 2000 U.S. Census are not publicly available for them. Instead we must rely on 1 percent sample data, which have a larger margin for error and therefore must be interpreted more cautiously.

The U.S. Census counted 67,733 South Africans and 12,148 Zimbabweans in 2000, up from 37,713 South Africans and 5,222 Zimbabweans in 1990 and

18,180 South Africans and 3,920 Zimbabweans in 1980. Other southern and central African immigrant groups are smaller in number but exhibit similarly high rates of growth between 1980 and 2000. Table 2 shows that legal immigration from both South Africa and Zimbabwe remained fairly stable over the 1990s (at approximately 2,000 and 300 per year, respectively), dipping somewhat in the late 1990s and then rising again in the early 2000s. Also notable is that immigration from the Congo increased significantly over the 1990s.

In 2000 the majority of legal immigrants from South Africa (58.0 percent) entered the country under employment-based preferences, while a third (33.1 percent) entered as immediate relatives of U.S. citizens and a small fraction (6.0 percent) entered through the Diversity Immigrant Visa Program, which was enacted in 1990 to increase immigration from countries with low rates of immigration to the U.S. (see Table 3). Figures for legal immigrants from Zimbabwe are similar, although a lower proportion (36.5 percent) entered under employment-based preferences, a higher proportion (50.0 percent) entered as immediate relatives of U.S. citizens, and a slightly higher proportion (9.8 percent) entered through the Diversity Program. Legal immigrants from Zambia, Malawi, Mozambique, and Madagascar (and to a lesser extent Angola and Botswana) exhibit similar entry profiles. However, higher proportions of legal immigrants from the Congo, Rwanda, and the Democratic Republic of Congo (formerly Zaire) have entered as refugees or asylees or through the Diversity Program. Little information about them is available in the

Table 2   Number of Central and South African immigrants admitted to the United States, by country of birth and year of entry, 1989–2002

Year	South Africa	Congo	Zimbabwe	Zambia	Rwanda	DRC (Zaire)	Burundi	Angola
2002	3,880	678	492	312	217	178	121	92
2001	4,100	313	476	296	148	148	79	95
2000	2,833	191	323	211	73	124	28	88
1999	1,580	190	184	143	98	88	16	57
1998	1,904	118	186	213	52	155	51	66
1997	2,093	31	274	262	170	414	59	75
1996	2,966	23	385	226	118	433	36	125
1995	2,560	11	299	222	41	355	26	81
1994	2,144	11	246	198	16	237	14	75
1993	2,197	10	308	225	25	233	13	92
1992	2,516	9	296	210	10	196	11	92
1991	1,854	22	261	228	12	238	11	107
1990	1,990	9	272	209	6	256	16	132
1989	1,899	10	230	259	7	140	5	141

Source: U.S. Immigration and Naturalization Service, Statistical Yearbook, 2002, Table 3 (Washington, D.C.: U.S. Department of Justice). Figures for Botswana, Comoros, Lesotho, Madagascar, Malawi, Mauritius, Mozambique, Namibia, Seychelles, and Swaziland are negligible.

Table 3   Percentage of immigrants admitted by selected class of admission, by country of birth, 2002

Country of birth	Number of immigrants	Percentage of immigrants admitted by selected class of admission				
		Family-sponsored preferences	Employment-based preferences	Immediate relatives of U.S. citizens	Refugee and asylee adjustments	Diversity programs
All countries	1,063,732	17.6	16.4	45.7	11.9	4.0
All Africa	60,269	4.6	10.3	35.4	22.3	27.1
South Africa	3,880	2.5	58.0	33.1	0.2	6.0
Congo	678	2.8	6.3	16.5	50.3	24.0
Zimbabwe	492	3.7	36.4	50.0	0.2	9.8
Zambia	312	9.9	32.7	43.6	2.2	11.5
Rwanda	217	—	6.0	4.6	86.2	3.2
DRC (Zaire)	178	1.1	7.3	19.7	71.9	—
Angola	92	14.1	12.0	65.2	8.7	—
Malawi	56	5.4	30.4	53.6	—	10.7
Mozambique	55	14.5	25.5	49.1	5.5	5.5
Madagascar	43	2.3	25.6	65.1	—	7.0
Botswana	30	6.7	20.0	46.7	6.7	20.0

Source: U.S. Immigration and Naturalization Service, Statistical Yearbook, 2002, Table 3 (Washington, D.C.: U.S. Department of Justice).

U.S. immigration literature, and more research on their experiences in the U.S. is warranted.

For the most part, South Africans and Zimbabweans in the U.S. today are recent immigrants. Table 4 shows that 51.8 percent of white South Africans, 50.5 percent of black South Africans, and 83.4 percent of black Zimbabweans living in the U.S. in 2000 had migrated to this country in the previous decade. Notably, a higher proportion of white than black Zimbabweans migrated to the U.S. in the 1970s and 1980s than in the 1990s; this difference is likely a product of the great white exodus from Zimbabwe between the 1970s and the mid-1980s, which was followed by increasing black frustration and emigration during the 1990s. Also notable is the relative recency of immigration from other southern and central African countries; approximately 80 percent of immigrants from Rwanda and Mauritius, 75 percent of immigrants from the Congo, and over 60 percent of immigrants from Malawi living in the U.S. in 2000 had migrated in the 1990s. All of these southern and central African immigrant groups have a younger median age than foreign-born immigrants in general (with the exception of immigrants from Mozambique, many of whom entered the U.S. in the 1980s). The sex ratios among these groups are either roughly equal (in the case of immigrants from South Africa, Zambia, the Congo, Rwanda, Mauritius, and Malawi) or more heavily male- than female-dominated (in the case of immigrants from Zimbabwe, the Democratic Republic of Congo, An-

Table 4   Age, sex, citizenship status, and decade of entry characteristics, selected foreign-born Central and South African groups, 2000

National origin	Median age	Percentage male	Percentage noncitizen	Percent arriving by decade					
				1990–2000	1980–1989	1970–1979	1960–1969	Before 1960
5 percent sample								
All foreign-born	37.0	49.8	56.3	41.7	26.7	15.3	8.6	7.7
South Africa	35.0	49.3	58.3	52.6	24.5	14.7	4.3	3.9
White (82.3%)	36.0	49.2	55.5	51.8	23.9	15.2	4.8	4.4
Black (5.9%)	34.0	48.3	62.3	50.5	32.3	12.7	2.4	2.1
Zimbabwe	32.0	54.6	65.9	61.2	18.6	13.2	5.2	1.8
White (40.9%)	39.0	59.4	48.7	36.4	30.0	20.9	8.8	3.9
Black (48.7%)	27.0	49.8	79.2	83.4	8.5	5.7	2.4	—
1 percent sample[a]								
DRC (Zaire)	30.0	58.4	48.0	58.4	28.3	6.1	4.3	2.9
Zambia	36.0	51.9	53.0	54.1	17.9	23.8	4.2	0.0
Congo	35.0	50.2	77.8	74.1	20.5	1.0	1.9	2.5
Angola	35.0	57.9	63.5	48.7	21.5	27.0	2.8	0.0
Rwanda	29.0	49.4	70.3	79.0	12.1	4.7	4.2	0.0
Mauritius	31.0	51.4	64.0	79.0	12.6	8.4	0.0	0.0
Malawi	32.0	48.6	58.6	63.6	12.0	24.4	0.0	0.0
Mozambique	38.0	60.0	40.0	51.6	31.4	8.4	8.5	0.0

Source: U.S. Census Bureau, 2000 Census, 5% Public Use Microdata Sample, weighted data.

a. Because of small population sizes, 2000 figures are available only from the 1% Public Use Microdata Sample and have a larger margin for error than figures from the 5% sample. Figures for Botswana, Burundi, Comoros, Lesotho, Madagascar, Namibia, Seychelles, and Swaziland are not available.

gola, and Mozambique). Rates of U.S. citizenship vary, with high proportions of immigrants from the Congo, Rwanda, Zimbabwe, Mauritius, and Angola still not naturalized in 2000. Greater numbers of black than white South African and Zimbabwean immigrants lack U.S. citizenship.

South Africans and Zimbabweans are among the most highly skilled and professionally employed immigrants in the U.S. today (see Table 5). Among South African immigrants in 2000, 57.4 percent had a bachelor's degree or higher, while only 4.8 percent had not completed high school; among Zimbabwean immigrants, the corresponding figures were 50.3 percent and 3.0 percent, respectively. Also among South African immigrants in 2000, 59.1 percent were employed in professional or managerial occupations, while just 4.5 percent were employed in service occupations and 8.6 percent in production, craft, and repair occupations; among Zimbabwean immigrants, the corresponding figures were 50.7 percent, 7.9 percent, and 11.8 percent. These figures are consistent with the contention that highly skilled professionals are leaving southern Africa to pursue higher education and professional opportunities elsewhere.

At the same time, important racial disparities are evident within both national-origin groups, with white South African and Zimbabwean immigrants faring significantly better along socioeconomic indicators than their black counterparts. Whereas 59.9 percent of white South African immigrants and 53.7 percent of white Zimbabwean immigrants had a bachelor's degree or higher in 2000, only 45.2 percent of black South African immigrants and 45.0 percent of black Zimbabwean immigrants did. Conversely, whereas only 3.2 percent of white South African immigrants and 2.0 percent of white Zimbabwean immigrants had not graduated from high school in 2000, 11.3 percent of black South African immigrants and 4.5 percent of black Zimbabwean immigrants had not. In terms of occupational concentration, whereas 61.6 percent of white South African immigrants and 52.4 percent of white Zimbabwean immigrants were employed in professional or managerial occupations in 2000, only 43.8 percent of black South African immigrants and 41.5 percent of black Zimbabwean immigrants were. Conversely, whereas only 3.9 percent of white South African immigrants and 4.7 percent of white Zimbabwean immigrants were employed in service occupations in 2000, and only 7.9 percent of white South African immigrants and 10.9 percent of white Zimbabwean immigrants were in production, craft, or repair occupations, 7.7 percent of black South African immigrants and 13.4 percent of black Zimbabwean immigrants were employed in service occupations in 2000, and 17.7 percent of black South African immigrants and 17.0 percent of black Zimbabwean immigrants were in production, craft, or repair occupations. In terms of median wage/salary income, whereas white South African and Zimbabwean immigrants earned an average of $39,900 and $38,000 in 1999, respectively, black South African and Zimbabwean immigrants earned averages of $28,000 and $25,600, respectively. Finally, whereas only 2.8

Table 5   Selected labor market characteristics, selected foreign-born Central and South African groups, 2000

National origin	Percentage with a bachelor's degree or higher	Percentage employed in managerial/professional occupations	Percentage employed in service occupations	Median wage/salary income, 1999	Percentage living below the poverty line
5 percent sample					
All foreign-born	26.0	29.7	16.3	$21,000	10.9
South Africa	57.4	59.1	4.5	$36,000	3.5
White (82.3%)	59.9	61.6	3.9	$39,900	2.8
Black (5.9%)	45.2	43.8	7.7	$28,000	7.1
Zimbabwe	50.3	50.7	7.9	$32,070	7.3
White (40.9%)	53.7	52.4	4.7	$38,000	4.2
Black (48.7%)	45.0	41.5	13.4	$25,600	13.2
1 percent sample[a]					
DRC (Zaire)	35.6	41.2	2.9	$32,000	0.0
Zambia	40.5	55.5	13.2	$20,000	0.0
Congo	39.8	50.9	23.8	$13,200	29.3
Angola	28.7	28.3	29.4	$24,000	0.0
Rwanda	54.0	50.5	12.8	$15,000	29.4
Mauritius	21.4	42.8	27.3	$19,800	0.0
Malawi	44.6	57.4	12.5	$38,000	11.0
Mozambique	24.8	32.2	0.0	$45,000	0.0

Source: U.S. Census Bureau, 2000 Census, 5% Public Use Microdata Sample, weighted data. Figures for education are for persons aged 25–64; figures for labor market, for persons aged 25–64 in the labor force.

a. Because of small population sizes, 2000 figures are available only from the 1% Public Use Microdata Sample and have a larger margin for error than figures from the 5% sample. Figures for Botswana, Burundi, Comoros, Lesotho, Madagascar, Namibia, Seychelles, and Swaziland are not available.

percent of white South African immigrants and 4.2 percent of white Zimbabwean immigrants were living below the poverty line in 1999, 7.1 percent of black South African immigrants and 13.2 percent of black Zimbabwean immigrants were.

Race even differentiates these groups' residential patterns in the U.S., with white South African and Zimbabwean immigrants more geographically dispersed in 2000 than their black counterparts. For example, not only did more white than black South African and Zimbabwean immigrants live in nonmetropolitan areas, but among those who did live in metropolitan areas—that is, in U.S. central cities and suburbs—whites lived in a broader range of them than blacks did. Moreover, there were slight differences in the concentration of white and black immigrants in their top U.S. metropolitan destinations. Whereas in 2000 white South African immigrants lived primarily in the greater metropolitan areas of Los Angeles (6.7 percent), San Diego (5.4 percent), New York (4.0 percent), Houston (3.1 percent), Orange County, California (3.0 percent), Atlanta (2.9 percent), and Dallas–Fort Worth (2.9 percent), black South African immigrants lived primarily in the greater metropolitan areas of New York (13.5 percent), Washington, D.C. (11.0 percent), Philadelphia (7.1 percent), Los Angeles (6.7 percent), Houston (4.9 percent), Chicago (4.9 percent), and Boston (4.8 percent). (Notably, these figures are more dispersed than they were in 1970, when Stanley Moss found that half of all nonwhite immigrants from South Africa lived in New York City.) Similarly, whereas white Zimbabwean immigrants lived primarily in the greater metropolitan areas of Los Angeles (6.4 percent), San Diego (5.5 percent), Philadelphia (3.7 percent), Dallas–Fort Worth (3.6 percent), Houston (3.3 percent), Tampa (3.0 percent), and Atlanta (2.7 percent) in 2000, black Zimbabwean immigrants lived primarily in the greater metropolitan areas of Washington, D.C. (10.5 percent), Atlanta (6.1 percent), Dallas–Fort Worth (6.0 percent), Benton Harbor, Michigan (5.4 percent), Charlotte, North Carolina (4.5 percent), Baltimore (4.1 percent), and Indianapolis (3.6 percent). This residential dispersion probably reflects the high degree of educational attainment and professional occupational concentration among immigrants from South Africa and Zimbabwe, especially whites.

Because most immigrants from South Africa and Zimbabwe speak English upon arrival, either alone or in addition to another language, they exhibit very low levels of linguistic isolation in the U.S. In fact, 97.4 percent of white South African immigrants, 90.3 percent of black South African immigrants, 96.2 percent of white Zimbabwean immigrants, and 89.3 percent of black Zimbabwean immigrants reported speaking English "only" or "very well" in 2000. These rates are high despite the fact that 21.9 percent of white South African, 17.1 percent of black South African, and 9.2 percent of white Zimbabwean immigrants reported speaking Dutch in their homes, and over 70 percent of black Zimbabwean and over 30 percent of black South African immigrants reported speaking a "Nilotic" language (the term used by the 2000 Census) in their homes.

Whereas Stanley Moss found no evidence of white South African associations in the U.S. in the 1970s, and political activity and organization mainly among black South African immigrants working for majority rule in South Africa during the apartheid era, a host of South African cultural and social associations exists today, welcoming members of all backgrounds. Social and sport clubs exist across the country, from the South African Club of Atlanta and South African Tarheels in North Carolina to the Arizona Springbok Club in Phoenix, the Provo Cricket Club in Utah, the NYNJ Springbok Club in New York/New Jersey, Amaboston in Boston, the South Africa Association of Indiana, the Springbok Club of Kentucky, the Braai Connection in Orlando, South Africans in Austin, and the Baybokke Springbok Club and Sacramento South Africans in northern California. These associations illustrate an incipient social organization among South African immigrants in the U.S., who are coming together in groups where they can share information and provide each other with social support in their new country. Additionally, South African restaurants, bars, and other businesses have opened up across the U.S. They cater primarily to South African immigrants longing for home country activities and tastes—for example, by showing rugby and cricket games on TV, serving boerewors, or selling Marie biscuits and Mrs Ball's chutney—but most are open to the general public as well. Southern African immigrants in the U.S., although relatively small in number, are increasingly making a social and cultural as well as an economic impact on American life.

Bibliography

Brown, Mercy, David Kaplan, and Jean-Baptiste Meyer. 2001. "Counting Brains: Measuring Emigration from South Africa." Southern African Migration Project (SAMP), Migration Policy Brief No. 5, www.queensu.ca/samp.

Chikanda, Abel. 2005. "Medical Leave: The Exodus of Health Professionals from Zimbabwe." Southern African Migration Project (SAMP), Migration Policy Series (no number), www.queensu.ca/samp.

Dodson, Brenda. 2002. "Gender and the Brain Drain from South Africa." Southern African Migration Project (SAMP), Migration Policy Series No. 23, www.queensu.ca/samp.

Haldenwang, B. B. 1996. Migration Processes, Systems, and Policies: With Special Emphasis on South African International Migration. Occasional Paper No. 25. Bellville, South Africa: University of Stellenbosch, Institute for Futures Research.

Mattes, Robert, and Wayne Richmond. 2000. "The Brain Drain: What Do Skilled Africans Think?" In Jonathan Crush, ed., "Losing Our Minds? Skills Migration and the South African Brain Drain," pp. 9–35. Southern African Migration Project (SAMP), Migration Policy Series No. 18, www.queensu.ca/samp.

McDonald, David, and Jonathan Crush. 2002. "Thinking About the Brain Drain in Southern Africa." Southern African Migration Project (SAMP), Migration Policy Brief No. 8, www.queensu.ca/samp.

Moss, Stanley. 1980. "South Africans." In Stephan Thernstrom, Ann Orlov, and Oscar Handlin, eds., *The Harvard Encyclopedia of American Ethnic Groups,* pp. 942–44. Cambridge: Harvard University Press.

Polonsky, M. J., D. R. Scott, and Hazel T. Suchard. 1989. "A Profile of Emigrants from South Africa: The Australian Case." *International Migration Review* 23, 4: 933–44.

Tevera, Daniel S. 2005. "Early Departures: The Emigration Potential of Zimbabwean Students." Southern African Migration Project (SAMP), Migration Policy Series No. 39, www.queensu.ca/samp.

Tevera, Daniel S., and Jonathan Crush. 2003. "The New Brain Drain from Zimbabwe." Southern African Migration Project (SAMP), Migration Policy Series No. 29, www.queensu.ca/samp.

Van Rooyen, Johann. 2000. *The New Great Trek: The Story of South Africa's White Exodus.* Pretoria: Unisa.

Zinyama, Lovemore M. 1990. "International Migrations to and from Zimbabwe and the Influence of Political Changes on Population Movements, 1965–1987." *International Migration Review* 24, 4: 748–67.

Canada

Donna R. Gabaccia

Although 820,000 people born in Canada lived in the United States in 2000, few would identify themselves as "new Americans." Some are not even immigrants and hold temporary visas. Most Canadians who enter the U.S. to live or work already regard themselves as Americans; most probably resent the fact that for over two centuries the U.S. and its citizens have uncritically appropriated the term "American" for their own nationality. Nor do citizens of the U.S. typically view Canadians as different enough from themselves to qualify either socially or culturally as "real" foreigners, even when legally they are among the immigrant groups most likely to retain their original citizenship. With the current attention of the U.S. fixed firmly on economic relations along the border with Mexico, few worry much about the much older northern border, which has both divided and joined Canada and the U.S. and their respective residents.

Nevertheless, Canada has provided one of the most important and persistent streams of immigration into the U.S. Only in the past half-century have the numbers of Canadians fallen drastically—to below fortieth place—in census counts of foreign-born residents of the U.S. Although scholars have characterized the Canadian border as one of ongoing exchange—Marcus Lee Hansen and Robert Bremner in 1940 labeled it a "mingling" of two peoples—Canadians have viewed the exchange as decidedly unbalanced, while their southern neighbors have remained unaware of it.

A Short History of the "Mingling" of Canadians and U.S. Americans

In 1900, when Canada's resident population numbered scarcely 5 million, over a million people born in Canada lived south of their border, making Canadians slightly more than 10 percent of the foreign-born population of the U.S. The much smaller numbers of U.S. citizens living in Canada at the time accounted for one third of Canada's immigrants. While Canadians clustered in the northeastern U.S., American citizens in Canada lived disproportionately in the prairie provinces. Together, these mobile North Americans exemplified the economic integration that had occurred first along the St. Lawrence and the Great Lakes and then extended westward with the construction of transcontinental railroads. Little remarked today, the U.S.-Canada borderland has been important to the development of both countries. Still, the particularly rapid development of the much larger U.S. and its greater success in attracting European immigrants left many Canadians wondering about the survival and future of their huge but sparsely populated new nation.

Throughout the 19th and early 20th centuries, most Canadians, and most Canadian immigrants to the U.S., lived along a 200-mile-wide swath of land on either side of the U.S.-Canada border. In 1920 over half of Canadian-born people who lived in New England were French-speakers; elsewhere along the border English-speaking Canadians far outnumbered *les canadiens français*. In New England, francophone Canadians worked overwhelmingly in industry, as most other immigrants did. But farther west, English-speaking Canadians were a much more diverse and prosperous group, including not only factory workers but also managers, professionals, and even industrialists in Detroit, lumber workers, tradesmen, and transport workers around the Great Lakes, and farmers in the Midwest and far West. English-speaking Canadian immigrants rarely organized along ethnic lines. French-speakers, by contrast, pursued *survivance* (ethnocultural and religious survival) by forming ethnic organizations.

In the early 1900s, Canadian migrations went largely unregulated and unnoticed in the U.S. In any given year of the first decade of the 20th century, immigrants from Canada and Mexico together rarely exceeded 3 percent of new arrivals. And a third of the immigrants entering the U.S. from Canada were neither citizens nor natives of Canada; they, too, were Europeans, who had merely arrived in Canadian ports or worked briefly in Canada before choosing to continue on to the U.S. Overall, cross-border commuting, temporary and circular migration between the two countries, and the constant division and reformation of families on both sides of the border made for a kind of comfortable familiarity in the Canada-U.S. borderland. This may also help to explain the low naturalization rates among Canadian-born people who lived in the U.S. Still, in an era of nativist calls for the "Americanization" of immigrants, the Catholic parishes, foreign-language newspapers, and mutual aid societies of the French Canadians occasionally fueled comparisons of this group to the hated Chinese immigrants of the West Coast.

Immigration restrictions enacted in the U.S. between 1917 and 1924 excluded Asians and imposed restrictive quotas on the southern and eastern European groups that had made up a large proportion of immigrants before World War I. The numbers of immigrants from Mexico and Canada (along with the "great migration" of

African Americans from southern states) surged strongly in the wake of immigration restriction, as the development of U.S. industry and agriculture now depended on North American workers.

Entries from Canada peaked at over 200,000 in 1924, and they remained strong—well over 50,000 yearly—until the Great Depression diminished economic opportunities in the U.S. Canadians thus constituted about 20 percent of the immigrants entering during the years of most intensive restriction. After dropping to less than 10,000 annually during World War II, new arrivals from Canada rose again to about 30,000 yearly during the 1950s. The numbers were still climbing slowly during the early 1960s.

Unlike Mexicans recruited as *bracero* contract laborers between 1942 and 1963, Canadians might have struck U.S. citizens as exactly the kind of immigrants the country needed, especially as the representation of French-speaking (and typically Catholic) Canadians declined. But precisely because immigrants from Canada seemed well educated, English-speaking, Anglo-American in culture, and familiar with democratic governance—in short, much like U.S. Americans—they were more often ignored than celebrated. In Canada, however, neither nationalists nor disgruntled French-speakers in Quebec were pleased with the outflow. Like their predecessors, Canadian observers in the 1950s and 1960s worried about the long-term costs of raising and educating citizens only to lose them to the U.S. Equally discouraging, Canada worked hard to recruit immigrants of its own in the postwar years, and the so-called new Canadians made up fully one third of people emigrating from Canada to the United States.

The Immigration Act of 1965

Longstanding if unbalanced mingling along the Canada-U.S. border was significantly altered by a series of new immigration laws and treaty negotiations in the last third of the 20th century. The 1965 reforms had particularly complex consequences in the Western Hemisphere, because they not only imposed numerical restrictions on Mexico and Canada for the first time but did so just as the U.S. terminated the *bracero* program, which had delivered large numbers of seasonal agricultural workers from Mexico.

The numbers of both "new Canadian" and Canadian-born immigrants entering the U.S. began to drop almost immediately after passage of this law. Whether this reflected anti-American sentiments sparked by the war in Vietnam or the related economic "stagflation"—a combination of falling employment and rising inflation—the U.S. attracted fewer than 10,000 Canadians annually during the 1970s. (U.S. citizens moving to Canada, including those who did so to evade military service, briefly outnumbered Canadians entering the U.S.) Complicating matters still further, in 1976 the U.S. imposed a 20,000-person annual limit on immigrants entering from any single country, including Canada. This may not have produced hysterical outcries in the U.S. about "illegal immigrants," but restrictions do generally generate violations, and Canadians evaded the restrictions, as others did. Scholars estimate that 25,000 Canadians (out of a total Canadian-born U.S. population of about 900,000) lived illegally in the U.S. in 1980; 20 years later, the number was estimated at 120,000, making Canadians the fourth largest group of undocumented immigrants in the country. Qualitative evidence also suggests that people from other nations who lacked proper documentation found it easier to enter the U.S. from Canada than from Mexico (as U.S. concern about terrorism in 2000 and 2001 revealed). Still, whether discussing Mexican or Canadian migrations, few commentators troubled themselves with how many U.S.-bound immigrants, legal or illegal, intended actually to settle in the country or become naturalized U.S. citizens. Again, qualitative evidence suggests that rates of return to Canada and circular migration between Canada and the U.S.—including the seasonal "snowbirds" so well known in Florida—were significant, further muddying efforts by both nations to make clear distinctions between immigrants, emigrants, and resident populations.

Without sparking much negative commentary in either Canada or the U.S., Canada's migrants, like those of many other groups during the restriction era, had also quietly feminized. In 1950 women made up 60 percent of the Canadians entering the U.S.; in 1970 the proportion was slightly more balanced, at 54 percent. The cause of this transition from the numerically male-dominated migrations of the early 20th century to the more balanced or even female-dominated migrations of the late century is still unclear. Perhaps a changing job market—notably the rise in demand for clerical, "pink-collar" service workers and those in traditionally female professions such as nursing and teaching—made the U.S. more attractive to women. Probably, however, restrictive immigration laws encouraged large numbers of women and children to enter under family visa categories.

The numbers of Canadians immigrating to the U.S. increased only slightly during the 1980s and closely followed the ups and downs of the U.S. economy as it deindustrialized and deregulated its industries and as both its business enterprises and its immigrant population globalized. More than ever, most Canadian immigrants seemed invisible. In the U.S., attention focused intensively on the southern border, on the incorporation of new immigrants from Mexico, Asia, Latin America, Africa, and the Middle East, on new hopes for a multicultural nation, and on fantasies and fears about the possible skin color of the average American citizen of the 21st century. In this context, it seems likely that Americans perceived the "new Canadians," a substantial number of whom had been born in Asia, Africa, and the Middle East before emigrating from Canada to the U.S., as immigrants of color and not as Canadians at all.

Invisible Immigrants, 1965–1990

Restrictive regulations of immigration by the U.S. did little to alleviate Canadian nationalists' fears about the loss of Canadian workers. Of the adult workers who entered the U.S. from Canada between 1950 and 1960, roughly a third were relatively well-educated professionals, technical workers, business people, administrators, or managers. By the end of the 1980s, it was obvious that the U.S. continued to attract highly qualified Canadians because it rewarded them well: 45 percent of Canadians in the U.S. were working in highly skilled occupations. Canadians living in the U.S. regularly reported better incomes, more job satisfaction, and lower taxes than they had experienced in Canada. Nurses and engineers were the two largest occupational groups. By the mid-1990s, demographers working with U.S. census data confirmed earlier portraits of Canadians in the U.S.: on almost every measure, they represented an elite subsection of Canada's population, and they were doing extremely well. Canadian immigrants were better-educated and had higher incomes than average Canadians; they worked in greater proportions as professionals, technical workers, and small- and large-business people than average Canadians did. Only in the 1990s did demographic research reveal that much the same could be said about U.S. immigrants living in Canada. Apparently the mingling of peoples noticed half a century earlier continues but is now more characteristic of the upper echelons of the populations of both countries.

In part because the largest Canadian migrations occurred earlier in the century and the Canadian-born thus constituted an aging population, and in part because of the more balanced sex ratios among recently arrived immigrants, women outnumbered men among Canadian immigrants in the U.S. during the 1990s. The 2000 Census confirmed the persistence of patterns already obvious in the previous two decades. The majority of Canadian immigrants are female, whereas males predominate among U.S. citizens living in Canada, especially among the most recently arrived. As is typical of almost all migrant populations, working-age people among both groups are much better represented than they are in populations of Canadians or U.S. Americans in their home countries.

Furthermore, Canadians are no longer settled exclusively along the long Canada-U.S. border. While the border states of Washington, Maine, Vermont, and New Hampshire and nearby Massachusetts and Rhode Island could still claim the highest proportions of resident Canadians in 1980, by 2000 states as diverse and far-flung as Connecticut, California, Florida, Nevada, and Oregon had joined the border states of Michigan, North Dakota, and Montana in claiming between 5.0 and 9.9 Canadians per 1,000 residents. One hundred and sixty-four Canadians living on the West Coast (most of them in California) who were interviewed in the late 1970s resembled Canadian immigrants nationwide in their high levels of education and highly skilled work. While the largest numbers admitted that jobs and improved prospects had attracted them to the U.S., a surprising 40 percent noted that family ties and friends fueled their immigration, and an even more surprising 23 percent admitted that they were dissatisfied with conditions in Canada.

By moving in increasing numbers to the Sunbelt in the 1970s and 1980s, Canadian immigrants behaved very much like their U.S.-born neighbors. Like middle-class U.S. Americans, Canadians have small families, low fertility rates, and high rates of home ownership. Yet because they resemble the American "majority" celebrated in myths about upward mobility, Canadians do not easily function as a "model minority." That role is instead filled by the formerly demonized Chinese and other Asian immigrants.

Although very much like the middle-class American majority, Canadians now show less interest in becoming U.S. citizens than they did in the past—a pattern found among many immigrant groups. This remains the case even though in 1977 Canada allowed its emigrants to retain Canadian citizenship after naturalization in the U.S. The proportion of naturalized U.S. citizens among Canadian-born people residing in the U.S. declined to just over half in 1980; by 1990 it had dropped still further, and in 2000 it was only 40 percent (although this figure also reflects a population affected by new visa options opened under NAFTA). Canadians in the U.S. may resemble their U.S. counterparts in many ways, but they also seem to want to maintain their Canadian national affiliations and identities. Their nationality carries a significance for them that U.S. citizens often cannot see, as it seems unmarked by either culture or color.

The Impact of NAFTA

The signing of the U.S.-Canada Free Trade Agreement in 1989, followed by the implementation of the North American Free Trade Agreement (NAFTA) in 1994, again altered the options of Canadians who wanted to live or work in the U.S. Unlike international agreements intended to unify the separate states of Europe politically in the 1980s and 1990s, NAFTA made no provisions for complete freedom of movement across the U.S.-Canada or U.S.-Mexico borders. It did, however, allow for relatively free cross-border movement by business people and certain professionals who are citizens of Mexico or Canada. The list of occupations eligible for the so-called TN or temporary (one-year) NAFTA visas includes many professional, scientific, and technical jobs, along with most business positions—everything from accountants to pharmacists to zoologists.

NAFTA allowed Canadians with the proper qualifications to apply for TN visas at the border and to renew them indefinitely. Meanwhile, the numbers of Canadian immigrants seeking permanent residence and naturalization in the U.S. also rose in the 1990s (although it remained well below the limit of 20,000 annually). Apparently well-educated Canadians increasingly prefer temporary visas to immigrant status; those who enter on temporary visas may not be particularly interested in eventual naturalization and citizenship. In any case, naturalizing is not an option for holders of TN visas. In 2004, Canadians held 71,878 such visas—97 percent of all the TN visas that had been issued.

By 1999 angry Canadians revived the argument that Canada was again bleeding its human resources to the behemoth to the south, this time under NAFTA. The supposedly large numbers of Canadian students seeking higher education in the U.S. remains a pressing concern. Approximately 20 percent of the graduates of Canada's top private high schools receive higher education in the U.S. Numbering under 20,000 in 1991, Canadian undergraduates in the U.S. reached 26,500 (compared with about 600,000 studying in Canada) by 2002. Intermittently in the 1980s and more vociferously after the passage of NAFTA, journalists and some social scientists have portrayed Canadians pursuing advanced degrees in the U.S., especially in science and engineering, as a "brain drain" much like those of third world countries. Alarmists point to the fact that half of Canadians who had received Ph.D.'s in technical fields in the U.S. were still working in the U.S. in 1995; others insist that Canadians with American Ph.D.'s in science and engineering are only slightly above the average among foreign students in having firm plans to remain in the U.S. Careful recent studies reveal that relatively few Canadians who left university in the mid-1990s (1.5 percent) moved to the U.S. after graduation, and Canadian statisticians have provided evidence that foreigners entering Canada with technical expertise and degrees outnumber Canadians leaving for the U.S. by a factor of four.

Melodramatic portraits of Canada's brain drain tend to ignore what oral historians and journalists recognize—that highly educated Canadians living in the U.S. have little interest in abandoning either Canada or Canadian citizenship. (While the U.S-imposed limit on immigration from Canada went unfilled in most years, Canadians opted for temporary visas as NAFTA permitted.) Of the 1995 graduates mentioned above, 90 percent who went to the U.S. did so with temporary visas, and 20 percent of them had returned to Canada by 1999. In the U.S., too, labor activists and some professional societies have expressed their unease with issuing so many temporary visas to highly educated professional, technical, and business workers. While few suggest that these are the 21st century's equivalent of Mexican *braceros,* Canadians' increasing use of temporary visas rather than immigration, permanent residency, and "green cards" merits further consideration.

Well-educated Canadians, who move about freely, if only temporarily, without changing their nationality, are in some ways the North American counterparts of Europeans who seek employment within the European Union. And for Canadians living in the U.S.—whether as naturalized citizens, permanent resident aliens, or temporary workers renewing their TN visas each year—the challenge of American life is not so much finding a way to accommodate culturally but maintaining a sense of Canadian nationality in a country that rarely recognizes its existence or significance. Despite the falling proportion of naturalized citizens among the Canadian-born population, there is little evidence that their sense of connection to Canada encourages them to form the kinds of ethnic and national organizations common among other immigrant groups. French Canadians still sometimes organize along ethnic lines, as in the Association des Québecois en Californie, and one can find websites like From Canada to the Twin Cities, but for most Canadians, invisibility and frequent border-crossing remain more important in defining life than ethnic solidarity within the U.S. does. At the same time, the unwillingness of the U.S. to recognize Canadians or to single them out as model immigrants may hold the key to Canadians' sturdy sense of connection to their homeland. Ironically, American citizens' easy acceptance of Canadian immigrants, along with their refusal to acknowledge cultural or social differences between the two mingled peoples, strike many Canadians as arrogant. Canadians do not want to become Americans if becoming American too easily subsumes or envelops rather than accepts their Canadian roots.

Bibliography

Brox, James A. "Migration between the United States and Canada: A Study in Labor Market Adjustment." *International Migration* 21, 1 (1983).

Cooper, Betsy, and Elizabeth Grieco. "The Foreign Born from Canada in the United States." *Migration Information,* Aug. 1, 2004.

Dorante, Catalina Amuedo, and Wei Chiao Huang. "Unemployment, Immigration, and NAFTA: A Panel Study of Ten Major U.S. Industries." *Journal of Labor Research* 18, 7 (Fall 1997).

Granatstein, J. L. *Yankee Go Home? Canadians and Anti-Americanism.* Toronto: Harper-Collins, 1996.

Hansen, Marcus Lee, with John Bartlet Brebner. *The Mingling of the Canadian and American Peoples.* New Haven, Conn.: Yale University Press, 1940.

Inglehart, Ronald, Neil Nevitte, and Miguel Basañez. *The North American Trajectory: Cultural, Economic, and Political Ties among the United States, Canada, and Mexico.* New York: Aldine De Gruyter, 1996.

Lines, Kenneth. *British and Canadian Immigration to the United States since 1920.* San Francisco: R & E Research Associates, 1978.

Ramirez, Bruno. *Crossing the 49th Parallel: Migration from Canada to the United States, 1900–1930.* Ithaca, N.Y.: Cornell University Press, 2001.

Samuel, T. John. "The Migration of Canadians to the United States: The Causes." *International Migration* 7 (1969): 106–16.

Sheppard, Robert. "The Magnetic North: A Group of Very Smart Young People Wrestle with How to Keep Talent Like Theirs in Canada." *Maclean's,* July 1, 2001, p. 81.

Simpson, Jeffrey. *Star-spangled Canadians: Canadians Living the American Dream.* Toronto: HarperCollins, 2000.

St. John-Jones, L. W. "Emigration from Canada in the 1960's." *Population Studies* 33, 1 (1979): 115–24.

U.S. Bureau of the Census. Current Population Reports. Series P-23, no. 161. *Migration between the United States and Canada.* Washington, D.C.: U.S. Government Printing Office, 1990.

Central America

Guatemala, Honduras, Nicaragua

Norma Stoltz Chinchilla and Nora Hamilton

Over the past 30 years the number of Central Americans coming to the United States has grown significantly, as a result of political upheavals in several Central American countries during the 1980s, the effects of Hurricane Mitch and other natural disasters in the 1990s, and deteriorating economic conditions in the region, as well as a demand for immigrant labor in certain U.S. labor markets. While this sudden growth can be directly linked to specific conditions in Central America, the trajectories that have guided immigrants to certain regions and employment niches in the U.S. have been shaped by those who came in previous decades.

The most dramatic upsurge in Central American migration occurred in the 1980s. Between 1980 and 1990, for example, the Salvadoran-born population in the U.S. increased nearly five times, from 95,800 to 472,393, while the number of foreign-born Guatemalans and Nicaraguans more than tripled (to 227,998 and 171,004, respectively) and the number of foreign-born Hondurans increased almost three times.

The foreign-born Central American population in the U.S. continued to grow throughout the 1990s, when the number of Guatemalan and Honduran immigrants more than doubled. Salvadorans continued to be the major subgroup of Central American immigrants (with 823,832 people, according to the U.S. Census), but Guatemalans increased to 487,288, Hondurans to 287,470, and Nicaraguans to 228,346. As of 2000, nearly 50 percent of Nicaraguan immigrants and over 60 percent of Guatemalan and Honduran immigrants in the U.S. had come in the 1990s.

Central America is characterized by the diversity of its population and of the histories of the countries that make up the region. Not surprisingly, immigrants from Central America also are diverse. The countries they come from—Belize, Costa Rica, El Salvador, Guatemala, Honduras, Nicaragua, and Panama—exhibit notable contrasts in geography, national histories, and migratory traditions. The populations of these countries are racially and ethnically diverse (indigenous, African-origin, European-origin, and mestizo) and have different socioeconomic characteristics, motivations for migration, places of destination, and access to legal status in the U.S.

The population of Guatemala, for example, is over 50 percent indigenous, with some 28 different ethnic and linguistic groups among the dominant Mayan population. All of the major groups are now represented in the U.S., where Q'anjob'al, Quiche, Mam, and others from a particular village in Guatemala form networks that link the village to American communities, jobs, and housing. In Los Angeles, for example, immigrants arriving from the Q'anjob'al village of San Miguel Acatlán in Huehuetenango are assisted by prior immigrants in finding housing, often in the same apartment buildings, and jobs in the nearby garment factories.

Afro-Caribbean groups from the coasts of Central America are also an important component of migration flows to the U.S. One such group is the Garifuna, descendants of Africans who landed on the Caribbean islands of St. Vincent and Dominica when the ships bringing them to slavery in the Americas were wrecked, and of Amerindians from South America who had previously migrated to these islands. The Garifuna were expelled from the islands by Britain and migrated to the Caribbean coastal areas of Central America beginning in the late eighteenth century.

Migration Trends and Trajectories

As with other migratory flows, that of different Central American populations results from the intersection of the personal histories of individual migrants with the broader context of historical events that shape relationships between their points of departure and places of settlement. Before the 1980s, most Central Americans were drawn to the U.S. primarily for economic or personal reasons (such as family reunification). Migration trajectories were frequently influenced by relations established through U.S. economic or political intervention in the region.

For example, Honduran migration in the early 20th century was linked to the banana trade, which resulted from the investment of U.S. companies in the region. The expansion of commerce between U.S. and Central American ports brought Hondurans and other Central Americans to seaboard cities such as New York and, notably, New Orleans, which had the largest Honduran population in the U.S. before the 1980s and continues to be an important center for Hondurans and Honduran Americans. Central Americans from several countries who worked in construction on the Panama Canal and subsequently for U.S. shipping lines were recruited to work in shipyards in San Francisco during World War II. Hondurans were hired by the United Fruit Company for the merchant marine, which reinforced migration to U.S. port cities. According to our interviews with Guatemalan and Salvadoran immigrants in Los Angeles, some Central Americans claimed Mexican nationality in order to work legally in agriculture under the *bracero* program during the 1940s and 1950s.

The 1960s and 1970s brought another surge in migration, parallel to the growth of U.S. investment in the region as a result of the creation of the Central American Common Market and the existence of manufacturing and service sector jobs available to immigrants in cities such as Los Angeles and Chicago. In contrast to Mexican migrants, the majority of Central American immigrants before the 1980s were women, reflecting, in many cases, the relative ease with which women could find jobs in the service sector and were able to establish networks with other prospective female immigrants, as well as their "availability" to migrate, because of their marital situation and/or their previous (paid) work experience. As discussed by Zentgraf, marital situations conducive to migration include single women without children who need to contribute to the income of their family of origin, female heads of household who need to support their children, and married women with children whose family income is inadequate, often because of a husband's unemployment, disability, or alcoholism. In 1980, 56.7 percent of Salvadoran immigrants, 54.4 percent of Guatemalan immigrants, 58.9 percent of Honduran immigrants, and 60.9 percent of Nicaraguan immigrants were women, according to the U.S. Census.

In the 1970s and 1980s, revolutionary movements against de facto dictatorships and the reaction of repressive governments and counterrevolutionary forces to the growth of a revolutionary movement or, in the case of Nicaragua, the emergence of a revolutionary (Sandinista) government were important factors in the dramatic increase in internal, regional, and international migration, particularly in and from Nicaragua, El Salvador, and Guatemala. In Nicaragua, the overthrow of the Somoza regime initially brought Somoza supporters to the U.S., notably Florida; they were later followed by Nicaraguans opposed to the Sandinista government and/or suffering from the political and economic impact of the U.S.-sponsored contra war. In El Salvador, persecution of political, labor, peasant, and student activists by the government and death squads, as well as the violence of the civil war between the revolutionary and government forces, were major factors in the increase in migration to the U.S., primarily to Los Angeles and to a lesser extent to Houston, San Francisco, and the Washington, D.C., area. This led to the migration of Guatemalans across borders into Mexico and the U.S., where they settled primarily in Los Angeles, followed by New York, Chicago, and parts of Florida.

The 1980s also brought a change in the gender composition of migrants. Salvadoran and Guatemalan men began to outnumber women, and the number of women in each group declined to 48.4 percent and 49 percent, respectively. This shift appears to be the result of conditions related to war, in which slightly more men than women felt the need to flee the region. Our 1995 survey of Salvadorans and Guatemalans in Southern California, for example, found that a majority of men who came during the 1980s ranked "political conditions" as the most important reason for their migration, while most women gave "economic reasons" their highest ranking.

Despite official peace agreements and democratic elections in the 1990s, Central American immigration to the U.S. continued to grow. The devastation caused by the wars, the inability of government economic and social policies to resolve the problems of poverty and joblessness, and the growth in crime and personal insecurity motivated many Central Americans to leave for better opportunities elsewhere. Taking advantage of existing networks, most came to the U.S. Conditions leading to migration were aggravated by natural disasters such as Hurricane Mitch, which resulted in the death of an estimated 15,000 people and left millions homeless.

Salvadoran and Guatemalan men continued to predominate in the migration flows from these two countries during the 1990s, with women making up 48.5 percent of Salvadoran and 44.8 percent of Guatemalan immigrants in the 2000 Census. Women continued to predominate among Hondurans and Nicaraguan migrants (50.3 percent and 53.2 percent, respectively), although the margin of difference between absolute numbers of men and women from each group was significantly reduced.

While settlement patterns were shaped by conditions in the sending countries and the U.S., individual migration histories also influenced the collective trajectories, often through the establishment of networks by "pioneers"—initial immigrants who came to particular communities or regions and subsequently found job opportunities for their relatives, friends, and neighbors, often in the same business or company, resulting in a process of chain migration. A particularly successful example of an individual pioneer eventually establishing a migrant chain, described by Hagan and Rodriguez, was Juan Xuc, a Maya from the village of San Pedro in the department of Totonicapán in Guatemala, who found a job for himself and subsequently for dozens of family members and, ultimately, residents of his own and other villages in a major supermarket chain in Houston. Women from these villages formed networks and recruited compatriots to work as housekeepers or child-care workers for friends of their own employers.

Patterns of Settlement and Incorporation

As noted, Central Americans coming in the 1980s tended to concentrate in areas where there was already a Central American population. California was a major destination, with 71.4 percent of the Salvadorans and 56.8 percent of the Guatemalans in the U.S. in 1980. California continues to be the principal destination of Central Americans, but by 1990 the proportion of Salvadorans living there had declined to 60 percent, while that of Guatemalans, including indigenous groups, had increased to 60.2 percent. In 2000, California was still the major center of Salvadoran and

Guatemalan immigrants, but the proportion had been further reduced to 43.9 and 43.8 percent, respectively. The top cities in terms of Central American population were Los Angeles (238,191), particularly Salvadorans and Guatemalans; New York City (99,099), particularly Hondurans and Guatemalans; Houston (60,642), notably Salvadorans; Miami (40,158), primarily Nicaraguans; San Francisco (23,367), particularly Salvadorans and Nicaraguans; Chicago (23,339), especially Guatemalans; Washington, D.C. (15,803), mainly Salvadorans; and Dallas (14,972).

A trend toward dispersion that began in the 1980s became increasingly pronounced in the 1990s, as immigrants moved from areas of first settlement to or arrived directly in other parts of the country. In addition to California, traditional destinations such as New York and Illinois saw a decline in the proportion of Central Americans, although the actual numbers increased in many cases. This was particularly dramatic in the case of Hondurans in New York, where the proportion dropped from 27 percent to 15 percent in the 20-year period between 1980 and 2000, and Guatemalans in Illinois, which shifted from 9 percent to 1.6 percent in the same period. In contrast, areas of growth included Florida, particularly among Hondurans, who increased from 12 to 18 percent of the total number of Honduran immigrants, and Nicaraguans, who increased from 18.8 to 44 percent between 1980 and 2000; and Texas, where the proportion of Salvadorans increased from 2.6 to 12.2 percent and that of Hondurans from 3.7 to 11.9 percent.

Hondurans have continued to be among the most dispersed of the Central American populations in the U.S. As indicated, Honduran immigration to this country dates back to the early 20th century, particularly in major port cities. Hondurans continued to be concentrated in New York (27 percent), California (18.2 percent), and Louisiana (14.5 percent) as of 1980. By 2000, however, Florida was their major destination, with 18 percent, followed by California, New York, and Texas. Only 4.5 percent of the Honduran immigrant population was in Louisiana, although New Orleans contains a large population of Honduran Americans.

In the case of Nicaraguans, the fall of the Somoza regime in 1979, the reforms initiated by the Sandinista government, and the contra war were important factors in increased out-migration during the late 1970s and early 1980s. Members of the Somoza family and its associates came to Miami, where they were welcomed by the established Cuban community. They were subsequently joined by professionals and business people, workers, and young men escaping from the draft resulting from the contra war. Salvadoran landowners and Honduran business people also immigrated to the Miami area. While Miami has continued to attract the wealthiest Central American migrants, many of whom settle in the suburbs, it is also the home of some of the poorest Central Americans.

A very different stream of migration to Florida was that of the indigenous people of Guatemala. Initial migrants found jobs in agriculture in and around Indiantown, a community in Palm Beach County, which grew substantially as a result of this influx. Subsequently they diversified into other types of jobs, such as landscaping golf courses, and dispersed to other parts of Florida and other states of the Southeast, where they found work in construction and industries such as poultry processing.

Immigrants from indigenous and Afro-Caribbean groups tend to form networks distinct from those of others from their countries of origin, even when they settle in the same states or cities. In Los Angeles, for example, not only do the Maya have separate settlement patterns, but these often vary according to specific ethnic and village origins. In New York, nonindigenous Hondurans tend to be located in predominantly Central American neighborhoods in Brooklyn, Queens, and Long Island, while the Garifuna live mostly in central Harlem and the South Bronx, along with African Americans, Dominicans, and Puerto Ricans.

In terms of socioeconomic status, Central American immigrants tend to be among the most disadvantaged of foreign-born U.S. workers, with socioeconomic characteristics only slightly better than those of foreign-born Mexicans. There are important distinctions among Central American immigrants, however. Nicaraguans tend to be better off than Guatemalans, Hondurans, and Salvadorans. According to the 2000 Census, the median family income of first-generation Nicaraguans is $40,200, compared with approximately $35,900 for Salvadorans, Guatemalans, and Hondurans. Only 16.1 percent of Nicaraguans, compared with 34 to 43 percent of the other three populations, have an eighth-grade education or less, while 14.6 percent of Nicaraguans, compared with 8.3 percent of Hondurans, 6.3 percent of Guatemalans, and 5.1 percent of Salvadorans, have a B.A. or an advanced degree. Nicaraguans are almost twice as likely to be employed in managerial, professional, technical, or sales positions (45.3 percent versus 19 to 27 percent for the three other groups) and, conversely, are less likely to be employed in production or service jobs (53.1 percent, compared with 67 to 73 percent of the other groups). Nicaraguans also score slightly higher on English-language ability, with nearly 61 percent speaking English well or very well, compared with 50 percent or fewer of the other three groups. They are also more likely to be U.S. citizens (33.1 percent versus 24 to 27 percent of the other groups).

The fact that a substantial number of Central American immigrants are undocumented constitutes an important obstacle to their economic success, limiting the kinds of jobs available to them and resulting in frequent exploitation of their labor. In contrast to Cubans and Vietnamese, Salvadorans, Guatemalans, and Nicaraguans were not accepted as refugees during the 1980s, and very few were able to obtain asylum. Some Central Americans benefited from the amnesty provisions of the Immigration Reform and Control Act (IRCA) in 1986, but relatively few had arrived before the cutoff date of January 1982. Salvadorans and Nicaraguans finally obtained temporary protected status (TPS) as part of the 1990 Immigration Act, which allowed them to remain in the U.S. until the end of civil strife in their respective countries, and this was extended in various forms until 1996. In December

1990 a legal decision in a landmark case brought by religious, refugee, and legal rights groups (*American Baptist Churches* v. *Thornburgh,* known as the ABC case) required that cases for Salvadorans and Guatemalans who had applied and been rejected for asylum during the previous decade be reopened and that others be able to apply.

Like other immigrants, Central Americans were affected by growing hostility toward immigrants during the 1990s, manifested in the 1996 Illegal Immigration Reform and Immigrant Responsibility Act. Among its other provisions, this law increased the requirements for applying for a stay of deportation based on character, length of stay in the U.S., and personal hardship. However, the 1997 Nicaraguan Adjustment and Central American Relief Act (NACARA) permitted Salvadorans and Guatemalans who had been in the U.S. since 1990 to apply for a stay of deportation under the previous conditions, and at the same time provided for the cancellation of deportation for Nicaraguans and Cubans who had arrived before 1995. Subsequent efforts to extend these conditions to Salvadorans and Guatemalans, as well as Hondurans and Haitians, have had limited success. Several bills providing for amnesty have been proposed, but to date none have passed. In the meantime, TPS was extended to Hondurans and Nicaraguans in 1999, following Hurricane Mitch, and to Salvadorans after two major earthquakes in El Salvador in early 2001.

Despite the high percentage who are undocumented, many Central Americans have been active politically. This was particularly true of Salvadorans and Guatemalans during the late 1970s and 1980s, when they participated actively in organizations oriented to securing the rights of immigrants and refugees in the U.S., opposing U.S. policy in Central America, and supporting revolutionary and progressive groups within their respective countries. At the same time, many Nicaraguan refugees and immigrants supported groups in Nicaragua opposed to the Sandinista government. Increasingly in the 1990s, Central Americans and their advocates focused particularly on securing legal status for their respective national groups. Along with other immigrants, Central Americans have been in the forefront of the new labor organizing, beginning in the late 1980s, especially among such groups as building cleaners (janitors) and hotel and restaurant workers. The successful Justice for Janitors campaign in Los Angeles, for example, relied on a combination of astute organizational leadership, on the one hand, and labor militancy spearheaded by Central Americans and other immigrants and activists, on the other.

Cultural Impact and Issues of Identity

By the mid-1980s, Central American immigrants had begun to transform the neighborhoods in which they settled. Guatemalan, Honduran, Nicaraguan, and Salvadoran restaurants, grocery stores, and bakeries catered to these new populations. Travel agencies featured trips to Guatemala City, San Jose, Costa Rica, and ultimately other major Central American cities, while express mail and transport services offered inexpensive and relatively secure means to send money, letters, and packages to families in the region. Weekly newspapers appeared in major centers of Central American immigrant settlement, featuring events in the respective countries of origin and their communities in the U.S. Salvadorans, Guatemalans, and Hondurans, often from a particular location, formed soccer teams and even their own soccer leagues. Nicaraguans, like Cubans, typically established baseball teams in areas where they predominated.

Religion is central to the culture and settlement process of Central Americans, as it is for many other immigrant groups. Most are Roman Catholic by birth, although Protestant evangelicalism has made significant inroads among Central Americans in the U.S. as well as in their countries of origin. For both Catholics and evangelicals, the church plays an important role, especially among recent immigrants. Churches that previously offered only English-language masses have introduced masses in Spanish and incorporated cultural elements familiar to the new immigrants. Catholic as well as Protestant churches and synagogues became part of the sanctuary movement in the 1980s, working to provide safe haven for Guatemalan and Salvadoran refugees. National religious feast days, such as La Purissima, a Nicaraguan festival that commemorates the conception of the Virgin Mary, are celebrated with songs and processions, and Guatemalans in Los Angeles make pilgrimages to a replica of the famous Black Christ of Esquipulas. Central Americans have their own traditions for religious holidays such as Christmas and Holy Week as well as for births, baptisms, and deaths.

Evangelical churches have won converts among Central Americans, including the Guatemalan Maya, some of whom were members of these churches in their home country. In contrast to some of the Catholic and mainstream Protestant churches, these do not typically engage in overtly political work but concentrate more on individual needs and the advancement of evangelical issues. The demands evangelical churches tend to place on members are high (tithing, proselytizing, and frequently attending church), but members receive substantial psychological and material support from church groups and each other, and the strong networks formed in such communities often facilitate access to jobs and other services.

Many Central American immigrant communities celebrate independence day in mid-September, the anniversary of the date that the region of the viceroyalty of New Spain—subsequently Mexico and Central America as well as parts of the United States—achieved its independence from Spain. The Maya and Garifuna have their own days of celebration. Q'anjob'al, Quiche, and other Mayan groups from particular villages celebrate their town's saint's day with music, processions, parties, and other events, in some cases bringing marimba bands and elaborate costumes and masks from their home communities.

The Garifuna celebrate various days associated with their immigration from

Dominica and St. Vincent to the Central American coastal areas. In New York, where the majority of Garifuna are from Honduras, the Honduran American Cultural Association sponsors a reenactment of Arrival Day, commemorating the arrival of the Garifuna on the Caribbean coast after they were expelled from the islands by the British. The Garifuna in Los Angeles are for the most part from Belize, although Tomas Zuniga, the president of their association, the Garinagu Empowerment Movement, or GEM, is a Guatemalan. GEM sponsors an annual street festival on April 12, and the Los Angeles City Council approved a resolution proclaiming April 12 Garifuna Day in Los Angeles.

As with other immigrant groups, first-generation Central American immigrants often have a bifurcated identity. On the one hand, they see the U.S. as providing economic opportunities lacking in their home countries and are particularly concerned that their children succeed here. On the other hand, they maintain a nostalgia for their home countries, which may be nourished by trips home by those who are documented or, conversely, by the longings of those who are undocumented and unable to visit for fear of not being able to return. Some who came from war-torn countries in the 1980s play down their origins. Others, particularly the Maya and Garifuna, have tried to maintain their traditions among their children. As with other immigrant groups, music is an important medium for bridging the gap between U.S., Latino, and/or indigenous cultures. The Maya and Garifuna have combined their traditional music, including the marimba (an important element of Maya culture) and *punta* (traditional drumming associated with Garifuna ceremonies), with contemporary Western forms of rock, reggae, hip-hop, rap, and so on.

One example of migrant efforts to retain traditional customs is the Escuelita Maya, established in Palm Beach County, which, as noted, is a major center of the Guatemalan Maya population. The Escuelita Maya provides after-school classes in Mayan art, culture, music, and dance as well as assistance with homework for children aged five to twelve. Established in 1995, the program is very popular; the classes are always full, and there is a long waiting list. The program cultivates pride in the Mayan heritage, and students, many of whom have never been to Guatemala or left at a very young age, express a wish to visit or eventually live there.

Many Central Americans, including those who have been in the U.S. for some time, retain contacts with their families and communities back home. Recent immigrants frequently send a substantial proportion of their earnings to their families, especially for the care of children or other relatives left behind. In several immigrant communities, Central Americans from a particular country or even a particular village have formed organizations to help families when a member has died, including funds to send the body back to their homeland for burial. Central Americans, especially Salvadorans and Guatemalans, have formed numerous hometown associations linking communities of origin with their compatriots in U.S. communities; their support ranges from providing medical supplies or sending an ambulance to building sports facilities and constructing potable water systems.

Sociologists and other scholars who have studied immigration generally reject the dichotomy between assimilation and marginality as the options for immigrants coming to the U.S. For second-generation immigrants in particular, assimilation can mean assimilation into an underclass in disadvantaged neighborhoods. Central Americans in impoverished, deteriorating, and densely populated areas such as Pico Union in Los Angeles live in an environment characterized by above-average high school dropout rates and youth involvement in drugs and gangs. Those immigrant or second-generation children who combine access to education and English-language skills with strong personal and cultural attachments to families and the immigrant community often fare better than their more "assimilated" peers.

Another form of "segmented assimilation" and reactive identity is that acquired by students of Central American ancestry who go to college and are exposed to U.S. Latino and/or Latin American history, sociology, anthropology, and ethnic studies classes. As is the case with other immigrant groups, it is often in the context of college classes, programs, and groups that such students discover, redefine, or reinvent an identity that incorporates elements of the place of origin of their parents. It was in the context of the Chicano/Latino studies program at California State University at Northridge, for example, that students of Central American ancestry first raised demands to have classes that focused on their history, culture, and current situation and eventually established the first Central American studies program in the nation. Conferences concerned with Central American literature and culture—in the U.S. and in the region—organized by graduate students and faculty have raised the profile of Central Americans within U.S. Latino culture, as have poetry and performance groups such as Epicentroamerica in California.

Central Americans are among the most rapidly growing immigrant populations in the U.S. Like other migration experiences, those of Central Americans are shaped by the intersection of individual decisions and broader conditions and events. Early migration trajectories were often influenced by relations established by the U.S. with the sending countries; later migrants often followed these trajectories and used networks established by the pioneers. The political upheaval and violence in several Central American countries during the 1970s and 1980s resulted in a dramatic upsurge in the level of Central American–U.S. migration during the 1980s, which has continued into the 21st century.

In addition to being among the fastest-growing immigrant populations in the U.S., Central Americans are among the most diversified, coming from seven different countries with distinct historical backgrounds and including a diversity of indigenous, Afro-Caribbean, European, and mestizo populations. Settlement patterns tend to reflect these differences. While the majority of Central Americans, particularly Salvadorans and Guatemalans, still come to California, it is Florida, and especially the Miami area, that is the major destination for Nicaraguans. During the

1990s many Central Americans sought out job opportunities in cities and rural areas outside the initial zones of settlement, resulting in more diversified locations.

Central Americans come from a variety of socioeconomic backgrounds, although most are disadvantaged, having relatively low levels of education, working in low-paying production and service jobs, and often lacking documents. Nevertheless, Central Americans have had an important impact in the U.S. through stores and services in their neighborhoods, religious and cultural practices, and art and music. Many, particularly the Maya and Garifuna, have sought to maintain their traditional languages and culture among their children, establishing language schools, developing musical forms combining U.S with Latino and/or indigenous traditions, and providing classes in art, culture, and dance. Many retain ties with their home countries, often sending a substantial part of their earnings to families back home and in some cases forming hometown associations which collect funds for various civic projects in their communities of origin. First- and second-generation Central Americans have sometimes become interested in their Central American origin and issues of identity in college, through classes and other programs, and in some cases have formed their own cultural groups.

The continuing influx of new immigrants and communications with relatives and friends back home indicate that the culture and traditions of Central American groups in the U.S. will continue to grow and evolve. At the same time, Central American immigrants, along with other immigrant communities, tend to come together around issues of legal status, access to quality education and health care for their children, and improvements in wages and working conditions, which suggests that they will play an increasingly important role in local and national political campaigns, unionization drives, and education programs. We can therefore anticipate that Central Americans will become more integrated into the political, economic, and social life of the U.S. while maintaining strong social, economic, and cultural ties with their countries of origin.

Bibliography

England, Sarah. 2000. "Creating a Global Garifuna Nation? The Transnationalization of Race, Class, and Gender Politics in the Garifuna Diaspora." Ph.D. dissertation, University of California, Davis.

Hagan, Jacqueline Maria. 1994. *Deciding to Be Legal: A Maya Community in Houston*. Philadelphia: Temple University Press.

Hamilton, Nora, and Norma Stoltz Chinchilla. 2001. *Seeking Community in a Global City: Guatemalans and Salvadorans in Los Angeles*. Philadelphia: Temple University Press.

Loucky, James, and Marilyn M. Moors, eds. 2000. *The Maya Diaspora: Guatemalan Roots, New American Lives*. Philadelphia: Temple University Press.

Mahler, Sarah J. 1995. *American Dreaming: Immigrant Life on the Margins*. Princeton, N.J.: Princeton University Press.

Menjívar, Cecilia. 2000. *Fragmented Ties: Salvadoran Immigrant Networks in America.* Berkeley: University of California Press.

Portes, Alejandro, and Rubén G. Rumbaut. 2001. *Legacies: The Story of the Immigrant Second Generation.* Berkeley: University of California Press.

Rodriguez, Nestor P., and Jacqueline Maria Hagan. 2000. "Maya Urban Villagers in Houston: The Formation of a Migrant Community from San Cristobal Totonicapán." In James Loucky and Marilyn M. Moors, eds., *The Maya Diaspora: Guatemalan Roots, New American Lives,* pp. 223–30. Philadelphia: Temple University Press.

Zentgraf, Kristine. Forthcoming. "Why Women Migrate: Salvadoran and Guatemalan Women in Los Angeles." In Enrique C. Ochoa and Gilda Laura Ochoa, eds., *Latina/o Los Angeles: Global Transformation, Migrations, and Political Activism.* Tucson: University of Arizona Press.

China: People's Republic of China

Xiao-huang Yin

Chinese Americans are a diverse ethnic group, made up of U.S.-born Chinese and immigrants from all over the Chinese world. As of 2000, their population totaled 2,858,291. Among them, more than 1 million are immigrants from China (PRC), or "mainland Chinese." They are not only the largest subgroup in Chinese America but also constitute a fast-growing population. Statistics indicate that between 2000 and 2004, approximately another 307,000 PRC immigrants were admitted to America. One recent study claims that including clandestine immigration, the number of mainland Chinese in the U.S. has actually exceeded 2 million, turning them into the second largest new American group, next to Mexicans.

What are the characteristics of these immigrants? What unifies them as a community and helps them identify with Chinese America? In what ways do their experiences in U.S. society reflect changes in post-1965 immigrant communities? This essay is an attempt to find some answers to these questions.

Historical Background

Although there were individual Chinese in America in the 18th century, large-scale Chinese immigration to the U.S. did not begin until the Gold Rush in 1849. By 1860 the U.S. Census reported some 33,000 Chinese in the U.S. The following decades saw a steady growth of the Chinese population, and by 1880 the census counted 105,465 Chinese, mostly young men, on the U.S. mainland. In the next two years 50,000 more entries helped the Chinese American population reach about 150,000. If we include those who returned to China, some 322,000 Chinese took the trip across the Pacific from 1849 to 1882.

Chinese immigration soon came to an end, however. Following public clamor and intensive anti-Chinese campaigns, Congress passed the Chinese Exclusion Act in 1882, barring Chinese immigrants from entering the U.S. This act remained in effect for the following 60 years, during which time loopholes were eliminated and its provisions became stricter. Exclusionary policies and social discrimination also severely constrained Chinese living in America, turning them into predominantly a bachelors' society, with little reproduction. As a result, the Chinese population in the U.S. shrank sharply. It was not until after 1943, when Congress repealed the Chinese exclusion laws, that a significant increase in the Chinese American population took place.

Post-1965 Immigration

The 1965 Immigration Act inaugurated another turning point in Chinese American history. The new law removed racial criteria from U.S. immigration policy, providing an equal allotment to each nation-state throughout the world. As Table 1 shows, the influx of Chinese immigrants since then has led to a more than tenfold growth in the Chinese American population. In fact, over 70 percent of all Chinese Americans were born overseas, with 76 percent of the immigrants arriving only in the past 20 years.

Because of the hostility between Beijing and Washington, however, most Chinese immigrants to the U.S. during the post–World War II era came from Taiwan, Hong Kong, and Southeast Asia. Those who identified themselves as China-born in census studies were actually secondary migrants who had moved overseas before the founding of the People's Republic in 1949. Only a few individuals were able to emi-

Table 1   Chinese population in the U.S., 1900–2000

Year	Population	Male/female ratio	U.S.-born (percentage)
1900	118,746	14:1	9.3
1910	94,414	9.3:1	20.7
1920	85,202	4.7:1	30.1
1930	102,159	3.0:1	41.2
1940	106,334	2.2:1	48.1
1950	150,005	1.7:1	53.0
1960	237,292	1.3:1	53.5
1970	435,062	1.1:1	46.9
1980	812,178	1:1	36.7
1990	1,645,472	0.99:1	30.7
2000	2,858,291[a]	0.99:1	29.1

Source: U.S. Census Bureau, General Population Characteristics; We the People: Asians in the U.S.: Census 2000 Special Reports (2004); http://www.census.gov.

a. Includes 435,321 individuals with mixed heritage who identified themselves as Chinese on the Census questionnaire.

grate from China to America after the communist revolution. One of them was Charles Bing Wang, the founder of Computer Associates International, who came from Shanghai as a child with his parents in the early 1950s. Bette Bao Lord, the author of the bestseller *Spring Moon* (1979), mentioned that her family managed to bring her younger sister from Beijing to New York in 1963.

Arrival of PRC immigrants. President Richard Nixon's historic visit to Beijing in 1972 normalized U.S.-China relations. The vast majority of PRC immigrants, however, did not arrive until after 1979, when Congress granted China, Taiwan, and Hong Kong separate annual immigration per-country limits. Immigration was further spurred by political and economic reforms in China during the post-Mao era, when Beijing relaxed its emigration restrictions, making it easier for Chinese to go abroad. As Table 2 shows, PRC immigration to America soon gained momentum, and it quickly surpassed immigration from Taiwan and Hong Kong.

Federal records reveal that immigration from China has continued to increase, and the number of mainland Chinese entering the U.S. in recent years has been four times that from Taiwan and Hong Kong combined. In 2002 alone, for example, 61,282 immigrants from China were admitted, while only 9,836 from Taiwan and 6,090 from Hong Kong were admitted.

Changes in places of origin. Today's Chinese immigration not only far outstrips that of earlier eras in size but also represents a varied profile in places of origin. Until the late 1940s, 90 percent of the Chinese in America came from the Pearl River Delta in Guangdong (Canton) Province; in 2000 the Cantonese accounted for only 8 percent of total PRC immigrants; the rest come from virtually every major part of China.

Such a dramatic change reflects the impact of chain migration sponsored by the growing number of PRC immigrants who have obtained U.S. citizenship. The first PRC immigrants to arrive in the early 1980s mostly originated from Guangdong, because of the province's strong historical connection with Chinese America. Since then immigrants from other regions have taken the lead. Like their predecessors, the new immigrants have kept close ties with their relatives in China while putting down roots in the U.S. After they obtain citizenship or legal alien status, they invite family members to join them.

Table 2   Country of birth of the foreign-born Chinese population, 1980-2000

Year	China (PRC)	Taiwan	Hong Kong
1980	297,780	81,300	81,480
1990	542,204	256,558	150,740
2000	1,011,805	335,787	206,903

Source: U.S. Census Bureau, 2000 Census, 5% Public Use Microdata Sample, weighted data.

It is noteworthy that the surge of PRC immigration to the U.S. was aided in part by special legislation in 1990. As a gesture of sympathy with the student victims in the Tiananmen incident on June 4, 1989, President George H. W. Bush issued Executive Order No. 12711, which led Congress to pass the Chinese Student Protection Act, granting PRC citizens who entered the U.S. between June 4, 1989, and April 11, 1990, permission to apply for permanent residency. More than 60,000 PRC citizens adjusted their status under this act. They too sponsored family members to immigrate to America.

Interestingly, even the adoption of children from China by American families since the 1980s has helped alter demographic characteristics of PRC immigrants. Totaling more than 60,000 as of 2005, these adopted children, mostly baby girls, have come from orphanages throughout China, especially in rural regions. Raised by parents who are overwhelmingly Caucasian, they have contributed to the cultural diversity of the Chinese American community.

No accurate figures are available for the distribution of PRC immigrants by origin. Estimates vary widely, but all agree that Fujian Province has replaced Guangdong as the most popular sending source for U.S.-bound immigrants. Numbering half a million by some estimates, Fujianese now account for the single largest speech group among PRC immigrants. In fact, the heavy concentration of Fujianese in "Little Fuzhou," in the two-block stretch between East Broadway and Division Street in New York City, has made the area the most densely populated Chinatown outside Asia. Even in traditionally Cantonese-dominated urban Chinatowns, such as those in California, the vast majority of residents now represent various Mandarin speech groups.

Despite immense demographic changes in their sending sources, immigrants from China resemble the early generations in their selection of residency destinations in the U.S. They often choose to settle in metropolitan areas on the West Coast and in the Northeast. California and New York continue to attract the most Chinese immigrants. As of 2000, 1.12 million Chinese were living in California and 420,000 in New York, accounting for more than 50 percent of the Chinese American population.

Student immigrants. The past two decades have also witnessed a growing presence of PRC professionals in the U.S., especially student immigrants—those who enter on a student/scholar visa but transfer to immigrant status after graduation. The number of PRC students attending American institutions of higher learning has been consistently on the rise since the 1980s. Totaling 61,765 in the 2003–2004 academic year, their presence makes China the leading nation in sending students to colleges and universities across the U.S.

Many PRC students have succeeded in adjusting their status, aided by their strong educational credentials. According to Chinese sources, of the nearly 400,000 PRC citizens who studied in the U.S. between 1978 and 2003, only around 20 percent returned home after they completed their education. Most eventually settled in the U.S. Immigration data also show that PRC immigrants have taken a very large percentage of the H-1 visas (for professional temporary workers) available every year since the mid-1980s. In 1999, for example, around 10 percent of all H-1 visas issued went to mainland Chinese.

PRC student immigrants have been highly successful in pursuing U.S. careers, partly because they concentrate heavily in science and technology. Having adapted well to the mainstream American job market, they are primed for success. For instance, thousands of former PRC student immigrants serve on the faculties of American colleges and universities. Many have established themselves as leading authorities in their fields. Together with their counterparts from Taiwan and Hong Kong, they have produced a disproportionately large number of America's scientists and scholars. Gang Tian, a mathematician on the faculty of Princeton University, and Lu Chen, who teaches neurobiology at the University of California, Berkeley, are two examples. Tian, who has received many top prizes in mathematics, has made his way to the pinnacle of mathematics studies, whereas Chen, a MacArthur Foundation "genius" grant recipient, has distinguished herself in the study of how brain cells communicate with one another through synapses.

By aiming at cultural integration and synthesizing Chinese ideas in an American context, some PRC student immigrants have also achieved prominence in art, music, film, and literature in mainstream society. Ha Jin (Jin Xufei), who came from north China to study at Brandeis University in 1985, won the National Book Award and the PEN/Faulkner Award with his novel *War Trash* (2002), about the suffering of Chinese POWs during the Korean War. Joan Chen (Chen Chong), a student immigrant from Shanghai, is well known as a Hollywood actress. To some extent, the striking success of many Chinese student immigrants has helped fuel the new stereotype of Asians as a "model minority" in U.S. society.

Undocumented immigrants. Ironically, while the PRC community boasts a strong presence of professional and student immigrants, it is also known for having a disproportionately large percentage of undocumented immigrants. Although there are no reliable figures, it is estimated that around 500,000 Chinese have illegally entered the U.S. from the PRC since the late 1980s.

The vast majority of undocumented immigrants come from a small number of townships surrounding Fuzhou, the capital of Fujian Province, especially from Changle County. With a population of 700,000, Changle has sent about 200,000 immigrants to the U.S. since the late 1980s. It is telling that most of the 286 smuggled Chinese on board the ill-fated *Golden Venture,* which ran aground off New York in June 1993, and nearly half of the 58 Chinese immigrants entombed in a tomato truck in England in the summer of 2000, were natives of Changle. A popular saying in Fujian vividly portrays how Changle has become a synonym for human trafficking to the U.S.: "Shijie Pa Meiguo, Meiguo Pa Changle"—"The world is afraid of Americans, but Americans are scared by Changle [because of its waves of human cargo]."

Illegal immigrants from the PRC began arriving in America in the late 1980s. They were nicknamed "18K Travelers" (*Wanba Ke*) because they typically paid $18,000 each to the heads of the smuggling rings (called "snakeheads" in Chinese) to get into the U.S. The cost increased to $40,000 in the mid-1990s, however, and has jumped to as much as $60,000 in recent years. Half of the fees must be handed to a snakehead as down payment, and the rest is collected after the prospective immigrant's "safe" arrival in the U.S. Because of the heavy debt, it is common for a newcomer to hold several jobs and work 70 to 80 hours a week until he meets his financial obligations.

Undocumented immigrants are customarily involved in the service industry, the restaurant business being the most popular choice for labor and investment. A report in *Time* claims that Chinese food is the second most frequently consumed ethnic food, following Italian food. As a result, the food business has become the standard occupation for newcomers from China, ranging from street carts selling fried rice and noodles to tiny takeout eateries serving American-style Chinese meals. According to several studies, there are around 50,000 restaurants owned by Fujianese alone in the U.S., with about 400,000 employees. In recent years, however, an increasing number of Fujianese immigrants have shifted to work in the construction industry, taking advantage of job opportunities created by the booming housing and real estate market.

Most Chinese Americans view the undocumented immigrants from China with a mixture of sadness, disengagement, and sympathy. The suffering of these people, especially given graphic pictures of the bodies of Chinese stowaways washed to the shore or suffocated in crammed containers after their odyssey across the Pacific, has shocked the community and disturbed many. Some Chinese Americans are also concerned with the rise of crime rates in Chinatowns. Differing from other contemporary Chinese immigrants yet resembling the early generations, undocumented immigrants have customarily left their families at home and live a bachelor's life in the U.S. until they can afford to bring their loved ones over. This has fostered a flourishing underground Chinatown economy peppered with prostitution and other lawless practices. For this reason, many Chinese view human trafficking as a serious crime that tarnishes the image of Chinese America and divides the community.

Others argue, however, that undocumented immigrants deserve sympathy and support because they are subject to social prejudice in both Chinese America and the larger society. They point out convincingly that despite the "humble background" of many Fujianese, their migration is propelled by the same desire for a better life that leads many affluent and educated Chinese to this country. If the rich can afford legal passage with their business investments and student immigrants can settle in the U.S. with the help of their educational credentials, the impoverished villagers of Fujian should also have the right to realize their dreams with hard work, even if they come illegally. Serving as a critical element for the growth of the Chinese American economy, these undocumented immigrants have brought new life to urban Chinatowns and played a crucial part in the development of the Chinese American community. In reality, it is their valuable service, however "cheap" it might be, that reduces the price of Chinese food and enables many professional Chinese immigrants to live comfortable lifestyles. Therefore, their presence and contributions should be recognized by both Chinese America and mainstream society.

A Bimodal Community

The fact that PRC immigrants come from a wide spectrum of socioeconomic conditions has left deep marks on their American experience. The two ends of this spectrum have resulted in two distinct groups: the "uptown" and the "downtown" Chinese. The former are professionals and other affluent immigrants, who tend to reside in suburban towns and are well integrated into mainstream society; the latter are predominantly working-class immigrants who are trapped in poverty-stricken urban ghettos. With limited resources and few readily transferable skills, these downtown Chinese have to struggle on the fringes of society. The striking division between the two groups has in effect transformed Chinese immigrants into a bipolar society. Measures of educational attainments, occupational patterns, and personal as well as family income all point in this direction.

As Table 3 indicates, there exists a wide gap in the educational attainments of PRC immigrants. As a group, they are better educated than the U.S. population as a whole. The 2000 Census shows that 46.7 percent of PRC immigrants aged 25 to 64 earned a bachelor's degree or higher; the percentage is almost twice that of the general population. What is equally striking, however, is that more than a quarter of PRC immigrants had less than a high school education, a much larger percentage than that in other groups.

Table 3 Educational distribution of the foreign-born Chinese and U.S. populations, persons aged 25–64, 2000 (percentages)

National origin	Bachelor's degree or higher	Less than high school
China (PRC)	46.7	25.6
Taiwan	67.9	4.9
Hong Kong	51.9	14.4
Total U.S. population[a]	24.4	19.6

Source: U.S. Census Bureau, 2000 Census, 5% Public Use Microdata Sample, weighted data.
a. *Source:* "Highlights from the Census 2000 Demographic Profiles," U.S. Census Bureau; http://factfinder.census.gov.

The disparity in educational achievement among PRC immigrants is consistent with their English-language ability. Although PRC immigrants are overrepresented in academia and education in U.S. society, nearly 40 percent of those above the age of four cannot speak English at all or do not speak it well; the corresponding rates for immigrants from Taiwan and Hong Kong are 16 percent and 14 percent, respectively. The consequences of lack of English-language ability cannot be ignored. As is commonly known, language barriers hinder upward mobility in American life and lead to prejudice: 60 percent of Chinese immigrants report that their difficulty with English is a reason for the discrimination they have encountered.

Similarly, occupational patterns of PRC immigrants highlight the polarization of their community. Thanks to the prominence of student immigrants, almost half (44.4 percent) of the working population is employed in managerial and professional occupations. This exceeds the rate among the U.S. population as a whole (33.6 percent). While PRC immigrants' career advancement is impressive, however, their success is not universal. As Table 4 shows, PRC immigrants are also more concentrated in unskilled occupations. In reality, more than one third of all the PRC immigrants in the labor force are employed in manual occupations—a much higher proportion than among their counterparts from Taiwan and Hong Kong.

The bimodal socioeconomic structure of the PRC community is also reflected in its income levels. Although their per capita and median household income is considerably greater than that of the general population, PRC immigrants have a larger percentage of individuals living in poverty. As Table 5 reveals, PRC immigrants earn 15 percent more in median personal income annually ($25,000) than their comparison group in the larger society ($21,587), and their annual median household income is almost $10,000 more than that of the general population. At the same time, however, the percentage of PRC immigrants who live below the poverty line is almost double that of their counterparts from Taiwan and Hong Kong.

The disparity in personal income of PRC immigrants is even more striking. In

Table 4   Occupational distribution of the foreign-born Chinese population, persons aged 25–64 in the labor force, 2000 (percentages)

Occupation	China (PRC)	Taiwan	Hong Kong
Managerial/professional	44.4	59.8	49.8
Technical/sales/administration	20.8	27.0	28.9
Service	16.7	6.3	10.3
Production/crafts/operators/fabricators	17.4	6.3	10.7
Other occupations[a]	0.7	0.5	0.4

Source: U.S. Census Bureau, 2000 Census, 5% Public Use Microdata Sample, weighted data.
a. Includes farming/forestry/fishing, active military, and unemployed/not classified.

Table 5   Income distribution, the foreign-born Chinese and total U.S. populations, 2000

National origin	Median household income	Median personal income	Percentage below the poverty line
China (PRC)	$51,060	$25,000	9.1
Taiwan	$65,000	$40,100	5.0
Hong Kong	$65,000	$38,090	4.6
Total U.S. population[a]	$41,994	$21,587	NA[b]

Source: U.S. Census Bureau, 2000 Census, 5% Public Use Microdata Sample, weighted data.

Note: Figures for median personal income and percentage below the poverty line pertain to persons aged 25–64 in the labor force, while figures for median household income pertain to all households. In 1999 dollars.

a. *Source:* "Profile of Selected Economic Characteristics," U.S. Census Bureau, *http://factfinder.census.gov.*

b. Nationwide, 13.5 percent of all Chinese Americans, including PRC immigrants, live in poverty compared with 12.4 percent of the total U.S. population. *Source: We the People: Asians in the U.S.: Census 2000 Special Reports,* 2004; *http://www.census.gov.*

1999, 20 percent of PRC immigrants aged 25 to 64 in the labor force made more than $56,000 a year, but another 20 percent earned less than $10,000 annually; and 40 percent of all PRC immigrants in this same bracket had an annual personal income of less than $20,000. Since earning power is considered a significant indicator of social status, these data suggest that PRC immigrants lag behind their peers from other parts of the Chinese world in this key aspect of American life. They also present a more complex picture of the Chinese experience in the U.S.: affluent immigrants have raised the median income level of the Chinese American community as a whole, obscuring the large numbers of Chinese Americans who struggle with very low incomes.

Transnationalism and Circular and Reverse Migration

As their community is constantly replenished with newcomers from China, most PRC immigrants naturally express interest in China-related affairs and maintain ties with their old home. Their involvement in networking across the Pacific is also a product of new and emerging trends in immigrant life in the age of globalization.

China's stunning transformation in recent years from a "backward" agricultural country into the "world's manufacturing floor" has buoyed its image among PRC immigrants, prompting them to view their former homeland with greater enthusiasm. Even those who do not benefit from a rising China have felt hope and satisfaction from knowing that their native land is no longer a miserable victim of Western colonial powers. It allows them to collect what W.E.B. DuBois would have called a "psychological wage." This is perhaps why 75 percent of 354 Chinese Americans who were randomly polled in 2004, including immigrants from all over the Chinese world as well as U.S.-born Chinese, viewed China favorably.

As China's vibrant economy grows, it also attracts many business-savvy PRC immigrants who have settled in the U.S. to return to their old country for work. These transnational migrants see China's attempt to move from a centrally planned economy to a free market one as an extraordinary opportunity to advance their careers. Indeed, even business people from Taiwan, who used to belong to the staunch anti-China camp, are anxious to cut lucrative deals with Beijing. Perhaps this is why 60 percent of all foreign investment and 70 percent of all joint ventures in China come from or are owned by diasporic Chinese.

More significantly, with the rapid expansion of U.S.-China economic networks, American-based multinational companies have been aggressively recruiting Chinese transnational professionals to run programs in China. Most of these are PRC students who came to study in the U.S. and have stayed on to work for American companies or institutions. Having lived in both Chinese and American societies, they not only possess knowledge and expertise in areas that are central to transnational business activities but also can bridge the cultural gaps that may frustrate bids by U.S. companies to crack the China market.

As a result, circular and reverse migration has become a viable strategy among transnational PRC professionals who are concerned with maximizing resources and opportunities. Dubbed "reverse gold seekers" or "sea turtles" in Chinese, they have been instrumental in setting the standard for China's market reforms and in expanding U.S.-China economic relations. One study shows that by 1996, among those who ran foreign businesses or managed joint ventures in Beijing, 50 percent were Chinese transnational migrants, including those from the U.S.

The circular and reverse migration of PRC transnational professionals also reflects the recent trend of thousands of Chinese immigrants returning to their native lands to work after settling in Western countries. For example, between 1985 and 1997 around 600,000 Hong Kong residents emigrated to the West, but by 2003 one third of them had moved back to Hong Kong or to China to take advantage of better employment opportunities.

Returning to take better-paying jobs or run lucrative businesses in China, however, does not mean that PRC immigrants have gone back to their old home for permanent resettlement. Chinese circular and reverse migration today rarely involves the entire family. Often the family stays in the U.S. while the husband returns to work in China, after obtaining permanent residency or American citizenship. He periodically flies back to visit his family; such a frequent air traveler is referred to as a "spaceman" or *taikuren* in Chinese, meaning "his wife is not by his side." Such commuting is facilitated by the more than two dozen daily flights that link major U.S. cities with various urban centers in China.

Chinese-language publications and news networks. The existence and expansion of transnational Chinese publications and news networks have contributed to the rise of transnationalism among PRC immigrants. Extensive and prompt coverage of events in China raises immigrants' awareness of what occurs in their old country and generates interest in transnational activities. According to a recent survey, for example, more than two thirds of Chinese immigrants in the U.S. report that they have paid very close or fairly close attention to events in their former homeland. Furthermore, Chinese-language publications have promoted a sense of "Chineseness" and ethnic solidarity among immigrants in American society.

As we have seen, Chinese immigrants in the U.S. are a highly diverse population, made up of people from all over China. While spoken Chinese comprises a variety of mutually incomprehensible dialects, written Chinese crosses linguistic lines and is recognized as a common heritage by all Chinese. Thus publications give Chinese immigrants a sense of community, reinforce their ethnic consciousness, and function as an identity tool that unites the diverse population in the new country.

Chinese-language publications have also served as a bridge between PRC immigrants and the larger society. They have furnished an interpretive prism through which most newcomers receive and share information. Ordinary Chinese immigrants must rely on them for knowledge about U.S. society because of their inability to understand English. Even those who are highly proficient in English find Chinese-language publications a significant and convenient way to exchange impressions of and communicate feelings about American life.

Conversely, the prominence and popularity of Chinese-language publications owe much to the growing number of Chinese immigrants. The influx of newcomers and the subsequent increase in the size of the Chinese-speaking population in the U.S. has brought new life to these publications. As Table 6 shows, Chinese is now the second most popular non-English language spoken in America, and today more than 70 percent of Chinese Americans speak Chinese at home.

The thirst of immigrants for publications in their mother tongue has resulted in the flourishing of Chinese-language journalism in America. At present at least four major transnational Chinese-language dailies are circulating throughout the U.S., most of them subsidiaries of major media networks in China, Taiwan, and Hong Kong. With a daily circulation of more than 250,000, *Shijie Ribao* (*Chinese Daily News*) stands out as the largest newspaper in the Chinese American community, followed by *Qiao Bao* (*China Post*), *Xingdao Ribao* (*Sing Tao Daily*), and *Guoji Ribao* (*International Daily News*). Although each of the newspapers has its own subscriber

Table 6   Five non-English languages most frequently spoken at home, 1990 and 2000

Language	Number of speakers, 2000	Number of speakers, 1990	Percentage change
Spanish	28,101,052	17,339,172	+62.1
Chinese	2,022,143	1,249,213	+61.8
French	1,643,838	1,760,216	−6.6
Tagalog	1,224,241	843,251	+45.2
Vietnamese	1,009,627	507,069	+99.1

Source: U.S. Census Bureau, Summary File 3 (SF 3), 2003. Figures pertain to speakers aged 5 and older.

group among immigrants from China, Taiwan, and Hong Kong, they tend to cater to the taste of readers across group lines to seek a larger share in the highly competitive Chinese publishing market in America. There are also numerous smaller regional and local Chinese dailies and weeklies in virtually every American town with a substantial Chinese population. The Southern California Chinese community alone supports more than 15 different Chinese-language newspapers, in addition to a dozen TV and cable TV programs as well as radio stations that cover China-related news.

Breakthroughs in technology have moved China closer to PRC immigrants in America in another way: they enable newcomers to stay in touch with their friends and relatives easily through telephone calls, e-mail correspondence, website information, and other advanced means of communication. For example, 31 percent of Chinese immigrants in Los Angeles report that they contact relatives and friends in their places of origin weekly. This is an impressively high rate measured by any standard. As the media outlets keep newcomers attuned to developments in their native land and advances in communication reduce the sense of distance across the Pacific, they have stimulated and sustained interest among Chinese immigrants in transnational activities. As scholars generally agree, immigrants feel much more involved if their old home is just on the other side of the border.

Transnational community organizations. The past two decades have also witnessed the emergence and expansion of many new transnational organizations. Founded by immigrants along functional lines and in response to perceived common identities, these business, family, cultural, native-place, and professional organizations have provided social stability for new arrivals in the U.S., played a vital part in binding the PRC community together, and served as powerful and effective ways for immigrants to develop and maintain close ties with China. The activities and missions of many contemporary hometown societies set up by PRC immigrants are a case in point.

Historically, community organizations founded by Chinese immigrants in America, such as clan associations or native-place societies—the *tang* (tong) or *hui* (association)—were always transnational in their activities. Created by merchants and scholars in China for mutual support on trips outside their home areas, these organizations were transplanted to America's Chinatowns by early Chinese immigrants. They served to unite the Chinese community, especially during the exclusion era, and functioned as active channels to help immigrants reach their folks in China. The transnational hometown societies established by recent PRC immigrants, called *tongxianhui*, can be viewed as a continuation of these traditional organizations.

The new transnational organizations are different in many important aspects, however. Compared with the old native-place societies in America's Chinatowns, for example, *tongxianhui* are not only highly diversified in activities and missions but also more open in membership eligibility. While traditional *tang* and *hui* are customarily composed of immigrants who share the same lineage, belong to similar speech groups, or come from the same place, *tongxianhui* have expanded the concept of hometown to include anyone who worked, studied, or lived in that place in China before emigrating to the U.S. This reflects the fact that increasingly large numbers of PRC immigrants no longer feel the same loyalty to their birthplaces as those of earlier generations did, and they are likely to identify with localities in China that they are most familiar with rather than their actual hometowns. Beijing Tongxianghui (Beijingers' Association), Shanghai Tongxianghui (Shanghaiers' Society), and Daxinan Tongxianghui (Association of Southwestern Regions of China) in Southern California are a few outstanding examples.

The development of such new societies as well as other kinds of transnational associations reveals that the majority of recent PRC immigrants do not join traditional Chinatown organizations, which cater mainly to the Cantonese. In addition, they find it difficult to gain assistance and support from traditional Chinatown hierarchies such as the Chinese Consolidated Benevolent Association (CCBA), which until recently was affiliated with the regime in Taiwan. Consequently, although they share cultural identities with other Chinese, PRC immigrants tend to establish their own community organizations, creating a subgroup within Chinese America.

The hometown societies founded by PRC immigrants have typically expanded their China-related activities. The traditional Chinatown organizations were mostly concerned with building connections and strengthening ties between their members in America and people in their birthplaces, but the new societies aim for broader goals. The events they have sponsored are more diversified and often involve the entire Chinese society, ranging from organizing professional conferences on China-related affairs to facilitating cultural exchanges, celebrating Chinese festivals, sponsoring U.S.-China trade fairs, initiating transnational philanthropy, and arranging business and other service-related tours to China.

Another significant group of new players in transnational Chinese organizations are the alumni associations founded by PRC student immigrants in the U.S. Leading Chinese universities such as Beijing, Tsinghua, and Nanjing have thousands of alumni in the U.S., thanks to their academic prominence and long history of sending graduates to study abroad. Alumni associations of these institutions are registered nonprofit organizations in America and are based on voluntary participation, democratic elections, and transient membership. In addition to sponsoring alumni reunions and employment fairs in the U.S., they have spearheaded transnational academic activities. For example, they frequently organize China-related scholarly conferences, encourage their members to volunteer to teach at their alma mater, and arrange lecture tours to underdeveloped regions of China.

The large-scale and highly diversified immigration to the U.S. from the People's Republic of China since the 1970s has had an enormous impact on Chinese American life. On the one hand, the immigrants' success and accomplishments have challenged the idea that the Chinese cannot be culturally and socially assimilated into American life. On the other hand, the plight of the "downtown" Chinese, particularly undocumented immigrants, indicates that a disproportionately large number of politically disfranchised and economically disadvantaged Chinese have been marginalized rather than integrated into American society.

Furthermore, the facts that PRC immigrants have strengthened rather than weakened ties with China and maintained extensive involvement in both societies after their adjustment to American life indicate a new type of settlement pattern. By establishing and promoting transnational linkages, they have proved how immigrants in our rapidly changing era can improve their socioeconomic status through borderless networks. Because it constitutes a remarkable divergence from traditional models of immigration, PRC immigration has redefined not only the Chinese American experience but also the discourse of diasporic studies in a dramatically shrinking global village.

Bibliography

Chin, Ko-lin. *Smuggled Chinese: Clandestine Immigration to the United States.* Philadelphia: Temple University Press, 1999.

Koehn, Peter H., and Xiao-huang Yin, eds. *The Expanding Roles of Chinese Americans in U.S.-China Relations: Transnational Networks and Trans-Pacific Interactions.* Armonk, N.Y.: M. E. Sharpe, 2002.

Li, Ming-huan. "Qiaoxiang shehui ziben jiedu: Yi dangdai Fujian kuajing yiminchao weili" (Social Capital of Overseas Chinese Hometowns: A Case Study of Contemporary Transnational Migration in Fujian Province). In *Huaqiao huaren lishi yanjiu (Overseas Chinese History Studies)* 18, 2 (Summer 2005): 38–49.

Lien, Pei-te. "Taking a Pulse of Chinese Americans at the Dawn of the 21st Century: Results from the Multi-Site Asian American Political Survey." In *Chinese America: History and Perspectives,* 1–38 (forthcoming).

Liu, Eric. *The Accidental Asian: Notes from a Native Speaker.* New York: Random House, 1998.

Pan, Lynn, ed. *The Encyclopedia of the Chinese Overseas.* Cambridge: Harvard University Press, 1999.

Reeves, Terrance, and Claudette Bennett. *We the People: Asians in the United States: Census 2000 Special Reports.* Washington, D.C.: U.S. Census Bureau, 2004.

Yin, Xiao-huang. *Chinese American Literature since the 1850s.* Urbana: University of Illinois Press, 2000.

———. "A Case Study of Transnationalism: Continuity and Changes in Chinese American Philanthropy to China." *American Studies* 45, 2 (Summer 2004): 65–99.

———. "Between Worlds: Chinese Immigrants as a Diversified Population and Transnational Community." Paper presented at the Immigration and Urban History Seminar, Massachusetts Historical Society, Boston, Oct. 27, 2005, pp. 1–53.

Zhao, Xiaojian. "The 'Spirit of Changle': Constructing a Chinese Regional Identity in New York." In Madeline Hsu and Suchang Chan, eds., *Heterogeneity of Chinese Identities*, pp. 1–39. Minneapolis: University of Minnesota Press, forthcoming.

Zhuang, Guotu. *Huaqiao huaren yu zhongguo di guangxi (The Relationship between Overseas Chinese and China)*. Guangzhou: Guangdong gaoden jiaoyu, 2001.

China: Outside the People's Republic of China

Jennifer Holdaway

Today the vast majority of foreign-born Chinese in the U.S. are from the People's Republic of China (PRC), but this was not always the case. Until migration from the PRC opened up in the late 1970s, most Chinese immigrants came from (or through) Taiwan and Hong Kong/Macao. Others were ethnic Chinese from Southeast Asia (Singapore, Malaysia, Vietnam, Thailand, and Indonesia), and from the Caribbean and South America.

In 1980 over half a million foreign-born people gave China as their primary ethnic ancestry, but only just over half—close to 300,000—were from the PRC. As Table 1 shows, in some cases ethnic Chinese comprised the majority of migrants from other countries, and in others only a small percentage. However, the overall result of these multiple migration streams is that people of Chinese descent from outside the PRC are very diverse in terms of their place of origin, dialect, social class, religion, and political affiliation. Their arrival over the postwar period transformed what was previously a fairly homogeneous Chinese American community into one that is extremely heterogeneous.

Chinese from Taiwan and Hong Kong/Macao are considered separately because these territories, while formerly part of the Chinese state and populated predominantly by ethnic Chinese, have been separate political entities for much of their history. Hong Kong was a British colony from 1842 until 1997, and Macao was ruled by the Portuguese from 1557 to 1999. Taiwan was under Japanese control from 1895 to 1945 and then (after a brief period of reconnection to the mainland, from 1945 to 1949) governed by the exile regime of the Kuomintang (KMT). Now a democracy, Taiwan remains in a tense relationship with the PRC, economically increasingly entwined but politically separate. As a result of these historical circumstances, Chinese in Hong Kong and Taiwan have inhabited quite different political

Table 1 Chinese ancestry among selected foreign-born groups, by place of birth, 1980–2000

Country of birth	1980			1990			2000		
	Population	Reporting Chinese ancestry		Population	Reporting Chinese ancestry		Population	Reporting Chinese ancestry	
		Number	Percent		Number	Percent		Number	Percent
All foreign-born	15,152,261	517,378	3.4	21,537,663	979,466	4.5	33,055,462	1,446,364	4.4
China (PRC)	297,780	265,000	89.0	542,204	488,120	90.0	1,011,805	877,276	86.7
Hong Kong	81,480	73,540	90.3	150,740	135,881	90.0	206,903	162,059	78.3
Taiwan	81,300	59,520	73.2	256,558	138,686	54.1	335,787	201,568	32.3
Vietnam	243,780	40,960	16.8	551,692	110,307	20.0	1,004,401	119,942	11.9
Philippines	548,880	10,640	1.9	1,001,174	17,629	1.8	1,455,328	2,4231	1.7
Thailand	62,620	5,460	8.7	120,055	6,648	5.5	180,693	9,977	5.5
Malaysia	11,000	5,000	45.5	32,716	15,475	47.3	51,510	23,535	45.7
Indonesia	30,820	4,620	15.0	49,786	11,617	23.3	76,983	20,162	26.2
Singapore	6,240	2,880	46.2	14,438	7,278	50.4	23,779	9,419	39.6
Cambodia	18,620	2,920	15.7	120,955	13,010	10.8	138,565	13,527	9.8
Macao	2,900	2,460	84.8	4,919	4,150	84.4	NA	NA	NA
Korea	305,280	2,760	0.9	660,379	4,924	0.7	907,457	7,618	0.9
Laos	51,960	1,520	2.9	178,382	4,575	2.6	208,300	5,804	2.8
Total		477,190			957,875			1,465,141	

Source: U.S. Bureau of the Census, 1980, 1990, and 2000 Censuses, 5% Integrated Public Use Microdata Sample, weighted data.

and economic environments from citizens of the PRC, and this influenced their motivation and ability to migrate, the policies under which they entered the U.S., and the resources they brought with them. Because they are more numerous, and because ethnic Chinese from elsewhere are not distinguished from non-Chinese of their national origin in many sources, this essay focuses on immigrants from Hong Kong and Taiwan, with only a brief discussion of Chinese immigrants from Southeast Asia and elsewhere.

Politics, Policy, and Migration Flows

Flows of Chinese migration have shifted in complicated ways over the postwar period in response to changing migration policies and economic and political conditions. U.S. foreign policy has also played an important role both in creating incentives for migration and in shaping the laws under which Chinese were admitted to the U.S.

Although the Chinese Exclusion Act, which had prohibited Chinese migration since 1882, was repealed in 1943, the official quota remained at 105 people per year, so that very few Chinese were able to come to the U.S. in the immediate postwar years. Chinese women married to U.S. servicemen were able to join their husbands in the U.S., and a number of diplomats and students from elite families who were unwilling to return to China after the communist revolution in 1949 were allowed to remain as refugees. They were joined by others—including many of the Kuomingtang elite—who fled to Taiwan after the victory of the Chinese Communist Party but saw better opportunities in the U.S. once it became clear that a rapid return to China was very unlikely.

Restrictions on migration from the PRC meant that nearly all Chinese who came to the U.S. in the 1950s and 1960s did so through Hong Kong and Taiwan, even if they were born in mainland China. With the communist revolution, Taiwan and Hong Kong assumed new and significant roles in the political economy of the region. Although the U.S. leaned toward recognition of the PRC immediately after 1949, the Korean War led it to see Taiwan as a bulwark against communism in Asia, and between 1953 and 1964 the U.S. government poured $1 billion in aid into that country. Cut off from China, the KMT pursued first import substitution and then an export-oriented development strategy that brought rapid growth. Hong Kong, which had been a relative backwater before the war, also saw a huge influx of people, capital, and skills from China in the 1940s and 1950s. This, along with investment by the colonial government in infrastructure and public services, led to Hong Kong's emergence as the financial center of Asia and the development of a manufacturing sector that exported garments and consumer goods to markets in the U.S. and Europe.

When the Immigration Act of 1965 ended race-based quotas and allocated

20,000 visas to each country, a number of factors had also combined to stimulate migration from Hong Kong and Taiwan. Politically dependent on the U.S. and Britain and economically dependent on international markets, both places were outward-oriented, and citizens were knowledgeable about opportunities overseas. Growing education at the secondary level coupled with limited opportunities for postsecondary and graduate education led many Hong Kong and Taiwanese Chinese to consider enrolling in foreign universities. Taiwan's educational system in particular had been restructured along American lines, and prestigious institutions groomed their top students to enter U.S. graduate schools.

Political factors also contributed to emigration from the two areas. The PRC's admission to the United Nations in 1971, followed by President Nixon's visit and the Shanghai Communiqué in 1972 and the U.S. recognition of China in 1979, led to fears that the U.S. would withdraw its support for Taiwan and rendered the island's status even more insecure. Applications for U.S. visas spiked in 1971 and 1979. Hong Kong experienced political instability in the late 1960s after riots related to the Cultural Revolution rocked the colony, but the bigger impetus came in 1984, when China and Britain reached an agreement for the return of Hong Kong to China in 1997. In response to uncertain futures, many families moved at least some of their assets to the U.S. and established the basis for residency, although not all planned to settle abroad permanently.

Initially many immigrants from Hong Kong and Taiwan were born in China and had left in the years following 1949. As Ronald Skeldon notes, statistics on migration from Taiwan and China were not recorded separately until 1982, but it is likely that most of the 9,657 immigrants from China in the 1950s and the more than 34,000 during the 1960s were secondary migrants from Taiwan. As these populations aged and migration out of the PRC was restricted, the percentage of step migrants has fallen. In 1982 about 18 percent of those admitted to the U.S. from Taiwan were not born on the island; by 2000 only 300 immigrants—nearly all admitted as dependent parents—were born elsewhere. The shift among immigrants from Hong Kong has been similar, although not so pronounced because migration from the mainland to Hong Kong continued in fits and starts throughout the postwar years. Nonetheless, the percentage of Hong Kong immigrants who were born in China fell from about 70 during the 1960s to less than 40 by the 1990s. These factors partly explain the falling percentages of immigrants from both places who give "Chinese" as their primary ancestry (Table 2), but they also reflect the strained relations between Hong Kong, Taiwan, and the PRC, which have led to the development of strong local identities, particularly in the political sphere.

Table 2   Changing ancestry responses of the foreign-born population from Hong Kong,
          Taiwan, and the PRC, 1980–2000 (percentages)

National origin	Chinese	Taiwanese	Hong Kong	Cantonese	Asian
Taiwan					
1980	73.2	14.5	0.0	0.1	0.3
1990	40.8	54.1	0.0	0.0	0.2
2000	32.3	60.0	0.0	0.1	0.5
Hong Kong					
1980	90.3	0.0	0.0	0.6	0.5
1990	90.1	0.2	2.6	0.0	0.6
2000	78.3	0.5	5.9	3.8	0.8
PRC					
1980	89.0	0.0	0.0	0.2	0.5
1990	90.0	1.2	0.1	0.0	0.4
2000	86.7	0.8	0.1	1.4	0.6

Source: U.S. Bureau of the Census, 1980, 1990, and 2000 Censuses, 5% Integrated Public Use Microdata Sample, weighted data.

Immigrants from Taiwan

The majority of Taiwanese—about 72 percent of the population—are descendants of people from Fujian and Guangdong Provinces in China who migrated to Taiwan in increasing numbers during the 16th and 17th centuries. Hakka people who moved to the south from central and northern China and migrated to Taiwan at around the same time account for another 14 percent. Although having little in common beyond their early settlement in Taiwan, these two groups and their off-spring are referred to as *bendiren* or *benshengren* (literally, "people of this place" or "province"). Another 13 percent are supporters of the KMT who retreated to Taiwan with Chiang Kai-shek's army in 1949. They and their offspring are referred to as *waishengren* ("from other provinces"). With the support of the U.S., *waishengren* dominated the political and economic landscape of Taiwan until the normalization of U.S.-China relations in 1979 led to a decline in the power of the KMT.

The first wave of migration from Taiwan included native Taiwanese who resented KMT rule, which imposed a Mandarin-only language policy in schools, compulsory military service for young men, strict censorship of the media, and indoctrination in KMT ideology. These early arrivals included a small number of dissident activists and many elite mainlanders who thought their prospects would be better in this country. Most of the small number who immigrated before 1965 came as students and attended graduate schools on the East and West Coasts or in Chicago. Because of the stiff competition to enter U.S. universities and the expense involved, most of them came from upper-middle-class families and were graduates of prestigious Taiwanese universities. Both their elite status and the fact that they mostly spoke Mandarin and/or Taiwanese meant that they remained largely separate from the Cantonese-speaking Chinese American community. After graduation, many settled in white suburban areas.

The 1965 Immigration Act increased the per-country limit of Chinese immigrants to 20,000 and provided for family reunification applications outside of it. This generally benefited longer-established Cantonese Chinese, but it did enable some Taiwanese students who had already settled and taken out citizenship to bring first their immediate and then their extended families to the U.S. More importantly, the legislation established preferences for migrants with technical and scientific skills, which enabled many Taiwanese professionals to apply.

The next wave of migration was the result of a change in U.S. foreign policy. The Taiwan Relations Act of 1979, which redefined U.S. policy toward Taiwan in the wake of normalization of relations with the PRC, stipulated that the island would receive an independent per-country limit of 20,000 per year. This decision, which took effect in 1982, reduced pressure on applications and enabled the chain migration of relatives. The Taiwanese government liberalized its emigration policy in 1980, which allowed ordinary citizens to travel more freely.

Although migrants from Taiwan in general continued to be better-educated than those from the PRC, the second wave was more diverse than those who had come earlier. In addition to many students, it included business people and some working-class families, thereby blurring the previous division between working-class Cantonese and "uptown" Taiwanese professionals.

Immigrants from Hong Kong

Hong Kong has always been the major port of departure for migrants from south China, many of whom lived for years in the colony before migrating again, making it hard to draw a clear distinction between Hong Kongers and mainland Chinese from Hong Kong in the U.S. As Ronald Skeldon recounts, the single largest wave of mainland migration into the colony took place between 1945 and 1950, when the population grew from 600,000 to 2.4 million, as both wealthy entrepreneurs and working-class refugees flooded in. Although the border was closed in 1953, the "touch-base rule" allowed immigrants who managed to set foot on Hong Kong Island or Kowloon to remain as refugees, and about 40,000 people a year managed to enter Hong Kong from China during the 1950s. Tighter emigration controls reduced this to 10,000 a year for most of the 1960s (with the exception of 1962, when 120,000 people arrived after the famine in China). Numbers rose again with economic reform and increased internal migration in the PRC in the late 1970s, and 400,000 mainland Chinese entered Hong Kong between 1976 and 1981. This led to the imposition of strict limitations on migration in 1980, and only 27,000 mainland Chinese entered Hong Kong in the following decade.

Some Chinese migrated directly on to the U.S. and other destinations in the 1940s, fleeing war, political upheaval, and then the communist government in China. Over the following decades migration from Hong Kong continued to include both step migrants who had been born in China, and, increasingly, residents born in the colony, which had its own quota of 600 visas. The 1965 Immigration Act facilitated both chain migration of China-born relatives of Chinese Americans living in Hong Kong and migration of students and skilled professionals. It also included a refugee preference that benefited Chinese who had fled China in 1949.

Following the Sino-British Declaration of 1984, the admissions limit for natives of Hong Kong was increased from 600 to 5,000 per year in 1986, then to 10,000 in 1990 and 20,000 in 1995. The U.S. also instituted a special preference for Hong Kong citizens who invested in the U.S., but few took advantage of this option. Emigration from Hong Kong rose from 22,400 in 1980 to 30,000 in 1987. Panic induced by the violent suppression of pro-democracy demonstrations in the PRC in 1989 led emigration to rise again, peaking at about 66,000 people a year between 1992 and 1994. Although this wave continued to include working- and middle-class families seeking to join relatives, it also included a much larger proportion of professionals and wealthy people who entered as students, skilled workers, or investors, often bringing considerable assets with them.

Characteristics of Immigrants from Taiwan and Hong Kong

Considering that Hong Kong and Taiwan are small territories, immigrants from these places are actually remarkably diverse. Although the bulk of Taiwanese migrants speak Mandarin and native Taiwanese also speak the southern Min dialect, the fact that the *waishengren* who fled to Taiwan in the 1940s came from all over China means that they have a range of regional identities and speak numerous dialects. Although the percentage of Hong Kong–born, Cantonese-speaking migrants from Hong Kong has grown over the years, refugees from China hail from many parts of the country. Although it is impossible to establish precise figures, it seems that Shanghainese are overrepresented among those who left the colony for the U.S., probably because of their relatively high socioeconomic status and international business connections.

Immigrants from Hong Kong span a greater range in terms of class origins, but on average immigrants from both Taiwan and Hong Kong over the past two decades have been more highly educated than those from the PRC. In 2000 more than 90 percent of Taiwanese Americans and over 85 percent of those from Hong Kong had at least a high school degree, compared with only a quarter of those from the PRC. Reflecting the fact that so many came as students or under limits for skilled professionals, Taiwanese are the most highly educated: in 2000, 67.9 percent had at least a B.A., compared with 51.9 percent of immigrants from Hong Kong. Nearly all have lived much of their lives in urban settings, they often have experience in business or trade, and they generally speak good English on arrival. In the 2000 Census, over 75 percent of both groups said they spoke English well or very well.

Given the high selectivity of these migration flows, it is not surprising that Taiwanese and Hong Kong Americans have higher median incomes ($65,000 for both groups in 2000) than immigrants from the PRC ($51,000). Reflecting their higher educational credentials, a higher percentage of Taiwanese (59.8) were in managerial or professional occupations in 2000, compared with 44.4 percent of those from the PRC and 49.8 percent of those from Hong Kong, who are more often business owners.

Like earlier Chinese immigrants, those from Taiwan and Hong Kong have settled predominantly on the two coasts, with nearly half living in California because of the superior transportation links to Asia. The New York metropolitan area, including suburban New Jersey, is the other major destination area for both groups. Substantial numbers of Taiwanese professionals have also settled in the Midwest and the South, forming sizable communities in Texas and Illinois.

Economic Impact on Chinese American Communities

Before 1960, Chinatowns in the U.S. were shrinking as Chinese American families who could afford it moved to the suburbs, leaving behind a dwindling community of the elderly. Chinese American businesses were predominantly laundries, restaurants, and small stores.

The arrival of middle-class and wealthy Hong Kong and Taiwanese Chinese brought about a revival of fading Chinatowns in East and West Coast cities. Although precise figures are not available, Hong Kong bankers estimated that between the mid-1980s and the mid-1990s, roughly 100,000 Hong Kong migrants took at least $3 billion in direct investments to Vancouver, Canada, and the figures are likely similar for U.S. cities. Meanwhile, growing foreign exchange reserves, coupled with political uncertainty over the island's future, led to similar capital flight from Taiwan—as much as $2 billion to $3 billion each year from the late 1970s to the early 1990s. Reports from Taiwan's Ministry of Economic Affairs said that $1.5 billion of Taiwan capital went to the Los Angeles area alone each year between 1985 and 1990.

Although many immigrants opened small retail businesses or entered the trades, those with more resources began to invest in manufacturing—particularly garments—and in import-export businesses, building on previous experience and connections in Hong Kong and Taiwan. By the mid-1960s, 90 percent of garment factories in New York that employed Chinese women were owned by Chinese. Lin found that by 1990, the total number of enterprises in New York's Chinatown had increased eightfold, as new immigrants set up not only factories but also a wide range of service-oriented businesses, including accountants' and real estate offices, doctors and lawyers' offices, beauty parlors and travel agencies. The new immigrants also invested heavily in real estate, buying up buildings and converting aging housing into office space or expensive housing. Some began to invest in businesses outside the ethnic economy, including hotels and clothing lines. Chan reports that by the end of the 1980s, Chinese buyers reportedly had acquired 10 percent of downtown San Francisco.

This economic activity was accompanied by the establishment of community banks. By 1986 two thirds of the 26 banks in New York's Chinatown were Chinese-owned. They handled remittances back to China but also provided loans to businesses and mortgages to homebuyers. This made it possible for immigrants with little credit to borrow money, but it also fueled a dramatic rise in real estate prices that drove poor residents and small businesses out of the area, propelling the development of new Chinatowns in outlying areas such as Brooklyn's Sunset Park.

Given the high proportion of Hong Kong and Taiwan immigrants who entered on student or professional visas, it is not surprising that they have been concentrated in professions in the hard sciences and engineering. Taiwanese in particular are also highly visible in the computer and information technology industry, the most famous example being Jerry Yang, the cofounder of Yahoo. Kwong and Miscevic report that between 1980 and 1998, 17 percent of all high-tech companies started in Silicon Valley were led by Chinese, mostly from Taiwan, and in 1998, 2,000 Chinese-run firms were employing over 40,000 people in the area.

Although many Hong Kong and Taiwanese Chinese have started businesses that serve a Chinese clientele, they often choose to live outside traditional downtown Chinatowns and have been responsible for the growth of what Li Wei termed "ethnoburbs." The Taiwanese community in New York City, for example, is centered around Flushing in Queens and has gradually expanded into Bayside and Whitestone in Long Island as well as areas of Queens closer to Manhattan. The picture is similar in California. Chan reports that from 1980 to 1990, the number of ethnic Chinese in Los Angeles County who lived in the suburbs grew to about 70 percent, and they were changing the demographics of the areas in which they settled. In 1990, the population of Monterey Park, for example, was 35 percent ethnic Chinese, and two thirds of the residential and business properties were owned by people with Asian names. Although there is some overlap, more affluent Hong Kong and Taiwanese immigrants often settle in different—and more expensive—neighborhoods from Chinese Americans of Cantonese descent who left Chinatowns in search of cheaper housing outside urban centers.

Although the infusion of capital and entrepreneurs into Chinatowns has undoubtedly generated a new vitality, there have also been negative effects. Speculation in real estate has driven prices up to a level that few small businesses can afford, displacing many former residents and diverting funds that could have been invested in more productive ways. Meanwhile, although garment factories offer work to non-English-speaking immigrants from the PRC who have few alternatives, workers are paid well below the legal minimum and often work excessively long hours in unsafe conditions. Employers take advantage of the fact that government regulators and labor unions show little interest and threaten to report their mostly undocumented employees to the government if they complain. Taiwanese and Hong Kong gangs are also implicated in the trafficking of illegal immigrants from the PRC, as well as in narcotics smuggling.

Cultural, Religious, and Political Life

The new immigrants from Taiwan and Hong Kong have also had a profound impact on the cultural, religious, and civic life of Chinese America. As Franklin Ng describes, this is seen immediately in the Chinese-language media, in which Taiwan and Hong Kong companies continue to play a major role. The *Singtao Daily* (*Xingdao ribao*), based in Hong Kong, was the first Chinese newspaper to start a North American publication in the 1960s, followed in 1976 by the *World Journal* (*Shijie ribao*), a Taiwan paper affiliated with the *United Daily News* (*Lianhe bao*) in Taipei. Widely read beyond the Taiwanese community, the *World Journal* had an estimated circulation of 300,000 in 1996 in the U.S. and Canada, with local editions for the East and West Coasts and Hawai'i. The company also owns a chain of bookstores selling Chinese-language magazines, books, periodicals, and educational texts. In addition to reporting on events in China, Hong Kong, Taiwan, and Asia, the newspaper carries articles on American politics and particularly on topics of interest to the Chinese immigrant community, including cases of discrimination against Chinese and information about how to navigate the American educational system. By making such information available to any immigrant who can read Chinese, these newspapers provide an important community resource.

The immigrants' impact is also evident in the cultural sphere. Hong Kong and Taiwanese immigrants have provided the resources and numbers necessary to support musical, theatrical, and film productions for a Chinese-language audience. They have also entered the American cultural mainstream and in many cases mingle Chinese and Western influences in their work. Ang Lee directed not only *The Wedding Banquet,* which explores the romantic dilemmas and intergenerational tensions of modern Taiwanese, but also the Jane Austen classic *Sense and Sensibility* and *Crouching Tiger, Hidden Dragon,* which brought Chinese martial arts to a mainstream American audience. Cellist Yo-Yo Ma, whose parents are from Taiwan, became famous for his mastery of the classical repertoire but has since traced links between Chinese and Western traditions in his Silk Road Project.

The religious landscape of Chinese America has also been affected by the presence of immigrants from Hong Kong and Taiwan. While Cantonese Chinese American families often have shrines to traditional gods in their homes or businesses, temples and public places of worship are rare, probably because of a lack of resources and time to maintain them as well as the shrinking size of the community. Ng points to the series of large Buddhist temples founded by affluent Taiwanese immigrants, including Hsi Lai Temple in Los Angeles and Chuang Yen Monastery in Carmel, New York. Immigrants from Taiwan and Hong Kong have also added to the number of Chinese Christians. Although Christians in Hong Kong and Taiwan make up a small percentage of the total population, the religion has had a disproportionate influence because of the prevalence of Christians among the elite, particularly professionals and educators. Temples and churches also serve as places to find companionship and as networking venues for professionals, and different congregations have grown up to serve different subsets of the community, including speakers of various dialects and the largely English-speaking second generation.

During the 1960s and 1970s, when most Chinese Americans spoke Cantonese and there were few migrants from the mainland, Taiwanese immigrants formed a quite separate community, divided by differences in dialect, social class, occupation, and political concerns. They lived in different neighborhoods and generally formed their own civic organizations, many of which still exist. When Taiwan was under KMT rule and many immigrants did not yet have citizenship, the primary focus was Taiwanese politics. Many Taiwanese organizations today have their roots in the late 1970s, when *benshengren* mobilized in support of the democratic movement and independence in Taiwan. For example, the Formosan Association for Public Affairs, founded in 1982, has chapters all over the country and lobbies Congress in support of Taiwan's accession to international organizations such as the World Health Organization and against the U.S. policy in favor of one China. Immigrants from Taiwan and Hong Kong have also formed alumni, professional, and student organizations and joined broader Chinese American or Asian American organizations. These organizations have served as vehicles for advancing professional careers and also for sustaining ethnic identity through social and cultural events.

Despite an active associational life, Chinese Americans overall have historically had low rates of formal political participation. There are indications that this may be changing, however. As they have become more established and reached a critical mass in some suburban communities, Taiwanese Americans in particular have become more visible in local politics, and a number have won elected office at the local level. John Liu, the first Asian American to be elected to the New York City Council, is Taiwanese American, and Taiwanese Americans are now well represented on local councils in Californian suburbs such as Monterey Park. David Wu, who came from Taiwan as a child, is the only Chinese American in the U.S. Congress. Taiwanese Americans have also held high-profile roles in the executive branch and include Elaine Chao, secretary of labor in the George W. Bush administration, and John Huang, assistant undersecretary of commerce in the Clinton administration.

The growing involvement of Taiwanese and Hong Kong Chinese in politics is made possible by their rising rates of citizenship and by their high levels of education and income. On questions of foreign policy—toward Taiwan and China, and on cross-straits relations—marked divisions exist among Taiwanese Americans who support independence for Taiwan, the continuation of the status quo (currently the majority position in Taiwan), and reunification with the PRC (currently the minority position). Although political affiliations span the party divide, there is more consensus on domestic issues, particularly on the need to respond to anti-Asian discrimination. Chinese Americans have organized to counter white residents who have resented their growing presence in some suburban neighborhoods, as well as to protest quotas limiting the number of Asian students in elite schools and universities. Discriminatory investigations carried out against the Taiwan-born engineer Wen Ho Lee and what many feel to be the unfair amount of attention given to Chinese American contributors to political campaigns have also provoked a strong response.

The Second Generation

If the first generation of immigrants from Hong Kong and Taiwan have mostly made a quiet contribution to American society, their children face a different future. As Vivian Louie shows, the parents' skills and resources enable them to position their offspring for success in school and in the labor market. Highly educated themselves, they know how to evaluate schools and are able to send their children to the best ones. They supplement their children's education with tutoring or additional classes at cram schools, sharing information about educational opportunities through social networks and the Chinese-language media. Children are motivated to study through comparisons to the successful children of relatives and friends, and parents also push cultural activities, including classical music, ballet, and tennis.

Although the children of working-class Chinese have also done well educationally, the children of professionals from Taiwan were the first to give the Chinese their reputation as a "model minority." Although new migration from China is blurring the distinction, differences are still apparent. My recent analysis of educational outcomes of second-generation immigrants in New York City shows that 75 percent of second-generation Taiwanese who attended public school in the 1990s went to schools ranked in the top quintile, compared with 48 percent of those with parents from Hong Kong and 37.8 percent of those with parents from mainland China. Nearly half (48 percent) of those who attended university were at colleges ranked in the top or second tier in the nation, compared with 35 percent of those with parents from Hong Kong and 40 percent of those with parents from the PRC.

Of course, Chinese American students are also outperforming the majority of whites, and their success has brought resentment. In California political battles have broken out over the high percentage of Chinese children (many of Taiwanese background) attending prestigious public schools like Lowell in San Francisco, as well as the University of California and other top institutions, including MIT, referred to as Made in Taiwan.

Immigrant parents still tend to encourage careers in science, engineering, medicine, or law over those in the humanities because these are seen as more lucrative and secure, professions where their children may more easily avoid discrimination or glass ceilings. Nevertheless, their American-born children are increasingly entering an expanding range of professions, including finance, business, and the arts. As they progress in their careers, they will make Chinese Americans far more visible and influential than they have been in the past.

Chinese, American, and International Lives

Chinese immigrants from Hong Kong and Taiwan and some parts of Southeast Asia are well equipped to make successful lives for themselves in the U.S. But at the same time, developments in Hong Kong, Taiwan, and the PRC are providing an incentive to maintain strong ties to Asia. Despite political tensions, the transition to Chinese rule in Hong Kong has proceeded without serious economic consequences, and since the PRC has tacitly accepted dual citizenship, many Hong Kong Chinese have been tempted to return. Estimates of the number of returnees range from about 12 percent to as high as 30 percent. Because opportunities for political participation are limited and China has ruled out the possibility of direct elections in the near future, returnees are active mostly in the economic sphere.

In Taiwan, the development of the economy has expanded opportunities in higher education, technology, and business, which have attracted many to return to the island. The Taiwanese government has mounted a very successful campaign to recruit skilled return migrants as part of its effort to develop its high-technology sector. These efforts have paid off. Chan reports that between 1989 and 1993 alone, 7,500 individuals, most of whom held postgraduate degrees and were either scientists or managers, returned. Taiwanese universities have also seen an influx of returning talent. The best-known academic return migrant is probably Yuan T. Lee, the former president of the University of California at Berkeley and a Nobel laureate in chemistry, who now heads the prestigious Academia Sinica in Taipei.

The democratization of Taiwan opened up political opportunities for native Taiwanese, and after the grip of the KMT began to loosen in 1987, many political exiles began to return. They played an active role in the rise of the Democratic Progressive Party from an illegal opposition group to victory in the 2000 presidential election. Since the end of one-party rule, many ordinary Taiwanese have taken advantage of dual citizenship to participate in elections (as many as 10,000 Taiwanese Americans voted in the 2000 presidential election—a significant number in that closely fought race), and all the major Taiwanese political parties have branches and campaign actively in the U.S.

Hong Kong and Taiwanese Americans have also played a role in linking the U.S. to the PRC, serving as intermediaries for foreign investment and trade. Given their concentration in the hard sciences and technology, they are particularly prominent in these areas, and top professionals are much sought after.

These patterns of return and circular migration, which are facilitated by the ease of transportation and communication links, mean that many middle-class Hong Kong and Taiwanese American families are now engaging in transnational lifestyles that were formerly common only among the very wealthy. In some cases the father is an "astronaut" (*taikongren*) who, after establishing his wife and children in the U.S., flies frequently back and forth to work in Taiwan, Hong Kong, or China. Also common are "parachute" kids, who live alone or with relatives in the U.S. while both parents continue to work in Asia. Often members of these families engage in what Aihwa Ong has termed "flexible citizenship," holding multiple passports that enable them to take advantage of changing opportunities for education, employment, and investment.

Ethnic Chinese from Southeast Asia, South America, and the Caribbean

In addition to immigrants from Taiwan and Hong Kong, a smaller but significant group of ethnic Chinese have migrated to the U.S. after living, sometimes for many generations, in countries in Southeast Asia, Latin America, and the Caribbean. The majority are the descendants of Chinese from the southern provinces of Fujian, Guangdong, and Hainan Island who went to work as contract laborers in Southeast Asia in the late 19th century, when colonial powers were recruiting workers. Because people from the same native place tended to migrate through networks to the same destinations, ethnic Chinese in particular countries tend to be from the same part (or parts) of China: those in Bangkok from Chaozhou, those in Vietnam from Guangdong, and so on.

Initially used by colonial governments as contract laborers or middlemen, some Chinese were extremely successful and eventually became independent entrepreneurs, running mines, mills, and banks; the majority became owners of small retail and service businesses. Their relationship with local populations varied considerably. In Thailand, ethnic Chinese became highly assimilated into the social elite and even married into the royal family, while in other countries, including Vietnam and Indonesia, they were resented by local populations and some suffered severe discrimination.

Ethnic Chinese from Southeast Asia have migrated to the U.S. for different reasons. The wealthy came to pursue educational opportunities or because of political and economic uncertainty or discriminatory policies. These individuals often arrived with considerable assets and had opportunities similar to those of Hong Kong or Taiwanese Chinese. In other cases, ethnic Chinese were forced to leave, as was the case with refugees who fled Vietnam in the late 1970s and early 1980s. In 1990, after particularly large waves of ethnic Chinese migration from Southeast Asia, 47 percent of Malaysians, 20 percent of Vietnamese, and 23 percent of Indonesians in the U.S. gave their ancestry as Chinese.

Chinese from Southeast Asia are too different from each other to be considered a community, but they do share certain characteristics. Generally speaking at least one dialect of Chinese in addition to their national language and often English, they straddle communities and add strength to the idea of a panethnic American identity. At the same time, they often maintain connections to networks of Chinese in their countries of origin as well as in China.

A much smaller number of Chinese, also mostly from Guangdong Province, migrated to Latin America and the Caribbean when these regions were colonized by European countries, making their way in particular to Peru and Cuba but also to Brazil, Mexico, British Guiana, and Dutch Surinam. The earliest migrants worked as long-term contract laborers on sugar plantations, in mines, or on railroad construction, but smaller numbers of artisans and traders followed in the early 20th century. Because these communities were not sustained by ongoing migration, there was considerable intermarriage with and assimilation into local populations over time. Nonetheless, Chinese in these countries were generally relatively wealthy by local standards and often left in the wake of political independence or revolutionary movements that would have jeopardized their position. Although surveys—and the presence of Cuban Chinese restaurants—indicate that a number of these people have come to the U.S., they often do not speak Chinese and have at most a tenuous relationship with the Chinese community. More information about these groups can be found in the *Encyclopedia of the Chinese Overseas*.

Bibliography

Chan, Wellington. 1999. "Chinese American Business Networks and Trans-Pacific Economic Relations since the 1970s." In Koehn and Yin, *Expanding Roles*.

Chen, Hsiang-shui. 1992. *Chinatown No More: Taiwan Immigrants in Contemporary New York*. Ithaca, N.Y.: Cornell University Press.

Hamilton, Gary, ed. 1999. *Cosmopolitan Capitalists: Hong Kong and the Chinese Diaspora at the End of the Twentieth Century*. Seattle: University of Washington Press.

Koehn, Peter, and Xiao-huang Yin, eds. 2002. *The Expanding Roles of Chinese Americans in U.S.-China Relations: Transnational Networks and Trans-Pacific Interactions*. New York: M. E. Sharpe.

Kwong, Peter, and Dusanka Miscevic. 2005. *Chinese America: The Untold Story of America's Oldest New Community.* New York: New Press.

Ma, Lawrence J. C., and Carolyn Cartier, eds. 2003. *The Chinese Diaspora: Space, Place, Mobility, and Identity.* New York: Rowman and Littlefield.

Ng, Franklin. 1998. *The Taiwanese Americans.* Westport, Conn.: Greenwood.

Pan, Lynn, ed. 1998. *The Encyclopedia of the Chinese Overseas.* Cambridge, Mass.: Harvard University Press.

Skeldon, Ronald, ed. 1994. *Reluctant Exiles?: Migration from Hong Kong and the New Overseas Chinese.* New York. M. E. Sharpe.

———. 1996. "Migration from China." *International Affairs* 49, 2 (Winter).

Williams, Jack F. 2003. "Who Are the Taiwanese? Taiwan in the Chinese Diaspora." In Ma and Cartier, *The Chinese Diaspora.*

Wong, Siu-lun. 1999. "Deciding to Stay, Deciding to Move, Deciding Not to Decide." In Hamilton, *Cosmopolitan Capitalists.*

Colombia

Luis Eduardo Guarnizo and Marilyn Espitia

Since 1970, Colombians in the U.S. have constituted the leading immigrant group from South America, and they are now the fifth largest Latin American immigrant group in the country. Although their presence can be traced back to the early 20th century, the rapid growth in the number of Colombian immigrants in the past two decades has made them more visible. Colombians are an intriguing group to study, as their socioeconomic profile has consistently been closer to that of mainstream U.S. society than to that of the Latino population in general (with the exception of Cubans). Yet in the U.S. public and official imaginations, Colombians are mostly associated with international commerce in illicit drugs and the unremitting violence affecting their homeland. U.S. media coverage and official attitudes have only helped cement this impression. Portrayals of Colombia and of what happens there have effectively been "narcotized," with most news and official information about the country focused on the drug trade. Moreover, the U.S. State Department has included on its list of foreign terrorist organizations Colombia's two major leftist guerrilla groups, the Revolutionary Armed Forces of Colombia (FARC) and the National Liberation Army (ELN), as well as a large right-wing paramilitary group, the United Self Defense Forces (AUC). Consequently, Colombia has become the recipient of the third largest amount of U.S. military aid in the world, after Israel and Egypt.

Using official U.S. and Colombian data as well as findings from previous studies, we will present a general, historically informed portrait of Colombians' migratory circumstances and experience in the U.S. Then we delve into their changing demographic and socioeconomic profile and their transnational modes of incorporation in the host society.

The Colombian Immigrant Presence

The mass arrival of Colombians in the United States began in the late 1960s, although Colombians were already present in significant numbers by the late 1940s. As Table 1 indicates, the number of legal immigrants skyrocketed during the second half of the 1960s. Since then it has followed a pattern of decennial jumps, peaking in the late 1970s, late 1980s, and early 2000s. By 2000, U.S. Census data show that there were approximately 526,000 Colombian immigrants in the U.S. However, the Colombian Ministry of Foreign Relations estimates that the population is over twice that large, including undocumented migrants.

Despite its long presence in the U.S., the Colombian population is mostly made up of recent arrivals. By 2000 nearly 45 percent had arrived in the previous decade. Another 28 percent arrived between 1980 and 1990, leaving approximately one

Table 1   Colombian immigration to the United States, 1936–2004

Year	Number	Year	Number	Year	Number
2004	18,678	1980	11,289	1956	1,576
2003	14,777	1979	10,637	1955	1,226
2002	18,845	1978	11,032	1954	1,202
2001	16,333	1977	8,272	1953	1,322
2000	14,498	1976	5,742	1952	1,140
1999	9,966	1975	6,434	1951	750
1998	11,836	1974	5,837	1950	592
1997	13,004	1973	5,230	1949	431
1996	14,283	1972	5,173	1948	470
1995	10,838	1971	6,440	1947	449
1994	10,847	1970	6,724	1946	467
1993	12,819	1969	7,627	1945	334
1992	13,201	1968	6,902	1944	266
1991	19,702	1967	4,556	1943	126
1990	24,189	1966	9,504	1942	168
1989	15,214	1965	10,885	1941	232
1988	10,322	1964	10,446	1940	170
1987	11,700	1963	5,733	1939	168
1986	11,408	1962	4,391	1938	137
1985	11,802	1961	3,559	1937	129
1984	11,020	1960	2,989	1936	95
1983	9,658	1959	2,524		
1982	8,608	1958	2,891		
1981	10,335	1957	1,961		

Sources: U.S. Immigration and Naturalization Service, *Statistical Yearbook of the Immigration and Naturalization Service,* 1960–2001; U.S. Department of Homeland Security, *Yearbook of Immigration Statistics, 2003–2004.*

quarter of Colombian immigrants as long-term residents who have lived in the U.S. for at least twenty years.

The interaction of several structural factors helps explain this growth pattern, including conditions in the receiving and sending countries, a changing economic global context, and the cumulative effects of the social networks built by the migration process. Coupled with the myth of the U.S. as the land of limitless opportunity, the Immigration Act of 1965 in particular had a significant influence on would-be migrants. The 1965 reform introduced a worldwide visa system with nondiscriminatory per-country limits and a family reunification clause, opening up the doors to a heterogeneous immigrant population. This new legal framework facilitated the entry of Colombians not only as individual, independent applicants but also as relatives of earlier immigrants and naturalized citizens. In fact, family reunification has become the most common legal mechanism used by Colombians to immigrate to the U.S. This option is being used by more Colombians, who seem unwilling to face an apparently uncertain future in a society marred by political and economic instability.

According to existing studies, until the late 1950s the vast majority of Colombian immigrants were well-off, including intellectuals, artists, international students, people with degrees from American universities (especially physicians, dentists, and engineers), and international bureaucrats who decided to stay on at the end of their official missions. Such social homogeneity was eventually disrupted as the immigrant inflow grew in size. The growth of Colombian immigration in the 1960s was strongly associated with the insecurity and uncertainty generated by *La Violencia,* a vicious conflict that pitted militants and sympathizers of the two main political parties (liberal and conservative) against each other, which ravaged the country from the mid-1940s to the mid-1960s. *La Violencia* prompted a migration outflow that was much more socially diverse.

Structural changes since the 1960s have molded Colombian immigration in a cyclical pattern. The jumps in the number of Colombians migrating to the U.S. since the 1960s have sprung from the country's economic instability and political crises. Structural instability has stemmed from several factors, including declining commodity prices in the international market, increasing political violence associated with an internal conflict between the state and leftist guerrillas since the late 1960s, the emergence and harmful effects of drug trafficking in the 1980s, and neoliberal economic reforms introduced in the early 1990s. Coffee, the main source of foreign exchange for the country for most of the 20th century, has faced a volatile global market characterized by declining prices since the mid-1970s. The persistent coffee crisis has fed high inflation, unemployment, and poverty rates, fueling a massive out-migration from the coffee region as people headed to North America and Europe.

Yet during the 1980s (the so-called lost decade in Latin America), despite adverse economic conditions engendered by low coffee prices and high inflation, Colombia did not suffer the severe recession and negative growth rates experienced by most Latin American countries. Analysts have attributed this to a then-novel external factor, namely, the inflow of large amounts of laundered money from the international drug trade. Nonetheless, during the 1980s and 1990s, drug trafficking and the state-sponsored restructuring of the national economy produced an array of unintended consequences that exacerbated the trend toward out-migration. While the economic effects of the drug trade first appeared to be positive, filling out the income gap left by the dwindling coffee revenues, in the long term it has produced disastrous social, political, and economic costs. The drug trade greatly contributed to the propagation of violence and insecurity in the country, introducing new kinds of violence and exacerbating existing political conflicts. Tens of thousands of Colombians were victimized or at least felt threatened and insecure enough to make the decision to emigrate. Also, a significant number of people emigrated precisely because of their connections with the illicit trade: drug cartels actively recruited personnel to work in the complex smuggling, protection, distribution, and money laundering activities associated with the business. Still others were recruited while already living abroad in areas where the traffickers had set up shop.

In addition, at the end of the cold war, the Colombian government introduced a drastic economic restructuring plan. Seeking to satisfy the country's international financial obligations, it followed an orthodox script provided by the International Monetary Fund. Through this and other policies it adopted in the early 1990s, the government also sought to alleviate the country's persistent political, social, and economic crises and reposition the country in the global political economy. Quite unintentionally, however, these measures ended up increasing the pressures for many to emigrate. The radical economic reforms adopted by the administration of President César Gaviria (1990–1994) included the privatization of state-owned enterprises, cuts in public expenditures, the elimination of social subsidies and programs, and the total opening of the economy to international markets and capital, including a sharp reduction in import tariffs and measures to facilitate the repatriation of earnings by foreign investors. The results of this shock treatment were disastrous. Thousands of firms, unable to compete with the influx of cheap imported goods, went bankrupt, and unemployment and poverty rates soared—especially aggravated by the large number of public employees who were laid off. At the same time, yielding to pressures from Washington to clamp down on drug trafficking and money laundering, the government unleashed an intensive campaign of repression against illegal drugs. The partial success of this policy led to a decline in revenues coming from the illicit business during the 1990s. The net revenue from illicit drugs dropped from a peak estimated at 6 percent of the Colombian GDP in 1990 to 2.3 percent by 1998.

By mid-1995, in the face of the new economic climate created by neoliberal reforms and the collapse of the main drug cartels, key economic sectors in advanced regions of the country witnessed a drastic decline. The effects of these changes were extraordinary, increasing out-migration from metropolitan areas such as Cali, Pereira, Medellín, and the capital, Bogotá. It is from these areas, the most urbanized and prosperous in the country, that the majority of the latest wave of emigrants to the U.S. and Europe have come.

However, the increase in Colombian immigration to the U.S. since the 1960s cannot be fully accounted for by macro structural factors alone. Social networks are central, as the majority of Colombians who enter the country legally have family connections here. For example, since the second half of the 1990s, nine of every ten new documented arrivals from Colombia have entered as family-sponsored migrants. Moreover, during that same time period, close relatives of U.S. citizens have constituted the bulk of the new admissions; around two thirds of the new immigrants (an annual average of 62 percent) have been immediate relatives of U.S. citizens, a kind of admission that is not subject to numerical caps. Compared with the 1970s, when family-sponsored immigrants accounted for 27 percent of the total, the current figure is remarkably high. The rising significance of this form of admission since the early 1990s is related to the growing number of Colombians who are naturalizing as U.S. citizens, which in turn is closely associated with Colombians' new dual citizenship rights, included in the 1991 Colombian constitution.

But not all Colombians in the U.S. have legal permission to remain in the country. According to the Immigration and Naturalization Service (INS), by 2000, 141,000 undocumented Colombians constituted the fourth largest group of unauthorized immigrants in the U.S. and accounted for 2 percent of the undocumented population nationwide. Recent journalistic and academic accounts indicate that the proportion of undocumented Colombians is increasing as the sociopolitical and economic situation in Colombia worsens. It is clear that the hardening of U.S. immigration policies since the early 1990s has meant that a growing number of middle- and upper-middle-class people who hold nonimmigrant tourist, business, or student U.S. visas and who want to immigrate now overstay their visas once they are in the country. Combined figures from the INS and the Department of Homeland Security show that the total number of nonimmigrant-visa holders arriving from Colombia between 1961 and 2004 has increased significantly, rising from 134,257 in the 1961–1965 period to approximately 1.8 million in the 2001–2004 period. Moreover, six out of every ten of these entered the U.S. after 1991. Meanwhile, during these four decades, four out of every ten documented immigrants were admitted after 1991.

Although there are no official data on the number of non-immigrants who overstay their visas, it is plausible to argue that given the worsening conditions in Colombia, a significant proportion of these temporary visitors have done so. Having lost their legal status, these unauthorized immigrants have been forced to take low-paying, dead-end jobs in the secondary labor market, a situation that, David Collier shows, has constrained their socioeconomic conditions and possibilities of integration, regardless of their human capital. Of course, like their documented conationals, undocumented Colombians also depend on the contextual conditions they encounter where they decide to settle to give them the opportunity to succeed.

Geographical Distribution

The greater New York metropolitan area has historically been the top destination of Colombians. Roughly half of Colombian immigrants to the U.S. lived there in 1980. Twenty years later, however, the area housed only slightly over one third of them. The steady decline of the tri-state region's geographical primacy has been accompanied by the growing importance of Florida, especially its southern counties, as Colombians' primary state of destination (31 percent lived there in 2000). Other new top destination states have emerged. Georgia and Pennsylvania are the most significant additions, with Atlanta emerging as the home of a relatively small yet rapidly growing and dynamic Colombian population. Some of this new distribution is due in part to internal migration, as people decide to move to areas where labor competition is less acute and living conditions are less crowded and more culturally amenable. In this sense, southern Florida—particularly Miami, which has been informally dubbed the Latin American capital of the U.S.—offers undeniable advantages.

Changing Demographics

Partly because of various waves of immigration, Colombian Americans are a socially diverse and dynamic group. They include established professionals who arrived before 1970, those from more diverse and lower-class backgrounds who came in the 1980s, and, most recently, post-1990 migrants from middle- and upper-class backgrounds who are fleeing political and economic turmoil. This social makeup is corroborated by several demographic and socioeconomic indicators. Nevertheless, official U.S. data reveal that in spite of the significant dominance of recent arrivals, who are usually worse off initially than long-term residents (see Table 2), Colombians fare well in terms of their socioeconomic incorporation into the U.S.

In terms of Colombian immigrants' demographic characteristics, three important factors illustrate their particular mode of incorporation: sex composition, age, and race. Unlike the sex composition of all Latin American immigrants in the U.S., the Colombian community has a larger proportion of females (55 percent) than males. This pattern seems likely to predominate in the near future; recent data from the Department of Homeland Security show that the sex ratio of legal Colombian immigrants has increasingly favored women, rising from 59 percent in 1998 to 62.9 percent in 2001 (the last fiscal year in which sex was reported). This pattern mat-

Table 2   Demographic characteristics of foreign-born Colombians, 1980–2000

	1980[a]	1990[a]	2000 Colombians[a]	2000 Latin Americans[b]
Total population	151,100	303,093	525,881	16,086,975
Period of U.S. entry				
1990–1999			45.1	44.8
1980–1989		52.0	27.9	29.9
1970–1979	54.1	25.8	14.5	25.3
1960–1969	35.7	18.4	10.2	—
Before 1960	7.4	3.8	2.2	—
N/A	2.8	—	—	—
Sex (percentage)				
Female	53.2	52.9	54.9	47.8
Male	46.8	47.1	45.1	52.2
Age				
Median age (years)	32.0	34.0	38.0	34.2
55 and older (percentage)	8.5	12.2	16.9	13.1
Race (percentage)				
White	71.2	63.8	62.9	42.2
Black	1.6	2	1.3	9.3
American Indian	0.01	0.03	0.04	0.1
All other races	27.1	33.9	35.4	48.4

a. *Source:* U.S. Bureau of the Census, 1980, 1990, 2000 U.S. Censuses, 5% Integrated Public Use Microdata Samples, weighted data.

b. *Source:* U.S. Bureau of the Census, *Census 2000 Special Tabulations* (STP-159). Does not include children "born abroad of American parents." Periods of U.S. entry are 1970–1974, 1980–1989, and 1990–2000.

ters: previous studies have demonstrated that women tend to settle permanently in the U.S. more than men do. They are also more likely to naturalize and to engage in local civic activities than their male counterparts, who tend to focus more on transnational activities and maintain a desire to return to their home countries. Consequently, this may favor Colombian settlement in U.S. society.

As Table 2 indicates, the median age among Colombians increased from 30 years in 1980 to 38 years in 2000. This figure is higher than that of all Latin American immigrants (34.2 years) and of the total U.S. population (36.3). The proportion of Colombian immigrants 55 years old and older doubled between 1980 and 2000 (from 8.5 percent to 16.9 percent). Meanwhile, the proportion of new Colombian immigrants legally entering the U.S. who are under 20 years of age (most likely the children of Colombians legally residing in the country) dropped from 28.2 percent in 1998 to 22.3 percent in 2001. Explaining this aging process requires further and more detailed investigation. However, it is plausible to argue that the trend is the result of the combined effect of the natural maturation process of the group and family reunification. Adult children who have naturalized as U.S. citizens are bringing their aging parents to live with them to escape the worsening conditions in their country of origin. In addition, this older composition of Colombians may favor their integration, as it may signal stronger economic stability via completed education and more years of work experience.

Another important factor that differentiates Colombian immigrants from the larger Latin American immigrant population in the U.S. is their racial composition. Specifically, the vast majority of Colombians identify themselves as "white," although the proportion decreased from 71 percent in 1980 to 63 percent in 2000. Still, 63 percent is closer to the racial profile of the entire U.S. population (76.8 percent "non-Hispanic white" in 2000) than to that of all Latin American immigrants, only 42 percent of whom identified racially as "white" in 2000. The combination of their racial and class background gives Colombians an edge vis-à-vis other immigrants and native minorities in the racialized U.S. labor market. Consequently, notwithstanding the negative drug stigma attached to them, Colombians' socioeconomic mobility may follow a pattern similar to those of Cubans and Asians. They appear less likely to experience the kind of racial discrimination that predominantly nonwhite Latinos such as Mexicans, Puerto Ricans, and Dominicans face.

Socioeconomic Incorporation

The socioeconomic status of Colombians, as measured by their English fluency, levels of formal education, income, and labor force participation, further suggests that their incorporation in the U.S. is more favorable than those of other Latin American immigrants—although increasing social inequality and class polarization within the group are becoming more visible. Table 3 shows that three fifths of Colombian immigrants (60 percent) report that they can speak English well or very well, compared with 52 to 53 percent among Mexican, Cuban, and Dominican immigrants. Nonetheless, another third of the Colombian population described their English-language ability as nonexistent or "not fluent."

Similarly, Colombians possess high levels of formal schooling, which positions them closer to the educational attainment levels of the native U.S. population than to the total Latin American immigrant population. By 2000, 23 percent of Colombians aged 25 to 64 had graduated from college, a figure similar to that of U.S. natives (25 percent). This sharply contrasts with the educational attainment of all Latin American immigrants aged 25 and older, only 9.5 of whom had graduated from college. Table 3 also shows that the proportion of Colombian immigrants with postsecondary education (some college, associate degrees, B.A. degrees and higher) has increased significantly over the past two decades. By 2000 almost half (49 percent) of all Colombian immigrants aged 25 to 64 had reached that level of schooling. Concomitantly, the proportion of Colombian immigrants aged 25 to 64 with less than a high school education dropped from 34 percent in 1980 to 25

Table 3 Socioeconomic incorporation of Colombian immigrants, 1980–2000

			2000	
	1980[a]	1990[a]	Colombians[a]	Latin Americans[b]
English-language ability (percentage)				
Speak very well	59.3	60.1	58.8	n/a[c]
Speak not well or not at all	31.4	30.6	33.0	n/a[c]
Less than 5 years old or native English speaker	9.3	9.3	8.2	n/a[c]
Naturalization rate	24.5	27.4	39.5	30.2
Education (percentage)				
Less than high school	33.6	31.7	25.0	56.1
High school graduate	30.1	26.9	26.0	19.0
Associate degree or some college	20.3	25.2	25.9	15.3
Bachelor's degree and higher	16.1	16.3	23.2	9.5
Median household income	$18,215	$33,700	$43,600	$35,519
Median total personal income	$9,505	$15,000	$20,000	$15,607
Labor force status				
Employed	70.9	72.1	63.0	55.6
Unemployed	4.6	6.1	4.8	5.4
Not in labor force	24.4	21.8	32.3	38.8[d]
Class of worker				
Private salaried	85.9	77.0	74.5	86.7
Government employee	7.4	7.9	8.5	7.3
Self-employed	6.6	10.2	11.9	5.7
Nongovernmental organization employee	0.0	4.4	4.9	—
Occupation				
Managerial/professional	16.5	17.9	25.5	14.3
Technical/sales/administration	22.6	25.0	23.2	17
Service occupations	14.7	21.4	21.3	25.3
Farming/forestry/fishing	0.4	0.8	0.3	3.8
Production/crafts/repairs/ operators/fabricators	45.3	34.4	28.5	39.6
Not classified	0.4	0.5	1.2	—

a. *Source:* U.S. Bureau of the Census, 1980, 1990, 2000 U.S. Censuses, 5% Integrated Public Use Microdata Samples, weighted data. In this source, English-language ability and naturalization rate data pertain to all persons; education and labor force status data pertain to persons aged 25–64; median total personal income, class of worker, and occupation data pertain to persons aged 25–64 in the labor force; and median household income data pertain to all households.

b. *Source:* U.S. Bureau of the Census, *Census 2000 Special Tabulations* (STP-159). In this source, naturalization rate data pertain to all persons; education data pertain to persons aged 25 and older; labor force, median total personal income, class of worker, and occupation data pertain to persons aged 16 and older; and median household income data pertain to all households. This source does not include children "born abroad of American parents."

c. English-language ability not presented due to different measurement categories from those in the 5% Integrated Public Use Microdata Samples.

d. 0.2 percent of the population in the labor force is employed in the military.

percent in 2000. In contrast, over half (56 percent) of all Latin American immigrants aged 25 and older had not finished high school in 2000.

Colombian immigrants' occupational attainment since 1980 parallels the changes observed in their level of education. In 1980, only 39 percent of Colombian immigrants aged 25 to 64 and in the labor force were employed in jobs classified as managerial, professional, technical, sales, or administrative. Twenty years later, nearly half (49 percent) were. Comparatively, just one sixth (16 percent) of all Latin American immigrants aged 16 and older were employed in such occupations by 2000. In contrast, consistent with the structural transformation of the U.S. labor market in the past decades, the proportion of Colombian immigrants aged 25 to 64 and in the labor force working in blue-collar production occupations declined sharply (from 45 percent in 1980 to 29 percent in 2000), while the proportion working in service occupations increased (from 15 percent in 1980 to 21 percent in 2000).

The rate and conditions of Colombian labor participation have also changed significantly over the past two decades. Specifically, while the proportion of Colombian salaried workers employed in the private sector has shrunk (from 86 percent in 1980 to 75 percent in 2000), the proportion of self-employed Colombians and those employed by the government and by nongovernmental organizations (NGOs) has grown. Notably, the self-employment rate among Colombians nearly doubled between 1980 and 2000 (from 7 to 12 percent), so that it is now roughly double the self-employment rate among all Latin American immigrants. Evidently these trends reflect some of the structural changes occurring in the U.S. economy more generally, but they are also a function of the most recent immigrants' high levels of human capital. Meanwhile, the data in Table 3 also point to shrinking labor force participation among Colombians. While their general occupational outlook appears to have improved, the proportion of Colombians who are not economically active has increased significantly, from 24 percent in 1980 to 32 percent in 2000. Although this trend calls for further research, particularly in regard to its implications for social policy, it is plausible to argue that it is partly a result of the aging process and the larger proportion of women among Colombians, who may stay at home and not participate in the labor force.

In contrast to this relatively positive look at Colombians' general socioeconomic profile, their income distribution offers more cause for concern. Whether measured at the household or the individual level, Table 4 shows that the trend is one of sharper economic polarization and inequality over time, as income is increasingly concentrated in the top quintile of earners. The ratio of the income of households in the top-earning 20 percent to those in the bottom-earning 20 percent doubled between 1980 and 2000, from 8.3 to 17.3. A similar pattern, although less extreme, is observed in the distribution of Colombian immigrants' individual incomes; the ratio of the income of individuals in the top-earning quintile to the income of those in the bottom-earning quintile almost doubled between 1980 and 2000, from 12.7 to 21.8. If anything, this polarization is likely to increase, and perhaps even acceler-

Table 4 Social inequality among foreign-born Colombians, 1980–2000

	1980	1990	2000
Household income quintile distribution			
20	9,005	17,000	20,000
40	15,010	28,000	35,830
60	21,530	40,000	53,300
80	31,029	59,069	81,100
99	75,000	194,140	345,000
Ratio top 5th to bottom 5th	8.3	11.4	17.3
Personal income quintile distribution			
20	4,685	7,000	8,500
40	7,885	12,000	16,000
60	11,010	18,000	25,000
80	16,397	27,600	39,300
99	59,466	123,515	185,000
Ratio top 5th to bottom 5th	12.7	17.6	21.8
Below the poverty line (percentage)	9.2	10.1	12.5

Source: U.S. Bureau of the Census, 2000, 1990, and 1980 U.S. Censuses, 5% Integrated Public Use Microdata Sample, weighted data. Total personal income and poverty data pertain to persons aged 25–64 in the labor force, while median household income data pertain to all households. In 1979, 1989, and 1999 dollars.

ate, given the occupational and socioeconomic characteristics of current Colombian immigrants, the increasing number of newcomers, and the rapidly changing U.S. labor market.

Not surprisingly, this social restructuring among Colombian immigrants mirrors that among other Americans over the past few decades. It could lead to increased poverty rates, reversing the upward trend that Colombians have experienced of late and placing them closer to the economic position of other Latin American immigrants. Still, this would be a new type of poverty—among well-educated people coming from abroad. But such an impoverished, well-educated population will probably not be socially and politically alienated. Many of them could strengthen their connections to their homeland, as has been observed among other poor immigrant populations, including Mexicans, Dominicans, and Salvadorans. This would lead to new forms of transnational political, economic, and even social organizations.

Also critical to the well-being of the Colombian population in the U.S. is the status of their U.S.-born children—the second generation. According to a recent study by the sociologist Rubén Rumbaut, there were an estimated 151,803 Colombian Americans in 2000, who comprise 23.4 percent of the total Colombian origin community in the U.S. Their socioeconomic profile suggests that Colombian Americans have an advantage relative to other second-generation Latino groups, coinciding with what has been found among the first generation. For example, 84.5

percent of second-generation Colombians reported speaking English well, compared with 71.8 percent of Mexicans, 80.3 percent of Puerto Ricans, and 72.7 of Salvadorans and Guatemalans. They have also surpassed second-generation Cubans in the proportion of college-educated individuals (38.3 percent of second-generation Colombians have a college degree, as compared with 34.2 percent of second-generation Cubans). Correspondingly, Colombian Americans also have a substantial proportion of individuals in professional, technical, and managerial positions (40.3 percent). It is worth noting, however, that another 23.5 percent are employed in low-wage labor jobs. Given the present income disparity among the Colombian immigrant population, it appears that this may also be prevalent among U.S.-born Colombians. In addition, compared with foreign-born Colombians, U.S.-born Colombians have shown improvement in socioeconomic indicators, suggesting continuous upward mobility for this community.

Immigrant Incorporation and Transnational Engagement

The 1990s opened with a remarkable change to the Colombian legal order, which included the granting of novel political rights to overseas citizens. In 1991 a new national constitution was approved, replacing the one adopted in 1886. For the first time, the constitution recognized Colombia as a multicultural and multiethnic nation and embraced Colombians residing abroad as active and permanent members of the nation. Of the new constitutional rights, dual citizenship (which allows Colombians to adopt any other citizenship without losing their original one) and the right of migrants abroad to elect a representative to the Colombian Congress, appear to be the most consequential, especially for Colombians seeking to position and incorporate themselves in new receiving societies. The 1991 constitution also ratified the right of overseas Colombians to vote in national elections. In 1997 migrants were granted the right to run for congressional seats and vote for regional representatives to the Colombian Senate and House of Representatives. These transnational rights are important for understanding Colombians' mode of incorporation in the U.S., in particular their changing rates of naturalization and political incorporation. In fact, since 1991, Colombians have naturalized at higher rates than before. Indeed, Francesca Mazzolari found a strong correlation between the approval of dual citizenship rights in 1991 and Colombian immigrants' increasing rates of naturalization.

A higher rate of naturalization implies a faster process of formal political incorporation. At the same time, naturalized citizens help maintain a steady flow of newcomers, since, as we saw earlier, naturalized Colombians are very likely to use their status to help bring in their close relatives. As U.S. citizens, these individuals do not face the immigration per-country limits that nonnaturalized immigrants who want to reunite their families in the U.S. do. Additionally, naturalized citizens' higher levels of economic mobility, social status, and access to resources facilitate transnational

Table 5   Local and transnational engagement of Colombian immigrants in New York City,
           1999

Measure of engagement	U.S. citizen (percentage)	Non-U.S. citizen (percentage)	Total
Local political participation			
Has voted in U.S. elections	63.2	3.4[a]	45.6
Gives money to U.S. parties	23.9	7.0	16.4
Transnational political participation			
Active member of party in Colombia	23.5	14.9	18.7
Gives money to party in Colombia	8.1	2.9	5.1
Participates in political activities in Colombia	14.7	8.0	10.6
Active member of Colombian civic association	22.1	14.9	18.0
Gives money for community projects in Colombia	23.5	14.9	18.7
Active member of Colombian philanthropic organization	40.4	21.7	29.9
Transnational socioeconomic relations			
Sends remittances	60.3	69.7	65.6
Invests in Colombia	18.9	12.6	15.3
Has bought real estate in Colombia	53.7	42.9	34.3
Has members of nuclear family in Colombia	9.8	31.4	22.0
Visits Colombia	15.7	12.1	32.0

Source: Adapted from Luis Eduardo Guarnizo, Alejandro Portes, and William J. Haller, "Assimilation and Transnationalism: Determinants of Transnational Political Action among Contemporary Migrants," *American Journal of Sociology* 108, 6 (2003).

a. Noncitizens are allowed to vote in local school board elections.

relations with Colombia. Data from a recent study of Colombians in the New York metropolitan area demonstrate that naturalized citizens are the most likely to be engaged in multiple transnational activities with their country of origin (see Table 5).

As Table 5 shows, naturalized Colombians are not only more likely to participate in local politics than their nonnaturalized counterparts (that is, voting and contributing monetarily to U.S. political parties), they are also more likely to be engaged in transnational political and socioeconomic activities. Their high engagement in local political action seems to signal increasing political voice and empowerment—but this still requires further investigation. Countering common wisdom, naturalized citizens are also more likely to be active politically in Colombia, as active members of political parties, civic associations, and charitable organizations and as business investors and tourists. Not surprisingly, they are less active than their nonnaturalized compatriots in terms of sending remittances back to Colombia, since members of their families are less likely still to reside in their homeland.

This suggests a positive correlation between U.S. incorporation and transnational engagement rather than a zero-sum game of contradictory loyalties. In this sense, Colombians, like many other new immigrant groups, are developing new ways of being incorporated into U.S. society while remaining part of their country of origin. In fact, Colombians can maximize their political influence as they are able to lobby two governments to have their needs addressed and solidify their claims. With an active political community that engages both the United States and Colombia, new possibilities emerge for the future incorporation of Colombian immigrants and especially of their children. For example, one study of second-generation Colombians and other South Americans in New York City found engagement in transnational practices such as visiting their parents' country of origin, sending remittances, and participating in ethnic organizations. This suggests that ties with the country of origin are maintained across generations, rather than abandoned, as suggested by the assimilation paradigm.

Overall, the rapidly changing demographic, socioeconomic, and transnational characteristics of Colombian immigrants signal internal social division. For example, studies have shown how the drug stigma damages and fragments Colombians' levels of social organization and levels of trust of one another. The data presented here also suggest a possible scenario in which there are at least two kinds of Colombian immigrants. One, with legal status and high levels of human capital, is well situated to participate in many mainstream U.S. social institutions and able to maintain active transnational ties. The other, without legal status and with lower levels of human capital, is confined to the Spanish-speaking enclave and limited in its transnational engagement. These two trajectories may very well lead to different socioeconomic outcomes among Colombians.

A particularly complicated question emerges in relation to the large group of new, well-educated Colombian immigrants who are undocumented. With the Colombian economy and violence continuing to be push factors for emigration, this population may continue to grow. Although the Colombian president, Alvaro Uribe, and the Colombian Congress have publicly and repeatedly asked the U.S. government to grant temporary protected status (TPS) to these immigrants, the restrictive political climate created by the September 11, 2001, attacks (including a strong anti-immigration lobby) has worked against this petition. The lack of legal status will undoubtedly stigmatize this cohort, limiting their options to participate fully in both societies. Still, given the strategic position of Colombia in the region, TPS remains an open possibility that could help ameliorate the chronic immigration crisis in the country as well as facilitate the incorporation of Colombian newcomers into the United States.

Bibliography

Collier, Michael W. 2004. "Colombian Migration to South Florida: A Most Unwelcome Reception." Latin American Caribbean Center Working Paper No. 9. Miami: Florida International University.

Cruz, Carmen Inés, and Juanita Castaño. 1976. "Colombian Migration to the United States (Part 1)." In *The Dynamics of Migration: International Migration.* Occasional Monograph Series 5.2, pp. 41–86. Washington, D.C.: Smithsonian Institution, Interdisciplinary Communications Program.

Escobar, Cristina. 2004. "Dual Citizenship and Political Participation: Migrants in the Interplay of United States and Colombian Politics." *Latino Studies* 2 (1): 45–69.

Guarnizo, Luis Eduardo. 2001. "On the Political Participation of Transnational Migrants: Old Practices and New Trends." In Gary Gerstle and John Mollenkopf, eds., *E Pluribus Unum? Contemporary and Historical Perspectives on Immigrant Political Incorporation,* pp. 213–63. New York: Russell Sage Foundation.

Guarnizo, Luis Eduardo, and Luz M. Diaz. 1999. "Transnational Migration: A View from Colombia." *Ethnic and Racial Studies* 22 (2): 397–421.

Guarnizo, Luis Eduardo, Arturo Ignacio Sánchez, and Elizabeth M. Roach. 1999. "Mistrust, Fragmented Solidarity, and Transnational Migration: Colombians in New York City and Los Angeles." *Ethnic and Racial Studies* 22 (2): 367–96.

Jones-Correa, Michael. 1988. *Between Two Nations: The Political Predicament of Latinos in New York City.* Ithaca, N.Y.: Cornell University Press.

Mazzolari, Francesca. April 2005. *Determinants of Naturalization: The Role of Dual Citizenship Laws.* Working Paper 117. La Jolla, Calif.: Center for Comparative Immigration Studies, University of California, San Diego.

Ricourt, Milagros. 2003. *Hispanas de Queens: Latino Panethnicity in a New York City Neighborhood.* Ithaca, N.Y.: Cornell University Press.

Rumbaut, Rubén. 2004. "Hispanics in the United States: A Portrait of a People." *La Vanguardia* (Madrid): 18–26.

Cuba

Lisandro Pérez

Cuban Americans are one of the most visible immigrant groups in the U.S., despite their relatively modest numbers. The 1.3 million people identified by the 2000 Census as being of Cuban origin or descent represented less than 4 percent of the total Hispanic population of the country. But their conspicuousness within that population, as well as within the larger national political and economic landscape, has been the result of a unique combination of factors that have given the Cuban presence in the U.S. a notable and exceptional character.

One of these factors is that the majority of the contemporary Cuban American population is composed of migrants who have arrived in the U.S. in successive waves since the Cuban revolution in 1959; more than 70 percent of the Cuban-origin population is Cuban-born (see Table 1). Those waves of migration took place within the shifting contexts of an internal class struggle, a cold war confrontation, a socialist transformation, the entrenchment of an autocratic political order and an austere economic system in the island, a persistent climate of hostile relations with the U.S., and, at least initially, a favorable, even welcoming reception in this country. Those contexts produced a Cuban American population in which the upper- and middle-class white sectors of Cuban society have been traditionally overrepresented and in which the ethos of exile continues to be a powerful force. That ethos involves an uncompromising opposition to the island's government and a commitment to the recovery of the homeland. The national visibility of Cuban Americans is due, at least in part, to their success in influencing, even determining, the continuation of a hostile U.S. stand toward Cuba, playing a role, as few immigrant groups have been able to do, in the formulation of U.S. foreign policy. Consequently, most Americans have an image of Cuban Americans as not only an economically successful group but also an influential conservative force whose politics are still rooted in the cold war.

Table 1   Cuban-origin and Cuban-born population in the U.S., 1970–2000

Year	Cuban-origin[a]	Cuban-born
1970	543,000	456,600
1980	822,120	623,940
1990	1,058,497	751,917
2000	1,241,685	883,439

Source: U.S. Bureau of the Census, 1970, 1980, 1990, and 2000 Censuses.
a. Includes both foreign-born and U.S.-born persons.

The profile of Cuban Americans has been enhanced by another fundamental characteristic of the group: its concentration in southern Florida, where nearly 60 percent of the Cuban-origin population of the U.S. now lives. That concentration has enabled Cuban Americans to maximize the strength of their relatively modest numbers at the national level by becoming the largest single ethnic group in Miami, the most populous metropolitan area in a key electoral state and America's gateway to Latin America and the Caribbean. In greater Miami, Cubans have not only created a strong ethnic enclave but also occupied most of the leadership positions in political, economic, educational, and cultural institutions. The influential presence of Cubans in an important electoral state has served to further elevate the visibility of the group at the national level. Since a majority of Cuban Americans are conservative and Republican, it can be argued that they were the critical factor in determining the outcome of the Florida presidential vote in 2000 and hence of the entire election.

Cubans in 19th-Century America

Although the contemporary Cuban American population is rooted in the postrevolutionary migration from the island, the Cuban presence in this country is much older, going back to the early 19th century, when the island was still a Spanish colony. The most important Cuban American communities in those days owed their origins and development to two related factors: the bourgeoning commerce between the U.S. and Spain's island colony, and the long struggle to extricate Cuba from Spanish control. Key West, New Orleans, and New York housed the earliest and most numerous communities of Cubans in the U.S. Although these communities were modest in size (none probably exceeded 2,000 in population), they played a prominent role in the economic and political history of Cuba and its relations with the U.S.

As the closest U.S. land point to Cuba, Key West became practically an extension of the island's cigar industry within U.S. territory. As early as the 1830s, factories owned and staffed by Cubans were rolling tobacco leaves imported from Cuba to produce cigars that were shipped to New York for distribution around the world.

Living beyond the control of Spain, and with a tradition of political activism, Key West's cigar workers were at the forefront of the efforts to end Cuba's colonial status.

The New Orleans community was based on the heavy traffic that developed during the first half of the 19th century between that city and Havana. Those were decades in which Cuba became a top world producer of sugar and Louisiana was at the forefront of the development of the technology for extracting and refining the product of the sugar-cane stalk. The closeness of those commercial relations had political implications during the years before the Civil War, as Louisiana sugar interests supported the island's annexation to the U.S. as a slave state. Those interests even helped to fund an expedition to Cuba that unsuccessfully attempted to wrest control of the island from Spain.

The Civil War disrupted the Louisiana-Cuba connection and the New Orleans Cuban community declined rapidly. After the war, New York became the most important Cuban community for most of the remainder of the century. In fact, during the 1870s and 1880s, Cuban New Yorkers constituted the largest community of Latin Americans east of the Mississippi. The commercial connections between New York and Cuban ports started early in the 19th century, spurred by the importance of both the tobacco and sugar-refining industries in Manhattan and Brooklyn. By midcentury, New York had become an important place for Cubans, not only economically but also culturally, as members of the island's elite became frequent visitors to the city, sometimes staying for the summer to shop in Manhattan or vacation in Saratoga. Notable Cuban writers and artists also spent long and productive sojourns in the city. An increasing number of tobacco workers arrived, lured by the many cigar factories established in lower Manhattan. For nearly 30 years, starting in 1823, New York was the home of one of the most prominent Cuban intellectuals of the time, Félix Varela y Morales, a Catholic priest who was a strong voice on behalf of Cuban separatism as well as an important figure in the New York diocese.

The outbreak of the first war for Cuban independence in 1868 was a watershed event in the history of Cuban migration to New York. Many landowners and businessmen who supported the Cuban cause found themselves persecuted by the Spanish authorities, and their properties were confiscated or embargoed. They flocked to New York, where they had business contacts and even financial accounts. The 1870 Census showed that many of the prominent Cuban landholding families were living in Manhattan that year, creating for the first time a Cuban community of exiled elites. They were eventually joined by cigar makers, craftsmen, and professionals as the conflict in Cuba dragged on. The war finally ended in 1878 without achieving independence, and many families chose to return to the island. Most, however, elected to stay in greater New York, where the 1880 Census counted 2,220 Cuban-born persons.

Starting in 1886, another Cuban American community rapidly rose to prominence with the opening of cigar factories in Ybor City, just outside Tampa. Ybor City was the creation of Vicente Martínez Ybor, a Spanish-born cigar manufacturer who had fled from Cuba during the 1868 conflict. In the 1870s he reestablished his business with great success in Key West and New York. By the mid-1880s, however, Martínez Ybor sought to move his operations to a location with better land and sea connections than Key West and far from the organizing efforts of the growing cigar makers' unions. He purchased a large tract of land outside of Tampa and built not only his factory but an entire community, with public buildings and housing for the workers. Ybor City became, in effect, an immigrant "company town," as Martínez Ybor succeeded in attracting other cigar manufacturers to open factories in his new development. Ybor City became a major center for the manufacture of cigars, importing both tobacco leaves and workers from Cuba. The Cuban population of the area boomed, and by the 1900 Census it was the largest Cuban American community in the U.S., with more than 3,500 Cuban-born people.

Ybor City and Key West became hotbeds of revolutionary activity during the second war of independence, which broke out in 1895 and eventually involved the United States in a conflict with Spain that led to the end of Spanish rule in the island. The war was initiated by a longtime resident of New York, José Martí, who from the U.S. crafted a civilian movement that was successful in taking the armed struggle to Cuba. Martí counted heavily on the revolutionary spirit of the cigar workers in the Florida communities for the critical financial support for his movement.

During the 19th century the development of Cuban American communities followed a pattern that continued well into the 20th century: migration was initiated by the alienated or persecuted upper sectors of Cuban society, followed by other social classes, creating communities marked by an active interest and participation in movements to change the political status of the homeland. That pattern would be repeated by the Cuban migrants after 1959.

Migration during the Cuban Republic (1902–1958)

At the start of the 20th century, Cuba was undergoing a transition toward self-government. Many longtime Cuban residents of the U.S. returned to the island in the ensuing years. Ybor City started to decline in the 1920s, when Havana regained its primacy as the center of cigar manufacturing and many workers went back home.

During the Depression and World War II, Cuban migration to the U.S. reached all-time lows. But the close economic, political, and cultural ties between the island and the U.S., as well as the geographic proximity, resulted in a high volume of traffic back and forth between the two countries. By 1948 more than 200,000 Cubans a year were visiting the U.S., the largest number of arrivals from any country in the world, representing 20 percent of U.S. passenger arrivals that year. Americans went to the island for business and pleasure, and Cubans came to the U.S. on a temporary basis to develop their careers, either in U.S. schools, in music, in the entertainment industry, or in professional sports, notably baseball and boxing. The international popularity of Cuban music was in large measure the result of the connections Cuban musicians made in the U.S., especially in New York, with its entertainment venues and recording companies.

After World War II and during the early 1950s, Cuban migration increased substantially. This was largely a labor migration spurred by employment opportunities in New York, a phenomenon with similar origins to and characteristics as the migration of Puerto Ricans to New York during the same period. By the mid-1950s, the political climate in Cuba had worsened under the dictatorship of Fulgencio Batista, and many left for political reasons. By 1957 more than 12,000 people were leaving the island every year, mostly immigrating to New York but also to the fairly new winter resort city near Cuba: Miami.

By the time of the Cuban revolution in 1959, there was already a well-established, century-old migration path from Cuba to the U.S. During the next five decades, however, that revolution propelled an exodus from Cuba that dwarfed any previous human flows from the island to the U.S.

Migration Waves since 1959

There have been four major migration waves from Cuba to the U.S. since the rise of the present Cuban government was established in 1959. Although those waves have differed a great deal, they have all been the result of a protracted international conflict that has utilized migration as a political tool. A climate of hostility and an absence of normal relations between the two countries, combined with the fact that Cuba is an island, have made migration difficult and generally unavailable except when the two governments, unilaterally or bilaterally, have made politically based decisions that allow migration to take place.

The first wave occurred from 1959 to October 1962. The approximately 200,000 individuals who made up this wave were automatically granted refugee status by the U.S. government and thus exempted from the restrictions imposed on most other nationality groups. A federal program was established in 1961 to assist in the resettlement and economic adjustment of the new arrivals.

Cuba's displaced elite was disproportionately represented in this wave. The contentious transition to socialism affected first and foremost, although not exclusively, the upper sectors of Cuban society. Many of those alienated from the revolutionary process were especially fearful of the implications of the political changes for their children in the wake of the nationalization of private, especially Catholic, schools in 1960. Families of upper socioeconomic status with children under 18 years of age

Table 2   Year of arrival of foreign-born Cubans, since 1959

Years of arrival	Number	Percentage of Cuban-born U.S. population
Before 1960	65,602	7.4
1960–1964 (early exiles)	133,992	15.2
1965–1974 (airlift)	247,726	28.0
1975–1979	29,508	3.3
1980–1981 (Mariel)	101,837	11.5
1982–1993	130,337	14.8
1994–1996 (rafter crisis)	96,168	10.9
1997–2000	78,269	8.9
Total	883,439	100.0

Source: U.S. Bureau of the Census, 2000 Census, 5% Integrated Public Use Microdata Sample, weighted data.

were therefore overrepresented in this wave. In fact, the concern with the fate of children in Cuba created a migration of more than 14,000 unaccompanied children, who upon arrival were cared for by religious charities, primarily in southern Florida, until their parents could leave the island. This was dubbed "Operation Pedro Pan."

This initial wave was singularly important in shaping the character of the Cuban presence in the U.S. Those arriving at this time had the skills and education to facilitate their adjustment to life in the U.S. and give them a lasting political and economic hegemony within Miami's Cuban American community. Known as the "golden exiles," these are the people who have been most economically successful. They have regarded themselves as reluctant migrants, compelled into exile as they lost the class conflict that led to the entrenchment of the socialist order. They have therefore been the principal standard-bearers in the sustained struggle against the Cuban government. Because so many in this wave were children, they have had an enduring demographic presence despite the fact that more than four decades have passed since their arrival. Even as late as the year 2000, nearly a third of the Cuban-born population of the U.S. had arrived in the 1960s.

The second wave started in the fall of 1965, when, to defuse internal discontent with the growing economic austerity, the Cuban government allowed persons from the U.S. to go to Cuba in boats to pick up their relatives. Some 5,000 people left from the designated port, Camarioca, before the U.S. government halted the operation and agreed to an orderly airlift. Also known as the "freedom flights" or "aerial bridge," the airlift brought 260,500 individuals in twice-daily flights from

Varadero, Cuba, to Miami before both governments agreed to end it in 1973. It was the largest of all the waves, but more orderly than the others and much less intense, taking place over eight years.

During the airlift the Cuban government selected the emigrants from a large pool of applicants, favoring women and the elderly and excluding males of military age, which resulted in a demographic profile that was hardly typical of international migrants. In its first few years, the airlift brought the remnants of Cuba's upper classes, especially the elderly parents of those who arrived in the earlier wave. But by the late 1960s, with sustained austerity in Cuba, the airlift started peeling away at the middle sectors of the island's class structure, bringing small entrepreneurs, skilled and semiskilled workers, and white-collar employees. As with the earlier wave, the airlift arrivals were automatically granted refugee visas, facilitating their entry into the U.S.

Looking to defuse tensions in the island once again, the Cuban government in 1980 opened another port, Mariel, to allow unrestricted emigration. What became known as the Mariel boatlift lasted for six months and brought more than 125,000 Cubans to the U.S. It was a disorganized exodus on private vessels that went to Cuba from Florida to pick up relatives of those already living in the U.S. Other people boarded the boats, however, resulting in a wave with a profile that is closer to that of the overall Cuban population, with significant representation from Cuba's lower socioeconomic and nonwhite sectors as well as writers, artists, professionals, and even government officials. Also arriving in the boatlift were convicted felons and inmates of mental institutions, placed on the boats by the Cuban government. Public attention in the U.S., especially in the press, focused on those felons and inmates among the arrivals. Those classified as criminals and therefore "excludable" from the U.S. were detained. In the end, however, only about 2,500 of the 125,000 people who arrived during the boatlift were deemed "excludable" by the U.S. government. Nearly 1,400 of those were eventually deported to Cuba under an agreement with the Cuban government. In 2006, about six hundred "excludables" were still in prison. After more than twenty-five years, regardless of whether they are currently detained, these "excludables" are still subject to deportation to Cuba whenever the next opportunity arises to send them back. They have never been admitted legally to the U.S.

The Mariel boatlift was a dramatic migration. Thousands of arrivals without U.S. relatives were interned in refugee camps until sponsors could be found for them. Despite the negative press that the Mariel arrivals received, the bulk of the *marielitos* made successful and productive adjustments to life in this country. But after the boatlift was finally halted, it was clear that the welcome that the U.S. had always extended to Cubans had worn thin.

The fourth wave, in 1994, faced unprecedented barriers to entering the U.S. Throughout the 1980s and into the early 1990s, relatively few Cubans were admitted each year through visas issued by the U.S. consulate in Havana. On August 11, 1994, responding to an alarming rise in unauthorized and even violent departures from the island, the Cuban government announced that it would not detain anyone trying to leave on a raft or other vessel, thus initiating the fourth wave. Remembering the Mariel experience, however, the Clinton administration was unwilling to hold the door open for Cubans. Rescued rafters were sent to camps at the U.S. Naval Base at Guantánamo, Cuba, with the expectation that they would never be admitted to the U.S. Nearly 37,000 Cubans were rescued by the U.S. Coast Guard, and most were interned in Guantánamo. Eventually the U.S. admitted these people, owing to the lack of alternative destinations for them as well as deteriorating conditions in the camps.

What became known as the Rafter Crisis of 1994 was halted after only a month when the two governments negotiated an agreement whereby the U.S. committed itself to admitting at least 20,000 Cubans a year through the normal visa process. The Cuban government in turn agreed to accept the return of any future unauthorized migrants interdicted by the U.S. Coast Guard before reaching U.S. shores. This has become known as the "wet-foot, dry-foot policy." Because of the 1966 Cuban Refugee Adjustment Act, which granted any Cuban already in the U.S. the right to apply for permanent residence, those Cubans who step on U.S. soil (dry-foot) are allowed to remain even if they have entered in an unauthorized manner. But if the Coast Guard interdicts them at sea, even a few feet from shore (wet-foot), they are returned to Cuba under the terms of the 1995 agreement.

This agreement continued to govern U.S.-Cuba migration into the 21st century. Some 20,000 Cubans arrive each year through the normal visa process. In addition, a limited number of unauthorized migrants continue to enter, usually with the help of smugglers with powerboats who bring them across the Strait of Florida and deposit them directly on U.S. soil. The rickety vessels and rafts that used to bring Cubans to the U.S. are no longer effective, since now the migrants need to elude not only the Cuban authorities but the U.S. Coast Guard as well.

An Atypical and Diverse Profile

The different waves of migration from Cuba set the stage for the development of a Cuban American population with profound demographic, socioeconomic, and even political contrasts. Cubans in the U.S. cannot be regarded as a homogeneous group.

One characteristic common to all waves, however, is a low birthrate. Cuba has long been a country infused with modern and secular values that tend to depress fertility levels. Once in the U.S., Cubans tend to aspire to fairly high levels of economic achievement, a factor leading to high rates of female labor force participation. High economic expectations and female employment have resulted in repro-

Table 3   Selected characteristics of foreign-born Cubans, 2000

Age	
Median age	49.0
Percentage 15 and under	3.8
Percentage 65 and over	26.1
Gender	
Sex ratio (males per 100 females)	95.6
Percentage of women ages 25–64 without children	41.6
Percentage of women ages 25–34 who are divorced	11.1
Employment	
Median family income	$36,800
Percentage ages 25–64 in labor force	66.9
Percentage ages 25–64 who are self-employed	13.1
Socioeconomic status	
Percentage ages 25–64 in labor force who are below the poverty line	8.5
Percentage who are not U.S. citizens	38.7

Source: U.S. Bureau of the Census, 2000 Census, 5% Integrated Public Use Microdata Sample, weighted data.

ductive levels for Cubans that are among the lowest among U.S. immigrant groups. In 2000, more than 40 percent of all Cuban-born women between the ages of 25 and 64 were childless.

Besides a low birthrate, one result of the relative absence of traditional family norms among U.S. Cubans is the high percentage of Cuban-born women who are divorced. In 2000, 11 percent of all Cuban women aged 25 to 34 were divorced, the highest percentage for all major U.S. immigrant groups. After age 35, the percentage climbs steadily and remains among the highest among all foreign-born groups in the U.S. The high incidence of divorce is another factor that contributes to lowering the birthrate.

The continued demographic importance of the waves that arrived in the 1960s and 1970s and the migration of many middle-aged and elderly persons during the airlift have combined with the low birthrate to make Cubans the oldest of all foreign-born populations in the U.S., with a median age of 49 in 2000. Only 3.8 percent of the Cuban American population was under 18 years of age, while 41.6 percent was over 55. No other foreign-born nationality in the U.S. comes close to such an atypical age profile.

The prevalence of older persons among U.S. Cubans has no doubt contributed to one of their most visible characteristics: political conservatism and an abiding commitment to changing the political status of the homeland. The older exiles arrived during the period of cold war confrontation with the Cuban government and are more likely than younger Cubans to embrace the dream of recovering the homeland, using the lens of exile to shape their political perceptions. Opinion surveys among Cuban Americans, however, consistently show a sharp contrast in political attitudes between older exiles and more recent arrivals. Those who arrived more than two decades after the establishment of the current socialist government are not as likely to embrace the exile ethos of the recovery of the lost homeland, placing a greater priority on their struggle to adjust successfully to life in the U.S. They are also more likely than the older exiles to have close family members still in Cuba, so their priority is not to isolate the island but to fulfill their family obligations through visits and remittances. A poll taken in Miami by Florida International University in 2000 showed, for example, that on the critical question of support of the decades-old U.S. embargo on Cuba, 54 percent of those arriving since 1984 favored lifting it, while less than a third of those arriving in the 1960s and 1970s did so.

The position of the earlier and older exiles, however, has tended to predominate in the Cuban American community. One basis for their hegemony is their economic position. The income differentials between the arrival waves are significant. The socioeconomic selectivity that operated in the earlier wave, joined with a very favorable reception by the U.S. government, facilitated their economic adjustment. In contrast, the characteristics of the later waves, along with a much less favorable reception, have conspired to make their economic adjustment much more difficult. The image of Cubans as successful immigrants is therefore not accurate for all groups. Since the 1980s, Cuban median family income has declined in relation to that of other immigrant populations; by 2000 it was $36,800, substantially below the U.S. median and below that of many other groups. Among those 25 to 64 years of age and in the labor force, 8.5 percent of the Cuban-born were below the poverty line.

Socioeconomic differences among Cuban Americans are likely to prevail in the near future. Research on the second generation has shown that the academic achievement and aspirations of Cuban American children mirror the socioeconomic disparities between the arrival waves.

Racially, the Cuban American population is far from being representative of the population of the island. In 2000 nearly 90 percent of Cuban-born persons in the U.S. identified themselves as white, while at least half of Cuba's population is estimated to have African ancestry. Of all the migration waves, only the 1980 Mariel boatlift brought a significant number of Afro-Cubans to the U.S.

Cuban Miami: An Ethnic Enclave

Miami has become the undisputed center of the Cuban presence in the U.S. Unlike most immigrant groups, which tend to concentrate initially in one metropolitan area and then disperse over time to other localities, Cubans have shown the inverse tendency, concentrating in Miami after a process of initial dispersion during the 1960s and early 1970s. At that time the U.S. government, through its Cuban Refugee Program, resettled some 300,000 immigrants as they arrived from Cuba. This voluntary program provided incentives such as housing, assistance, and other support through local religious charities throughout the U.S. in order to ease the pressures Miami was facing with the Cuban exodus. In 1970, at the height of the program, only about 40 percent of the Cuban-born population lived in southern Florida.

The resettlement program was still in effect when many resettled Cubans started returning to Miami. Sizable Cuban communities in the Northeast, the Midwest, and the Pacific Coast lost many of their members to the Miami-bound flow during the 1980s and 1990s. In addition, newer migrants from the island, arriving after the termination of the resettlement program, showed a disposition to remain in Miami after they arrived. In Miami-Dade County, people of Cuban origin are now the largest single ethnic group, larger than either white non-Hispanics or African Americans, representing nearly 30 percent of the total population and accounting for a majority of the Hispanic population.

The community Cuban Americans have created in Miami is the foremost example of an ethnic enclave in the United States. It is characterized by a broad range of highly differentiated immigrant entrepreneurial activity. The foundation of the Miami enclave was laid by the immigrants who arrived in the 1960s, who possessed the combination of skills, experience, and attitudes that eventually made it possible for them to undertake various means of self-employment. In 2000, 11 percent of the Cuban-born population aged 25 to 64 years was self-employed, one of the highest percentages among U.S. immigrant groups. The wide range of services available within the community makes possible the enclave's institutional completeness— that is, the community's members, if they wish, can live out their lives within its boundaries. In Miami's Cuban community, members provide each other with virtually every service, from medical and legal needs to sales, craft and repair work, and even access to public institutions such as government and schools. Private bilingual schools are owned and operated by fellow Cubans. Firms, large and small, owned or operated by Cubans enable new arrivals from the island to enter the labor market within a familiar culture and language. From cradle to grave, maternity ward to funeral home, Cubans in Miami are afforded the opportunity to live entirely within the world they have created in southern Florida.

A strong ethnic enclave favors the maintenance of the culture and language of the home country, slowing down the process of acculturation. Miami is de facto a bilingual city, with both English and Spanish used to conduct a broad range of public business. Even the second generation of Cuban Americans, while preferring to use English, know and are competent in their parents' native language. Bilingualism is viewed as a requisite for employment in most sectors of Miami's service economy.

The enclave is one reason that the ethos of exile has remained so entrenched among Cuban Americans. A discourse of opposition and hostility toward the Cuban government and the commitment to overthrowing that government has been echoed through the years in the media of the enclave. Local Spanish-language television and especially radio stations have been largely owned and/or operated by Cubans and reflect the exile discourse. Especially combative are various talk radio stations that have been a favored vehicle for communicating a vehement and militant message in opposition to the Cuban government and to those within the exile community who advocate a moderate position.

Within the enclave one can also find a large number of ethnic associations based on economic activity. These organizations provide networks for their members' economic advancement. Of particular note are the associations that Cubans have formed to bring together those engaged in construction and real estate development, the sector of Miami's economy in which the most economically successful Cubans have made their fortunes. A strong ethnic network is critical to the successful operation of the many levels of contracting and subcontracting that permeate that industry. The associations serve to expand and reinforce that network.

In Cuban Miami, religious organizations are not as important as those based on economic activity. This is largely a result of Cuba's long history of secularism and the institutional weakness of the Roman Catholic Church in the island, going back to the earliest colonial times. Most Cubans in Miami are Roman Catholic, but for many religion is not a vehicle for connecting with their community. Furthermore, significant numbers of Cubans in Miami, reflecting the island's diverse religious traditions, belong to Protestant denominations, and in Miami Beach there is a Cuban synagogue. With the arrival of many Cubans of African descent during the Mariel boatlift, there was a visible increase in Afro-Cuban religious sects such as Santeria, whose traditions originated in West Africa. Because of these sects' inherently secretive nature, it is difficult to know how many adherents they have in Miami, but it is clear that followers can be found even among white Cubans.

Looking to the Future

The Cuban revolution launched in 1959 and the U.S. response to it created and shaped the contemporary Cuban presence in the U.S. For the past five decades, the conditions that created the exodus from Cuba have remained fundamentally unchanged: a government headed by Fidel Castro is still in power in Havana, Cubans in Miami maintain the exile dream of overthrowing it and recovering the homeland, and the U.S. still backs the exiles by fostering a policy of hostility and isolation toward that government.

When that enduring situation finally changes and the relationship between the U.S. and Cuba is normalized, Cubans in the U.S. will face a profound transformation in their group identity as they find that they can no longer define themselves as exiles. Despite the avowed exile goal of recovering the homeland, relatively few will actually return to Cuba to live, especially since many of the older exiles, those who were most likely to return, have already passed away. One poll has consistently found that only about 20 percent of Cuban-born people in Miami say that they will return to the island to live, and only under favorable political and economic conditions.

The Cuban presence in the U.S. will endure beyond the end of the current Cuban government. Even if returning permanently is not an option for most Cuban Americans, visiting their homeland and their relatives will certainly take place on an enormous scale. The volume of air traffic across the Strait of Florida may well reach the levels that now exist between, say, New York and Washington, D.C., as Cubans in the U.S. become a true transnational community. After all, Miami is closer to Havana than it is to Disney World.

Bibliography

Garcia, Maria Cristina. *Havana USA: Cuban Exiles and Cuban Americans in South Florida, 1959–1994.* Berkeley: University of California Press, 1996.

Grenier, Guillermo J., and Lisandro Pérez. *The Legacy of Exile: Cubans in the United States.* Boston: Allyn and Bacon, 2003.

Masud-Piloto, Felix Roberto. *From Welcomed Exiles to Illegal Immigrants: Cuban Migration to the U.S., 1959–1995.* Lanham, Md.: Rowman and Littlefield, 1996.

Ojito, Mirta. *Finding Mañana: A Memoir of a Cuban Exodus.* New York: Penguin, 2005.

Pérez, Lisandro. "Growing Up in Cuban Miami." In Rubén G. Rumbaut and Alejandro Portes, eds., *Ethnicities: Children of Immigrants in America.* Berkeley: University of California Press, 2001.

Pérez Firmat, Gustavo. *Life on the Hyphen: The Cuban-American Way.* Austin: University of Texas Press, 1994.

Portes, Alejandro, and Robert L. Bach. *Latin Journey: Cuban and Mexican Immigrants in the United States.* Berkeley: University of California Press, 1985.

Portes, Alejandro, and Alex Stepick. *City on the Edge: The Transformation of Miami.* Berkeley: University of California Press, 1993.

Poyo, Gerald E. *"With All, and for the Good of All": The Emergence of Popular Nationalism in the Cuban Communities of the United States, 1848–1898.* Durham, N.C.: Duke University Press, 1989.

Stepick, Alex, Guillermo J. Grenier, Max Castro, and Marvin Dunn. *This Land Is Our Land: Immigrants and Power in Miami.* Berkeley: University of California Press, 2003.

Torres, Maria de los Angeles. *In the Land of Mirrors: Cuban Exile Politics in the United States.* Ann Arbor: University of Michigan Press, 1999.

Dominican Republic

Peggy Levitt

Dominican migration to the United States began in earnest in the mid-1960s, increased steadily during the 1970s and 1980s, and declined slightly in the mid-1990s. Between 1961 and 2001, 850,026 Dominicans were admitted to the continental U.S., more than from any other Caribbean country, with the exception of Puerto Rico, and second only to Mexicans as the principal immigrant group entering from the Western Hemisphere. Dominicans have also established sizable communities in over a dozen countries, including Spain, Venezuela, Curaçao, Aruba, the U.S. Virgin Islands, Italy, the Netherlands, Switzerland, Canada, Panama, and Martinique.

Historical Background

Political and economic interdependence between the U.S. and the Dominican Republic has a long history. The U.S. occupied the Dominican Republic in 1916. By the time American forces withdrew in 1924, U.S. dominance in the region had been firmly established and the Dominican Republic was irrevocably integrated into the system of global economic relations that later precipitated both internal and international migration.

The root causes of internal migration began during the dictatorial regime of Rafael Leónidas Trujillo (1930–1961), when government expropriation of large tracts of land for sugar, cacao, and coffee export production created a large labor surplus. When Trujillo loosened restrictions on internal movement in the 1950s, many Dominicans left the countryside for urban areas.

By the late 1950s, however, economic growth driven by the agricultural export sector was on the decline. There was also increasing opposition to the almost daily torture and killing of political prisoners to which Trujillo resorted to maintain power. The 1960 assassination of the Mirabal sisters, national heroines who actively opposed the Trujillo regime in the face of harsh political repression, drew sharp international criticism. That same year the Organization of American States imposed sanctions on the Dominican government and froze many of its financial assets. President Kennedy withdrew his support after his election in 1960. Trujillo was assassinated in 1961.

As economic conditions deteriorated and political instability took hold, U.S. leaders feared that a communist takeover like that in Cuba would occur. A U.S.-backed provisional government was organized to hold presidential elections. A progressive leader, Professor Juan Bosch, was elected in 1963, and a democratic constitution was ratified. Seven months later a group of military officers ousted Bosch from office and formed an unstable alliance with large landowners, industrialists, and international trade merchants. In April 1965 a military faction broke from the alliance and tried to reinstate Bosch; their rebellion quickly escalated into a popular uprising. Four days later, 40,000 U.S. Marines landed in Santo Domingo to prevent what President Johnson claimed was an imminent communist revolution.

Before the 1960s, few people emigrated from the Dominican Republic. Trujillo severely restricted movement out of the country, fearing that his opponents would organize against him from abroad. Migration to the U.S. increased from a yearly average of almost 1,000 people during the 1950s to nearly 10,000 people per year during the first half of the 1960s. Many of the first to emigrate were Trujillo supporters fleeing the country before and following his death. They feared Bosch's left-leaning policies, whereas later migrants feared the instability plaguing the country after Bosch's defeat.

The overthrow of the Bosch government, the civil unrest that followed, and the subsequent U.S. intervention created a pool of potentially volatile antigovernment opponents. According to Christopher Mitchell, the U.S. government increased the numbers of visas it granted to prevent these individuals from further heightening instability. Migration acted as a political safety valve that would weaken opposition and stabilize the Dominican political scene. Most of these migrants went to New York City, but many settled in San Juan, Puerto Rico. These politically motivated flows were encouraged by the two regimes that followed, which failed to modernize agriculture and bestow the benefits of greater industrialization on labor. Frustration grew among the middle class.

Dominican migration to the U.S. increased steadily during this period, rising from 9,250 in 1968 (after an initial high of 16,503 in 1966) to 13,858 in 1973. Similarly, the number of Dominicans admitted to Puerto Rico increased, from 1,751 in 1968 to 2,735 in 1974. This sustained exodus complemented the industrialization strategy pursued by President Joaquín Balaguer by diminishing the large numbers of unemployed workers who would have remained behind.

In 1978, tired of Balaguer's repressive policies and their diminishing economic gains, the Dominican public elected the Partido Revolucionario Dominicano (PRD) candidate, Antonio Guzmán, in what was considered the country's first democratic election. Despite several important economic and political reforms, the PRD's first term coincided with the country's harshest economic crisis in years. By 1982 declining sugar prices and increasing oil prices and interest rates worsened conditions even more. Growing unemployment and underemployment, the rising cost of living, a chaotic transportation system, and the near collapse of basic services were all powerful incentives to move abroad. Under a reelected Balaguer, the country pinned its hopes on export processing zones (EPZs), tourism, and nontraditional agricultural exports. Although these resulted in rapid economic growth during the 1990s, they did little to improve living conditions for most Dominicans.

During the 1990s, EPZs and tourism became the two most important economic sectors. Revenues from tourism increased from $368.2 million in 1985 to $1.046 billion in 1992. Between 1980 and 1988 firms in the EPZs increased the country's exports from $117 to $517 million. These gains, however, were fragile and driven by forces outside the republic. President Leonel Fernández, elected in 1996, introduced a bold reform package aimed at creating a market-oriented economy that could compete internationally. Though many reforms stalled in the legislature, the economy grew vigorously in 1997 and 1998. By 2001, however, growth once again stagnated. In 2003 alone, economic growth declined by 5 percent, two of the three main political parties experienced internal divisions, and the government's approval rating fell to less than 15 percent. Three major banks collapsed, the head of the presidential security services was arrested, and peso devaluations paralyzed public and private investment.

Thus, recent migration largely resulted from economic restructuring and the high levels of rural and urban unemployment that followed. In addition, public opinion shifted, transforming those who emigrated to the U.S. from traitors into brethren living outside the country. High birthrates and lower mortality rates also encouraged migration. Better communication and transportation networks, the spread of private domestic telephone service, and Dominicans' acquisition of radios and television sets brought the outside world to nonmigrants and converted emigration into a ubiquitous norm. At present, emigration has a self-perpetuating momentum.

Dominicans in the United States

Scholars have long debated the socioeconomic background of migrants from the Dominican Republic, especially their regional and class composition. In the early 1970s, several authors portrayed migrants as rural, poor, and illiterate. Antonio Ugalde, Frank Bean, and Gilbert Cárdenas first challenged this view when their analysis of the 1974 DIAGNOS National Study revealed that while over 53 percent of the Dominican population resided in rural areas, only 24 percent of international migrants left from the Dominican countryside. Subsequent studies also indicated that most Dominicans held skilled blue-collar or white-collar positions prior to migration. As Max Castro found, although all classes were represented, emigrants came primarily from the working class. By the 1990s, however, Dominican emigration—both documented and undocumented—included a broad cross-section of the sending society, drawn largely from the urban working classes rather than from the middle class or the peasantry. Recent data from the Immigration and Naturalization Service (INS) suggest a bimodal distribution in the occupational background of Dominicans legally admitted to the U.S. On the one hand, reports Jorge Duany, one out of four migrants held a relatively skilled and well-paying job in the Dominican Republic during the period from 1996 to 2000. On the other hand, more than half were employed in low-skilled and low-paying occupations, particularly as operators, fabricators, laborers, and service workers. The small numbers who identify as agricultural workers suggest that the majority are not rural dwellers leaving areas now dependent on remittances.

Researchers using 2000 U.S. Census data and data from the Current Population Survey (CPS) arrive at different figures for the number of Dominicans living in the U.S. According to the census, there were 799,768 persons of Dominican ancestry in the U.S. mainland in 2000; just under 70 percent (545,262) were foreign-born. They represented 2.1 percent of the total U.S. Hispanic population and were the fourth largest Hispanic group. Between 1980 and 2000, the population of foreign-born Dominicans in the U.S. grew by 315 percent. Analyses of the CPS place these numbers somewhat higher. According to Max Castro and Thomas Boswell, there were 1,014,879 Dominicans in the country, while John Logan, using CPS and census data, places the number at 1,121,257, thereby increasing the Dominican share of the Hispanic population to 3.2 percent. In addition, the 2000 Census counted 57,003 residents of Puerto Rico with Dominican ancestry. More than 90 percent were foreign-born.

Gender relations structure the process of migration and are transformed by the migration process. In 2000 the numbers of Dominican females (54.6 percent) surpassed the numbers of males (45.4 percent). Dominicans are relatively young; their median age was 36 years, up from 30 years in 1980. A quarter of the population was less than 25 years old; 46 percent were between the ages of 25 and 44. Just over half of women between the ages of 25 and 54 were married. While the proportion of women aged 25 to 34 who were divorced or separated stood at about 20 percent, this figure increased to approximately one third for women between 25 and 64. Just over 50 percent of Dominican households in the U.S. are female-headed, compared to about 25 percent for the nation overall. Immigrants' marital status is in part a reflection of the widespread practice of common-law marriages throughout the Caribbean. It also reflects changing gender dynamics and enhanced opportunities for women living in the U.S. versus the island. While only 49 percent of men between 25 and 34 were married, the rate increases for older men (67 percent for those between 45 and 64). Almost half (49 percent) of the women between the ages of 25 and 64 had two children, while 21 percent had between three and five offspring.

Dominicans are by and large relatively recent arrivals. Forty-three percent entered the country between 1990 and 2000. An additional 32 percent came during the 1980s. Of these foreign-born Dominicans, only 36 percent were naturalized U.S. citizens by 2000. Combined with the second generation, 68 percent of all the Dominicans in the U.S. are citizens. Twenty-three percent claim they are white, 8 percent choose black as their racial classification, and 58 percent select the "other race" category.

Individuals of Dominican ancestry continue to be highly concentrated in the New York/northern New Jersey metropolitan area (67 percent), but there are also important clusters in the Miami/Fort Lauderdale area (7.7 percent) and around Boston, Massachusetts (4.1 percent), and Providence, Rhode Island. In 2000 the top metropolitan areas of settlement for Dominicans were New York City (406,806), San Juan (44,444), Miami–Fort Lauderdale (36,454), Bergen-Passaic, New Jersey (36,360), and Boston (25,057). Some of these cities—especially New York and San Juan—have more people of Dominican origin than many places in the Dominican Republic. For some time now, for example, New York City has had more Dominican residents than Santiago de los Caballeros, the second largest city in the Dominican Republic.

Dominicans in the U.S. face significant challenges. Most arrive without the occupational and language skills demanded by the changing U.S. labor market. The number of well-paying, unionized jobs for unskilled laborers who do not speak English is on the decline. Consequently, while 46.5 percent of all foreign-born Dominicans were employed in manufacturing in 1979, only 35.7 percent worked in the sector by 1989.

As a result, in 2000, foreign-born Dominicans ranked lower than the U.S. population as a whole in terms of occupational status, education, and income. Just 10 percent have a college or advanced degree. While 41 percent of all Dominicans graduated from high school, 49 percent did not receive a high school diploma. Fourteen percent of all Dominican men between the ages of 25 and 44 and 21 percent of all women lived below the poverty line. Only 61 percent of males and 48 percent of females classified themselves as employed. They worked in blue-, gray-, and pink-collar jobs in the service sector (18 percent), in technical, sales, or administrative positions (18.5 percent), or as operators, fabricators, and handlers (30 percent). Fifteen percent held managerial or professional positions.

Dominicans also fare worse than most other Latino groups. While the 25 percent of all Cubans who were professionals and managers nearly equaled the rates for the nation as a whole (29 percent), only 17 percent of Puerto Ricans and 11 percent of

Dominicans held comparable positions. Similarly, the mean personal income for a full-time worker in the U.S. was $40,645, again nearly matched by Cubans ($40,056) but not by Puerto Rican ($31,851), Dominican ($27,258), and Mexican workers ($23,727). Finally, while one quarter of the general population and of Cuban immigrants had college degrees or higher, only 13 percent of Puerto Ricans, 10 percent of Dominicans, and 6.2 percent of Mexicans had college degrees.

Hispanic segregation as a whole, as measured by the Index of Dissimilarity, is intermediate between those of blacks (about 14 points higher) and Asians (about 9 points lower). Dominicans have the lowest exposure to whites; the average Dominican lives in a neighborhood where only one of eight residents is a non-Hispanic white, prompting the sociologist John Logan to conclude, "Dominicans are clearly the least successful as well as the most segregated." Furthermore, 37 percent of Dominican households were considered "linguistically isolated." Nearly 42 percent of census respondents classified themselves as speaking English "not well" or "not at all."

While the immigrant generation is faring poorly, second-generation Dominicans are exhibiting educational and occupational gains, as revealed by Castro and Boswell's comparison of U.S.-born Dominicans with those who arrived before 1990. Only 9 percent of U.S.-born Dominicans 25 years and older did not complete high school, compared to 53 percent of the pre-1990 cohort. In addition, the proportion of second-generation Dominicans who completed a college degree (22 percent) is more than three times as high as the pre-1990 immigrant cohort (7 percent). The median income for full-time U.S.-born Dominican workers ($26,125) surpasses the $20,000 earned by comparable workers who arrived before 1990. Finally, U.S.-born Dominicans are almost twice as likely to be employed as professionals and managers (18 percent) than their pre-1990 counterparts (10 percent) are.

The sustained proportion of female-headed households presents a continuing challenge. While the number of Dominican men in the labor force who were at or below the poverty line decreased slightly from 1990 to 2000, there was actually an *increase* for working women over the same period. Clearly, this contributes to levels of poverty among the second generation, especially those growing up in female-headed households, and remains a cause for concern—just over 10 percent of the U.S. population of Dominican ancestry is under 18 and lives at or below the poverty level.

Dominicans are also well represented among the ranks of small business owners. While the vast majority (61.5 percent) are private salaried employees, an additional 7.2 percent are self-employed in such businesses as groceries and restaurants, beauty parlors and insurance/travel agencies, gypsy cab companies, and finance firms that cash checks or transfer remittances. In fact, a 1992 study by Alejandro Portes and Luis Guarnizo revealed that Dominicans owned 70 percent of all bodegas in New York City, with estimated annual sales of $1.8 billion.

Finally, the media have paid a good deal of attention to Dominicans involved in drug trafficking. While some individuals clearly do participate in these kinds of activities, they represent only a small fraction of the community. The vast majority of Dominicans are law-abiding citizens whose reputation has been tarnished by a few.

Dominicans exhibit one of the lowest naturalization rates among recent migrants. In 1999 only 13 percent of all Dominicans admitted to the U.S. since 1961 had become U.S. citizens. Pamela Graham and Greta Gilbertson, among others, attribute this to the republic's proximity to the U.S., the relative ease and low cost of transportation, the multiple, widespread transnational ties spanning the U.S. and the island, and the current citizenship regime. In 1996, however, when immigration reforms severely restricted services to noncitizens, more than 27,000 Dominicans naturalized, almost tripling the number who had naturalized the previous year. Despite these gains, according to the Dominican American National Roundtable (DANR), Dominicans have less political power than their numbers would suggest. In 2003 only 18 Dominicans held elected state and city government offices.

Dominicans seem to be finding their political voice. In 2003, 45 percent of the naturalized Dominicans in New York City were registered to vote; they make up 20 percent of the city's registered Latino voters. No candidate can run for statewide or municipal office in New York without seeking the support of the Dominican community. In addition, several New York–based Dominicans have been appointed to important advisory positions. A large statewide Conference on Dominican Affairs was held at Rutgers Law School in Newark, New Jersey, in February 2001. It aimed to bring together Dominicans living throughout the state to discuss shared concerns about social and economic development. The political opportunity structure and socioeconomic context in which Dominican migrants are embedded clearly influence their political advancement. While Dominicans have also made gains in small cities like Lawrence, Massachusetts, and Providence, Rhode Island, they have not enjoyed comparable success in Boston.

Despite their limited formal political mobilization, Dominicans have been prolific organizers of community-based groups. The Centro Cívico Cultural Dominicano was established in New York City in 1962. Since then a series of service-delivery and advocacy organizations has been founded, including the Community Association of Progressive Dominicans (ACDP) and Alianza Dominicana in New York, Quisqueya in Action in Providence, and the Dominican American National Foundation in Florida. DANR, founded in 1997, is a nonpartisan, nonprofit corporation seeking to bring together the different voices of all people of Dominican origin in the U.S. and Puerto Rico. Dominicans 2000 was a national youth organization established to create a national agenda for Dominicans living in the U.S.

Another place that Dominicans make their mark is in religious institutions. By the end of this decade, researchers predict that Latinos will make up more than 50 percent of all Catholics in the U.S., outnumbering their Irish and Italian coreligionists. The vast majority of Dominicans are Catholics, meaning that being Catholic and being Dominican are often synonymous. Dominican Catholicism generally mixes formal ritual with many informal, popular, home-based practices. Small numbers are also joining Pentecostal, Adventist, Episcopalian, and other Protestant denominations.

Dominicans have also made significant cultural contributions. Authors like Junot Díaz and Julia Alvarez are key members of a growing cadre of first- and second-generation authors writing about the immigrant experience. The American musical scene has been strongly influenced by imports like merengue and bachata and singers like Juan Luis Guerra, Pedro Tavarez, and Victor Victor. Dominican designer Oscar de la Renta made an indelible mark on the fashion world. And the Dominican Republic has produced many of the U.S.'s favorite baseball stars, including Sammy Sosa, Pedro Martinez, Felipe Alou, and Manny Ramirez.

Finally, a word about race. Dominican conceptualizations of racial identity do not fit neatly into the binary classification systems that have prevailed in the U.S. According to Silvio Torres-Saillant, nearly nine out of ten Dominicans could be classified as mulatto or black by U.S. standards based on their skin color alone. Yet Dominican national identity generally reflects an amnesia about the island's Taino and African inhabitants and instead emphasizes its Spanish roots. Persistent Dominican-Haitian tensions are evidenced by the deprecating way in which many Dominicans refer to Haitians as black, in contrast to their own reluctance to self-identify as *negro* (black).

Enduring Homeland Involvements

Many Dominicans remain active in the economic, religious, and political life of the island at the same time that they are making a place for themselves in the U.S. A growing share of the Dominican population lives abroad (at least 10 percent in the year 2000). In 2001 migrant remittances represented the second leading source of foreign currency in the Dominican Republic, after tourism. Dominicans living outside the country are entitled to dual citizenship and voted in the 2004 presidential election. The constant flow of money, people, goods, and social remittances circulating between the island and places abroad blurs the boundary between American and Dominican life, creating a seamless social space that combines both contexts.

Accurate data on actual economic flows are notoriously difficult to come by. In 2002 between $1.9 and $2.1 billion U.S. were sent to the country in remittances—over half the value of its exports and a 16.9 percent increase from 2001. Transnational business owners, whose enterprises depend on regular cross-border exchanges of goods, labor, and money, make important contributions to the Dominican economy. Island businesses catering to consumption patterns created by migration also form part of this transnational social field. Dominican economic policy takes into account, albeit unofficially, that emigration reduces local unemployment and generates additional income for those who remain behind.

Dominican political life has also become transnational. In the past three decades, the U.S., and New York City in particular, has become a critical staging ground for Dominican political battles. All three of the principal political parties have well-established organizations along the eastern seaboard. Guarnizo, Portes, and Haller found that nearly 13 percent of the Dominicans they interviewed belonged to a political party in which they participated regularly, while an additional 23 percent occasionally participated. The political scientist Pamela Graham estimated that between 15 and 30 percent of the funding for the 1994 presidential campaign came from emigrants, who also strongly influence how nonmigrant family members vote.

The Dominican Revolutionary Party (PRD) provides one example of transnational political mobilization. It creates community-level committees, aggregated into municipal zones, which are then grouped into regional sections in New England, New Jersey, Florida, Puerto Rico, and Washington, D.C. In 1992 the party also approved the creation of base-level committees for Dominicans who became naturalized U.S. citizens and for second-generation Dominican Americans. Four members of the U.S. sections represent the migrant community on the party's National Executive Committee in Santo Domingo. The party also appointed a coordinator for all U.S.-based activities, whose job is to facilitate cooperation between party members at all levels on the island and in the U.S.

As the party's financial dependence on migrant contributions increased and migrant members made their conditions for remaining active supporters clear, leaders reinvented the party's relationship with its U.S. constituency. They recognized that the PRD needed to pursue an agenda that simultaneously addressed the needs of migrants and furthered Dominican national interests. If the party encouraged migrants to integrate politically in the U.S., the immigrant community would in turn be better positioned to advocate for Dominican national concerns in New York City and Washington. In exchange, the party would support policies that migrants favored, such as lowering taxes on the goods they brought back into the country, dual citizenship, and the expatriate vote.

The 1996 constitution gave full citizenship rights to Dominicans who opt for a second citizenship. The new constitution also granted citizenship to those born outside the country to Dominican parents, thus ensuring the formal inclusion of the second generation and beyond. The right to vote from abroad was approved in 1997, although not implemented until the 2004 election. More than 24,000 Dominicans in New York were among the estimated 52,000 registered voters who cast their ballots.

Despite migrants' enormous economic and political influence, the Dominican state has done little to systematically ensure their continued involvement, compared to countries such as Mexico and El Salvador. There are some signs that this too is changing. The government no longer refers to Dominicans abroad as *migrantes* (migrants) or the deprecating *Dominicanyorks* but as *dominicanos residentes en el exterior* ("Dominicans living abroad"). Such changes strategically signal that the state recognizes emigrants' success and their continued economic and social role in the Dominican Republic. Today people of Dominican birth or ancestry do not have to buy a tourist card when they enter their country of origin. They pass through customs in the same line as individuals residing on the island. Dominican customs policies have been revised so that return migrants can import a portion of their belongings duty-free. The government has placed customs officers at several consulates to help migrants fill out the papers they need before they return home. During the first Fernández administration, any housing project built by the government included a quota of houses to be sold to emigrants. Prospective buyers could deposit their down payments in dollars or in pesos at Banco Popular branches in the U.S. or on the island. Emigrants paid the remaining costs over a 15-year period at an interest rate below market value.

Politics and economics are not the only arenas where Dominicans continue to express their membership in two places. A third important arena for transnational activism is the hometown club—a social or cultural association based on its members' regional origins. Guarnizo and his colleagues report that nearly 10 percent of the Dominican migrants in their study participated regularly in a hometown association, 9 percent frequently contributed money to community projects, and 6 percent supported sending-country charitable organizations. Nearly 20 percent reported that they occasionally engaged in these activities. These clubs generally organize trips back home, donate medical supplies to their compatriots, and promote the celebration of special occasions. Of interest again is the Dominican government's lack of coordinated efforts to encourage these activities, despite their very important contributions to rural and urban development.

Religious institutions also serve as sites of dual belonging. The Catholic Church is perhaps the prime example of a transnational institution that welcomes its members wherever they are. Migrants circulate in and out of home- and host-country parishes, creating local-level ties between specific churches. These relationships are reinforced by those developing in response at higher levels of the church hierarchy. As more and more priests and seminarians interact, money and supplies are donated, and labor-sharing arrangements are formalized, the interrelationship between Dominican and U.S.-based religious life grows stronger. Increasing numbers of Dominicans around the world are also joining Protestant congregations that form part of global religious networks. For example, Jorge Duany found that Dominicans in Puerto Rico belonged to Adventist, Baptist, Episcopalian, Lutheran, and Pentecostal denominations. A homegrown Puerto Rican church, La Iglesia de Mita, has even expanded into the Dominican Republic and other Latin American countries.

Finally, transnational migration transforms fundamental aspects of social and cultural life, as I found in my study of migration between Miraflores (a pseudonym for a village in the Dominican Republic) and Boston. Migration from Miraflores began in the late 1960s, when the commercialization of agriculture and unequal land tenure patterns made it harder for people to earn a decent living by farming. In

1994 almost 60 percent of the nearly 500 households in Miraflores had relatives in the greater Boston metropolitan area. Fashion, food, forms of speech, and appliances and home decorating styles reflected these strong connections. In Miraflores, villagers often dressed in T-shirts with the names of businesses in Massachusetts printed on them and proudly served coffee with Cremora or juice made from Tang to their visitors. The local *colmados* stocked SpaghettiOs and Frosted Flakes. And almost everyone, including older community members who could count on their fingers how many times they had visited Santo Domingo, could talk about "La Mozart" or "La Centre"—Mozart Street Park and Centre Street in Jamaica Plain, two focal points of the Miraflores community in Boston.

In Boston, Mirafloreños have recreated their premigration lives as much as their new physical and cultural environment allows. Particularly during the early years of settlement, but even today, a large number of migrants live within the same 20-block radius. There are several streets where Mirafloreños occupy an apartment in almost every triple-decker house. Community members leave their doors open, so that the flow between households is as easy and uninhibited as it is in Miraflores. Women continue to hang curtains around the doorframes; in the Dominican Republic, these provide privacy without keeping in the heat, but in Boston they are merely decorative. Because someone is always traveling between Boston and the island, there is a continuous circular flow of goods, news, and information. As a result, when a community member becomes ill, cheats on a spouse, or is finally granted a visa, the news spreads quickly in both countries.

During their visits and phone conversations and through the videotapes they send home, migrants introduce those who remain behind to the ideas and practices they observe in the U.S. Nonmigrants gradually begin to adopt these behaviors and develop U.S. cultural and consumer styles. This steady infusion of social remittances, combined with migrant and nonmigrants' heightened social and economic interdependence, further encourages transnational village formation and perpetuation.

Other transnational villages span the Dominican Republic and the U.S. Migrants from Tenares, who have settled in Lawrence, Massachusetts, also maintain strong ties to one another. People from Sabana Iglesias who moved to Queens, New York, have stayed strongly connected to their sending community. But cultural change also occurs among migrants whose sense of connection is to a broader, diasporic Dominican community. In Washington Heights, New York, for example, Duany found that many Dominicans expressed enduring connections to their homeland by renaming streets and schools, establishing businesses with the same names as those in the home country, redecorating public and private spaces, and organizing parades and festivals based on Dominican folk traditions.

More and more Dominicans and migrants from other parts of the globe continue to be active in the economic, social, and political lives of their homelands while they put down roots in the countries that receive them. Their activities challenge conventional notions about immigrant assimilation and about the relationship between migration and development, because class, diversity, and democracy are no longer solely determined by what happens in the U.S. Some problems beg for binational cooperation, but how that can happen remains uncertain. When individuals belong to two countries, even informally, are they protected by two sets of rights and subject to two sets of responsibilities? Which states are ultimately responsible for which aspects of their lives?

Transnational migration, for example, raises questions about how the U.S. and other host nations should address immigrant poverty. Should transnationals qualify for housing assistance at the same time that they are building houses in their communities of origin? What about people who cannot fully support themselves in the U.S. because they are supporting family members in their homelands? Should sending-country social and community development programs distinguish between those who receive remittances from the U.S. and those who have no such outside support?

The factors giving rise to transnational migration are unlikely to decline anytime soon. For one thing, the conditions that precipitate migration, such as wage differentials, labor market segmentation, and economic globalization, are showing no signs of disappearing. Unlike the early 1900s, when immigration restrictions meant that ethnic identities were shaped largely by forces at work inside the U.S., immigration today has continued largely unabated since the mid-1960s. Constant new infusions of sending-country languages, values, and practices arrive each day, reinforcing homeland ties and providing migrants with the elements with which to shape transnational livelihoods. The social networks through which these flow are so strong and widespread that some scholars consider them impervious to immigration restrictions.

Critics in the U.S. will say that if migrants earn their living in America, their income, skills, and philanthropic efforts should remain here. In sending countries, they may argue that emigrants have no right to political voice because they have abandoned ship and lost touch with the day-to-day realities. These are valid concerns. There are no easy answers about how to balance transnational migrants' rights and responsibilities. The challenge is to figure out how individuals who live between two cultures can best be protected and represented and what we should expect from them in return. To meet it, we need to acknowledge the interdependence between the U.S. and sending countries and to begin to solve problems by looking outside the nation-state box. Rather than seeing remittance flows as a drain on the U.S. bank account, we can regard them as a way to rectify years of uneven development. Rather than seeing transnational political groups as suspect for their dual agendas, we can see them as strengthening democracy at home and fostering immigrant political integration into the U.S. Instead of seeing immigrant entrepreneurs who outsource as part of homeland brain drain, we can seek ways to turn their efforts into brain gain.

Bibliography

Castro, Max, and Thomas D. Boswell. 2002. "The Dominican Diaspora Revisited: Dominicans and Dominican-Americans in a New Century." *The North-South Agenda,* Paper 53. Miami: North-South Center, University of Miami.

Duany, Jorge. 1994. *Quisqueya on the Hudson: The Transnational Identity of Dominicans.* CUNY Dominican Studies Institute Monograph. New York: CUNY Press.

Espinal, Rosario, and Jonathan Hartlyn. 1999. "The Long and Difficult Struggle for Democracy in the Dominican Republic." In L. Diamon, J. Hartlyn, J. Linz, and S. M. Lipset, eds., *Democracy in Developing Countries,* pp. 469–518. Boulder, Colo.: Lynne Riemmer.

Georges, Eugenia. 1990. *The Making of a Transnational Community.* New York: Columbia University Press.

Grasmuck, Sherri, and Patricia Pessar. 1991. *Between Two Islands: Dominican International Migration.* Berkeley: University of California Press.

Guarnizo, Luis E., Alejandro Portes, and William Haller. 2004. "Assimilation and Transnationalism: Determinants of Transnational Political Action among Contemporary Migrants." *American Journal of Sociology* 108, 6: 1211–48.

Levitt, Peggy. 2001. *The Transnational Villagers.* Berkeley: University of California Press.

Pacini-Hernandez, Deborah. 1995. *Bachata: A Social History of Dominican Popular Music.* Philadelphia: Temple University Press.

Portes, Alejandro, William Haller, and Luis Guarnizo. 2002. "Transnational Entrepreneurs: The Emergence and Determinants of an Alternative Form of Immigrant Economic Adaptation." *American Sociological Review* 67: 278–98.

Sagas, Ernesto, and Sintia E. Molina. 2004. *Dominican Migration: Transnational Perspectives.* Gainesville: University of Florida Press.

Torres-Saillant, Silvio. 1998. "The Tribulations of Blackness: Stages in Dominican Racial Identity." *Latin American Perspectives* 25, 3: 126–46.

Torres-Saillant, Silvio, and Ramona Hernández. 1998. *The Dominican Americans.* Westport, Conn.: Greenwood.

El Salvador

Cecilia Menjívar

Migration has been an enduring feature of Salvadoran history. At different times, economic policies and political decisions have generated migration flows with their own dynamics and characteristics, mainly to adjacent countries. But Salvadorans also have been migrating to the United States for at least 100 years. Until recently, however, they remained relatively invisible, "passing," or being mistaken, for Mexicans. Until the 1980s Salvadoran immigrants constituted a relatively small group; 95,800 Salvadorans were enumerated in the 1980 Census, as compared with 2,242,100 Mexicans. According to the 2000 Census, approximately 85 percent of Salvadorans in the U.S. immigrated between 1980 and 2000. Most of those who arrived before 1980 left a relatively peaceful country and faced U.S. immigration laws that were relatively relaxed. For those who arrived after 1980, this situation changed dramatically. They emigrated in the midst of a civil war. Many left their country at a moment's notice or in extreme danger, and they often had to travel by land, which made their journeys costly and perilous. The numbers bound for the U.S. increased exponentially, and the class composition of the flows was transformed. In addition, stiffer U.S. immigration policies shaped their reception and subsequent incorporation in American society.

Early waves of Salvadoran migration to the U.S. can be linked to the commercialization of coffee in Central America and to U.S. industries in need of labor during World War II. Initially, members of El Salvador's coffee-producing elites settled around San Francisco, the chief processing center for coffee from Central America in the first years of the 20th century. Initial contacts were limited to coffee growers and business people, but during and after World War II, labor-scarce shipyards and wartime industries recruited other Central Americans who had worked on the Panama Canal. These job prospects attracted many Salvadorans and accounted for a significant increase of Salvadorans in San Francisco during the 1940s. By 1950,

Salvadorans and other Central Americans (mainly Nicaraguans) outnumbered the Mexican-born in San Francisco. And Salvadorans have continued to arrive, making San Francisco the U.S. city with the longest continuous history of Salvadoran immigration.

Though Salvadoran immigration has continued, its size, composition, and geographical concentration have changed substantially since the mid-20th century, particularly since 1980. The number of Salvadorans in the U.S. increased from 34,000 in 1970, to 95,800 in 1980, to 565,081 in 1990, to 823,932 in 2000. Thus, whereas in 1980 El Salvador did not make the list of the top 25 sending countries, in 1990 it was in eleventh place, and in 2000 it moved up to eighth place. Also, the U.S.-born Salvadoran population is estimated to be about half a million. Independent estimates place the number of Salvadorans in the U.S. much higher, with at least 1 million already in 1990, indicating that the census undercounts this group. Conceivably, between one sixth and one fifth of El Salvador's 6 million inhabitants currently reside in the United States.

Salvadoran immigrants to San Francisco at the beginning of the 20th century tended to be upper-middle-class or upper-class business people, and those who arrived in the 1940s came mostly from middle-class backgrounds. In contrast, the flow from the 1980s onward encompassed all sectors of Salvadoran society, as the political upheaval in their country weighed heavily in individuals' decision to emigrate. The civil war in El Salvador meant that urban migrants from the working, lower-middle, and middle classes left the country, as did upper-class Salvadorans. Still, the most impoverished Salvadorans (who make up the majority of the country's population) were rarely able to move to the U.S. Instead they migrated internally, remained in El Salvador as displaced persons, or migrated to neighboring countries like Costa Rica and Guatemala and particularly to refugee camps in Honduras and Mexico.

Salvadorans have established communities across the U.S., notably in Los Angeles, Miami, Houston, New York, Chicago, Atlanta, Seattle, Phoenix, and several midwestern cities as well as in mid-sized towns. Though San Francisco has the longest history of Salvadoran migration, Los Angeles is home to the largest concentration of Salvadorans anywhere outside of San Salvador, estimated at close to half a million, or about 60 percent of the total number of Salvadorans in the U.S. The Washington, D.C., metropolitan area is a relatively new destination, and the overwhelming majority of Salvadorans there have arrived in the past two decades (there were 6,887 Salvadorans in Washington, D.C., in 1990 and 15,886 in 2000). Yet Washington is the only U.S. city where Salvadorans make up the majority of the Latino population (10.5 percent). Salvadorans also have settled in other immigrant-receiving cities all over the country, the majority having arrived either directly from El Salvador or from California in the 1990s.

Gender has played an important role in the formation of some of these communities. Whereas mostly men arrived to work in war-time industries in San Francisco in the 1940s, women are believed to be the pioneers of the migration to Washington, D.C., as those who worked as domestics for U.S. diplomats in El Salvador in the 1960s were hired to continue their work in the U.S. Across the country, these diverse configurations affect Salvadorans' perceptions of themselves, their participation in the local community and relations with other groups, and their continued relationships with their communities in El Salvador.

Legal Status and Its Ramifications

For many Salvadorans, the journey to the United States is not a straight line from origin to arrival; it is often plagued with uncertainty and danger, as many undertake the trip by land. The crossing of at least three international borders, often without documents, makes the trip a long and arduous process. Traveling by land often involves complicated arrangements with *coyotes* (smugglers) as well as robberies, assaults, and extortion by local authorities. Thus, the journey usually takes a couple of months, sometimes longer. Stiffer immigration laws and the militarization of the U.S.-Mexico border since the mid-1990s have made it even more costly, both physically and financially. But Salvadoran migrants have had powerful reasons for undertaking such perilous journeys: to escape persecution, generalized violence, and/or harsh conditions brought about by years of civil war and its aftermath.

After the civil conflict in El Salvador officially ended, in 1992, migration to the U.S. continued. The rigid socioeconomic structures that led to the civil war and to significant migration are still in place, and in the aftermath of the war, El Salvador has been subject to waves of violence—the homicide rate is one of the highest in the hemisphere—and high levels of unemployment and underemployment. These factors continue to create structural and social conditions that prompt emigration, but they alone do not explain why so many Salvadorans specifically come to the U.S. The social networks already established in this country have played a central role. However, these networks have been forged over a long history of U.S. political, military, economic, social, and cultural influence in El Salvador.

In the United States, Salvadorans have faced a cumbersome web of legal obstacles and confusing and intractable immigration laws. Although many left their country because of the civil war and the detrimental effects of its trauma on their lives (confirmed by research), they were not officially recognized as refugees by the U.S. government, largely owing to U.S. foreign policy toward El Salvador. During the war, the Salvadoran government fought the opposition with substantial U.S. support, making it impossible for the U.S. government to legally recognize refugees fleeing from the conflict.

Once on U.S. soil, Salvadorans could apply for political asylum, but they did not fare well, and less than 3 percent were granted asylum. Those who arrived before

January 1, 1982, applied for amnesty under the Immigration Reform Control Act (IRCA), but the thousands who arrived in the 1980s, at the height of the political conflict, were ineligible. Immigrants' rights groups lobbied on the Salvadorans' behalf, and eventually, in 1990, Congress granted temporary protected status (TPS) to all Salvadorans. This special dispensation allowed Salvadorans to live and work in the U.S. for a period of 18 months; it was extended a few times and finally ended in 1994.

In the same year, Salvadorans whose asylum applications had been turned down, as well as TPS beneficiaries, were allowed to resubmit asylum applications. Initially 28 percent of these applications were successful, but the number has since declined to earlier levels, around 3 percent. Some Salvadorans were included as beneficiaries of the 1997 Nicaraguan Adjustment and Central American Relief Act (NACARA). Salvadorans who entered the country before September 1990 could be granted a "cancellation of removal" (cancellation of deportation), which meant that those who had already been placed in deportation procedures and were therefore required to appear before an immigration judge could request that their status be readjusted to that of a permanent resident. Immigrants' rights groups have lobbied to extend to Salvadorans the benefits that NACARA confers to Nicaraguans and other nationals, including adjustment to legal permanent residence without a hearing on a case-by-case basis. In October 1998, however, Congress voted to deny Salvadorans such benefits. After the devastating earthquakes of 2001 in El Salvador, the United States once again provided TPS to Salvadorans for a period of nine months, a dispensation that has been extended twice and as of this writing is due to expire in September 2007.

Given the difficulty of obtaining legal status, it is not surprising that, according to the 2000 Census, only about one quarter of Salvadoran immigrants have naturalized and a large proportion remain undocumented. The Immigration and Naturalization Service estimated in 1998 that close to 60 percent of Salvadorans were in the country without documents or were in the process of obtaining them. As a result, Salvadorans have been depicted as one of the most vulnerable immigrant groups in America. The question of legality is paramount for any immigrant group, but for Salvadorans it has become a constant struggle that reverberates in all aspects of their lives, including work, family, and community.

Labor Force Participation

The majority of Salvadorans in the U.S. participate in the labor force—62.1 percent in 2000, with an unemployment rate of only 4.9 percent—but their lack of legal status and generally low educational levels have limited their job opportunities. According to the 2000 Census, about two thirds of Salvadorans do not have a high school diploma, nearly one third are high school graduates, and about 5 percent have a bachelor's degree or higher; close to half speak English well or very well. In general, Salvadorans have found jobs in manufacturing, retail trade, and personal services industries. In 2000 just over 40 percent worked as operators and laborers, 15 percent worked in technical occupations and sales, and just over 30 percent worked in service occupations. Better-educated men have found white-collar jobs, whereas those with lower educational levels have found work in construction, landscaping, restaurants and hotels, and janitorial services. In times of economic downturn, many turn to day labor and can be found congregated on street corners looking for work in cities like Los Angeles, San Francisco, New York, and Phoenix as well as in suburbs across the country.

Better-educated women work in clerical and administrative jobs, while women with lower levels of education work as housekeepers, caretakers for the elderly and children, hotel chambermaids, and janitors. These distinctions are not always clear-cut, since even those with skills and/or high educational levels (including college graduates) and substantial work experience usually find themselves in low-level jobs when they are undocumented or in a legal limbo. Some Salvadorans have opened businesses that cater mostly to compatriots and other Latino clientele, and a growing proportion are self-employed. Many are street vendors, and in Los Angeles they have organized to lobby for the legalization of street vending.

Job opportunities for Salvadorans also vary by location. For instance, jobs in construction are plentiful in Washington, D.C., during certain times of the year and tend to be better-paying than in other cities. There have been reports of Salvadoran men who travel from Los Angeles to Washington every spring for the construction season and then return to Los Angeles during the winter. The jobs that women traditionally perform, such as baby-sitting, are usually available even during recessionary times, and in some cities, like Los Angeles, Salvadoran (and Guatemalan) women are much more likely than other immigrant women to work as domestics, cleaners, and child-care workers.

Wages among Salvadorans in the United States are generally low. Their average personal income in 2000 was $17,000, and their median household income was $42,000, a figure that can be explained by the high proportion of Salvadorans—nearly 50 percent—who live in households of four or more. Importantly, their already low incomes have to be stretched substantially and in different directions, as many send remittances to their families back home (estimated to be about $1 billion annually). The average Salvadoran sends between $100 to $150 three to four times each year, and approximately one third of households in El Salvador receive remittances.

Gender and Family

At the time of the 2000 Census, 52 percent of Salvadorans in the U.S. were men, a ratio that has remained relatively unchanged during the post-1980 migration. Still,

Salvadoran women have figured prominently in this migration, sometimes as pioneers. Some came to reunite with or accompany husbands, parents, or other relatives, but others came on their own. According to a study by Repak in Washington, D.C., two thirds of the Central American women interviewed (mostly Salvadorans) made the decision to migrate on their own, without the collaboration or assistance of male partners or fathers, demonstrating an unusual degree of autonomy.

Immigration law, theoretically gender-neutral, affects men and women differently, and often the legal status of a woman is tied to reunification with a husband or family group. In fact, more Salvadoran women than men are undocumented or in the process of regularizing their status. In spite of their lack of legal status, Salvadoran women have been able to find work relatively more easily than men, even when the economy is not strong, but this has not translated into higher incomes, as Salvadoran women generally earn less than men do. And although we would expect that earning an income would lead to more equitable relations in the home, this has not happened for all Salvadoran women. Sometimes women's steady employment ends up reinforcing gender subordination, as women make efforts not to upset their male partners at home.

Some Salvadorans arrive single and establish families in the U.S., arrangements that do not always work out smoothly. Others leave their families back home, as traveling by land can be dangerous for children, or worry that they will have little time to supervise their children once they are in the United States. Some bring their families, but given the high crime rates and the high prevalence of drugs in the neighborhoods where many Salvadorans live, many send the children back to El Salvador (though this practice may change in the face of the current high crime rates and violence in that country). For these families, parents labor in the U.S. to send money for the school supplies and other necessities of children who are in the care of relatives back home. This means that many Salvadorans live in "transnational families," separated by distance but remaining closely in touch through various forms of modern technology. The uncertain legal status of many family members makes it difficult for them to see each other regularly, as they cannot travel back and forth if they are undocumented or in the process of regularizing their status. Not surprisingly, when they finally reunite, sometimes parents and children cannot find the family of their memories and cannot even physically recognize each other. Thus, family separations among Salvadorans cannot simply be celebrated as part of the immigrants' enduring links with their communities of origin, as these separations often involve heavy costs, including anxiety, dislocation, and alienation.

Approximately 6 percent of Salvadorans in the U.S. are 15 years old or younger. Many Salvadoran youngsters face the triple burden of entering adolescence, adjusting to a new society, and living in a reconstituted family, which puts pressure on them and other family members. Many have also been exposed to the ravages of war, witnessing the abduction or murder of family members, tortured bodies in the streets, bombings, crossfire, and other forms of violence. Those who did not witness such atrocities have heard their family members talk about such experiences, and thus for many, memories of the civil war and its aftermath have shaped who they are and how they relate to their parents' home country. Once in the U.S., many Salvadoran children also are burdened with adult duties that sometimes interfere with their schooling and emotional development. Because they often acquire English-language skills and become familiar with U.S. culture before other family members do, they frequently act as translators and interpreters of the new culture for their parents. In these roles they acquire new authority and status, a situation that can exacerbate or spur intergenerational conflict. In spite of many adversities, however, many Salvadoran youngsters exhibit remarkable resilience and contribute meaningfully and in diverse ways to their communities, schools, and families.

Older Salvadorans also face challenges in the United States. Even though only 3.5 percent of Salvadorans in the 2000 Census were 65 and over (a small percentage compared to the number of older people in other immigrant groups), they constitute an important presence in their families and face a particular set of obstacles. It is typically impossible for them to find jobs, and they seldom master the English language; as a result they become dependent on relatives for the practicalities of life. Although cultural dictates among Salvadoran migrants call for children to support parents in old age, older immigrants become especially dependent on their children for financial, material, informational, and emotional comfort. The high cost of health care is a primary concern among older migrants who lack access to health insurance or the financial means to pay out-of-pocket. They may have labored hard in their home country, but they are not guaranteed security in their old age either there or in the U.S. However, older Salvadorans contribute in important ways to their communities and families. They often care for their grandchildren, and they are important transmitters of culture, providing key emotional and moral support and advising and comforting younger family members.

Church and Community

The church is one of the most important places for Salvadorans to interact with others. Through the church they are often able to remain connected to their home country, as churches create institutional spaces that link the migrants with communities back home. Salvadorans attend Catholic and mainline Protestant churches as well as evangelical and Pentecostal ones, often traveling substantial distances to get to their places of worship. In El Salvador religious congregations were pivotal before, during, and after the civil war. In the United States, in the absence of government assistance, the Catholic Church and the main Protestant denominations have filled the vacuum for these de facto refugees and have been actively involved in improving their lives by providing a range of services. Churches have created sanctuaries to protect Salvadorans (and Guatemalans) from deportation, provided settlement assistance, championed the legal struggle that eventually granted to Salvadorans temporary protected status and an opportunity to resubmit asylum applications, and issued pastoral calls to ask coreligionists to welcome immigrants into their communities. Evangelical churches have not created a similar infrastructure of support and lack the institutional organization that permits the Catholic and mainline Protestant churches to coordinate larger efforts to protect and press for change. Nonetheless, their role in immigrants' lives has been central, and church members obtain help with employment, health, and housing from coreligionists. Newcomers themselves establish many of these smaller churches and open up new temples to welcome their brothers and sisters in need.

Salvadorans also find themselves participating in the heavily Latino communities where they often live, interacting with neighbors, coworkers, and bosses from a variety of national backgrounds. Such interactions have led to different forms of coalition-building, although at times these relations have been fraught with tension and competition. One important component of these interactions, and ultimately of how Salvadorans will become part of the larger American population, is their self-identification. In the 2000 Census, in response to the question on race, one third of Salvadorans identified themselves as "white alone," but 57 percent identified as "some other race alone" and 6.5 percent as "two or more races." Such self-identification will undoubtedly shape the way they behave with others and become incorporated into the larger society as well as the kinds of links they create and maintain with El Salvador.

Bibliography

Hamilton, Nora, and Norma Stoltz Chinchilla. 2001. *Seeking Community in a Global City: Guatemalans and Salvadorans in Los Angeles.* Philadelphia: Temple University Press.

Landolt, Patricia, Lilian Autler, and Sonia Baires. 1999. "From Hermano Lejano to Hermano Mayor: The Dialectics of Salvadoran Transnationalism." *Ethnic and Racial Studies* 22, 2: 290–315.

Lopez, David E., Eric Popkin, and Edward Telles. 1997. "Central Americans: At the Bottom, Struggling to Get Ahead." In Roger Waldinger and Mehdi Bozorgmehr, eds., *Ethnic Los Angeles,* pp. 279–304. New York: Russell Sage Foundation.

Mahler, Sarah J. 1995. *Salvadorans in Suburbia: Symbiosis and Conflict.* Boston: Allyn and Bacon.

———. 1999. "Engendering Transnational Migration: A Case Study of Salvadorans." *American Behavioral Scientist* 42, 4: 690–719.

Menjívar, Cecilia. 2000. *Fragmented Ties: Salvadoran Immigrant Networks in America.* Berkeley: University of California Press.

———. 2003. "Religion and Immigration in Comparative Perspective: Salvadorans in Catholic and Evangelical Communities in San Francisco, Phoenix, and Washington, D.C." *Sociology of Religion* 64, 1: 21–45.

————. 2006. "Liminal Legality: Salvadoran and Guatemalan Immigrants' Lives in the United States." *American Journal of Sociology* 111, 4: 999–1037.

Menjívar, Cecilia, Julie Davanzo, Lisa Greenwell, and R. Burciaga Valdez. 1998. "Remittance Behavior of Filipino and Salvadoran Immigrants in Los Angeles." *International Migration Review* 32, 1: 99–128.

Repak, Terry A. 1995. *Waiting on Washington: Central American Workers in the Nation's Capital.* Philadelphia: Temple University Press.

Europe: Western

Germany, Italy, Ireland, Portugal, Greece, Spain

Donna R. Gabaccia

Once the vast majority entering the United States (notably during the period of the so-called mass migrations, between 1850 and 1930), immigrants from Europe have declined since 1965 to only a small minority—less than 15 percent—of newcomers. Dwindling immigrant populations have been most obvious among those western European countries that once sent the largest numbers of immigrants to the U.S., notably Germany, Italy, and Ireland.

A century ago, few Americans would have thought of Germany, Italy, Ireland, Portugal, Greece, and Spain as a logical grouping. Immigrant populations from Germany and Ireland, the two largest groups among the so-called old (northern European) immigrants, had peaked in 1890 and were declining. By contrast, the numbers of Italians and others from southern and eastern European countries—the so-called new immigrants—rose rapidly after 1890. At that time, people born in the Mediterranean countries were regarded as racially quite different from northern Europeans such as Germans, and they were treated that way under U.S. immigration policy and its restrictive national-origins quotas until 1965. Since 1965, however, as the European Union (EU) has become an economic and increasingly also a political reality, Americans' perceptions of immigrants from Europe have changed fundamentally. Today immigrants from all six countries seem more like each other and more like the Euro-American majority population of the U.S. than they did in the past.

Still, white Europeans from the relatively prosperous countries of the EU appear as a homogeneous group mainly only when contrasted racially to the much larger and typically darker populations of recent immigrants from Asia and Latin America. At least at present, the existence of the EU has not obliterated national sentiments among Europeans or among European immigrants living in the U.S. Sizable cultural differences between the latest arrivals from Europe and those who arrived earlier in the 20th century (along with their children and grandchildren) also reveal how class and occupational differences discourage the formation of a single panethnic or Euro-American identity in the 21st century.

A Brief History of European Immigration

Immigration laws passed by the U.S. Congress in 1917, 1921, and 1924 placed severe restrictions on immigration from many European countries and essentially ended immigration from Asia. Reducing the numbers arriving from southern and eastern Europe was perhaps the main goal Congress hoped to achieve with this legislation, since Europeans were the overwhelming majority (as high as 95 percent) of immigrants in the years before World War I. In restricting immigration from Europe, legislators drew on the racial science of the late 19th century, which distinguished between "Mediterranean," "Alpine," and "Nordic" European races, but implemented restriction through highly discriminatory and differential national quotas. Quotas for each nation were determined by calculating 2 percent of each nationality group's population in the U.S. in 1890. Under this system, for example, only 3,500–5,000 Italians could hope to enter the country yearly after 1929, while quotas from Britain and Germany were much larger and often went unfilled. Unlike residents of Britain and Germany, the Jewish, Catholic, and Eastern Orthodox "new" immigrants from southern Europe struck American restrictionists as peoples unlikely to assimilate to American culture. Restrictive laws allowed the close relatives of naturalized aliens (and later permanent resident aliens) to enter the U.S. outside the quotas; nevertheless, the numbers of Italians and Greeks entering the U.S. plummeted. In the 1930s and 1940s, depression and war reduced immigration further.

However, the numbers of immigrants entering the U.S. from Europe did rise sharply, if temporarily, in the early to mid-1950s, before dropping again by the early 1960s (see Table 1). Clearly, patterns of migration after 1945 differed sharply by national group. Displaced persons from Germany swelled numbers in the immediate aftermath of the war. The Immigration Act of 1952 introduced immigration policy changes (including the admission of refugees, the lifting of Asian exclusions, and the creation of preferences for skilled workers) but left discriminatory national-origin quotas in place and thus provided little relief for unskilled workers, especially those from southern Europe. Germans, who were less affected by restrictive quotas, remained the largest single group of immigrants from Europe, followed by the more heavily restricted Italians and Greeks, who were nevertheless able to take some advantage of provisions for family reunification. Responding to American restrictions, many prospective immigrants from Italy and Greece chose destinations other than the U.S. after World War II. In the 1950s and 1960s, for example, more Italians migrated to Canada than to the United States. By the late 1950s, furthermore, as the German, French, and British economies recovered with assistance from the U.S.-funded Marshall Plan, Greek, Italian, Spanish, and Portuguese mi-

Table 1   Western European immigration to the U.S., by country of birth, 1945–2002

Year	Country of birth					
	Ireland	Germany	Greece	Italy	Portugal	Spain
1945–1949	20,355	65,153	6,592	45,721	3,877	1,954
1950–1954	23,923	168,117	16,503	51,395	5,913	3,464
1955–1959	39,336	176,790	29,380	131,505	8,628	5,989
1960–1964	32,199	138,530	20,625	86,860	19,710	10,136
1965–1969	16,321	83,534	56,943	109,750	53,385	17,950
1970–1974	8,528	36,971	64,999	106,572	57,283	20,170
1975–1979	6,158	32,110	40,508	43,066	51,998	12,052
1980–1984	5,181	33,933	18,394	20,128	25,977	8,076
1985–1989	16,979	28,106	10,175	11,793	14,696	6,263
1990–1994	58,172	38,194	10,003	13,290	15,557	8,172
1995–1997	8,047	18,708	3,810	6,714	7,264	4,221
1998–1999	1,756	10,673	1,590	3,361	2,607	1,917
2000–2002	4,262	26,485	3,189	4,262	4,354	4,366

Sources: Table BCS.C.4 in Robert E. Barde, Susan B. Carter, and Richard Sutch, "Immigration." In Susan B. Carter, Scott S. Gartner, Michael R. Haines, Alan L. Olmstead, Richard Sutch, and Gavin Wright, eds., *Historical Statistics of the United States, Millennial Edition* (New York: Cambridge University Press, 2006). *Statistical Yearbook of the Immigration and Naturalization Service,* 2002 (Washington, D.C.: U.S. Department of Justice, U.S. Immigration and Naturalization Service).

grants provided the labor power for northern European economic recovery. By the late 1950s and 1960s, Italy's own "economic miracle" revealed itself as southern Italians flocked to jobs in the northern part of the country.

Postwar immigrants from Europe settled unevenly throughout the United States. Irish and Italian immigrants clustered in New England and in mid-Atlantic cities; Portuguese immigrants settled mainly in New England. Greeks and especially Germans scattered more widely. Especially for the heavily restricted immigrants from the Mediterranean, postwar community life continued to revolve around church and family, with local grocery stores, cafés, mutual aid associations, and newspapers in their native tongues signaling their continued "foreignness" to American neighbors, even when those neighbors viewed them—as they increasingly did after World War II—as racially white.

Immigrants from Europe were also outspoken critics of discriminatory U.S. immigration policy. Throughout the 1950s ethnic organizations such as the American Committee on Italian Migration supported legislative reform, and intellectuals of recent immigrant parentage argued that the U.S., as a "nation of immigrants," should abandon the racist policies of the past, eliminate quotas, and again open its doors to the downtrodden. Both the American labor movement and legislators from large northern cities were among the strongest supporters of the Hart-Celler Immigration Act, passed in 1965. Aging European immigrants and their children expected that the law, which included provisions for family reunification, would lead to a new surge of immigration from those parts of Europe that had in the recent past sent large numbers to the U.S. Supporters of immigration reform were rather quickly surprised to discover that this would not be the case.

European Immigration since 1965

By the time the U.S. eliminated national-origin quotas in 1965, Europe's postwar economic recovery was no longer limited to northern Europe but was changing life around the Mediterranean as well. Germany had become a major importer of foreign labor through its guest worker programs, but after 1960 it increasingly drew on Turkey rather than Yugoslavia, Italy, Spain, and Portugal for its workers. Around the Mediterranean, economic development had surged. By the mid-1970s the numbers of Italians leaving Italy equaled the numbers of foreigners seeking homes and jobs in Italy; thereafter, Italy attracted more workers than it lost. And within three decades, Spain and Greece also became attractive to immigrant workers from Asia, Africa, and (after 1989) the formerly communist countries of eastern Europe. The impact on U.S. immigration of such economic and political change in Europe was predictable. To the surprise of congressional representatives who had made family reunification one of the strongest grounds for allotting visas (thereby hoping to attract the relatives of earlier European immigrants), far fewer Europeans than expected took advantage of these provisions. Under the 1965 law, unskilled potential immigrants continued to experience difficulties obtaining visas for entry to the U.S., and Asians and Latin Americans quickly replaced Europeans as the main sources of U.S. immigration.

Migrations from Europe did not end, of course. The numbers of European students, temporary visitors, and tourists entering the U.S. grew steadily. And even after 1965, with discriminatory quotas eliminated, southern and northern European immigrants continued to respond to the attraction of the U.S. in somewhat diverse ways, as Table 1 suggests. Migration from Germany dropped sharply and immediately, from 24,000 in 1965 to less than 7,000 yearly throughout most of the next three decades. Italians, Greeks, and Portuguese outnumbered Germans as immigrants throughout the 1970s. Declines in Irish migration were equally precipitous, from a relatively modest high of 5,500 in 1965 to around 1,000 yearly in the 1970s; in the late 1980s and early 1990s, however, Irish immigration temporarily rose dramatically—to 17,256 in 1994—before dropping to earlier levels. In rather strong contrast, migrations from Italy remained stable, and those from Greece increased significantly in the decade after 1965 before declining after 1974. Migrations from Portugal and Spain increased and remained fairly strong until the late 1970s; small increases in the 1980s then gave way to sharp reductions in the 1990s.

As this suggests, homeland conditions may have driven emigration decisions as much as any magnetic appeal of the U.S. did. In the case of Ireland, for example, a deep recession in the 1980s generated a legal migration of highly skilled workers to the U.S.; they were accompanied by significant numbers of unskilled people who were unable to acquire visas in a system that privileged the highly skilled and who traveled without proper documentation and became "illegal" immigrants. (Anecdotal evidence suggests that large numbers of both groups may have returned to Europe when employment opportunities opened in the EU.) Since 1990 other European destinations have become more attractive than the U.S., especially for young, unskilled Irish people seeking to go abroad.

The populations of European immigrants living in the U.S. today are still substantial. At the time of the 2000 Census, aliens and naturalized citizens born in Germany numbered over 700,000; those born in Italy were almost half a million. The comparable figure for Portugal was over 200,000; for Ireland and Greece, over 150,000 each; and for Spain, somewhat under 90,000. Recent arrivals now outnumber the even more sharply declining populations of elderly immigrants who arrived in the U.S. during the period of racially and nationally based immigration quotas between 1920 and 1965.

European immigrants today no longer fit the portrait of the "huddled masses" that Americans associate with Ellis Island and with immigrants from Europe in the past. Some Europeans arriving over the past four decades came to the U.S. to join their families. Many more, however, have entered with visas allotted under a preference system that privileges highly skilled immigrants over blue-collar workers. The lottery system for "green cards" introduced by the U.S. may also privilege Europeans by requiring facility in English and higher levels of education than can easily be obtained in poorer countries.

As an examination of the patterns of work, education, and ethnic association of each European immigrant nationality indicates, class differences now divide most European nationality groups. The differences between the more affluent new arrivals and the older working-class and lower-middle-class generations is particularly pronounced among the largest groups—Italians, Germans, and Irish—whose migrations and immigrant populations peaked before World War II; these groups were not well positioned to use family reunification provisions to build on older local, regional, or familial migrations in the new century. Well-educated newcomers often speak standard versions of their national languages, something that earlier immigrants, long separated from their homelands, cannot do, thus exacerbating class differences between the two groups.

German Immigrants

Today German immigrants to the U.S. are only slightly more numerous than the very large group (over 500,000) of American citizens born in Germany of American parents (many of them serving in the U.S. military). Because so many of this population of immigrants arrived decades ago, and because Germany is home to so many military bases (where American servicemen often marry German women), females significantly outnumber males among German immigrants. In just forty years, as older immigrants aged and the number of new arrivals dwindled, immigrant populations from Germany have dropped by one third.

Far more than in the past, German immigrants today live scattered throughout the U.S. The rural Midwest is no longer home to the largest group; rather, the southeastern Atlantic states (including Florida), where almost a quarter now live, are dominant. As this suggests, German immigrants are like longtime Americans in finding the Sunbelt states attractive for both employment and retirement; they have also settled in significant proportions in states along the Pacific coast. Germans are like native-born white Americans in many other respects, too. They are homeowners in a nation that values property ownership. Their families are very small, with high rates of childlessness; the typical German immigrant woman, like her American counterpart, gives birth to only one or two children.

The opportunity to work still attracts small numbers of Germans to the U.S. Among working-age Germans, unemployment in 2000 was only 2 percent. But the kind of work available has changed dramatically over the past century. Of German immigrant men between 25 and 64 years old, four in ten worked in managerial and professional fields and another 20 percent earned salaries in technical, sales, or administrative positions. Eighty percent of working-age German immigrant women also work in these fields, albeit disproportionately in the second category. Immigrant women were more likely to work in the U.S. than their agemates in Germany—just a third were outside the American labor force in the year 2000.

The rise of Europe as a major regional economy in a globalizing world has affected identity formation among German immigrants in significant ways. Although some immigrants work for German corporations in the U.S. and send their children to German "Saturday schools" in the expectation that they will return home, Germany's postwar prosperity has neither prevented emigration nor encouraged significant rates of return. Most Germans immigrants in the U.S. consider themselves to have integrated or assimilated rather quickly, even if they continue to speak German at home and to maintain transnational contacts through visits and frequent communication with relatives in Europe. In 2000 two thirds of German immigrants were naturalized U.S. citizens. Since this proportion has dropped slightly from previous decades, it may reflect a slow reorientation in Germans' assessments of the benefits of U.S. citizenship or a growing preference for long-term life in the U.S. as resident aliens and for transnational lives.

In entering the U.S., recent arrivals from Germany take up residence in a country where almost a quarter of the population claims descent from the German immigrants of the past. The societies, religious practices, and celebrations of ethnic German Americans—from Steuben Day parades to Oktoberfests featuring beer-drinking, men dressed in lederhosen, and women in dirndls or *trachten;* from the conservative Lutheran churches of the Missouri Synod to immigrant mutual aid, musical, and gymnast groups—do not typically appeal to well-educated and cosmopolitan newcomers. Like most middle-class European professionals and white-collar workers, German immigrants are secular in outlook; they have considerable lived experience in contemporary Germany and thus little understanding of the celebrations and organizations that met the needs of earlier immigrants—many of them farmers, working-class people, and rural dwellers—or that represented a Germany of an earlier time. Having lived closer to the historical presence of the Third Reich and the Holocaust, today's Germans may also see less to celebrate in the German past than the descendants of earlier immigrants do.

Italian Immigrants

Because so many Italian immigrants arrived many decades ago, their numbers too are declining—by over half in the past forty years. Earlier Italian migrations were heavily male-dominated, so the current immigrant population is relatively more gender-balanced than some other groups, even as it ages. And unlike Germans, who have scattered more widely recently, almost half of Italian immigrants still live in the mid-Atlantic states (with New York City and its Long Island, New Jersey, and Westchester suburbs housing the largest cluster); another 12 percent live in New England.

In contrast to a group that was once overwhelmingly working-class and unskilled or semiskilled, today less than 40 percent of working-age immigrant Italian men and only 14 percent of working-age immigrant Italian women are employed in manufacturing. Levels of employment in managerial and professional work among men have risen steadily, but service work still outpaces employment in white-collar technical, sales, and administrative positions. By contrast, the numbers of Italian immigrant women working in these lower white-collar fields now challenges those in manufacturing and far outstrips women in service jobs. Italian immigrants were once known (however inaccurately) for their particularly patriarchal family and gender ideologies and for their stay-at-home wives and mothers, but working-age Italian immigrant women now typically work for wages. Forty percent, however, remain outside the labor force—a figure somewhat higher than among their German or Irish counterparts. Fertility among immigrant Italians has dropped in recent years as marriage rates, childless marriages, and women bearing only one or two children have increased. The number of Italian immigrant women with more than three children has declined from 38 percent to only 11 percent since 1980.

For Italian immigrants entering the U.S. under provisions for family reunification, the persistence of chain migrations from particular villages and regions, blue-collar employment, and settlement in the urban Northeast has guaranteed some continuity in identity between older and newer arrivals. The Catholic Church, an Italian-language press, societies such as the Sons of Italy, and local ethnic organizations continue to provide assistance and fellowship during the initial years of adjustment, especially for blue-collar immigrants. The same cannot be said for the better-educated and more highly skilled Italians who have arrived in growing numbers in the past two decades. More secular in orientation, urban in origin, and left-wing in their politics, these newer immigrants are comfortable with cosmopolitan identities as Italians and Europeans. They are less enthusiastic about older immigrants' stereotypes of Italy as an impoverished land of high unemployment, their use of dialect, their blue-collar lifestyles, and their "Italian" food, which rarely resembles the cuisines of modern Italy. Professional immigrants are also more likely to contemplate a return to Italy and to maintain their Italian citizenship; joining together with the 4.5 million *italiani all'estero* (Italians abroad), they are more likely to pressure Italy's government for representation and the right to vote in elections there than their older immigrant counterparts were. Although three quarters of Italian immigrants were naturalized U.S. citizens at the time of the 2000 Census, that proportion has dropped very slightly in subsequent years. This suggests that for recent, highly skilled immigrants from Italy, like those from Germany, transnational lives as Italians or as Europeans may be producing different identities from the ethnic Italian American ones favored by earlier immigrants and their children and grandchildren.

Portuguese Immigrants

Alongside the dramatic political changes that accompanied decolonization and the transition to democracy in Portugal, migrations from this country exhibit considerable continuity with the past. Portuguese immigrants to the U.S. have come fairly continuously from the Azorean Islands, now an autonomous region of Portugal. (It has been estimated that 80 percent of today's Portuguese immigrants originated in the Azores.) Cape Verdeans, who also formed an important component of past Portuguese migrations to the U.S., no longer appear in census listings as being of Portuguese origin, since their island homeland became independent in 1975.

Like those who preceded them, recent Portuguese immigrants cluster in a few locations in New England, where most have worked in manufacturing. At the time of the 2000 Census, almost half of Portuguese immigrants still lived in New England, where they concentrate in towns such as New Bedford, Fall River, and Boston, Massachusetts. Another quarter live in the nearby mid-Atlantic states, and over 10 percent live in longstanding communities in the Pacific coast states—for example, in Santa Clara, California. Especially among working-age male immigrants, furthermore, manufacturing remains important: over half of Portuguese men work in manufacturing or crafts. Their blue-collar jobs are probably an indication of their still limited education.

Nonetheless, there are signs that Portuguese immigrants have changed in recent years, most notably in their gender and family patterns. Whereas only two decades ago a small but significant minority (7.5 percent) of Portuguese women had given birth to more than six children, the comparable figure in the 2000 Census was con-

siderably less than 1 percent. Working-age Portuguese women are actually somewhat less likely to be in the labor force today than was the case 20 years ago, perhaps
because their families have greater financial stability and because higher, more secure wages are earned by other family members. Portuguese women are nevertheless
still more likely to hold jobs than their Italian or Greek immigrant counterparts.
Those women who do work are also much less heavily concentrated in manufacturing and blue-collar jobs (less than one third) than are the men of their families. Almost as many Portuguese women work in technical, sales, and administrative positions as in industrial production, and almost one in five is employed in service
work, many in restaurants, hospitals, and cleaning services.

The life of Portuguese immigrants, much like that of their Italian counterparts,
continues to revolve around church and community organizations. For the majority
of working-class immigrants, the social distance between the majority who arrived
before 1960 and the newcomers is often not great. Unlike Italians, however, Portuguese have relatively low rates of naturalization; only slightly more than half have
become citizens. Return visits to the Azores are very common, and longtime immigrants continue to sponsor and provide assistance to newcomers to their settlements
in New England.

Greek Immigrants

A smaller group than either the Italians or the Portuguese, whom they otherwise resemble both demographically and socially, Greek immigrants in the U.S. stand out
for communities that still revolve to a considerable degree around distinctive Greek
Orthodox churches. The most recent arrivals may be more secular in orientation
than past immigrants, but churches continue to unite newcomers and old-timers,
especially in smaller cities and towns where small numbers of Greeks have lived
since the early years of the 20th century. In addition to conducting religious services, Greek churches support year-round language and cultural programs for their
members, attended not only by first-generation immigrants but by their bilingual
children and grandchildren, too. Many Greek churches sponsor an annual festival
that raises funds by inviting American and immigrant neighbors to learn about
Greek food, history, and culture.

As this suggests, Greek communities continue to strike their neighbors as distinctive. In part this reflects the fact that Greek immigrants are less concentrated in a
few major northeastern cities than either the Catholic Italians or the Portuguese are.
At the time of the 2000 Census, less than half of all Greek immigrants lived in the
Northeast, and Greeks were also better represented in the Upper Midwest and the
Southeast than other southern European groups. Their wider dispersal reflects a
long history of work in small business, which sent Greeks in search of clients for
their services as candy-sellers, grocers, or restaurateurs in the years before World
War II. The persistence of visible and distinctive, if scattered, communities should

not, however, be mistaken for a lack of interest in American life. Rates of naturalization among Greeks are comparable to those for Italians.

Alone among the southern European immigrant populations discussed here, Greek immigrant populations still show vestiges of the strongly male-dominated migrations of the past. Men continue to outnumber women, albeit by much smaller margins than in the past. Work in small businesses—restaurants, diners, produce stores, and the like—also seems to have created a more effective springboard into white-collar work for Greeks than for other southern European immigrants. The 2000 Census found that over half of working-age Greek men earned a living in either managerial or professional fields (39 percent) or technical, sales, and administrative positions (15 percent). Greek women are rather evenly divided among service, professional, and other kinds of white-collar work; relatively few work in factories. Still, working-age Greek women were the most likely of all European immigrants to remain outside the workforce. Whether this reflects conservative gender ideologies or the relative prosperity of Greek immigrant families cannot easily be measured. In any case, Greek immigrant women do not, on average, have significantly larger families than the other immigrants from the Mediterranean.

Irish Immigrants

A relatively privileged group under the restrictions based on national origins, Irish immigrants faced greater hurdles to migration after 1965—notably their genealogical distance from relatives, who could not sponsor them under provisions for family reunification, and their employment in blue-collar or service work, which limited access to visas. While a surge in undocumented and legal migration occurred in response to Irish recession in the 1980s, studies suggest that many Irish professionals returned to Ireland, a country that (like Spain, Greece, and Italy) is now experiencing a net inflow of migrants. The rise of a powerful European economy, to which the Irish now have full access, along with the end of the conflict in Northern Ireland, may help to explain why large numbers of Irish immigrants in the U.S. (almost 40 percent) have not taken up U.S. citizenship. However, Irish immigrants seem more likely than their German counterparts to participate in the festivals and ethnic societies founded by earlier immigrants. A strong sense of oppositional and exile Irish nationalism, often rooted in a shared Catholicism, continues to bridge immigrant generations.

In most respects, though, the once stigmatized Catholic Irish now blend easily into American life. Although most are Catholic, their parishes are now multiethnic, and their families are actually smaller than those of Americans and other northern European immigrants. While the large representation of women seeking work as domestic servants once distinguished Irish from other, more male-dominated migrations, Irish gender ratios today are less imbalanced than those of German immigrants. Once known for their high rates of poverty, most Irish men now work in white-collar professions or other salaried positions. Irish women are no more likely to work in service than other immigrant women, and they are actually more likely to hold professional positions than Irish men are.

Spanish Immigrants

The small American population of immigrants from Spain stands out for its geographical concentration, the recentness of its arrival, and its low rates of naturalization. This reflects the fact that the largest group of Spanish immigrants (almost a third) arrived in the U.S. only in the past thirty years. In addition, only a third of the immigrants who have come from Spain in the past forty years are of Spanish descent. Who, then, are these people?

Although the U.S. has long attracted very small numbers of immigrants from Spain, it is likely that a very high proportion of today's immigrant Spanish population is of Cuban descent, either exiles who fled after the Cuban revolution of 1959, when Fidel Castro came to power, or their children born in Spain. Thus, it is probably no accident that immigrants from Spain resemble Cuban immigrants more generally in clustering heavily in two regions of the U.S. Almost a quarter live in the mid-Atlantic states (notably in New Jersey, which also has a large Cuban population) and in the southeastern Atlantic states (notably in Florida, which has a large Cuban community in Miami).

Immigrants from Spain resemble the profile of Cubans in the U.S. in many other ways, too. Although Spanish immigrants have in recent years been somewhat more likely than other European immigrants to fall below the poverty line, rates of workforce participation for both men and women are higher than for the longer-settled Italian and Greek immigrant populations. Like Cuban immigrants, large proportions of working-age Spanish men (42 percent) and women (47 percent) work in professional and managerial positions, suggesting high levels of education. Adding technical, sales, and administrative occupations to the professionals and managers reveals that 60 percent of immigrant men and almost 80 percent of immigrant women are white-collar workers.

Since Spanish immigrants of Cuban descent are able to merge almost invisibly into the much larger community of Cubans living in the U.S., little is known about them. Many probably share the exile identities of Cuban refugees and continue to work toward or hope for the end of Castro's regime. As in the case of other recently arrived refugees, homeland orientation affects rates of naturalization. Over half of Spanish immigrants living in the United States at the time of the 2000 Census had not become U.S. citizens.

At the turn of the 21st century, immigrants from Europe remain a diverse group, sharply divided between those hailing from NATO countries and those from former Warsaw Pact (communist) countries. Despite the formation of the EU, migration and settlement patterns, work experiences, and family and demographic characteristics continue to differ among northern and southern Europeans—groups that were long treated differently under U.S. immigration policies. In a multicultural America, where both northern and southern European immigrants are now perceived by their American neighbors as whites en route to (or having already achieved) full assimilation and citizenship, most immigrant community organizations formed or joined by recent European immigrants nevertheless continue to emphasize their distinctive national origins. Sometimes these link older and newer immigrant generations (as is more typical among working-class and southern European groups); sometimes, as in the case of the *italiani all'estero,* organization among the more prosperous newcomers takes a more diasporic or transnational turn (with a corresponding diminished interest in U.S. citizenship). Finally, for many highly educated, secular, and cosmopolitan European professionals, life in the U.S. may no longer encourage the kind of "ethnicization" or the adoption of hyphenated ethnic identities that so characterized the Americanization of the European immigrants of the past. At least at present, however, the western European immigrants described here show few signs of creating the kind of panethnic (Euro-American) identity adopted by the children and grandchildren of immigrants from Asia and Latin America. How the further consolidation of the European Union or the response of secularized European immigrants to American expectations of strong religious and racial ("white") identifications will affect the ethnic options of European immigrants remains unsettled. Euro-Americans may very well emerge from the new world melting pot even before a comparable pan-national identity coalesces in the European Union.

Bibliography

Almeida, Linda Dowling. *Irish Immigrants in New York City, 1945–1995.* Bloomington: Indiana University Press, 2001.

Bloemraad, Irene. "Portuguese Immigrants and Citizenship in North America." *Lusotopie* 5 (1999): 103–20.

Cuddy, Dennis. *Contemporary American Immigration: Interpretive Essays (European).* Boston: Twayne, 1982.

Gabaccia, Donna R. *Italy's Many Diasporas.* University College of London Press, 2000.

Kessner, Thomas, and Betty Boyd Caroli. *Today's Immigrants, Their Stories: A New Look at the Newest Americans.* New York: Oxford University Press, 1981.

Kunkelman, Gary A. *The Religion of Ethnicity: Belief and Belonging in a Greek-American Community.* New York: Garland, 1990.

Lobo, A. P., and J. J. Salvo, "Resurgent Irish Immigration to the U.S. in the 1980s and Early 1990s: A Socio-demographic Profile." *International Migration Review* 36, 2 (1998): 257–80.

Williams, Jerry R. *And Yet They Come: Portuguese Immigration from the Azores to the United States.* Staten Island, N.Y.: Center for Migration Studies, 1982.

Europe: Central and Southeastern

Bulgaria, Former Czechoslovakia, Hungary, Romania, Former Yugoslavia

Simone Ispa-Landa

Immigration from Bulgaria, Romania, Hungary, and the former Czechoslovakia since 1965 has comprised diverse groups and falls into two major categories: those who arrived in the U.S. before the end of Soviet influence in their countries of origin and those who have come since the fall of the Berlin Wall in 1989. Despite their many differences, people from these countries are united by their collective history of incorporation into the Soviet sphere of influence. Most of these immigrants—perhaps because of their white skin and good education—have received sympathetic treatment from American employers, educators, and the media and have been quickly incorporated into American middle-class society.

Immigrants from the former Yugoslavia consist primarily of refugees, and the majority have arrived within the past 15 years. Refugees from the Yugoslav wars differ in major ways from immigrants from the other socialist countries: the majority had little time to prepare for life in the U.S. and came not in search of a new citizenship or a better way of life but as a last hope for physical survival in the face of genocide.

Recent Immigration from Central and Southeastern Europe

Most immigrants from Hungary, Bulgaria, Czechoslovakia, and Romania who arrived in the U.S. in the 1960s, 1970s, and 1980s were educated urban people who were motivated to emigrate by disgust with corrupt governments, mandatory atheism, and the prohibition on open criticism of the regimes in their countries of origin. Many sought asylum as refugees. As they had generally earned college degrees before emigrating, they often established themselves as professionals in large cities on the East and West Coasts.

During those years, the Soviet satellite countries had closed border policies. Once a citizen left, he or she was considered a traitor who had betrayed socialist ideals. Former citizens were not allowed to return, and friends and relatives from the homeland who remained in contact were suspected of anticommunist activities. As a result, political dissidents who immigrated to the U.S. expected to make this country their permanent home and usually cut off ties with friends and relatives behind the Iron Curtain. These factors weakened opportunities for their children to learn their native languages and inhibited their children's knowledge of—and interest in—political and cultural events in their countries of origin.

After the collapse of socialism, most immigrants from Hungary, Bulgaria, Czechoslovakia, and Romania were still college-educated, but the primary motivating factor for migration became the search for economic opportunity. In addition, as borders opened, immigrants arrived fully expecting to keep in touch with friends and family at home. Recent immigrants visit their homelands, invest in businesses there, and keep in constant communication with those they left behind. Some plan to retire or move back when conditions are propitious.

In the decades before 1990, the experience of Yugoslav immigrants—primarily Croats and Serbs—was somewhat different. During the communist years, Yugoslavs had more intellectual freedom than the residents of most of central Europe, and in 1961 the head of the government, Marshal Tito, lifted restrictions on emigration. Tito's open border policy meant that emigrants were able to maintain strong ties to Yugoslavia even if they were opposed to the regime there. Unlike their compatriots from the Soviet satellite countries, Yugoslavs who came to the U.S. before the collapse of socialism were prone to view this country as a site of temporary exile and a base from which to promote national independence from the Yugoslav communist federation. They could use a reliable airmail system to communicate with their families back home and could legally call relatives on the telephone. In addition, low-cost air charters facilitated a flow of people between Yugoslavia and the West. Continuous and effective exchanges with Yugoslavia promoted language fluency among the children and grandchildren of immigrants.

Refugees from the Yugoslav wars of the early 1990s who were resettled in the U.S., however, differ in major ways from those who immigrated for political reasons. Unlike immigrants, they typically did not take English classes or think about their financial survival here, as they left their homeland abruptly. Moreover, their transition to life in the U.S. has been complicated by the physical and psychological aftereffects of a brutal war.

Characteristics of Central European Immigrants

Bulgaria. Bulgarians made up a small part of the great wave of immigration of the late 1800s and early 1900s, but those who did come, mostly peasants from the countryside, generally settled in smaller industrial towns in the U.S. Though few

Table 1   Selected characteristics of foreign-born population from former Soviet-bloc states, 2000

	Bulgaria	Czechoslovakia	Hungary	Romania
Total population	35,090	83,080	92,015	135,965
Median age	34.4	54.9	61.1	42.6
Percentage with bachelor's degree or higher	53.8	31	30	35.9
Employment (percentages)				
Managerial, professional, and related	40.6	38.9	44.5	41.0
Service	17.1	17.7	12.2	15.4
Sales and office	18.3	19.3	20.6	18.1
Farming, fishing, forestry	0.2	0.3	0.2	0.2
Construction, extraction, maintenance	8.1	12.8	9.7	10.3
Production, transportation, and material moving	15.7	11.1	12.8	15.1
Median earnings, men 16 and older in the labor force	37,216	41,285	49,154	40,078
Median earnings, women 16 and older in the labor force	27,866	30,760	31,089	29,176

Source: U.S. Bureau of the Census, 2000 Census, Special Tabulations (STP-159).

immigrants came between the early part of the 20th century and World War II, immigration slowed further after the war, and only 8,085 entered the U.S. between the establishment of Bulgaria as a Soviet satellite in 1946 and 1989. Most of these were well-educated, professional political refugees and asylum-seekers who opposed the Soviet takeover of their country. They tended to settle in urban areas.

Of the total population of foreign-born Bulgarians in the U.S. today, 77 percent (27,005 out of 35,090) entered between 1990 and 2000. Like the political refugees who arrived during the communist era, most of today's Bulgarian immigrants are young, college-educated people from urban areas (according to the 2000 Census, 54 percent of Bulgarian immigrants hold a bachelor's degree or higher, compared with 27.8 percent of native-born Americans; see Table 1). However, although they are demographically similar to their politically motivated predecessors, recent immigrants cite the impoverishment of professionals in Bulgaria as the main reason for their immigration.

After the fall of socialism, Bulgaria began the transition to a market economy, which quickly resulted in widespread poverty. In 1990, wages there were lower than in any other post-socialist country. For example, average earnings of the more than 7,000 professors and researchers who emigrated from Bulgaria in 1995 were $50 per month. Highly skilled workers moved to the U.S. in the hope of parlaying their skills into earnings, and to a large degree they have succeeded. Of foreign-born Bulgarians in the country in 2000, 41 percent were employed in professional or managerial positions, 18 percent in sales and office work, and 16 percent were unskilled laborers. The median income for men over 16 years of age in the workforce was $37,216, well above the national median of $27,239 for all foreign-born Americans.

Most Bulgarians today live in urban areas, primarily in New York (15 percent), California (14 percent), Florida (10 percent), Illinois (9 percent), and New Jersey (7 percent). Bulgarians who have arrived in the past 15 years have established cultural centers, churches, and cafés where they can associate with others who speak Bulgarian and who share their experiences. Professional immigrants have established cultural organizations to preserve Bulgarian culture and provide places to socialize; for example, the Bulgarian Society of Atlanta, established in 2001, helps newcomers with practical advice on seeking employment and buying houses and cars. Annual cultural festivals featuring Bulgarian music and dance are common, and proceeds from these events are used to raise money to help the needy in Bulgaria.

Many Bulgarian immigrants hope to raise bilingual children, and some efforts have been made to establish community-wide organizations so that second-generation Bulgarians will continue to speak the language and be familiar with customs in the homeland. For example, a Bulgarian Eastern Orthodox church in Boston established a Sunday school aimed at teaching Bulgarian language, literature, history, and geography to the children of immigrants in the Boston area. In addition, Bulgarian-language newspapers, such as the *Macedonian Tribune,* published in Chicago, and an international émigré newspaper, *Nedelnik,* unite immigrants living in all fifty states.

Czechs and Slovaks. Over half (57 percent) of the current foreign-born population from Czechoslovakia arrived in the U.S. before 1980. These people were mostly well-educated political dissidents from urban areas. Some were dissidents who were given refugee status after the Soviet invasion of Czechoslovakia in 1968; others were Jews who were granted asylum after pogroms racked the country in that same year. Like other immigrants from closed border socialist countries, these immigrants arrived with little prospect of ever returning home. They were quick to find employment and social acceptance in the international milieus of American cities and universities in the 1970s. For the most part, they kept their distance from other Czech and Slovak Americans, whom they saw as provincial, politically backward, and overly assimilated into the American mainstream.

Immigration from the post-Soviet Czech Republic and Slovakia (established in 1993) has slowed, primarily because of the high standard of living in these states since the collapse of socialism. The Czech Republic and, to a lesser degree, Slovakia are more politically stable and economically successful than most central and southeastern European countries. As a result, the foreign-born Czech and Slovak population in the U.S. today consists of a relatively older, well-educated group of professionals living in large cities on the East and West Coasts. The states with the largest concentrations are New York (19 percent), California (18 percent), Florida (11 percent), New Jersey (8 percent), and Ohio (6 percent). Thirty-nine percent of people from the former Czechoslovakia hold professional and managerial positions, and 31 percent have a bachelor's degree or higher.

The majority of Americans with Czech or Slovak ancestry are the descendants of immigrants from the turn of the 20th century, when great numbers of these groups settled in the Midwest and were chiefly employed in manufacturing and industrial jobs. While those with such ancestry once made up 40 percent of all foreign-born immigrants in the U.S., their proportion had dwindled to less than 3 percent of the population by 1990. Czech- and Slovak-speakers are becoming increasingly rare in the U.S., as those from earlier waves of immigration die out and their children, grandchildren, and great-grandchildren assimilate into the white American mainstream. Slovak and Czech Catholic and Lutheran churches founded in the 1920s have declining attendance; many now serve majority Polish or Hispanic congregations.

During the "ethnic revival" of the 1960s and 1970s, Americans began to study the everyday life of immigrant Slovaks and Czechs. Historians, anthropologists, and sociologists sought to describe the life of the early Slovak and Czech pioneers and produced monographs on Slovak religious institutions, labor organizations, and community life. Czech descendants of the early wave of immigrants in Nebraska, Iowa, and Texas issued publications to document their history and explain their culture to younger generations. The Czech Heritage Foundation and a Czech Council for the Arts in Cedar Rapids, Iowa, established a museum and archive, which documented early Czech immigrant life. In 2003 the Czech-Slovak Heritage Society was established to help descendants of Czech and Slovak immigrants from Virginia learn about their forebears, and in 2004 Houston saw the establishment of a Czech Cultural Center.

Czech heritage festivals are popular in Texas, Kansas, Minnesota, Iowa, Ohio, Pennsylvania, and Nebraska. Participants enjoy polka music, folk dancing, and contests to make and eat kolache. The Czech center in Houston brings together the descendants of immigrants from Bohemia, Moravia, Silesia, and Slovakia and claims the largest Czech American membership in the country. Such groups are usually active in charitable causes to benefit their homelands. For example, many Czech and Slovak historical societies solicited donations to assist in the rebuilding of Czech towns and cities hit by floods in 2002.

Hungary. Like Czechs and Slovaks, Hungarians joined the great migration of the late 1890s and early 1900s in significant numbers. From the later 1890s until World War I, more than 450,000 Hungarians came to the U.S. in search of economic opportunity. The last significant wave of Hungarian immigration to the U.S. occurred in 1956, when Soviet troops and tanks entered Budapest in order to subdue Hungarians' attempts to liberate themselves from Soviet rule. Roughly 190,000 Hungarians subsequently fled the country. The U.S., as part of its cold war strategy, accepted roughly 35,000 of them, primarily young single men. In Hungary they had been intellectuals; in the U.S., they entered the middle and top ranks of American industry, universities, and hospitals. Like other émigrés from Soviet satellite countries, Hungarians who left socialist Hungary could not travel back, and communication with relatives remaining in the homeland was difficult.

After 1956, a modest number of Hungarians entered the U.S. each year until 1989, but the robust post-socialist Hungarian economy has stalled immigration. According to the 2000 Census, only 14,045 Hungarians have arrived since 1990, and over half of these entered on family reunification visas. As a consequence, the median age of foreign-born Hungarians is 61.1 years—the highest of any of the eastern and southeastern European groups.

Thirty percent of Hungarian immigrants hold a bachelor's degree or higher, and 45 percent are in managerial or professional careers. Probably because of the 1956 cohort's ability to take advantage of the strong American economy at the time of their arrival, median earnings for Hungarian-born men are quite high, at $49,154.

In the late 1960s, Hungarian enclaves in St. Louis, Chicago, New York City, Cleveland, New Brunswick, New Jersey, and Allentown, Pennsylvania, began to lose significant portions of their populations because of the aging of the immigrants who had built them, "white flight," and the failure of these neighborhoods to attract recent Hungarian arrivals. In the past ten years, many Hungarian Roman Catholic and Eastern Orthodox churches have closed as aging parishioners have died and their children, if they are religious, have chosen to attend English-language services. Nevertheless, a few Catholic, Baptist, Pentecostal, Calvinist, and Presbyterian churches established by immigrants continue to offer services in Hungarian. They are concentrated in areas that had significant Hungarian populations at the turn of the 20th century: California, New Jersey, New York, Ohio, and Pennsylvania.

Ethnic preservation efforts are under way across the U.S.: Hungarian heritage societies and museums have been established to inform the public about the lives of early immigrants, and Hungarian festivals featuring ethnic foods, folk dancing, and fencing are held in cities that once held large Hungarian populations.

Romania. Life for most citizens in Nicolae Ceaușescu's Romania (1965–1989) was exceptionally harsh. In the 1970s, many members of Romania's political and intellectual elite fled to the U.S. in fear of retaliation from the regime for publicizing human rights violations and were allowed to enter as refugees. By the 1980s, the Romanian Securitate, or secret police, had developed networks of indigent citizens who would spy on friends, neighbors, and even family members for money. The government made life unbearable for those who were found to be involved in religious organizations with anti-Ceaușescu overtones, and so Romanian refugees who arrived in the U.S. in the 1980s were likely to be members of underground religious (often Protestant) organizations.

After revolution erupted in 1989 and Ceaușescu and his wife were executed by a firing squad, the U.S. continued to accept Romanians as refugees for a time, but since the early 1990s refugee status has seldom been granted, and most Romanian immigrants are now sponsored by relatives or employers. Others apply for a green card in the lottery system.

Romanians are one of the few European immigrant groups whose numbers have been rising in recent decades. The number of Romanian speakers more than doubled between 1980 and 1990, from 24,058 to 53,493. According to the U.S. Census, 135,965 foreign-born Romanians were in the country in 2000. This figure is likely to be an underestimate; the Maritime Security Council estimates that between 3,000 and 5,000 Romanians enter the country illegally each year, mostly sealed in freight containers on ships. Moreover, Romanians who immigrate to the U.S. from neighboring countries are often not identified as Romanian in the census, despite the fact that many of them speak the language and consider themselves Romanian.

Romanians who have entered the U.S. since the early 1990s are mostly economic migrants, fleeing the low wages and high unemployment rate that have plagued the post-Ceauşescu labor market. Not surprisingly for a new and growing population composed of those subjected to religious persecution, they have been quick to establish or revitalize Orthodox, Pentecostal, and Seventh-Day Adventist churches in the U.S. Churches appear to be the main providers of services to new immigrants: members help newcomers with loans and language lessons, and pastors act as community liaisons and often announce job or housing opportunities during Sunday services. Nonetheless, the immigrant community appears to have been rent by suspicions that some of their number were involved with the Securitate. In 1995 the *St. Louis Dispatch* reported that at a dance held to unite the city's 15,000 Romanian refugees, individuals wondered aloud which of their fellow guests had worked for Securitate. And as late as 2002, the *Phoenix New Times* reported that parishioners of the Elim Romanian Pentecostal Church accused their pastor of having spied for the Securitate's Neo-Protestant Cults Department while attending seminary in Romania.

Twenty-eight percent of Romanian immigrants do not speak English fluently, and this group is more likely to be linguistically isolated than other central European immigrants. In spite of that, Romanians are concentrated in managerial and professional occupations (41 percent), followed by sales and office work (18 percent). Median earnings for Romanian-born men over age 16 are $40,078.

The largest Romanian communities can be found in New York (22 percent), Illinois (14 percent), California (12 percent), Michigan (8 percent), and Ohio (7 percent). Areas with large Romanian populations have Romanian-language newspapers, television stations, and radio programs.

Former Yugoslavia: Bosnia-Herzegovina, Croatia, Macedonia, and Slovenia. Many Yugoslav immigrants in the period from 1965 to 1990, like those from the other socialist states, were highly educated political dissidents. Unlike other socialist states, however, Yugoslavia had relatively open borders after 1960. Airmail was fast and reliable, telephone calls were legal, and low-cost charter flights transported émigrés back and forth. Even those who opposed the Yugoslav government were in constant contact with the country. The government's active courtship of emigrants fortified these ties. Slovene American choral societies and bands went on annual tours to Slovenia, travel bureaus in Serbia encouraged émigré families to spend their summers at Serbian resorts, and the government subsidized Croatian-language lessons for émigré children visiting Croatia. Furthermore, the Yugoslav government permitted the American embassy in Belgrade to forward Social Security checks to retirees living in Yugoslavia, so that many of those who had emigrated earlier spent their retirement years in their homeland. Similarly, the children of emigrants were frequent visitors to Yugoslavia. They were more likely than other second-generation central European immigrants to speak their parents' native languages fluently and to be familiar with the rites and customs of their homeland.

The communist republic of Yugoslavia occupied and united territories that had previously been under the rule of the Austro-Hungarian and Ottoman empires and incorporated members of the Roman Catholic, Eastern Orthodox, and Muslim faiths. We do not know how many immigrants from Yugoslavia identified themselves as belonging to a particular territory, since the U.S. Census lumped them all together as "Yugoslav." However, their political and religious activities suggest that most were from Serbia, Croatia, Slovenia, and Macedonia. Serbian Orthodox churches and Croatian and Slovenian Catholic churches were revitalized by a flow of immigrants after 1960, and a Macedonian Orthodox church was established in the 1960s and 1970s by immigrants who wanted to promote the idea of an independent Macedonia. Croatian and Macedonian fraternal organizations in the U.S. were active in supporting nationalist movements. In Chicago, a large sign on 53rd Street in Hyde Park reminded passersby that "Croatia is dying to be free." And Macedonian organizations encouraged the U.S. government to recognize an independent and unified Macedonia.

In 1991, Yugoslavia began to disintegrate as its constituent republics declared sovereignty and war broke out. Diaspora communities collected funds to help their compatriots. Some (mostly male) immigrants returned home to participate in the war, and some returned to the Balkans and became political leaders there.

During the Yugoslav wars, which lasted from 1992 to 1995, immigration from the former Yugoslavia changed. The proportion of immigrants from Croatia, Macedonia, and Slovenia—areas that were relatively unaffected by the conflict—shrank, while the number of migrants from the war zone of Bosnia-Herzegovina soared. According to the U.S. State Department, more than 143,000 refugees resettled in the U.S. between 1993 and 2003, most of them from Bosnia-Herzegovina. Although the American government granted all refugees the option of asylum, a small percentage have since returned home.

The wars disrupted educational attainment, vocational training, and professional development, a fact reflected in statistics on Bosnian refugees in the U.S.: less than 14 percent hold a bachelor's degree, and median earnings are the lowest of all the groups covered here—$24,904 for men and $18,729 for women (see Table 2). Forty percent of refugees work in production, transportation, and moving.

These refugees qualify for a number of special federal and state benefits in the health, business, and human service sectors. Special trauma centers have been established to help them cope with depression, anxiety, and post-traumatic stress syndrome. They are usually sponsored by a local church or civic organization, and sponsoring groups play a vital role in helping refugee families adjust, finding them housing, paying the first months' rent, transporting them to and from schools and medical appointments, and helping them find employment. Some churches cooperate with local companies to train and hire refugees; for example, the Virginia Council of Churches found jobs for Bosnian refugees at carpentry shops in Richmond. Managers in some workplaces have had to adjust to foreign cultures. For example, the influx of refugees employed at a steel fabrication plant in Virginia meant that management has had to get accustomed to employees asking to take time off for Ramadan. Supervisors sometimes ask more experienced workers to act as interpreters and teachers for newer employees.

Most refugees arrive knowing little or no English. At first they find minimum-wage jobs where English fluency is not required. Many work as cooks, servers, busboys, hosts, bartenders, dishwashers, and factory workers. Social workers report that well-educated refugees who held high-status positions in their home countries struggle to maintain a sense of self-worth in their new circumstances.

The extent to which immigrants from the former Yugoslavia cooperate with one another appears to depend on the communities in which they settle. In small cities such as Dayton, Ohio, cooperation between immigrants from different regions of their homeland is commonplace. In large cities such as Chicago, Detroit, and St. Louis, refugees appear to be highly residentially concentrated according to their place of origin. The south St. Louis neighborhood of Bevo Hill, for example, is often referred to as "Little Bosnia" or "Little Sarajevo" because of its high concentration of Bosnians and the refugee-owned and -operated businesses that cater to them. (Estimates of the Bosnian population in St. Louis range from 35,000 to 60,000.) Few Yugoslav immigrants who are not Bosnian live in the area. Similarly, in 1998 the *New York Times* reported that a bar owned by Croatian immigrants in Astoria, Queens, was full of people speaking Serbo-Croatian who had gathered to watch Croatia's first appearance at the World Cup, and Bosnian cafés cater to a Bosnian and American clientele—but not to refugees from other parts of the former Yugoslavia.

Soccer matches appear to mute tensions between members of different republics. In cities with large refugee populations, Albanian and Bosnian Muslims, Orthodox

Table 2 Selected characteristics of foreign-born population from former Yugoslavia, 2000

	Yugoslavia[a]	Bosnia-Herzegovina[a]	Croatia[a]	Macedonia[a]	All foreign-born[b]	All Americans[b]
Total population	113,985	98,765	40,910	18,680	28.4 million	281 million
Median age	51.0	30.3	48.6	40.8	38.1	35.3
Percentage with bachelor's degree or higher	19.7	13.7	22.3	13.7	26	24.4
Employment (percentages)						
Managerial, professional, and related	27.9	13.1	31.3	17.5	24.7	33.6
Service	22.8	20.1	16.1	24.3	19.2	14.9
Sales and office	17.9	17.1	19.3	15.3	—	26.7
Farming, fishing, forestry	0.1	0.2	0.4	0.3	4.5	0.9
Construction, extraction, maintenance	10.1	9.7	12.3	10.9	—	9.4
Production, transportation, and material moving	21.2	39.8	20.6	31.3	—	14.6
Median earnings, men 16 and older in the labor force	39,633	24,904	45,064	37,531	27,239	37,057
Median earnings, women 16 and older in the labor force	27,522	18,729	27,807	24,389	22,139	27,194

a. Source: U.S. Census Bureau, Census 2000 Special Tabulations (STP-159).

b. Sources: "Profiles of the Foreign-Born Population in the United States: 2000," Current Population Reports, Special Studies, P23-206 (December 2001); "The Foreign-Born Population in the United States," Current Population Reports, Population Characteristics, P20-534 (January 2001).

Serbs, and Catholic Croats are happy to play with and against each other in public soccer leagues.

Refugee children sometimes require special psychological care because of the unique trauma of war, and they have a high incidence of health problems rarely seen in the U.S. that require special medical attention. Many young people were kept out of school during the wars, which has made their adjustment to American education quite difficult. Some schools have worked to meet these children's needs by hiring teacher's aides who are bilingual, increasing the availability of ESL classes, and hiring psychologists who specialize in childhood trauma.

In high schools with large and diverse refugee populations, violence has flared between Orthodox Serbs, Bosnian Muslims, and Kosovar Albanian refugees. School administrators have taken a range of measures to stop the violence, from seeking police intervention to separating students by national origin. In cities with large refugee populations, talented boys have reinvigorated high school soccer teams and public soccer programs. The factors pushing migrants out of Bulgaria, Czechoslovakia, Hungary, and Romania have changed drastically since the collapse of Soviet socialist rule. Before that, the majority of immigrants were well-educated professionals who objected to the suppression of intellectual and religious freedoms. In the U.S., they entered occupations that gave them access to mainstream American middle- and upper-middle-class life.

After the collapse of Soviet rule in central and southeastern European communist states, migration began to follow economic logic: immigration from the poorer countries (Bulgaria and Romania) has swelled, while the more prosperous countries (the Czech Republic, Slovakia, and Hungary) are sending fewer migrants than ever before. In general, immigrants from former socialist states have done well in the American labor market and have found rapid acceptance in the United States.

Bulgarian and Romanian newcomers have been quick to establish churches that provide for members' spiritual, social, and economic needs. In contrast to their predecessors, for whom emigration meant a complete severance of ties to their homelands, most current central and southeastern European immigrants travel freely back and forth, use telephones and the Internet to keep in touch with those they left behind, and send remittances to members of their former communities.

People coming to the U.S. from communist Yugoslavia have experienced immigration very differently from those fleeing the Soviet bloc states, in part because of Marshal Tito's open borders policy. For them, emigration was less a final departure than a state of exile punctuated by frequent visits to the homeland. They were also more likely to engage in political activism directed at their former government than immigrants from countries whose governments considered them traitors for leaving.

Refugees from the Yugoslav wars have often arrived in the U.S. with little or no preparation for life in America. Moreover, they carry with them the tremendous losses incurred by the wars. They thus have little in common with either the political refugees or the economic migrants from neighboring countries.

Bibliography

Altankov, Nikolay G. 1979. *The Bulgarian-Americans.* Palo Alto, Calif.: Ragusan.

Barton, Josef J. 1975. *Peasants and Strangers: Italians, Rumanians, and Slovaks in an American City, 1890–1950.* Cambridge, Mass.: Harvard University Press.

Chada, Joseph. 1981. *The Czechs in the United States.* Washington, D.C.: SVU Press.

Govorchin, Gerald Gilbert. 1961. *Americans from Yugoslavia.* Gainesville: University of Florida Press.

Manojlović ar ković, Radmila, ed. 1996. *I Remember/Sjećam Se: Writings by Bosnian Women Refugees.* San Francisco: Aunt Lute Books.

Novak, Michael. 1973. *The Rise of the Unmeltable Ethnics: Politics and Culture in the Seventies.* New York: Macmillan.

Padgett, Deborah. 1989. *Settlers and Sojourners: A Study of Serbian Adaptation in Milwaukee, Wisconsin.* New York: AMS Press.

Schnabel, Albrecht, and Ramesh Chandra Thakur. 2000. *Kosovo and the Challenge of Humanitarian Intervention: Selective Indignation, Collective Action, and International Citizenship.* New York: United Nations University Press.

Várdy, Steven Béla. 1985. *The Hungarian-Americans.* Boston: Twayne.

Zivich, Edward Andrew. 1990. *From Zadruga to Oil Refinery: Croatian Immigrants and Croatian-Americans in Whiting, Indiana, 1890–1950.* New York: Garland.

Haiti

Lisa Konczal and Alex Stepick

In October 2002, more than 200 Haitian immigrants jumped from a 50-foot wooden freighter off the coast of Miami, waded ashore, and rushed onto a major highway. They came from the poorest country in the Western Hemisphere, with a per capita gross national income of $380, an infant mortality rate of 79 per 1,000, and an average life expectancy of 52 years, according to figures from the World Bank in 2004. News of immigrants reaching the Florida shores via makeshift, over-crowded vessels is not unusual. Over the years thousands of Haitians have braved the risky 700-mile voyage to the U.S. It is not only the circumstances of the long voyage that are perilous; what happens after their arrival can also be dangerous, since Haitians are often either deported back to their politically repressive and economically destitute country or received negatively on both individual and institutional levels.

Haitian immigrants in the U.S. share many of the characteristics of other new immigrants: they are perceived as nonwhite, they seek refuge from a nation in political and economic turmoil, and those who are young often end up caught between the values of their parents and their need to construct a new identity. Whatever their similarities to other immigrants, however, Haitian Americans undergo exceptional experiences in terms of reception. They are sometimes referred to as *triple minorities*. First, they are dark-skinned and in the U.S. are automatically labeled as black. Second, they speak an unfamiliar language, Haitian Creole, unique to their country of birth. Finally, they are immigrants. The weight of the immigrant stigma is perhaps heavier for Haitians than for any other group, because of the prolonged burdens of differential immigration policy toward them.

Context of reception is therefore highlighted throughout this essay as a principal factor shaping the fate of Haitians in the U.S. The first section is an introduction to demographic trends, past and present, of Haitians coming to the U.S. The following section identifies the chronological sequence of institutional struggles Haitians have faced both in their island homeland and within the U.S. Finally, this essay provides a narrative of Haitian American culture in terms of language, religion, education, identity, and socioeconomic outcomes.

Demographic Trends and History

According to the 2000 U.S. Census, approximately 429,848 foreign-born Haitians are residing in the U.S., and 632,680 persons described themselves as Haitian. However, because the U.S. Census has had a difficult time counting Haitians, it is impossible to know precisely how many there really are. For example, in 1990 the census counted nearly 300,000 people who acknowledged their primary ancestry to be Haitian, but some estimates put that figure at 450,000. And in Miami–Dade County, the census missed as many as 50 percent of some neighborhoods' residents.

Table 1   Select areas of Haitian settlement by year, 1980–2000 (percentages)

	1980	1990	2000
Total number	92,960	225,639	429,848
State[a]			
Florida	18.5	37.4	42.8
New York	60.7	38.7	29.7
New Jersey	5.2	6.6	8.2
Massachusetts	5.3	8.4	7.8
Connecticut	1	1.6	1.8
Georgia	0.1	0.3	1.5
Pennsylvania	1	0.4	1.4
Maryland	0.8	1.3	1.2
California	1.5	1.2	0.9
Illinois	2.8	1.3	0.9
Texas	0.5	0.5	0.4
Delaware	0	0	0.4
Virginia	0.3	0.2	0.4
Rhode Island	0	0.3	0.3
North Carolina	0.2	0.1	0.3
Metropolitan Areas[b]			
New York-Northeastern NJ	29.2	57.8	23.1
Miami-Hialeah, FL	23.7	14.3	18.2
Ft. Lauderdale-Hollywood-Pompano Beach, FL	8.1	2.5	11.3
West Palm Beach-Boca Raton-Delray Beach, FL	5.8	0.4	7.2
Boston, MA	7.4	5.1	6.5
Newark, NJ	4.8	3.6	5.2

a. *Source:* U.S. Bureau of the Census, 1980, 1990, 2000 Censuses, 5% Public Use Microdata Sample, weighted data.

b. *Source:* U.S. Bureau of the Census, 1980, 1990, 2000 Censuses, authors' own 5% Public Use Microdata Sample, weighted heavily.

Table 2   Arrival of foreign-born Haitians

Years	Percentage	Number
Before 1965	3.0	12,771
1965–1969	5.0	21,676
1970–1974	7.7	33,205
1975–1979	8.4	36,002
1980–1984	18.9	81,034
1985–1989	17.0	73,183
1990–1994	19.0	81,757
1995–1999	19.3	82,756
2000	1.7	7,464
Total	100.0	429,848

Source: U.S. Bureau of the Census, 2000 Census, authors' own 5% Public Use Microdata Sample, weighted data.

Despite the uncertainty of the numbers, however, the Haitian population undoubtedly grew from 1990 to 2000.

Florida is the primary destination for these immigrants, but that has not always been the case (see Table 1). New York was the first and until the 1990s the major location of Haitian settlement in the U.S. The eradication of black-white segregation in the South broadened the geographic landscape for black immigrant settlement, and between 1990 and 2000, Florida surpassed New York as the destination of choice. Haitians also settle primarily in central city areas (Miami, New York City, and Boston).

From Haiti's founding as a French colony and then after independence, the country's largest immigration flows were to France, as well as to former French colonies in Africa and to French-speaking Canada. Until the latter half of the 20th century, most Haitian immigrants followed these colonial links. Only about 500 Haitians permanently migrated to the U.S. each year before the late 1950s, while another 3,000 came temporarily as tourists, students, or business people. After François "Papa Doc" Duvalier assumed power in 1957, the U.S. became more involved in Haitian affairs, and as a result Haitians began immigrating to the U.S. in greater numbers than they did to other nations (see Table 2). The first to leave were upper-class people who directly threatened Duvalier's regime. Around 1964 the middle class began to leave. The 1965 Immigration Act, which permitted family members to bring close relatives into the U.S., broadened the base. By the late 1960s, nearly 7,000 Haitians each year became permanent immigrants and approximately 20,000 more came with temporary visas. This influx resulted in a visible Haitian presence in New York City, along with smaller communities in Chicago, Boston, and Montreal, Canada.

The first detected boatload of Haitian refugees arrived in September 1963. When they requested political asylum, the Immigration and Naturalization Service (INS) summarily rejected their claims and dispatched them back to Haiti. The second boat did not appear until 1972, and by the end of the 1970s between 5,000 and 10,000 Haitians risked their lives each year in attempts to reach the U.S. by sea. The U.S. media stigmatized Haitians as desperately poor and pathetic people who were washed onto south Florida's shores. Since then the U.S. government has conducted a resolute campaign to keep Haitian refugees from coming to Florida by boat.

Institutional Barriers

The Haitian interdiction program was established in 1981 by the Reagan administration to stem the movement of undocumented Haitians by boat to the U.S. Under this program, U.S. Coast Guard vessels are authorized to stop and board Haitian and unflagged vessels on the high seas, determine whether their passengers are undocumented aliens bound for the U.S., and if so return them to Haiti. Also in 1981 the INS began systematically detaining Haitians entering the U.S. until they had a hearing and their status was determined. This marked a departure from the established policy of detaining only those aliens who were determined likely to abscond or to pose a threat to public safety or national security. Haitians were the only persons who were detained regardless of whether they were deemed likely to abscond or pose a public threat.

Those Haitians who managed to settle in the U.S. (including Haitian youth) encountered other forms of prejudice. A strong stigma stuck to the community from its earliest days. During the early 1980s the Centers for Disease Control (CDC) in Atlanta identified Haitians as a primary group at risk for AIDS. They were later removed from that list, but the Food and Drug Administration (FDA) continued to refuse to accept blood from Haitian donors. In response, 5,000 Haitian protesters rallied in front of the FDA offices in a Miami suburb, indicating that there was indeed a Haitian political presence.

The U.S. government justified its differential policy toward Haitian immigrants by claiming that they were economic migrants rather than political refugees. Most obviously, they were regarded as different from Cubans who came to the U.S. fleeing from the regime of Fidel Castro. The double standard was most evident during the Mariel boatlift of 1980, when 125,000 Cubans were welcomed with open arms while an estimated 25,000 Haitians who came around the same time were denied asylum and threatened with deportation.

After the cold war ended in 1989, U.S. policy toward Cubans became less welcoming, but so did policy toward Haitians. In 1994, when the government of Haiti became more stable with the return of the exiled, democratically elected president Jean-Bertrand Aristide, the U.S. government returned to Haiti an estimated 15,000 Haitians detained in the U.S. naval base at Guantánamo Bay, Cuba, along with an estimated 150,000 living in the U.S. with temporary work permits.

The 1996 Welfare Reform Act restricted access to social benefits for recent immigrants. Under the 1996 act, immigrants entering after August 22, 1996, are barred from most federal means-tested services for a period of five years. The 1998 Haitian Refugee Immigration Fairness Act exempted from these restrictions some Haitian asylum-seekers and unaccompanied Haitian minors. A 2003 study on welfare reform, however, found that Haitians who are eligible for Temporary Assistance to Needy Families (the new term for federal welfare payments) usually do not enroll for the services because they are afraid of being labeled a "public charge"—that is, a noncitizen who establishes a pattern of systematic use of government benefits, which can result in the refusal of an immigrant's citizenship application or denial of an application to sponsor other immigrants. Haitians, who are consistently threatened with deportation, have reason not to enroll in the new, albeit limited TANF program.

At the turn of the 21st century, the Bush administration restricted the ability of arriving immigrants to claim asylum, apparently in response to fears of a mass exodus of Haitians to the shores of south Florida. These gatekeeping practices have focused not only on limiting new inflows of Haitian asylum-seekers but on expediting the removal of asylum-seekers currently residing in the U.S. In August 2001, for example, approximately 10,000 Haitian families in south Florida were being considered for removal by the U.S. government.

Political instability in Haiti intensified in 2001, particularly in December, when an armed attack on the National Palace in Port-au-Prince led to widespread violence. Departures of unauthorized migrants from Haiti increased significantly at the end of that year. Despite the increased violence in Haiti, the U.S. continued to treat Haitians as economic migrants rather than political refugees. During 2001 the coast guard interdicted nearly 2,000 Haitians at sea and returned almost all of them to Haiti. In December alone, the U.S. interdicted 500 Haitians—more than in any other month in at least five years. In 2003 violence escalated as supporters of President Aristide attacked demonstrators who demanded his resignation. That same year the U.S. Coast Guard interdicted more than 2,000 Haitians at sea, up more than 35 percent from the year before, and repatriated almost all of them. In 2004 armed militants associated with Aristide's Lavalas movement and the former Haitian military seized most of the country. In response, the U.S. and France pressured Aristide to leave on February 29, 2004, leaving the government in the hands of interim prime minister Gerard Latortue.

Socioeconomic Characteristics

Over a quarter of Haitians who immigrated to the U.S. during the first major wave in the 1960s were professionals. In 1980, before most of the second wave of Haitian immigrants had arrived in south Florida, 55.9 percent of all the Haitians in the country had graduated from high school and nearly 10 percent had completed four years of college. Although these immigrants could not immediately make use of their human capital when they arrived in the 1960s, by the 1980s they were able to obtain higher education or their children had done so. In contrast, most Haitians in the second wave, that is, after 1980, had much less human capital to begin with. Stepick's study of Haitians arriving in south Florida during the 1980s revealed that only 5 percent had graduated from high school, and none of the study participants had completed a four-year college degree.

Current figures on educational attainment show that about 35 percent of Haitian immigrants do not have a high school diploma, which is about the same as among the total immigrant population and 15 percentage points more than among the total U.S. population (see Table 3). However, those who do graduate from high school are likely to go on to achieve at least some higher education, although usually they do not attain a bachelor's degree or higher. Completion of a college degree is relatively infrequent among Haitian immigrants compared to both the U.S. population as a whole and the total immigrant population.

Table 3 also shows Haitian unemployment rates (5.9 percent for those aged 25 to

Table 3   Educational and economic status of foreign-born Haitians, the total foreign-born population, and the total U.S. population, 2000

	Foreign-born Haitians[a]	Total foreign-born[a]	U.S. population[b]
Total number	429,848	22,034,522	281,421,906
Educational attainment (percentage)[c]			
8th grade or less	13.0	20.4	7.5
9th to 12th grade	22.3	14.6	12.1
High school graduate, GED	24.0	19.0	28.6
Some college, AA degree	26.3	19.9	27.4
Bachelor's degree	9.7	15.2	15.5
More than bachelor's degree	4.6	10.9	8.9
Employment (percentage)[c]			
Not in labor force	27.8	30.6	17.7
Employed	66.3	65.4	77.6
Unemployed	5.9	4.0	3.7
Economic situation			
Median family income[d]	$36,100	$41,000	$50,046
Percent below poverty line[e]	13.6	10.9	4.1[f]

a. *Source:* U.S. Bureau of the Census, 2000 Census, 5% Public Use Microdata Sample, weighted data.

b. *Source:* U.S. Census Bureau, Census 2000 (U.S. Summary 2000: Census 2000 Profile), July 2002.

c. Persons aged 25–64.

d. All households.

e. Persons aged 25–64 who are in labor force.

f. U.S. Department of Labor, Bureau of Labor Statistics, "A Profile of the Working Poor," table 2 (Washington, D.C.: Government Printing Office, 2002).

Table 4   Socioeconomic characteristics of foreign-born and U.S.-born Haitians, 2000
(percentages)

	Foreign-born	U.S.-born
Total number	412,300	207,100
Age		
Percentage of children under 18	11.3	71.0
Median age	38.0	12.0
English-language ability[a]		
None	3.9	0.2
Does not speak well	15.8	4.0
Speaks well	30.0	11.6
Speaks very well	43.5	61.0
Speaks English only	6.8	23.2
Educational attainment[b]		
No high school diploma/GED	35.4	15.5
High school graduate/GED	25.2	19.6
College (some to postgraduate degree)	39.4	64.9
Occupational attainment[c]		
Low-wage labor (SEI < 25)	55.2	25.8
High-status jobs (SEI > 50)	19.5	33.8
Income/poverty		
Median wage/salary income	$19,400	$14,000
Percentage at or below poverty threshold	19.4	22.4

Source: U.S. Bureau of the Census, 2000 Census, authors' own 1% Public Use Microdata Sample, weighted data.

a. Persons aged 5 and older.

b. Persons aged 25–64.

c. Percent of those employed, ages 25–64. SEI = Duncan Socioeconomic Index. High-status occupations (professional, managerial, technical) have SEI scores above 50. Low-status jobs with SEI scores below 25 include laborers, operators, fabricators, and low-wage service jobs. Not shown are mid-status white-collar and skilled blue-collar jobs with SEI scores between 25 and 50.

64 years) and the number of Haitians living below the poverty line (13.6 percent for persons aged 25 to 64 in the labor force), which is higher than among the total foreign-born population. Accordingly, median family income for foreign-born Haitians ($36,000) is lower than the medians for both the total foreign-born population ($41,000) and the total U.S. population ($50,000).

In the early 1980s, the first surveys of recently arrived Haitian immigrants in southern Florida revealed extraordinarily high unemployment rates. As many as 80 percent of females and nearly 50 percent of males claimed to be unemployed and looking for work. Besides lack of legal status, unfounded rumors of health problems (tuberculosis and AIDS) among Haitians made it difficult for them to find work. To survive, they turned to the informal sector and engaged in low-paying tasks such as dressmaking, child care, hairdressing, and construction work. As fears of disease subsided, Haitians incorporated themselves into the local economy, particularly in "back-of-the-house positions" as cooks and busboys at restaurants. According to the U.S. Census, Haitians hold low-level positions, with the largest segment working in restaurants, over one third working in services (especially in hotels), and over one fourth working as low-skilled laborers.

The data presented in Table 4, which compares the occupations of foreign-born and U.S.-born Haitians, show that more than 50 percent of foreign-born Haitians work in low-wage jobs. U.S.-born Haitians appear to have improved their status, with only one quarter employed at those low levels. They have also outperformed their foreign-born counterparts in education. The 2000 Census data show that 64.9 percent of U.S.-born Haitians (aged 25 to 64) have at least some college education, compared with only 39.4 percent of foreign-born Haitians. However, those born in the U.S. have a lower median wage/salary income and a higher percentage of persons living at or below the poverty threshold. That can partially be explained by discrepancies in ages: the U.S.-born population is much younger, with over 70 percent under the age of 18 (compared with 11.3 percent under 18 for the foreign-born). The median age for foreign-born Haitians in 2000 was 38, while the median age for U.S.-born Haitians was only 12.

Reinventing Culture and Identity

Besides institutional barriers, differential treatment emerges at a more basic level. At local high schools in Miami, Haitian students are stigmatized for being Haitian, or, as one student put it, "American people are always pickin' on Haitians." In the early 1980s, when Haitians first started entering the Miami high school closest to "Little Haiti" in significant numbers, conflict periodically convulsed the school. Students ridiculed and beat up anyone who looked Haitian or who spoke Creole or accented English. African American, Anglo, and Hispanic students severely mocked newly arrived Haitians during sports events. After years of research in the south Florida Haitian community and schools, Stepick and his associates found that Haitians are more likely than other immigrant groups to say they have felt discrimination (especially from other students). Furthermore, they are more likely than their counterparts from other countries to agree strongly that racial discrimination exists in the U.S. and that people will discriminate regardless of education.

The Children of Immigrants Longitudinal Study (CILS) provides otherwise unavailable data on Haitians in the U.S., particularly in southern Florida (see Table 5). In sum, this study supports other studies which show that Haitian immigrants and their children experience *cultural dissonance,* manifested in young people's covering up or hiding their home culture, including language.

Cultural dissonance. Whereas immigrants of the late 19th and early 20th centuries were described as experiencing one-way assimilation characterized by the adoption of middle-class, white, Protestant values (which would inevitably lead to

Table 5   Selected characteristics of Haitians (Children of Immigrants Longitudinal Study)

Nativity and age	
Mean age at 1992 survey	14.3
Mean age at 2001–2003 survey	24.0
Father's education (percentage)	
Less than high school	43.6
College graduate	16.9
Mother's education (percentage)	
Less than high school	40.4
College graduate	19.2
Achievement tests, 1991	
Math (national percentage)	48.85
Reading (national percentage)	30.01
Academic GPA, 1995	2.32
Education by age 24 (percentage)	
Some high school	3.6
High school graduate	8.3
Some college	60.7
College graduate	17.9
Graduate school	1.2
Language acculturation (percentage)	
Preferred English, 1992	84.1
Preferred English, 1995	84.9
Preferred English, 2002	66.3

Source: Children of Immigrants Longitudinal Study (CILS), 1991–2003.

upward mobility), new immigrants face new challenges. New immigrants may experience "dissonant acculturation," in which ties between children and the immigrant community are severed, depriving young immigrants of privileged sources of material and moral support while leaving them exposed to the challenges of the larger society and therefore an increased likelihood of downward mobility. This path is attributed to communities of nonwhite immigrant workers living in the inner city, as is often the case with Haitians settling in poor African American neighborhoods.

In contrast, immigrants who retain the norms of their coethnic community may achieve upward mobility. Maintaining close ties to one's ethnic community leads to positive results, helping immigrants achieve middle-class status. Scholars such as Alejandro Portes describe this process as *selective acculturation,* in which immigrants learn American ways while maintaining strong bonds with the ethnic community. Selective acculturation is found in immigrant enclaves and is positively associated with the size and resources of these communities. For example, Cuban immigrants in Miami, who had a comparatively positive reception in the U.S., gained the resources and capital to create private bilingual schools where children were taught

English but preserved Spanish and a strong attachment to Cuban history. In other words, they preserved some of their community's characteristics. Because of this preservation (rather than despite it), educational attitudes were positive. The selective acculturation of second-generation Cuban Americans who were able to preserve their language and ties to Cuban culture led to positive educational attitudes among those children.

The CILS data show that compared with other immigrants in Miami, and unlike the Cubans, adolescent Haitian students were ambivalent about their cultural roots as a result of prejudice. Researchers such as Stepick have found that this manifests itself in frequent conflict with parents, a claimed ignorance of Haitian Creole, and consequently a poor academic orientation—in sum, an effort to distance themselves from their roots.

Language and cultural identification. The CILS data show that Haitian students claimed less knowledge of a foreign language (for them, this would be Haitian Creole) than other south Florida respondents. Yet an ethnographic study that accompanied the large-scale survey contradicted the students' claim and found that the respondents were underestimating their Creole abilities. Furthermore, while the Haitian youngsters claimed that English was the predominant language used at home, their parents claimed that Haitian Creole was in fact usually spoken at home.

The differences in reported language ability reflect broader alienation of the Haitian students from their parents and the culture their parents represent. Haitians were significantly more embarrassed by their parents and reported higher levels of parent-child conflict than other students in the CILS survey.

Studies of Haitians in New York by Flore Zéphir confirm these findings. Results of approximately 125 in-depth interviews of Haitian Americans in New York document the rejection of Haitian identity (including Haitian Creole) and the adoption of American identities by members of the 1.5 and second generations, particularly those from lower socioeconomic backgrounds. However, the opposite is true for higher-income second-generation Haitians in New York. They are more likely than their peers of lower status to retain a Haitian ethnic identity. While hiding immigrant origins helps young people avoid the stigma of Haitian roots, the American identity available to Haitians—being African American—can carry other stigmas. In south Florida this is apparent in the chosen self-identification of Haitians in predominantly African American schools. The CILS data show that Haitian adolescents in predominantly black schools were somewhat more likely to label themselves as Haitian American or Haitian and correspondingly less likely to call themselves African American than those in nonblack schools.

Identity choices of Haitian Americans become even more complex when we consider patterns of culture such as language and religion in the homeland, where speaking French is associated with the upper class and speaking Creole with the lower class. Haiti has cultural roots in Africa and France, although the French language and religion (Catholicism) were historically associated with a small elite class. For years French was the official language in Haiti. The Haitian constitution of 1957 reaffirmed French as the official language but permitted the use of Creole in certain public functions. It was not until the late 1980s that Creole became the official language, even though the majority had spoken it exclusively for years. The roots of Creole are complex, but according to most scholars, it developed as a pidgin French used as a means of communication among African slaves of many languages and their colonial masters, mostly French. In addition, northern Haiti was one of the geographic concentrations of pirates. Pirates, or buccaneers, the French-derived word for pirates, were multiethnic and multinational and thus contributed to the diverse etymological roots of Haitian Creole.

In the U.S., Haitian language choices reflect class identities carried over from the homeland. While New York Haitians use Creole most frequently with close family, friends, and intimates, sometimes they choose French during interactions with Haitians who are not members of their intimate circle. Haitians use French as a tool to express information about their social class, and once this information is conveyed (usually at the beginning of an interaction), there is no need to continue speaking French to carry on a conversation. This may be especially true for Haitian populations in the northern states, which are home to a distinct wave of upper-class Haitians who migrated during the 1960s and 1970s, many of whom are now second generation.

In south Florida too there is evidence of class segmentation. The more recently arrived "boat people" come from the impoverished peasantry and laboring classes. Middle-class Haitians, many of whom are secondary migrants from New York, have created most of the formal businesses in the fledgling ethnic economy. They admit that they are Haitian but usually speak French and differentiate themselves from the darker, Creole-speaking "boat people." Leaders of the community include the activist priest Gerard Jean-Juste and other ministers as well as business and professional people who struggle to consolidate a viable ethnic enclave. These class divisions keep the group from developing a community that can sustain solidarity and trust. For example, in the 1990s thousands of Haitians rallied to demand the reinstatement of the disposed Haitian president Jean-Bertrand Aristide. However, middle-class Haitians, especially entrepreneurs and business managers, vehemently opposed him.

Religion. Although the vast majority of Haitians are devout Christians, North Americans often associate Haitians with voodoo and associated negative stereotypes. In fact, Haitians are among the most devout Christians in the U.S. In the 1980s nearly 70 percent of Miami's Haitians reported attending church at least once a week. Little Haiti's streets are lined with churches, and the most important religious institution in Miami is the Haitian Catholic Center, which literally overflows with people on Sundays. Since the early 1980s the church has been a political and social center, where Haitians in Miami unite not only for worship but for health care, language classes, and child care.

Roman Catholicism is the official religion of Haiti, but Protestantism has been growing both in Haiti and among Haitians in the U.S. At least 40 percent of Miami's Haitian community identify as Protestants. Storefront Protestant churches abound in Little Haiti, and a few Protestant churches have had explosive growth. One Baptist church has converted a huge former textile plant into an impressive church with a congregation of over 1,000.

Although Americans associate Haiti and Haitians with voodoo, they often have a misconception about the religion. Because of the overlap in Christian and African beliefs, some aspects of voodoo pervade all of Haitian culture. For example, a Christian who goes to church regularly may possess a pillow embroidered with the name of Ezili, the voodoo goddess of love. From an anthropological perspective, voodoo's primary thrust is ancestor worship, reflecting Haitians' ancestral roots in Africa. In fact, in Haitian Creole the name of the religion, *sevi lwa,* translates as "serving the spirits." While using spirits to affect the lives of others negatively is a component of voodoo, it is a very minor component. The focal point is the appeal to the spirit world for assistance in one's own life.

In general, voodoo practice is less visible in the U.S. than in Haiti. Here voodoo rituals are likely to occur in basements and involve only those who are personally invited. Some Haitians have attempted to counteract negative stereotypes of voodoo. The Miami-based Haitian cultural group Sosyete Koukouy held a well-publicized conference in 1996 on the history of the religion and its impact on Haitian culture. More recently, voodoo, and Haitian culture in general, have found acceptance in the world of Western music. Groups like Boukman Eksperyans and the most popular Haitian group, the Fugees, especially its member Wycliffe Jean, have found wide acceptance among American audiences.

Haitians in the U.S. have probably suffered more prejudice and discrimination than any other contemporary immigrant group, ranging from the U.S. Coast Guard interdiction and the jailing of those who do make it to U.S. shores to the mislabeling of Haitians as carriers of AIDS and schoolyard accusations that Haitians eat cats. These stereotypes say much more about Americans' perceptions of Haitians than they do about Haitians themselves. The data cited here reveal the diversity among Haitians. Many, especially among those born in the U.S., have completed college and have relatively high-status jobs. Furthermore, Haitians have made political strides in just the past few years. Various Haitians have become city councilors in south Florida municipalities, and in 2000, Phillip J. Brutus became the first Haitian American elected to the Florida state legislature and only the second Haitian immigrant to hold an elected state office in the nation. Yet regardless of such accomplishments, Haitians continue to struggle against the negative stereotypes that too many Americans maintain.

Bibliography

Loescher, G., and John Scanlan. 1984. *U.S. Foreign Policy and Its Impact on Refugee Flow from Haiti.* New York: New York Research Program in Inter-American Affairs.

Masud-Piloto, Felix Roberto. 1996. *From Welcomed Exiles to Illegal Immigrants: Cuban Migration to the U.S., 1959–1995.* Totowa, N.J.: Rowman and Littlefield.

Portes, Alejandro, and Alex Stepick. 1993. *City on the Edge: The Transformation of Miami.* Berkeley: University of California Press.

Stepick, Alex. 1989. "The Haitian Informal Sector in Miami." In A. Portes, M. Castells, and L. Benton, eds., *The Informal Economy: Studies in Advanced and Less Developed Counties,* pp. 111–31. Baltimore: Johns Hopkins University Press.

———. 1998. *Pride Against Prejudice: Haitians in the United States.* Boston: Allyn & Bacon.

Stepick, Alex, and Alejandro Portes. 1986. "Flight into Despair: A Profile of Recent Haitian Refugees in South Florida." *International Migration Review* 20, 2 (Spring/Summer): 329–50.

Stepick, Alex, and Carol Dutton Stepick. 1992. *Ethnographic Evaluation of the 1990 Decennial Census Report Series, Report No. 8, Final Report for Joint Statistical Agreement 90-08.* Washington, D.C.: U.S. Bureau of the Census.

Stepick, Alex, Carol Dutton Stepick, Emmanuel Eugene, Deborah Teed, and Yves Labissiere. 2001. "Shifting Identities and Inter-Generational Conflict: Growing Up Haitian in Miami." In R. Rumbaut and A. Portes, eds., *Ethnicities: Children of Immigrants in America,* pp. 229–66. Berkeley: University of California Press.

Zéphir, Flore. 1996. *Haitian Immigrants in Black America: A Sociological and Sociolinguistic Portrait.* Westport, Conn.: Bergin & Garvey.

———. 2001. *Trends in Ethnic Identification among Second-Generation Haitian Immigrants in New York City.* Westport, Conn: Bergin & Garvey.

India

Karen Isaksen Leonard

Immigrants from India, now termed "Asian Indians" in the U.S. Census, have been coming to the U.S. since the 1890s, and many things have changed for them. First, India's external boundaries have changed. Before 1947, Britain's colonial empire of India included present-day India, Pakistan, and Bangladesh; India and Pakistan gained their independence in 1947, and East Pakistan split off in 1971 to become Bangladesh. The new term "South Asian," being used on campuses and in political coalition-building, reaches back to that broader unit and even beyond, including Sri Lanka, Nepal, Bhutan, and, according to some, even Burma and Afghanistan.

Second, although the geographic base from which Indian immigrants come has narrowed to India, the profile of the immigrants has broadened dramatically with respect to numbers, regions of origin, class, gender, and religion. The "old" and "new" (post-1965) Asian Indian immigrants differ in many ways. The old immigrants constituted a relatively small group, between 2,544 in the 1910 Census and 2,398 in the 1950 Census, as the earlier immigrants began to age and die off. They were also a very homogeneous group, almost all men and almost all from the Punjab province, along the northwestern frontier with Afghanistan. These men all spoke the Punjabi language, but they were religiously diverse, being Sikhs, Hindus, and Muslims (although most were Sikhs). The Punjabis were overwhelmingly from farming backgrounds, and they settled in California and worked in agriculture. Between 60 and 77 percent of Indian immigrants were in California between 1910 and 1940.

These pioneer Indian immigrants encountered discriminatory laws that effectively ended immigration in 1917 and affected their rights to gain citizenship, hold agricultural land, and marry whom they chose. These federal policies and laws included the Immigration Act of 1917, barring most Asians from legal immigration; the Immigration Act of 1924, setting a quota of 105 immigrants per year from In-

dia; and the 1923 *U.S. v. Bhagat Singh Thind* decision, declaring Indians to be Caucasians but not "white" and therefore ineligible for U.S. citizenship. State policies
and laws included California's Alien Land Laws of 1913, 1920, and 1921, which
prohibited noncitizens from owning and leasing agricultural land and were copied
by other states. Various states also had anti-miscegenation laws that prohibited marriages between people of different races.

The pioneer Punjabi men were called "Hindus" by others in their localities,
meaning "people from Hindustan," or India. Because of the legal constraints,
most of them married women of Mexican ancestry; the Punjabi men and Mexican
women looked racially similar to the county clerks who issued marriage licenses.
These immigrant couples produced a generation of Mexican-Hindu children with
names like Maria Jesusita Singh and Jose Akbar Khan, who were usually bilingual in
English and Spanish. They were mostly Catholic (their mothers' religion) but called
themselves Hindu and were extremely proud of their Indian heritage. Later Asian
Indian immigrants, unable to imagine the conditions in which the Punjabi pioneers lived, have found it hard to acknowledge their mostly Sikh descendants as
"Hindus."

Asian Indian immigration opened up again slightly after 1946, when political
changes at the national level in both the U.S. and India made it possible for the old
immigrants to reestablish connections with their homeland and for new immigrants
to come. In 1946, successful lobbying by the Indians in the U.S. secured the passage of the Luce-Celler Act, which gave Asian Indians the right to become naturalized U.S. citizens and allowed access to the immigration quota of 105 per year set
by the 1924 Immigration Act. Once they had become American citizens, the pioneers could revisit their villages and sponsor relatives as immigrants. Their pride in
their newly independent nations was an impetus to reconnect in these ways, but the
numbers of immigrants were still severely limited.

The great inflow of new immigrants from India began with the 1965 Immigration Act, legislation that vastly increased the numbers of immigrants from Asia and
set preferences favoring those who were highly educated professionals. According to
the 2000 Census, the number of immigrants from India rose from 8,736 in 1960,
to 387,223 in 1980, to 623,940 in 2000. More than half of current immigrants
(54.7 percent) came in the decade from 1990 to 2000. These people come from all
of India's regions, displaying the diversity of the Indian subcontinent. English, not
Punjabi, is the common language of these educated immigrants, yet they come
from many vernacular-language backgrounds and Indian states (India has 19 major
vernaculars, and internal state boundaries were realigned in 1956 to reflect linguistic ones). In the U.S., the most numerous linguistic groups are Gujaratis, Punjabis,
and Malayalis (from the states of Gujarat, Punjab, and Kerala, respectively). The
post-1965 immigrants are predominantly well-educated urban professionals, migrating in family units including men, women, and children. They represent many

religions and include Hindus, Muslims, Christians, Sikhs, Parsis (Zoroastrians), and Buddhists. Also, many traditional caste and community categories still have some significance in their lives, particularly in regard to marriage.

Asian Indians not only come from all over India but are settled all over the U.S., and they are doing very well. Like other Asians, they favor California (Asians formed some 10 percent of the state population in 1993), with New Jersey, New York, Illinois, and Texas next in popularity. Of the foreign-born groups in the 2000 Census, immigrants born in India had the third highest median household income (behind only South Africans and those from the United Kingdom), the second highest median family income (behind South Africans), and the second highest median per capita income (behind those from the U.K.). As in 1990, Asian Indians in 2000 had the highest percentage of immigrants with a bachelor's degree or higher and were among the highest percentages in managerial and professional fields. Many South Asian professionals are doctors, with one estimate in the 1990s putting the number at more than 20,000, or nearly 4 percent of the nation's medical doctors. The largest ethnic doctors' association in the U.S. is the American Association of Physicians from India. In terms of family stability, immigrants from India have one of the highest rates of marriage and the lowest rates of separation and divorce. There are slightly more men than women, 53.9 percent to 46.1 percent. Fertility is low, with 59 percent of Indian immigrant women having only one or two children and only 9 percent having more than three children.

In the 2000 Census, most Asian Indians (93 percent) identified themselves racially as "Asian"; 4.1 percent regarded themselves as "mixed," 1.5 percent as "white," 1.1 percent as "other," and 0.3 percent as "black." (Interestingly, Pakistani immigrants, whose profile is similar to Indians' in many ways, identified themselves as "Asian" 82.7 percent of the time, with "mixed" at 13.4 percent, "white" at 3 percent, "other" at 0.5 percent, and "black" at 0.3 percent.) Asian Indians are not clustered in residential areas but dispersed, with residential patterns very much like those of the white population. In the census, 11.1 percent recorded themselves as native speakers of English, and 62.5 percent said they spoke English well (among the foreign-born, only nonnative English-speakers from Uganda, Ghana, and Kenya were higher, with 65.3 percent, 63.5 percent, and 62.8 percent, respectively, claiming to speak English very well). English was the home language of 9.6 percent of Indian immigrant households, with another 71.3 percent speaking Indo-European (North Indian) languages and 17.7 percent speaking other Asian (presumably Dravidian or South Indian) languages.

Post-1965 immigrants achieved a high level of socioeconomic success, although those arriving in the mid-1980s temporarily brought down the averages and medians. Many of these later arrivals came in under family preferences and were not as well qualified as their predecessors, and recessions in the U.S. economy had a further negative effect. In the 1990 Census, those arriving since 1985 showed a much lower percentage in managerial and professional jobs, a much lower median income, and a much higher unemployment rate. Thus the percentage of South Asian families in poverty was also high in 1990, putting Indian immigrants twelfth on the lists of both families in poverty and individuals in poverty. The U.S. Immigration Act of 1990 reversed this downward trend, however, since it sharply increased the numbers of highly skilled immigrants from India (and Asia generally) at the expense of unskilled workers and unemployed parents and spouses of citizens. The effects of the setbacks in the computer industry at the end of the 20th century and of the post-9/11 immigration policies and regulations on Asian Indians are still uncharted.

Political participation has been a goal for both early and later Indian immigrants. After the Luce-Celler Act made the Punjabi pioneers eligible for citizenship in 1946, they helped elect Dalip Singh Saund from California's Imperial Valley in 1956, the first congressman born in India. After initial hesitation, the post-1965 immigrants are becoming naturalized citizens and engaging in politics, and they are active in both Democratic and Republican funding and campaigning. In 2004, Bobby Jindal, a Republican and a Catholic of Indian descent, won a congressional seat from Louisiana's first district, and others of Indian descent won seats in state legislatures. The 2000 Census shows that 37.7 percent of Indian immigrants are naturalized citizens, slightly lower than previously because more than half of all Indian immigrants are recent arrivals, having come since 1990. Also, until the past few years Indians have had to give up their Indian citizenship to take U.S. citizenship, because India, unlike the U.S., did not allow dual citizenship, although it always actively encouraged what it calls NRIs, or nonresident Indians, to invest financially in the homeland. In late 2003 India finally decided to allow dual citizenship, but only for Indians in selected (Western or developed) countries; the details are still being worked out.

Asian Indian organizations have changed over time, starting with the Gadar Party, formed by California's Punjabis in the early 20th century to hasten India's independence from Great Britain. South Asian immigrants, still small in numbers, then formed organizations based on national origin (India, Pakistan, Sri Lanka) or ecumenical religious categories that incorporated them into Christian churches or Muslim mosques. As the Indian immigrant population has grown, linguistic associations, ethnic organizations, and sectarian or guru-centered religious groups have proliferated. Some of these reproduce divisions that are important back in India, but at the same time, the organizations are mobilizing in the U.S. on the basis of Indian ancestry. The four leading national associations are the Association of Indians in America, the National Federation of Indian Associations (NFIA), the Indian American Forum for Political Education, and the National Association of Americans of Indian Descent. These competing federations reflect not only rivalry among leaders but uncertainty over the best term for the community. "Asian Indian" is the census term, while "Indian American" and "Indo-American" are also favored denominations. Now there is an international organization, the Global Organization of People of Indian Origin, led by Indians from the U.S.

Indian American political strategies include building coalitions with other groups, such as Asian Americans and Muslim Americans. Among Asian Americans, Indians are moving from being the fourth largest group, after the Chinese, Filipinos, and Southeast Asians, to the third largest. The Indian group (expanded to South Asian, including Indians, Pakistanis, Bangladeshis, Sri Lankans, and Fijians and Guyanese of Indian origin) has lagged behind most other Asian American groups in participation in educational and political coalitions, but that situation is changing fast. Similarly, Islam either already is or will soon be the largest non-Christian religion in the U.S., and it has been argued that South Asian Muslims provide much of the intellectual and political leadership for Muslim Americans.

Indo-American political mobilization is sometimes based on issues involving race and class in the U.S., such as crimes against South Asians, individual or institutional discrimination in higher education and business, and problems with municipalities. Thus merchants may fight to achieve preferential minority business status or to name a business area Little India, while religious leaders seeking to establish Hindu temples or other institutions act to secure local permission. Sometimes these efforts encounter thinly veiled prejudice. For example, in the 1990s in Norwalk, California, zoning regulations required those building a Hindu temple to adopt Spanish mission architecture to obtain construction approval.

After September 11, 2001, Indians (and South Asians) of all religions have found that many native-born Americans are unable to distinguish among them, and they have built coalitions to fight media scapegoating, harassment, and attacks based on a general fear of terrorism. Turban-wearing Sikhs have been singled out and have mobilized along with Indian Muslims. Other political issues focus on class, gender, and generational issues. Women's groups have been particularly active in addressing issues of domestic violence; important groups include Apne Ghar in Chicago, Sakhi in New York, and Manavi in New Jersey.

Most first-generation Indian immigrants are in the U.S. to stay, and not only their political participation but their businesses and popular culture reflect that. Their children are moving into the American mainstream, while elderly parents are leaving India to join their families in the U.S. This latter trend is a mixed blessing for the parents, bereft of their old friends and former lives and usually isolated in the suburbs. Often they serve as babysitters, phone answerers, and perhaps even cooks for their working adult children.

However, these trends undoubtedly help make Indian culture more widely available, working to set a standard for Indian restaurants and contributing to the explosion of Indian fast foods and packaged foods being distributed in South Asian ethnic groceries throughout the country (for business reasons, the "South Asian" label is often used to attract a broader market or audience). "Indian groceries," owned by anyone from South Asia, supply full lines of ethnic food, toiletries, and often videos. Boutiques and shops now supply almost everything needed to produce Indian weddings satisfactorily in America, and this is a booming market niche.

Art, cultural performances, and writing linked to India or those of Indian origin not only abound in the U.S. but show varying degrees of integration into the American cultural landscape. Religious and cultural festivals are observed, but their timing is adjusted to those of American holidays. Indian dance and music teachers have started schools all over the U.S. Indian dance academies offer classical Bharatanatyam and regional folk dances like Punjabi *bhangra* and Gujarati *giddha,* along with dances from Hindi films and "hip-hop bhangra." In northern California, Ali Akbar Khan's College of Music enrolls many Euro-American students, and the master musician Ravi Shankar has settled in Southern California. The literary scene is active, too, as both first- and second-generation immigrants are producing widely acclaimed prose and poetry. Cities like New York host a second-generation youth party scene, as young "desis" (countrymen, as in ABCDs, "American-born confused desis") congregate enthusiastically, drawing on both American (sometimes urban black American) and Indian culture.

Among the post-1965 immigrants, Asian Indian religious activity has intensified. Transnational networks can be strong, as religious figures from India tour the U.S., lecturing and sometimes raising funds for religious or political activities. Sikh *gurdwaras,* Hindu temples, South Asian mosques, Parsi fire temples, and other religious institutions are being established in America's urban centers, fueled by relative prosperity and the ease of securing the necessary materials, as well as the craftsmen, artisans, and religious specialists to put them together, in this era of global trade and travel. Especially for Indian Hindus, changes from homeland practices are occurring in temples and religious spaces, as people from different linguistic, caste, and sectarian backgrounds come together in the American setting. Although Hinduism has not been promoted as a universal or world religion, it has had a major impact on American popular culture through yoga and new-age meditation movements, which are so hybridized that they are no longer recognizably religious or Indian in nature.

Interactions between immigrant and indigenous followers of religions from the Indian subcontinent have become part of the process of settlement in the U.S. Hindus and Sikhs are primarily immigrant communities, still strongly oriented toward India but also flourishing in the U.S. North American converts form very small parts of the two communities, and American converts to Sikhism and Hinduism— the members of Yogi Bhajan's Sikh Dharma (also called "white" or "gora" Sikhs), the Ramakrishna Mission, the Transcendental Meditation movement, and the Hare Krishnas—often differ strikingly from immigrants. Converts' beliefs and practices can be considered either hybrid or more "authentic," in the sense of being text-based, than those of immigrants.

The Sikh immigrant community in the U.S. sees itself as a diaspora community, and many of its members also recast the pioneer "Hindu" or Punjabi immigrants to North America as "the Sikh diaspora." Indian Sikhs have a public profile marked by sharp public disagreements over their place in India and the nature and extent of Sikh religious authority. Their minority status (they constitute some 2 percent of India's population) and specific grievances in India exploded in the 1986 demand for a homeland, or Khalistan, by many Canadian and U.S. Sikhs. The centralizing institutions of Indian Sikh governance tried to exercise supreme authority at home and abroad, and militant takeovers of North American Sikh *gurdwaras,* associations, and media followed. But Sikh moderates resisted, and some Sikhs in the U.S. have turned successfully to American courts, arguing that *gurdwara* congregations have always exercised local control. Thus Western legal systems are being used to resist religious law extended from India.

The decline of the Khalistan movement has facilitated a closer integration of the Punjabi immigrant Sikhs with the small group of American converts, and that, along with converging second-generation conceptions of Sikhism as a world religion, has had impacts back in the Punjab. The Sikh Dharma group has become active in India, setting up a school in Amritsar and sending their children there to learn Punjabi culture. Meanwhile, pressure for gender equity, promised by Sikhism, has increased, partly because of convert expectations. Sikh Dharma women recently won the right for all Sikh women to perform certain previously male-only duties in the Golden Temple in Amritsar (Sikhism's holiest site).

Hindus, least in number among the early Indian immigrants, are probably the largest and most privileged of the new South Asian religious populations in the U.S., and are overwhelmingly immigrants. As in India, those who follow Hindu beliefs and practices are extremely diverse. The religious beliefs and practices designated as Hinduism have relied primarily on family- and caste-based rituals, and new temples in the U.S. have been financed, at least initially, by regional and sectarian groups. However, some new congregations and temples combine deities, architectural styles, or language groups seldom combined in India. Hindu immigrants tend to have strong and continuing allegiances to India, and some neo-Hindu, or Hindutva, groups are undeniably important with respect to politics in the homeland. But there is little in the way of Hindu politics focused on goals in North America, and efforts to build a unified Hindu community in the U.S. appear insignificant. Some of the many linguistic, regional, caste, occupational, and educational associations to which Hindus in the U.S. belong cross religious lines, but others reinforce sectarian or caste boundaries, regulating marriages and conduct in the diaspora as in the homeland.

Hindu religious authority is decentralized in the U.S., as in India, and gender issues are important. Some sectarian or caste groups in India extend authority over members overseas, and Hindu religious specialists recruited from India staff the new temples in America. There are parallels to the Sikh court cases involving contested leadership of particular Hindu temples, but such cases are not part of a national or transnational pattern contesting the nature and extent of religious authority exercised from India. While changes in beliefs and practices involving gender are occurring among American Hindus, it is hard to generalize. Some scholars find women's empowerment and greater gender equality in the new context, while others see Hindu families and communities instituting more inegalitarian and restrictive models of womanhood than they do in India.

Buddhist and Muslim immigrants from India are extremely diverse in terms of national origin, class, language, and race and ethnicity. In both cases, there are significant numbers of American-born coreligionists, and Muslims in particular are making efforts to unify believers across the many internal boundaries. Buddhists from India make up a very small proportion of American Buddhists. While monks from India's neighbor, Sri Lanka, with their English-language ability, strong educational backgrounds, and the backing of prosperous Sri Lankan immigrants, have been conspicuous in Buddhist institution-building and interfaith efforts, Buddhists from India are primarily Dalits, or untouchables. They are mobilizing in the U.S. to help their caste-fellows back in India, where a small-scale conversion movement of Dalits to Buddhism is under way.

Muslims from India are also only a part, but a large and very important part, of America's emerging Muslim community. The first Muslims in the U.S. were African Americans, and they still make up about a third of the American Muslim population. Interestingly, it was Ahmadiyya missionaries from British India who helped the African American Muslim movement by bringing an English translation of the Quran in 1920, publishing the first English-language Muslim magazine in the U.S., and telling America's black Muslims about the five pillars of Islam, thus heading them toward mainstream Sunni teachings.

After the 1965 Immigration Act, new Muslim immigrants came from many countries, including India. These immigrants rank high in terms of educational and socioeconomic status, and by the 1990s South Asian Muslim men had begun to take the national political leadership of American Muslims away from earlier Arab Muslim immigrants. Many first-generation Indian Muslims work to expand the basic definition of America's civic religion, the Judeo-Christian tradition, to the Abrahamic (Judeo-Christian-Muslim) tradition. American Muslims also write about the compatibility between Islam and democracy and increasingly pay attention to the political sphere.

Indian American Muslims, like Sikhs and Hindus, wrestle with issues of religious authority and gender. Since September 11, Muslims of all backgrounds may battle together against the stereotyping of Muslims as terrorists, but they acknowledge no single source of religious authority. American Muslims follow divergent beliefs and practices rooted in many countries and many sectarian traditions. Leading scholars of *fiqh,* or Islamic jurisprudence, agree that Muslim mobilization in the U.S. involves the development of *fiqh* in the new context rather than transnational applications of *fiqh* from various homelands. Gender issues are prominent in American Muslim community discourses. Patriarchy and gender complementarity (different roles for males and females) in family and community are generally upheld.

Indian Christians in the U.S. are also very internally diverse, representing communities ranging from Roman and Syrian Catholics to members of Jacobite, Mar Thomite, Nestorian, and many Protestant denominations. They have sometimes joined mainline American Christian congregations and sometimes retained their ethnic or national-origin identities. Like Muslims from India, Christians from India and Pakistan have asked for help not only from coreligionists but from other immigrants from their homelands as anti-Christian attitudes and actions in India and Pakistan have threatened their ancestral communities.

In the U.S., Parsis, or Zoroastrians, from India find themselves confronting Zoroastrians from Iran. The Indian Parsis are providing trained priests to American congregations even where they are outnumbered by Iranians (in Los Angeles, for example), because the religion has weakened in Iran. Both populations are doing extremely well economically, and the Gujarati- and English-speaking Parsi immigrants are working hard with the Persian-speaking Iranian immigrants to build an integrated North American community of Zarthustis, the name on which they have agreed.

The Zarthustis, too, debate issues of religious authority and gender. In a religion where conversion has not traditionally been possible, priests in India refuse to marry Parsi women to non-Parsi men, and they refuse to baptize the children of mixed marriages. But in North America such practices are becoming accepted as concern grows about the declining numbers in the community. New Zarthustrian religious centers in the U.S. are also cultural centers, intended to strengthen second-generation attendance and encourage marriages among the young people. Inter-marriages and baptisms of "mixed" children raise the possibility of conversion, at least in this country.

Gender issues loom large in Indian immigrant life, with most communities and religious leaders seeing the dominant American values of gender equality and freedom of sexual expression as serious threats to ordered social life. There is fear that "American individualism," interpreted not as a moral ideal but as egoism, will lead to family and societal breakdown. Whether certain practices, such as wearing the turban (for Sikhs) or the *hijab* (headscarf, for Muslim women), are religiously required or simply matters of culture is often vigorously debated.

Not only gender but generational tensions are shared to some extent by immigrant Sikhs, Hindus, Buddhists, Muslims, Christians, and Parsis, as immigrants worry about emerging "problems" involving their children. Despite all the signs of their own adaptation to and, indeed, impact on American life, some immigrants are concerned that their children will "lose their culture." This concern, and perhaps a feeling that they themselves cannot ever be more than second-class citizens of the U.S., leads some older Indian immigrants to retire to India, where housing complexes are being built for senior citizens returning from the U.S.

Worries about children of Indian descent being raised in the U.S. are reflected in ethnic newspapers, conference sessions, public talks, and private conversations. "The youth problem" is discussed endlessly in the ethnic press. Parents have high ambitions for their offspring, and children are encouraged to undertake higher education and professional training, particularly in medicine and engineering. Parents may stress the retention and transmission of the home culture over the adoption of American culture, which places their children, who are products of their American cultural context and comfortable in this context in ways that their parents are not, in a difficult position. The second generation's participation in American culture, in all its diversity and intensity, is borne out in many ways. In campus youth conferences, discussion topics always include interracial marriage, South Asian coalition-building, hip-hop culture, homosexuality, premarital sex, and violence against women, as well as identity formation, discrimination in corporate America, and racism.

While the experience of growing up in America is not uniform, most youngsters of Asian Indian descent go through a cycle of early identification with American culture and then, later, identification with Indian culture. Yet even after they become more interested in their heritage, these young people do not necessarily see themselves as part of a larger community of Asian Indians. But one writer asserts that they do have one thing in common with other Indo-Americans: their "overinvolved, overworried, overprotective" parents.

Some of the concern over the "youth problem" comes from religious leaders and organizations. This concern is ostensibly about the continuity of family, caste, and community religious traditions, but just as clearly it is about sexuality and marriage, in particular about parental arrangement of marriages and parental control of family life. Asian Indian religious leaders and parents often oppose dating on the grounds that it inevitably leads to either consensual sex or date rape, and it is the young women of Asian Indian background, not the young men, who are of most concern.

Sexuality is a major theme in powerful new writings by younger people of Asian Indian descent in America—not only heterosexual feelings and activities but gay and lesbian ones as well. A strategy of not telling one's parents about the significant choices one is making in life is common. With respect to marriage, gender and generational differences become magnified, and marriage is sometimes the occasion for crisis in Asian Indian immigrant families. Because of parental opposition to dating and "love marriages" (marriages in which women and men choose each other, rather than traditional arranged marriages), the children of immigrants are usually put into an either-or situation. They must trust their parents to arrange their marriages, or they must trust themselves. They know of many arranged marriages that have not worked out, and divorce is now a distinct possibility for Indo-Americans. The frequently transglobal marriage and family networks add international legal complications to the emotional costs of divorce for Asian Indians.

The experiences of the Punjabi pioneers and their Punjabi-Mexican families, experiences that emphasized the flexibility of ethnic identity and culture, are clearly relevant to the post-1965 Indian immigrants. The new immigrants, too, are witnessing the historical construction and reconstruction of their identities in Indian, American, and global arenas. Time and place are very important components, as changes in the historical context have had powerful consequences for individual, family, and community identity. Just as the turnabouts in U.S. citizenship and immigration policies in the 1940s and 1960s had dramatic consequences for Indian immigrant life in California, the changing global economy and society at the start of the 21st century are having dramatic consequences for the much larger and more diverse population of Asian Indian immigrants in the U.S. Just as identities and communities have been changing over time back in India, new concepts of identity and community are being produced in the U.S. by Asian Indian immigrants and their descendants in conjunction with other Americans.

Bibliography

Bhardwaj, Surinder M., and N. Madhusudana Rao. "Asian Indians in the United States: A Geographic Appraisal." In Colin Clarke, Ceri Peach, and Steven Vertovec, eds., *South Asians Overseas: Migration and Ethnicity,* pp. 197–218. New York: Cambridge University Press, 1990.

Fenton, John Y. *Transplanting Religious Traditions: Asian Indians in America.* New York: Praeger, 1988.

Helweg, Usha, and Arthur Helweg. *An Immigrant Success Story: East Indians in America.* London: Hurst, 1990.

Jensen, Joan. *Passage from India.* New Haven, Conn.: Yale University Press, 1988.

Koshy, Susan. "Category Crisis: South Asian Americans and Questions of Race and Ethnicity," *Diaspora* 7 (1998): 285–320.

Leonard, Karen Isaksen. *Making Ethnic Choices: California's Punjabi Mexican Americans.* Philadelphia: Temple University Press, 1992.

———. *The South Asian Americans.* Westport, Conn.: Greenwood, 1997.

Maira, Sunaina. *Desis in the House: Indian American Youth Culture in New York City.* Philadelphia: Temple University Press, 2002.

Williams, Raymond. *Religions of Immigrants from India and Pakistan: New Threads in the American Tapestry.* New York: Cambridge University Press, 1988.

Women of South Asian Descent Collective. *Our Feet Walk the Sky: Women of the South Asian Diaspora.* San Francisco: Aunt Lute Books, 1993.

Iran

Mehdi Bozorgmehr

Iranian immigrants are sometimes referred to by others as Persians, since "Iran" and "Persia" are used interchangeably in the U.S. Many Iranian immigrants call themselves Persian, in an effort to conjure up images of the old Persian empire and disassociate themselves from the Islamic Republic of Iran. The label "Iranian" is more inclusive, however, because "Persian" excludes non-Persian religious and ethnic minorities from Iran. Since Iran is the largest Shia Muslim country in the world, many assume that all Iranian immigrants are Muslim. Despite Iran's relative religious homogeneity (about 98 percent of its population in 1976 was Muslim), the full spectrum of its religious minorities is represented in relatively large numbers in the U.S. These include Christian Armenians and Assyrians, Baha'is, Jews, Zoroastrians, and Sunni Kurds. Because of selective migration, many of these minorities left Iran as a result of the 1978–1979 revolution and the establishment of the Islamic Republic in 1980.

Immigration Trends

Only 130 Iranians are known to have immigrated to the U.S. from the mid-19th century to the beginning of the 20th century. From 1925 to 1950, fewer than 2,000 Iranian immigrants were admitted. An additional 12,000 were admitted from 1950 to 1969. Table 1 shows the number of Iranian immigrants admitted annually from 1965 to 2004, including individuals who arrived to become permanent residents as well as those already in the U.S. who adjusted to permanent resident status. The number of Iranian immigrants steadily increased for most of this period, from less than 2,000 in 1970 to a peak of almost 25,000 in 1990. The peak year does not correspond to the peak of Iranian immigration to the U.S. (1978), however, because of a lag between arrival and adjustment of status. The total number of annual

Table 1 Iranian immigration, 1970–2004

Year	Number admitted
1965–1969	5,935
1970	1,825
1971	2,411
1972	3,059
1973	2,998
1974	2,608
1970–1974	12,901
1975	2,337
1976	3,731
1977	4,261
1978	5,861
1979	8,476
1975–1979	24,666
1980	10,410
1981	11,105
1982	10,314
1983	11,163
1984	13,807
1980-1984	56,799
1985	16,071
1986	16,505
1987	14,426
1988	15,246
1989	21,243
1985–1989	83,491
1990	24,977
1991	19,569
1992	13,233
1993	14,841
1994	11,422
1990-1994	84,042
1995	9,201
1996	11,084
1997	9,642
1998	7,883
1999	7,203
1995–1999	45,013
2000	8,519
2001	10,497
2002	13,029
2003	7,251
2004	10,434
2000–2004	49,730

Sources: U.S. Immigration and Naturalization Service, *Annual Reports, 1970–1977,* and *Statistical Yearbooks,* 1978–1986. U.S. Department of Homeland Security, *Statistical Yearbook of the Immigration and Naturalization Service, 1986–2004.*

Iranian immigrants admitted has declined since 1990, but it is still at much higher levels than during the prerevolution period.

Few Iranians had immigrant status upon arrival; most were admitted as students (before the revolution) or as visitors (during the revolution and afterward). In the decade between 1980 and 1990, obtaining refugee or asylee status was the most common way for Iranians to achieve permanent residence in the U.S. It was relatively easy to get a U.S. visa in Iran before the seizure of the American embassy in Tehran in 1979. Since the embassy closed, Iranians have been forced to go abroad to obtain a U.S. visa, and many have gone to Turkey, which does not require visas for Iranians to visit for up to three months.

Nonetheless, it is incorrect to call all Iranian immigrants exiles or political refugees. Many emigrated for educational reasons, as a result of Muhammad Reza Shah's industrialization drive, which began in the 1960s and took off in the mid- to late 1970s with rising oil revenues. Unlike some other oil-producing but underpopulated countries in the Middle East, which imported skilled workers, Iran relied on its own large population for labor. However, because there were relatively few universities in Iran, studying abroad became the only viable way to obtain the skills workers needed in a rapidly industrializing economy. Iranian students traveled to several countries in pursuit of higher education, but their favorite destination was the U.S.; about half of the student population abroad was in the U.S. in the mid-1970s. Because English was the foreign language commonly taught in Iranian high schools, their chances of being admitted to American universities were fairly good. Moreover, universities in the U.S. offered state-of-the-art education in technical fields such as engineering. Many of these students chose to remain in the U.S. after the revolution, in what may be construed as self-imposed exile. Immediately after the revolution, other members of the elite classes and the most modernized segments of Iranian society made up the first real wave of exiles.

Population Size and Settlement Patterns

The United States is by far the favored destination of the global Iranian diaspora. The Iranian population in the U.S. has increased substantially since 1980. Despite persistent claims by some Iranians that their population in the U.S. exceeds 2 million, the 2000 Census counted only 338,000 Iranians, including persons born in Iran as well as those of Iranian ancestry born in the U.S. and other countries. It is possible that this number is an undercount because it is based on an open-ended question about ancestry on the long form of the census questionnaire. Self-reported data tend to increase error and nonresponse. Whatever the true number, the undocumented Iranian population is small, though some do overstay their visas.

About half of the Iranians in the U.S. live in California. Iranians, including those born in the U.S., tend to prefer cosmopolitan regions, and in 2000 over half resided

Table 2   Selected demographic and socioeconomic characteristics of foreign-born Iranians in the U.S., 2000

Characteristic	Percentage
Age	
24 and younger	12.3
25–34	14.9
35–44	27.3
45–54	21.3
55 and older	24.2
Decade of immigration	
1990–2000	26.5
1980–1989	33.5
1970–1979	32.2
Before 1969	7.7
Education[a]	
Up to high school graduate	22.6
Some college	22.5
Bachelor's degree	29.4
More than a bachelor's degree	25.5
English proficiency	
Speak English very well or well	74.6
Speak English not well or not at all	15.9
Not applicable (under 5 years, native speaker)	9.5
Citizenship	
Citizen	61.6
Noncitizen	38.4
Labor force participation[a]	
Employed	70.5
Unemployed	3.3
Not in labor force	26.2
Occupation[b]	
Managerial/professional	50.2
Technical/sales/administration	22.5
Service	7.5
Operators/laborers	12.0
Unemployed or not classified	0.8
Self-employment rate[b]	
Not incorporated	11.8
Incorporated	9.6
Unpaid family worker	0.4
Total	21.8

Source: U.S. Bureau of the Census, 2000 Census, 5% Public Use Microdata Samples, weighted data.
Note: Percentages do not add up to 100 because of rounding.
a. Persons aged 25–64.
b. Persons aged 25–64 in the labor force.

in four metropolitan areas: greater Los Angeles (31.1 percent), the San Francisco Bay area (10 percent), metropolitan New York (9 percent), and the Washington, D.C., area (8 percent).

While 80 percent of the Iranian population was foreign-born in 1990, by the year 2000 only 68 percent was foreign-born. This suggests that Iranian immigration has slowed down. The figures also show the coming of age of second-generation Iranian Americans: 12.3 percent of the total Iranian population is now under 24 years of age (post-revolution children), and another 14.9 percent is between 25 and 34 (see Table 2).

Social and Economic Adaptation

The combination of former college students and elite exiles makes Iranians one of the best-educated immigrant groups in the U.S. According to the 2000 Census, 29.4 percent of foreign-born Iranians 25 years and older hold a college degree, and another 25.5 percent hold more than a bachelor's degree (see Table 2). This means that over half (54.9 percent) of immigrants from Iran have a college degree or higher, a rate twice as high as that among all foreign-born people (26 percent). Foreign-born Iranians consistently rank among the most highly educated large immigrant groups (over 100,000 persons) in the U.S. The five top groups with a bachelor's degree or higher are Asian Indians (71.3 percent), Taiwanese (67.9 percent), Russians (59.9 percent), Nigerians (58.4 percent), and Iranians (54.9 percent). The Islamic Republic of Iran suffers from one of the highest levels of brain drain in the world.

Reflecting their high levels of educational attainment, Iranian immigrants rank very high in percentage of the population working in professional occupations. With a rate of 50.2 percent, they lead all Middle Eastern groups in managerial/professional occupations. By comparison, 29.7 percent of all foreign-born people hold similar white-collar occupations (e.g., physicians, engineers, accountants, and supervisors) in 2000. Not surprisingly, 75 percent of foreign-born Iranians report that they speak English well or very well, as opposed to 51 percent of all foreign-born people (see Table 2).

With a self-employment rate of 21.8 percent in 2000, Iranians are also one of the most entrepreneurial groups in the U.S. At their peak, in 1990, Iranians ranked third, after Greeks and Koreans, in self-employment among the 35 largest immigrant groups in the U.S. Unlike immigrants who turn to self-employment because of disadvantages in the labor market (e.g., language barriers among Koreans), Iranians generally opt for self-employment because some were self-employed before migration, especially members of classic middleman minorities such as Armenians and Jews. The availability of capital and the presence of highly skilled self-employed professionals such as doctors, dentists, and lawyers further contribute to the high self-employment rate of Iranians. Iranian businesses, like their residences, are typically not geographically concentrated. Iranians do not really have what sociologists call an "ethnic enclave economy," that is, a spatial clustering of enterprises. There are no Little Tehrans or Irantowns. Instead, Iranians call Los Angeles "Irangeles" or "Tehrangeles."

The combination of salaried and self-employed professionals, as well as managers, accounts for the generally successful economic adaptation of Iranian immigrants. This success, however, is qualified by the downward mobility, at least initially, of exiles, and the discrimination Iranians as a whole face in the labor market. Exiles in particular have had more difficulty than economic migrants in transferring their Iranian occupation to the U.S. economy, owing to the incompatibility of their qualifications with those needed in the U.S. According to 1990 Census data, an earnings gap existed between foreign-born Iranians and native-born whites in greater Los Angeles. The severe psychological problems that Iranian exile families sometimes face when they are confronted with downward mobility were dramatically portrayed in the Hollywood movie *House of Sand and Fog.*

Unlike their male counterparts, Iranian immigrant women have a low labor force participation rate (56.1 percent as compared to 82.3 percent) in spite of their relatively high educational levels. A number of factors account for this phenomenon. First, many women did not engage in paid work prior to migration and continue to remain out of the labor force. However, this trend has declined with the passage of time and the coming of age of the second generation. Second, many Iranian immigrant women remain at home because of a common family strategy that ensures that children get full parental attention in their formative years while the professional or self-employed breadwinner spends long hours at work. Third, while in Iran household tasks, child-rearing duties, and home maintenance are often shared by live-in extended family members and maids, the burden of these responsibilities falls largely on the shoulders of Iranian women in the U.S. Last, whenever Iranian husbands' incomes are high enough to support the family, wives tend to be full-time homemakers despite their generally high levels of education. When Iranian women work, as is the case of Armenians, whose employment has increased in the U.S., it changes the traditional household and gender roles.

Immigrants who have high levels of educational and occupational achievement as well as English proficiency are expected to integrate rapidly into American society. While some Iranians in the U.S. are indeed well integrated—especially students who arrived before the revolution, subsequently married Americans, and settled down in college towns where there are few other Iranians—most postrevolution exiles are not. Congregated in the Los Angeles, San Francisco, New York, and Washington metropolitan areas, they have resisted pressures to assimilate. This is particularly the case among religious minorities, who prefer to live, work, and interact with their coethnics or coreligionists. For instance, Armenian and Jewish Iranians in Los Angeles have maintained many of their traditions.

Dissatisfaction with the Islamic Republic explains why most Iranian Muslims in the U.S. are secular, though visible segments of religious Iranian Muslims can be found in the U.S. Low religiosity is likely to increase Iranians' integration, but exile status, a strong sense of Iranian nationalism, and attachment to the homeland hinder that outcome.

Iranian Americans remain preoccupied with the homeland. The Persian-language media reflect the interests of their audience in the diaspora and even in Iran. Los Angeles boasts numerous television stations, satellite channels, and radio stations that transmit directly to Iran on a daily basis. Shortly after Iranian television stations were established in the U.S. in the 1980s, they produced more programs than any other ethnic TV in Los Angeles, with the obvious exception of Hispanic programming (many Asian programs were produced overseas). This extensive programming rarely focuses on issues confronting the community in the U.S. There are also numerous Iranian expatriate Internet sites (e.g., Gooya.com, Payvand.com, and Iranian.com), which are additional sources of news about Iran. Iranian.com is especially oriented toward the Iranian American community and the second generation.

The Persian New Year, Now Ruz, brings most Iranian immigrants together and contributes to their sense of national identity. Of all Persian holidays, Now Ruz is the only one that is observed by all Iranian Americans, regardless of religious and ethnic background. Appropriately, the Persian New Year always begins on the first day of spring, March 21. Historically, Zoroastrians celebrated the creation of life by offering their god, Ahura Mazda, seven trays full of symbolic objects representing truth, justice, good thoughts, good deeds, prosperity, virtue, immortality, and generosity. To commemorate their heritage, Iranian Americans set a table with seven objects whose names start with the Persian letter *s* (a coin for prosperity, a candle for light, live fish in a bowl for life, a blossom for birth, and so on).

Discrimination and Prejudice

Very few social problems are associated with Iranian immigrants, yet they are more often subject to discrimination and prejudice than other high-status immigrant groups. The survey of Iranians in Los Angeles in the late 1980s showed that 20 percent of the respondents had experienced discrimination in finding a job and getting promoted. The perception of prejudice was even higher, at 50 percent.

Anti-Iranian prejudice has been primarily provoked by the actions and policies of the Islamic regime that took over the country following the revolution in 1980. During the Iranian revolution, anti-American feelings ran high, culminating in the Iran hostage crisis in 1979–1981, when 52 Americans were held hostage in the American embassy for 444 days. In the U.S., the crisis prompted a presidential order referred to as the "Iranian Control Program." It screened almost 57,000 Iranian students, at the time the single largest group of foreign students, to make sure that they had legal status. Each student was required to register with the Immigration and Naturalization Service (INS) by mid-December 1979, have a valid visa, and provide proof of full-time school enrollment; those who were out of legal status were subject to deportation.

Several Iranian students sued the U.S. government to have the presidential decree overturned. Arguing that Iranians had been unfairly singled out, they cited protection of personal rights under the Fifth Amendment. In its defense, the government argued that the regulation served "overriding national interests." The district court dismissed this claim, finding dubious any connection between protecting the lives of American hostages in Iran and singling out Iranians for registration with the INS. The court held that the regulation seemed mainly to serve the psychological purpose of appeasing the American public's demand for governmental action in response to the hostage crisis. When the government appealed, the U.S. Court of Appeals for the Washington, D.C. Circuit reversed the lower court's order, noting that the Immigration and Nationality Act of 1965 had given the attorney general broad authority to screen aliens of certain nationalities.

Although fewer than a thousand Iranians were actually deported, government policy targeted and scapegoated Iranian immigrants. Ironically, some of them had been persecuted by the very regime that perpetrated the hostage crisis. Every time conflict breaks out between Iran and the U.S., Iranian immigrants experience tensions in their adopted country. Many Iranians perceive that there is prejudice against them in the U.S. After September 11, 2001, Iranians were singled out in the National Security Entry-Exit Registration System (NSEERS) initiative. Special registration resulted in the arrest of several hundred Iranians in Los Angeles who were deemed in violation of their visas. In response, Iranians staged large demonstrations outside the Federal Building in the Westwood area of Los Angeles in 2002. When President George W. Bush designated the Islamic Republic of Iran as part of the "axis of evil," individuals bearing Iranian passports were denied visas, even though Iran and Iranians had nothing to do with the terrorist attacks.

Since 9/11, three grassroots advocacy organizations have emerged with the goal of mobilizing the Iranian American community against anti-Iranian legislation. These are the National Iranian American Council (NIAC), the Iranian American Political Action Committee (IAPAC), and the Iranian American Bar Association (IABA). These organizations were sorely needed in the Iranian community, which has a very limited organizational infrastructure. Although IABA was founded before the terrorist attacks, its programs and activities were accelerated afterward. IABA published an important report on the implementation of the special registration program in 2004, detailing the violation of the rights and abuse of 34 Iranians who were detained.

IAPAC was established after post-9/11 legislation made it more difficult for Iranian nationals to obtain visas to come to the U.S. The founders felt that the most effective way for Iranians to have a voice in the American political system was through campaign financing and donations to political candidates. IAPAC raises money from the community to distribute to candidates running for political office. Its mission is to encourage the civic participation of Iranian Americans and support candidates for office who are responsive to the needs of the community. It has campaigned to get candidates elected, and has also worked with elected officials to address immigration issues and to defend civil liberties against initiatives such as NSEERS, which resulted in the detention and mistreatment of Iranian nationals.

Iranian Americans have come to realize that the strategy of passing as non-Iranians or disassociating themselves from the Iranian regime does not protect them against hostility in the U.S. Despite Iranian Americans' high rate of citizenship (58.9 percent), they have little involvement in American politics. It is likely that this will change as the second generation reaches maturity.

With the possible exception of religious minorities, Iranians do not have adequate organizations to address the needs of the community in the U.S., even in areas of high concentration. The main explanation for this is cultural: voluntary associations were rare in Iran under the Shah's dictatorship. The striking shortage of voluntary associations among Iranians can also be attributed to class resources (education, knowledge of English, occupational skills), which obviate the need for collectivism or mutual assistance. Indeed, few Iranian associations are set up with the objective of mutual assistance. Iranians seem to follow a trajectory of individualistic, as opposed to collectivist, adaptation. The overall wealth of Iranians further mitigates their need for voluntary associations. The overarching goal of the majority of Iranian associations is the preservation of Iranian culture, not political activism or advocacy.

Since the closure of the American embassy in Iran, the U.S. and the Islamic Republic of Iran have had no diplomatic relations. In lieu of an embassy, the Iranian Interests Section operates under the auspices of the embassy of Pakistan in Washington, D.C. Data collected by the section show that more than 130,000 Iranians contacted this agency for passport-related services from 1996 to 2004, indicating a high degree of transnationalism, as Iranian Americans visit Iran.

Iranian ethnicity is becoming increasingly symbolic and recreational, enacted through family relations, cuisine, music, and the arts. There are significant generational shifts between immigrants and the native-born. While the first generation is resistant to integration because of its preoccupation with homeland issues and seeming lack of interest in American politics, the second generation is more American. As they come of age, this generation and their children are more likely to invest socially, politically, and emotionally in their American birthright. Changes in Iran are also likely to affect Iranians' sense of national identity in the U.S., especially among the second generation. However, the future of religious minorities from Iran has much less to do with events in Iran (since repatriation is not an option) than with assimilative forces within American society. The effects of all of these factors on Iranian ethnicity, identity, and community in the U.S. remain to be seen.

Bibliography

Ansari, Aboudolmaboud. *Iranian Immigrants in the United States.* New York: Associated Faculty Press, 1988.

Bozorgmehr, Mehdi, ed. "Iranians in America." *Iranian Studies* 31, 1 (special issue, 1998): 3–95.

Bozorgmehr, Mehdi, and Georges Sabagh. "High Status Immigrants: A Statistical Profile of Iranians in the United States." *Iranian Studies* 21, 3–4 (1988): 4–34.

Dallalfar, Arlene. "Iranian Women as Immigrant Entrepreneurs." *Gender and Society* 8, 4 (1994): 541–561.

Der-Martirosian, Claudia. "Economic Embeddedness and Social Capital of Immigrants: Iranians in Los Angeles." Ph.D. dissertation, University of California, Los Angeles, 1996.

Fathi, Asghar, ed. *Iranian Refugees and Exiles Since Khomeini.* Costa Mesa, Calif.: Mazda, 1991.

Hannasab, Shideh, and Romaria Tidwell. "Intramarriage and Intermarriage: Young Iranians in Los Angeles." *International Journal of Intercultural Relations* 22, 4 (1998): 395–408.

Karim, Perssis, and Mehdi M. Khorrami, eds. *A World in Between: Poems, Stories, and Essays by Iranian-Americans.* New York: George Braziller, 1999.

Kelley, Ron, and Jonathon Friedlander, eds. *Irangeles: Iranians in Los Angeles.* Berkeley: University of California Press, 1993.

Mobasher, Moshen. "Migration and Entrepreneurship: Iranian Ethnic Economy in the United States." In Leo-Paul Dana, ed., *Handbook of Research on Ethnic Minority Entrepreneurship.* Cheltenham, U.K.: Edward Elgar, 2006.

Naficy, Hamid. *The Making of Exile Cultures: Iranian Television in Los Angeles.* Minneapolis: University of Minnesota Press, 1993.

Shavarini, Mitra K. *Educating Immigrants: Experiences of Second-Generation Iranians.* New York: LFB Scholarly, 2004.

Jamaica

Milton Vickerman

Jamaicans are prominent in the current immigrant upsurge into the United States, accounting for almost half of all West Indian immigrants and propelled by an entrenched tradition of migration and economic hardship. An indicator of their propensity to travel is that worldwide, migrant Jamaicans are a third of Jamaica's population of 3 million. Moreover, their emigration rate—the likelihood of leaving a country, taking population size into consideration—is notably high. In 2001 it measured 59.2, making Jamaicans the second most likely population (after Bosnians) to migrate from their homeland to the U.S. Additionally, in polls Jamaicans repeatedly express a high desire to migrate, and at times the Jamaican government has actively promoted emigration as a means of coping with poverty and other economic problems. Traditionally, Jamaican immigrants have maintained close contact with the island, and this pattern has intensified in recent years, facilitated by cheaper travel and communications technology. These ongoing ties influence how Jamaican immigrants adjust to American society.

Although Jamaican migration to the U.S. dates back to the 19th century, as Kasinitz notes in *Caribbean New York* it began in earnest at the beginning of the 20th century and has come in three waves. The first lasted until the 1920s and was ended by a combination of restrictive immigration policies and the Great Depression; the second occurred in the 1940s and 1950s; and the third was spurred by Jamaica's achievement of independence in 1962, which enabled it to take advantage of liberal provisions in the 1965 Immigration Act. The most recent wave is the most significant in terms of numbers. For instance, based on Ira Reid's estimates in *The Negro Immigrant* and assuming that 50 percent of West Indian immigrants are Jamaicans, about 70,000 Jamaicans came to America during the first migration wave. In contrast, U.S. Citizenship and Immigration Services (USCIS) data show that between 1971 and 2004, 571,265 Jamaicans entered the country.

Residentially, Jamaicans are concentrated in cities along the East Coast, with New York City alone accounting for 47 percent of all foreign-born Jamaicans in the U.S. Various cities in south Florida—especially Miami—account for another 28 percent. Other, smaller concentrations are in Connecticut (chiefly Bridgeport), New Jersey, greater Washington, D.C., and Atlanta. Jamaicans' residential concentration is even more marked than these numbers indicate. For instance, most Jamaicans in New York City live in a few neighborhoods, including Crown Heights and Flatbush in central Brooklyn; Laurelton, Springfield Gardens, and St. Albans in Queens; and Wakefield, Williamsbridge, and Baychester in the Bronx.

Jamaicans in the Economy

Like most other immigrants, Jamaicans come to America for economic reasons and display a high labor force participation rate. In 2000 this rate was 69 percent for women and 74 percent for men over 16 years old. Individual Jamaicans often hold multiple jobs, and their households often contain multiple job-holders. In Florida, for instance, 22 percent of Jamaican households contain three or more individuals who are active in the workforce, compared to 13 and 15 percent of white and African American households, respectively. Culturally speaking, this propensity to hold multiple jobs has become one of the stereotypes that native-born Americans apply to Jamaicans. Pragmatically speaking, the tendency compensates for the immigrants' low personal income by boosting total household income.

Overall, 6 percent of Jamaican immigrant households earn less than $20,000 per year, 45 percent earn between $20,000 and $49,999, 25 percent earn $50,000 to $100,000, and 14 percent earn over $100,000. The wealthiest Jamaicans—who also tend to be U.S. citizens—live in the suburbs of New Jersey, Maryland, and Atlanta. In New Jersey, for example, 21 percent of Jamaican households earn over $100,000 per year. These areas are also home to the most highly educated Jamaicans. The general pattern of economic polarization reflects Jamaicans' tendency to migrate out of central cities to the suburbs as they become more prosperous. Although levels of income are lower in Florida than in other regions of settlement along the East Coast, that state is particularly popular among Jamaicans who migrate from other parts of the U.S., who often perceive it as offering a good compromise between living in America and enjoying a climate and lifestyle similar to those in Jamaica. It should also be noted that the small percentage of Jamaicans who live in nontraditional areas of settlement (e.g., California) tend to be wealthier and better educated than those along the East Coast. Also, many Jamaicans view home ownership as the primary symbol of economic success, and 64 percent (compared to 73 percent of all Americans) own their own homes.

Jamaican culture idealizes high-status jobs—notably in medicine and law—as key markers of success, and higher education as the prescribed method for attaining such jobs. A sizable number of immigrants—18 percent—work at management and professional jobs. However, owing to a combination of their low human capital, cultural proclivities, and gender norms, most Jamaican immigrants work in the service sector. Men are fairly evenly distributed along the occupational spectrum, but women are highly concentrated in health care; 34 percent of female immigrants work either as health-care professionals (especially nurses) or as health-care aides. Only 4 percent of males are so employed. Like their female counterparts, the majority of male Jamaican immigrants work in the mainstream economy. Self-employment is less evident among these immigrants than is popularly believed, but it is a factor, and males are more apt to be self-employed than females.

A few large ethnic businesses exist, and these primarily serve the ethnic community. For example, VP Records of Jamaica, Queens—the leading independent producer of dancehall, the very popular reggae/hip-hop hybrid—reported revenues of $5 million in 2002. Most Jamaican-owned businesses operate on a much smaller scale than this and are concentrated in the service field. Typically, they include restaurants, bakeries, travel agencies, and record stores. A notable addition is the private transportation industry in New York City, where Jamaican men are active, operating cars and vans that compete with the public transportation system.

Jamaican American Communities

Typically, Jamaican immigrants live in the same neighborhoods as other immigrants from the British West Indies and, increasingly, Haiti (but not the Hispanic Caribbean). Consequently, the culture of these neighborhoods is blended, but the Jamaican influence tends to stand out because Jamaicans make up almost half the total West Indian population. Moreover, the American popular media have taken symbols of Jamaican culture—notably Rastafarianism and reggae music—and used them to represent all West Indians. It is important to note that Jamaican–West Indian neighborhoods are significantly shaped by racial segregation. As an indicator, Logan and Deane have shown in a 2003 study that West Indian–white segregation in New York City stands at 82.7 (where 100 represents complete segregation). Class is also an issue. As noted, upwardly mobile Jamaican immigrants often migrate to New Jersey, Maryland, and Georgia, but stratification is also evident within urban areas. For instance, in New York City, Jamaicans living in Queens and the North Bronx are wealthier than those living in central Brooklyn.

Ethnic foods and displays are part of the cultural life that binds Jamaican immigrants together. Experiences, behaviors, modes of thought, and expectations that are rooted in Jamaican culture are transmitted through socialization to the American-born children of these immigrants. Transnationalism reinforces this culture by continuously circulating people, ideas, symbols, and material objects between Jamaica and the United States through travel and electronic technology. For instance, imported copies of the *Daily Gleaner,* Jamaica's premier newspaper, can be found in many Jamaican-owned businesses, along with North American editions of this paper and others, such as the *Carib News.* Public festivals, the most visible manifestation of Jamaican/West Indian–American culture, are now held in a number of cities around the country. Usually associated with Independence Day celebrations in Jamaica (August 6), annual festivals are held in Washington, D.C., Jacksonville, and, most famously, Brooklyn.

On a day-to-day basis, Jamaican immigrant life revolves around jobs, informal gatherings in voluntary associations and homes, the church, and, most importantly, the family. We have already noted the centrality of work to Jamaicans' sense of self. Also of importance is another institution, rotating credit associations, which bridge the gap between the public economic sphere and the private sphere of personal relationships. "Partners," in Jamaican parlance, are informal groups that practice a form of enforced saving. These groups, ranging in size from 5 to 20 people or more, consist of friends who designate one of themselves as the "banker." Each week members of the group deposit a specified sum with the banker, who in turn gives all the contributions to a designated member. The process of depositing funds ("throwing a hand") and receiving proceeds ("getting a draw") continues until each member of the group has had a chance to receive a payoff from the banker. For instance, in a group of five people, each of whom contributes $50 per week, each member receives $250 once every five weeks. The purpose of "partners" is economic, since Jamaicans use their payoffs to buy consumer goods and houses or start businesses, but the practice of "partnering" strengthens ethnic bonds among Jamaicans (and sometimes other West Indians), because it is based entirely on trust. This is especially true of the banker, in whom group members must have utmost confidence. Not surprisingly, members of rotating credit associations were often friends in Jamaica, and new members are recruited through word of mouth.

If rotating credit associations effectively strengthen the immigrant community, Jamaican volunteer associations serve both local and international functions. These organizations, primary locations for ethnic bonding, combine socialization, aid for Jamaican causes, and, to a lesser extent, political activity. Alumni associations, a popular institution among Jamaican immigrants (as opposed to second-generation Jamaicans), are typical in many of these respects. They developed to create networks among immigrant graduates of various Jamaican high schools and colleges. Their formal goal is to aid the namesake alma mater, and to this end alumni associations hold regular meetings and fundraising events. A case in point is the Excelsior Alumni Association in Brooklyn, which, according to its publicity material, held 11 formal meetings, an annual raffle, a citywide fund drive, and 3 formal dinner-dances in 2003 to support the financially strapped namesake high school in Jamaica. More than 12 such organizations exist in the New York City area alone, and similar bodies can be found in other cities with high concentrations of Jamaicans.

Religion is even more important than voluntary associations in integrating Jamaican American communities. In Jamaican terms, "religion" usually means Protestant Christianity, but Roman Catholicism is also well represented among Jamaican immigrants. In New York's West Indian neighborhoods, many churches often exist within a few blocks of each other. Some consist primarily of Jamaican (and other West Indian) worshippers, and in such cases the churches may actively promote West Indian culture. In Brooklyn, a good example is St. Mark's Episcopalian in Crown Heights, which has established a primary school catering to West Indian parents who decry perceived lack of discipline in U.S. public schools. In other instances, Jamaicans attend mainstream churches with largely white congregations. Such worship is facilitated by the popularity of televised American religious programs and personalities in Jamaica. Rastafarianism, the major alternative to Christian religious expression, has had an enormous impact on Jamaican culture, but very few Jamaicans or Jamaican immigrants are practicing Rastafarians. Those who are often worship in one of two major Rastafarian churches in America, the Twelve Tribes of Israel and the Ethiopian Orthodox Church.

The family—the most important institution in the Jamaican American community—reflects a mixture of pre- and postmigration ideals and practices as well as the influence of American culture. Jamaicans idealize the nuclear family, but in reality many (mostly lower-class) Jamaicans practice two alternative family forms: common-law marriage, and visiting relationships in which males maintain a number of households and spend time with each one in turn. Middle- and upper-class Jamaicans are more likely to live in nuclear families, but this does not prevent some of these men from engaging in the other family forms as well. Conversely, since Jamaican culture idealizes the nuclear family, common-law marriage partners often officially sanction their relationship in formal marriage after many years of living together.

Immigration both transmits and complicates these relationships. Thirty-seven percent of Jamaican American families are nuclear, and an equal proportion (38 percent) are headed by single women. The latter number reflects Jamaicans' practice of serial immigration, in which an adult member of a family—usually a woman—moves to the United States alone. After becoming financially stable, over months or even years, the immigrant reunites her family by facilitating their entry into the U.S. This practice extends the pattern of female headship evident in visiting relationships but accords women more power by endowing them with financial independence. Despite this, the evident benefits of living in a two-parent household, combined with Jamaican and American society's focus on the nuclear family, moves many Jamaican American families toward this cultural ideal.

In America, some Jamaican men continue their pattern of serial relationships and persist in holding on to traditional gender roles within their households. This creates contradictions for Jamaican American women, who gain enhanced autonomy through migration but must also deal with the double burden of fulfilling traditional sex roles while working full-time. Similar continuities and modifications of Jamaican traditions occur in child-rearing. Jamaican American parents, like their Jamaican counterparts, emphasize obedience, politeness, respect for elders, and pursuit of education in their children. They also continue to practice corporal punishment. However, since American society rejects such punishment, immigrant Jamaicans have deemphasized the practice—especially since children, aware of American norms, will sometimes accuse their parents of child abuse to authorities.

Adjustment to American Society

Like other immigrants, Jamaicans' adjustment to American society is an interactive process, involving not only the attributes that they bring but, more importantly, the way the society receives them. As immigrants, Jamaicans enjoy advantages, because broad similarities between Jamaican and American culture help minimize the initial difficulties of adjustment. Because of a common British origin, Jamaican culture (and that of other British West Indians) approximates its American counterpart. This means that Jamaicans are already familiar with a range of basic institutions, from a legal system based on common law to a capitalist economy. Jamaicans also speak English, and even if it is mixed with a patois (depending on level of education and social class), most immigrants readily comprehend standard written and oral communications in the U.S. All this is magnified by America's global influence, which has deeply penetrated the Caribbean through investments (e.g., in Jamaican bauxite), tourism, and media. When added to the constant circulation of people between the Caribbean and the U.S., these realities give Jamaicans broad premigration exposure to American culture and ease their adjustment to American society.

Jamaican culture's broadening influence on American society also facilitates adjustment. This influence stems in part from the simple fact that the immigrant population is large. But the 1972 release of the Jamaican film *The Harder They Come*, and well-received reggae songs by the established American artists Paul Simon and Johnny Nash in the same year, affected the culture more specifically by introducing reggae music to American audiences. Guitarist Eric Clapton's 1975 recording of Bob Marley's "I Shot the Sheriff" opened the doors even wider, acquainting Americans with the Rastafarian trappings of reggae. Later in the same decade, the British group the Police introduced the British version of reggae, along with ska—1960s Jamaican popular music—to American audiences. Reggae, and especially ska, are now well established in American popular music. By the end of the 1970s Jamaican immigrants had taken another reggae variant, "toasting," which involves singers talking over music tracks, to New York City. It became popular among American youth in the South Bronx and mixed with black culture to emerge as hip-hop. By the 1990s, hip-hop and reggae had grown together to produce dancehall, which was a hit with both American youth and second-generation West Indians. By 2005 the Puerto Rican version of dancehall, reggaeton, had been introduced to the U.S. and increasingly drew adherents from all Hispanic groups as well as urban youth from other racial and ethnic backgrounds.

Despite these influences, Jamaicans still face significant difficulties in adjusting to American society. Some relate to Americans' changing view of Jamaicans, but race is by far the main problem. Traditionally, Americans regarded Jamaicans—notably those in the first and second immigration waves—as a "model minority," adept at creating businesses, attaining professional credentials, and achieving outstanding success as leaders of the black community. Colin Powell's rise from the child of obscure immigrant Jamaican parents to become U.S. secretary of state is a good illustration. More recently, this view has changed somewhat, in response to the rising numbers of Jamaican immigrants, declines in their socioeconomic status, the popularity of elements of Rastafarian culture, and the marketing of Jamaica as a hedonistic paradise. Today Americans are as likely to see Jamaican immigrants as drug traffickers and easygoing pleasure-seekers as social strivers. In the 1980s, political turmoil in Jamaica forced the emigration of politically connected criminals to the U.S., and the activities of this group and drug smuggling from the island fused with the panic over crack cocaine. Some law enforcement officials in America came to see Jamaican "posses"—whom they erroneously linked to Rastafarians—as particularly potent crack dealers, and these criminal gangs negatively affected the public image of the larger Jamaican American community.

Race is more important than all these factors, because it remains a key organizing principle in America, although Jamaicans experience it differently from Americans. Race pervades American society and blacks are stigmatized, but certain factors mitigate the centrality of race in present-day Jamaica, despite its historical importance there. Essentially, black Jamaicans' demographic predominance has retarded the development and dissemination of full-blown racist ideologies, preventing their full institutionalization, as in the U.S. Moreover, the Jamaican state projects an effective and influential image of the island as a haven of multiracial tolerance, best summed up in its official motto: "Out of Many, One People." In practice, multiracialism easily slips into nonracialism, since the political system and mass media studiously ignore race. The island's long history of slavery, colonialism, and present-day social inequality ensure that race remains an issue on some levels, but other factors work to submerge it. Notably, Jamaicans have historically eschewed rigid, American-style racial dichotomies in which people are classified as either "black" or "white," opting instead for a complex system in which a multiplicity of factors (e.g., ancestry, complexion, social standing, and education) determine "race." Consequently, on a day-to-day basis, Jamaicans hardly think about race—especially since all their role models (both social failures and the society's leaders) are black. This detachment of race from achievement becomes a major problem for Jamaican immigrants, since Americans usually link these concepts. Jamaicans' adjustment to American society can be summed up in one question: Will they assimilate as blacks and face racial discrimination, or will they sidestep such discrimination and achieve full acceptance by identifying as Jamaicans or West Indians?

Research on this question is inconclusive, producing data supporting both sides of the equation. First- and second-wave Jamaicans exhibited high levels of nationalism but found Jim Crow racism too entrenched to overcome and eventually assimilated as African Americans. Third-wave Jamaicans face somewhat more favorable social conditions; though racism is still widespread, the rigidities of the Jim Crow system have abated. Moreover, the most recent group of immigrants is much larger than the previous two. These factors, together with the growth of multicultural ideology and intensifying transnationalism, have allowed Jamaican immigrants to create a viable ethnic identity that is semi-independent of the African American community. Social circumstances allow them to express their nationalism in ways that were not possible for earlier Jamaican immigrants. Yet since antiblack racism is widespread, they are just as likely as African Americans to experience discrimination. Consequently, Jamaicans typically are tugged in opposite directions by social pressures: to express an ethnic (nationalistic) identity that emphasizes the immigrant values of achievement and Jamaican experiences that minimize race, or to express a racial identity that focuses on solidarity with African Americans. In practice, Jamaican immigrants express both tendencies, vacillating between distancing themselves from and identifying with African Americans. To a large extent this dynamic pivots around a private/public distinction, where ethnic identity is predominant in the home and the ethnic neighborhood but a broader racial identity expresses itself more readily as they venture out into the larger society. In that sphere, Americans typically do not distinguish among blacks along the lines of ethnicity, and phenotype is unquestionably the basis for accepting or rejecting individuals. Ultimately, Jamaican immigrants would prefer to resolve this dilemma by establishing an understanding of "blackness" like the one that prevails in Jamaica: namely, that African ancestry and socioeconomic achievement are compatible. But this optimistic viewpoint must contend with entrenched stereotypes of blacks as inferior. Consequently, though these immigrants increasingly empathize with African Americans as they reside in America for longer periods of time, they will probably continue their pattern of vacillating between an ethnic and a racial identity.

Growing political clout is a natural corollary to ethnic concentration, but despite Jamaican society's high level of politicization, notable first-wave immigrant political activism (especially through Marcus Garvey), and the involvement of Jamaican-connected activists in the civil rights movement (e.g., Harry Belafonte), third-wave Jamaican immigrants have largely subordinated politics to economic advancement. They do, however, participate in the normal political process and can become quite energized when certain issues are at stake. Research by Vickerman shows that the 55 percent of Jamaican immigrants who are citizens typically reflect African American voting patterns and support the Democratic Party. Though they are socially conservative and may personally agree with the viewpoints typically associated with the Republican Party, race makes the difference. Like African Americans, Jamaican immigrants tend to believe that Democrats better represent the interests of blacks than Republicans do. A good example of this, and one that also demonstrates how particular circumstances can energize Jamaicans, was the political campaign to elect David Dinkins mayor of New York City. Because he was a black candidate with a serious chance of winning that high office, Jamaicans (and other West Indians) voted for him in large numbers.

More important in terms of their political participation is the fact that Jamaicans have begun to practice ethnic (as opposed to racial) politics. Most evident where they are highly concentrated, this politics derives from a number of sources, including the gradual realization that Jamaicans and West Indians have special interests that do not necessarily overlap with those of African Americans. This realization fits the political culture of places such as New York City, which have a long history of ethnic politics. Consequently, mainstream (often white) politicians have reached out to these immigrants as ethnics, further solidifying their self-awakening. As a result, Jamaicans have begun to enter mainstream politics. A good example of this in New York City is Una Clarke, who represented her largely West Indian district on the city council and whose slot was taken over by her daughter when she retired.

In addition to these factors, community activists whom the sociologist Philip Kasinitz has termed "ethnicity entrepreneurs" have taken it upon themselves to strengthen the political clout of Jamaicans and other West Indians. For instance, following passage of the three harsh 1996 immigration acts, ethnicity entrepreneurs seized on disquiet among West Indian immigrants and urged them in a series of public forums to become citizens. Traditionally, many of these immigrants had been content with being legal permanent residents, but while this status conferred many quasi-citizenship benefits, it also limited their political power. Vickerman, for instance, found that over 40 percent of Jamaican immigrants were "green card" holders, who typically took as long as 10 years to become citizens. Other Jamaicans had lived in the U.S. for almost 30 years and were still legal permanent residents. Fundamentally, this reluctance to become citizens stemmed from Jamaican immigrants' elevation of economic over political interests. In opposition to this point of view, ethnicity entrepreneurs argued that the 1996 immigration acts severely undercut the security offered by legal permanent residency, thereby exposing West Indians to deportation. This argument received wide circulation in the North American edition of the *Daily Gleaner* and persuaded at least some Jamaican immigrants to become citizens.

It should also be noted that the Jamaican illegal immigrant population is sizable, estimated by the USCIS to be about 40,000 (about 7 percent of the total Jamaican population in the U.S.) in 2005. Naturally, these individuals are even more strongly motivated than legal permanent residents to strengthen the security of their status, and they have been known to achieve legal permanent residency through the use of lawyers.

The Second Generation

Questions of assimilation weigh most heavily on second-generation immigrants, because they indicate the path Jamaicans will take in America in the future. Despite the cross-pressures affecting them, identity is a fairly settled issue for immigrant Jamaicans, since most view themselves as "Jamaican" or "West Indian." Second-generation immigrants face a more complex situation. They are American citizens, but as blacks they face racial discrimination. Moreover, research has shown that immigrant parents consciously socialize their children into Jamaican culture, believing that this will help them achieve at higher levels. As a result, ethnic identification is fundamentally important to the second generation. What is less clear is how these various identities interact to help determine their future. The research indicates that degree of racial discrimination, social class, and residential location influence their choices.

In a seminal study, Waters argued that second-generation West Indians fall into three main groups: the American-identified, the island-identified, and the ethnic-identified. The first group lives primarily in resource-poor inner-city areas and experiences wide-ranging racial discrimination, which results in the development of pessimistic attitudes and the formation of an oppositional identity. At the other end of the spectrum are the ethnic-identified, who cultivate a sense of ancestry, believing that it facilitates upward mobility. Generally speaking, they have wealthier parents than the American-identified, enjoy more and better resources, and are more optimistic about their chances of attaining success in America. The third group, the island-identified, Waters argues, are so oriented toward the West Indies that the question of having an American identity does not even occur to them. Ultimately, this identity is unsustainable, and she expects that in the long run second-generation West Indian identity options will resolve to a choice between being American- or ethnic-identified.

The 2000 Census and other research lends support to Waters's thesis. Among individuals claiming Jamaican ancestry who were born in the U.S., residents of the suburbs enjoy greater wealth than urban dwellers. In this respect, it is useful to compare New York City and its suburbs, because large numbers of Jamaicans live in these areas and their quality of life varies noticeably. For instance, second-generation Jamaicans in Nassau County, Long Island, live in households with a median yearly income of $90,000. The median household income of those residing in another suburb, Yonkers, New York, is $71,000. This contrasts with $45,000 for similar individuals living in New York City and $38,000 for those residing in Newark, New Jersey. The data show that, consistent with greater wealth, suburbanized second-generation Jamaicans are somewhat more likely to attend private schools than their urbanized coethnics. Whereas 14 percent of second-generation Jamaican youth in New York City attend private school, 17 percent of males and 22 percent of females in Nassau County do so.

The difference between wealthy and poorer second-generation young people lies not so much in the messages transmitted to them by their immigrant parents as in the efficacy of the messages. Regardless of income, Jamaican parents stress values emphasizing respect, hard work, education (especially in the professions), and material success. For example, in research comparing second-generation youth in California and Florida, the sociologist Rubén Rumbaut found that Asians and Jamaicans display the highest educational aspirations of all the groups studied. Also, Jamaicans exhibit the highest grade-point average of any non-Asian group. While these results point to the efficacy of certain values and cultural advantages (e.g., speaking English) enjoyed by Jamaicans, it is also true that poorer parents often lack the resources to make their goals for their children a reality. Poor Jamaican homes are more likely to be headed by single parents than those in suburban areas, and this is associated with lower household income. In New York City, 68 percent of Jamaicans live in single-parent households of one type or another, whereas in Nassau County the figure is 52 percent. The median income of these New York households is $38,980, compared to $71,160 for similar households in Nassau County.

The implication is that structural conditions facilitate socioeconomic success for affluent West Indian youth but inhibit it for poorer coethnics. In some urban environments, poor schools, low expectations, discrimination, and negative peer influences combine with fewer household resources to further dampen West Indian parents' aspirations for their children. A good example is situations in which recently arrived Jamaican youth, resentful at being left behind in Jamaica when their parents originally came to the U.S., find themselves in inner-city environments where single parents have little time to devote to them because of a heavy workload or because they work as live-in domestics in distant suburbs. Underachieving peers can then wield significant influence, leading to delinquent behavior and downward mobility. Despite this, evidence indicates that many Jamaican American young people still associate socioeconomic success with being Jamaican and attempt to apply the norms and values they link with a Jamaican identity to overcome discrimination.

In the long run, the circulation of people and culture between Jamaica and Jamaican American communities will significantly influence the process of assimilation into American society. First- and second-wave Jamaican immigrants displayed a strong—and often criticized—tendency to hold on to their ethnic identity. However, many of these immigrants became an integral part of the larger black community and their children became African Americans. Third-wave immigrants may be different. The racial pressures pushing them to integrate into the African American community are still quite potent and will probably remain so for the foreseeable future. However, these pressures are increasingly being challenged by a growing Jamaican immigrant population. Crucially, this growth is augmented by transnational processes that add "authenticity" to Jamaican American culture by faithfully replicating the Jamaican way of life in the United States. This allows Jamaicans to feel increasingly comfortable in their culture even while living in a foreign country. Their cultivation of this culture to enhance upward mobility further strengthens it and sharpens divisions with non–West Indians. As in the past, Jamaican culture will continue to exert disproportionate influence on the larger West Indian community because of the weight of numbers and Americans' tendency to conflate "Jamaican" with "West Indian." But to say that ethnic identity is challenging entrenched American views about race (notably antiblack racism) is not to say that ethnicity is supplanting race. It remains to be seen whether Jamaicans will be able to sustain a distinct ethnic identity. In this respect, the outcome of the second generation will be especially instructive. Race remains the potent factor looming over all Jamaican efforts to assimilate into American society.

Bibliography

Chevannes, Barry. *Rastafari: Roots and Ideology.* Syracuse, N.Y.: Syracuse University Press, 1994.

Foner, Nancy. *Islands in the City: West Indian Migration to New York.* Berkeley: University of California Press, 2001.

Henke, Holger. *The West Indian Americans.* Westport, Conn.: Greenwood, 2001.

Kasinitz, Philip. *Caribbean New York: Black Immigrants and the Politics of Race.* New York: Cornell University Press, 1992.

Kasinitz, Philip, and Milton Vickerman. "Ethnic Niches and Racial Traps: Jamaicans in the New York Regional Economy." In Hector R. Cordero-Guzman, Robert C. Smith, and Ramon Grosfoguel, eds., *Migration, Transnationalization, and Race in a Changing New York,* pp. 129–211. Philadelphia: Temple University Press, 2001.

Model, Suzanne. "West Indian Prosperity: Fact or Fiction?" *Social Problems* 42, 4 (Nov. 1995): 535–52.

Palmer, Ransford. *Pilgrims from the Sun: West Indian Migration to America.* New York: Twayne, 1995.

Reid, Ira De A. *The Negro Immigrant.* New York: Columbia University Press, 1939.

Rumbaut, Rubén. "Turning Points in the Transition to Adulthood: Determinants of Educational Attainment, Incarceration, and Early Childbearing among Children of Immigrants." *Ethnic and Racial Studies* 28, 6 (Nov. 2005): 1041–86.

Vickerman, Milton. *Crosscurrents: West Indian Immigrants and Race.* New York: Oxford University Press, 1999.

Waters, Mary. *Black Identities: West Indian Dreams and American Realities.* Cambridge: Harvard University Press, 1999.

Korea

Pyong Gap Min

As a result of the significant immigration of Koreans in the post-1965 era, the Korean population in the United States increased from approximately 70,000 in 1970 to about 1.1 million in 2000. Korean immigrants have maintained strong ethnic attachment and solidarity—probably more so than other Asian groups—because of their homogeneity, their affiliation with and frequent participation in Korean immigrant churches, and their concentration in small businesses.

Immigration before 1965

The first wave of Korean immigration to the U.S. took place between 1903 and 1905, when famines in Korea and the effective intermediary role of Dr. Horace Allen, an American Presbyterian missionary, encouraged many Korean men to go to Hawai'i to work on sugar plantations. About 40 percent of these pioneer immigrants were converts to Christianity, and they chose to come to Hawai'i for religious freedom as well as for a better economic life. Although the plantation owners needed more workers, Japan's political domination of Korea soon put a stop to the immigration, though about 2,000 additional Koreans came to Hawai'i and California between 1905 and 1924, most of them as "picture brides" of the earlier immigrants. Another 600 were political refugees and students involved in the anti-Japanese independence movement, and most of these studied at universities in New York and other East Coast cities. A small number of these students constituted the core of the Korean community in New York, whereas the pioneer labor migrants and their families made up the majority of the Korean population in Honolulu, San Francisco, and Los Angeles.

Immediately after Korea gained independence from Japan in 1945, the country suffered from internal political conflict and U.S.-Soviet struggles for hegemony over it. In 1948, Korea was divided into two political entities, a rightist government in South Korea supported by the U.S. and a communist government in North Korea supported by the Soviet Union. The first ideological armed conflict, known as the Korean War, took place between 1950 and 1953, and since then the U.S. has been deeply involved in South Korea militarily, politically, and economically. The strong links between the two countries contributed to a steady increase in the number of Korean immigrants; between 1950 and 1964, approximately 15,000 Koreans came to the United States. An overwhelming majority of these were Korean women married to U.S. servicemen stationed in South Korea or Korean orphans adopted by American citizens.

Immigration after 1965

The Immigration Act of 1965, which liberalized U.S. immigration policy, led to a dramatic increase in the number of Asians coming to the U.S. As shown in Table 1, the flow of Korean immigration steadily rose after this law was passed. About 30,000 Koreans were arriving annually by the latter half of the 1970s, and the flow reached its peak in the late 1980s, when about 35,000 came per year. In the 1980s, South Korea was the third largest source country of immigrants to the U.S., after Mexico and the Philippines. But the flow significantly dropped in the 1990s, before increasing slightly in the first three years of the 21st century.

Lack of economic opportunity, social and political insecurity in South Korea, and the difficulty of sending children to colleges and universities pushed many Koreans to emigrate to the U.S. in the 1970s and 1980s. In those years many high school graduates had difficulty gaining admittance to a decent college or university

Table 1   Immigration of Koreans by five-year periods, 1950–2002

Period	Number of immigrants
2000–2002	57,593
1995–1999	75,579
1990–1994	112,215
1985–1989	175,803
1980–1984	163,088
1975–1979	155,505
1970–1974	93,445
1965–1969	18,469
1960–1964	9,521
1955–1959	4,490
1950–1954	539

Source: U.S. Immigration and Naturalization Service, *Annual Reports* and *Statistical Yearbooks,* 1950–2002 (Washington, D.C.: U.S. Dept. of Justice).

in Seoul, prompting many parents to immigrate to the U.S. to give their children a second chance for higher education. But Korean parents' zeal for education also sent too many young people to college, so about half of college graduates could not find jobs. Consequently, these unemployed college graduates also emigrated. Many intellectuals also sought refuge from the ruling Korean military dictatorships between 1961 and 1987.

Strong U.S.-Korean ties stimulated immigration as well. Because the U.S. has stationed a large military force in South Korea for many years, Korean women have married American servicemen and come to the U.S. with their husbands when they return home. Moreover, many Korean orphans have been adopted by U.S. citizens since the Korean War. Close U.S.-Korean ties, the presence of American forces, and the postgraduate training of many Korean intellectuals in the U.S. popularized American culture in South Korea and led many middle-class Koreans to view America as a country of affluence and prosperity.

As a result of the influx of immigrants, the Korean American population has increased dramatically over the past thirty-five years. In 1970 there were only about 70,000 Korean Americans, the majority of them native-born. This population increased to 354,000 in 1980, to 800,000 in 1990, and to about 1.1 million in 2000. In addition, about 150,000 people defined themselves in the 2000 Census as Korean and one or more other ethnic/racial categories, suggesting that they are children of Korean intermarriages.

Settlement Patterns

Following the general pattern of Asian Americans' settlement, Korean Americans are highly concentrated in California. In 2000 approximately 346,000 Korean Americans, or 32 percent of the Korean population in the U.S., lived in California. New York is the second largest state, with 11 percent of Korean Americans. New Jersey experienced a fourfold increase in the Korean population—the highest rate of increase among all states with concentrations of Koreans—between 1980 and 2000. In 1980, Illinois, Texas, and Washington had more Korean Americans than New Jersey, but by 2000, New Jersey had the third largest concentration, with over 65,000 Koreans (6 percent).

Table 2 shows the six consolidated metropolitan statistical areas (CMSAs) with the largest Korean populations. About 60 percent of Korean Americans are concentrated in these six areas. Southern California, comprising Los Angeles, Orange, and three adjacent counties, had over a quarter million Korean Americans in 2000 and was the largest Korean population center outside of Korea. Almost one out of four Koreans in the United States lives in that area, which also has the largest Asian American population in the U.S., approximately 1.7 million in 2000.

According to Yu and his associates, Korean immigrants established their community in Los Angeles as early as 1904. In 1970, Los Angeles County, with 8,811 peo-

Table 2   Top six Consolidated Metropolitan Statistical Areas (CMSAs) with a large Korean
population, 2000

Rank	CMSA	Number	Percentage
1	Los Angeles–Riverside–Orange County	257,975	24.0
2	New York–New Jersey–Long Island	170,509	15.8
3	Washington–Baltimore	74,474	6.9
4	San Francisco–Oakland–San Jose	57,386	5.3
5	Chicago–Gary–Kenosha	46,871	4.4
6	Seattle–Tacoma–Bremerton	41,169	3.8

Source: U.S. Census Bureau, 2000 Census, Summary File 1, QT-P3.

ple of Korean background, was the largest Korean population center, and growth since then has been exponential. About 47,000 of these people live in Koreatown, approximately three miles west of downtown Los Angeles. Covering about 25 square miles, Koreatown is the residential and commercial center of life for Los Angeles Koreans. They made up only 20 percent of its population in 2000—Hispanics, primarily Mexicans, accounted for the majority—but the Korean residents of Koreatown composed 18 percent of the Korean population in the five-county Southern California area and over half of the Korean population in the city of Los Angeles.

The New York/New Jersey/Long Island area is the second largest Korean population center, with about 170,000 people, 16 percent of Korean Americans in 2000. In 1960 only about 400 Koreans lived in New York City, many of them students enrolled in universities in the area. The vast majority who came in the late 1960s and early 1970s came under an occupation preference, including a large number of medical professionals. Approximately 6,200 Korean medical workers immigrated to the U.S. between 1965 and 1975, and about one third of these (36 percent) settled in New York, New Jersey, and Connecticut.

More than 70 percent of Korean Americans in New York City itself (numbering about 87,000 in 2000) have settled in Queens, with 25 percent in Flushing. Koreans immigrants have established a residential and commercial center in downtown Flushing, and numerous businesses with Korean-language signs are dotted along the main street. Koreans refer to this area as Haninsanga (the Korean business district). In addition to Flushing, such middle-class white communities as Bayside, Little Neck, and Douglaston in Queens have large numbers of Korean immigrants.

Self-Employment in Small Businesses

In contrast to many other ethnic groups, Korean immigrants often choose to run small businesses rather than work for others in the U.S. Table 3 presents the top nine entrepreneurial groups based on 1980, 1990, and 2000 Census data. In 1980, 18 percent of Korean immigrants in the labor force were self-employed. In that

Table 3   Self-employment rates of the nine most highly entrepreneurial immigrant groups, 1980, 1990, and 2000 (percentages)[a]

Country of origin	1980	1990	2000	Total number of workers in 2000
Greece	23.3	26.8	26.0	84,226
Syria	20.9	23.1	25.5	26,191
Israel/Palestine	22.9	23.6	24.1	63,110
Korea	18.0	26.5	23.4	418,407
Jordan	24.2	23.1	23.2	25,794
Paraguay	11.6	20.4	23.1	5,722
Iran	20.1	21.3	23.1	160,539
Lebanon	20.0	19.2	21.4	59,006
Hungary	16.0	18.1	19.0	35,387

Source: U.S. Census Bureau, 1980, 1990, 2000 Censuses, 5% Public Use Microdata Samples, weighted data.
a. Persons aged 25–64 in the labor force.

year, Korean immigrants had one of the highest self-employment rates among all immigrant groups. The self-employment rate of Korean immigrants increased to 26.5 percent in 1990. In that year, only Greek immigrants recorded a higher self-employment rate, at 26.8 percent. In 2000, the self-employment rate of Korean immigrants slightly fell to 23.4 percent. This may be due to the increase in the number of professional immigrants since 1990.

Because the Korean immigrant population is much larger than that of any of the other highly entrepreneurial groups included in Table 3, Korean immigrants hold a significant place as a trading minority. Korean-owned businesses are far more visible to the American public than, say, Greek- or Pakistani-owned businesses. Since both Greek and Pakistani immigrants are heavily concentrated in New York City, their businesses are highly visible there. By contrast, Korean-owned businesses attract public attention in Los Angeles, New York, Chicago, Washington, Philadelphia, Atlanta, and many other cities.

Census surveys based on respondents' self-reports underestimate the extent of self-employment for a number of reasons. A survey conducted in Los Angeles and Orange counties in 1986 reveals a much higher self-employment rate among Korean immigrants than the 1990 Census data show. The majority of Korean male respondents and more than one third of female respondents in the two Southern California counties were self-employed. Forty-five percent of Korean workers in Southern California (including the respondents, their spouses, and other working family members) were self-employed, in contrast to the 35 percent cited by the census. The 1986 survey revealed that 53 percent of the respondents' households owned at least one business.

Korean immigrants are heavily concentrated in several labor-intensive small businesses, such as grocery or greengrocery stores, fish stores, shops selling manufactured goods imported from Asian countries, dry cleaning and manicure services, and garment manufacturing. The retail grocery-and-liquor business is the most popular one in all major Korean communities in the U.S. As of December 1991, there were approximately 25,000 Korean-owned grocery and/or liquor stores in the U.S. and Canada, including 2,800 in Southern California. In the New York/New Jersey area, selling produce as well as groceries is a popular Korean business line, with about 1,800 stores in 1994.

Another popular business for Korean immigrants is the retail and wholesale of manufactured goods imported from South Korea and other Asian countries—wigs, handbags, clothing, costume jewelry, hats, and shoes. Taking advantage of their native language and connections with South Korea, many immigrants established import and wholesale businesses in the 1960s and 1970s. By the early 1990s, there were approximately 600 Korean-owned import businesses in the Los Angeles/Long Beach area and 500 in the New York/New Jersey metropolitan area. Korean importers in Los Angeles and New York supply Korean- and Asian-made goods to other Korean wholesalers, who in turn distribute mainly to Korean retailers all over the country.

Dry cleaning is another favored Korean business line, partly because it is very suitable for family work and partly because it requires shorter hours of labor and less physical strength than other kinds of retail businesses. There are approximately 1,500 Korean-owned manicure shops and 700 fish retail shops in New York, but these two businesses are not common in other major Korean communities.

Business-Related Interactions with Other Groups

In the U.S., Korean immigrants can be considered a "middleman minority"—a group that bridges two other groups in a stratified society by distributing the products made by the ruling group to minority customers. Chinese in Asian countries, Asian Indians in African countries, and Jews in medieval Europe are representative of middleman minorities. Similarly, Korean merchants in the U.S. depend on low-income minority customers, especially blacks, to a greater extent than is expected by chance, largely because structural factors encourage Korean immigrants to run small businesses in minority neighborhoods.

Two kinds of Korean businesses are common in black neighborhoods. One is the grocery and liquor business. Predominantly white neighborhoods have major grocery chains and therefore do not need small Korean-owned grocery stores. But few grocery chains locate in low-income black neighborhoods, since the low spending capacity of the residents, high crime rates, and vandalism discourage them from investing in these areas. Moreover, many people in these neighborhoods do not own cars, so they depend on small neighborhood grocery stores for much of their grocery shopping. Accordingly, independent Korean grocers do not encounter as much competition in low-income black neighborhoods as those in predominantly white areas.

The other major Korean business in minority areas is the fashion business. Korean storeowners have the advantage of easy access to Korean suppliers and importers. Whereas American buyers distribute these imported manufactured goods to department stores in white neighborhoods, Korean importers provide them directly to Korean retailers. Korean owners of fashion stores in minority neighborhoods, like Korean small grocers, have a competitive advantage, because there are no department stores in these neighborhoods.

Regardless of what kind of business they run, Korean entrepreneurs depend largely on Mexicans and other Latino employees to operate their stores. For example, in the 1986 survey, Mexican workers made up 48 percent of employees in Korean-owned businesses in Los Angeles and Orange counties, outnumbering Korean employees (40 percent). In a survey of Korean businesses in black neighborhoods conducted in 1992, Latinos made up 42 percent of the employees, followed by blacks (31 percent) and Koreans (23 percent).

In addition, Korean merchants depend heavily on white landlords, especially Jewish ones. For example, the Korean Small Business Service Center estimated that less than 10 percent of Korean merchants in New York City own the buildings where their businesses operate; the others usually have white landlords, who are mostly Jewish.

Conflicts with the black community. Korean merchants in black neighborhoods have been subjected to several forms of hostility and rejection. They have experienced verbal and physical assaults, press attacks, murder, arson, boycotts, and looting. Patrick Joyce's comparison between New York City and Los Angeles reveals that New York experienced more and longer boycotts from 1981 to 1995, while Los Angeles had more cases of severe violence, including shootings and arson. Fourteen boycotts of Korean stores occurred in New York during this period. The longest, the Brooklyn boycott of two Korean produce stores between January 1990 and May 1991, drew national and even international media attention and became the subject of several books. It started after a scuffle between a Haitian immigrant woman, who paid only two dollars for a three-dollar item, and the Korean manager of the store, who allegedly beat her.

In the 1980s, Korean immigrants in Los Angeles maintained better relations with blacks than their counterparts in New York did. However, black-Korean tensions were heightened there in the spring of 1991 when a 14-year-old black girl was shot to death in a Korean-owned grocery store while struggling with the female owner over an unpaid-for bottle of orange juice. When Du Soon Ja, who shot the girl, was given five years' probation, blacks were angrier about the court decision than about the incident itself. Unfortunately, five months later, a jury acquitted four white police officers accused of beating a black motorist, Rodney King, sparking riots in Los

Angeles. Approximately 2,300 Korean stores in South Central Los Angeles and Koreatown became targets of destruction and looting. Korean merchants absorbed property damages of more than $350 million, about 45 percent of the total damages incurred during the Los Angeles riots.

Conflicts with other groups. Korean grocery, liquor, produce, and fish store owners depend on white suppliers, and their relationships with these suppliers involve inherent tensions as both groups attempt to maximize their profits. Korean merchants have encountered discrimination from white suppliers in terms of price, quality of merchandise, item selection, speed of delivery, parking allocations, and overall service. For example, Korean produce retailers and produce delivery truck drivers in New York buy fruits and vegetables at Hunts Point Market, the largest wholesale produce market in the U.S. Korean retailers visiting the market have had altercations with employees of wholesalers, and some Korean merchants have been severely beaten. Many times Korean retailers have not been allowed to exchange merchandise or have been forced to buy items they do not want.

Korean merchants' dependence on Latino employees also leads to friction. New Latino immigrants and illegal residents often work in Korean-owned stores because they are severely disadvantaged in the general labor market in terms of language, educational level, and legal status. In my research, Korean merchants told me that they prefer Latino employees to black employees mainly because they are perceived to be "hardworking, cheap, and docile." But for the very same reasons Koreans can be charged with exploiting Latino employees.

Tension between white landlords and Korean renters is inevitable, because their goals are in sharp conflict. Korean merchants can generally change suppliers if they do not like their prices and/or services, but they cannot change landlords as easily, and that opens the door to exploitation. Many Korean immigrants buy a failing business or open a new one and then turn it into a thriving business within a few years. As Korean-owned businesses become more successful, some landlords raise rents by a significant margin over a short period of time.

Ethnic Attachment and Solidarity

Ethnicity involves two interrelated but basically different phenomena. One, which we might call "ethnic attachment," indicates the extent to which members of an ethnic group are culturally, socially, and psychologically integrated with their group. The other phenomenon, whose meaning can be captured by the term "ethnic solidarity," is the degree to which members use collective actions to protect their common interests. Korean immigrants have maintained high levels of both ethnic attachment and ethnic solidarity. It may be safely said that these are the defining characteristics that distinguish Korean immigrants' adjustment to life in America from that of other Asian immigrant groups.

Three factors have contributed to Korean immigrants' high levels of ethnic attachment and solidarity: the homogeneity of the group, their high rate of affiliation with and frequent participation in ethnic religious congregations, and their high concentration in small businesses.

Group homogeneity. Korean immigrants are more homogeneous in their cultural background and homeland than any other Asian immigrant group. One important factor is that they share one language, which gives them a big advantage over multilingual Asian immigrant groups such as Indians and Filipinos in maintaining their identity as Koreans. For example, Korean immigrants, who can speak, read, and write the Korean language fluently, depend mainly on Korean-language newspapers and TV and radio programs for news, information, and leisure activities. This dependence on ethnic media strengthens their ties to the ethnic community and the home country.

The Korean ethnic media, which have been highly developed and are very effective because of immigrants' monolingual background, have contributed to ethnic solidarity as well. For example, community leaders in New York have effectively used ethnic media to educate Koreans about the importance of participating in school-board elections and the 2000 Census. Through Korean-language television, radio, and newspapers, they have been able to publicize community political issues widely.

Church participation. Christians are a minority population in South Korea; in 1999, 18 percent of Koreans were affiliated with Protestant churches and another 7 percent with Roman Catholic churches. But approximately three quarters of Korean immigrants are affiliated with Christian churches in the U.S.—55 percent with Protestant churches and 20 percent with Catholic churches. This is partly because of the selective migration of Korean Christians. Results of surveys conducted in New York, Los Angeles, and Chicago found that slightly over half of Korean immigrants belonged to a Christian church in Korea, and a majority are urban, middle-class people, a segment of the Korean population in which Christianity is strong. Korean Christians are more likely to emigrate to the U.S. than are Buddhists or those with no religion. In addition, many people who were not Christians in Korea decide to attend a Korean church in the U.S. for such practical reasons as the church's immigration orientation, fellowship, and ethnic education for their children. Because there is an abundance of pastors, there are approximately 4,000 Korean immigrant churches in the U.S.

The church participation rate among Korean immigrants is exceptionally high, much higher than that of other Christian groups. Kim and Kim's analysis of the Presbyterian Racial and Ethnic Panel surveys shows that 78 percent of Korean Presbyterians attend their congregations' Sunday worship every week, compared with 28 percent of white Presbyterians, 34 percent of African Americans, and 49 percent of Latinos. Most Korean immigrant churches hold one or two weekday services in addition to the main service on Sunday, and a significant proportion (about 35 percent) of Korean Protestant immigrants participate twice a week or more often.

Korean churches organize many social activities that contribute to fellowship and networking among congregants, including full lunch or refreshments after Sunday's service, committee activities, family retreats, birthday parties for elderly members and children, and, most important, the district meeting, or *guyuk yebae*. This is a monthly meeting held in a private home, including a short worship service and a long fellowship over dinner, for a small neighborhood group (usually 12 families). Immigrant churches also help Koreans preserve their cultural traditions by celebrating Korean festivals and national holidays several times a year. All Korean churches celebrate Chuseok, the Korean version of Thanksgiving Day, by serving traditional food, and many women wear traditional Korean dress (*chimajeagori*). Large churches have established schools to teach children the Korean language and cultural traditions. Whether they have a school or not, all Korean churches try to teach children Korean etiquette and Korean values through formal and informal activities.

Korean immigrant churches have also enhanced ethnic solidarity by providing an institutional basis for collective and political activities. During the 1990–1991 African American boycott of two Korean stores in Brooklyn, many Korean churches mobilized their members to shop in groups at the boycotted stores to give the owners moral support and collected donations to provide financial support.

Concentration in small business. Korean immigrants' high level of concentration in several kinds of small business has also contributed to their strong ethnic attachment. Since the vast majority of Korean immigrants work in the ethnic economy as business owners, unpaid family members, or paid employees, they speak the Korean language and practice Korean customs at the workplace and often interact socially almost exclusively with other Koreans. Their experiences are significantly different from those of immigrant groups with low self-employment rates. For example, only 5 percent of Filipino immigrants are self-employed, so the vast majority have to speak English and follow American norms at the workplace. They also have more opportunities than Korean immigrants to establish close friendships with workers outside their own ethnic group.

Conflicts with black customers, white suppliers, Latino employees, white landlords, and government agencies have also contributed to Korean immigrants' feelings of solidarity. In particular, the serious threat of hostility from African Americans, in the form of armed robbery, physical violence, murder, arson, boycotts, and riots, has a profound effect. By establishing local business associations, Korean merchants in black neighborhoods have collectively tried to solve problems with black customers and residents. Although a number of incidents of business-related conflict have enhanced Koreans' solidarity, the 1990–1991 boycott of two Korean stores in New York City and the destruction of many Korean stores in the 1992 Los

Angeles race riots significantly affected the Korean community in terms of ethnic solidarity and political consciousness.

The Brooklyn boycott occurred about one year after another black boycott, led by the same activists, had successfully forced a nearby Korean store to close. Korean community and business leaders agreed that if the two boycotted stores were also forced to close, another Korean store would soon be targeted. Therefore, they made every effort to support the two produce stores financially until the boycott was abandoned. The Korean Produce Association of New York and the local business association in Brooklyn raised funds, mostly from their members, to help their fellow storeowners. The Korean Association of New York, other Korean business associations, and many Korean churches quickly followed them in raising funds from the Korean community. Approximately $150,000 was raised during the first year of the boycott, providing each boycotted storeowner with about $7,000 per month. Although the sales volume of each store was reduced to almost nothing during that year, both were able to stay open, mainly because of community contributions.

Koreans also used political means to terminate the boycott. Korean community and business leaders in New York visited the Brooklyn borough president, the mayor, the New York State Legislature, and even the U.S. president and pressured them to take effective measures to break the boycott. In particular, they asked Mayor David Dinkins to enforce the court order that picketers stay 50 feet away from the boycotted stores. When the mayor, a black man, did not actively intervene to terminate the boycott, the Korean Association of New York organized a mass demonstration in front of city hall. About 7,000 Koreans participated. The Korean American Senior Citizens Center mobilized its members, many of whom came in traditional dress. The Council of Korean Churches of Greater New York encouraged its members to mobilize as many congregants as possible, and many came to the rally in church vans.

While Korean merchants' conflicts with blacks have contributed to solidarity among all Koreans, their conflicts with white suppliers have brought them together as a group and enhanced political skills among themselves. By establishing business associations, Korean merchants have acted together to protect their economic interests against white suppliers through demonstrations, boycotts, group purchases, and other collective actions. All major Korean business associations, including the national and local Korean American Grocers Association (KAGRO), have used collective actions against wholesalers or suppliers. The collective activities of the Korean Produce Association of New York (KPANY) are representative.

As noted, Korean produce retailers in New York have encountered different forms of unfair treatment by white suppliers. The KPANY, established in 1974, has used more demonstrations and boycotts than any other Korean business association in New York. Its office is located at Hunts Point Market, where Korean produce retailers purchase fruits and vegetables every day. Whenever a retailer encounters unfair treatment by a supplier, he or she is supposed to report the incident to the

KPANY, which immediately sends a troubleshooter to the scene to resolve the conflict. Since Korean produce retailers make up the majority of the wholesalers' customers, the KPANY has used boycotts as an effective strategy to defend Korean merchants from unfair actions by suppliers. Between 1977 and 1991, the KPANY organized five boycotts as well as five demonstrations against suppliers.

Mainly because of the language barrier and their unfamiliarity with the U.S. labor market, many Korean immigrants cannot find professional and other white-collar occupations commensurate with their high educational levels. As an alternative to blue-collar occupations, they have chosen to become entrepreneurs, often in grocery and liquor retail, produce retail, wholesale and retail of Asian-imported manufactured goods, dry-cleaning services, and manicure services. Most of their retail businesses are dependent on white suppliers and on lower-income minority customers. Consequently, Korean immigrants have played the role of middleman merchants, serving as a bridge between white corporations and minority customers. They are also highly dependent on Latino employees and white landlords for their business operations. As a result, Korean immigrant merchants have encountered a great deal of business-related conflict with other ethnic groups. Economic segregation and business-related conflicts have contributed to ethnic solidarity, as have Korean immigrants' active participation in Korean churches, homogeneity, and monolingual background. These factors have led to Korean immigrants' segregation from the mainstream society but to a strong sense of attachment to their Korean background.

Historically, middleman groups have usually functioned to bridge a gap in status in societies in which social mobility is difficult. However, American society has usually enabled immigrants to achieve social mobility and thus does not need a permanent middleman minority to serve as merchants in lower-income minority neighborhoods. The 2000 Census shows that few native-born Korean Americans are self-employed; the vast majority participate in the general economy. This means that Korean Americans experience a radical intergenerational transition in occupation—a more radical transition than that of any other Asian ethnic group. It also suggests that by virtue of their occupational assimilation, native-born Korean Americans maintain much lower levels of ethnic attachment and solidarity than immigrants do. Similarly, second-generation Korean churches have eliminated many Korean cultural traditions and downplayed their Korean identity as they have become incorporated in the white evangelical movement.

Bibliography

Joyce, Patrick D. 2003. *No Fire Next Time: Black-Korean Conflicts and the Future of America's Cities.* Ithaca, N.Y.: Cornell University Press.

Kim, Claire J. 2000. *Bitter Fruits: The Politics of Black-Korean Conflict in New York City.* New Haven, Conn.: Yale University Press.

Kim, Illsoo. 1981. *New Urban Immigrants: The Korean Community in New York.* Princeton, N.J.: Princeton University Press.

Kim, Kwang, Chung Kim, and Shin Kim. 2001. "The Ethnic Role of Korean Immigrant Churches in the United States." In Ho-Youn Kwon, Kwang Chung Kim, and Stephen. R. Warner, eds., *Korean Americans and Their Religions: Pilgrims and Missionaries from a Different Shore,* pp. 71–94. University Park: Pennsylvania State University Press.

Light, Ivan, and Edna Bonacich. 1988. *Immigrant Entrepreneurs: Koreans in Los Angeles.* Berkeley: University of California Press.

Min, Pyong Gap. 1988. *Ethnic Business Enterprise: Korean Small Business in Atlanta.* Staten Island, N.Y.: Center for Migration Studies.

———. 1992. "The Structure and Social Function of Korean Immigrant Churches in the United States." *International Migration Review* 26: 352–67.

———. 1996. *Caught in the Middle: Korean Communities in New York and Los Angeles.* Berkeley: University of California Press.

Min, Pyong Gap, and Dae Young Kim. 2005. "Intergenerational Transmission of Religion and Culture: Korean Protestant Immigrants in New York." *Sociology of Religion* 66: 263–82.

Patterson, Wayne. 1988. *The Korean Frontier in America: Immigration to Hawaii, 1896–1910.* Honolulu: University of Hawaii Press.

Yu, Eui-Young, Peter Cha, Sang Il Hen, and Kimberly Yu. "Emerging Diversity: Los Angeles' Koreatown, 1990–2000." *Amerasia Journal* 30, 1: 25–52.

Mexico

Albert M. Camarillo

People of Mexican origin occupy a unique status in contemporary American society: they are among the newest and oldest of ethnic groups within the U.S. The roots of permanent settlement by people of Spanish and Mexican origin in what is now New Mexico dates back nearly 400 years, to the founding of Santa Fe two years after the Jamestown colony was founded. While some New Mexicans can claim to be 16th-generation Americans, others crossed the U.S.-Mexico border yesterday. Indeed, people from Mexico have continuously migrated north and in the process have shaped and reshaped the demographic contours of the nation's second largest ethnic minority. Especially over the past 100 years, Mexican immigration, in four successive waves, reinforced the group's geographic concentration in the American Southwest, where the great majority of Mexican-origin people have always lived. Yet the constant flow of international migration and the internal migration of Mexican-origin people have resulted in a diaspora that extends into the Midwest, the Pacific Northwest, and, within the past two decades, the Southeast and Northeast. The past 30 years constitute a high-water mark of immigration from Mexico, a phenomenon that has propelled the Mexican-origin population to unprecedented numbers. This fourth wave of immigration has contributed to the formation of one of the most diverse and fastest-growing groups in contemporary America.

Origins of Mexican American Society in the Southwest

Before the mid-19th century the trek north from Mexico was made by settlers seeking a new life in the far northern frontiers of New Spain and Mexico. Though the circumstances prompting migration, both in Mexico and within the U.S., have changed drastically over the centuries, one unifying theme binds all who moved northward: improving their quality of life and searching for opportunity. These basic desires motivated Spanish colonists and Mexican citizens alike to relocate from the early 17th century through the first half of the 19th century. Today these same desires drive hundreds of thousands of Mexicans each year to enter the U.S., legally and clandestinely, in search of opportunities unavailable to them at home.

An obvious historical benchmark to begin any discussion about Mexican Americans is the U.S.-Mexico war of 1846–1848, which was settled by treaty and resulted in the annexation of a vast territory and its people by the U.S. Both Mexican settlers and indigenous tribal societies were encompassed within the "new" Southwest after 1848. But to make this the legal point of departure for the origins of Mexican American history is to miss an important context for understanding subsequent migrations, immigrations, and settlement patterns. Though Spanish explorers had trekked through what is now the Southwest in the 1540s, it was not until the 1580s that Spain embarked on establishing permanent colonies in the region. Paranoia and religious fervor combined to set in motion the settlement of northern New Spain. The perceived military need to fortify a defensible area between the center of the colonial empire in Mexico and foreign threats to the north (English, Russian, and later American) prompted Spain to move soldiers and recruit civilians to settle on the frontier. Military and civilian personnel alike were given incentives of land grants and other resources to relocate. They were joined by Catholic missionaries sent to harvest Indian converts, a cornerstone of Spain's colonizing efforts throughout the Americas. The few thousand hardy souls who carved out settlements stretching from Texas to California migrated north in part because new opportunities were promised by superiors. Mexican Americans' heritage in the region thus dates from the Spanish colonial period, but it continued after Mexico's independence from Spain in 1821.

The fledgling colonies of the Spanish borderlands were small but viable settlements despite their great distance from the political center of Mexico. Subject to colonial administration under Spain and later by provincial governments under Mexico, they were largely self-sufficient and insular, guided by Catholic traditions and familial networks tied to kinship. The change in sovereignty from Spain to Mexico affected land ownership and governmental oversight, and introduced new settlers from Mexico, but the most important change was the lifting of the ban on foreign trade and immigration of American settlers into Mexico. These new developments caused irrevocable demographic and political changes that culminated in Americans, and a handful of their Mexican allies, proclaiming an independent Texas in 1836, an event that precipitated war with Mexico a decade later.

As the ink on the Treaty of Guadalupe Hidalgo dried in 1848, approximately 100,000 Mexican citizens had the option of remaining on their native land and becoming American citizens. Few, if any, actually opted to move south of the imaginary border that now separated the U.S. from Mexico. For generations Mexicans in the region traveled freely between provinces and settlements on both sides of the

Rio Grande, and U.S. sovereignty did nothing to halt this practice. Indeed, the movement of Mexicans north increased when gold was discovered in California in 1849, as about 10,000 prospective miners from Sonora set out for the Sierra Nevada foothills. After being driven out by Americans who detested the competition of Mexicans and other foreign miners, many drifted back to Mexico. Others settled among compatriots in the pueblos (towns), neighborhoods that afforded both shelter and a buffer zone as Americans gained numerical ascendancy in California and throughout much of the region.

Aside from the fortunate few who managed to hold on to some wealth and political influence in the decades following the war, Mexican Americans were subject to a racial ideology and a sociopolitical environment in which most were cast as inferior nonwhite people and thus excluded from the culture and institutions that Americans brought with them to the Southwest. Confined to the pueblos-turned-barrios in the burgeoning towns and rural villages across the arid region, Mexican Americans became a submerged ethnic subculture. The borderlands of the Southwest—a region where most people of Mexican origin continued to live and work as a marginalized ethnic minority—persisted through the late 19th century, serving as cultural and linguistic links for millions of immigrants from Mexico, who continued to migrate north during the 1900s and into the 21st century.

The First Great Wave of Immigration

Mexicans crossed the U.S. boundary line in relatively small numbers during the last two decades of the 19th century, but during the first three decades of the new century, especially after the Mexican Revolution began in 1910, the trickle turned into a tsunami. As much as a tenth of the entire population of Mexico, perhaps as many as 1.5 million people, relocated to the U.S. The devastating effects of civil war in Mexico together with the prospect of employment in the U.S. prompted the wholesale movement of people from the central plateau and northern states of Mexico. The great majority entered through Texas border towns and cities; El Paso was the most widely used port of entry. Those who opted to formalize their status paid a head tax of a few dollars at an immigration station, but those who wished to enter without paying simply walked across the border or waded across the Rio Grande. Before the establishment of the U.S. Border Patrol in the late 1920s, the 2,000-mile international boundary was unguarded; well into the 1940s, those wanting to enter illegally could do so easily.

The overwhelming majority of Mexican immigrants settled in cities, towns, and small agricultural colonies in the Southwest. The regional economic boom in the agricultural and transportation industries relied heavily on Mexican labor at the time, especially during and after World War I. Texas was the preferred state of settlement for Mexican immigrants and Mexican Americans during this period, with

Arizona, California, and Colorado far less favored destinations (historically, relatively few immigrants have settled in New Mexico). Over time, however, California began to attract an ever-increasing share. A small number of Mexican immigrants—probably fewer than 5 percent—also ventured to more northern destinations, especially in the Great Lakes region. For example, small communities of Mexicans began to appear in Chicago, Detroit, and Gary, Indiana, during the 1920s. In addition, Mexicans settled in smaller agricultural towns in the Great Plains and in cities such as Omaha and Kansas City.

During the interwar period, more and more Mexican immigrants opted for city life and the opportunities that urban areas afforded them. Rural-to-urban migrations continued to fuel the growing populations in Texas cities such as San Antonio and Houston and California ones such as San Diego and Los Angeles. For several generations San Antonio was home to the single largest concentration of Mexican-origin people in the U.S., a distinction eclipsed during the 1920s by Los Angeles, a city with a population of over 100,000 Mexicans by 1930.

The number of Mexican immigrants paled in comparison to that of European immigrants during the first two decades of the 20th century. Between 1910 and 1914, Mexicans accounted for less than 2 percent of all immigrants in the U.S. However, between 1925 and 1929 they accounted for 16 percent of the total, as a result of the Immigration Act of 1924, a policy that effectively halted immigration from Europe and reinforced restrictions against Asian immigration. In the Southwest, Mexican-origin people constituted the largest ethnic group, a distinction they have held to the present day.

Like other immigrants, Mexicans adapted to life in the U.S. in a variety of ways. They formed mutual aid societies and associations to provide social and cultural cushions as they adjusted to living in America. They attended church services in an increasing number of Catholic parishes established in and near barrios. Their children attended mostly segregated schools or classrooms, but despite this racial separation, became Mexican American. They incorporated many of the characteristics that increasingly defined them as American into their daily lives—the English language, popular culture in the form of music and entertainment, clothing styles, and other features that set the young apart from their elders.

Adaptation to American life also brought restrictions of the kind that set Mexicans apart from most of their white immigrant counterparts. Educational segregation was only one manifestation of a type of "Jaime Crow" discrimination and ethnic isolation directed at Mexicans in the Southwest. It was common in the pre–World War II era, for example, for Mexican Americans to face restrictions that kept them from patronizing certain restaurants, community swimming pools, movie theaters, and other public places, which effectively put them on the opposite side of the color line from whites. Housing segregation became more acute as racially restrictive covenants in deeds of sale determined who could and could not buy property in certain neighborhoods. Social discrimination was most severe during the 1930s and early 1940s, when Mexicans were targeted as contributors to the economic problems of the Great Depression and as dangers to the health and welfare of American citizens. The response to these perceived problems was a large-scale voluntary repatriation and an involuntary deportation program orchestrated by the U.S. Department of Labor and local police and welfare relief agencies. As a result, perhaps as many as 750,000 Mexican immigrants and their American-born children left the region during the worst years of the depression. During the so-called Zoot Suit Riots in Los Angeles in June 1943, white military personnel from area bases descended on downtown and East Los Angeles (where the large majority of Mexican Americans lived) and provoked the largest race-related riots in the West before the Watts riots in 1965.

Braceros and "Wetbacks": The Second and Third Waves

The economic troubles of the Great Depression and the deportation of hundreds of thousands of Mexican-origin people during the 1930s coincided with a cessation of further immigration from Mexico. But World War II and the postwar years gave rise to two new waves of immigration. The first was regulated; it became commonly known as the *bracero* program (the term is derived from the Spanish word *brazo* and refers to those who work with their arms). The war drained much-needed labor from agricultural industries during a time when farmers were expected to expand production to meet wartime exigencies. Looking to its neighbor to the south, the U.S. entered into an agreement with Mexico to supply workers on a seasonal, temporary basis to meet the demands of the emergency. The Mexican government recruited the workers while the U.S. guaranteed transportation, housing, and other resources to support the program. However, as American farming interests grew dependent on Mexican *braceros,* the U.S. Congress extended the wartime measure of 1942. The number of workers during the war years was modest, reaching about 50,000 by 1945, but by the mid-1950s the program supplied nearly half a million workers annually to agribusiness, primarily in southwestern states.

The *bracero* program was not terminated until 1964, and by that year some 5 million *braceros* had entered the U.S. as temporary workers. Though most returned to Mexico, as called for in the agreement, many thousands left the program before their designated time in the U.S. expired and drifted to towns and cities where they could easily be absorbed into large Mexican American communities. Many thousands more married Mexican American women and legalized their status.

Unintentionally, Congress's cessation of the *bracero* program fostered a new wave of immigrants from Mexico, the vast majority undocumented. The termination of the program left hundreds of thousands of workers in Mexico seeking employment in the U.S. In addition to the former *braceros,* there were tens of thousands of others who had been turned away from the labor-recruiting centers in Mexico. Problems in Mexico spurred an ever-increasing number of people to consider crossing the border illegally in search of wage labor. The land reforms instituted after the Mexican Revolution never reached their intended goals of providing land and resources so poor rural Mexicans could make a go of family farming. Furthermore, Mexico's attempt to industrialize attracted far more workers to its cities than could be incorporated into their labor markets, thus creating even more pressure for workers to venture north. The introduction of irrigated large-scale farming in the northern Mexican states attracted thousands of eager workers, most of whom were disappointed when work did not materialize. Many headed to the burgeoning border cities. These factors, combined with the relative ease of crossing the border illegally in the 1950s, led to the first large wave of undocumented immigration when the U.S.-Mexico border was a guarded boundary line.

One way to gauge the extent of illegal immigration from Mexico is to look at the data from the Immigration and Naturalization Service's "Operation Wetback" program during the early 1950s. "Wetback" was a derogatory term referring to those who crossed the border illegally—literally, those who crossed the Rio Grande and emerged on the U.S. side with wet backs. (In fact, most undocumented immigrants did not cross the river at this time; instead they entered through the arid regions along the California-Mexico border.) In 1953 alone, some 875,000 Mexicans were caught by the INS and deported as illegal immigrants. For many, if not most, the return to the other side of the border prompted another attempt to enter illegally. Despite the efforts of the INS, tens of thousands of unauthorized Mexicans found their way to the towns and cities of the Southwest. There they joined an increasing number of immigrants from Mexico who were admitted legally in the post–*bracero* program era (for example, between 1955 and 1959 some 214,000 Mexicans were admitted, 15 percent of all immigrants). These were the pioneers of the largest immigration of Mexicans in the 20th century—a movement of people that has continued unabated for over 40 years.

The Fourth Great Wave

In 1970 the population of Mexican Americans was about 4.5 million. In 2005 that figure stood at over 25 million (see Table 1). Mexican-origin people constitute the great majority—about 63 percent—of the 40.4 million Hispanics in the U.S. Obviously, the last third of the 20th century witnessed a spectacular rise in the Mexican-origin population, a product of sustained mass immigration and natural increase. According to the 2000 Census, over 9.3 million people indicated their country of birth as Mexico, a group that constituted 37.2 percent of all Mexican-origin people in the U.S. By contrast, in 1960 only about 15 percent of all Mexican-origin people in the Southwest were foreign-born. Since 1970 the number of immigrants from

Table 1   Mexican-origin population, 1960–2005

Year	Number	Percentage of U.S. population
2005	25,467,000	8.8[a]
2000	21,207,000	7.5
1990	13,393,000	5.4
1980	8,740,000	3.9
1970	4,532,000	2.2
1960	1,736,000[b]	1.0

Source: Adapted from Frank D. Bean and Gillian Stevens, *America's Newcomers and the Dynamics of Diversity* (New York: Russell Sage Foundation, 2003).

a. Figure from *Hispanics—A People in Motion* (Washington, D.C.: Pew Hispanic Center, January 2005).

b. Number calculated as a sum of the Mexican-born population and natives of Mexican parentage.

Mexico has steadily increased each decade, accounting for a huge part of the demographic explosion of Mexican Americans. For example, of all Mexican immigrants in the U.S. as of 2000, nearly half (48.7 percent) entered the country during the 1990s. About 29 percent entered during the 1980s, while 15 percent immigrated in the 1970s and a mere 5 percent in the 1960s. Unprecedented rates of immigration were matched by high fertility rates among Mexican-origin women, rates that are among the highest of any major immigrant population in the U.S.; in 1995, for example, the fertility rate for Mexican American women was 60 percent higher than for U.S. women in general. This demographic trend is revealed in the number of families with five or more people: 31 percent of all Mexican American households, as compared with only 11 percent of non-Hispanic white households.

Any profile of the Mexican immigrant population must consider both those who are in the U.S. legally and those who are not. In 1966, two years after the *bracero* program was terminated and one year after the Immigration Act of 1965 (which eliminated the long-standing quota system based on national origins established in the 1920s) was passed, slightly more than 45,000 Mexican immigrants were admitted legally. The number of Mexican workers granted legal immigrant status soared in subsequent decades. About 680,000 immigrants from Mexico entered the U.S legally during the 1970s, but in the first half of the 1990s alone, some 2.2 million Mexicans obtained legal documents to work in the U.S. The volume of those who entered illegally was nearly as large. In 2005 it was estimated that about 57 percent of the roughly 11 million unauthorized immigrants currently in the U.S. were born in Mexico. This number rose from 1,310,000 in 1980 to 5,900,000 in 2005 (see Table 2).

As the total population of Mexican-origin people skyrocketed, the demographic distribution of this group began to shift. Before 1940, Texas was the primary gateway state and home to the largest proportion of Mexican immigrants; California

Table 2   Unauthorized Mexican immigrants as percentage of Mexican foreign-born and
Mexican-origin populations, 1980–2005

Year	Estimated number of unauthorized Mexican immigrants	Percentage of Mexican foreign-born population	Percentage of Mexican-origin population
2005	5,900,000	53.0	23.2
2000	3,900,000	45.9	18.6
1996	2,700,000	40.4	15.0
1990	1,321,000	30.7	9.9
1980	1,131,000	51.4	12.9

Sources: Jeffrey S. Passel, *Estimates of the Size and Characteristics of the Undocumented Population* (Washington, D.C.: Pew Hispanic Center, March 21, 2005); Frank D. Bean and Gillian Stevens, *America's Newcomers and the Dynamics of Diversity* (New York: Russell Sage Foundation, 2003).

and Arizona were far behind. These three southwestern states accounted for 85 percent of all immigrants from Mexico, a percentage that held fairly constant through 1960. But by the 1940s, California had reached near parity with Texas, and between 1950 and 1960 it surpassed the Lone Star State as the most popular destination among Mexican immigrants and Mexican Americans. The emergence of California as the principle gateway state and as the home to the largest population of Mexican-origin people is attributable to three developments. First, a disproportionately large number of *braceros* worked in California agriculture (2 million were employed between 1942 and 1960). As a result, after thousands regularized their immigration status, they settled there and were joined by thousands of other former *braceros* who crossed backed into the U.S. as illegal immigrants. Second, the majority of undocumented immigrants, who had not been employed in the *bracero* program, also headed for the Golden State. Finally, California became a desirable location for transplanted Texas Mexican Americans, a trend that accelerated during and after World War II. Outside the Southwest, Illinois gained importance as a receiving state as both Mexican Americans and Mexican immigrants were attracted to industrial jobs in and around Chicago (6 percent of the Mexican-origin population lived in Illinois in 1960).

The surge of Mexican immigration after the late 1960s cemented California's preeminence as the center of the Mexican-origin population in the U.S. By 1970, for example, California's Spanish-surname population (the vast majority of Mexican origin) numbered nearly 2.4 million, while Texas had 1.8 million. With regard to immigrants, as the proportions declined in all other states, California continued to be the primary destination for new migrants, claiming 57 percent of the total by 1980. Southern California cities and counties in particular experienced dramatic increases in the Mexican-origin population. Los Angeles has been the epicenter of demographic change since 1970. By 1980, Los Angeles County contained nearly half of the state's 4.5 million Hispanics. Hispanics made up 28 percent of the county's total population.

By 2000 nearly 8.5 million Mexican Americans lived in California, 5 million resided in Texas, and 1.1 million lived in Arizona (the numbers were significantly smaller in the other southwestern states, with 450,000 in Colorado and 330,000 in New Mexico). Other important demographic trends manifested themselves during the 1990s, especially the growth of Mexican-origin communities outside the Southwest. Four factors help explain this diaspora. First, in the wake of the Immigration Reform and Control Act (IRCA) of 1986, two new policy directions signaled a change for substantial numbers of new immigrants from Mexico. Given increased sanctions against employers who knowingly hired undocumented immigrants and the saturation of traditional labor markets as a result of the amnesty provision of the law (which gave some 2.8 million former illegal immigrants from Mexico documented status), many Mexican immigrants began to favor destinations beyond the usual cities. Second, increased surveillance and patrol of the border by the INS made it more difficult and costly to enter California illegally. Third, an increasingly hostile environment for undocumented immigrants developed in California. This was reflected in Proposition 187, spearheaded by Governor Pete Wilson in 1994, which prohibited education, health care, and welfare services to these immigrants. Such developments sent a strong message to immigrants that other destinations were perhaps more amenable to those seeking work in the U.S. Last, the lingering economic recession of the early 1990s, which hit California particularly hard, encouraged immigrants to settle elsewhere in the nation. All of these factors tended to direct immigrants away from California and Texas, especially in the wake of a devaluation of the peso that resulted in a deep economic recession in Mexico, a development that drove even more Mexican workers to seek employment in the U.S.

Thus while California had been the magnet for Mexican immigrants for nearly 50 years, by the 1990s the percentage of immigrants in California dropped appreciably, the numbers in Texas also dipped, and the largest increases in Mexican immigration were recorded in areas outside the Southwest. For example, Illinois continued to attract immigrants, a fact that helped push the number of Mexican-origin people in that state past the 1 million mark by 2000. In addition, states that had very few Mexican immigrants in 1980 experienced marked growth. Florida, Georgia, and North Carolina together had a total population of people born in Mexico below 17,000 in 1980, but in 2000 the number of Mexican immigrants in these states surpassed 550,000—more than a 3,000 percent increase over two decades. Though many states in the Midwest did not experience comparable rates of increase, the gains were nonetheless impressive. Illinois is now home to the largest Mexican immigrant population in the Midwest, but Michigan also witnessed gains over the course of two decades (from about 11,000 Mexican-born residents in 1980 to nearly 61,000 in 2000). Mexican immigrants also ventured to states elsewhere in the nation where few Mexican immigrants had lived before. In 1980 Nevada and Utah had a combined Mexican immigrant population of about 14,000; by 2000 it was 181,000. Similarly, in 1980 New York and New Jersey had a combined Mexican immigrant population of 14,000; by 2000 they were home to over 237,000 people born in Mexico. Even New Mexico, Arizona, and Colorado recorded sharp increases during the last two decades of the 20th century. Never before had nontraditional, non-gateway states attracted such a large percentage of immigrants from Mexico. In the 21st century, the second largest ethnic minority group in the U.S. is distributed nationally, not just regionally.

Still, when considering the total number of Mexican-origin people in the U.S., and not just those born in Mexico, it remains true that the great majority of Mexican-origin people continue to live in the Southwest, with California and Texas accounting for 65 percent of the total. When Arizona, New Mexico, and Colorado are included, nearly 75 percent of all Mexican Americans and their immigrant counterparts live in this region.

A Profile of Mex-America Today

The phenomenal increase in immigration from Mexico since the 1960s added immensely not only to the total population of Mexican-origin people in the U.S. but to the diversity of the group as well. Any socioeconomic profile of Mex-America today must take into account this growing diversity. Forty or 50 years ago, observers of Mexican American society often identified major defining characteristics of this ethnic group. First and foremost, although they were a people of immigrant origins, by 1960 those origins were distant, as about 85 percent were U.S.-born. Second, the great majority (79 percent) were urban dwellers in 1960, and they were the most rapidly urbanizing group in the Southwest in the post–World War II decades. Although large pockets of Mexican Americans lived in rural areas, especially in south Texas and New Mexico, the growing trend was toward residence in the largest urban centers. Mexican Americans were also highly concentrated in the southwestern states, where over 90 percent resided in 1950. Third, in 1960, Mexican American educational achievement and jobs in higher-level occupations lagged far behind those of non-Hispanic whites. For example, 60 percent of women and 64 percent of men of Mexican origin held unskilled and semiskilled jobs in 1960. Some modest levels of occupational mobility appeared in the postwar years, but when compared to their white counterparts, Mexican Americans were disproportionately represented on the bottom rungs of the Southwest's labor market. In schooling, they seemed to be even further behind their white and nonwhite counterparts in the Southwest; the median school years completed for Mexican Americans in 1960 was 7.1, while for whites it was 12.1 and for nonwhites 9.0. Although some of these socioeconomic trends have been slow to change, Mex-America has experienced a profound reshaping, not only because of renewed mass immigration from Mexico but because of social changes that deeply affected the recent history of the group.

The arrival of large numbers of new immigrants in existing Mexican American communities was reminiscent of the first three waves of immigration. New immigrants had an impact on how Mexican Americans viewed themselves and how they were viewed by the larger society. New immigrants strengthened ties to families and communities on both sides of the border and reinforced the use of the Spanish language and cultural traditions from Mexico. They also often competed with their U.S.-born counterparts for low-wage work, for low-cost housing, and for other resources tied to education, health care, and welfare. Though tensions and mistrust often characterized relations between native-born and foreign-born, over time the larger Mexican American population absorbed new immigrants. The fourth-wave immigration of the past 30 years has continued these historical patterns, but the volume of immigrants has set in motion some new dynamics as well. Three developments stand out: the growing internal diversity of the group, the restriction of immigrant populations to barrios, and the educational and occupational stratification of newcomers.

Perhaps the most obvious impact of the fourth wave of immigration from Mexico involves the internal diversity of people of Mexican origin. Many generations of native-born and foreign-born people now coexist in the U.S., creating more diversity than in any previous era. Mexican American generational cohorts, for example, include elders who immigrated in the early 20th century and their children, grandchildren, and great-grandchildren, who comprise at least three or four generations of native-born Mexican Americans. In addition, those who immigrated during the *bracero* program and in the 1950s, both legal and undocumented, also produced two or three generations of Mexican American offspring. To this diversity we must add the millions of immigrants who have arrived since the late 1960s. However, we cannot lump all these newer immigrants together, for they arrived during different decades, and each successive wave was larger in number than the preceding one. For example, of the over 11 million immigrants from Mexico who resided in the U.S. in 2004, 56 percent were estimated to have entered during the 1990s. Obviously, the social and economic adaptation of these immigrants and their children is at a different stage than that of those who immigrated during the 1970s. Indeed, mass immigration over the past 30 years (1980s–2000s) has contributed further to the differentiation of various native-born Mexican American cohorts. It is not surprising, therefore, that terms used by Mexican-origin people today, more than at any time in the past, reflect the growing diversity of this population. Those who still hold deep attachments to Mexico may call themselves "Mexicanos" or "Mexicans," while others prefer "Mexican American" or "Chicano" (a historical term revived during the 1960s as a term of political and social/cultural awareness, especially for younger people who rejected assimilation). Others prefer "Hispanic" or "Latino," terms that include all Spanish-origin people in the U.S. Some identify with multiple terms, while others reject any label that references national origin or ethnic identity. As immigration from Mexico continues on a large scale, the great diversity that characterizes Mexican-origin people will surely continue.

Another important development is the geographical and demographic profile of Mex-America. Three patterns are noteworthy. First, although prior immigrants maintained connections to sending communities in Mexico as they traveled and settled in the U.S., the fourth wave of immigrants has maintained stronger binational orientations owing to chain migration and routine visits to see family in Mexico. Despite the expense and difficulty of going to Mexico and back on a regular basis—especially for illegal immigrants—immigrants now more than ever are members of an increasingly international community renewed and rejuvenated by constant travel across the border. Second, in the past immigrants not only tended to migrate to the towns and cities where Mexicans historically resided but were involved in establishing new communities of Mexican-origin people in agricultural areas, rural towns, and metropolitan suburbs in western cities. Much smaller numbers coalesced in neighborhoods in cities of the Midwest. Most recent immigrants have contributed to these patterns, though with some modification. They too have settled in existing Mexican American urban barrios and towns, primarily in the Southwest, but they are also prime movers in the establishment of newer metropolitan barrios throughout major urban areas of the Southwest and Midwest. For example, in East Los Angeles, an area that historically has had the highest proportion of Mexican-origin residents in the U.S., newer immigrants initially settled there but moved to suburbs throughout greater Los Angeles and were joined by those with the means to move to neighborhoods with better schools and housing. A new development attributable primarily to immigrants after 1970 is the establishment of ethnic neighborhoods in small towns and cities in the Southeast and Northeast (about 25 percent of all Mexican-origin people now live outside the Southwest). The availability of steady low-wage and service-sector jobs fed this geographical distribution. The increasing concentration in and distribution of the Mexican-origin population within metropolitan regions (in 1990, Mexican Americans, and Hispanics in general, were among the most highly concentrated ethnic groups within metropolitan areas and central cities) has led some observers to label this phenomenon the "browning" of America. Indeed, both the growth and the distribution of the Mexican-origin population lend some credibility to this metaphor. Between 1990 and 2000, for example, the Mexican-origin population increased by 53 percent (58 percent for all Hispanics), whereas the rate of increase for the U.S. as a whole was 13 percent. In addition, the percentage of Mexicans among all immigrants in the U.S. has steadily risen since the 1970s (Mexicans accounted for 22 percent of all immigrants who entered during the 1980s, 27 percent between 1991 and 1996; in 2004 they constituted about one third of all immigrants). Considering the increases of the Hispanic population in general over the past 40 years (from 3.9 percent of the total U.S. population in 1960 to 13.3 percent in 2000) and projections that it will account for about 25 percent of the nation's total population in 2050, the "browning" of American society is not a farfetched notion.

Unlike most immigrant groups in U.S. history, which tended to enter in one or two large waves during a concentrated period of years or decades, mass immigration from Mexico spans an almost uninterrupted period of nearly a century. Successive waves of Mexican immigrants thus make any analyses of group progress over time complicated and complex, unless very specific cohorts are considered based on such factors as nativity, time of immigration, age, citizenship, language, and other variables. With regard to social class profiles, using household income and occupation as two important indicators, aggregate analyses reveal that people of Mexican origin as a group have median family household incomes and occupational distributions that are significantly lower than those of non-Hispanic whites. For example, in 1996, 23 percent of all employed Mexican-origin males 16 years and older held professional, administrative, and sales-related jobs, while 77 percent were employed in service, skilled, and unskilled jobs. The distribution in these same occupations for non-Hispanic whites was 51 percent and 49 percent and for blacks 34 percent and 66 percent, respectively. However, because most immigrants enter the U.S. with little education and few occupational skills and are handicapped by lack of English-language ability, most social indicators for the group as a whole are lowered as a result. When we measure educational achievement, a similar trend is revealed. In 2002, for example, Mexican-origin people had the lowest percentage (50.6) of all Hispanic adults 25 years and older who had at least a high school education. The percentage for non-Hispanic whites was 88.7 percent. However, when we consider U.S.-born Mexican Americans, the percentage that completed high school increased to 67 percent, according to data published in 1997.

Though the social class and educational profiles surely improve when the second and subsequent generations are considered, there is still debate among scholars about how much mobility Mexican Americans have achieved over time in education, occupation, and income. There are also questions about how much progress Mexican immigrants and their children are likely to make in American society, given that certain avenues of mobility are less available today than in the past. For example, the increasing segregation of Mexican immigrant children and Mexican Americans in poor, minority-majority public schools is sure to have negative consequences for occupational mobility beyond low-wage, low-skill jobs.

As new immigrants from Mexico continue to enter the U.S. and as various cohorts of native-born Mexican Americans mature, this group will continue to experience dynamic growth and increasing diversity. To be sure, Mexican immigrants today enter an American society that is substantially different from the one their predecessors entered in the 1920s or 1940s. As a result of the civil rights struggles of the 1950s and 1960s in general and the Chicano civil rights movement in particular, as well as subsequent social reforms that opened doors of opportunity previously shut to Mexicans, the life chances of Mexican Americans today are genuinely better than during any previous era. Immigrants now have access to legal services, health care, and other important resources that their peers even a generation ago could not have imagined. And yet a critical question remains about the future direction of the group: Will Mexican Americans over time be fully incorporated into the fabric of U.S. society, or will socioeconomic and educational disparities continue to characterize large segments of the group?

Bibliography

Chavez, Leo R. *Shadowed Lives: Undocumented Immigrants in American Society.* Fort Worth: Holt, Rinehart and Winston, 1992.

Cull, Nicholas J., and David Carrasco, eds. *Alambrista and the U.S.-Mexico Border: Film, Music, and Stories of Undocumented Immigrants.* Albuquerque: University of New Mexico Press, 2004.

Gamio, Manuel. *Mexican Immigration to the United States.* Chicago: University of Chicago Press, 1930.

Gutiérrez, David G., ed. *Between Two Worlds: Mexican Immigrants in the United States.* Wilmington, Del.: Scholarly Resources, 1996.

Hondagneu-Sotelo, Pierrette. *Gendered Transitions; Mexican Experiences of Immigration.* Berkeley: University of California Press, 1994.

Massey, Douglas, S. Jorge Durand, and Nolan J. Malone. *Beyond Smoke and Mirrors: Mexican Immigration in an Era of Economic Integration.* New York: Russell Sage Foundation, 2002.

Portes, Alejandro, and Rubén Rumbaut. *Legacies: The Story of the Immigrant Second Generation.* Berkeley: University of California Press, 2001.

Sánchez, George J. *Becoming Mexican American: Ethnicity, Culture and Identity in Chicano Los Angeles, 1900–1945.* New York: Oxford University Press, 1993.

Suárez-Orozco, Marcelo M., ed. *Crossings: Mexican Immigration in Interdisciplinary Perspectives.* Cambridge, Mass.: Rockefeller Center for Latin American Studies, Harvard University, 1998.

Zúñiga, Víctor, and Rubén Hernández-León, eds. *New Destinations: Mexican Immigration in the United States.* New York: Russell Sage Foundation, 2005.

Middle East and North Africa

Steven J. Gold and Mehdi Bozorgmehr

The Middle East stretches from Morocco on the west to Afghanistan on the east. Although many countries are usually considered to be part of this region—Turkey, Syria, Lebanon, Israel/Palestine, Jordan, Iraq, Iran, Saudi Arabia, Yemen, Oman, United Arab Emirates, Qatar, Bahrain, Kuwait, and Egypt, Libya, Tunisia, Algeria, Morocco, and Mauritania in North Africa—here we include the major countries in the Middle East and North Africa but exclude those with few immigrants to the U.S.

Middle Eastern immigrants to the U.S. are diverse, representing many nationalities, ethnicities, and religions. They have widely varying social characteristics, ranging from highly educated urban professionals to agricultural workers; they speak various languages and dialects; and they maintain a broad array of lifestyles. Ethnic and/or religious minorities, driven out of the region by political, economic, and sectarian conflicts over the past century, make up a significant fraction. These include Armenians, Assyrians, Chaldeans, Copts, Druze, Jews, Kurds, Palestinians, and Shiites from Lebanon and Iraq. For many of these groups, ethnic and/or religious identities are often more deeply felt than national origins.

Members of the Arabic-speaking majority of many Middle Eastern countries, including some Christians, have emphasized a panethnic Arab identity both in their countries of origin and in the U.S. This has been especially the case since 1967, when collective opposition to U.S. policy on the Middle East unified these populations. However, Egyptian Copts, Iraqi Chaldeans, and some Lebanese Maronites have generally distanced themselves from an Arab identity, especially after September 11, 2001, because of its stigmatized status in U.S. society.

Patterns of identification continue to be diverse and malleable among Middle Eastern immigrants in the U.S. While some individuals and groups favor panethnic (e.g., Arab) identification, others emphasize national (Lebanese), ethnic (Armenian), or even subethnic (Armenian from Lebanon) affiliation. As is the case among other migrant populations, politically ambitious individuals may emphasize multiple identities—as Arab, Yemeni, Muslim, or Middle Easterner—according to the context in which they find themselves. Finally, Middle Eastern Americans often intermarry, either within or beyond the Middle Eastern population, further creating hyphenated identities in the second generation.

Immigration and Settlement

The migration history of Middle Easterners to the U.S. can be divided into two major waves, from the 1880s until World War II and from that war to the present. The vast majority of early arrivals were Christian—over 100,000 people, who were enumerated as Syrians—who came to the U.S. between 1885 and 1941 from what is now Lebanon. They included Maronites (Lebanese Christians who follow the pope), Antiochan Orthodox, Melkite, and other Christian sects who claimed that persecution of minorities by the ruling Ottoman empire was the motivating factor. Recent research, however, has shown that on the whole, the Ottoman administration was more accommodating than oppressive to the population in Mount Lebanon. Therefore, the origins of the Christian Lebanese migration were more economic than political. But this was clearly not the case for Armenians, who fled the Ottoman massacres at about the same time. These mass killings and deportations practically depleted today's Turkey of its Armenian population. Unlike Arabic-speaking immigrants in the Ottoman empire, who had aspirations of returning home (and some did), Armenian refugees did not have the option to go back to their homeland.

Given that national boundaries have altered significantly in the Middle East since the 19th century, historical records on the origins of immigration lack consistency. For example, depending on their time of arrival, people entering the U.S. from Beirut might be identified as Turkish, Syrian, or Lebanese. In immigration records until 1899 and U.S. Census records until 1920, all Middle Eastern immigrants were labeled, along with Turks and Armenians, as "Turks in Asia," because residents of Syria were subjects of the Turkish Ottoman empire until 1918. After 1920, the growth of the Middle Eastern immigrant population warranted the creation of a separate classification for Syrians. The region was collectively called Greater Syria until the independence of Lebanon, Syria, and Palestine. Although the pioneering immigrants are frequently referred to as Syrians, they are more correctly Lebanese, because they came from the region of Ottoman Syria called Mount Lebanon, which became independent from France in 1943. Having fled from Israel after 1948, people of Palestinian origin who have arrived in the U.S. from several countries in the Middle East continue to identify as Palestinians.

Many of the early immigrants sought economic advancement and settled in the northeastern and midwestern U.S. While they found employment in a variety of occupations, including farming and factory work, this group showed a remarkable proclivity for self-employment, a trend that is still evident among the Lebanese in particular and the Middle Eastern American population more generally. The earliest arrivals were pack peddlers who sold, among other items, religious articles from "the Holy Land" to rural Americans. Later these Syrio-Lebanese immigrants concentrated in food and garment businesses, establishing Haggar and Farrah, well-known brands of men's ready-to-wear clothing. While Syrio-Lebanese Christians were the largest group, their Muslim counterparts also arrived during this period. Later Muslim migrants established a community in Highland Park, Michigan, where many worked in the growing automobile industry. In 1921, Turks residing in the Detroit area established the Kizil Ay (the Red Crescent Society, the Muslim equivalent of the Red Cross), which raised funds for the homeland. Some of these Turks came from the Balkans after the collapse of the Ottoman empire.

The lives of early Middle Eastern migrants were not very different from those of the southern and eastern Europeans who settled in the U.S. at the turn of the 20th century. In 1916 the Ford Sociological Department enumerated 555 Arab men among its workforce. Disproportionately male and Christian, these migrants remained single or married Christian women of European extraction, although some arranged to marry picture brides or returned home to find coethnic wives. Intermarriage, coupled with the dispersion that resulted from peddling, contributed to a relatively rapid assimilation of the pioneers into American society. Indicating a highly imbalanced sex ratio, 93 percent of the 22,085 "Turks" (the generic term for all Middle Easterners at that time) who entered the U.S. between 1900 and 1925 were male. Despite this tendency, the Syrian population enumerated by the Dillingham Commission in the first decade of the 20th century was more balanced in terms of sex ratio. The 361 Syrian households surveyed, totaling 1,370 people, were 53.7 percent male and 46.3 percent female.

The second wave of Middle Eastern migrants began to enter the U.S. following World War II, largely because of several political and economic factors in the region but also because of the Immigration Act of 1965, which made it easier for non-European migrants to enter the U.S. Political factors included the formation of the State of Israel in 1948, which displaced Palestinians, and the flight of ethnic and religious minority groups from nationalist regimes that sprang up in Egypt, Syria, Iraq, and Yemen in the 1960s. Among the economic factors, the oil boom of the 1970s provided both states and families in oil-producing countries with the wherewithal to send their children abroad to obtain higher education. Given the limited educational infrastructure in the region, students applied to universities abroad, and the Middle East quickly became the largest source of foreign students in the U.S.

The oil boom also brought about massive social change and triggered political instability in the region, further contributing to the exodus of refugees, exiles, and migrant workers. The vast majority of the Middle Eastern–born population in the U.S. immigrated in the 1970s, 1980s, and 1990s. Some groups, like Afghans, Kuwaitis, Saudis, and Algerians, are mostly new arrivals (post-1980), whereas Israelis, Palestinians, Syrians, Turks, Egyptians, and Moroccans have been in the U.S. longer. The percentage of the population arriving before 1969 for most of the Middle Eastern groups is roughly equal to or lower than that of the total foreign-born population in the U.S. (see Table 1).

The 2000 Census added Palestine to Israel to create an "Israel/Palestine" national-origin category; 21.4 percent of this population, or about 24,000 people, are of Arab ancestry and/or speak Arabic, while the remaining 78.6 percent—close to 100,000—are presumably Jews (the U.S. Census is prohibited from collecting data on religion). While there are limited data on Israeli Arabs in America, the 1990 Census enumerated 20,026 Palestinians. Israeli Arabs in the U.S. are highly educated and skilled, often Christian, and unlikely to return. Political and economic difficulties and violence in Israel and the occupied territories, especially during the era of the Al Aqsa Intifada (2000–2006), have increased the emigration of Jews, Christians, and Muslims.

Table 1   Population size and immigration patterns of foreign-born Middle Eastern and North African groups, 2000

National origin	Population	Decade of immigration (percentage)			
		Before 1969	1970–1979	1980–1989	1990–2000
Afghanistan	44,690	3.1	7.7	53.7	35.5
Iraq	93,565	8.7	20.9	18.4	52.0
Israel/Palestine	125,325	17.2	17.9	28.8	36.2
Jordan	50,193	10.7	19.6	30.1	39.5
Kuwait	22,600	1.0	8.0	26.8	64.1
Lebanon	112,702	9.9	27.2	33.7	29.2
Saudi Arabia	27,819	4.5	3.8	19.5	72.3
Syria	55,500	11.8	19.2	32.2	36.9
Turkey	93,245	19.1	15.0	20.8	45.1
Yemen Arab Republic	19,672	5.1	14.2	21.2	59.5
Egypt	118,081	15.7	18.1	25.9	40.3
Algeria	11,664	11.6	8.5	16.6	63.4
Morocco	39,995	18.6	11.9	21.6	48.0
All foreign-born	33,055,462	16.3	15.3	26.7	41.7

Source: U.S. Bureau of the Census, 2000 Census, 5% Public Use Microdata Sample, weighted data.
Note: Data are not available for Tunisia.

The second wave of Middle Eastern migrants to the U.S. is noted for its high educational attainment. This is partly due to the fact that the Immigration Act of 1965 granted preference to skilled immigrants. In addition, as noted, a considerable number of Middle Easterners came as students who attended American universities and stayed on after graduation. Others entered the U.S. as de facto or de jure refugees fleeing such social, political, and economic conflicts as the civil war in Lebanon, the Iran-Iraq war, and the wars in Afghanistan and Iraq. From 1975 through 1991, about 132,000 refugees from the Near East/Asia entered the U.S.; the largest nationalities among those entering from 1983 through 2001 were Iraqis (41,103) and Afghans (27,447).

Unlike the pioneers, recent arrivals are predominantly Muslim and far more diverse in their national origins. They have encountered a contradictory and often hostile political climate characterized by a dominant ideology of cultural pluralism on the one hand and the scapegoating of Middle Easterners in response to the anti-American hostility in the Middle East on the other. These newcomers' pattern of adaptation has involved ethnic attachment and solidarity and is less assimilationist than the first wave. In fact, the arrival of many recent migrants from the Middle East is credited with reinvigorating the ethnic and national identity of the American-born component of the Middle Eastern population. For instance, Armenian Americans had pretty much assimilated when a new wave of Armenians arrived in the 1970s and 1980s, converging in Los Angeles, not far from Fresno, California, a major early Armenian settlement.

Given that recent Middle Eastern immigrants are more dedicated to retaining traditional outlooks and are confronting a host that is often hostile to them, many express serious concerns about their ability to find a place in American society. Accordingly, unlike nearly every other immigrant group with a long record of immigration, integration is arguably more problematic now than it was for entrants of the past century. Even though recent arrivals are well educated and entering a society that champions tolerance, they describe a degree of alienation rare in accounts of the first wave.

Population and Characteristics

In the late 19th and early 20th centuries, Middle Eastern immigrants established communities in the northeastern and midwestern U.S., where they found factory jobs as well as consumer demand for their entrepreneurial pursuits. To some degree this pattern persists, as Middle Easterners, especially Iraqis, Yemenis, and Lebanese, continue to settle in places like Detroit. Israelis, Yemenis, Turks, Syrians, Jordanians, Moroccans, and Egyptians reside in the middle Atlantic region of New York and New Jersey. Finally, western states, notably California, are growing areas of concentration.

According to the 2000 Census, there are five nationality groups from the Middle

East, excluding Iranians, whose population approaches or exceeds 100,000 (see Table 1): Israelis/Palestinians (125,325), Egyptians (118,081), Lebanese (112,702), Iraqis (93,565), and Turks (93,245). The two next largest groups are Syrians, with a population of 55,500, and Jordanians, with a population of 50,193; Afghans number 44,690. As noted, a large fraction of Syrians have similar origins to the Lebanese, while a significant proportion of Jordan's population is Palestinian. Hence, a considerable number of Syrians and Jordanians might be included within other national groups rather than be considered autonomous.

Since approximately 40 percent of Israel's population is foreign-born, census figures based on nativity rather than prior citizenship do not accurately reflect the number of Israelis living in the U.S., which exceeds 200,000. Finally, people from several other Middle Eastern nations, including Morocco, Bahrain, Kuwait, Qatar, Saudi Arabia, United Arab Emirates, Yemen, Algeria, and Libya, reside in the U.S. In each case, their population is less than 40,000.

Middle Eastern Americans are a well-educated group. With 62.9 percent completing a bachelor's degree or higher, Egyptians are the most highly educated of all Middle Eastern nationalities, and one of the best educated in the U.S. Over 35 percent of all other Middle Eastern groups, except for Yemenis, Iraqis, and Afghans, have completed college or graduate school, compared with 26 percent of all foreign-born people (see Table 2).

Table 2 Educational attainment of foreign-born Middle Eastern and North African groups, 2000

National origin	Population	Bachelor's degree only (percentage)	More than a bachelor's degree (percentage)	Total bachelor's degree or more (percentage)
Afghanistan	30,076	19.7	11.4	31.1
Iraq	65,708	14.3	8.9	23.2
Israel/Palestine	88,629	23.1	20.4	43.5
Jordan	38,745	23.8	11.4	35.2
Kuwait	13,190	35.3	18.9	54.2
Lebanon	86,150	22.2	19.6	41.7
Saudi Arabia	10,405	31.5	20.4	51.9
Syria	40,001	18.0	19.4	37.4
Turkey	61,726	22.8	23.4	46.2
Yemen Arab Republic	11,490	10.6	4.5	15.1
Egypt	86,567	39.0	23.9	62.9
Algeria	8,932	23.9	28.9	52.8
Morocco	31,764	25.9	12.0	37.9
All foreign-born	22,034,522	15.2	10.8	26.0

Source: U.S. Bureau of the Census, 2000 Census, 5% Public Use Microdata Sample, weighted data.
Note: Population 25–64 years old. Data are not available for Tunisia.

Patterns of Economic Incorporation

Middle Easterners have long been noted for their high rates of entrepreneurship. The Dillingham Commission, which surveyed 10,000 urban immigrant households in the first decade of the 20th century, found that among migrants in New York City, Syrians had the highest rate of self-employment of all populations sampled. Among foreign-born male heads of households, 70 percent were self-employed. While a relatively high number of Syrian women "remained at home" (56 percent), an additional 33.5 percent were employed in trade. Working as peddlers, Syrians fanned out and interacted, even intermarried, with English-speakers.

A century later, Middle Easterners continue to exhibit high rates of entrepreneurship. According to the 1990 Census, six Middle Eastern groups (Israelis, Palestinians, Egyptians, Lebanese, Armenians, and Iranians) ranked among the top ten ancestry groups in self-employment rate. As shown in Table 3, nearly all recent Middle Eastern nationalities have total rates of self-employment (not incorporated, incorporated, and unpaid family worker) that exceed the 10.8 percent average for all foreign-born Americans. The groups with the highest rates are Israelis/Palestinians (33.4 percent), Syrians (26 percent), Jordanians (23.4 percent), Lebanese (22

Table 3   Self-employment rates of foreign-born Middle Eastern and North African groups, 2000 (percentages)

National origin	Not incorporated	Incorporated	Unpaid family worker	Total self-employed
Afghanistan	9.9	5.0	0.0	14.9
Iran	11.8	9.6	0.4	21.8
Iraq	9.6	8.6	0.3	18.5
Israel/Palestine	12.0	12.1	0.3	33.4
Jordan	13.6	9.6	0.2	23.4
Kuwait	5.0	6.5	0.6	12.1
Lebanon	10.6	10.8	0.6	22.0
Saudi Arabia	4.1	6.5	0.3	10.9
Syria	15.8	9.7	0.5	26.0
Turkey	8.7	7.0	0.4	16.1
Yemen Arab Republic	11.0	6.5	1.2	18.7
Egypt	7.9	6.2	0.4	14.5
Algeria	5.9	3.6	0.2	9.7
Morocco	6.4	4.8	0.3	11.5
All foreign-born	6.8	3.7	0.3	10.8

Source: U.S. Bureau of the Census, 2000 Census, 5% Public Use Microdata Sample, weighted data.
Note: Population 25–64 years old in the labor force. Data are not available for Tunisia.

percent), Yemenis (18.7 percent), and Iraqis (18.5 percent). (Iranians are covered in a separate entry, and Armenians are an ancestry group, not a national-origin group.) Even Saudis' rate of self-employment, at 10.8 percent, is on a par with that of all foreign-born people. Algerians and Moroccans, two North African groups, are the only Middle Eastern nationalities with below-average self-employment rates.

Yemenis, who have the lowest educational achievements of all Middle Eastern nationalities, tend to be more involved in unskilled occupations than others from the region. They find employment as industrial laborers in the factories of Detroit/Dearborn, Michigan, and Buffalo/Lackawanna, New York, and as agricultural laborers in California, and they run restaurants and grocery stores in New York City. According to the 2000 Census, almost 40 percent of Yemenis are employed in retail enterprises.

Iraqi Chaldeans have a concentrated niche in the ethnic economy. Chaldeans are an Eastern Rite Catholic group who speak an Aramaic language and are predominantly from Iraq. They have a strong tradition of self-employment in both Iraq and the U.S. They own 80 to 90 percent of the retail businesses in Detroit, where grocers' and gas station owners' associations are largely Chaldean in membership. The group also maintains an entrepreneurial settlement in El Cajon, a suburb of San Diego, California. In the mid-1990s, the Chaldean community published a single business directory that listed enterprises in these two cities, which are some 2,000 miles apart.

Because of their high rates of self-employment in African American neighborhoods, Chaldeans are sometimes involved in conflicts with local activist groups similar to those experienced by Jews and Koreans who run businesses in America's inner cities. Since late 2003, Detroit has engaged in a crackdown against small businesses that have violated various regulations. Feeling targeted, the Chaldean community has responded by organizing, holding community forums, writing letters to local newspapers, and meeting with the mayor.

In addition to their remarkable levels of self-employment, many Middle Eastern groups are professionally employed. Israelis/Palestinians have the highest rate of professional/managerial employment in this group, at 50 percent. Turks, Lebanese, Egyptians, Saudis, Algerians, and Kuwaitis reveal rates of professional employment in 40 excess of percent. Syrians, Jordanians, and Moroccans rank in the high 30 percent range, while Iraqis and Yemenis have rates of professional employment in the teens and twenties. For purposes of comparison, the average rate of managerial/professional employment for all foreign-born people in the U.S. in 2000 was 29.7 percent. Rates of employment as technicians, salespeople, and administrators are also in the 20–40 percent range for nearly all Middle Eastern groups. The rates for operators/laborers range from the teens to the thirties. Relatively few Middle Easterners work in service occupations (see Table 4).

Reflecting their cultural orientation and high earnings in the U.S., foreign-born

Table 4 Occupations of foreign-born Middle Eastern and North African groups in the
United States, 2000

National origin	Population[a]	Occupation (percentage)			
		Managerial/ professional	Technical/sales/ administration	Service	Operators/ laborers
Afghanistan	19,283	30.5	32.1	14.7	21.4
Iran	161,774	50.2	29.5	7.5	12.0
Iraq	43,337	24.4	34.2	9.9	30.7
Israel/Palestine	63,342	50.0	31.1	6.7	11.7
Jordan	25,965	33.0	38.1	18.2	14.9
Kuwait	8,902	48.9	36.0	4.1	10.3
Lebanon	59,399	44.4	29.9	8.9	16.1
Saudi Arabia	5,299	44.0	32.0	5.7	15.6
Syria	26,343	37.3	31.5	8.3	22.3
Turkey	44,252	43.4	25.8	10.6	19.3
Yemen Arab Republic	7,116	16.6	45.3	11.6	25.0
Egypt	62,687	47.4	26.1	9.9	15.6
Algeria	6,384	44.1	24.7	12.1	18.5
Morocco	24,430	34.6	28.5	17.7	18.1
All foreign-born	15,299,536	29.7	22.2	16.3	29.0

Source: U.S. Bureau of the Census, 2000 Census, 5% Public Use Microdata Sample, weighted data.

Note: Data are not available for Tunisia. The total percentage of occupations do not add to 100 percent
due to the omission of military, farming/forestry/fishing, and unemployed or not classified.

a. Population aged 25–64 in the labor force.

Middle Eastern women have low rates of labor force participation. In particular,
immigrant Arab women have some of the lowest rates of labor force participation
among all immigrant groups. While Middle Eastern families in the U.S. are quite
diverse, they tend to be patrilineal and extended. They are regarded as the central
bases of security and stability for their members. Religiosity, endogamous marriages, and women's responsibility for maintaining traditional families are among
the main factors accounting for women's low employment rate.

Relatively Westernized and highly educated populations such as the Turks, Lebanese, Israelis/Palestinians, Moroccans, Algerians, and Egyptians have the highest
rates of female labor force participation (in the 50–60 percent range), which ap-
proximate those of foreign-born women generally. However, even highly educated
women from the Middle East often remain outside the labor market. Interestingly
enough, Israeli women reveal a lower labor force participation rate in the U.S. than
they do in their country of origin. This can be attributed to the greater earnings of
their husbands in the U.S. and the domestic and communal responsibilities associated with raising their children in an unfamiliar environment.

Religion

Religion is a source of both solidarity and conflict within Middle Eastern American populations. Even though a considerable part of the population is largely secular, many communal activities are organized along religious lines. Community members represent several religious affiliations, including Lebanese Christians of Maronite, Melkite, Syrian, and Greek Orthodox faiths as well as Sunni and Shia Muslims; Palestinians/Jordanians of Catholic, Protestant, Greek Orthodox, and Sunni Muslim belief; Yemenis of Shafei and Zeidi Muslim persuasions; and Iraqis of the Eastern Rite Catholic Chaldean sect. Other religious affiliations include Judaism, Druze, and Alawi.

Muslim immigrants arrived in the U.S. at the turn of the 20th century along with their Christian compatriots. A significant number were from Syria and Lebanon, but there were also some Muslim Turks. These proportions have changed since the 1960s, with Muslims outnumbering their Christian counterparts. Many North Africans, especially Moroccans, have come through the Diversity Visa Lottery, a program open to countries that have sent fewer than 50,000 immigrants to the U.S. in the past five years.

In a relatively short time, the Muslim American community has created numerous places of worship (over 1,200 mosques) and organizations. Unlike Christianity and Judaism, however, Islam is not a congregational religion. Muslims are not required to attend mosques regularly to practice their faith. In fact, despite the exaggerated portrayal of Muslims in the U.S. media (depicted as overly observant veiled women and bearded men), a relatively small segment of this population attends mosques regularly. The homogenized media portrayal ignores the segment of Muslim immigrants who are cultural Muslims, since Islam is both a religious and a cultural tradition. These nominal, or sometimes even secular, Muslims are a byproduct of "push" factors of migration, migrant selectivity, and the assimilation process. Arguably, the American context has absorbed many different Muslim nationalities, allowing for a wide range of Muslim practices and therefore resulting in a uniquely American Islam. The visual representation of this is evident among Muslim youth who comply with religious requirements while participating in American popular culture, including music, sports, and fashion. For example, young women in Dearborn, Michigan, often wear the *hijab* (Muslim headscarf) along with the team jerseys of their favorite NBA players.

Between 1899 and 1926, over 50,000 Jews from the Ottoman empire, specifically Turkey, Syria, Greece, and the Balkan region, settled in the U.S., largely in New York City, with additional concentrations in Atlanta, Los Angeles, and Seattle. Culturally, their traditions, diet, language, and social practices were distinct from those of Ashkenazi (northern European) Jews, who make up the majority of the American Jewish population. While many of the descendants of Middle Eastern

Jews have assimilated into the larger Jewish American community, some, like the Syrian Jews residing in New Jersey and Brooklyn, have established an ethnic economy, maintain several synagogues, and continue to marry within their own group. This has permitted them to retain cultural, religious, and liturgical traditions. Since the 1950s and 1960s, a new wave of Middle Eastern Jews has arrived, primarily from Israel, Iran, and the Arab countries (Iraq, Egypt, Lebanon, Syria). In the mid-1990s, the number of Middle Eastern Jews in the U.S. was estimated to be between 200,000 and 300,000.

Ethnic Organizations

In spite of a growing population and high levels of educational and occupational achievement, Middle Eastern immigrant communities are only now developing a thriving organizational infrastructure. Moreover, most of these organizations are relatively new. Few ethnic/religious organizations were founded before 1969, which coincides with the large influx of immigrants from the Middle East and North Africa in the 1970s. Compatriotic societies were more typical in the early 20th century.

Most Middle Eastern and Muslim organizations are oriented toward a panethnic constituency and have been established since the 1970s, reflecting the relatively recent origins of the population. The majority of these are in major metropolitan areas such as New York, Los Angeles, Chicago, and Detroit, where significant populations congregate. The Arab Community Center for Economic and Social Services (ACCESS) and the Arab American Institute (AAI) are examples of local and national Arab American organizations, respectively. Based in Dearborn, Michigan, ACCESS is the oldest (established in 1971) and largest community center and provides a range of services, including social, legal, employment, health, cultural, and educational, predominantly to Arab Americans. It is undeniably the premier Arab American human services center and grassroots organization. Its budget exceeds $10 million a year, its programs are comprehensive, it serves over 50,000 clients, and it comes into contact with about a quarter of a million people annually.

The AAI was established in 1985 to represent the interests of Americans of Arab descent in politics and to foster their civic and political empowerment through policy, research, and public affairs services. AAI has been active in challenging negative stereotypes of Arabs and Arab Americans in the media and American society at large. Since 1996 the Arab American Institute Foundation has been supporting public information and education programs as well as sponsoring outreach in order to promote a fuller and deeper public understanding of the Arab American community.

The American-Arab Anti-Discrimination Committee (ADC), another leading

Arab American organization, is committed to defending the civil rights of people of Arab descent and promoting their cultural heritage. Founded in 1980 by the former U.S. senator Jim Abourezk, ADC features an advisory board that includes prominent Arab Americans from several nationalities, ideological positions, and walks of life and has members in all 50 states. Its legal department handles over 2,000 complaints and cases annually.

Other Middle Eastern Americans organize themselves on the basis of nationality, religion, and place of birth. For example, Palestinians have created several organizations with both local and international agendas. The lives and social activities of Chaldeans and Copts are oriented toward church-based and business or professional associations. Israelis have developed an array of social, cultural, and political organizations, some in consort with American Jews or the Israeli government, in major cities such as New York, Los Angeles, Chicago, and Miami, where many reside. Middle Eastern groups frequently publish newspapers, such as *Forum and Link,* the *Arab American News,* and *Al-Jadid,* which are mailed to a wide audience. Along with print publications, a variety of cable and satellite TV services connect members of Middle Eastern American communities with each other and their countries of origin. Nationalities with relatively small populations in the U.S., such as Moroccans and Tunisians, have developed websites to share contacts and information.

Stereotypes and Discrimination

In the beginning of the 20th century, the pioneers' appearance and dress, as well as cultural practices and language, set them apart. Children were harassed by teachers because of their "unpronounceable" names, while peers derided them with epithets such as "camel jockey" and "sand nigger," though most often they called them "Turks." This label was particularly infuriating to these immigrants because they were fleeing the corrupt and decaying regime of the Ottoman Turks.

Prejudice against Middle Easterners was also reflected in official government policies. In 1910 the U.S. Census Bureau classified Middle Easterners as "Asiatics" (that is, nonwhite), making their right to naturalization questionable. Several cases came before the courts to argue that the Syrians/Lebanese, Armenians, and other immigrants from the Middle East were indeed Caucasians, and people of Middle Eastern ancestry are now officially classified as white. As a consequence, these people have been rendered invisible in official records. Scholars contend that Middle Easterners' racial status remains unclear to various American groups and to themselves, making analysis of their situation nearly impossible. As aptly put by Therese Saliba, "Arabs are labeled Caucasian, Asian, Afro-Asian, non-European, Semitic, Arab, black, or 'of color' as racialized formulations shift with political struggles." This misclassification has also made Middle Eastern Americans ineligible for affirmative action programs, although they regularly encounter prejudice and discrimination.

The popular media—including Hollywood movies, inflammatory news shows, talk radio, and the tabloid press—have been especially prone to perpetuating negative stereotypes of Middle Easterners. Scholars, notably the late literary critic Edward Said of Columbia University, have argued that anti–Middle Eastern racism, which he called "Orientalism," is pervasive and institutionalized in the U.S. These stereotypes are not only tolerated but condoned and manipulated by the government and politicians to support U.S. policy in the Middle East. With few exceptions, politicians remain indifferent to the fate of Middle Eastern Americans. Since this group is relatively small in number and lacks political power, it was not able to counter such attacks, ironically, until after 9/11.

The stereotype of Middle Easterners as terrorists, Muslim fundamentalists, and nationalist zealots has become so sensationalized and institutionalized in the U.S. that any time an act of terrorism is perpetrated against Americans in the region, Middle Eastern Americans suffer repercussions. The long list of events that have incited the American public include the hostage crisis at the 1972 Munich Olympics, the 1973 Arab oil embargo, the 1979–1981 Iran hostage crisis, the 1983 suicide bombing of the U.S. Marine barracks in Beirut, the 1985 hijacking of TWA Flight 847 to Beirut, Libya's confession to the 1988 Pan Am bombing over Lockerbie, Scotland, and the 1990–1991 Gulf war. In fact, many Middle Eastern immigrants are refugees, asylum-seekers, and exiles whose presence in the U.S. can be traced to their own victimization by factions carrying out violent and repressive actions in their region of origin.

The cumulative effect of a series of terrorist events has manifested itself in a hostile environment, resulting in negative stereotypes, prejudice, and discrimination toward those of Middle Eastern origin. But nothing compares to the Al Qaeda–sponsored terrorist attacks on America of September 11, 2001. It is important to distinguish between two kinds of backlash from these attacks. The first consists of hate crimes and bias incidents, such as murder, arson, and acts of harassment, perpetrated by ordinary Americans against fellow citizens who are believed to be Middle Eastern. The second encompasses various official directives, initiatives, and laws carried out by the U.S. government at the federal, state, and local levels and the resulting consequences for Middle Eastern American communities.

In terms of hate crimes, the FBI confirmed four murders and inconclusively investigated another seven cases as directly related to the 9/11 attacks. In its 2001 annual hate crimes report, the FBI noted an increase of 1,600 percent in incidents against Muslim individuals, institutions, and businesses (there were 28 cases in 2000, compared to 481 in 2001). Hate crimes and bias incidents were particularly prevalent at airports, the entry points of hijacking terrorists. Physical markers such as the *hijab* and, ironically, the Sikh turban (Sikhs are neither Arab nor Muslim) made individuals particularly susceptible to harassment. Ethnic businesses and places of worship were also vulnerable, but police presence and protection prevented major violence there.

Concluding that "Arab Americans suffered a serious backlash following September 11, 2001," the American-Arab Anti-Discrimination Committee tabulated over 700 violent incidents and more than 800 cases of employment discrimination aimed at Arab or Muslim Americans in the first nine weeks after the attacks. These represent a marked escalation from previous years. The South Asian American Leaders of Tomorrow (SAALT) tallied some 645 incidents nationally during the first week after 9/11.

In addition to hate crimes and other forms of violence, several new government policies adversely affected Middle Eastern Americans. The most significant of these was the USA PATRIOT Act, a sweeping array of legislation passed with nearly unanimous support shortly after 9/11, which introduced broad changes in domestic law. Immigrants from Middle Eastern and/or Muslim countries became subject to arbitrary detention. If suspected of terrorism, detainees could be kept without charge for an extended time. Hearings could be "secure" (i.e., closed to the public), bond could be denied, and attorney-client communication privilege could be disregarded. Estimates on the number of detainees vary from 500 to over 1,200. Pakistanis made up the largest number of detainees, followed by Egyptians, Turks, and Yemenis, suggesting that both Arabs and non-Arab Muslims were targeted.

In addition, the Department of Justice required the FBI to enter into its database the names of about 6,000 male absconders (visa violators subject to deportation) who were Arab and/or Muslim nationals believed to be from countries that harbored Al Qaeda and to apprehend these men. The National Security Entry-Exit Registration System (NSEERS), another initiative that ended, obligated aliens from 26 predominantly Muslim countries to be registered, fingerprinted, and photographed upon arrival and periodically afterward. In addition, men older than 16 who were citizens of Iran, Iraq, Libya, Sudan, and Syria—allegedly terrorist-training countries—were required to register with the INS. By early May 2003, over 80,000 men had registered. Student and Exchange Visitor Information System (SEVIS), another policy, was intended to track all foreign student enrollments in the U.S., though it was not limited to people from Middle Eastern and Muslim countries. The attorney general ordered the FBI to conduct "voluntary" interviews with some 5,000 men aged 18 to 33 who had entered the U.S. between January 2000 and November 2001 from countries suspected of Al Qaeda presence or activity, once again targeting a population whose profile matched that of the hijackers.

The U.S. government also tightened controls over international financial transactions in order to impede sources of funding for terrorist organizations. As part of this initiative, the government accused three large Muslim charitable organizations—the Holy Land Foundation for Relief and Development, the Benevolence

International Foundation, and the Global Relief Foundation—of money-laundering and froze their assets. As a consequence, Muslim Americans have been concerned with the government's interference in their religious obligation to *zakat* (tithe).

A full accounting of the post-9/11 measures has never been released by the U.S. government. Accordingly, the actual number of those detained, interviewed, registered, or deported is unknown. Civil libertarians have criticized these policies as both ineffective and in violation of the equal protection clause of the U.S. Constitution, perhaps the reason why they were terminated. While Middle Eastern and/or Muslim immigrant men and their families suffered the most from these policies, their ethnic/religious communities were left feeling extremely vulnerable.

These overwhelmingly harsh restrictions on travel and financial transfers have hindered Middle Eastern Americans from engaging in patterns of long-distance nationalism and exchange of support and information that have long sustained contacts with their countries of origin. Under current conditions, transnational communication, travel, entrepreneurship, activism, and family relations have become much more difficult or even impossible.

Having settled in the U.S. for over a century, Middle Eastern Americans are currently confronting new issues regarding their adaptation and communal identity. Growing in size, sophistication, and political power, their communities have the potential to become major actors on the local, national, and international scene. Despite their dissimilar origins, many are united by shared notions of national, cultural, linguistic, and religious identity as well as their reactions to U.S. Middle East policy and the scapegoating, hostility, and profiling to which they have been subjected, especially since September 11, 2001.

In reaction to recent events, Arab and Muslim Americans have made concerted efforts to become more organized and active. They have developed numerous communal activities and organizations, conferences, and cultural groups. Among these is the 38,500-square-foot, $13 million Arab American National Museum, which opened in Dearborn, Michigan, in May 2005.

Prominent Middle Eastern American figures, such as political activist Ralph Nader, National Institutes of Health director Dr. Elias Zerhouni, actress Salma Hayek, designer Joseph Abboud, and tennis star Andre Agassi, visibly contribute to American culture and society. At the same time, less renowned Middle Easterners also contribute in their own way. While the current political climate has made the lives of many Middle Eastern Americans challenging, if not difficult, this diverse, dynamic, and growing population is endowed with education, skills, and experience. Drawing on these resources, the Middle Eastern American population will continue to play a vital role in the advancement of the U.S., just as they have done in the past.

Bibliography

Abraham, Nabeel, and Andrew Shryock. *Arab Detroit: From Margin to Mainstream.* Detroit: Wayne State University Press, 2000.

Bakalian, Anny. *Armenian Americans: From Being to Feeling Armenian.* New Brunswick, N.J.: Transaction, 1993.

Bakalian, Anny, and Mehdi Bozorgmehr. "Backlash 9/11: Mobilizing Middle Eastern and Muslim Americans." Unpublished manuscript, 2006.

Bozorgmehr, Mehdi, and Alison Feldman, eds. *Middle Eastern Diaspora Communities in America.* New York: Kevorkian Center for Near Eastern Studies, New York University, 1996.

Gold, Steven J. *The Israeli Diaspora.* Seattle: University of Washington Press, 2002.

Khater, Akram Fouad. *Inventing Home: Emigration, Gender, and the Middle Class in Lebanon, 1870–1920.* Berkeley: University of California Press, 2001.

McCarus, Ernest, ed. *The Development of Arab-American Identity.* Ann Arbor: University of Michigan Press, 1994.

Mirak, Robert. *Torn between Two Lands: Armenians in America, 1890 to World War I.* Cambridge, Mass.: Harvard University Press, 1983.

Naff, Alixa. *Becoming American: The Early Arab Immigrant Experience.* Carbondale: Southern Illinois University Press, 1985.

Read, Jen'nan Ghazal. *Culture, Class, and Work among Arab-American Women.* New York: LFB Scholarly, 2004.

Shaheen, Jack G. *Reel Bad Arabs: How Hollywood Vilifies a People.* New York: Olive Branch, 2001.

Suleiman, Michael W., ed. *Arabs in America: Building a New Future.* Philadelphia: Temple University Press, 1999.

Pacific: Fiji, Tonga, Samoa

Cathy A. Small

Fijians, Tongans, and Samoans share a geographical space in the western Pacific and an interactive history that includes centuries of intermarriages, wars, and trade. In the U.S. they are part of a category called "Pacific Islanders," representing more than 25 different peoples who are lumped together by U.S. government bureaucracy into the broad, almost meaningless designation "Asian-Pacific Islanders." But even among just Fijians, Tongans, and Samoans, the interplay of culture, language, ethnic or racial categorization, nationality, and political and legal statuses within the U.S. illustrates the complexity of, and the problems imposed by, these designations.

Fijians are actually members of two different broad ethnic groups: native Fijians, a Melanesian people with strong cultural and historical ties to the Polynesian Samoans and Tongans, and Indo-Fijians, themselves divided ethnically and linguistically, who were taken from India to Fiji in the 19th century by British colonialists to work as indentured laborers on sugarcane plantations. Over the years, the relationship between the two groups became increasingly strained as Indo-Fijians became the country's primary business owners while native Fijians solidified their control over land and political power. The majority of recent immigrants to the U.S. are Indo-Fijians who left Fiji after 1987, when a series of political coups—the last in 2000—severely limited their political rights and sense of future. They continue to speak Hindi, as they did in Fiji, and to follow many Indian family and religious patterns, although most Indo-Fijians have never seen India and certain key customs, such as the caste system, have been discarded. About half the U.S. immigrants from Fiji are indigenous Fijian and half are Indo-Fijian, and the statements we can make about Fijian Americans differ markedly depending on which subgroup we are referring to.

Samoans, who include Western (independent) and American Samoans, have a common language and culture, but their statuses as migrants are distinct. American

Samoa became a territory of the U.S. in 1900 and remains so, while Western Samoa, once a German colony, became a trusteeship of New Zealand in 1914 and achieved independence in 1962. (In 1997, Western Samoa changed its name to Samoa.) Migration patterns have tended to follow these colonial routes. American Samoans, who have the status "U.S. nationals," have primarily migrated to the U.S. mainland because of their unrestricted legal access, while (Western) Samoans have gone to New Zealand. Those (Western) Samoans who come to the U.S. often do so by moving first to American Samoa, as Michael Levin has documented, blurring the lines between these Samoan groups in the U.S. Here, statements about "Samoans" generally include both independent and American Samoans.

Tongans share a Polynesian heritage with Samoans, but Tonga is an independent kingdom and a former protectorate of Great Britain whose citizens began migrating to the U.S. after 1965, in response to growing land shortage, limited wage labor and educational opportunities, and a more inviting U.S. immigration policy.

The migration flows of different Pacific Islander groups to the U.S. are also distinct historically; there were significant inflows of Samoans before 1980, of Tongans between 1980 and 1989, and of Indo-Fijians after 1989.

Pacific Islanders in the U.S.

Despite their many differences, many Pacific Islanders show similarities. First, 92 percent of Fijians, Tongans, and Samoans (hereafter referred to as PIs) live in the western U.S., a result of a system of chain migration. In every family, initial migrants arranged plane fare, visas, and temporary housing for relatives, who in turn set up independent households and brought over more relatives to the same areas. One obvious result of this process is that PI populations have come to be concentrated in certain key states: 86 percent reside in California, Utah, Hawai'i, and Washington, and secondary communities are found in Arizona and Texas.

Another, less obvious result is that certain towns, counties, and regions within the key states have impressive numbers of Pacific Islander residents. Although Samoans, Fijians, and Tongans combined make up a minuscule portion of U.S. immigrants—less than one hundredth of one percent—they are a formidable presence in these areas of concentration. In the 2000 Census, Pacific Islanders (including Hawai'ians) were half of one percent of the Bay Area population, according to the *San Francisco Chronicle*, but this represented more than 36,000 people, with some California counties having almost 10,000 documented PI residents. Many more undocumented PIs are living in these communities, because overstaying one's visa is a common practice among them.

A Tongan, Samoan, or Fijian will not find his or her entire California neighborhood made up of Pacific Islanders, but there are enough countrymen in the area to have social, business, and church activities that cater to Polynesian tastes and needs.

Living in San Mateo or Daly City, California, Tongans or Samoans will be able to attend a church service in their native language, to participate in one of the 88 Polynesian dance troupes currently in northern California, or to use a travel agent who is a countryman to arrange a trip home. In Sacramento, Indo-Fijians can attend services at a Hindu temple funded and built largely by other Indo-Fijians. It is not hard to find a Pacific Island grocery store, probably owned by an Indo-Fijian family, that sells taro, yams, dried octopus, and other island fare as well as tinned biscuits, canned corned beef, and familiar snacks that are often imported to the islands. Tongan men can readily find kava-drinking clubs on Friday nights, while Fijian men might attend a weekly cricket match.

"The community's presence," the *San Francisco Chronicle* reports, "is increasingly felt"—in the growing number of Polynesian restaurants and food markets in the Bay Area (now more than 20), in the proliferation of hula dance groups, and in the more than 10,000 people who reportedly participated in Samoan Flag Day celebrations in San Francisco. Likewise, a visit from the king of Tonga can draw 10,000 Tongans in northern California and more than 2,000 in Phoenix or Salt Lake City.

This concentration of the PI population enables a number of related developments in these key geographical areas: the growth of supervisory and sales jobs to serve these immigrants; the development of ethnically based churches, wards, and religious services; and the existence of a dense and supportive social network. Within the key states we can find enclaves of island culture that favor larger, more extended families and a high degree of language retention. Ninety-four percent of foreign-born PIs in the four key states speak their native language in the home, and more than 30 percent of their households have six or more family members—almost seven times the national average. These big households often represent extended families in which, as in the islands, grandparents or siblings of the householder and their families have come to live. The result is that a PI resident in these areas can live a life of marriages, funerals, first birthdays and church dedications, and cricket matches that only peripherally involve people outside the ethnic group.

Transnationalism

PI migrants' strong connections to their culture, language, and family is a corollary of their transnational life, that is, the vibrant and ongoing relationships they maintain with island villages, institutions, and people. Indeed, we cannot understand PI life in the U.S. without recognizing the flows of information, wealth, and people that pass between the U.S. and the islands.

Ethnographic and economic evidence from all three cultures indicate that migrants send money and goods to relatives back home at very high rates—high enough that many Pacific island economies stay afloat because of these remittances. (After the Fijian coup, however, there have been some reports of negative remittance flows among Indo-Fijians.) Everything from cash for school fees, church donations, and family feasts to truck-sized boxes stuffed with clothing, furniture, and appliances (from hair dryers to stoves) is sent home to the islands. A Pacific cyclone will result in a formidable influx of overseas funds to help victims, relatives and nonrelatives alike. The islands in turn send a steady stream of traditional wealth and ceremonial items—Samoan fine mats, Tongan tapa cloth, and Fijian kava bowls—which are used in social and ceremonial events in the U.S.

More than material wealth goes back and forth. Photographs and full-length videos of marriages, funerals, and other ceremonies frequently cross the ocean; in homes both on the islands and in the States, it is common to see a designated shelf stacked with videotapes of family events, which household members watch over and over again. PI migrants regularly fill the planes to the Pacific for holidays and special island events, and in the opposite direction, visiting Samoan *malaga* (traveling ceremonial groups), Tongan royalty, and native Fijian dignitaries are brought in to grace ceremonial events held in the U.S. Island children needing education or English-language training come to stay for a year or more, while children resident in the U.S. who are in trouble in school or are beginning to mix with the "wrong" friends are sent to the islands for discipline.

Becoming a Minority

The strength of Pacific Islander culture in pockets of the U.S., together with strong and frequent home island connections, may give the impression that island culture is faithfully recreated in the U.S. In truth, though, it is not, in large part because the reproduction of customs and culture is taking place in a very different national context, in which "Pacific Islander" has new and distinct meanings as well as repercussions.

For one thing, Pacific Islanders are minorities in this culture, and they are, as Ilana Gershon has pointed out for Samoans, "minor" minorities at that. Like most other minorities, they have a much dimmer educational and economic picture than that of the majority. In the 2000 Census, Pacific Islanders' average per capita income (based on those aged 25 to 65 in the labor force) was $28,124, 67 percent of what it was for white Americans, and only 47 percent owned their own homes, compared with 67 percent for the nation at large. (This ranges from a low of 36 percent among Samoans to a high of 61 percent among Fijians.) In 1999, 17.7 percent of Pacific Islanders lived below the poverty threshold, compared to 12.4 percent of the entire U.S. population.

It is job category rather than participation in the labor force that best explains PIs' narrow slice of the economic pie. PIs are overrepresented in lower-paying categories such as service, construction, production, and transportation industries. Conversely, only 18.5 percent of Pacific Islanders were in management and professional occupations, compared with 33.7 percent of the national population. Many Pacific Islanders are employed in lower-status jobs in the U.S. than they had in their home country, a drop they endure because of the wage differentials between the islands and their adopted home at the time of migration. The teacher becomes a teacher's aide, the independent farmer becomes a suburban tree trimmer or a janitor, the homemaker becomes a nursing home attendant. David Dixon argues that economic indicators by age group suggest that PIs have decidedly less upward mobility than Americans at large do. With lower incomes and less mobility come their American corollaries: lower educational achievement and higher gang activity, especially in urban centers such as Los Angeles and Salt Lake City, where Samoan and Tongan gangs are active.

Although many PIs migrate for educational opportunities, only 10 percent actually are able to earn their bachelor's degrees, less than half the national average. And even educated PIs do not have the same job outlook as other Americans. Of those 25 and older with bachelor's degrees, only 55 percent are in professional and management areas, compared with 73 percent of college-educated whites. College-educated PIs are overrepresented in sales, office, and service jobs. The statistical outlook for Fijians, who have a high concentration of recent professional immigrants, is more positive and the highest of PIs', but they still do not compare well with whites on economic and educational measures.

Pacific Islander culture and social networks can serve as a buffer against these harsh U.S. realities. PI households in the four key states are 80 percent larger than the average U.S. household and more than five times as likely to contain more than one family unit. These extended and multiple family living arrangements, involving several adults who work and contribute to the household, enable PI household income in these areas, at $54,620, to approximate the average household income for the general population ($55,681), even when PI *per capita* income is only two thirds the national average. Islanders beyond the household also offer a dependable network of economic support to new immigrants and an ongoing system of mutual aid. An immigrant's first residence and first job typically come from a countryman, along with information about where to shop, bank, and get airline tickets or a medical checkup. Money for a big purchase is often loaned through local networks rather than a bank, where a migrant may have no credit history or encounter credit problems. Because PIs are often concentrated in certain occupations, islanders who need extra time off or wish to work part-time can look to one another for job sharing or shift tradeoffs.

Being a "Pacific Islander," like being a member of any minority in America, is a double-edged sword, providing both a vehicle for support and identity and a source of difference and discrimination. Dixon and Small determined that states with the heaviest concentration of PIs, and consequently the most visible and vibrant PI cultures, are simultaneously those with the biggest income differentials between PIs and whites. And "culture," as many PI youth are quick to see, has its costs as well as its benefits. Fulfilling obligations to extended kin for numerous life-cycle events, which are sometimes more opulent than those on the home island, may be onerous, requiring significant cash outlays, travel costs, and missed work time. These events, coupled with church or temple donations and remitted cash and goods sent home by the "rich" Americans to their island villages and relatives, require a huge investment of time and resources that places a constant demand on PI families. It can be a particular drain for wealthier families, who may bear the brunt of family requests, and for poorer families, whose contributions take away from already meager resources.

Trends

These complexities and contradictions of being ethnic and minority, islander and American, shape many daily realities in the lives of Pacific Islanders in the U.S. and are manifest in the following key trends and issues.

Identity. Both geographically and ethnically, the identities of Tongans, Fijians, and Samoans are widening. Initially, this meant the blurring of family and village boundaries as islanders took up residence in the U.S. As Joan Ablon wrote of earlier Samoan migrants, "The mere fact of origin in Samoa sufficed to qualify the individual for aid no matter what his family and village connexions." This applies to Tongans and Fijians of the same ethnic background as well.

Particularly among young people, this sense of community has extended from a common national homeland or ethnicity to a more pan-Polynesian (or pan–Pacific Islander) purview, as seen in this statement by a Samoan man in California, cited in the *San Francisco Chronicle:* "If I see a Hawai'ian brother or a Tongan brother, we say, 'How you doing?' . . . We consider ourselves flesh and blood. We're like cousins." Polynesian dance troupes, described by Amy Stillman, which have become prolific in many western states, attract youth from different island backgrounds, including Filipinos and others outside of Polynesia; their repertoires typically include dances from five or more island heritages.

We see the same merging of interests and associations in student and political groups, as Polynesians join with Pacific Islanders, Pacific Islanders with Asians to form associations such as the Pacific American Foundation, the Pacific Islanders Cultural Association, and the Asian Pacific American Labor Alliance. In the U.S., PIs now regularly ally themselves with other, often more numerically prominent racial minorities—including not only Asians but "people of color"—to further their community agendas.

Perhaps as a result of these social, residential, and political connections, the census reveals pockets of PIs who speak Spanish or Vietnamese or Filipino; frequent intermarriages with other Pacific Islanders as well as other U.S. minorities; and a number of PI youth who have adopted hip-hop styles and black urban dialects of English, as in this Internet posting from a middle-class Tongan: "I just wanted 2 c wat y'all doin in college/highskool or wateva. I know 4 a fact that there are so many Tongan peepz out dea doin drugs and sh!t on da streets, which is Y I wanted 2 explore da other side." The force of such "other" identification among PI young people can be formidable, as April Henderson has documented for the Samoan hip-hop scene.

Of these new identity alliances and allegiances—expressed in areas as diverse as marriage patterns, linguistic use, joint academic and political projects, and music—some hold more long-term promise than others. Indo-Fijians, despite their long island history, may identify more with India and others in the Indian diaspora than with South Pacific Islanders; tensions with indigenous Fijians in their homeland, coupled with shared Indian religion, language, and food, strengthen an affinity to India and Asia. Samoans, Tongans, and indigenous Fijians may find little culturally or experientially in common with others identified as Asian, as Paul Spickard has argued, and may forge uneasy alliances with the blacks and Chicanos with whom they share neighborhoods and economic status. Spickard, watching the ways many migrants from the region and their children are coalescing in the U.S., believes that a new identity is on the cusp of being formed: not Tongan American, Samoan American, Fijian American, Polynesian American, or Asian American but Pacific Islander American.

Mobility. American-born PIs are more likely to move outside the population centers, and those who do so show a pronounced tendency toward cultural change, including language loss and smaller families. It is unclear why American-born PIs are more mobile—whether it is because there is less of an anchor to their countrymen, greater opportunities in other areas, or other reasons. The fact remains that while less than 20 percent of foreign-born PI heads of household (aged 25 and older) live outside the main PI states, almost 40 percent of American-born PIs do so. Two out of every five American-born PI heads of household are thus raising families in states without large concentrations of their countrymen, and it is in their households that we see the most pronounced changes in cultural indicators, such as language retention and household size and composition.

In 65 percent of households in this group, a Polynesian language is no longer spoken in the home. Living outside the population centers has had a bigger "English only" effect—almost twice as much—on those born in the U.S. than on those born abroad, whose native language doesn't fade as readily outside the PI communities.

The loss of language is related not only to living outside a wider community of PI-speakers but also to changes in household composition, because language retention and household size are highly correlated. Among both foreign-born and American-born PIs, English only is spoken by less than 5 percent of households with more than six people. Yet among households headed by American-born PIs situated outside PI population centers, there are few with more than six people (only 8.7 percent), and the presence of subfamilies in this population is very small, at only 2.9 percent. Thus, while there are more outside pressures to speak English, there are also fewer countervailing influences, such as the presence of a non-English-speaking aunt, uncle, or cousin, to retain the native language.

The general picture of American-born Samoans, Tongans, and Fijians is not yet one of language or cultural loss, though. Although the total number of American-born PIs who speak only English in their homes is almost six times that of PIs born overseas, the majority of all American-born PIs still speak their parents' native language in the home. Many of these are children living in the households of immigrant parents. The indications are that as this new generation of American-born PIs comes of age, raises its own families, and continues to spread out across the U.S., this cultural continuity will not endure without a concerted effort by PI American householders to preserve the language and culture of their heritage.

Changing traditions. Most U.S.-born Pacific Islanders are embracing their cultural heritage and finding customs and traditions increasingly important, especially as they raise children. However, in the transnational context, the boundaries and definitions of traditional cultural life are changing. In more recent years, this network of identity has gone global, connecting PIs in the U.S. (often young PIs) with their counterparts on the islands and with Pacific Islander migrants living in Australia, New Zealand, India, and Canada. Organizations such as the International Congress for Fiji Indians (ICFI) seek to join Indo-Fijians around the world, while e-magazines such as *Little India* connect Indo-Fijian migrants to the wider and far-flung Indian diaspora. In a similar way, Samoans, Tongans, and indigenous Fijians have become part of a global village that includes their countrymen, other Polynesians, and other Pacific Islanders in many countries.

The Internet taps into and animates these global networks, which include family-based listserves and web pages, home island news sites, and international websites and chatrooms such as PolyCafe, the KavaBowl, Planet Tonga, Samoa Chat, Yahoo's Fiji chatroom, and BulaFiji. The cyberspace network of Pacific Islanders has become sizable over the past 10 years and is a major vehicle for people to keep apprised of news in their home country, issues of concern to young people, and ethnic events, music, and interfamily messages. New forms of culture, such as PI rap groups, thrive in these Internet venues and bind migrants and island youth together. Movies from Bollywood are beamed via satellite to Indo-Fijian households, and music from "home," now located more virtually in cyberspace, is downloaded onto portable CD players.

It is primarily the young adult children of migrants who are making family web pages that display photos and family news to those around the world and who are communicating with PIs in countries other than their own. Their websites are the way that some extended family members who live in different countries meet one another and exchange photos and family lore.

The discourse in these diverse global forums is telling, in terms of both subject areas and language. Although family announcements, dating, and sexual banter pepper online conversations, cultural and political issues remain an important component of many sites and discussion groups. Young PIs born in the U.S., Australia, and New Zealand are vocal, both in ethnographic accounts and in Internet chatrooms, in debating the pros and cons of traditional commitments and the local politics of their "home" islands: How much should one give overseas? Or to the church? How many days should a ceremony last? Is Fijian policy toward Fijian Indians fair? Which Samoan villages were damaged in the last hurricane? Should Tongan nobility allow for more democracy?

Discussion postings are typically found in English or the island language, but often chatroom talk reflects a fusion of dialects or languages. For instance, in Tongan sites it is typical to find English words interspersed with Tongan words and phrases to form a sort of "Tonglish," intelligible only if you speak both languages to a reasonable degree.

Such pidgin discourse is an apt metaphor for the way that PI Americans, particularly the young, understand their lives. Pacific Islanders, feeling the pull of both their personal heritage and their native U.S. (or New Zealand, Canadian, or Australian) cultures, talk about selecting and blending aspects of their dual enculturation. American-born PIs, like their counterparts in other countries, are actively picking and choosing the aspects of their culture that they will nurture and emphasize. They are using their background as Americans to filter, hone, and question Pacific Island ways, often modifying customs related to social hierarchy, punitive child-rearing practices, and excessive church and ritual expenditure. At the same time, their traditions as Islanders become a platform for critically questioning American values, which deemphasize families, generosity, ceremony, and the importance of obligations to others. Drawing from both traditions, PI youth believe they can find the best of both worlds.

Bibliography

Grieco, Elizabeth. 2002. *The Native Hawaiian and Other Pacific Islander Population: 2000.* Washington, D.C.: U.S. Census Bureau.

Janes, Craig. 1990. *Migration, Social Change, and Health: A Samoan Community in Urban California.* Stanford, Calif.: Stanford University Press.

Small, Cathy. 1997. *Voyages: From Tongan Villages to American Suburbs.* Ithaca, N.Y.: Cornell University Press.

Spickard, Paul, Joanne L. Rondilla, and Debbie Hippolite Wright, eds. 2002. *Pacific Diaspora: Island Peoples in the United States and across the Pacific.* Honolulu: University of Hawaii Press.

Pacific: Japan, Australia, New Zealand

Nana Oishi

Immigrants from the Asia-Pacific region—Japan, Australia, and New Zealand—share such characteristics as high educational attainment, occupational profile, income, and intermarriage rates. However, they also greatly differ in immigration history, ethnic identity, and community development. Here we will highlight the similarities and differences of these three groups. Australians and New Zealanders are considered together, partly because of the limited availability of information but also because of their similarity in immigration patterns and community formation.

Japanese Immigration

The early period. While the arrival of Japanese fishermen in Hawai'i dates back to 1841, major Japanese immigration to the U.S. began only in the late 19th century. It was a period of radical change in Japan, when the rule of the Tokugawa shogunate ended and the Meiji government initiated drastic modernization processes. In the midst of such sociopolitical confusion, 150 Japanese workers were informally recruited by an American businessman and sent to Hawai'i in 1868 to work on sugar plantations. A group of political refugees also arrived in northern California and established a small colony in 1869. The Japanese government initially banned emigration of its citizens, but it reopened the channel in 1885 because of overpopulation and poverty in rural areas. Between 1885 and 1899, 65,045 Japanese—mostly single men—migrated to Hawai'i. The Japanese population on the mainland also grew significantly after the U.S. annexed Hawai'i in 1898; between 1900 and 1910, over 35,000 Japanese moved from Hawai'i to California, Oregon, and Washington, and another 35,000 came directly from Japan.

Early Japanese immigrants, however, faced difficulties soon after their arrival. Anti-immigrant sentiments had already grown, particularly on the mainland, as indicated by the passage of the Chinese Exclusion Act in 1882, which suspended immigration from China. Racial hostility was similarly extended to Japanese immigrants, who confronted job discrimination, school segregation, and racial violence. Because of concerns about security and the impact on diplomatic relations, the U.S. and Japan concluded the Gentlemen's Agreement in 1907–1908, by which the U.S. agreed to solve the problem of school segregation in San Francisco and the Japanese promised to halt the immigration of laborers to the U.S.

The only exception to this rule was Japanese women. Under the so-called Ladies' Agreement, Japanese women were allowed to immigrate as the wives of Japanese residents in the U.S. The early Japanese American community was dominated by men, as most of the immigrants were either single or had left their families back home. Many Japanese bachelors in the U.S. had a marriage arranged by their families in Japan through the exchange of photographs. The arrival of the "picture brides," which continued until 1920, significantly improved the gender balance of the Japanese American population and increased their community through immigration and reproduction.

When World War II began, the fate of Japanese Americans took another turn. President Roosevelt issued Executive Order 9066 on February 19, 1942, which resulted in the internment of thousands of people of Japanese descent living on the West Coast, including part of Arizona. Almost 120,000 Japanese Americans were relocated to remote camps between 1942 and 1945, despite the fact that almost 70 percent of them were U.S. citizens. Segregated in concentration camps across the desert areas of Arizona, California, Utah, Idaho, Colorado, and Wyoming, Japanese Americans lived in substandard housing with inadequate nutrition and health care. This experience had a tremendous impact on community development and ethnic identity among Japanese Americans on the mainland after the war.

It should be noted that Japanese Americans in Hawai'i had a different experience. Although the Japanese military attacked Pearl Harbor, the vast majority of Japanese Americans on the islands were not interned, although 900 aliens were evacuated to the mainland. There were approximately 150,000 Japanese Americans in Hawai'i in 1941, making up one third of the total population, and evacuating all of them would have been too costly. Another factor was Hawai'ian society, which has long been highly multiracial and thus was less prone to racism. The islands' official policy of interracial unity remained intact during the war years.

The postwar period. After the harsh internment experience, about 5,000 Japanese Americans chose to return to Japan. Most remained in the U.S., but 45 percent resettled outside the West Coast. Those who returned to the West Coast decided to live in suburbs instead of the Japantowns they had formerly inhabited, fearing anti-Japanese sentiments. At the same time, after the Immigration Act of 1952 removed racial restrictions on immigration, new immigrants began to arrive from Japan. Most were the family members of Japanese Americans and war brides of American soldiers. Approximately 63,000 Japanese arrived in the U.S. between 1952 and 1964, making Japanese Americans the largest group of Asians. However, Japanese immigration has decreased since then, as economic development opened new career opportunities in Japan. In contrast, the number of other Asian immigrants—Chinese, Koreans, Indians, Filipinos, and Vietnamese—rapidly increased after the Immigration Act of 1965. As a result, the overall presence of Japanese Americans has declined over the past three decades. By 2000, Japanese Americans were only the sixth largest Asian American group.

In the postwar period, Japanese Americans made strenuous efforts to become assimilated to the mainstream American society so that they and their offspring would not experience persecution again. Many of the Nisei—second-generation Japanese Americans—even avoided retaining their Japanese language and cultural heritage by speaking mostly English to their children and espousing an "American" lifestyle. Their emphasis on education resulted in high rates of college graduates among themselves and their children, which pushed Japanese Americans up the socioeconomic ladder. Many of the Sansei (third generation) entered universities, became professionals, and earned significantly higher incomes than the national average. Their overall success and upward mobility gave rise to the myth of a "model minority" after the late 1960s. This myth, which was later extended to other Asian Americans, emphasized traits such as strong values regarding family, education, and hard work. While it has misleading and problematic aspects, it symbolizes a positive shift of public perceptions toward Japanese Americans. Furthermore, during the cold war the U.S. and Japan developed a strong political alliance, which has continued to date. While trade frictions have surfaced from time to time, the existence of a solid political partnership between the two countries has helped win the trust of native Americans and improved Japanese Americans' image as a group.

The redress movement. As the civil rights movement spread across the country in the 1960s, many younger Japanese Americans began to reexamine the unjust treatment that their parents and grandparents received during World War II. Many also questioned the legality of imprisoning so many innocent U.S. citizens without clear evidence of disloyalty.

With the cooperation of multiple generations, the Japanese American community first pressured the government to issue a formal apology, which came from President Ford in 1976. The community then worked to obtain financial compensation for the victims, who lost almost everything because of the internment. As a result, the Commission on Wartime Relocation and Internment of Civilians (CWRIC) was established in 1980 to gather information. Eventually the CWRIC recommended that a formal apology be issued by the Congress and that each surviving victim receive compensation of $20,000. These recommendations were implemented in 1988, when President Reagan signed House Resolution 442, providing redress payments to surviving internees, education funds, and a formal apology from the U.S. government. The government admitted that the internment had violated the basic constitutional rights and civil liberties of Japanese Americans. The Office of Redress Administration was then set up to administer individual payments to 82,220 Japanese Americans (it closed in 1999). This was a historic achievement for the Japanese American community.

The emergence of "new Japanese Americans." The overall structure of the Japanese American community has been rapidly changing for the past few decades. The impact of intermarriage is particularly significant, because Japanese Americans have by far the highest intermarriage rate among Asian Americans. In the New York City region, Liang and Ito found that about 80 percent of U.S.-born Japanese men and women were married to members of other ethnic groups. This was in stark contrast to Chinese (33 percent of men and 45 percent of women), Indians (45 percent of men and 24 percent of women), and others. The 2000 Census also shows that Japanese Americans have the highest percentage of multiple ethnic origins (30.7 percent) of all Asian Americans—another effect of the high intermarriage rate. Japanese Americans with mixed racial backgrounds also compose a significant segment of *hapa*—individuals of part Asian or Pacific Islander ancestry—who have been gradually organizing themselves as a new "ethnic" group for the past decade.

Another new component of Japanese American communities is immigrants who arrived after the 1980s. The globalization of the economy and the resulting expansion of multinational corporations led to an increase in the immigration of Japanese businessmen, their families, and students. Reflecting the burst of the "bubble economy" in Japan in 1991, the number of Japanese who arrived in the U.S. between 1990 and 2000 tripled in comparison to the previous three decades, and these immigrants now make up 42.4 percent of all foreign-born Japanese in the country. Although no systematic research has been conducted on these newcomers, available evidence shows that many of them arrived as businessmen and students and chose to stay because of stronger economic growth and more appealing career opportunities in the U.S. These are highly skilled people who were not necessarily "pushed" from their country because of economic difficulties but were "pulled" by better career opportunities in the U.S.

Overall, Japanese immigrants have privileged socioeconomic profiles: 47.1 percent of them have a bachelor's degree or higher; 48 percent hold managerial or professional positions. Japanese with fewer qualifications often work in the expatriate community, mainly catering to Japanese businessmen, their families, and students. However, the median household income of all Japanese in the U.S. is still $56,700, significantly higher than the national average and the average of all immigrants. Contrary to the stereotype, Japanese immigrants are not linguistically isolated; 76.3 percent speak both English and Japanese at home.

Last, one of the most important characteristics of the most recent immigration flow from Japan is its feminization. Women were a minority (47.9 percent) among foreign-born Japanese in the U.S. in 1980, but their presence increased to 59.6 percent by 2000, which is significantly higher than the average of all immigrant groups (50.2 percent). Their socioeconomic achievement has also been noteworthy. While Japanese women were slightly better qualified than those of other ethnic groups in 1980, by 2000 they far exceeded the average of immigrant women: 40.4 percent held a bachelor's degree or higher. Furthermore, 43.1 percent worked in managerial or professional positions. A large number of these women are not the spouses of Japanese businessmen but independent migrants who sought better career or educational opportunities.

The growing feminization of Japanese immigration highlights the exacerbation of gender inequality in the Japanese labor market, especially since the burst of the "bubble economy" and the economic stagnation that followed. In Japan, despite the increase in women's educational level, women's share of full-time employment has been declining. Their career opportunities have also remained limited: only 15 percent of Japanese women hold managerial or professional positions. The gap between women's growing aspirations and the inequality in the labor market seems to be the main cause of the feminization of immigration from Japan.

The future of the Japanese American community. The Japanese American community faces many challenges as its population diversifies. The most critical concern derives from the demographic transition. Many Nisei—the primary supporters of local cultural institutions—have retired from community activities. Integrating new immigrants into the community has been a major challenge, as they do not share the old-timers' history, including internment and the redress movement. Many of the newcomers are not even aware of the history of the Japanese American community. Because of the lack of a common background and the language barrier, they tend to establish their own communities, often centered on Japanese-speaking churches, language schools, business circles, and so on. Some Japanese shops and restaurants also serve as the locus of networking and help community-building. Such separation is particularly salient in the Midwest and South and on the East Coast (except New York), where Japanese Americans do not have a strong community base.

Apart from unifying the group, perhaps the biggest challenge for the survival of the Japanese American community is the decline in strong ethnic identity among younger generations of Japanese Americans and those with mixed racial backgrounds, who are beginning to regard themselves panethnically, as Asian Americans. While their cultural and linguistic ties with Japan are rather weak, they share many sociopolitical challenges with other Asian Americans, or *hapa,* with whom they identify more closely.

The political leaders of the Japanese American community have also recognized that their ethnic politics has lost its force since the success of the redress movement and needs to become more inclusive. The Japanese American Citizens League

(JACL), which was established to represent Japanese Americans in U.S. politics, now acknowledges the need to reexamine its roles and adapt to demographic diversification and the changing needs of the community. Recognizing the growing Asian American populations and the challenge of insuring their rights and well-being, the JACL is now officially committed to protecting the civil rights of all segments of the Asian Pacific American community. Its concern for Asian Americans had emerged by 1982, when a Chinese American, Vincent Chin, was mistakenly identified as Japanese and murdered. The need to incorporate the cause of Asian Americans is now more generally acknowledged and even extended to non-Asian groups. The JACL has politically supported Arab Americans since September 11, 2001, when anti–Arab American sentiments began to grow in the country. Its membership is now open to anyone, of Japanese or non-Japanese descent.

The survival of geographic bases for Japanese Americans is another major challenge. The remaining three ethnic enclaves—Japantowns in San Francisco and San Jose and Little Tokyo in Los Angeles—which used to be thriving, have been gradually transformed into mere sightseeing spots, with limited cultural connections to Japanese Americans. Most Japanese American shop owners have moved to suburbs, and Japanese corporations began to leave in the 1990s because of the economic slowdown back home. Their businesses are now run by Koreans and Chinese, who hire many Hispanics and other ethnic minorities as their staff, further reducing the "Japanese-ness" in Japantowns.

The high rate of intermarriage and assimilation and these disappearing geographical bases could indeed endanger the cohesion of the community in the future. However, many community members also see an opportunity to expand the ethnic boundary. Despite some initial reluctance to include those who are not "pure" Japanese Americans in the traditional sense, the community has gradually accepted individuals of partial or no Japanese ancestry as its members. For instance, the Nisei Week Japanese Festival in Los Angeles, one of the largest Japanese American events in the U.S., has chosen six "queens" and more "princesses" who do not carry Japanese surnames and are of partial Japanese descent. Furthermore, some Japanese American organizations on the West Coast have begun to make efforts to overcome the barrier between new and old immigrants. For instance, the Japanese Cultural and Community Center of Northern California has been offering various programs for both groups. An affiliated group, Japanese Newcomer Services (Nobirukai), provides bicultural and bilingual assistance for newly arrived immigrants, students, business people, and their families. Prefectural associations (Kenjinkai) also offer various activities for young and old who come from the same prefecture in Japan.

A Japanese American Community Conference in 1998, "Ties That Bound," was a major milestone for community development. This three-day national event, which aimed to redefine and strengthen the Japanese American community, explored the dynamic changes within the community and sought new directions and priorities for the future. The Declaration for the Nikkei Community, an outcome of the conference, was particularly noteworthy in that it officially celebrated the community's growing diversity, accepting Japanese nationals, those of partial Japanese descent, and any other groups who wish to identify with the Japanese American community. A follow-up conference, "Nikkei 2000: Empowering Our Community in the 21st Century," held in San Francisco in 2000, also identified "inclusivity and diversity" as a common community vision.

Since these conferences a number of virtual communities have been established on the Internet, which bring together young people across the country to discuss issues such as identity, culture, intermarriage, and the future of their community. These virtual communities help connect those who live in the Midwest and on the East Coast, where fewer Japanese American cultural events and social activities are available.

Another successful outcome of recent community efforts has been increased political and financial support for the physical survival of Japantowns. In 2001, Governor Gray Davis approved U.S. Senate Bill 307, which created the California Japantown Preservation Pilot Project, giving a one-time grant to San Francisco, San Jose, and Los Angeles to help preserve historic Japanese neighborhoods. Proposition 40, which was passed in 2002, allocated further resources for the preservation of Japantowns. These events have instilled new inspiration and energy into the Japanese American community.

Last, the impact of globalization on the Japanese American community is worth noting. Japanese Americans have been establishing transnational contacts with Nikkei—people of Japanese descent—for the past three decades. Since they established the Pan American Nikkei Association (PANA) in 1979 with Nikkei in North, Central, and South America, they have been promoting solidarity and sharing experiences across national borders. The Pan American Nikkei Convention has been held every two years since 1981. These institutional links have been expanded and strengthened in recent years. For instance, at the Nikkei 2000 conference, participants from Canada, Brazil, and Peru discussed the challenges they have in common as Nikkei. The networks have also been extended to Asia. The JACL now has a Japan chapter in Tokyo, which attempts to strengthen political, economic, and cultural ties between Japanese Americans and Japanese citizens and works with Japanese Brazilian and Peruvian return migrants, who face discrimination and exploitation within Japanese society. Such networking has been gradually forming a transnational Nikkei community, and suggests that the identity of Japanese Americans is not simply disappearing or in the process of becoming panethnic but holds the possibility of developing a new dimension as a transnational Nikkei.

Australians and New Zealanders

The histories of Australians and New Zealanders in the U.S. have not been well documented so far. One of the reasons could be their relatively small numbers. According to the 2000 Census, only 107,112 Australians and 36,415 New Zealanders live in the U.S., constituting only 0.4 percent of the foreign-born population.

According to Churchward, the first wave of Australian immigration dates back to the late 18th century, when many Americans began to trade with Australia as an appendage to the China trade. As American whaling ships started operating off the coast of Australia and New Zealand in the 1790s, commercial relationships gradually became established. At that time the British government, which intended to populate Australia, imposed restrictions on Australians' emigration. However, some American captains and merchants recruited a small number of Australians, and except during the American Revolution, when Australia sided with Britain, emigration flows continued despite the British restrictions.

A major wave of Australian immigration to the U.S. occurred at the time of the Gold Rush in California, in 1848. Between 1849 and 1851, 4,000 to 5,000 Australians arrived in California. They included not only laborers but also middle-class families who preferred to settle in the U.S. because of the stable government, better security for property, and liberal land laws. Although some Australians returned home after gold was found in their own soil in 1850, more continued to move to the U.S.

One small but notable Australian immigrant group in the early period consisted of Mormons. After American missionaries established the Australian mission in 1851, many people converted to Mormonism and left for the "Land of Zion"— Utah. Some were religiously motivated, but many had mixed motivations, taking advantage of church-sponsored immigration and the availability of cheap land in the U.S. According to Newton, between 45 and 55 percent of Australian Mormons emigrated to the U.S. in the 19th century. However, the total number was small: the record shows that 442 emigrated between 1853 and 1859, most settling in California instead of Utah. While the data for other years are not available, the overall immigration level in the late 19th and early 20th centuries is assumed to be low.

A Mormon connection has also existed between New Zealand and the U.S., since Mormon missionaries arrived in New Zealand in 1854. While many early converts were British, the majority of later converts were the indigenous Maori. No data are available on the emigration of Maori, but Newton found that the missionaries were instructed to teach them to "flee out of Babylon [New Zealand] to Zion [Utah]." Given the influence of missionaries in those days, we can assume that some Maori did immigrate to the U.S. The whaling business is also assumed to have resulted in some emigration from New Zealand. Apart from such linkages, the immigration history of New Zealanders in this period has not been documented. There were few economic "push" factors for New Zealanders' emigration after the late 1850s, because of the discovery of gold in that country and the development of a flourishing sheep-farming industry, which allowed for economic self-sufficiency.

Immigration flows from Australia and New Zealand to the U.S. were small for most of the early 20th century and continued to be so in the first few decades after World War II. Of the resident population in the 1980 Census, 11,250 Australians and 2,460 New Zealanders had arrived before 1950. Even after the war, according to the INS, the average annual immigration remained around 1,000 from Australia and 400 to 500 from New Zealand until the end of the 1960s.

The large majority of Australians and New Zealanders arrived after the 1970s; 76 percent of Australians and 82 percent of New Zealanders in the U.S. came between 1970 and 2000. The immigration upsurge has been particularly notable since 1990, reflecting rapid U.S. economic growth, particularly in the information technology and financial sectors. Between 1990 and 2000, the number of Australians and New Zealanders in the country increased by 46.2 percent and 49.6 percent, respectively.

California is the most popular destination for both groups, but their remaining geographical distributions differ slightly. Many Australians have settled in New York, Texas, and Florida. For New Zealanders, Utah is the second major destination; more New Zealanders live in Utah than in New York, one of the major destinations for all immigrants. A sizable proportion of New Zealanders in Utah are thought to be Maori who converted to Mormonism. Utah also has a relatively higher percentage of Australians than other immigrant groups. These data suggest that the Mormon links from the prewar period continue.

Overall, postwar immigrants from Australia and New Zealand are highly educated. According to the 2000 Census, 51.3 percent of Australians and 44.5 percent of New Zealanders hold a bachelor's degree or higher, and 58.3 percent and 53.1 percent, respectively, have managerial or professional positions, compared to the national average of 33.6 percent. The median household income of Australians in 2000 was $69,400, which is the highest among all immigrant groups. The median income of New Zealanders, $63,300, is also significantly higher than the national median of $41,994. While the majority of these immigrants are young and middle-aged professionals (25 to 44 years old), there are a significant number of senior business executives as well. The list of directors, advisers, and staff members of the Australian American Association, for instance, includes many influential corporate leaders of Fortune 500 companies and large multinational corporations. The association's fundraising activities and business mentor programs indicate a strong presence of senior business professionals in the Australian American community.

In a survey carried out by the Australian Senate in 2003–2004, many Australians in the U.S. stated that they had intended to return home after they completed their studies or gained some work experience, but after they established a career and a family, returning became more difficult. In addition, more limited employment opportunities, lower salaries, higher tax rates, and bureaucratic red tape back home have hindered many Australians' return. While many still plan to retire in Australia, the difficulty in transferring social security benefits and other assets is a major concern.

Ethnic and coethnic communities. Community-building among Australians and New Zealanders in the U.S. started in 1948, when the Australian American Association (AAA) was established by prominent business leaders such as the chairman of J. P. Morgan and a founding partner of Morgan Stanley, among others. Though the name of the organization represents only Australians, it includes New Zealanders and Americans as its members. In fact, the most notable aspect of this community is its inclusiveness. Unlike many other ethnic organizations, which focus on one group, Australians and New Zealanders form coethnic communities, partly because of the close socioeconomic and cultural ties between Australia and New Zealand and partly because of their small numbers. The community's thin dispersion across the country necessitates joint membership in order to establish a sizable organization.

Community development has shown remarkable progress in the past decade, reflecting the large influx of new immigrants. Not only have coethnic organizations in Los Angeles, San Diego, and Seattle expanded, but ethnic-specific organizations have emerged since the late 1990s. New Zealanders now have their own community organizations in New York, Atlanta, San Francisco, and Los Angeles. However, these groups are also open to those who are not New Zealanders; for instance, many of these organizations include Americans with no New Zealander heritage as their core members or directors.

In addition to these organizations, virtual communities have also been emerging, ranging from personal and associational groups to business and networking groups. Those established in recent years tend to be the latter kind. Even long-standing nonvirtual organizations, which have focused more on social activities, have gradually diversified their activities to accommodate the needs of newly arrived young professionals, who need networking and mentoring for their career development.

Ethnic identities. Australians and New Zealanders are highly assimilated groups in terms of socioeconomic characteristics. Coming from multicultural societies with an Anglo-Saxon heritage, most of them have faced few linguistic or cultural problems and easily blend into American society. Even Maori are well integrated, as they were accustomed to Anglo-Saxon culture in New Zealand. A senior official of the New Zealand consulate in Los Angeles commented to me, "They [New Zealander immigrants] just fit right in. The language is the same; the attitude is the same . . . The intermarriage rate is also high. Asians in Silicon Valley get together because they feel different and uncomfortable. Kiwis [New Zealanders] don't feel that way." Unlike Japanese Americans, most Australians and New Zealanders have never faced overt discrimination as a group and find the American perception of Australia and

New Zealand to be positive. While some individuals have gone through uncomfortable experiences because of slight linguistic or cultural differences, most feel accepted by U.S. society.

Nevertheless, my limited interviews with Australians and New Zealanders in California and my analyses of nationwide virtual discussion groups suggest that both groups still retain distinct ethnic identities. The sources of their identities vary; newcomers tend to recognize more differences between their countries and the U.S. than earlier immigrants did, particularly in linguistic expressions (e.g., "gas" instead of "petrol"), distinctive accents, political stances, and other subtle cultural distinctions. Strong identity is partly related to the short period of these immigrants' residence, since over one third arrived between 1990 and 2000. The majority of Australians and New Zealanders also have not acquired U.S. citizenship. In fact, a large number have not decided where to settle in the long run, because more generous medical care and social security systems in their homelands hold appeal for their old age. The number of dual citizens might increase in the future, since both Australia and New Zealand now allow dual citizenship.

The relationship between the acquisition of dual citizenship and the retention of ethnic identity among Australians and New Zealanders requires further research. As seen in the case of Japanese Americans, ethnic identity retention among later generations will be a complex issue. The high intermarriage rate among these groups may weaken ethnic identities in the future, leaving only "symbolic ethnicity" behind. More importantly, the definitions of "Australians" and "New Zealanders" are being called into question as their home countries continue to undergo transformation into multiethnic societies. Hugo and others have pointed out that over half of the immigrant population in Australia wishes to emigrate to the U.S. or elsewhere eventually, suggesting that these people have a relatively weak Australian identity. More research will be needed to examine secondary migration patterns among these ethnic Australians and New Zealanders and their subsequent identity formation processes.

As we have seen, Japanese, Australians, and New Zealanders are at the top of the socioeconomic ladder among new immigrants in the U.S. Their high levels of education, professional or white-collar backgrounds, and high intermarriage rates have facilitated their successful integration into U.S. society. However, Japanese Americans have historically undergone greater difficulties owing to racial discrimination, which culminated in internment during World War II. Against this backdrop, Japanese Americans are more highly engaged in ethnic politics and civil rights issues than Australians and New Zealanders. Their sociopolitical concerns have been extended to Asian Americans (and more recently to Arab Americans), who have increased in number and experience common problems. In recent years, many Japanese Americans have also developed a hybrid or panethnic identity because of intermarriage and weakened sociocultural ties with Japan. With more recent immigration from Japan, the community is now trying to adapt to the needs of diverse groups and bridge differences between them. At the same time it is reaching out to Nikkei communities across national borders, forming transnational Nikkei networks. While more research is needed to evaluate the long-term impact of these initiatives, they seem to be successful in helping expand ethnic boundaries, reinvigorate the Japanese American community, and redefine their ethnic identity.

Australians and New Zealanders have been generally well received by Americans and have never faced any outright discrimination. Nevertheless, many of them retain a strong ethnic identity, partly because the majority still hold citizenship in and maintain strong ties with Australia and New Zealand. Research on ethnic identity retention among the second and third generations, particularly those with mixed racial backgrounds, will be needed. The small numbers and cultural proximity of Australian and New Zealander immigrants have also resulted in the establishment of coethnic communities. While the recent increase in both groups has given rise to separate organizations, their membership has been open to both groups and any others who are interested in joining. Questions remain, however, about whether second- and third-generation Australians and New Zealanders will retain their ethnic identity and remain active in community affairs. And as secondary migration increases, those with ethnic minority backgrounds (such as Indian Australians and Chinese New Zealanders) might affiliate with their original ethnic communities rather than Australian/New Zealander communities upon their arrival in the U.S. In any case, despite their small numbers, Australians and New Zealanders deserve more scholarly attention, given their strong social and economic influence in the country.

Bibliography

Churchward, L. G. 1979. *Australia & America 1788–1972: An Alternative History.* Sydney: Alternative Publishing Cooperative.

Daniels, Roger. 1990. *Asian America: Chinese and Japanese in the United States since 1850.* Seattle: University of Washington Press.

Hirabayashi, Lane Ryo, Akemi Kikumura-Yano, and James A. Hirabayashi. 2002. *New Worlds, New Lives: Globalization and People of Japanese Descent in the Americas and from Latin America in Japan.* Stanford, Calif.: Stanford University Press.

Hugo, Graeme, Dianne Rudd, and Kevin Harris. 2001. *Emigration from Australia: Economic Implications.* CEDA Information Paper No. 77.

Liang, Zai, and Naomi Ito. 1999. "Intermarriage of Asian Americans in New York City: Contemporary Patterns and Future Prospects." *International Migration Review* 33, 4: 876–901.

Newton, Marjorie. 1987. "The Gathering of the Australian Saints in the 1850s." *BYU Studies* 27, 2: 1–11.

Okamoto, Dina G. 2003. "Toward a Theory of Panethnicity: Explaining Asian American Collective Action." *American Sociological Review* 68 (Dec.): 811–42.

Parliament of Australia. 2005. "Inquiry into Australian Expatriates." www.aph.gov.au/senate/committee/legcon_ctte/expats03.

Spickard, Paul. 1996. *Japanese Americans: The Formation and Transformation of an Ethnic Group.* New York: Twayne.

Takezawa, Yasuko I. 1995. *Breaking the Silence: Redress and Japanese American Ethnicity.* Ithaca, N.Y.: Cornell University Press.

Philippines

Catherine Ceniza Choy

Nurse. Navy steward. Corazon Aquino. These are some of the images that come to mind when Americans think of Filipinos. Yet beyond the visible presence of Filipino nurses in U.S. hospitals, the high concentration of Filipino Americans in the U.S. armed forces, and the dramatic rise of the housewife who would become Philippine president, many Americans are unaware of how and why the new immigration from the Philippines has transformed U.S. society.

Located southeast of China and northeast of Indonesia, the Philippines is an archipelago of more than 7,000 islands. Since the 1980s it has been the second leading sending country of immigrants to the U.S., behind Mexico. According to the 2000 U.S. Census, the foreign-born population from the Philippines numbered approximately 1.4 million, and the total Filipino American population comprised 2.36 million people, making Filipino Americans the second largest Asian American group in the U.S.

The Immigration Act of 1965 inadvertently ushered in these demographic changes. The act's new ceiling system replaced previous restrictive immigration legislation aimed at Filipinos specifically and Asians more broadly. Although U.S. legislators expected the act to increase European immigration, Filipinos effectively utilized its preference system, which favored skilled labor and family reunification. Partly as a result of the act's occupational preference visas, many of the new Filipino immigrants are highly educated professional workers.

The skilled backgrounds of these new Americans have resulted in Filipino American socioeconomic mobility. According to a 2000 Census special report, Filipino Americans have the smallest percentage (6.3) of individuals living below the poverty line of all Asian groups. In 1999 their median family income was $65,200, up from $25,310 in 1989. The median total personal income of persons aged 25 to 64 in the labor force was $30,000, an increase from $20,800 in 1990. The economic re-

Table 1   Education of foreign-born Filipinos, persons aged 25–64, 1980–2000

Year	Total number	Less than high school		High school graduate		Bachelor's degree or higher	
		Number	Percentage	Number	Percentage	Number	Percentage
1980	338,200	58,920	17.4	110,140	32.6	169,140	50.0
1990	670,492	78,125	11.7	279,399	41.7	312,968	46.7
2000	1,042,376	93,091	8.9	447,670	42.9	501,615	48.1

Source: U.S. Census Bureau, 1980, 1990, and 2000 Censuses, 5% Integrated Public Use Microdata Sample, weighted data.

sources of the majority of foreign-born Filipino Americans (87.1 percent) placed them two or more times above the poverty line, which in 1999 was $17,029 for a family of four.

The educational backgrounds and English-language ability of the new immigrants from the Philippines have contributed to their high employment rates. In 2000, 77 percent of foreign-born Filipino American men and 71 percent of women were employed; only 3.7 percent of the men and 2.5 percent of the women were unemployed, while 19.3 percent and 26.5 percent, respectively, were not in the labor force. Overall, the new immigrants from the Philippines are a highly educated group (see Table 1). In 2000, 48.1 percent of foreign-born Filipino Americans possessed a bachelor's degree or higher; an additional 32.6 percent were high school graduates. Among all Filipino Americans, 54.3 percent reported that they spoke English "very well" and an additional 23.4 percent responded "well."

Reflecting the prominent role that immigration has played in the current Filipino American population, 83.9 percent of all Filipino Americans in 1990 reported that they spoke another language at home, in contrast to the 16.1 percent who spoke English only. According to U.S. Census data from 1980, 1990, and 2000, Tagalog and English were the top two languages spoken by Filipino Americans. Tagalog was spoken by the majority (79.1 percent) in 2000. Filipino Americans also spoke Ilocano, Visayan, Spanish, and Chinese, reflecting the regional and linguistic diversity of the archipelago (where over 80 dialects are spoken), the history of Spanish as well as U.S. colonialism, and the historical presence of Chinese in the country. However, the percentages of speakers of these languages among Filipino Americans have been quite small in recent decades. In 2000 only 1.2 percent of all Filipino Americans spoke Spanish and only 1.1 percent spoke Chinese.

New immigrants from the Philippines, like previous generations, have generally settled in the Pacific and West Coast regions of the U.S. In 2000, 59.8 percent of foreign-born Filipino Americans resided there, while only 10.7 percent lived in the Middle Atlantic and Northeast regions. In recent decades California has been home to the largest majority (47.7 percent in 2000). Hawai'i, Illinois, New York, and New Jersey also have significant Filipino immigrant populations. According to a 2003 Migration Policy Institute report, the states that experienced the greatest increases in their Filipino immigrant populations between 1990 and 2000 were Nevada (271 percent) and North Carolina (156 percent). Utah, Arizona, Idaho, Georgia, and Indiana also saw significant increases.

The upwardly mobile image of the new immigrants from the Philippines, however, belies the existence of a diverse Filipino American community across generational, political, and socioeconomic lines. A community profile based on U.S. Census data obscures, for example, the presence of a multigenerational Filipino American community in Louisiana, the post-1972 immigration of Filipinos fleeing the political oppression of martial law under the dictator Ferdinand Marcos, and the continuing challenge for highly educated Filipino immigrants to find employment commensurate with their training.

While the 1965 Immigration Act greatly influenced the composition of the contemporary Filipino immigrant community, many other factors have shaped this immigration. These include the history of Spanish and U.S. colonialism, U.S. labor recruitment of Filipino health-care workers and military personnel after World War II, and the contemporary Philippine labor export economy, which has made the Philippines the leading government-sponsored labor-exporting nation in the world. Although these time periods are often treated separately in Philippine as well as American studies, they need to be studied together if we are to appreciate the transnational and global dimensions of contemporary Filipino migrations, of which post-1965 Filipino immigration to the U.S. plays one important part.

Colonial Crossroads

In 1898, Philippine nationalists found themselves at a colonial crossroads between two empires: Spain and the United States. Although resistance to European exploration of the islands had begun as early as 1521, when Ferdinand Magellan died in a clash led by the chieftain Lapulapu, Spain colonized the archipelago beginning in the 1570s. Spanish imperialism informed early Filipino migrations to the Americas. During Spanish colonial rule, galleons manned by crews that included Philippine natives traveled between Manila and Acapulco. Some Philippine natives accompanied the explorer Pedro de Unamuno when he landed on the California coast at Morro Bay in 1587. In 1883, Lafcadio Hearn, writing in *Harper's Weekly,* reported that Malay fishermen from the Philippine islands lived in the bayous of Louisiana. Although a direct link between these Filipinos and those who manned Spanish galleons has yet to be proven, some scholars believe that Filipino seafarers from the galleon trade fled from oppressive Spanish rule and settled in Louisiana. A multigenerational Filipino American community in Louisiana lives on in current times and is featured in Renee Tajima-Pena's 1997 documentary film on Asian American ethnic and regional diversity, *My America, or Honk If You Love Buddha.*

After three centuries of Spanish colonial exploitation and native revolts, a nationalist movement developed in the Philippines in the second half of the nineteenth century, culminating in a declaration of independence from Spain on June 12, 1898. But the beginnings of Asia's first republic coincided with the Spanish-American War. After Spain was defeated, the U.S. purchased the Philippines, along with Guam and Puerto Rico, for $20 million, and U.S. colonizers soon replaced Spanish ones. Filipinos continued to fight for their independence in the Philippine-American War, which cost hundreds of thousands of Filipino lives. Their efforts were unsuccessful, however, and the Philippines continued to be a U.S. colony until July 4, 1946.

The U.S. colonial presence in the archipelago produced larger flows of Philippine overseas migrations. Two major factors of the U.S. colonial project—racial uplift and economic exploitation—shaped the development of contrasting early migration flows. The vast majority of pre-1965 Filipino migrants came from agricultural and working-class backgrounds, although an early wave was made up of a privileged group. Beginning in 1903, the U.S. colonial government in the Philippines sponsored an elite group of Filipino students to study in the U.S. The vast majority of these students, called *pensionados,* were men who studied medicine, politics, and law; the few women who participated in the program primarily studied subjects related to domestic and care work. U.S. colonial ideologies about what constituted the proper roles for civilized men and women as well as Spanish and Philippine patriarchal beliefs informed this gendered division of labor, which persisted in post-1965 Filipino labor migration.

After the 1924 Immigration Act virtually banned Asian immigration by barring persons who were unable to naturalize, U.S. western agriculture turned to the Philippines as a new source for inexpensive labor. Since the Philippines was a U.S. colonial possession, Filipinos were able to enter as U.S. nationals.

Between 1920 and 1929, 37,600 migrants from the Philippines arrived on the U.S. mainland. In California, 93 percent of Filipinos were male, and 77 percent of them were single. Given the paucity of Filipino women, a prominent feature of the few Filipino American families formed during this time was their interracial composition. In some states, however, including California in 1933, the passage of anti-miscegenation laws prohibiting marriage between Filipinos and whites was one example of the racial animus that Filipinos experienced in this era.

Filipino men found employment in hotels and restaurants as domestics, bellmen, cooks, dishwashers, and janitors, but most followed the harvest as migrant agricultural laborers and worked in Pacific Northwest canneries during the canning season. Although they significantly contributed to the growth of California's economy by performing physically difficult labor that other Americans would not do, they were accused of displacing white workers and undercutting their wages. The Great Depression exacerbated anti-Filipino hostility and culminated in the passage of the 1934 Tydings-McDuffie Act, which provided for the gradual independence of the Philippines, transformed the legal status of Filipinos from U.S. nationals to aliens, and restricted their entry to 50 per year.

The demographic composition of this pre-1965 Filipino migrant population contrasts dramatically with that of the post-1965 immigrants in three major ways. First, before 1965, the numbers of Filipino migrants to the U.S. peaked during the 1920s, whereas post-1965 Filipino immigration shows no signs of abating. Between 1980 and 2000 the number of Philippine-born persons in the U.S. increased by approximately 165 percent. Second, the increase in post-1965 female immigration has balanced the sex ratio in Filipino American communities. In recent decades women have made up a slight but increasing majority of immigrants from the Philippines (see Table 2). From 1980 to 2000 the percentage of female immigrants increased from 53.6 percent to 57.6 percent. Third, in the post-1965 period, Filipinos have played a prominent role in professional immigration. Between 1966 and 1970, 17,134 Filipino professionals immigrated to the U.S., constituting almost one third of all Filipino immigrants. By contrast, worldwide professional immigration to the U.S. in 1970 was only 11 percent of the total.

While the occupational preferences for skilled labor codified in the 1965 Immigration Act facilitated the immigration of Filipino professionals, recent scholarship has explored how the U.S. colonial education established preconditions that enabled the mass immigration of Filipino nurses in the second half of the 20th century. One of the most enduring legacies of U.S. colonialism in the Philippines was the exponential growth of primary and secondary education, which included the study of English. Furthermore, while Spanish colonizers introduced the professional study of medicine to an elite group of Filipino men, the U.S. colonial government established the first Philippine nursing schools, which followed the academic trends of U.S. professional nursing and actively recruited young Filipino women into the profession.

Table 2   Sex distribution of foreign-born Filipinos, 1980–2000

Year	Total number	Men		Women	
		Number	Percentage	Number	Percentage
1980	548,880	254,680	46.4	294,200	53.6
1990	1,001,174	440,707	44.0	560,467	56.0
2000	1,455,328	617,736	42.4	837,592	57.6

Source: U.S. Census Bureau, 1980, 1990, and 2000 Censuses, 5% Integrated Public Use Microdata Sample, weighted data.

In the 1950s, American hospital labor recruiters started utilizing the U.S. Exchange Visitor Program to bring in foreign-trained nurses to alleviate critical nursing shortages. The Philippines became a popular labor source, since its nurses had been trained in an Americanized educational system and were fluent in English. Between 1956 and 1969, over 11,000 Filipino nurses participated in the program. Although the Exchange Visitor Program began as a cold war measure aimed at promoting a better understanding of the U.S. in other countries, it inadvertently facilitated the first mass wave of professional migration from the Philippines. Filipino engineers, scientists, and physicians also migrated to the U.S. in significant numbers as exchange visitors. Like the *pensionados* before them, Filipino exchange visitors fueled the collective imagination of future generations of Filipino immigrants through their stories about life in the U.S., told through letters, telephone calls, and packages to friends and family back home and in person when they returned. They popularized the notion that study and work in the U.S. was a form of adventurous travel as well as a way to achieve socioeconomic mobility.

Recent studies have also explored how the presence of U.S. military bases in the Philippines since the early colonial period has fostered the overseas migration of Filipino military personnel. Historically, Filipinos have been the only foreign nationals allowed to enlist in the U.S. armed forces, specifically in the U.S. Navy. During the Philippine-American War at the turn of the 20th century, the U.S. established its first military bases in the archipelago, and soon afterward the navy began actively recruiting Filipinos. By World War I, 6,000 Filipinos were enlisted in the U.S. Navy. After Philippine independence, the 1947 Military Bases Agreement gave the U.S. continued access to military installations in the Philippines and enabled the navy to recruit Philippine citizens. Their service in the U.S. armed forces was a path to U.S. citizenship.

Post-1965 Immigration

Professional, military, and family immigration make up three major streams of new immigrants from the Philippines. Although similarities in socioeconomic background and method of immigration bind these groups together, it is important to note that there is much internal diversity as well. The groups can overlap when professional and military immigrants, for example, participate in family chain immigration.

Filipino professionals. According to Yen Le Espiritu, since the 1960s the Philippines has sent the most professional immigrants to the United States. Professional immigration is very visible because although this group includes accountants and engineers, the majority are health-care professionals working in small towns as well as big inner-city hospitals. For example, an episode of the 2003 documentary film series *Searching for Asian America* features two Filipino immigrants, Jeffrey Lim and

Martin Bautista, who completed their medical degrees in the Philippines but work as physicians in Guymon, Oklahoma, a rural town of 12,000 people. Nursing has been and continues to be the major occupational niche of Filipino immigrant health professionals. Between 1966 and 1985 at least 25,000 Filipino nurses migrated to the U.S. By 1989, Filipino nurses made up the overwhelming majority (73 percent) of foreign nurse graduates in this country; Canadian nurses made up the second largest but a comparatively much smaller group (12 percent). Hospitals in New York, California, Florida, Texas, and Massachusetts have been the major recruiters of nurses from the Philippines. However, urban areas in the Midwest, notably Chicago, have also been major destinations.

Although occupational-preference immigrants from the Philippines did not surpass 4,100 in any year between 1977 and 1991, Filipino professionals immigrated through other means. For example, exchange visitors were initially supposed to remain in the U.S. for a maximum of two years. In 1970, however, U.S. legislation made it easier for exchange visitors to adjust their status and become permanent residents without having to return to their countries of origin. Between 1966 and 1978, 7,495 Filipino exchange visitors became permanent U.S. residents.

As Filipino professionals quickly utilized the occupational-preference visas of the 1965 Immigration Act, backlogs for these visas soon ensued. In 1970 a U.S. immigration amendment increased employment opportunities for foreign workers with temporary work visas—also known as H-1 visas—by allowing these workers to fill permanent positions. After 1976 temporary work visas became the primary means of entry for Filipino nurses. Like other forms of temporary work programs in U.S. immigration history, this led to more permanent migration. The 1989 Immigration Nursing Relief Act enabled H-1 visa holders who were present in the U.S. on September 1, 1989, and had worked for three years as a registered nurse to adjust their status to permanent resident. It also exempted these nurses and their immediate family members from current immigrant visa numerical limitations and backlogs.

Passage of the Immigration Act of 1990 substantially increased immigration through employment-based preferences. Under the 1990 act, 9,800 Filipinos can be admitted each year on the basis of job skills. Despite this increase, the Philippines is one of only two countries—the People's Republic of China is the other—that has a backlog of skilled workers awaiting admission.

The origins of the strong desires of Filipino professionals to immigrate to the U.S. are complex. In addition to aggressive recruitment by U.S. health-care institutions, limited employment opportunities in the Philippines and political instability motivate Filipino professionals to work abroad. In the 1960s, Philippine newspapers and nursing journals reported that high levels of professional unemployment, low wages, and poor working conditions in inadequate facilities caused the so-called brain drain. Furthermore, President Marcos's declaration of martial law in 1972 contributed to high levels of emigration. During his dictatorship, Marcos suspended the Philippine constitution and violently attempted to stamp out political dissent. Critics of his regime included Filipino professionals, some of whom immigrated to the U.S. in fear of political persecution. Anti–martial law movements in the U.S. and the Philippines contributed to the 1986 prodemocracy movement known as People Power that toppled the Marcos regime and led to Corazon Aquino's presidency. Finally, the U.S. is a favored destination for Filipino professionals as well as nonprofessionals because of major socioeconomic disparities between the two countries. Given the increasing devaluation of the Philippine peso in relation to the U.S. dollar, it takes several decades for a professional working in the Philippines to earn what he or she could earn in the U.S. in one year.

Although professionals are a privileged group, professional Filipino immigrants have faced various obstacles in the U.S. Professional boards have enacted regulations, such as additional testing requirements for those trained in other countries, that have limited opportunities for their employment. These boards have also collaborated with the INS and the Department of Labor to restrict professional immigration. Filipino immigrants have also encountered race, accent, and language discrimination in the workplace. In the late 1980s, the Filipino nurse Aida Dimaranan was demoted after challenging a no-Tagalog policy at Pomona Valley Hospital. In the mid-1990s, the Filipino nurse Aileen Villanueva reported that Woodbine Healthcare Center in Missouri required Filipino nurses to do the dirtiest jobs and the heaviest work and to perform unpaid overtime labor. Both women successfully sued these institutions, using civil rights legislation.

According to recent U.S. Census data, many Filipino immigrants continue to be concentrated in professional and managerial positions (39 percent in 2000) and technical, sales, and administrative positions (30.2 percent in 2000). While the continued U.S. recruitment of Filipino nurses to alleviate current critical nursing shortages helps explain why Filipino women in the U.S. have an even higher concentration in professional and managerial positions (44.5 percent in 2000) than Filipino men (31.8 percent in 2000), media and government reports have documented the trend in the new millennium of Filipino male physicians enrolling in accelerated nursing programs in order to work in the U.S.

Military personnel. According to a 2005 Migration Policy Institute report, almost one fourth of the foreign-born people in the U.S. armed forces were from the Philippines, making it the largest source of foreign-born U.S. military personnel. Partly as a result of its long-standing recruitment of Filipino nationals, the U.S. Navy had the highest number of foreign-born personnel of all military branches. During the 1960s an estimated 100,000 Filipinos applied to the U.S. Navy each year. Competition among these applicants was high, given the rate of Filipino reenlistment—94 to 99 percent, in contrast to a U.S. citizen reenlistment rate of less than 50 percent. By 1970 there were more Filipinos in the U.S. Navy (14,000) than in the Philippine Navy. It was not until the early 1990s, when the Philippine Senate rejected the renewal of the Military Bases Agreement, that the U.S. Navy's recruitment of Filipino nationals finally ended.

In the post-1965 period, immigration in connection with the navy has created Filipino American communities near naval bases and training facilities from San Diego, California, to Norfolk, Virginia, to Bangor, Maine. A primary challenge of Filipino American enlistees has been occupational advancement within the navy. A post–World War I ruling restricted Filipinos to work as stewards and mess attendants. Although a 1973 policy enabled Filipino enlistees to enter any occupational rating, during that year 40 percent continued to work as stewards, and the majority of the others were concentrated in clerical positions.

New Filipino immigrants have also had an important relationship to the U.S. Army. Section 450 of the Immigration Act of 1990 made naturalization available to surviving Philippine-born veterans of the U.S. armed forces in the Far East, the Philippine Army, the Philippine Scout Rangers, and recognized guerrilla units who served between September 1, 1939, and December 31, 1946. By 1998 over 28,000 of 70,000 eligible veterans became naturalized, and an estimated 17,000 came to the U.S. Although the legislation importantly acknowledged their military participation on behalf of the U.S. during World War II, it did not confer upon them full veterans' benefits, such as old-age pensions and free medical care in veterans' hospitals. U.S. media reports documented that upon their arrival, many veterans lived in poverty on Supplemental Security Income (SSI) payments. Filipino veterans' equity continues to be a political struggle for the Filipino American community.

It is also important to note that by the late 20th century, the U.S. Army had a few high-ranking Filipino American officers. Born in Sampaloc, Manila, Antonio M. Taguba immigrated to the U.S. when he was 11 years old. In 1997 he became the second Filipino American general in the history of the army. Major-General Taguba is well known for writing the 2004 report that detailed inmate abuse at the army's Abu Ghraib prison in Iraq.

Family reunification. In the post-1965 period, family reunification has enabled the vast majority of Filipinos to immigrate to the U.S. Although professional and military immigration played a key role in the establishment of Filipino American families in the decade after 1965, the numbers of Filipino family-preference immigrants soon dominated those of occupational-preference immigrants. From 1971 to 1975 those admitted for occupational preferences made up 51.5 percent of Filipino immigrants, while those admitted for family preferences made up 48.4 percent. From 1976 to 1980 the percentage of family-preference immigrants dramatically increased to 79.8 percent, while that of occupational-preference immigrants dwindled to 19.3 percent. This proportion persisted in the 1980s.

Compounding these numbers were Filipinos who were able to enter outside the preference system, such as spouses and minor children of U.S. citizens. In the 1970s and early 1980s, the numbers of these admissions exceeded the number of Filipino immigrants admitted through the preference system. Recent policy changes have restricted certain kinds of family immigration while encouraging others. The Immigration Act of 1990 reduced the number of immigrant visas for siblings of U.S. citizens and made these visas more difficult to obtain. However, it also increased the numbers of immigrant visas for spouses and children of permanent residents.

As a result of this dual stream of immigration, there is far more class diversity in the contemporary Filipino American community than before. It would be accurate to characterize the new immigration as having a dual nature in which both working-class and middle-class Filipinos have immigrated in large numbers. In 1992 the Children of Immigrants Longitudinal Study (CILS) surveyed approximately 800 Filipino students in the San Diego Unified School District and found that 43 percent of the fathers and 28 percent of the mothers were in blue-collar or low-wage service jobs such as custodial and assembly work.

Family reunification preferences have made it easier for contemporary Filipino American families to stay together. According to recent U.S. Census data, the median age of foreign-born Filipino Americans increased from 33 in 1980 to 41 in 2000. In 2000, 77.6 percent of foreign-born Filipino American women and 77.4 percent of men between the ages of 35 and 44 were married. The divorce rates for these groups were slightly higher for women (8.2 percent) than for men (5.4 percent), but quite low when compared to the estimated 50 percent divorce rate of the total U.S. population. Philippine religious beliefs as well as U.S. immigration policy affect this phenomenon, although more research in this area is needed. An estimated 85 percent of the Philippine population is Roman Catholic, and the Catholic Church continues to hold considerable influence over the country's politics and government. Recent attempts to legalize divorce in the Philippines have failed. Furthermore, post-1965 U.S. immigration policies favoring family reunification may also contribute to these low divorce rates.

Although the recent growth of the Filipino American population can be attributed to children born in the U.S. as well as new immigration, the fertility of foreign-born Filipino American women between the ages of 25 and 64 underwent significant changes between the 1990 and 2000 Censuses. The percentage of this group of women with no children increased from 26.1 percent to 38.8 percent, while the percentage of women with three to five children decreased from 25.9 percent to 13.8 percent. In 2000 less than 1 percent (0.3 percent) had six or more children, down from 5.6 percent in 1990. The highest concentration of women (47.1 percent) had one to two children.

A significant percentage of Filipino American families and their children continue to be interracial. After Japanese Americans, Filipino Americans report the highest percentage (21.8) of people of mixed heritage among Asian Americans. However, because of their larger numbers, the more than half a million Filipino Americans of mixed heritage form the single largest contingent of mixed-race Asian

Americans. Recent media reports have suggested that the high rate of intermarriage between Filipinos and Latinos may be attributed to similar religious beliefs and similar historical influences of Spanish culture. Furthermore, the end of anti-miscegenation laws in 1967, the settlement of Filipino immigrants in small towns with few other Filipinos, and the large numbers of Filipino women in the mail-order bride industry have also contributed to the growth of interracial families. A study by Roland Tolentino estimated that between 50 to 60 percent of mail-order brides are Filipinas and that there are approximately 50,000 Filipina mail-order brides in the U.S.

As a result of their large numbers and internal diversity, Filipino Americans face multiple challenges in the new millennium. Qualitative research has illuminated how the working-class lives of some of the new Filipino immigrants challenge the notion that increasing socioeconomic mobility has affected the entire community equally. A study conducted by the Centers for Disease Control in San Diego found that Filipino female students had extremely high rates of suicidal thoughts and actual suicide attempts.

Filipino Americans also continue to encounter racial prejudice. In 1999 a white supremacist fatally shot Joseph Ileto, a 39-year-old Philippine-born U.S. postal worker, because he was a nonwhite U.S. government employee. According to the 1992 CILS research, 69 percent of young Filipinos reported having experienced racial discrimination. Although a smaller percentage of Filipino parents (40 percent) claimed to have experienced racial discrimination, over 70 percent believed that white Americans considered themselves superior to Filipinos and 20 percent feared that their children would face resistance if they wanted to move into a white neighborhood or marry a white American. These attitudes have contributed to the strong persistence of ethnicity among Filipino immigrants and their children. Recent studies have documented how new Filipino American communities create spaces such as ethnic grocery stores, ethnic newspapers, and Filipino American community centers in order to claim a sense of belonging to both the U.S. and the Philippines as opposed to one or the other.

Transnational and Global Dimensions

Like earlier waves of Filipino immigrants, the new immigrants have responded to these contemporary challenges by forming a diverse range of Filipino American organizations. While Philippine regional, provincial, and linguistic differences continue to provide the basis for some of these groups, they are also organized along political and professional lines. A transnational mission that responds to members' concerns in both the U.S. and the Philippines informs many of these groups. In 1973, Filipino immigrants, many of whom had been political activists under the Marcos regime and left the Philippines after Marcos's declaration of martial law, founded the KDP (Katipunan ng mga Demokratikong Pilipino, or Union of Democratic Filipinos). What distinguished the KDP from other anti–martial law organizations was its focus on the dual nature of the Filipino American community, a community that was simultaneously linked to the history and culture of the Philippine nation and becoming increasingly aware of its position as a racialized minority group in the U.S. Until its dissolution in 1986, anti-imperialist activism in the Philippines and antiracist work in the United States were part of the KDP's political agenda.

Filipino immigrant health professionals have organized along professional lines, creating local organizations such as the Philippine Medical Society of Northern California (PMSNC) as well as national ones, such as the Philippine Nurses Association of America (PNAA). The mission of the PMSNC includes serving the needs of elderly and indigent Filipinos in the U.S. as well as conducting regular medical missions to impoverished areas in the Philippines. The objectives of the PNAA include facilitating the cultural and professional adjustment of Filipino nurses in the U.S. and collaborating with agencies and organizations in both the Philippines and the U.S. PNAA leaders are currently advocating making the Philippines an international test site for the U.S. National Council Licensure Examination, which is the final requirement for foreign-trained nurses who wish to practice in the U.S. However, concerns about Philippine national security caused the U.S. National Council of State Boards of Nursing to bypass the Philippines as an international test site, at least for the time being.

Political developments since September 11, 2001, have created new challenges for the Filipino American community. The Department of Justice has identified the Philippines as an "al Qaeda active nation" because of the presence of Abu Sayyaf terrorists on Basilan Island, in the southern region of Mindanao, the historical center of Muslim influence in the archipelago. This designation has led to increased scrutiny of the Filipino American community and resulted in record high numbers of Filipino deportations under the Justice Department's Absconder Apprehension Initiative and the Homeland Security Department's Office of Removal and Detention. Furthermore, although Filipino immigrants have sought U.S. citizenship in large numbers—in 2000, 58.1 percent were naturalized, up from 40.8 percent in 1980—those who have chosen not to naturalize or whose naturalization process has been delayed by backlogs have also suffered the consequences of new post-9/11 security measures. For example, the 2001 Aviation and Transportation Security Act required U.S. citizenship for certain kinds of employment, such as airport screeners. In the San Francisco Bay area, Filipinos made up approximately 75 percent of airport screeners at three major airports, and those who were not U.S. citizens were laid off.

While the Philippines' colonial history and post-1965 U.S. immigration policies provide two important contexts for understanding the dynamics of the new immigration from the Philippines, the contemporary global dimensions of Philippine overseas migration provide another. Beginning in the early 1970s, the people of the Philippines witnessed their government's growing commitment to an economy that actively promoted the export of Filipino laborers as well as goods. Originally inspired by the demand for Filipino men as loggers in Indonesia and as construction workers in U.S. military bases in Vietnam and Thailand, the Philippine government actively promoted labor migration in the mid-1970s in response to the demand for contract migrant labor in the Middle East. Philippine labor-export policies also targeted women for work overseas after Marcos observed the international demand for nurses, although the vast majority of Filipino female overseas contract workers today are domestic workers.

Subsequent Philippine government administrations have asserted that labor export is a short-term strategy, but they have continued to support this economy because remittances from overseas laborers are a major source of revenue, lowering the nation's unemployment rate as well as alleviating its international debt. In 2004 remittances from abroad totaled over $8.5 billion. As a result, the Philippines is the leading government-sponsored labor-exporting nation in the world, with 7 million Filipinos working in 187 countries. Saudi Arabia and Hong Kong are the major destinations, but the United States, Taiwan, Japan, and Singapore each account for 6 percent or more of this migrant flow.

These migrant labor flows contrast with the new Filipino immigration to the U.S. because of their temporary duration. Most overseas work contracts are two years in length, with the possibility of renewal. However, given that temporary forms of Filipino migration to the U.S. have historically resulted in more permanent migration, and given the continuing backlog of Philippine applications for immigrant visas, it seems likely that immigration from the Philippines will continue to shape American society in the new millennium.

Bibliography

Bonus, Rick. *Locating Filipino Americans: Ethnicity & the Cultural Politics of Space.* Philadelphia: Temple University Press, 2000.

Choy, Catherine Ceniza. *Empire of Care: Nursing and Migration in Filipino American History.* Durham, N.C.: Duke University Press, 2003.

Critical Filipina and Filipino Studies Collective. "Resisting Homeland Security: Organizing Against Unjust Removals of U.S. Filipinos." www.sjsu.edu/depts./sociology/living/removal.html.

Dela Cruz, Melany, and Pauline Agbayani-Siewert. "Filipinos: Swimming with and against the Tide." In Eric Lai and Dennis Arguelles, eds., *The New Face of Asian Pacific America: Numbers, Diversity & Change in the 21st Century,* pp. 45–50. San Francisco: AsianWeek, 2003.

Espiritu, Augusto. "Filipino Americans." In John D. Buenker and Lorman A. Ratner, eds.,

Multiculturalism in the United States: A Comparative Guide to Acculturation and Ethnicity. Rev. ed. Westport, Conn.: Greenwood, 2005.

Espiritu, Yen Le. *Homebound: Filipino American Lives across Cultures, Communities, and Countries.* Berkeley: University of California Press, 2003.

Espiritu, Yen Le, and Diane L. Wolf. "The Paradox of Assimilation: Children of Filipino Immigrants in San Diego." In Rubén Rumbaut and Alejandro Portes, eds., *Ethnicities: Children of Immigrants in America.* Berkeley: University of California Press, 2001.

Nakano, Satoshi. "Nation, Nationalism, and Citizenship in the Filipino World War II Veterans Equity Movement, 1945–1999." *Hitotsubashi Journal of Social Studies* 32 (2000): 33–53.

Ngai, Mae. "From Colonial Subject to Undesirable Alien: Filipino Migration, Exclusion, and Repatriation, 1920–1940." In Josephine Lee, Imogene L. Lim, and Yuko Matsukawa, eds., *Recollecting Early Asian America: Essays in Cultural History.* Philadelphia: Temple University Press, 2002.

Posadas, Barbara M. *Filipino Americans.* Westport, Conn.: Greenwood, 1999.

Tolentino, Roland. "Bodies, Letters, Catalogs: Filipinas in Transnational Space." *Social Text* 48 (Autumn 1996): 49–76.

Poland

Mary Patrice Erdmans

Two large waves of Polish immigrants arrived in the first and last decades of the 20th century, and a smaller but significant group came between them. As a result of these multiple waves, contemporary American Polonia—the community of Poles abroad—is a mosaic of diverse migrations and generations: Polish American descendants of those in the early wave, older World War II émigrés and their children and grandchildren, and the newest immigrants and their children. Moreover, Poland has changed considerably over the past century, and with it the causes for emigration and the characteristics of each cohort. Before World War I, Poland was an agrarian territory divided between Russia, Prussia, and Austria; between the wars it became an industrializing independent nation and, after World War II, a part of the communist bloc; and since the "revolution" of 1989 it has become a capitalist democracy. Peasant immigrants from agrarian Poland were quite different from the political refugees of the 1940s, who are different from contemporary undocumented laborers.

Despite these differences, Polish immigrants often resettle in cities with established Polish American communities, and because of these differences the settlement often produces some tensions. Conflict has occurred in organizations, churches, and the media, usually over leadership struggles, cultural and class differences, and divergent identity needs. One of the more contentious fault lines within the community is that between new immigrants and later-generation ethnics. This conflict first appeared in the postwar period, with the arrival of the new émigrés, and resurfaced at the end of the century with the newest immigrant cohort. Of the 9 million residents who reported some Polish ancestry in 2000, only 5 percent (484,464) were foreign-born Poles, but the majority of those were new immigrants, as 60 percent had arrived after 1980.

Early Immigration

Before World War I, an estimated 1.5 million people immigrated to America from the partitioned lands of Poland. While they included both ethnic Poles and Polish Jews, generally only ethnic Poles identified themselves and were identified as part of the Polish American community, Polonia. This early immigration was mostly labor movement, as rural farmworkers, dislocated by the transition from feudalism, moved to industrializing regions in the U.S. While the immigrants were generally uneducated peasants, often referred to as *za chlebem* (for bread) immigrants (especially those arriving after 1890), this migrant cohort included a small number of intellectuals, revolutionaries, and clergy (many of whom arrived before 1890). The institutional base of early Polonia was Roman Catholic parishes and large fraternal organizations such as the Polish Roman Catholic Union (1873) and the Polish National Alliance (1880). Fraternal organizations are a system of local lodges, with a centralized representative body, established for the purpose of mutual benefit. This early community is well described in W. I. Thomas and Florian Znaniecki's *The Polish Peasant in Europe and America.*

The Polish immigrant community matured into an ethnic community between the wars. By 1920 native-born Americans of Polish descent already outnumbered foreign-born Poles, and the restrictive quota laws widened this ratio. In several years before World War I, annual immigration exceeded 100,000, but beginning in 1930, Poles were allotted just 6,524 slots annually. By 1940 only a third of the community was foreign-born.

The Polish American identity was decidedly working class. The immigrants migrated to industrializing regions, and their communities abutted their worksites, as evident in the coal-mining towns of Pennsylvania, the Back of the Yards adjacent to the meatpacking industries in Chicago, and Hamtramck near the automobile factories in Detroit. The descendants of this early cohort continued to work in manufacturing industries, and with the help of unions they became high-priced skilled laborers well positioned to take advantage of the strong industrial economy in the midcentury. Polish Americans defined themselves and were defined as white, hardworking, religious, and disciplined people who celebrated a folk-based cultural attachment to their ancestral homeland but maintained a political loyalty to America.

The War Émigrés

After 1939, Polish immigrants were pushed out of their homeland by war, the realignment of geopolitical borders, and a repressive postwar communist regime. More than 200,000 ethnic Poles arrived through the Displaced Persons Act of 1948 and the Refugee Relief Act of 1953, including nearly 18,000 Polish soldiers who had served in the Allied armies in Europe. These involuntary exiles were often better educated, more cosmopolitan, and of a higher social class than the earlier immigrants and their descendants. Émigrés from middle-class backgrounds often achieved higher levels of education than Polish Americans (which as an aggregate lagged behind national averages until the 1970s) and moved into managerial and professional occupations (where Polish Americans were still underrepresented) and into suburban homes outside the old Polish neighborhoods. Their social class and heightened nationalism, influenced by Poland's 20 years of independence prior to the war, the war itself, and their foreign-born status, complicated their assimilation into working-class Polish American communities, which they criticized for not having organized a strong political lobby and disdained because of the folk-based nature of the Polonian "polka culture."

The new immigrants separated themselves occupationally, residentially, and culturally, and they created their own organizations to meet their own needs and interests. As refugees, they established self-help organizations such as the Polish War Refugee Association in the United States; as educated professionals, they helped organize (with the professional stratum of the Polish American community) the Polish American Historical Association and the Polish Institute of Arts and Sciences in America; and as ex-servicemen, they founded the Association of Veterans of the Polish Army and the Polish Veterans of World War II.

Over time these immigrants worked more cooperatively with Polish Americans on matters related to Poland. Both groups were fiercely anticommunist, and within the newly established Polish American Congress (1944), the political wing of Polonia, the newcomers dominated committees concerned with Poland's affairs.

The New Immigration

Contemporary Polish immigration is a result of economic and political conditions in Poland, strong social networks between Poland and Polonia, and liberal U.S. immigration policies. In the first half of the 1960s, roughly 7,000 Poles were admitted annually. After the 1965 Immigration Act, this rate was cut in half for the next 20 years, though the number of Polish newcomers rose steadily throughout the 1970s and 1980s, with the arrival of political refugees and an increase in temporary visitors.

The 1968 upheaval in Poland created a new wave of refugees. Unrest in the universities, initiated by intellectuals but manipulated by factions within the Polish Communist Party, led to an anti-Semitic and anti-reformist backlash. Most of the Jewish émigrés went to Israel, while ethnic Poles came to the U.S. A larger wave of refugees began arriving in the late 1970s. National strikes in Poland in 1976 and again in 1980 led to the formation of the trade union Niezalezny Samorzadny

Zwiazek Zawodowy (Independent Self-Governing Trades Union), known in Poland as Solidarnosc (Solidarity). In December 1981, the Polish state declared martial law, disbanded Solidarity, and jailed opposition activists. The U.S., always welcoming of dissidents fleeing communist governments, admitted more than 40,000 "Solidarity" refugees.

While rising political discontent in Poland became manifest in the U.S. as increased refugee admissions, growing economic dissatisfaction was reflected in the escalating number of temporary visitors, particularly "visitors for pleasure," known within the community as *wakacjusze* (vacationers) or *turysci* (tourists). The number of visitors for pleasure rose from an average of 24,000 annually in the 1970s, to 36,000 in the 1980s, to almost 50,000 in the 1990s. Many of these "vacationers" worked without authorization, and a significant number overstayed their visas (in some cases for decades). Estimates in the mid-1980s were that 95,000 Poles were living (and working) in the U.S. illegally—the second largest population of illegal immigrants. In 1992 in Chicago, 27 percent of all illegal immigrants came from Poland and 44 percent from Mexico (and in that same year, 1,141 Mexicans were deported but only 27 Poles were). Efforts to reduce this population through the 1986 Immigration Reform and Control Act gave amnesty to more than 16,000 Poles and 2,000 of their dependents. (Most of these amnesty recipients were officially "admitted" between 1989 and 1993, which explains part of the numerical surge in immigration in the 1990s.) In 1996 the estimate of the illegal population was down to 70,000, and Poland dropped to tenth among countries with illegal populations.

In addition to the temporary visitors/undocumented workers, 381,641 permanent Polish immigrants were admitted between 1960 and 2000, nearly half of them after 1989, the year marking the formal collapse of the communist system in Poland. The transitional capitalist market in Poland created unequal rates of development, high rates of inflation that outpaced increases in income, high rates of unemployment (15 percent for most of the 1990s), and, in consequence, a reserve immigrant labor force. While the great majority of Poles immigrated to Germany (71 percent in the 1990s), the U.S. continued to attract Poles, especially with the more expansive immigration policies in the 1990s. The Immigration Act of 1990 raised immigration ceilings, which benefited all countries, but Poles were helped particularly by the new "diversity visas," available to people from countries adversely affected by the 1965 Immigration Act. Between 1992 and 1997, 53,000 Poles were admitted under this program (known within the community as the "lottery") before the admission procedures changed.

Adding together the amnesty recipients, lottery winners, and general immigration, 180,035 Poles were admitted in the 1990s, more than twice the number admitted in the 1980s (81,578) and four times the number admitted in the 1970s

(42,378). With this surge in immigration at the end of the century, the Polish immigrant community is, in general, a fairly new migrant cohort.

Polish Immigrants in the American Labor Market

With the new admissions, the community has become younger and better educated. In 1980, when almost three quarters of the community had arrived before 1960, over half of the foreign-born population was over 64 years of age, and only 15 percent were between the ages of 25 and 34. By 2000 only a quarter was older than 64, and 31 percent were between 25 and 34. Most new Polish immigrants arrive with craft, technical, and professional skills, especially those emigrating from urban areas (83 percent of all emigrants from Poland in the 1990s came from urban areas). In 1980 a third of all Polish immigrants had at most an eighth-grade education, while only 15 percent had postsecondary degrees; by 2000 only 5 percent had an eighth-grade education or less, and a third had postsecondary degrees (similar to the native-born American population).

While being educated helps new immigrants secure better jobs, they still pay a price for their newness, expressed in the Polish phrase *emigracja to deklasacja* (emigration leads to downward mobility). While the drop in occupational prestige is generally offset by an increase in the material standard of living, new immigrants nonetheless feel a status decline when their occupations are not commensurate with their education. Compared to the Polish American population (which has rates similar to the general white population), Polish immigrants are more likely to work in semi- and low-skilled positions and the personal service sector (and almost twice as likely if they are new arrivals). Over time the immigrant population begins to resemble their ethnic population, although they still remain slightly overrepresented in service and manual labor occupations. According to the 1990 Census, a quarter of the Polish foreign-born worked in professional and managerial occupations; however, when broken down by time of arrival, 30 percent of those who arrived before 1980 worked in these occupations, compared to 17 percent of those arriving in the 1980s.

Even after the influx of a fairly well-educated cohort in the 1990s, Polish immigrants were still underrepresented in professional and managerial occupations and overrepresented in manual labor and service positions. According to the 2000 Census, 45 percent of Polish immigrants worked in professional, managerial, technical, and sales administration occupations (compared with 63 percent of the U.S. native-born population, as reported in the 2002 Current Population Survey), but Polish immigrant women were twice as likely to have these positions as men (56 percent compared with 26 percent). Polish men were more likely to be working in skilled and unskilled labor positions in the construction and manufacturing sectors: 50

percent of all Polish men worked in these industries. Polish women were more likely to work in the professional and personal service industries.

Incorporation of New Immigrants into Polonia and America

New immigrants often resettle near established Polonias. Over half of all foreign-born Poles live in Illinois and New York, and another fifth live in New Jersey, Connecticut, and Michigan, all states with established Polonian communities (e.g., in Chicago, Brooklyn, Buffalo, and Detroit). In addition, immigrants have built new communities in Florida and California. While these two states have only a small share of the total Polish immigrant population (10.6 percent), twice as many immigrants live there as in Pennsylvania and Massachusetts, states with established Polonias.

Recent immigrants, temporary migrants, and undocumented workers are the most likely to live in the older Polish neighborhoods in the inner city. These urban centers are best characterized as immigrant consumer service communities (rather than traditional ethnic neighborhoods), and they include retail shops, professional offices, restaurants, and businesses specializing in immigrant services (e.g., travel agencies, passport and visa services, translators, and shipping companies). Because of their limited English-language skills—in 2000, roughly a third of the Polish foreign-born population was living in linguistically isolated households—new immigrants supply a clientele for Polonia's commercial and professional community, which has grown significantly; for example, the Chicago Polish-language phone book had more than 1,500 pages in 2001. These consumer service centers are found in cities that have a steady flow of immigrants (e.g., Jackowo and Belmont/Central in Chicago; Greenpoint in Brooklyn; Broad Street in New Britain, Connecticut). In Jackowo, 90 percent of the businesses are owned by Poles and serve primarily Polish customers, most of whom do not live in the neighborhood.

Most Polish Americans have left these old neighborhoods and moved to the suburbs; for example, two thirds of Polish Americans in metropolitan Chicago live outside the city. An increasing number of new immigrants are also resettling in the suburbs. In Chicago, the destination for one third of all new Polish immigrants, the number of new arrivals listing a suburban zip code as their intended residence more than doubled, from 16 to 36 percent, between 1983 and 1998. In addition, more immigrants buy homes in suburban areas five to ten years after their arrival. The presence of immigrants in the suburbs is also evidenced by the growth of Polish Saturday schools, organized and funded by members of Polonia to teach Polish language, history, and culture to the children of immigrants. In 1983 there were 18 Polish Saturday schools in the Chicago metropolitan area, and all but one were located in the city; by 2002 there were 27 schools, 14 of them in the suburbs.

Polish immigrants move to the suburbs for the same reasons the general American population moves—the schools are better and housing is more affordable. Beginning in the 1920s, the growing presence of blacks in the cities increased contact and conflict between blacks and Polish Americans in neighborhoods, worksites, and public spaces. By the 1960s, Polish Americans and other whites began leaving urban areas because of the decentralization of the economy, which relocated industries outside the city; the construction of new suburban housing; fiscal crises that eroded city services (in particular, education) and depreciated the quality of urban life; and the increasing number of racial minorities. While the older generations often remained entrenched in their communities, their adult children bought homes in the suburbs.

When Polish Americans moved to the suburbs, they did so as later-generation ethnics who easily assimilated into the white landscape. In contrast, when the newest immigrants move, both assimilation and accommodation take place as the suburban space is transformed to meet their needs. Suburban immigrant communities look different from their urban counterparts. Rather than being in a concentrated consumer center, Polish video stores and delis in the suburbs are inserted into strip malls beside national chain stores. The community is more dispersed and integrated, so that Polish-speaking tellers, hygienists, and legal secretaries work in non-Polish banks, dentists' offices, and law firms to meet the needs of Polish-speaking clients. Their presence is also noticeable in the churches. Polish immigrants and Polish American ethnics are predominantly Roman Catholic. In urban ethnic neighborhoods, the community was built around the parish and the parish reflected the ethnic identity of the neighborhood. Today suburban parishes do not become "Polish" parishes but instead are Roman Catholic parishes accommodating the language needs of a Polish-speaking congregation. Polish is spoken not in an effort to preserve ethnicity but in order to sustain Catholicism.

Organizations of New Immigrants

Unlike the earlier waves of Polish immigrants, the newest migrant community is not formally organized, although there were efforts to organize the political stratum in the 1980s. The international Support of Solidarity organization, founded in 1982 by Solidarity refugees, created chapters in 13 countries, including 12 chapters in the U.S. and a dozen more affiliated organizations. Immigrants established these political organizations working to support Poland's independence in old Polonian centers such as New York, Chicago, Buffalo, and Detroit, as well as in places like Seattle and California (which had 7 chapters of Solidarity California). With the political and economic changes in 1989, however, this organizational structure collapsed, and no new national organization has replaced it.

The new immigrant community has taken advantage of modernization of communication. A national (and international) network of virtual associations has been created through a growing number of Polonian websites and listserves that provide information, venues for discussion, and social networks (such as Polish Global Village). New immigrants are also responsible for the revitalization and dramatic proliferation of Polish-language media. In the 1980s there were two Polish-language dailies in the U.S. By 2002 there were six Polish-language dailies (three in New York and three in Chicago) and dozens of weekly and monthly magazines. *Nowy Dziennik,* first published in 1971, had a circulation of 30,000 in 2003. In addition, the community has access to Polish radio and cable stations that broadcast Polish-language shows 24 hours a day in large cities, as well as several hours of Polish-language programming weekly in smaller cities. Some programs are produced in Poland (for example, *Wiadomosci*—the nightly news program) and broadcast through a direct satellite feed; others are produced in the U.S. for a Polonian audience. These media provide news from Poland, local news (in Chicago or New York), international news, and national news, generally in that order of importance.

While new immigrants have not created a large formal organization, they have organized locally around more specific interests. Polish immigrants are active in professional organizations such as the Polish Medical Alliance, the Polish Teachers' Association, and the Advocates Society. They have created small associational clubs as well, often named after a city or university in Poland (e.g., the Krakow Society, the Jagiellonian Society), for socializing. New immigrants also provided the impetus and expertise to develop Polish-language collections in public libraries, where they have also organized Polish book clubs. The Chicago Public Library, whose Polish-language collection dates back to 1883, was expanded and modernized in the 1990s and today has 15,000 Polish-language volumes in its collection.

Culturally, the new immigrants work mostly within their communities, but plays by Polish playwrights produced for an American audience (such as Janusz Glowacki's *Hunting Cockroaches*) and the reopening of the Chopin Theater in Chicago are examples of Polish theater marketed to a wider audience. In addition, art galleries featuring contemporary Polish artists were opened in the 1980s, and exhibits such as "The Independent Culture in Poland," on *samizdat* publishing, toured cities throughout the Midwest in the early 1990s. Moreover, Polish artists, actors, and musicians arriving for permanent and temporary stays have an increasing presence in mainstream venues in New York, San Francisco, and Chicago.

The present community is a transnational one, much as it was 100 years ago, when circular migration brought money, experience, and information to Poland and low-cost labor to America. Restrictive U.S. immigration policies in the middle of the century combined with cold war politics to limit contact between the two communities, but the collapse of the communist regime reopened transoceanic ties and made Poland more accessible to tourism, cultural exchanges, and business investments. At the same time, alterations in U.S. immigration policy made America more accessible to Polish tourists, temporary workers, and permanent immigrants. Advancements in communication and transportation (e.g., an increase in the number of air flights, computer banking procedures, and cell phones) also make it easier and more inexpensive for scholars to work together, capital to make business, families to stay in contact, and money to flow back to Poland (between 1994 and 1999, Polish workers' remittances totaled $4.41 million). Dense social networks will continue to encourage immigration, as will the instability of Poland's economic system and U.S. immigration policies designed to encourage a global labor force.

Bibliography

Blejwas, Stanislaus. 1981. "Old and New Polonias: Tension within an Ethnic Community." *Polish American Studies* 38, 2: 55–83.

Bukowczyk, John. 1987. *And My Children Did Not Know Me: A History of Polish-Americans.* Bloomington: Indiana University Press.

Erdmans, Mary Patrice. 2006. "New Polonia: Ghetto Immigrants, Professional Suburbanites, and Urban Cultural Actors." In John P. Koval et al., eds., *The New Chicago.* Philadelphia: Temple University Press.

———. 1998. *Opposite Poles: Immigrants and Ethnics in Polish Chicago, 1976–1990.* University Park: Pennsylvania State University Press.

Jaroszynska-Kirchmann, Anna. 2004. *The Exile Mission: The Polish Political Diaspora and the Polish Americans, 1939–1956.* Athens: Ohio University Press.

Kula, Marcin. 1996. "Emigration from a Communist Country—Both Economic and Political: A Post-Communist Perspective." *Journal of American Ethnic History* 16, 1: 47–54.

Lopata, Helena. 1976. *Polish Americans: Status Competition in an Ethnic Community.* Englewood Cliffs, N.J.: Prentice Hall.

Morawska, Ewa. 1985. *For Bread with Butter: The Life Worlds of East Central Europeans in Johnstown Pennsylvania, 1890–1940.* Cambridge, Eng.: Cambridge University Press.

Mostwin, Danuta. 1991. *Emigranci Polscy w USA* [*Polish emigrants in the USA*]. Lublin, Poland: Catholic University of Lublin Press.

Thomas, William, and Florian Znaniecki. 1958 [1918]. *The Polish Peasant in Europe and America.* Chicago: University of Chicago Press.

Russia

Steven J. Gold

Nearly 3 million people claimed Russian ancestry in the 1990 U.S. Census, while the 2000 Census reported that 388,178 residents of the U.S. were born in Russia. However, counting the American population of Russian origin is a complex matter, because of a number of changes in both the national boundaries of the country of origin and the meaning of Russian identity.

Changing Regional Definitions

The nations and geographical regions that have made up Russia have altered significantly since the 19th century. From 1922 until 1991, Russia was part of a much larger nation—the Soviet Union. As a consequence, depending on the year of entry, people immigrating to the U.S. from the same region may or may not be listed as being from the former Soviet Union or Russia.

Since the demise of the Soviet Union in 1991, several countries that were part of that nation, including Latvia, Estonia, Lithuania, Belorussia (now Belarus), Moldavia (now Moldova), Kirgizia, Uzbekistan, Azerbaijan, Kazakhstan, Tajikistan, Armenia, Georgia, Turkmenistan, and Ukraine, have declared their independence. In fact, according to the 2000 Census, the number of people born in just four of these former Soviet republics now living in the U.S.—409,569 from Ukraine, Belarus, Lithuania, and Armenia—exceeds those born in Russia by almost 20,000 (see Table 1).

Table 1 Population of foreign-born residents by country of origin, 2000

National origin	Number of residents
USSR (other USSR, Russia)	388,178
Latvia	27,907
Lithuania	28,569
Armenia	63,814
Azerbaijan	14,325
Byelorussia	38,859
Moldavia	22,031
Ukraine	278,327
Georgia	10,072
Uzbekistan	23,068

Source: U.S. Census Bureau, 2000 Census, 5% Integrated Public Use Microdata Sample, weighted data.

Definitions of Russian Identity

In addition to the difficulties involved in enumerating Russian Americans because of geopolitical changes, a problem is presented when we seek to determine who is included within the Russian ethnic identity. Russian ethnicity is associated with being a member of the Russian Orthodox Church and of Slavic national origins. Hence, people who live in Russia but maintain distinct national, ethnic, or religious identities—Jews, Poles, Germans, Armenians, and the like—are not generally considered to be Russian. In fact, less than 20 percent of people living in the U.S. who trace their origins to the former Soviet Union are ethnically Russian, while more than 80 percent are members of various minority groups.

Nevertheless, the wide-ranging policy of Russification, which involved the training and indoctrination of various non-Russian groups into the Russian language, culture, and identity, together with the establishment of Russian elites in non-Russian parts of the former Soviet Union, meant that immigrants who were not ethnically Russian were oriented toward Russian-speaking environments, were often identified by Americans as Russians, and frequently made significant contributions to Russian American life. As such, members of these Russified groups must be considered as important parts of the population. During the first decades of the 20th century, several nationality groups, including Germans, Poles, and Latvians, were enumerated as Russians in U.S. censuses. Further, since about 1900, over half of all Americans who trace their origins to the former Soviet Union have been Jews.

History of Settlement

A considerable literature documents the contemporary and historical experience of Russian Jews in the U.S. In contrast, there is a paucity of research on non-Jewish Russians. Accordingly, we will concentrate on the latter.

Unlike other European groups, which disembarked in the eastern U.S., the earliest Russians maintained a unique pattern of settlement oriented toward the West Coast, Canada, and Alaska. In fact, Russians were the first Europeans to explore this region. Crossing the Bering Strait (which was "discovered" by the Danish sea captain Vitus Bering, working in the service of Czar Peter the Great), they found that Asia and North America were separate continents and established a fur trade between them. The first permanent Russian colony was founded on Alaska's Kodiak Island in 1784. By the early 19th century, more than 25 settlements had been established from Alaska to Fort Ross, California, just 100 miles north of San Francisco. In addition to protecting fur traders, many of these encampments housed missionaries who sought to convert the local population to the Russian Orthodox Church. In 1861 there were 9 Orthodox churches and 35 chapels in the Russian territories on the west coast of North America.

After Russia sold Alaska to the U.S. in 1867, the center of Russian American activity moved from Alaska to California. The largest influx of Russians on the West Coast arrived during the first decades of the 20th century, when religious sectarians, especially Molokans, immigrated. As pacifists who rejected Orthodoxy, Molokans were reviled in the Russian empire and fled to the U.S. (as well as Iran) to escape conscription. Some 5,000 entered California between 1904 and 1912. Many settled in Los Angeles' Boyle Heights, a neighborhood later associated with Mexican, Jewish, and Japanese migrants, and in San Francisco. By 1970 about 20,000 Molokans resided in California.

Following the initial settlement on the West Coast, Russians came in several waves from European ports to New York and Boston. The first arrived between 1880 and 1914. In 1910 there were about 90,000 Russians in the U.S. Many originated in Galicia and Belorussia. (Illustrating the complexity of Russian migration, neither of these areas is currently part of Russia. Galicia spans Poland and Ukraine, while Belorussia [now Belarus] is a separate nation.)

Most of these early Russian immigrants were former peasants who found work in industrial mills, meatpacking, construction, and garment industries in large cities of the East, Midwest, and California. Others took employment in mines, railroads, food processing, and lumber enterprises in the Rocky Mountain and Western states. Russians also settled in rural areas like Sicily Island, Louisiana, and New Odessa, Oregon, where they created short-lived utopian communities. More successful agricultural colonies were established in southern New Jersey, Ohio, and Illinois. By 1925 approximately 30,000 Russians were engaged in farming.

The period from 1880 to 1920 also marked the arrival of Russian Jews. From 1881 to 1928, the U.S. Jewish population increased by 2,302,378; the overwhelming majority came from Russia. Those entering the U.S. from other countries (Germany, France, the United Kingdom, Canada, and Africa) were largely secondary migrants from eastern Europe. They settled in major cities of the Northeast and Midwest, especially New York. Their initial occupations were in factories, peddling, and trade. Many found work in the rapidly expanding ready-to-wear garment industry, which was largely under the control of coreligionists of German origin by the time the Russian Jews arrived. Russian Jews were more skilled, literate, and urban in origin than other southern and eastern European immigrants. Moreover, fleeing oppression in the Pale of Settlement (the region of Russia and eastern Europe where most Jews lived), they generally came as intact families and had low rates of return. As a consequence, they achieved rapid economic and educational mobility, which allowed them to enter public service and the professions and overcome discrimination to join the middle class in a relatively short period.

The next flow of Russians to immigrate to the U.S., numbering some 30,000, included many members of the Russian elite who opposed the Soviet system. They entered as refugees between 1920 and 1940, fleeing the Bolshevik Revolution (1917) and the Russian civil war (1918–1921) that established the Soviet Union. Another wave, consisting of displaced persons who had been sent to work in the Nazi war industry during World War II, came during the decade after the war. More skilled and educated than the first wave, they initially accepted low-status jobs but eventually found positions matching their skills, often in research, publishing, and security-related pursuits that utilized their cultural and linguistic skills to inform the U.S. about Soviet society. From about 1970 until 1988, over 100,000 Soviet refugees entered the U.S. Members of minority ethnic and religious groups made up a large fraction. The majority were Jews, but the group also included Catholics, Pentacostalists, and Armenians.

Finally, the most recent Russian migrants have come to the U.S. since 1989, their arrival precipitated by *glasnost* (a policy of openness initiated by Soviet premier Mikhail Gorbachev) and augmented by the end of the Soviet system. Highly educated, they have made rapid progress in adjusting to the U.S., finding professional and technical positions in medicine, engineering, computer fields, and small business. From 1975 until 1999, 527,297 refugees from the former Soviet Union entered the U.S., making them the second largest refugee nationality to enter the country (after the Vietnamese) during the last quarter of the 20th century. The peak year of arrival was 1992, when the Hebrew Immigration Aid Society (HIAS) resettled 45,871 refugees from the former USSR. Since 2000, about 7,500 refugees have entered the U.S. annually from the former USSR, but only a small fraction of these have been Jewish. In addition to those entering with refugee status, a number have arrived under various migrant statuses.

The Cold War

America's six decades of political conflict with the former Soviet Union (labeled "the evil empire" by President Ronald Reagan) have been the major force in shaping the experience of Russian Americans. Many Russian migrants chose to emigrate because of their opposition to communism and the Soviet way of life. Seeking to discredit its ideological and geopolitical opponents, the U.S. government welcomed Russian refugees with generous resettlement programs. A further impact of the cold war has been to shape Russian American assimilation. Because of the largely negative image of Russia in cold war America, few people of Russian ancestry have actively attempted to develop a Russian American ethnic community, as other American national- or ethnic-origin populations have, such as Greek Americans, Mexican Americans, and African Americans.

In the public mind, Russian Americans were frequently associated with socialism, anarchism, or communism and as such were considered to be both un-American and dangerous. During periodic "Red scares," especially those following the first and second world wars, the U.S. government undertook campaigns to crack down on domestic revolutionaries and those sympathetic to them. As a result, many Russian aliens were deported.

Before the 1920s, Russian Americans, including many of Jewish ancestry, played a dominant role in the growing American socialist movement, but after 1920, with the decline of American radical socialism and the influx of the new anti-Bolshevik immigrants, Russian American political activity became increasingly concerned with the country of origin rather than the American scene.

Because of the negative image of their homeland, many Russian Americans felt forced to forsake their heritage. Instead, like German Americans, who learned to mask their national origins because of hostility associated with the two world wars, Russians concealed their country of origin and instead emphasized a generic Euro-American identity. The consequences of this were ruinous for ethnic communal organizations, because public displays of Russian heritage became taboo.

Paradoxically, however, the cold war also provided benefits for Russian Americans. The "space race" (initiated by the Soviet Union's launching of a satellite in 1957, before the U.S. was able to do so), competition between the U.S. and the USSR to establish allegiances with newly independent nations, and the Soviet development of atomic weapons in the late 1940s made it a national priority to learn more about Russia. Accordingly, governmental efforts and funds fostered an expansion in Russian studies in American universities as well as the popularization of Russian culture through books, movies, and television programs. Educated Russian Americans, who were knowledgeable about Russian culture and language, found their skills in great demand.

Despite this trend, a combination of Russian Americans' religious and ideological diversity and the larger society's hostility toward the open expression of identification with Russia discouraged the organization and unification of the Russian American population. Only a few ethnic organizations and publications continue to exist. Among them are the Tolstoy Foundation, which has aided in the resettlement of thousands of Russian exiles, and the New York–based Russian-language daily *Novoe russkoe slovo* (*New Russian World*). Generally, however, the entire population reveals few links. Even academic research on the Russian American population is lacking.

Religion

Religion has been a major force in motivating Russian emigration to the U.S. and coordinating migrants once they arrive. The Russian Orthodox Church has provided the central focus of community life, organization, and linguistic and cultural preservation in the U.S. Early on, church schools taught Russian language and history, published newspapers, maintained theatrical groups, and (until 1917, when the czar was killed) encouraged loyalty to the Russian monarch. Such activities, along with dramatic religious ceremonies, played a vital role in teaching American-born children their national heritage.

As a consequence of political conflicts associated with the Russian Revolution, there have been three distinct venues wherein adherents of the Russian Orthodox Church can practice their faith in the U.S. Two maintain a specifically Russian character and emphasize Russian language and culture in services as well as publications, camps, and other activities, but have contrasting relations with the mother church in Moscow. A third, the Orthodox Church in America, maintains a multi-national approach to Orthodox Christianity and as such does not emphasize Russian culture. Of the two Russian-focused churches, the patriarchal parishes of the Russian Orthodox Church in the United States and Canada remain under the jurisdiction of the patriarchate of Moscow. Its rival is the Russian Orthodox Church Outside Russia (ROCOR), governed by the Synod Abroad. The collapse of the Soviet Union has not resolved conflicts between the two Russian-focused branches, which continue to battle, even establishing competing links to coreligionists in the former USSR.

In addition to those Russian immigrants who follow Orthodoxy, several other faiths, including Old Believers, Molokans, Dukhobors, and Pentacostalists, as well as Jews, are represented within the Russian American community. A small number of Russians in the U.S. have joined various Baptist and evangelical churches, and there are a few Russian Catholic parishes in New York City, Los Angeles, San Francisco, Chicago, and Portland, Oregon. Some have maintained close-knit enclaves in urban neighborhoods or religiously focused rural communities like Woodburn, Oregon. Most, however, have settled in the nation's largest states and cities, including New York, California, New Jersey, Massachusetts, and Illinois.

Demographic Characteristics

Patterns of family composition that have their roots in the Soviet Union reinforce intimacy and mutual involvement among Russian émigrés in the U.S. Because of

Soviet housing shortages and the desire to maximize available resources for children's mobility, family size in the Soviet era was typically small. Families rarely had more than one or two offspring. Those in the workforce retired early (women at 55, men at 60) and were often extensively involved in the lives of their children and grandchildren, with whom they lived. As immigrants, Russians often bring over elderly family members to care for children, and so the family remains intact in a more secure environment than that of the former USSR. Women outnumber men and are significantly older, indicating their greater life expectancy as well as the effects of World War II, which killed more men than women. A tendency toward early and close to universal marriage has been maintained in the U.S. The fraction of women born in the former USSR who are unmarried by age 40 (4 percent) is less than one third (14 percent) of that of all American women and substantially lower than that of other migrant populations, including women born in China and Latin America.

Economic Adjustment

Russians who arrived in the U.S. prior to the 1920s followed social patterns similar to those of other southern and eastern European migrants of the same period. Their children, like the young people of other groups, often moved away from ethnically defined urban neighborhoods and into suburban communities. Those who have entered the U.S. since 1970 are characterized by very high levels of education, often in technical and professional fields. Their economic progress has been impressive, yielding near-universal entry into the American middle class. Over 25 percent of people from the former USSR entering from 1994 to 1999 had a university or medical degree. A large number entered as refugees and hence had access to a package of benefits including health care, job and language training, housing, public assistance, and legal resident status. Many of these are Jews, who can use communal services provided by the American Jewish community, including Jewish Family Service, Jewish community centers, Jewish retirement homes, and other programs. Jews, Armenians, and other ethnically defined populations also have access to networks of native-born coethnics who often aid their resettlement by providing guidance, jobs, and various services. Consequently, they tend to prosper.

Like the native-born population of Russian origin, Russian immigrants are active in professions and entrepreneurship. According to the 2000 Census, 60 percent of USSR-born people aged 25 to 64 had a bachelor's degree or higher. Thus, they are much better educated than the total group of foreign-born people, 26 percent of whom have a bachelor's degree or higher. Their educational achievements also outstrip those of the native-born population. Reflecting their high levels of education, recent Russian immigrants experience rapid economic mobility. According to the 2000 Census, USSR-born men aged 25 to 64 who were in the labor force had a median income of $38,000 in 1999. For purposes of comparison, the median income for all foreign-born men in this group was $27,000. USSR-born women of the same age group had a median income of $24,500 in 1999; the median income for all foreign-born women was $19,400 in that year.

According to the 2000 Census, 73 percent of immigrants in this group were employed as managers, administrators, salesmen, professionals, or technical specialists, as compared with 54 percent of all foreign-born people. Other important occupational categories are gender-based: craftwork (frequently in construction and jewelry) for men and service occupations for women. One economic asset of recent Russian immigrants over natives and other immigrant groups is the high number of women with professional and technical skills—a product of the USSR's egalitarian educational system. As of 1981, 67 percent of Soviet women in the U.S. had been engineers, technicians, or other kinds of professionals before migration. In contrast, only 16.5 percent of American women worked in these occupations. According to the 2000 Census, 31 percent of Soviet-born women were college graduates—more than double the figure (15.1 percent) for all foreign-born women. In addition, 47.1 percent of Soviet women in the U.S. were employed as managers or professionals; in contrast, the figure for all foreign-born women was 33.2 percent. A smaller proportion of Russian immigrant men (45.5 percent) are employed as managers or professionals. Russian men are slightly more likely than other immigrants to be self-employed; 12 percent of Russians and former Soviets (14.9 percent of men and 9.0 percent of women) were self-employed. The rate of self-employment for all foreign-born people was 10.8 percent—11.9 percent for men and 9.3 percent for women (see Table 2).

While the average income of Russian migrants suggests a generally successful transition into the American middle class, the economic adjustment of this popula-

Table 2   Educational and economic characteristics of the foreign-born population, 2000

	Russian-/USSR-born		All foreign-born	
	Men	Women	Men	Women
Percentage with a bachelor's degree or higher[a]	61.1	58.8	27.2	24.8
Median total personal income[b]	$38,000	$24,500	$27,000	$19,400
Percentage in managerial or professional jobs[c]	43.5	47.1	27.1	33.2
Percentage self-employed[c]	14.9	9.0	11.9	9.3

Source: U.S. Census Bureau, 2000 Census, 5% Integrated Public Use Microdata Sample, weighted data.
a. Persons aged 25–64.
b. All households.
c. Persons aged 25–64 in the labor force. Self-employment unpaid family workers.

tion covers a wide range, from poverty to significant wealth. As might be expected, recently arrived refugees made much less in 1990 than those with longer tenure in the U.S. For example, about 30 percent of former Soviets who had been in the U.S. for a year or less in June 1991 were receiving cash assistance—an indicator of low income.

Recently arrived refugees also had higher unemployment rates and lower labor force participation rates than other refugee groups, except for Laotians and Cambodians. This can be attributed to the former Soviets' advanced age, poor health, limited English proficiency, relatively recent arrival, and the fact that their high educational profiles make some reluctant to accept entry-level jobs, which are the most readily available.

Social Adjustment

Education of immigrant children. School-aged Russian immigrants who have entered the U.S. since the 1970s generally have a strong educational background and do well in American schools. For example, in a 1991 comparison of the 12 largest immigrant groups attending New York City public schools (grades 3–12) who had been in the country three years or less, students from the former Soviet Union ranked first in reading scores, second in math, and fifth in English. Their reading and math scores were much higher than the average for all students, including the native-born. In addition, their mean increase in scores over the previous year was the highest of all groups in both reading and English and among the highest in math. Russian immigrants' educational accomplishments make sense, because many describe America's educational opportunities as a major reason for their immigration.

Social adaptation of recent migrants. Russian immigrants who entered the U.S. during the late 19th and early 20th centuries encountered forms of discrimination and prejudice because of their culture, religion (many were Jews), and leftist political leanings. In contrast, recent Russian immigrants find themselves among the upper echelon of all migrants because of their largely European origins, high levels of education, legal status, connections to established coethnics, and white skin. For example, Jewish émigrés often lose their public Jewish identity, since non-Jewish Americans simply see them as white foreigners and American Jews find them lacking in religious knowledge. An émigré interviewed by the sociologist Paul Ritterband in New York commented on his loss of minority status: "Here I feel less a Jew than in Russia . . . I live calmly and nobody bothers me . . . Nobody tells me I'm Jewish."

Relations with established coethnics. Recent Soviet immigrants often receive resettlement assistance from established coethnics and coreligionists—American Jews, Armenian Americans, and the like—who act as proximal hosts. While they are grateful for such services, they sometimes find that differences among those of the same ethnic background create conflict, reflecting their varying backgrounds, values, and outlooks.

Like turn-of-the century Jews, recent Jewish immigrants from the former USSR sometimes lock horns with the host community about the nature of group identity, religious involvement, and location of settlement. Admitting that conflicts between migrants and hosts have always taken place, Ritterband argues that current issues of contention are distinct from those of the past: "The 1880–1914 Russian Jewish immigrants were offered a network of settlement houses and other institutions designed by the earlier wave of German Jewish immigrants as a means of Americanizing their all too traditional and exotic co-religionists. By contrast, the contemporary American Jewish community, itself composed largely of descendants of earlier waves of East European immigrants, has attempted to Judaize the immigrants." In both periods, conflicts developed as hosts directed new arrivals toward patterns of adaptation that were not of their own choosing. Similar conflicts occur between Soviet Armenians and the established Armenian American population.

In order to maintain a measure of control over their adaptation to their new life, Soviet immigrants often gravitate toward their own enclaves, where they can interact in a familiar environment. This tendency is magnified because the population includes many elderly people who are limited in their ability to adjust to American life and the English language and hence are highly dependent on coethnic settings. Because Russian immigrants have relatively high rates of self-employment, their neighborhoods feature numerous ethnically oriented shops, restaurants, service providers, and media industries that provide ways to socialize and reconstruct an identity. While these communities have geographic, cultural, religious, and economic links with those of American coethnics, the conational preference often predominates. Further, such communities are themselves often stratified into subgroups on the basis of class, ideology, region of origin, occupation, religiosity, ethnicity, tenure in the U.S., and other factors.

Russian immigrant enclaves have a strong attraction for the broader nationally defined population, who often commute long distances to and from work in order to live among coethnics. Within these enclaves, a fairly high level of institutional completeness exists. For example, in West Los Angeles or Brooklyn, a Russian immigrant can interact with neighbors, shop for food, clothes, appliances, or medication, see a doctor or dentist, attend religious services, read a newspaper, watch cable TV, visit a local park to play dominoes, spend an evening in a nightclub, and interact with numerous acquaintances, all without speaking a word of English.

Russian and American Jews maintain distinct attitudes and social habits, which often reinforce the immigrants' desire to stay among their own. Immigrants generally think Americans are superficial and lacking in passion and warmth. Making this point, Mila, a Russian-born college student I interviewed in Los Angeles in

1994, contrasted an American wedding with a Russian one: "Big things like weddings, anniversaries, parties, are just done in a different way. A Russian wedding—I mean, you go all out. You have the whole synagogue. You have the wedding in the chapel and then there's a huge reception. Huge meals and appetizers and an emcee and a band and flowers and balloons and God knows what else. It's like a big occasion. Where Americans, they're like, 'Well, the wedding's at seven and we'll leave by nine and just have appetizers—cheese and crackers.'"

Russian Jews' shared dislike of American values and cultural patterns is a reason some turn away from American coreligionists. Having been admitted to the U.S. with refugee status from the discredited and now defunct Soviet Union, recent Russian immigrants continue to hold conservative political views and often join the Republican Party when they become naturalized citizens, whereas American Jews tend to be Democrats. Since the election of 1994, however, reports suggest that migrants from the former Soviet Union have begun to vote Democratic at higher rates, largely because Republican welfare reform policies reduced their eligibility for benefits.

Interestingly, some of the greatest differences between American Jews and Russian Jewish immigrants are found in their patterns of religious and ethnic identification—apparent commonalities that would seem to bring these groups together. This is because for most American Jews, Judaism is a religious identity, rooted in religious knowledge and practice. In contrast, in the atheistic Soviet Union, Judaism was regarded as a nationality. While the Russian word for "Jew" was inscribed in Russian Jews' passports, access to Jewish education and practice was severely limited. Accordingly, before 1990 Soviet Jews maintained a secular Jewish identity. Further separating American Jews from Russian immigrants is the fact that Reform and Conservative Judaism, Western denominations with which the vast majority of American Jews affiliate, are all but unknown in the former Soviet Union. Rejecting American denominations, many Russian Jewish migrants prefer to affiliate with Chabad, an ultra-Orthodox Hassidic movement considered exotic by mainstream American Jews. Although they lack religious training, Russian immigrants are drawn to Chabad's familiar ambiance and make use of its extensive immigrant-oriented programs, including Russian synagogues in major areas of settlement. These religious centers deliver social and religious services with Russian-speaking rabbis in a highly personal context.

Despite Russian immigrants' feelings of distance from American Jews, most see their eventual amalgamation with coethnic hosts as both positive and inevitable. Based on his analysis of the New York Jewish Population Study of 1991, Ritterband argues that "in many ways, the new immigrants, despite their lack of religious training and with few exceptions, score as high—or higher—on the religious, secular and affiliational dimensions of Jewishness as do other New York Jews."

While a large fraction of immigrants from the former Soviet Union in the 1970s and early 1990s were Jews, since that time members of other ethnic and religious populations—including Russians and Armenians—have arrived as well. For example, 7,565 refugees from the former USSR were admitted in 2000, with HIAS resettling 1,339, or about 18 percent. The reduction in the number of Russian Jewish refugees is a consequence of a decrease in the numbers of Jews who want to leave the former USSR, as well as the impact of the Lautenberg-Specter Amendment (which went into effect in 1990), which made refugees from the former USSR eligible for admission only if they have first-degree relatives here (spouses, parents and children, siblings, and grandparents and grandchildren).

The Russian American Community

Whether ethnically Russian or not, recent immigrants from Russia and the former Soviet Union are party to the Russian culture, language, and way of life to a greater extent than immigrants in the past. Because of their involvement with Russian culture, many develop ties to the greater Russian American community when they arrive in the U.S. Regardless of their ethnicity and religion, they tend to speak Russian and have similar tastes and cultural outlooks. As a consequence, enclaves have recently taken on a panethnic character. For example, in Los Angeles, Jews and Armenians reside near each other and patronize each other's stores along Santa Monica Boulevard. In Boston and New York City, non-Jewish Russians socialize in restaurants established by Jewish conationals.

At the same time, as larger numbers of immigrants from different parts of the former Soviet Union establish themselves in the U.S., they build their own communities reflecting cultural styles. The historian Annalise Orleck contrasts the adaptation of Bukharan and Georgian Jews from eastern regions of the former USSR to that of Jews hailing from the European USSR. The former, she reveals, were far less Sovietized than their conationals from Moscow, St. Petersburg, and Kiev. Accordingly, they have a higher percentage of entrepreneurial occupations and a much higher degree of religiosity than the latter. These ethnic resources have been put to use in the development of a prosperous enclave in Queens, New York.

Today Russian immigrants concentrate in the nation's largest cities, especially New York, Chicago, and Los Angeles. New York is the principal settlement. The Jewish Community Study of New York enumerated 202,000 people in Russian-speaking Jewish households in 1997. In contrast, emigrants from Armenia heavily favor LA, where over 81 percent of all Armenian-born people in the U.S. reside (see Table 3).

Given the large number of recent Russian immigrants, the cessation of cold war hostilities, and expanded opportunities to travel to and trade with Russia and other regions of the former Soviet Union, it stands to reason that in the coming years, the

Table 3   Ten cities with the highest populations of foreign-born Russians, 2000

	Russians			Ukrainians			Armenians		
Rank	City	Number	Percentage	City	Number	Percentage	City	Number	Percentage
1	New York	98,361	25.2	New York	72569	26.0	Los Angeles	51,832	81.3
2	Los Angeles	22,063	5.7	Chicago	19,663	7.0	New York	1,485	2.3
3	Chicago	19,304	5.0	Los Angeles	15,726	5.6	Boston	1,225	1.9
4	N/A[a]	16,678	4.3	Philadelphia	15,723	5.6	Sacramento	1,015	1.6
5	Boston	15,902	4.1	Sacramento	12,008	4.3	Fresno	791	1.2
6	Philadelphia	11,080	2.8	Seattle	9,740	3.5	Las Vegas	624	1.0
7	San Francisco	9,749	2.5	N/A[a]	8,844	3.2	(all others less than 1%)		
8	Washington, D.C.	9,454	2.4	Portland, Oregon	8,371	3.0			
9	Portland, Oregon	9,199	2.4	San Francisco	7,943	2.8			
10	Seattle	8,642	2.2	Boston	6,971	1.2			
Total West Coast		389,876	12.8		279,591	19.2		63,774	85.1

Source: U.S. Census Bureau, 2000 Census, 5% Integrated Public Use Microdata Sample, weighted data.
a. City not available, or household does not reside in a metropolitan area.

Russian American community will experience an unprecedented level of growth and vitality as well as ongoing transformation.

Bibliography

Glazer, Nathan. 1955. "The Social Characteristics of American Jews." *American Jewish Year Book* 56: 3–42.

Gold, Steven J. 1994. "Soviet Jews in the United States." *American Jewish Yearbook*: 3–57.

———. 1995. *From the Workers' State to the Golden State: Jews from the Former Soviet Union in California.* Boston: Allyn and Bacon.

Hardwick, Susan Wiley. 1993. *Russian Refuge: Religion, Migration and Settlement on the North American Pacific Rim.* Chicago: University of Chicago Press.

Hertzberg, Arthur. 1989. *The Jews in America: Four Centuries of an Uneasy Encounter: A History.* New York: Simon and Schuster.

Howe, Irving. 1976. *World of Our Fathers.* New York: Harcourt, Brace, Jovanovich.

Magocsi, Paul Robert. 1980. "Russians." In Stephen Thernstrom, ed., *Harvard Encyclopedia of American Ethnic Groups,* pp. 885–94. Cambridge: Belknap/Harvard University Press.

Markowitz, Fran. 1988. "Jewish in the USSR, Russian in the USA." In Walter P. Zenner, ed., *Persistence and Flexibility: Anthropological Perspectives on the American Jewish Experience,* pp. 79–95. Albany: State University of New York Press.

———. 1993. *A Community in Spite of Itself: Soviet Jewish Émigrés in New York.* Washington, D.C.: Smithsonian.

Morris, Richard A. 1991. *Old Russian Ways: Cultural Variations among Three Russian Groups in Oregon.* New York: AMS Press.

Orleck, Annalise. 1999. *The Soviet Jewish Americans.* Westport, Conn.: Greenwood.

Simon, Rita J. 1985. *New Lives: The Adjustment of Soviet Jewish Immigrants in the United States and Israel.* Lexington, Mass.: Lexington Books.

Wirth, Louis. 1928. *The Ghetto.* Chicago: University of Chicago Press.

South America

Ecuador, Peru, Brazil, Argentina, Venezuela

Helen B. Marrow

While South Americans have migrated to the United States for many decades—nearly ten times as many South Americans as Central Americans entered before 1900, and over 4,000 entered annually between 1910 and 1930—before the mid-20th century, most South American migration occurred within a single country or spilled over only into neighboring countries. According to INS statistics, just 132,103 South Americans entered the U.S. legally between 1891 and 1950, and according to U.S. Census statistics, only 33,623 South Americans lived in the country before 1930 (87,705 before 1965). Since the mid-20th century, however, South American immigration has increased dramatically.

Why? Major changes in politico-economic developments throughout South America increased the pressures for emigration, as many countries' dreams of successful modernization and industrialization ran aground by the 1970s, sometimes as early as the 1950s. South American immigration also rose because of rapidly expanding economic opportunities in the U.S., 1965 changes in U.S. immigration law (which began granting entry based on employment and family preferences rather than restrictive quotas), and the proliferation of American technology and capital flows, the English language, and American cultural and consumption models throughout the Western Hemisphere.

Historically, there have been fewer South Americans than other Latin Americans in the U.S. Sheer distance makes travel from South America more difficult than from elsewhere in Latin America and the Caribbean. But more importantly, the historical and structural roots of migration flows help explain this difference. Labor migration flows react to historic patterns of penetration, moving along them in the opposite direction—for example, from colonized countries toward their former colonial powers, or from countries affected by direct labor-recruiting practices or indirect economic and cultural influences toward the countries where these influences

Table 1 South American immigrants by selected class of admission and country of birth, 2002

Country of birth	Number of immigrants	Percentage admitted by selected class of admission				
		Family-sponsored preferences	Employment-based preferences	Immediate relatives of U.S. citizens	Refugee and asylee adjustments	Diversity programs
All countries	1,063,732	17.6	16.4	45.7	11.9	4.0
All South America	74,506	19.4	14.7	62.1	1.6	1.8
Colombia	18,845	13.0	8.6	75.9	2.0	—
Ecuador	10,602	17.2	11.8	68.1	0.4	2.1
Peru	11,999	16.8	9.1	64.0	3.4	6.1
Brazil	9,474	2.9	36.3	58.6	0.4	1.3
Guyana	9,962	66.8	2.7	30.2	0.1	0.1
Argentina	3,685	6.8	26.6	62.3	1.6	2.3
Venezuela	5,259	6.6	22.8	63.7	4.8	1.8
Chile	1,858	14.0	17.8	66.0	0.9	0.6
Bolivia	1,670	13.8	26.5	57.0	0.8	1.1
Uruguay	539	8.9	22.8	65.9	0.9	1.1
Paraguay	359	12.8	27.9	57.9	0.6	0.8
Suriname	248	21.0	31.0	46.4	0.8	0.4

Source: U.S. Immigration and Naturalization Service, *Statistical Yearbook, 2002*, Table 3 (Washington, D.C.: U.S. Department of Justice).

Table 2   Foreign-born South Americans, by country of birth, 1970–2000

| Country of birth | Population (percentage of total U.S. foreign-born population) | | | |
	1970[a]	1980	1990	2000
Colombia	84,921	151,100 (1.0)	303,093 (1.4)	525,881 (1.6)
Ecuador	49,491	89,960 (0.6)	143,006 (0.7)	299,106 (0.9)
Peru	35,450	60,440 (0.4)	151,837 (0.7)	282,264 (0.9)
Brazil	46,758	44,940 (0.3)	94,407 (0.4)	222,836 (0.7)
Guyana	N/A	51,740 (0.3)	121,567 (0.6)	216,172 (0.7)
Argentina	67,364	70,680 (0.5)	99,523 (0.5)	131,055 (0.4)
Venezuela	17,321	38,120 (0.3)	50,823 (0.2)	116,867 (0.4)
Chile	25,125	38,640 (0.3)	62,036 (0.3)	84,242 (0.3)
Bolivia	10,187	14,620 (0.1)	32,194 (0.1)	52,913 (0.2)
Uruguay	7,041	14,240 (0.1)	23,012 (0.1)	25,031 (0.1)
Paraguay	N/A	3,440 (0.0)	7,092 (0.0)	13,542 (0.0)
Suriname[b]	N/A	1,440 (0.0)	3,041 (0.0)	6,073 (0.0)

Sources: U.S. Census Bureau, 1980, 1990, and 2000 Censuses, 5% Public Use Microdata Samples, weighted data.

a. 1970 Census figures from S. Thernstrom, ed., *The Harvard Encyclopedia of Ethnic Groups* (Cambridge, Mass.: Harvard University Press, 1980), p. 210, based on figures from U.S. Bureau of the Census, *Census of the Population, 1970,* vol. 1, *Characteristics of the Population,* pt. 1, *U.S. Summary* (Washington, D.C., 1973), I, p. 598, Table 192.

b. 2000 Suriname figures available only from U.S. Census Bureau, 2000 Census, 1% Public Use Microdata Sample, weighted data.

originated. By this reasoning, fewer South Americans than other Latin Americans have migrated to the U.S. because American involvement and intervention in South America has paled in comparison to U.S. colonialist and neocolonialist activities in Central America and the Caribbean (Puerto Rico, Cuba, Mexico, Haiti, El Salvador, Nicaragua, and Guatemala).

In pointing this out, however, we do not forget that many South American professionals and technicians have immigrated under formal U.S. employment preferences and not as traditional labor migrants (in 2002, 36 percent of Brazilians, 28 percent of Paraguayans, and 27 percent of Argentines and Bolivians admitted fell into this category; see Table 1), nor that many specific international linkages and American activities in South America have helped create and maintain less-skilled labor migration flows. For example, the banana and Panama hat industries helped tie small villages in southern Ecuador to New York City, North American textile interests helped tie Peruvian towns and cities to northern New Jersey, and American mining and industrial efforts helped tie Governador Valadares, Brazil, to Framingham, Massachusetts. Similarly, America's current roles in the Colombian drug war, Argentina's financial crisis, and Venezuela's political troubles are helping to attract migrants from those countries.

Overall, South American immigration took its strongest hold in the 1980s and 1990s. According to INS statistics, 349,568 South Americans entered the U.S. legally between 1951 and 1970, followed by 295,741 between 1971 and 1980, 461,847 between 1981 and 1990, and 681,335 between 1991 and 2002. Aggregate U.S. Census statistics show similar strides: as shown in Table 2, approximately 2 million South Americans (both documented and undocumented) were living in the U.S. in 2000, and these figures are widely criticized as undercounts.

Leaving South America

When analyzing South American emigration trends, we need to consider important political "push" factors such as military repression in Chile, guerrilla and counter-guerrilla warfare in Peru, political instability in Venezuela, and the drug war in Colombia. But even more important are the massive social transformations generated by globalization and neoliberal economic development policies over the past few decades. Recent South American emigration has grown out of economic and political *aperturas* (openings), with their privatization of state-owned businesses, deregulation of markets, and cuts in public spending meant to integrate South American countries more competitively in a global world economy. South American countries have now experienced debt crises (1980s), trade deficits (early 1990s), new financial crises (late 1990s/early 2000s), and a host of aggravated social inequalities and increasing economic uncertainties affecting their middle classes.

Therefore, South Americans have "chosen" to emigrate based on declining economic standing relative to rising educational, political, social, and cultural expectations. They are considered to be voluntary economic migrants rather than forced political refugees (at least, they are treated this way by the U.S. government; as shown in Table 1, only 2 percent of South Americans were admitted in 2002 as refugees or asylum-seekers, with proportions reaching no higher than 5 percent among Venezuelans and 3 percent among Peruvians). As Marcelo Suárez-Orozco and Mariela Páez write in *Latinos: Remaking America,* "Globalization and economic restructuring have intensified inequality in Latin America, generating unemployment and underemployment—and hence new migratory waves." Substantial economic transformations in the past few decades have turned most South American countries into exporters of people and importers of capital—a stark contrast to what they were in decades and centuries past.

While these descriptions do not hold perfectly, a brief look at recent events illustrates the connection between emigration and struggling development policies in countries where average educational attainments have been rising and familiarity with American-style consumption practices have been expanding. In between periods of economic growth and democratization, periods of recession and decline have hindered progress and increased pressures to emigrate. In 2002 figures from the Economic Commission on Latin America and the Caribbean (ECLAC) showed a deterioration in economic activity in the South American Common Market (MERCOSUR) since 1998–1999, completing "half a lost decade for the region as a whole" between 1997 and 2002. Declining regional economic conditions worsened social ones; increases in poverty and joblessness were most severe in Argentina, Venezuela, Paraguay, and Uruguay, but even in Colombia and Ecuador, poverty levels were higher in 2000 than they were in 1990. In such situations, workers from professional, middle-class, and even manual-labor backgrounds have turned to international migration as their native countries' credit infrastructures and job markets have ceased to satisfy their personal expectations.

Ecuador. In 2000, Ecuadorians passed Peruvians in immigrant population size, making them the second largest South American group in the U.S., behind Colombians (see Table 2). There have been roughly three main phases of Ecuadorian immigration. In the first phase (late 1950s to 1970s), "pioneer" men from rural communities in the south-central highland provinces of Cañar and Azuay began migrating to New York and Chicago. To explain why Ecuadorians head overwhelmingly to New York, researchers point to the industrial influence of banana companies in coastal Guayaquil and to connections and business routes already established between New York and rural southern Ecuador's *paja toquilla* (Panama hat) economy earlier in the 20th century.

In the second phase (1980s to early 1990s), Ecuador's once-successful petroleum, agriculture, and *paja toquilla* economies suffered severe setbacks. Real income and foreign exchange declined while debt increased, oil prices plunged, and strict austerity measures and currency devaluations failed to overcome rising unemployment and inflation. These worsening economic conditions provoked substantial emigration, as more men (and increasingly women and children) began leaving the country. During this period, Ecuadorian immigrants to the U.S. remained disproportionately undocumented and from rural, poor, peasant backgrounds, while south-central Ecuador consolidated itself as the regional hub of emigration. By the early 1990s, the three largest Ecuadorian cities were unofficially considered to be

Guayaquil, Quito, and New York City (instead of Cuenca), and in southern Ecuador, New York City became known as "La YANY" (*Yo amo a Nueva York,* or "I love New York").

Never having recovered from the "lost decade" of the 1980s, Ecuador then suffered an even more acute economic crisis in the mid- to late 1990s (the third phase). During this period the country's GDP fell while poverty and unemployment rates increased. In 1995 a short border war with Peru hurt Ecuador's economy, and in 1997–1998 El Niño devastated crops and transportation infrastructure. In 1999 the International Monetary Fund froze dollar bank accounts, and Ecuador was recognized as having the highest inflation rate in Latin America. Finally, in 2000, President Jamil Mahuad dollarized the Ecuadorian currency amid large-scale social protests (especially from impoverished indigenous populations). The effects of these changes on recent international emigration flows have been enormous. In 1999 and 2000 more than 267,000 Ecuadorians left the country, and remittances to Ecuador increased from $643 million in 1997 to $1.7 billion in 2003. Building on the original peasant bases from Azuay and Cañar, newer U.S.-bound Ecuadorians continue to head primarily to New York, although other migrants increasingly originate from more diverse occupational and regional backgrounds and head to different countries (especially Spain).

Peru. There have been five broad phases of Peruvian immigration in the U.S. Peruvian laborers migrated to California during the Gold Rush, and then others were recruited to work in textile mills near Paterson, New Jersey, after World War II. In the third phase (late 1960s through 1980s), Peruvian immigration increased and diversified. Highly skilled professionals and technicians began migrating in response to the 1965 changes in U.S. immigration law and new employment-based economic policies. By the early 1980s, Peruvian immigrants exhibited great socioeconomic diversity. Most had migrated because economic and social mobility were becoming increasingly harder to attain in Peru.

The fourth phase (1980s to 1992) was both economic and political. Economically, Peruvian industrial, export agriculture, and *estancamiento* policies uprooted more manual workers, who had fewer skills and were more likely to come from mountainous regions in the Andes than their professional predecessors. During the "lost decade" of the 1980s, urban poverty in Peru was exacerbated by an acute economic crisis, rising unemployment and underemployment, and the overcrowding of cities because of continued internal migration. Politically, Peru witnessed a substantial increase in violence and human rights abuses, starting with the appearance of the Shining Path and Túpac Amaru revolutionary movements and then matched by the rise of a state-sponsored governmental opposition force. This guerrilla and counterguerrilla warfare terrorized the Andean highlands and urban Lima, resulting in thousands of deaths, huge rural displacements, and declines in ordinary Peruvians' confidence in their government. What Jorge Durand calls the "shock" of combined economic crisis and political chaos spurred "explosive" Peruvian emigration in the 1980s. Collected estimates stand somewhere between 200,000 and 600,000, mostly self-identified *andinos* (indigenous people of rural, lower-class origins). Most of these migrants headed to the U.S., including 40 percent of the 112,687 Peruvians who left between 1985 and early 1988.

The Peruvian military's capture of Shining Path's leader in 1992 ushered in a new period of hope and stability for Peruvians abroad, and many returned home. However, data from the Latin American Migration Project (LAMP) show emigration continuing through the 1990s (the fifth phase), largely in sync with the economic adjustments and crises of that decade. In the 1990s currency devaluations led to a 30 percent decrease in income levels, and 60 percent of Peruvians fell into poverty, squeezed into unemployment and underemployment by structural adjustments and privatizations. Peruvians never fully recovered from the "lost decade," known even in the indigenous language Quechua as *década de chaqwa* (decade of chaos). Peruvian and Ecuadorian emigration rates hit new highs in 1998, 1999, and 2000. In 2000 alone, 183,000 Peruvians left their home country, a figure more than double that of previous years.

Brazil. Historically, Brazil is best known as an immigrant-receiving country. The Portuguese colonized it in the 1500s, about 4 million African slaves were imported over the next three centuries, and during the 19th and early 20th centuries, Portuguese, Italian, Spanish, German, Japanese, and various other immigrant groups made Brazil their home. However, three broad phases of Brazilian emigration have dominated recent decades. During the first phase (World War II to the 1970s), Brazilian intellectuals, artists, and politicians migrated to the U.S. while labor migrants came to fill industrial demands. Emigration during this phase was primarily economic or cultural; only a small number of political refugees left during a military government.

In the 1980s (the second phase), extreme crises transformed Brazilian emigration into an exodus of "economic refugees." Hyperinflation (almost 3,000 percent in 1993), failed macroeconomic packages like the Cruzado Plan in 1986 and the Collor Plan in 1991, and falling real income and declining standards of living gave middle-class Brazilians greater incentives to look for mobility elsewhere. For the first time in Brazil's history, Brazilians began leaving en masse—primarily for the U.S., but also for Paraguay, Japan, Europe (mostly Portugal and Italy), Canada, Australia, and other South American countries. One estimate by Teresa Sales shows the number of Brazilians living outside Brazil increasing by approximately 20 percent each year in the 1980s. It was also during this phase that large-scale emigration from the states of Governador Valadares and Minas Gerais began to attract greater attention. Widely cited as a "pioneer" immigrant flow, the 1980s *valadarense* and *mineiro* migrants were building on the social networks of previous immigrants from the region (which had developed during World War II in conjunction with American military and business activity in Minas Gerais), as Ana Cristina Braga Martes points out.

The third phase of Brazilian immigration (mid-1990s to the present) began when then finance minister Fernando Henrique Cardoso released his Real Plan in 1994. The Real Plan reduced inflation and stabilized much of Brazil's economic crisis. Emigration levels also stabilized, operating more according to the internal dynamics of migrants' social networks than to economic "push" factors. However, starting in 1999, with the devaluation of the Real Plan following the Asian financial crisis, frustration over (President) Cardoso's economic policies, and uncertainty leading up to the election of Luiz Inácio Lula da Silva in October 2002, emigration increased again. The number of Brazilian immigrants admitted to the U.S. in 2000 rose 78 percent, to 6,959, up from 3,902 in 1999—the largest annual increase since 1990–1991. And although economic conditions in Brazil stabilized by 2005, social networks continue to sustain further migration; reports of undocumented Brazilians apprehended while trying to cross the Mexico-U.S. border have increased dramatically since 2000. As with Ecuadorian and Peruvian immigrants, U.S. immigration figures are not recent enough to document the new movement. Collected "extra-official" estimates put the Brazilian population in the U.S. somewhere between 800,000 and 1.2 million in 2004.

Argentina. Like Brazil, Argentina is best known as an immigrant-receiving country. Most of its past immigrants came from Spain and Italy, more recent ones from Bolivia and Paraguay. But beginning in the 1950s, Argentines began leaving their country in three major phases. The first (1950s–1970s) was primarily economic, when professionals left because of dissatisfaction with their working conditions, income levels, and standards of living after Argentine industrialization ran into its first major hurdles. The second phase was primarily political but also economic. A repressive military government during Argentina's "Dirty War" (1976–1983) and hyperinflation and economic deterioration during the 1980s provided all classes of Argentines greater motive to emigrate. While these emigration flows were composed primarily of manual laborers, their high proportion of professionals earned them a reputation as brain drains.

The third and current phase is primarily economic. In the early 2000s, Argentines began responding to a severe economic crisis and Argentina's default on over $100 billion in debt (December 2001) by leaving in rapidly expanding numbers and heading to Spain, Italy, the U.S., Canada, Australia, and Israel. The magnitude of the crisis reversed a century of economic stability in Argentina and made a middle-class lifestyle harder to protect. Whereas Argentina was one of the ten richest countries in the world in 1900, in 2001–2002 its GDP fell rapidly, joblessness stood at over 20 percent, and an estimated half of its population of 37 million had fallen into poverty. Although the economic situation improved by 2004, Argentina's National Migration Directorate cites an exodus of 255,000 Argentines between

2001 and mid-2003 (roughly six times the number of emigrants who left between 1993 and 2000), and a 2002 survey found that a third of the country's residents would emigrate if they could.

U.S. immigration figures are not recent enough to document the new movement among Argentines. Collected "extra-official" estimates showed somewhere between 40,000 and 180,000 Argentines in Florida in 2002, and various sources documented an increase in the number of visa requests made at the American embassy in Buenos Aires. In February 2002 the INS removed Argentina and Uruguay from its visa-waiver program in response to swelling numbers of Argentine and Uruguayan nationals overstaying their visas. The Argentine embassy also delivered a request to the American government to grant temporary protected status (TPS) to Argentines who had fled the economic crisis and were living in the U.S. illegally—although it was not granted.

Venezuela. Before the 1980s, Venezuela was a stable country with a center-left democratic system, a functioning upper-middle-class economy, and a petroleum industry that linked it successfully to first-world development plans. It was also primarily an immigrant-receiving country, having welcomed its own 20th-century immigrants from neighboring Colombia, Europe, the Caribbean, other South American countries, Asia, and the Middle East. Only recently has Venezuelan emigration received attention.

The shift occurred because various debt, banking, and currency crises and rising inflation and unemployment plagued Venezuela during the 1980s and 1990s, increasing the incentives for emigration. During the 1980s, Venezuela witnessed economic stagnation and political discontent as its petroleum industry—alongside Ecuador's—began to decline. On February 18, 1983, "Black Tuesday" marked the beginning of a long line of currency devaluations that culminated in riots in February 1989. During the 1990s, Venezuela witnessed two coups (1992), a presidential impeachment (1993), a major financial crisis (1994), and the gradual collapse of its traditional party system and election of the populist Hugo Chávez Frías as president (1998). Javier Corrales shows that real wages in Venezuela decreased almost 70 percent over two decades, the probability of being poor increased from 2.4 percent to 18.5 percent over one decade, and over two thirds of the population now lives below the poverty line. Politico-economic unrest has worsened in recent years, especially following an attempted coup against Chávez on April 11, 2002, continued declines in petroleum values, and labor strikes and protests.

As elsewhere in South America, these crises have made a middle-class lifestyle harder to attain and protect. As Venezuela painfully worked its way through not one but two "lost decades," emigration increased dramatically; a 2002 survey found that over half of Venezuelans under the age of 24 wished to leave the country. As with other South American immigrants, U.S. figures are not recent enough to document the new movement. Specific to post-1989 Venezuelan emigration are rising incentives for Venezuelan elites, entrepreneurs, and upper-level bureaucrats to emigrate in order to protect their personal property and capital investments, especially as Chávez and his populist policies have begun challenging them more seriously since 1998. In this respect, early analyses have likened Venezuelan emigration under Chávez's presidency to Cuban emigration under Fidel Castro.

In brief, international emigration from South America is tied to neoliberal development—policies based on privatization and deregulation. Growth in immigration flows from the region has built on the earliest immigrants' experiences and expanded through social networks both within and outside the framework of U.S. immigration policy. Chile sends fewer migrants to the U.S. than most South American countries today, primarily because its successful transition to free-market capitalism and greater economic stability encourage more residents to stay put. (In the early 2000s, Chile is struggling with immigration of its own, mostly from Argentina, Bolivia, Peru, and Ecuador.) Bolivia, Paraguay, and Uruguay send fewer migrants to the U.S. as well, although recent events in each of these countries suggest that neoliberal development will not occur independent of international migration.

Economic and Human Capital Characteristics

South Americans in the U.S. resemble Cubans more closely than they do other Latin American groups. On average, South Americans tend to be older and demonstrate more equal male-to-female ratios than these groups (see Table 3). U.S. Census data analyzed by John Logan show that on average, South American immigrants are better educated, earn higher incomes, have lower poverty rates and levels of unemployment, and are less likely to receive public assistance than Cuban immigrants (who in general fare better on such indicators than other Latin American immigrant groups, but not necessarily better than *all* U.S. immigrant groups).

Table 4 shows that on average, South Americans display higher educational attainments than most other Latin American immigrant groups. They also tend to be more heavily concentrated in white-collar managerial and technical occupations, to be less concentrated in service and blue-collar production/operation occupations, and to exhibit somewhat lower poverty rates and higher incomes. Together, these data confirm South American immigrants' different modes of economic incorporation and experiences in the U.S. labor market compared with other Latin American immigrant groups (although again, not necessarily with all U.S. immigrant groups).

Yet aggregate data hide important variation among South American groups by region and national origin, class, and legal status. On average, the Andean groups from Colombia, Peru, and Ecuador have lower educational attainments and less favorable occupations than their counterparts from the Southern Cone (defined as containing Argentina, Chile, Uruguay, and Paraguay), Brazil, and Venezuela (Boliv-

Table 3 Age, sex, citizenship status, and decade of entry of foreign-born South Americans, by country of birth, 2000

National origin	Median age	Percent male	Percent noncitizen	Percentage arriving by decade					
				1990–2000	1980–1989	1970–1979	1960–1969	Before 1960	
All foreign-born	37.0	49.8	56.3	41.7	26.7	15.3	8.6	7.7	
Colombia	38.0	45.1	58.5	45.1	27.9	14.5	10.2	2.2	
Ecuador	36.0	52.1	64.2	46.8	25.5	15.2	10.4	2.2	
Peru	38.0	48.2	60.8	46.4	31.8	12.5	7.0	2.4	
Brazil	33.0	45.9	73.7	63.3	21.0	6.5	6.4	2.9	
Guyana	39.0	41.0	39.7	34.6	41.8	17.0	5.4	1.2	
Argentina	42.0	49.6	51.3	36.8	20.7	17.0	18.6	6.9	
Venezuela	32.0	47.3	68.8	60.7	19.7	9.7	6.5	3.4	
Chile	39.0	49.5	55.3	36.9	26.0	21.7	10.3	5.1	
Bolivia	36.0	48.5	60.4	44.9	30.6	13.1	8.6	2.8	
Uruguay	42.0	50.9	48.4	28.5	31.8	23.8	13.6	2.4	
Paraguay	32.0	44.7	47.1	50.3	27.9	10.7	9.0	2.1	
Suriname[a]	36.0	41.6	49.1	57.6	21.8	8.2	6.8	5.6	

Source: U.S. Census Bureau, 2000 Census, 5% Public Use Microdata Sample, weighted data.

a. 2000 Suriname figures available only from U.S. Census Bureau, 2000 Census, 1% Public Use Microdata Sample, weighted data.

Table 4 Selected labor market characteristics among foreign-born groups from the Western hemisphere, by country of birth, 2000 (percentages)

National origin	Bachelor's degree or higher	Managerial and professional occupations	Service occupations	Median wage/salary income, 1999	Living below the poverty line, 1999
All foreign-born	26.0	29.7	16.3	$21,000	10.9
Canada	41.3	51.3	7.0	$34,000	3.5
Central America					
Mexico	4.5	9.2	22.8	$15,000	19.9
El Salvador	5.1	10.3	30.7	$15,600	14.7
Guatemala	6.3	11.8	27.9	$15,100	16.2
Honduras	8.3	13.6	24.7	$14,400	19.0
Nicaragua	14.6	18.7	20.0	$18,000	10.7
Panama	28.2	36.6	13.4	$26,000	5.8
Costa Rica	19.9	27.7	21.8	$20,800	11.7
Belize	13.8	28.7	17.1	$22,800	8.6
Caribbean					
Cuba	21.0	28.6	12.8	$22,000	8.5
Dominican Republic	10.1	18.7	21.4	$15,900	17.5
Jamaica	19.1	38.0	13.4	$26,000	7.0
Haiti	14.3	29.6	23.1	$19,000	13.6
Trinidad and Tobago	19.0	34.6	14.8	$26,000	8.3
South America					
Colombia	23.2	25.5	21.3	$18,200	12.5
Ecuador	13.7	17.6	19.4	$18,000	11.6
Peru	24.9	25.4	19.7	$20,000	8.3
Brazil	34.1	30.1	25.8	$20,000	11.7
Guyana	17.3	33.1	12.6	$25,000	6.9
Argentina	36.7	42.7	12.0	$26,700	7.5
Venezuela	46.4	41.7	11.2	$25,000	8.6
Chile	31.8	35.9	16.2	$24,000	7.2
Bolivia	25.8	30.3	21.0	$22,400	8.1
Uruguay	22.5	27.4	14.0	$25,000	5.8
Paraguay	26.1	29.2	26.0	$21,600	9.2
Suriname[a]	27.3	24.2	3.4	$10,400	7.0

Source: U.S. Census Bureau, 2000 Census, 5% Public Use Microdata Sample, weighted data. Economic categories reflect percentages among persons aged 25–64 in the labor force; education reflects percentage of persons aged 25–64.

a. 2000 Suriname figures available only from U.S. Census Bureau, 2000 Census, 1% Public Use Microdata Sample, weighted data.

ians are the exception, although their educational attainments have declined since 1980 to resemble those of other Andean groups more closely). For example, in 2000, 46 percent of Venezuelans and 37 percent of Argentines but only 14 percent of Ecuadorians aged 25 to 64 held a bachelor's degree or higher. Important class divisions also create variation between well-to-do, educated, and professional migrants and their less-educated, lower-status compatriots. Finally, undocumented immigration status is a crucial factor shaping the lives of many South American immigrants, whether they are upper-middle-class migrants who experience difficulty securing a visa or transferring a professional degree to the U.S. or migrants who started out lower on the social totem pole at home.

For example, even though the Argentine and Brazilian streams include high proportions of documented, educated, and professional migrants, each also includes a substantial number of undocumented, less-educated, and manual-laborer migrants. An August 2002 *Los Angeles Times* article cited Brazilians second only to Mexicans in the number of undocumented persons captured by the Border Patrol in San Diego County, and in 1988, Adriana Marshall showed that most Argentine migrants were manual laborers rather than professionals or technicians. In 2000, Colombians, Ecuadorians, Brazilians, and Peruvians ranked among the top 15 estimated undocumented immigrant populations in the U.S. (with estimates at 141,000, 108,000, 77,000, and 61,000, respectively). Illustrating the bifurcated and complex nature of many South American migration streams, Teófilo Altamirano estimates that nearly one out of three Peruvians and Ecuadorians in the U.S. is undocumented at the same time that highly skilled human capital emigration is becoming a serious problem in both sending countries. Thus, many South Americans do very well in the U.S., but others, especially the undocumented, fare less well. They can often be found in lower-level service and production occupations that are more isolated from mainstream Americans and that garner lower economic and social returns. They also confront various linguistic, psychological, and political hurdles that many of their compatriots do not.

Residential Patterns

For the most part, South Americans head for the major U.S. immigrant-receiving states and cities. In the 2000 Census, Colombians were concentrated in Florida (31 percent), New York (21 percent), and New Jersey (13 percent) and Peruvians in California (20 percent), Florida (19 percent), and New York and New Jersey (16 percent each). Ecuadorians were concentrated overwhelmingly in New York (46 percent) but also in New Jersey (18 percent) and Florida (10 percent), while Venezuelans were concentrated overwhelmingly in Florida (41 percent) but also in California (10 percent) and Texas (8 percent). Brazilians were concentrated in Florida (21 percent), Massachusetts (16 percent), California (11 percent), and New Jersey (10 percent), and Argentines in California and Florida (23 percent each) and New York (14 percent). Finally, Chileans were concentrated in Florida (20 percent), California (18 percent), and New York (16 percent) and Bolivians in Virginia (29 percent), California (15 percent), Florida (11 percent), and New York (10 percent).

Within these states South Americans are concentrated heavily in metropolitan areas; around half reside in the New York and Miami metropolitan areas alone.

And within these cities, South Americans settle in or near other Latin American communities. Many Colombians, Ecuadorians, and Peruvians reside near Mexicans, Cubans, and Dominicans in Queens, New York. Argentines, Brazilians, Colombians, and Venezuelans have settled throughout the greater Miami/Ft. Lauderdale area alongside other Latin Americans, while Bolivians and Peruvians rank among the principal Latino groups in the greater Washington, D.C., area, settling near Salvadorans and Mexicans. (Brazilians have also settled near established Portuguese-speaking communities in New England.) But on average, South Americans are more geographically dispersed than other Latin American groups. Several Central American and Caribbean immigrant groups are heavily concentrated in just one or two U.S. states, but only Ecuadorians and Venezuelans exhibit such concentrations at the state level. Their smaller numbers and greater geographic dispersal means that many South Americans settle outside established Latino communities, in suburban areas or alongside people who have similar class or educational but different national backgrounds. It also means that the South American communities that do exist are smaller as well as more closely linked to mainstream American society than those of other Latin American groups.

For example, it is not uncommon to hear South American names attached to settlements boasting high proportions of immigrants from a particular country or region—such as Little Colombia in Jackson Heights, Queens, Little Peru in Paterson, New Jersey, Little Brazil in Framingham, Massachusetts, Little Buenos Aires in upper Miami Beach, or Huancayo Chico, Callao City, and Quitolándia in heavily Andean settlements. However, the areas that these names describe are different from Little Havana in Miami and Dominican Heights in New York. Census data analyzed by John Logan show that on average, even though South Americans tend to live in neighborhoods where Hispanics outnumber non-Hispanic whites, "they often live in areas whose Hispanic flavor comes less from themselves than from the mélange of people from different parts of the Hispanic world." On average, South Americans are also less segregated from non-Hispanic whites and more segregated from African Americans than other Hispanic groups (with the exception of Cubans).

Social Characteristics

South American immigrants display a range of other characteristics. They come from Andean countries in central and western South America, coastal and plains areas in the north, all parts of Brazil, and countries making up the Southern Cone. They also come from distinct nation-states and are differentiated by regional origin and local ethnic affiliation within them. For example, Brazilian immigrants express local affiliations depending on their home state or town (i.e., *cariocas,* who hail from Rio de Janeiro, or *paulistas,* who hail from São Paulo). Peruvians come both from the Andean highlands and metropolitan Lima, and Ecuadorians come primarily from the southern states of Azuay and Cañar but also from coastal Guayaquil and the northern region surrounding Quito.

South American immigrants also differ by religion, language, and political affiliation. Although most are Catholic, many are traditional Protestant, evangelical, or Jewish. And although most speak Spanish, many enter the U.S. with a relatively good command of English. Furthermore, important regional and national differences exist among Spanish-speakers' dialects and vocabularies, and Brazilians speak Portuguese. Still other immigrants speak indigenous languages instead of or in addition to Spanish, such as Quechua or Aymara, which Ulises Juan Zevallos Aguilar argues is broadening traditional ethnolinguistic ideas of the "Andean archipelago" in South America. Finally, distinct political histories based on varying ethnic, racial, linguistic, and class struggles as well as distinct inter-American relations mean that South American immigrants exhibit no clear or unified political stance. To date there are few data on South American immigrants' political participation beyond naturalization rates (but see Michael Jones-Correa, 1998).

South American immigrants are also racially and ethnically diverse. Table 5

Table 5 Racial identification of foreign-born South Americans, by country of birth, 2000 (percentages)

National origin	White	Black/ Negro	American and Latin American Indian	Asian/ Pacific Islander	Other race	Two or more races[a]
Colombia	62.9	1.3	0.4	0.2	27.6	7.6
Ecuador	49.1	0.9	0.6	0.3	40.4	8.6
Peru	48.5	0.6	1.1	1.4	41.1	7.2
Brazil	69.7	1.9	0.1	1.3	15.4	11.6
Guyana	2.3	44.7	1.6	21.4	14.4	15.7
Argentina	84.4	0.4	0.1	1.0	9.1	5.0
Venezuela	70.4	2.1	0.3	1.4	19.1	6.7
Chile	73.6	0.4	0.3	0.3	19.5	6.0
Bolivia	60.9	0.7	1.0	0.3	29.1	8.0
Uruguay	80.5	0.2	0.0	0.5	11.3	7.4
Paraguay	65.8	1.1	1.5	3.6	21.0	6.9
Suriname[b]	12.2	41.3	0.0	18.1	22.7	5.7

Source: U.S. Census Bureau, 2000 Census, 5% Public Use Microdata Sample, 2000, weighted data.

a. The 2000 Census allowed all respondents to specify more than one major U.S. racial category for the first time; details on the specific racial categories marked by respondents who marked more than one are not provided here. In 2000 the U.S. Census's race question remained separate from its Hispanic origin/ethnicity question.

b. 2000 Suriname figures available only from U.S. Census Bureau, 2000 Census, 1% Public Use Microdata Sample, weighted data.

shows that most consider themselves white and trace their ancestry to European populations (Spanish, Portuguese, Italian, German, Polish, Ukrainian, etc.). A few (mostly from Guyana and Suriname, but also from Brazil, Venezuela, and Colombia) consider themselves black and trace their ancestry to African slaves brought to South America long ago. Still others consider themselves a mix of European, Amerindian, and/or African heritages, or trace their ancestry to Middle Eastern and Asian immigrants who migrated to South America in the 20th century (e.g., Brazilian and Peruvian migrants of Japanese heritage, Venezuelan and Paraguayan migrants of Lebanese or Korean heritage). As South Americans enter the U.S., their racial identifications often come into conflict with prevailing American ideas of race, which tend to force racial identifications into bounded categories, emphasize African and indigenous over European features, and impose a new racialized ethnic category (Hispanic/Latino) on all immigrants from Latin America. Many South American immigrants, especially Brazilians, are confused by their inclusion within this group, which they see as a derogatory label directed at poor and uneducated Mexican, Caribbean, and Central American minority groups rather than an accurate reflection of their own social, historical, political, and racial backgrounds. Many draw on their regional, national, and linguistic identities, as well as their relatively higher economic and political standing vis-à-vis other Latin American groups in the U.S., to distinguish themselves in a more positive manner. At the same time, the question of whether South Americans will "become" Hispanics/Latinos over time and generations is a topic that warrants more research.

Cultural Adaptations and Influences

In the U.S., South Americans' sense of identity and community frequently revolve around social and religious networks—sports and social clubs, church groups, music and dance festivals, and the like. These associations provide valuable social support to new immigrants, helping them maintain country-of-origin values, manage migration and adaptation pressures, collect money to remit home, and even organize politically. For example, Peruvians now have over 450 voluntary associations in the U.S., based on local and regional affiliations in Peru as well as socioeconomic and cultural concerns in this country, and since 1984 annual national conventions have brought these associations together. Other South American immigrant groups are less organized at the national level, but soccer leagues (Arlington Bolivian Soccer League in northern Virginia), restaurants (Confitería Buenos Aires Bakery/Café in Miami), immigrant advocacy groups (Brazilian Immigrant Center in Boston), cultural associations (Uruguayan Cultural Association in West Palm Beach), nonprofit organizations (Venezuelan American Brotherhood Foundation), music festivals and groups (Ecuadorian *sanjuanistas* and Argentine tango societies), immigrant newspapers (*The Brasilians* in New York), professional organizations (Peruvian American

Medical Society), and even political organizations (American Colombian Democratic Organization) provide institutional space for new immigrants to fraternize and organize along various lines.

Hemispheric Transformation

The U.S. has been South Americans' preferred destination for several decades. In 2002 almost half of Peruvian emigrants resided in the U.S., as did most Brazilian emigrants in 2000. In fact, according to recent research by David Kyle, recent Ecuadorian migrants in Spain still express a desire to end up in New York City, where they can earn their livings directly in American/Ecuadorian dollars. However, South Americans are increasingly heading to other countries, notably Spain and Japan. Using 2005 data from the Organization for Economic Cooperation and Development (OECD), the geographer Marie Price calculates that while over 60 percent of Peruvian, Bolivian, Colombian, and Guyanese immigrants going to OECD countries choose the U.S., only 40 to 60 percent of Venezuelan and Ecuadorian immigrants do so (and the percentage among Ecuadorians is decreasing), and less than 40 percent of Chileans, Argentines, and Brazilians do so.

The United States' role in South Americans' migration schemas plays out in several ways. An important one is that immigrant remittances are increasing, and by extension exerting more weight on South American countries' future economic and social development plans. The Multilateral Investment Fund at the Inter-American Development Bank reports that in 2003 remittances totaled $5.2 billion for Brazil, $3.1 billion for Colombia, $1.7 billion for Ecuador, $1.3 billion for Peru, $340 million for Bolivia, $247 million for Venezuela, $225 million for Argentina, $137 million for Guyana, and $42 million for Uruguay (figures are not available for Chile and Paraguay). Many remittances come from migrants in the U.S., although South American figures are distinguished from Mexican and Central American ones precisely because a higher proportion come from migrants outside the U.S.

At the dawn of the 21st century, South America faces a range of major economic, political, and social concerns. What merits theoretical attention about current South American emigrants, no matter where they go, is the fact that many of them come from countries once known for economic stability and immigration, not emigration. Today the U.S. is the only country in the Western Hemisphere that has not yet witnessed a major exodus of its own people.

Furthermore, demand-side changes in receiving countries are producing new incentives for emigration. To fill labor demands, employers in the U.S., Canada, and Europe are looking to Central and South America as sources of educated workers frustrated with their existing opportunities. Future trade agreements may help South American countries respond to current economic and social realities in the long run through major neoliberal adjustments. But there is little doubt that they will also encourage migration in the short run, by virtue of being "penetrative forces." Thus, given the relative recency of South American immigration in the U.S. and current instabilities throughout South America, the most important research on South American immigrants will be produced in years to come.

Bibliography

Altamirano, Teófilo. 1990. *Los que se fueron: peruanos en los Estados Unidos* [*Those Who Left: Peruvians in the United States*]. Lima: Pontifícia Universidad Católica del Peru, Fondo Editorial.

Berg, Ulla D., and Karen Paerregaard, eds. 2005. El quintosuyo: Transnacionalidad y formaciones dispóricas en la migración perunana [El Quintosuyo: Transnationalism and Diasporic Formations in Peruvian Migration]. Lima: Instituto de Estudios Peruanos.

Beserra, Bernadete. 2003. *Brazilian Immigrants in the United States: Cultural Imperialism and Social Class.* New York: LFB Scholarly.

Cordova, Carlos, and Raquel Pinderhughes. 1999. "Central and South Americans in the United States." In Elliott R. Barkan, ed., *A Nation of Peoples: A Sourcebook on America's Multicultural Heritage,* pp. 96–118. Westport, Conn.: Greenwood.

Grimson, Alejandro, and Edmundo Paz Soldán. 2000. *Migrantes bolivianos en la Argentina y los Estados Unidos* [*Bolivian Migrants in Argentina and the United States*]. La Paz: Editorial Offset Boliviana.

Jokisch, Brad, and Jason Pribilsky. 2002. "The Panic to Leave: Economic Crisis and the 'New Emigration' from Ecuador." *International Migration* 40, 4: 75–101.

Jones-Correa, Michael. 1998. *Between Two Nations: The Political Predicament of Latinos in New York City.* Ithaca, N.Y.: Cornell University Press.

Kyle, David. 2000. *Transnational Peasants: Migrations, Networks, and Ethnicity in Andean Ecuador.* Baltimore: Johns Hopkins University Press.

Latino Studies 3, 1. 2005. "Special Feature: *Los que llegaron:* South American Immigrants in the United States."

Margolis, Maxine. 1994. *Little Brazil: An Ethnography of Brazilian Immigrants in New York City.* Princeton, N.J.: Princeton University Press.

Marrow, Helen B. 2003. "To Be or Not to Be (Hispanic or Latino): Brazilian Racial and Ethnic Identity in the United States." *Ethnicities* 3, 4: 427–64.

Marshall, Adriana. 1988. "Emigration of Argentines to the United States." In Patricia R. Pessar, ed., *When Borders Don't Divide: Labor Migration and Refugee Movements in the Americas,* pp. 129–41. Staten Island, N.Y.: Center for Migration Studies.

Martes, Ana Cristina Braga, and Soraya Fleischer, eds. 2003. Fronteiras cruzadas: Etnicidade, gênero, e redes sociais [Crossed Frontiers: Ethnicity, Gender, and Social Networks]. São Paulo, Brazil: Paz e Terra.

Price, Marie. Forthcoming. "South Americans." In Ines Miyares and Christopher Airriess, eds., *Contemporary Geographies in America.* Lanham, Md.: Rowman & Littlefield.

Salazar, Miguel. 1998. "Talento venezolano en los Estados Unidos, Canada, y el Japón [The Highly-Skilled Venezuelan Diaspora in the United States, Canada, and Japan]." Colección Estudios No. 6. Caracas: Fondo Editorial Fundayacucho.

Zevallos Aguilar, Ulises Juan. 2000. "Hácia una topografía del archipiélago cultural andino [Toward a Topography of the Andean Cultural Archipelago]." *Socialismo y participación* 87 (May): 101–10.

South Asia

Pakistan, Bangladesh, Sri Lanka, Nepal

Nazli Kibria

Here we look at four contemporary immigrant groups, with origins in the countries of Bangladesh, Nepal, Pakistan, and Sri Lanka. Among the specific themes to be considered is the emerging nature and significance of the "South Asian" identification as a basis of political and cultural community for these populations. Within the U.S., Bangladeshis, Nepalese, Pakistanis, and Sri Lankans often face an ascribed or externally imposed identity as "South Asian," a rubric reflected in the available scholarship. As a result, the particular characteristics of these four groups remain largely unnoted, submerged within general discussions of South Asian immigrant life. This is particularly true given the far smaller numbers and more recent U.S. immigration histories of these groups in comparison with those of Asian Indians, whose experiences have defined understandings of the South Asian immigrant experience.

History of U.S. Immigration and Settlement

The shared histories of Bangladesh, Nepal, Pakistan, and Sri Lanka include British colonialism in the Indian subcontinent. As a consequence, for much of the 20th century, immigration from these countries to the West was primarily directed toward Britain. Facilitating this movement was the British Nationality Act of 1948, which allowed the citizens of its former colonies unrestricted entry into the country until its repeal in the 1970s. Since the 1970s, labor migration to the Middle East has also been an important feature of many of the South Asian national economies. Migrant remittances have become an important source of national revenue, and an institutionalized culture of international labor migration has emerged in many parts of South Asia.

It is only since the 1980s that the United States has become an important destination for migrants from Bangladesh, Nepal, Pakistan, and Sri Lanka. As is the case with international migrant flows in general, movements to the U.S. have no doubt been fueled by the forces of economic and cultural globalization and especially ongoing economic scarcities and inequities within the societies of these countries. More specific "push" factors include the decline in the 1990s of labor opportunities in the Middle East as well as the rise of civil unrest in many parts of South Asia. Of particular note is the situation in Sri Lanka, which was plagued by violence in the 1980s and 1990s owing to ethnic tensions between the Sinhalese majority and Tamil separatists. Conditions of instability have also marked Nepal since the mid-1990s because of a Maoist insurgency.

Scholars of South Asians in the U.S. have noted three immigration phases. The first and earliest phase took place in the late 19th and early 20th centuries and involved relatively small numbers of Sikh men from the state of Punjab in India. The second phase was marked by the passage of the 1965 Immigration Act and the dramatic growth in opportunities it created for people of Asian origin to immigrate to the U.S. In the second phase, which includes the decade and a half that immediately followed passage of the act, most South Asian immigrants were Indians and Pakistanis, with relatively few people of other nationalities. They also had an overwhelmingly middle-class profile, as the employment-based provisions of the 1965 act encouraged the entry of those with technical and professional skills.

The third phase of South Asian immigration began in the 1980s and continues to the present time. It is in this third phase that immigrants from Bangladesh, Nepal, and Sri Lanka have become notable elements of the South Asian inflow, although Indians continue to make up the numerical majority of South Asian immigrants. As reflected in Table 1, the last two decades of the 20th century were clearly a time of sharp growth in numbers for these four populations. Pakistanis are the largest group, followed by Bangladeshis, Sri Lankans, and Nepalese. The growth in numbers of Bangladeshis in the U.S. has been particularly notable, rising from

Table 1   Foreign-born South Asian population growth, 1980–2000

National origin	Number			Percentage growth, 1980–2000
	1980	1990	2000	
Bangladesh	5,880	21,749	92,235	1,469
Nepal	1,280	2,384	12,265	858
Pakistan	32,620	87,643	233,020	614
Sri Lanka	5,780	14,057	25,922	349
Total	47,540	127,823	363,442	

Source: U.S. Census Bureau, 2000 Census, 5% Public Use Microdata Sample, weighted data.

5,880 in 1980 to 92,235 in 2000. Among other things, these numbers suggest a high proportion of recent immigrants within these populations today.

U.S. Census data show the states of California and New York to be particularly important areas of settlement for immigrants from Bangladesh, Nepal, Pakistan, and Sri Lanka. According to the 2000 Census, 6,694 Sri Lankans (25.8 percent of all foreign-born Sri Lankans) and 32,998 Pakistanis (14.2 percent of all foreign-born Pakistanis) live in California. New York is home to 43,147 Bangladeshis (46.8 percent) and 51,895 Pakistanis (22.3 percent). While California and New York are the top-ranking states of settlement for all four groups, they do differ with respect to the concentrations of each group within them. The third-ranking state of settlement also varies across the four groups, including New Jersey for Bangladeshis, Virginia for Nepalese, Illinois for Pakistanis, and Massachusetts for Sri Lankans.

Table 2 presents information on entrants from the four countries from 1996 to 2002 by category of legal admission. With the exception of immigrants from Nepal, family-related admissions constitute the major mode of legal entry during this period. This is particularly so for Pakistanis, reflecting perhaps their longer history of settlement in the U.S. in comparison with the other populations. Employment-based preferences are particularly important for immigrants from Nepal and Sri Lanka, possibly indicating their use of the employment-related entry provisions, particularly for skilled labor, put forward under the Immigration Act of 1990. In the case of Sri Lankans, the ability to use these provisions has undoubtedly been facilitated by high levels of achievement in literacy and education in the country of origin. The H-1B visa program, under which three- to six-year visas are given to foreign workers whose specialized skills are sought by U.S. companies, is an important entry provision for Indians in technology fields.

Table 2 also shows that the 1986 Immigration Reform and Control Act (IRCA) and "refugee and asylee adjustments" have played a relatively minor role in recent admissions from Bangladesh, Nepal, Pakistan, and Sri Lanka. Of note, however, is the Diversity Program, popularly known as the green card lottery, which accounted for 30.5 percent of Bangladeshi admissions and 23.5 percent of Nepalese admissions during the period from 1996 to 2002. Designed to achieve diversity from countries with low levels of immigration to the U.S., the lottery, established in 1990, is open only to those from countries that have sent fewer than 50,000 people to the U.S. in the past five years. The immigration lottery programs of the 1980s were informally dubbed "the Irish Sweepstakes" because of their heavy use by Irish immigrants. Somewhat unexpectedly, however, the major beneficiaries of the program in the 1990s have included a number of the South Asian groups.

Observers of South Asian international migration flows have noted the numerical prevalence of men within them. As far as contemporary movements to the U.S. go, this idea receives some (albeit uneven) support from available census information on the relative numbers of men and women in the four populations. Among

Table 2   Immigrants by selected class of admission and country of birth, 1996–2002

Class of admission	Bangladesh	Nepal[a]	Pakistan	Sri Lanka	Total
Family-sponsored preferences and immediate relatives of U.S. citizens	29,559 57.4%	1,341 37.0%	84,128 75.9%	3,583 41.8%	104,568
Employment-based preferences	5,146 10.0%	1,417 39.0%	14,517 13.0%	3,093 36.0%	24,173
Refugee and asylee adjustments	863 1.6%	12 .3%	1,579 1.4%	341 3.9%	2,795
Diversity Program	15,700 30.5%	857 23.5%	10,105 9.1%	1,606 18.7%	37,292
RCA program	12 .02%	9 .2%	33 .02%	2 .002%	56
Other[b]	15 .3%	6 .1%	474 .4%	44 .5%	852
Total	51,447	3,633	110,836	8,557	227,050

Sources: U.S. Immigration and Naturalization Service, *Statistical Yearbooks,* 1996–2001, and *Yearbook of Immigration Statistics,* 2002 (Washington, D.C.: U.S. Dept. of Justice).
  a. Data for Nepal are from 1998–2002, owing to the unavailability of figures for 1996 and 1997.
  b. The "Other" row includes figures for the category "Cancellation of removal."

foreign-born Bangladeshis and Pakistanis, men strongly outnumber women. While the numbers of men and women are similar among foreign-born Sri Lankans, in the Nepalese population there are more women than men. This suggests a pattern of predominantly male migration in the Bangladeshi and Pakistani experience, a situation that is reversed in the Nepalese case.

In the aftermath of the 2001 terrorist attacks on the U.S., the legal and political context of contemporary South Asian American life has shifted, with potentially significant consequences for South Asian immigration to the U.S. South Asian immigrants, in particular men from the Muslim-majority countries of Bangladesh and Pakistan, have been subject to a variety of surveillance measures instituted by the U.S. government, including mandatory special registration and interviews with immigration authorities. Some analysts have suggested that these measures, coupled with a rise in general hostility toward Muslims, will work to depress rates of Bangladeshi and Pakistani immigration in the early part of the 21st century. Indeed, journalistic reports have noted the departure from the U.S. of many Bangladeshis and Pakistanis following 9/11, particularly among the undocumented and working-class sectors of these populations. While some of these former U.S. migrants have returned to their countries of origin, others have crossed the border to Canada, which is viewed as a less restrictive place for potential immigrants.

The full implications of the post-9/11 environment for patterns of South Asian immigration to the U.S. will become clear only in the years to come. Some support for the hypothesis that Bangladeshi and Pakistani immigration to the U.S. has fallen off, at least in the short term, is provided by data from the Immigration and Naturalization Service, which show a decline in the total number of immigrants legally admitted from these countries in 2002 in comparison with 2001. Thus, in 2001, 7,171 Bangladeshis and 16,448 Pakistanis were legally admitted to the U.S. In 2002 the comparable numbers were 5,492 and 13,743. Of note is the contrasting trend of a slight rise in Nepalese and Sri Lankan entrants, from 949 and 1,507, respectively, in 2001 to 1,138 and 1,534 in 2002.

Socioeconomic Adjustment

One of the popular images that has surrounded South Asian Americans in recent times is that they are a "model minority," with high levels of socioeconomic achievement. However, U.S. Census data reveal more complex and varied realities, which are masked by this image. For example, a significant and negative gap between the socioeconomic condition of foreign-born Indians and that of the four populations of study has emerged in recent times.

As shown in Table 3, about half of immigrants from Bangladesh, Pakistan, Nepal, and Sri Lanka are college graduates. This suggests a generally higher rate of educational attainment than that of the general U.S. population and of non-Hispanic whites. However, for all four of the groups, the rates are vastly surpassed by that of foreign-born Indians, 71.3 percent of whom are reported to be college graduates or

Table 3   Basic educational distribution of foreign-born South Asians, by country of birth, persons aged 25–64, 2000

National origin	Less than high school	High school graduate	College graduate or more	Total
Bangladesh	12,211	20,482	30,608	63,301
	19.3%	32.4%	48.4%	
Nepal	1,297	2,777	4,187	8,261
	15.7%	33.6%	50.7%	
Pakistan	28,426	51,115	84,691	164,232
	17.3%	31.1%	51.6%	
Sri Lanka	2,446	7,792	10,326	20,564
	11.9%	37.9%	50.2%	
India	76,786	150,069	563,989	790,844
	9.7%	19.0%	71.3%	

Source: U.S. Census Bureau, 2000 Census, 5% Public Use Microdata Sample, weighted data.

have postgraduate education. Within the Bangladeshi and Pakistani populations in particular, there are fairly high percentages (19.3 and 17.3, respectively) of people reporting less than a high school education, thus suggesting an emerging pattern of socioeconomic polarization within these communities. Census data from 1980 show a higher percentage of college graduates within these four populations than those indicated by the 2000 figures shown in Table 3. Possible explanations for this decline over time include the use of family reunification measures by skilled immigrants to bring less educated family members into the U.S., as well as the Diversity Program, which has provided U.S. migration opportunities to people from a wider array of socioeconomic backgrounds within the South Asian countries than in the past.

Table 4 offers information on several indicators of economic status for the four populations of study. According to the 2000 Census, median household income for the general U.S. population is $42,148 and for non-Hispanic whites is $45,904. In comparison, median household income among Bangladeshis and Nepalese is lower, a pattern that is reversed in the case of Pakistanis and Sri Lankans. However, the median household income for foreign-born Indians is $70,000, far surpassing that of foreign-born Bangladeshis, Nepalese, Pakistanis, and Sri Lankans. The presence of a significant economic gap between Indians and the four other South Asian populations is also suggested by the data on poverty rates. A far smaller proportion of Indians (5.0 percent) are below the poverty line, in comparison with Bangladeshis (16.3 percent), Nepalese (12.3 percent), and Pakistanis (11.2 percent). With the exception of Sri Lankans, the poverty figures for these populations also exceed that of the general U.S. population (9.4 percent).

In an apparent confirmation of the model minority image, many Bangladeshis,

Table 4   Indicators of economic status of foreign-born South Asians, by country of birth, 2000

National origin	Median household income[a]	Percentage of persons below the poverty line[b]	Percentage of men/women in managerial and professional occupations[b]	Percentage of self-employed persons[b]
Bangladesh	$40,000	16.3	30/35	9.1
Nepal	$32,050	12.3	42/27	6.6
Pakistan	$47,400	11.2	40/41	14.7
Sri Lanka	$62,200	7.2	56/54	12.1
India	$70,000	5.0	62/53	10.7

Source: U.S. Census Bureau, 2000 Census, 5% Public Use Microdata Sample, weighted data.

a. All households.

b. Persons aged 25–64 and in the labor force.

Nepalese, Pakistanis, and Sri Lankans in the U.S. today are employed in white-collar jobs. That is, the combined sectors of managerial/professional and technical/sales/administration occupy a majority of workers in these four populations. But the image is also challenged by the widespread presence of working-class occupations. Approximately 40 percent of foreign-born Bangladeshi men in the U.S. hold jobs in either the service sector or the production/manufacturing sector. Among foreign-born Nepalese women, 25 percent are in service sector jobs, and 23 percent of Pakistani men work in the production/manufacturing sector.

There are some notable differences across the four populations in the reported rates of women's labor force participation. Among foreign-born Sri Lankan women aged 25 to 64, 61 percent are in the labor force. This proportion is higher than that among Bangladeshis (48 percent), Pakistanis (46 percent), and Nepalese (43 percent). Table 4 shows the percentages of men and women in the labor force who are in managerial/professional occupations. We see that across the four populations, among men, the percentage of those in managerial/professional occupations is highest at 56 for Sri Lankans and lowest at 30 for Bangladeshis. For all four of the populations, these figures are lower than for Indian men, 62 percent of whom are in managerial/professional occupations. Comparing the percentages of women in these occupations, we see the concentration to be highest at 54 percent among Sri Lankan women. As for gender variations within the groups, the higher percentage of Nepalese men than women in managerial/professional occupations, a pattern that is reversed for Bangladeshis, is notable. Among Pakistanis and Sri Lankans, similar proportions of men and women in the labor force are employed in these occupations.

South Asian Ethnic Economies

Ethnic economies are an important feature of contemporary South Asian immigrant life. I use the term "ethnic economies" to refer to the clusters and networks of businesses that draw on ethnic ties for a variety of possible resources, including labor, capital, and clientele. South Asian ethnic economies in the U.S. today encompass a variety of businesses, ranging from stores that cater to South Asian consumers to those that provide services to the larger U.S. population. Besides their role in the economic adaptation of Bangladeshis, Nepalese, Pakistanis, and Sri Lankans in the U.S. today, these ethnic economies are important to intra–South Asian relations and potentially even to the development of a pan–South Asian community.

A variety of accounts suggest that South Asian business neighborhoods, such as the Jackson Heights area in New York City, are sites of entrepreneurial activity for people from all the South Asian countries. Although there is no doubt that Indian entrepreneurship is predominant, Pakistani businesses are increasingly important, as indicated by census data on rates of self-employment within the South Asian populations. As shown in Table 4, approximately 10 percent of foreign-born Pakistanis are self-employed. There are also reports that the cooperative exchange networks of business owners within these enclaves encompass South Asians of varied backgrounds, stretching across the divisions of national origins and religion. In addition, and perhaps most significantly, ethnic economies are a cross-ethnic source of employment for South Asians. It is far from uncommon for business owners and operators to employ South Asians who have a different background from their own. Of course, these employer-employee relations are not necessarily conducive to a sense of intra–South Asian amity and community, given the unequal context from which they emerge. This point is emphasized by the reported presence of systematic patterns to these relationships. Specifically, Bangladeshis and Nepalese are far more likely to be working for Indian and Pakistani business owners than the other way around. Those who are employed within these enclaves are particularly vulnerable to low wages and poor working conditions, given that they tend to be new immigrants, often with limited English-language skills and without legal status in the U.S.

The case of South Asians in the New York taxicab industry highlights some of the complex social dynamics of South Asian ethnic economies, including their potential role as a forum for cross-ethnic political organizing among these groups. Studies of this industry report that a majority of the drivers today are South Asian immigrants, of varied national origins. The South Asians who drive taxicabs are typically young, single, college-educated men, often with temporary or undocumented legal status. Driven by limited occupational alternatives, they often get into the business through networks of friends and kin. A common strategy is to coordinate day and night shifts with other cabdrivers to make maximum use of the cab rent they pay for twenty-four hours. The visibility of South Asian cabdrivers has made them a focal point for expressions of hostility against South Asian immigrants. Associations such as the Lease Drivers Coalition and the New York Taxi Workers Alliance have been formed, often through the leadership of progressive young second-generation South Asian Americans who have strived to be inclusive and multiethnic in their organizing efforts.

South Asian ethnic economies also bring South Asians together as consumers. As suggested by the common storefront sign INDO-PAK-BANGLA PRODUCTS SOLD HERE, businesses that are geared toward selling to South Asians, ranging from jewelry stores to travel agencies, typically and deliberately attract clientele of varied nationalities. In doing so, they both reflect and reinforce the presence of a pan–South Asian popular and consumer culture—what South Asians refer to as "desi" culture. Some analysts have argued that this emerging culture is diasporic, produced and consumed in multiple global sites. Desi culture both draws on and enhances shared South Asian cultural aesthetics and taste in food, clothing, music, and film. Of particular note in this respect is the famous blockbuster Bollywood movie industry, based in Bombay, India. Bollywood reaches an audience that stretches across South Asia and beyond. There is also bhangra remix, a music and dance style that originated among young Punjabis in Britain but now has fans of South Asian origin around the globe.

The Politics of Race and Identity

In 1974 the Association of Indians in America (AIA) successfully lobbied to have Asian Indians reclassified in the U.S. Census from the category "Other" (as they had been in the 1970 Census) to "Asian American." The success of their efforts has had consequences not just for Indians but for all immigrants from South Asia. Since the 1970s, South Asians have been included under the umbrella "Asian/Pacific Islander" category and have been granted official minority status.

Most observers would agree, however, that for immigrant South Asians, "Asian American" is for the most part an externally imposed label, affecting their own conceptions of identity in very limited ways. Indeed, available studies of race identity among South Asians in the U.S. today emphasize the prevalence of a strategy of disengagement from the racial order of the U.S. That is, as suggested by their experiences—in particular those of middle-class Indian immigrants, who serve as points of reference for these studies—South Asians resist incorporation into the racial order, especially as "nonwhites." They often actively work to draw attention to their national origin and/or religious affiliations and to deflect attention away from questions of racial identity.

There are reasons to believe that the strategy of racial disengagement is becoming increasingly difficult to sustain, in light of the growing complexity of the South Asian experience. For one thing, such disengagement is less feasible and effective for working-class South Asians, who tend to be more vulnerable to overt racist attacks. The post-9/11 environment has also been a challenging one for South Asians in the U.S. In the aftermath of the terrorist attacks, South Asians were the targeted victims of hate crimes and other hostilities because of a perception of their physical resemblance and thus presumed shared origins and affinity with the terrorists. Among South Asians, these attacks, in their profoundly indiscriminate nature, resulted in greater awareness of the significance of race in the U.S., and especially of their own vulnerabilities within the racial order. They have also resulted in a heightened consciousness of how South Asians are vulnerable to being "lumped together," of being seen as "the same," in the eyes of others. Of course, the exception is the situation of people from Nepal, who may be thought to look "Oriental" and thus phenotypically distinct from most people from the Indian subcontinent.

The post-9/11 era may thus be a particularly fruitful time for the development of pan–South Asian political solidarities, as South Asians of varied origins come together to tackle the shared challenges of the U.S. environment. But there is also the possibility that this will be a polarizing period, as some South Asians disidentify with or assert difference from Muslim South Asians in an effort to protect themselves from the widespread distrust and suspicion of Islam that exists in the U.S. A strategy of disidentification on the basis of religion is in some ways supported by the ongoing history of Hindu-Muslim divisions on the Indian subcontinent and the animosities that have emerged from it. It is possible that solidarities among South Asians will not be pan–South Asian but rather will develop primarily along religious lines. If this is the case, then the boundaries of national origin will be crossed as South Asian Hindus of Indian and Nepalese descent join together, differentiating themselves from South Asian Muslims of Indian, Pakistani, and Bangladeshi descent. But of course the possibility that such cross-national religious coalitions will form is itself tempered by the deeply felt national divisions of the Indian subcontinent.

Developments of Community Life

The shifting and multilayered quality of affiliations among South Asians is highlighted by the vast array of community organizations that mark their presence in the U.S. A growing number of these organizations are organized under a pan–South Asian banner. These range from social welfare groups such as Manavi (South Asian Women's Support Organization), which works against domestic violence, to political organizations such as SAALT (South Asian American Leaders of Tomorrow), which strives to foster the civic engagement of South Asians in the U.S.

Along with the creation of pan–South Asian groups, nationality-based organizations continue to be important. Among the specific consequences of 9/11 is the rapid development of organizations that are devoted to increasing the political participation and impact of their communities on the U.S. political system, particularly among Bangladeshis and Pakistanis. These include the Bangladeshi-American Foundation, Inc. (BAFI) and the National Council of Pakistani Americans (NCPA), which strives to protect the civil liberties of members. However, locally based cultural associations (for example, the Sri Lankan Association of Washington, D.C.) tend to dominate South Asian immigrant community life.

The cultural associations of South Asian Americans facilitate and encourage the practice of cultural traditions as well as fostering a sense of community. Their primary function tends to be organizing events to celebrate national holidays and festivals, but other common activities include fundraising for charitable causes in the country of origin and hosting social events that showcase homeland dignitaries. As most clearly shown in studies of Indian immigrant life, cultural associations can also be a focal point of conflict—a forum for the expression of established and emerging social fissures within the South Asian communities.

As one might expect, ethnic and regional conflicts from the country of origin (for example, the Sinhalese-Tamil conflict in Sri Lanka) are often part of the contentious internal politics of cultural associations. Other points of tension include alienation among second-generation community members, in response to feelings that only immigrant interests are reflected, and a sense of marginalization among working-class members, who keep their distance from the associations because of their elitist character and the dominance of middle-class male immigrants among their leaders. On a related note, there are growing expressions of concern about how cultural associations try to portray and promote an idealized version of the community's cultural traditions and experiences, often deliberately feeding the stereotype of South Asians as a model minority. Among the specific consequences of this strategy is the masking of social problems within the community, such as poverty and domestic violence.

A general and notable feature of South Asian community life is the simultaneous formation of associations that extend across boundaries of national origin and of others that affirm them. Thus, while the cultural associations of South Asians are often based on national origins, some also are organized by regional origins and language. The latter often include members from several countries. For example, Tamil cultural associations may bring together Tamil-speaking people from both India and Sri Lanka; similarly, Bengali cultural associations have Bengali-speaking members from both India and Bangladesh. These linguistic affiliations are also part of the vibrant South Asian immigrant media in the U.S., which often attract consumers from different national backgrounds through a shared language.

The pattern of the simultaneous presence of associations based on national origin with others that cross over national boundaries is evident also in the development of South Asian religious associations. Especially in areas of the country where there are significant numbers of a particular immigrant group, religious organizations that affirm the significance of national origins, such as Sri Lankan Buddhist temples and Pakistani mosques, have been established. At the same time, many religious organizations involve several South Asian nationalities as well as non–South Asians. For instance, the largely Hindu Nepalese immigrant population in the U.S. tends to attend Hindu temples that have been founded and organized by Indian immigrants. Among many Bangladeshis and Pakistanis as well there is growing participation in mosques and Islamic study groups that bring together Muslims of varied ethnic and national origins, including African Americans and Arab Americans.

In general, religion as a basis of organization and identity is increasingly prominent in contemporary South Asian American life. This may be particularly the case for the second generation—the children of South Asian immigrants—who may find religion to be a more compelling basis for community and identity than nationality or language. Indeed, studies of second-generation Muslim South Asians report a trend toward involvement in Islamic organizations and away from the nationality-based affiliations of their immigrant parents. These trends are part of the complex and emerging mosaic of contemporary South Asian American life.

Bibliography

Abraham, M. 2002. *Speaking the Unspeakable: Marital Violence among South Asian Immigrants in the U.S.* New Brunswick, N.J.: Rutgers University Press.

Baluja, K. F. 2003. *Gender Roles at Home and Abroad: The Adaptation of Bangladeshi Immigrants.* New York: LFB Scholarly.

Bhattacharjee, A. 2002. "Immigrant Dreams and Nightmares: South Asian Domestic Workers in North America." In S. Sarkar and E. N. De, eds., *Trans-Status Subjects: Gender in the Globalization of South and Southeast Asia,* pp. 289–308. Durham, N.C.: Duke University Press.

George, R. M. 1997. "From Expatriate Aristocrat to Immigrant Nobody: South Asian Racial Strategies in the Southern Californian Context." *Diaspora* 6, 1: 31–60.

Kurien, P. 2003. "To Be or Not to Be South Asian: Contemporary Indian American Politics." *Journal of Asian American Studies* 6, 3: 261–88.

Leonard, K. 1997. *The South Asian Americans.* Westport, Conn.: Greenwood.

———. 2000. "State, Culture, and Religion: Political Action and Representation among South Asians in America." *Diaspora* 9, 1: 21–38.

Maira, S. M. 2002. *Desis in the House: Indian American Youth Culture in New York City.* Philadelphia: Temple University Press.

Prashad, V. 2000. *The Karma of Brown Folk.* Minneapolis: University of Minnesota Press.

Williams, R. B. 1988. *Religions of Immigrants from India and Pakistan: New Threads in the American Tapestry.* Cambridge, Eng.: Cambridge University Press.

Southeast Asia

Laos, Cambodia, Thailand

Carl L. Bankston III and Danielle Antoinette Hidalgo

People with ethnic origins in Laos, Cambodia, and Thailand are members of some of the most rapidly growing groups in American society. Table 1 shows that there were only 114,210 Thai, ethnic Lao, Hmong from Laos, and Cambodians in the United States as recently as 1980. Two decades later, the Thai alone almost equaled that number, and these statistics refer only to those who gave Thai, Lao, Hmong, or Cambodian as their sole racial or ethnic background in the 1980 and 2000 Censuses. If we include all the Americans who claimed these ancestries in combination with others, the total for 1980 would not have changed significantly, but by 2000 those with backgrounds in central mainland Southeast Asia together came to about three quarters of a million people: 150,093 Thai, 196,893 Lao, 184,842 Hmong, and 212,633 Cambodians.

These groups are so new to the American population that in the 1990 Census, a majority of them had arrived only within the previous decade. By 2000, an estimated 86 percent of Cambodian Americans, 81 percent of Hmong Americans, and

Table 1   The Thai, Lao, and Cambodian populations in the U.S., 1980–2000

Detailed race category	1980	1990	2000
Thai	45,279	91,360	110,851
Lao	47,683	147,375	167,792
Hmong	5,204	94,439	170,049
Cambodian	16,044	149,047	178,043

Sources: U.S. Bureau of the Census, 2000 Summary File 4, 1990 Summary File 3, 1980 Asian and Pacific Islander Population in the U.S., Table 1.

Note: Includes both foreign-born and U.S.-born people.

74 percent of Lao Americans were either post-1980 immigrants or children who had been born since 1980. Only Thai Americans, the smallest of the groups in 2000, had a substantial minority (46 percent) who had been born abroad and arrived in the U.S. before 1980.

Connected Homelands

Americans of Laotian, Cambodian, and Thai origin come from three adjoining and culturally interlinked nations that form a cluster in the middle of Southeast Asia. The connections among the peoples of these nations go back centuries and have been renewed by events in recent history. The Thai and the Lao are particularly closely related, and their dominant ethnicities may be regarded as two branches of a single cultural and linguistic group, whereas Cambodians are culturally and linguistically distinct. Still, anyone who is familiar with Thai or Lao will often be struck by how many Cambodian words sound similar to words in the other two languages. This is not only a result of centuries of cultural and linguistic exchange, but also a consequence of the fact that the words and practices of the three nations often have a common Indian origin. Unlike Vietnam, which was more heavily influenced by China, Thailand, Laos, and Cambodia took India as their primary cultural model, and their peoples generally practice Theravada Buddhism, sometimes known as the southern school or Hinayana.

Another reason for the interconnection among these groups has been the modern history of warfare and exile in their region. The U.S. became heavily involved in this geographic area as a result of the Vietnam War. During the 1960s, the CIA recruited members of the Hmong, an ethnic group living in the mountains of Laos, to form a secret army to fight against leftist forces in Laos who were allied with the North Vietnamese and Vietcong.

Many refugees from the wars in Laos and Cambodia fled first to Thailand, which created linkages (and also tensions) between the Thai and the refugees. This migration has also complicated immigration statistics based on place of birth. Many first-generation Americans whose place of birth is listed as Thailand in census or Immigration and Naturalization Service (INS) statistics were born in refugee camps in Thailand to parents who had fled from Laos or Cambodia. Calculations from an individual-level sample of census data indicate that in 2000, over 8 percent of all Lao Americans, over 14 percent of all Hmong Americans, and about 6 percent of all Cambodian Americans were born in Thailand. If we concentrate only on immigrants and we remove the U.S.-born people from these calculations, then over 12 percent of immigrants in the U.S. of Lao ethnicity, more than 25 percent of immigrants of Hmong ethnicity, and about 10 percent of immigrants of Cambodian ethnicity were born in Thailand.

Resettlement in the United States

Lao and Hmong. Two thirds of people of Lao ethnicity and just over half (56 percent) of the Hmong in the U.S. in 2000 were born outside this country. Among people aged 30 or more, over 99 percent of both groups were foreign-born. With the fall of South Vietnam to North Vietnamese forces, the fall of Cambodia to the communist Khmer Rouge, and the assumption of power by communist forces in Laos in the spring of 1975, the U.S. Congress passed the Indochina Migration and Refugee Assistance Act in order to admit Southeast Asians who had been closely associated with American military activities. The ensuing first wave of refugees included 126,000 Vietnamese and 4,600 Cambodians, but only 800 refugees from Laos were admitted.

At the end of 1975, Congress agreed to accept more of the people from Laos who were languishing in refugee camps in Thailand. During the following year, the U.S. brought in 10,200 Laotian refugees who had been living in the Thai border camps. Most admitted at that time were family members of people who had been employed by the U.S. Agency for International Development, the U.S. Information Service, or the U.S. embassy in the Laotian capital, Vientiane.

In the late 1970s these numbers went down again, to 400 in 1977, but then rose to 8,000 in 1978, when war between Vietnam and Cambodia caused new, highly publicized waves of migration within Southeast Asia, bringing increased public attention to the region and creating a favorable environment for the admission of new Southeast Asian refugees. Refugee resettlement in the U.S. of people from Laos grew to 30,200 in 1979, 55,500 in 1980, and 19,300 in 1981, or about 105,000 individuals during this three-year period.

As shown in Table 2, refugee admissions from Laos never again reached the high point of 1980, and the admissions slowed to a trickle by the end of the 20th century. In addition, there was a shift from "refugee" to "immigrant" in the classification of arrivals from Laos, largely as a result of two trends: the gradual winding down of the movement of refugees from Southeast Asia and the growth of the Lao American population. Because U.S. immigration policy stresses family reunification, as U.S. citizens and residents of a given national or ethnic group increase in numbers, more people in that group are allowed into the country as family members.

Cambodians. Two thirds of all Cambodian Americans and over 99 percent of Cambodian Americans older than 30 were born outside the U.S., according to the 2000 Census. Most Cambodians arrived as refugees. From 1975 until the end of 1978, the brutal Khmer Rouge ruled Cambodia; war with Vietnam broke out in December 1978, and by January 1979 the Vietnamese had conquered the Cambodian capital, Phnom Penh. Under the Khmer Rouge, virtually all of Cambodia was turned into a collection of forced labor camps, and the war made it possible for

Table 2   Refugees and immigrants of Lao, Cambodian, and Thai origin admitted to the U.S., 1975–2001

Year	Lao origin[a]		Cambodian origin[a]		Immigrants born in Thailand[b]
	Refugees	Immigrants	Refugees	Immigrants	
2001	22	896	23	2,398	4,291
2000	64	672	0	2,106	3,785
1999	19	471	0	1,361	2,381
1998	9	502	7	1,377	3,102
1997	915	572	9	1,475	3,094
1996	2,203	692	5	1,358	4,310
1995	3,682	572	6	1,224	5,136
1994	6,211	607	15	847	5,489
1993	6,944	738	63	931	6,654
1992	7,285	670	163	878	7,090
1991	9,232	5,792	179	2,564	7,397
1990	8,715	6,364	2,329	3,577	8,914
1989	12,560	6,973	2,162	4,425	9,332
1988	14,597	6,037	2,897	7,098	6,888
1987	13,394	3,557	1,786	8,494	6,733
1986	12,313	4,239	9,845	9,013	6,204
1985	5,195	212	19,175	198	5,239
1984	7,218	185	19,727	193	4,885
1983	2,907	159	13,041	163	5,875
1982	3,616	130	6,246	129	5,568
1981	19,777	78	38,194	113	4,799
1980	55,500	179	16,000	148	4,115
1979	30,200	NA	6,000	NA	3,194
1978	8,000	NA	1,300	NA	3,574
1977	400	237	300	126	3,945
1976	10,200	163	11,000	126	6,923
1975	800	96	4,600	98	4,217

  a. *Source:* Southeast Asia Resource Action Center, Americans From Cambodia, Laos, and Vietnam: Statistics. Retrieved on January 27, 2003, from www.searac.org.

  b. *Source:* Immigration and Naturalization Service, Yearbooks of Immigration Statistics, 1975–2001.

thousands of Cambodians to flee to neighboring Thailand. The agonies of the Cambodian people were widely publicized and aroused international sympathies. At the same time, the plight of refugees fleeing from Vietnam also received media attention. In response, the U.S. government passed the Refugee Act of 1980, which led to the resettlement of thousands of Southeast Asian refugees.

Table 2 shows that large-scale refugee movement from Cambodia to the U.S. began in the year of the Refugee Act. In 1981 over 38,000 Cambodian refugees reached the U.S. By the end of the 1980s, numbers of Cambodian refugees began to decline. After 1995, 1,000 to 2,000 legal immigrants per year replaced the refugees from Cambodia.

Thai. Nearly eight of every ten people who identified themselves as Thai to the U.S. Census in 2000 were born outside the U.S. Almost one fourth of the foreign-born Thai Americans had arrived only in the previous five years, and well over one third had reached the U.S. during the 1990s. Unlike the Cambodians and the two groups from Laos, though, Thai Americans have arrived as immigrants, not refugees.

Small numbers of immigrants from Thailand began to arrive after the U.S. liberalized its immigration laws in 1965. Many of these early immigrants were highly skilled professionals in areas such as medicine and engineering, seeking opportunities that were unavailable in Thailand at that time. During the mid- to late 1960s, a larger number of immigrants came as a result of marriage with American military personnel stationed in Thailand for the war in Vietnam, Laos, and Cambodia. According to census data, women made up 62 percent of the Thai American population in 1980, 63 percent in 1990, and just over 60 percent in 2000.

Table 2 shows the numbers of immigrants born in Thailand admitted to the U.S. Some of these individuals were not Thai but members of the other Southeast Asian groups born in refugee camps in Thailand. It will be noted that immigration from Thailand varied much less than that of people from Cambodia and Laos and did not show the huge influx in the 1980s of these other two groups. As shown here, women have always outnumbered men among immigrants from this country, especially during the last years of American involvement in the Vietnam War.

Areas of Settlement and Ethnic Communities

Table 3 shows the distribution of the Southeast Asian groups among the states. Clearly, California has the largest number of Southeast Asian immigrants. In 2000, Los Angeles was home to over 30,000 Cambodians, and nearly 5,000 lived in neighboring Orange County. Within Los Angeles, Long Beach had the greatest concentration, with about 20,000 people of Cambodian ethnicity; by the mid-1980s, the area along 10th Street in Long Beach had become known among Cambodian Americans as the "New Phnom Penh." Lowell, Massachusetts, was home to the greatest concentration of Cambodians in the eastern U.S., with a population of about 11,000. In the Northwest, approximately 15,000 Cambodians lived in the Seattle area, mostly in Seattle itself.

The Los Angeles area was also home to nearly one out of every four Thai Americans in 2000, with 20,000 residing in Los Angeles County and over 3,000 in neighboring Orange County. At the beginning of the year 2000, the section of Hollywood Boulevard between Western and Normandie Avenues was officially designated "Thai Town." Other cities with fairly large Thai concentrations were

Table 3   Estimated distribution of the Lao, Hmong, Cambodian, and Thai people in U.S. states, 2000 (percentages)

State	Lao	Hmong	Cambodian	Thai
Alabama	0.9	0.0	0.4	0.4
Alaska	0.2	0.4	0.0	0.4
Arizona	0.9	0.0	0.6	2.2
Arkansas	1.3	0.5	2.4	0.2
California	35.0	43.7	35.2	38.0
Colorado	0.8	4.7	0.1	1.7
Connecticut	2.8	0.0	1.8	1.8
Delaware	0.1	0.0	0.1	0.4
District of Columbia	0.2	0.0	0.0	0.0
Florida	2.6	0.2	2.4	5.5
Georgia	4.0	1.1	0.5	2.1
Hawai'i	0.6	0.0	0.5	0.5
Idaho	0.0	0.0	0.0	0.1
Illinois	2.1	0.0	0.8	4.7
Indiana	0.0	0.0	0.4	0.6
Iowa	1.5	0.0	0.3	0.2
Kansas	1.3	0.6	0.6	0.4
Kentucky	0.5	0.0	0.4	0.1
Louisiana	0.5	0.0	0.0	0.7
Maine	0.0	0.0	0.7	0.0
Maryland	0.0	0.0	2.8	1.9
Massachusetts	1.8	1.2	13.3	1.7
Michigan	2.7	2.6	1.1	1.1
Minnesota	5.2	20.2	2.2	1.0
Mississippi	0.0	0.0	0.3	0.4
Missouri	0.1	0.0	0.1	0.7
Montana	0.0	0.0	0.0	0.0
Nebraska	0.0	0.0	0.0	0.6
Nevada	0.8	0.0	0.4	2.7
New Hampshire	0.4	0.0	0.1	0.0
New Jersey	0.2	0.3	0.6	1.6
New Mexico	0.4	0.0	0.0	0.1
New York	1.9	0.4	1.0	6.6
North Carolina	3.5	4.7	2.4	1.1
North Dakota	0.0	0.0	0.0	0.0
Ohio	3.5	0.0	1.2	1.3
Oklahoma	1.7	0.4	0.1	1.1
Oregon	1.7	1.1	2.1	0.5
Pennsylvania	1.7	0.1	2.6	1.8
Rhode Island	1.3	0.0	2.2	0.7
South Carolina	0.7	0.0	0.5	1.5
South Dakota	0.4	0.0	0.0	0.4
Tennessee	0.4	0.0	1.1	0.4
Texas	6.4	0.0	4.4	4.1

Table 3   Estimated distribution of the Lao, Hmong, Cambodian, and Thai people in U.S.
states, 2000 (percentages) (continued)

State	Lao	Hmong	Cambodian	Thai
Utah	2.1	0.0	0.9	0.5
Vermont	0.0	0.0	0.0	0.1
Virginia	2.8	0.0	3.2	3.0
Washington	4.7	2.6	12.6	4.3
West Virginia	0.0	0.0	0.0	0.0
Wisconsin	2.7	15.0	0.0	0.9
Wyoming	0.0	0.0	0.0	0.0

Source: 2000 U.S. Census, Summary File 4.
Note: Includes both foreign-born and U.S.-born people.

New York, which was home to over 4,500 Thai Americans in 2000, and Chicago, where about 2,700 Thai Americans lived.

The Hmong were especially determined to build ethnic communities in the U.S. Since many were initially resettled in Minnesota, the city of St. Paul became a magnet, and by the end of the 20th century Hmong was the single largest non-English language spoken in St. Paul's public schools. By 2000, Minneapolis and St. Paul together were home to an estimated 40,000 Hmong. Other Hmong sought to live in the warmer climate of California, seeking relatively rural areas. By the mid-1980s, about 20,000 had resettled in the three Central Valley counties of Merced, San Joaquin, and Fresno. U.S. Census data indicated that approximately 24,000 Hmong lived in Fresno, another 6,000 in San Joaquin, and 6,600 in Merced. Another 17,000 to 18,000 Hmong had settled in Sacramento County, bordering San Joaquin County on the north, by 2000.

The ethnic Lao were the least concentrated of the groups, often forming small communities in various parts of the U.S. Texas was home to a number of these, with populations of roughly 500 to 1,000 Laotians in Amarillo, Dallas, Euless, Houston, and Irving. An estimated 3,000 to 4,000 Lao Americans lived in St. Paul and Minneapolis, drawn by the support programs that also served the Hmong.

Despite their concentration in Los Angeles, Thai Americans were fairly widely distributed around the country, partly because large proportions of Thai immigrants arrived in the U.S. as the spouses of American citizens, as professional employees, or as students. Refugees from Laos and Cambodia, in contrast, were intentionally dispersed by the U.S. government, which initially planned to scatter them around the country in order to minimize the impact on receiving communities and integrate them into American society as quickly as possible. The government also made use of local voluntary agencies for support and assistance in resettling Southeast Asians. Therefore, Hmong, ethnic Lao, and Cambodians tended to go where there were agencies willing to help them and communities willing to receive them. To some extent, this undercut the plan to disperse them. Minnesota and Wisconsin, for example, took in Hmong refugees because church groups, particularly those connected to the Lutheran faith, offered to sponsor Hmong. Similarly, Massachusetts built a Cambodian community because voluntary associations in Lowell and other cities offered to sponsor Cambodians. After communities had been formed, later immigrants tended to go where family members had already settled. For example, although the State Department stopped sending Hmong refugees without family members in Minnesota to that state, Minnesota's Hmong population continued to grow as a result of family reunification. The desire to live with coethnics accordingly produced ethnic clusters in several seemingly unlikely places.

Theravada Temples

As mentioned, the Southeast Asian peoples described here except the Hmong are mainly Theravada Buddhists, and their homelands have close cultural identifications with Buddhism. (Most Hmong and many of the minority ethnic groups in Laos and Thailand practice animism.) Buddhist temples have therefore become cultural centers for Thai, ethnic Lao, and Cambodians in North America. According to Wendy Cadge, a scholar specializing in Thai American Buddhism, about 87 Thai temples, or *wats,* have been established in 29 states. These temples help to maintain transnational connections, since the monks have generally been trained in Thailand and the temples sometimes receive financial assistance from the Thai government. Further, Thai American children's participation in cultural events at the *wat* serves as an important link to networks in Thailand and to their cultural heritage.

Lao and Cambodian Americans often attend Thai temples. However, the refugee groups have also established their own temples. In the mid-1980s, the New York Cambodian community opened the first Cambodian Buddhist temple in the city in a converted two-story house in the Bedford section of the Bronx. By 2004 there were Cambodian American Buddhist temples in at least 15 states, with an estimated 15 temples in California—at least 6 in Long Beach alone—and 8 in Massachusetts. At the beginning of the 21st century there were at least 76 Lao temples in the U.S., in almost every state. California was home to an estimated 20 of these.

Status, Income, and Employment

Among the non-Vietnamese Southeast Asian groups in the U.S., the Thai were in the most favorable economic positions and the Hmong were in the least favorable, as shown by Table 4. One common measure of social and economic status is the Duncan Socioeconomic Index, which scores people according to their income, edu-

Table 4 Socioeconomic indicators among the Thai, Cambodian, Lao, Hmong, and total U.S. populations, 1990–2000

Indicator	All U.S.		Thai		Cambodian		Lao		Hmong	
	1990	2000	1990	2000	1990	2000	1990	2000	1990	2000
Median SES	44.0	44.0	44.0	42.2	18.0	34.8	18.0	26.7	18.0	32.8
Percentage SES <25	36.8	34.2	43.4	38.6	57.9	50.4	69.0	59.0	63.1	51.2
Percentage SES 26–50	28.2	31.2	29.3	24.8	26.5	26.7	21.9	26.8	26.2	27.4
Percentage SES 51–75	28.4	28.3	18.7	27.0	14.9	17.3	8.2	12.1	9.7	18.1
Percentage SES >75	6.6	6.3	8.6	9.6	0.6	5.6	0.9	2.1	1.0	3.3
Unemployment rate	6.2	3.7	5.3	2.5	13.3	3.6	9.7	5.0	26.1	7.1
Poverty rate	13.1	9.1	12.6	14.4	36.9	29.3	31.4	18.5	62.6	37.8
Percentage with public assistance	7.5	3.4	21.8	2.0	61.4	22.4	50.2	14.2	73.3	30.3
Median household income	$30,056	$41,994	$41,850	$40,329	$22,000	$36,155	$24,098	$42,978	$15,370	$32,076
As percentage of median U.S. income	—	—	139.0	96.0	73.2	86.1	80.1	102.0	51.1	76.4
Median per capita income	$14,420	$21,587	$11,587	$19,966	$3,520	$10,366	$4,274	$11,830	$2,101	$6,600
As percentage of median U.S. income	—	—	80.4	88.3	24.4	48.0	29.6	54.8	14.6	30.6
Home ownership (percentage)	64.2	64.4	65.4	64.2	26.8	46.0	30.4	56.9	11.5	41.2
Median home value	$78,500	$119,600	$137,500	$160,900	$95,000	$120,800	$62,500	$100,500	$67,500	$92,600

Sources: U.S. Bureau of the Census, 1990 and 2000 Censuses, authors' own 5% Public Use Microdata Sample, weighted data; U.S. Bureau of the Census, 2000 Summary File 4.

Note: Includes both foreign-born and U.S.-born people.

cational level, and occupational prestige. This index, which runs to just under 100, shows that on average, in 1990 and 2000, Thai Americans had a socioeconomic status about equal to that of other Americans. However, Thai Americans had somewhat higher proportions in both the highest and lowest socioeconomic levels than others did, suggesting inequality within the population. The three refugee groups show much lower socioeconomic levels than other Americans, but their socioeconomic positions improved markedly from 1990 to 2000.

In 1990, Cambodians and Hmong had very high unemployment rates, and the Lao had a rate of joblessness somewhat higher than that of the American population in general. By 2000 unemployment rates of the refugee groups had dropped dramatically, and the Thai continued to be the least likely to be out of work. Poverty rates followed similar patterns, although the Thai poverty rate had risen above that of the rest of the country by the end of the 20th century. The refugee groups had extremely high rates of poverty in 1990, but this dropped dramatically over the course of a decade. As the poverty rate dropped, dependence on public assistance also went down. Public assistance income decreased most among the Thai, from over 20 percent in 1990 to 2 percent in 2000. A large part of this decrease can also be attributed to welfare reforms in 1996, which eliminated many forms of public assistance to immigrants.

Statistics on income and home ownership tell similar stories. The Thai resemble the larger population, and the refugee groups have made rapid progress but continue to be disadvantaged. Thai household incomes were actually slightly higher than those of other Americans in both 1990 and 2000, and Lao household incomes had surpassed those of other Americans by 2000. Household income can be misleading, though, because some groups have larger households (see Table 5), with more people to support and more workers bringing in income. All of the Southeast Asian groups had median per capita incomes substantially below the national median. In the case of the Hmong, individual income was only 30 percent of the national median in 2000, despite substantial progress over a ten-year period.

Economic well-being includes assets as well as income, and for most Americans, a home is the primary asset. Home ownership was about as common among Thai Americans as among other people in the country, but the refugee groups were all much less likely to own homes, although again there was substantial progress over the decade shown here. By 2000 a majority of Lao Americans owned their own homes and close to half the Cambodians and Hmong were homeowners. The census statistics on home values are interesting, because the Thai and Cambodians generally owned homes with somewhat higher values than those of other Americans—probably because these Southeast Asians frequently live in urban areas on the coasts, where the cost of housing is much higher than it is in other parts of the country.

Table 5 Family and marriage characteristics among the Thai, Cambodian, Lao, Hmong, and total U.S. populations, 1990–2000

Characteristic	All U.S.		Thai		Cambodian		Lao		Hmong	
	1990	2000	1990	2000	1990	2000	1990	2000	1990	2000
Average family size	3.28	3.17	3.60	3.04	5.40	4.85	5.57	5.05	7.66	7.41
Fertility	2.89	NA	2.46	NA	3.82	NA	3.86	NA	5.75	NA
Percentage of multiple-family households	9.0	12.0	15.2	17.9	22.2	14.2	12.2	6.9	4.3	12.4
Percentage of single-mother households	11.9	10.9	9.7	7.3	19.5	17.0	7.7	10.1	5.3	13.6
Percentage of single-father households	2.4	3.5	2.2	4.1	3.9	3.9	4.6	5.4	2.5	2.0
Marital status (25 and older; percentage)										
Men										
Single	14.3	16.1	23.0	33.9	14.4	21.7	18.2	17.5	7.2	11.7
Married	72.0	68.2	67.7	58.2	78.5	71.6	75.7	75.0	88.7	82.2
Divorced	8.6	10.5	6.7	5.3	2.0	2.3	2.8	3.8	1.8	3.0
Separated	2.2	2.1	1.8	1.1	2.5	2.3	2.2	2.5	0.9	1.5
Widowed	2.9	3.1	0.8	1.6	2.6	2.0	1.1	1.3	1.4	1.5
Women										
Single	10.2	12.0	11.9	16.0	9.5	11.5	7.6	13.1	4.3	6.0
Married	62.1	60.2	73.1	64.7	61.8	64.3	75.9	70.7	71.2	69.2
Divorced	10.2	12.6	9.0	11.8	4.6	6.7	4.5	5.4	4.3	7.7
Separated	2.7	2.6	2.3	2.5	5.8	4.3	3.1	3.2	3.3	5.5
Widowed	14.8	12.5	3.7	5.0	18.3	13.1	8.9	7.6	16.9	11.5

Source: U.S. Census, 1990 and 2000, 5% Public Use Microdata Sample.

Family and Marriage

Table 5 shows that Thai American families tend to be similar in size to other American families, while the refugee groups all have larger families. This is particularly notable among the Hmong, who average over seven people per family. The 2000 Census did not provide information on how many children had been born to each woman, but the 1990 Census shows fertility rates consistent with family sizes: the average Hmong woman had given birth to nearly six children.

Over the course of the decade, the probability that Cambodians and Lao would live in multiple-family households decreased, probably because refugees gradually moved out of housing with friends and non-nuclear family members and established their own homes. The Hmong, in contrast, were far more apt to live in multiple-family households. This may be a result of the fact that the Hmong have engaged in substantial secondary migration and have been moving in with other group members as they arrive in new locations.

Single-mother households have been most common among the Cambodians. In part, the especially high rate of mother-only families in this group has been a result of a high rate of widowhood, especially in 1990, when many Cambodian Americans had newly arrived from the devastation of their homeland. Hmong rates of single motherhood went up dramatically from 1990 to 2000, probably as a result of the strains of American society on their traditional ways of life.

As for marriage, Thai men are the most likely to be single of all groups, despite the fact that marriage rates of Thai women have not differed greatly from those of other American women. The reason for this disparity is made clear by the intermarriage statistics in Table 6, which show that under half of Thai American women had Thai husbands, while nearly nine out of ten Thai American men had Thai wives. This trend toward intermarriage may help us understand some of the socioeconomic statistics we have considered: Many Thai Americans have similar socioeconomic characteristics to other Americans because they are in the same families as those other Americans.

The three refugee groups all have fairly low rates of out-group marriage, but these increased slightly over the decade. One interesting trend among all groups is the growing tendency to marry other Asians. This may reflect the growth of a pan-Asian ethnicity in the U.S.

Cambodian, Thai, Lao, and Hmong people come from societies that have substantially different ideas about family and gender from those of other Americans. Among all the Southeast Asian groups, women are expected to be subordinate to men and children are expected to be subordinate to parents. Because so many Thai Americans are married to white Americans, Thai Americans often need to negotiate differences with spouses from other cultures (see Table 6). Among the groups from Laos and the Cambodians, the experience of women working outside the home can

Table 6   Ethnicity of marriage partners of the currently married Southeast Asian population, 1990–2000

Ethnic groups	1990		2000	
	Husband	Wife	Husband	Wife
Thai	42.3	87.8	39.4	86.9
White	47.2	6.4	46.5	6.0
Black	3.9	0.3	3.3	0.3
Other Asian	5.2	5.1	10.6	6.6
Other	1.4	0.4	0.2	0.3
Cambodian	94.0	95.5	85.7	90.2
White	3.0	1.1	5.3	2.0
Black	0.1	0.0	0.5	0.3
Other Asian	2.2	3.3	8.5	7.5
Other	0.7	0.1	0.0	0.0
Lao	93.8	95.5	84.7	87.5
White	2.3	1.3	5.1	3.4
Black	0.2	0.0	0.6	0.1
Other Asian	3.4	2.9	9.6	9.0
Other	0.2	0.3	0.0	0.1
Hmong	98.4	98.8	92.1	95.5
White	0.4	0.0	1.3	0.4
Black	0.0	0.0	0.0	0.0
Other Asian	1.0	1.2	6.6	4.1
Other	0.2	0.0	0.0	0.0

Sources: U.S. Bureau of the Census, 1990 and 2000 Censuses, authors' own 5% Public Use Microdata Sample, weighted data; U.S. Bureau of the Census, 2000 Summary File 4.

Note: Includes both foreign-born and U.S.-born people.

be disorienting. Women generally have much more explicit power in their families in the U.S. than they had in their homelands. This shift in power is frequently also paired with a shift in power to children, especially among the refugee groups. The children must often act as translators for their parents, giving them a marked degree of influence in their families.

Education, Language, and Youth

Given the high average socioeconomic level of Thai Americans, it is not surprising that many of them also have fairly high levels of educational attainment, as shown in Table 7. In both 1990 and 2000 they were about as likely as other Americans to be high school graduates and much more likely to be college graduates. Looking at people in the 19-to-22 age range, of traditional college age, young Thai in America were far more likely than their peers to be in institutions of higher education, partly

Table 7   Selected characteristics relating to education, language use, and youth among the Thai, Cambodian, Lao, Hmong, and total U.S. populations, 1990–2000 (percentages)

Characteristic	All U.S.		Thai		Cambodian		Lao		Hmong	
	1990	2000	1990	2000	1990	2000	1990	2000	1990	2000
People aged 25 and over										
High school graduates (25 and over)	75.2	80.4	76.1	78.4	35.8	50.5	45.0	48.3	31.1	40.3
College graduates (25 and over)	20.3	24.4	29.4	41.4	5.5	10.2	3.9	7.6	4.9	10.0
People aged 19–22 attending college	38.3	42.5	67.9	71.7	50.5	52.2	40.0	34.2	32.6	32.1
Speak English well or very well										
Under 30	95.6	97.7	89.1	84.8	72.3	92.9	79.6	92.9	63.3	86.6
30 and over	96.1	97.2	81.4	93.3	39.6	66.1	39.3	65.4	30.9	62.3
Median age	33.0	35.4	32.0	34.7	17.0	23.8	19.0	26.1	11.0	16.3
People who are minors and U.S.-born[a]	95.5	94.9	33.8	73.6	59.5	83.6	60.0	79.4	41.2	69.5
And speak only English	89.9	86.2	44.5	30.6	14.2	18.1	12.1	14.9	1.3	6.5

Sources: U.S. Bureau of the Census, 1990 and 2000 Censuses, authors' own 5% Public Use Microdata Sample, weighted data; U.S. Bureau of the Census, 2000 Summary File 4.

Note: Includes both foreign-born and U.S.-born people.

a. Minors are aged 17 or younger.

because many people of Thai ethnicity have come to this country in order to study. INS statistics show that each year in the late 1990s and early 2000s, between 11,000 and 13,000 Thai citizens were granted temporary admission as students. This reflects the recent growth of a middle class in Thailand, particularly in highly urbanized areas such as Bangkok. Also, as the data show, far more Thai women are studying in the U.S. in 2000 than in 1980. A substantial number of these students, though, remain in the U.S. after finishing their studies, further contributing to the numbers of Thai American people at high socioeconomic levels.

All three refugee groups had comparatively low levels of educational attainment in 1990, when they were still quite new to the U.S., and all three made progress in ten years. The data show clear improvements in English-language skills over time and across generations. In 1990 most Lao, Hmong, and Cambodians over 30 spoke English poorly or not at all. Just 10 years later, most of those in this age group and almost all of the people under 30 in all the refugee groups spoke English well.

Compared to Thai Americans and all other Americans, the Cambodians, Lao, and Hmong were all very young, although the median age increased somewhat over the 10-year period shown here. This was especially true for the Hmong, half of whom were under 11 in 1990 and under 16 in 2000. The youth of these groups, combined with their high fertility rates, suggests that their native-born population will grow rapidly. By 2000 most children in all of the Southeast Asian groups had been born in the U.S. Despite this, the young people retained their ancestral languages, since only small minorities of Cambodians, Lao, and Hmong spoke only English in 2000, and the percentage of monolingual Thai American children actually decreased from 1990 to 2000, a fact that may be due to continued Thai immigration. However, it should be kept in mind that this does not include the approximately 40,000 Americans of mixed Thai ancestry.

An issue that has affected all of these groups, especially the refugees, has been the sharply contrasting experiences of children and parents. Parents are overwhelmingly foreign-born and arrived in the U.S. as adults, whereas their children have grown up in the U.S. and attended American schools with other American children.

The ethnic identification of these American-born children has been a complicated matter. Thai American children, particularly in the middle classes, have shown a strong tendency to adopt a primarily "American" identity. The children of the three refugee groups often identify as "Cambodian" or "Hmong" or "Lao," but their experiences are so different from those of their parents that they identify chiefly with coethnics of their own generation. The young people see themselves as members of American minority groups rather than as distinct nationalities. There has also been some movement toward a panethnic identification, especially since many Lao and Cambodians have settled in neighborhoods with heavy Vietnamese concentrations. This identification is still fluid, though, and young people will frequently describe themselves as "Asian" in one conversation and as a member of a specific group in another.

Problems in the United States

Despite rapid socioeconomic and educational progress over a short period of time, the Southeast Asian populations have experienced a number of serious problems. Thai Americans are, on average, fairly prosperous, and the economy of Thailand developed rapidly during the late 20th century. Still, Thailand continues to have many extremely poor people, and this has led to an often unrecognized problem of poor Thai Americans facing desperate circumstances and exploitation. The problem came to national attention in August 1995, when immigration officials staged a raid on a garment factory in El Monte, California. Surrounded by barbed wire, the factory held 72 workers from Thailand, kept in virtual slavery by coethnic employers. In a number of other cases, immigration officials have found Thai women brought illegally to the U.S. and forced to work as prostitutes.

Cambodian Americans have continued to be haunted by events in Cambodia, which have often had severe psychological and even physical consequences. A number of Cambodian Americans have lost the ability to see, apparently for no physiological reason. Settled in low-income urban neighborhoods, Cambodians have often encountered violence and hostility from their neighbors. During the 1980s and 1990s, Cambodian youth gangs developed in several of these neighborhoods. Adults often had trouble finding work, since most of them had been farmers in their native land and had few skills that were relevant to life in the U.S. They were also frequently separated from other Americans by differences in culture. In 1989, for example, two Cambodian American men in Long Beach were put on trial for slaughtering and eating a German shepherd puppy that a coworker had given them as a pet.

Given the vast cultural differences between the mountains of Laos and American cities, the Hmong have dealt with their transition with strength and resilience. They have developed self-help organizations, and many have achieved rapid upward mobility. Although their parents are from a largely nonliterate society, Hmong young people have achieved a reputation for academic excellence. Still, the Hmong have experienced some of the most serious problems in adapting to American society and have had to deal with some of the most negative reactions from other Americans. A number of localities have objected to their arrival. Concerned about the influx of Hmong in Minnesota, in 1986 Republican senator Dave Durenberger asked the U.S. State Department to restrict the number of Hmong sent to that state, saying that he believed they had few prospects for employment and were difficult to assimilate. Coming from a nonliterate culture, most adult Hmong saw the U.S. as an utterly alien world. Thus, most subsisted on public assistance or on low-skilled, low-paying jobs. The welfare reform enacted by Congress in 1996 posed a serious threat to them, since it denied them several forms of public assistance. When the Department of Agriculture began cutting their food stamps in 1997, many of the Hmong were in despair, and a number in California and Wisconsin committed suicide. The Hmong were bitter, since they felt that they were in this country as a result of their service as a U.S. secret army in Laos during the Vietnam War and that the Americans owed them a debt.

The Hmong practice of "bride capture" has led to clashes with U.S. authorities. A Hmong man will sometimes seize the woman he considers to be his future wife and carry her to his home, where the marriage is consummated. This became a legal issue in 1985, in the case of *People* v. *Moua,* when a Hmong woman who had more mainstream American cultural views filed charges against the man she saw as having imprisoned and raped her.

While the ethnic Lao have not experienced the severe problems of their Hmong compatriots, they have also had their difficulties. Lao youth gangs have appeared even in small ethnic communities, and there are often serious generation gaps between parents born in Laos and children born in the U.S. Language continues to be a problem for older people. Like the other Southeast Asian groups, the Lao have frequently settled in low-income urban neighborhoods and face all the difficulties presented by their surroundings.

Despite the many problems of these very new American ethnic groups, they are rapidly becoming part of the American landscape. Although Thailand is the only one of the Southeast Asian nations that continues to send fairly large numbers of immigrants to the U.S., the youth and relatively large family sizes of the other groups ensure that their numbers will increase. The future of the Southeast Asian groups remains unclear, since each has only begun to produce a native-born generation within the past few years.

Bibliography

Bankston, Carl L. III. "Sangha of the South: Laotian Buddhism and Social Adaptation in Rural Louisiana." In Min Zhou and James V. Gatewood, eds., *Contemporary Asian America,* pp. 357–71. New York: New York University Press, 2000.

Cadge, Wendy. *Heartwood: The First Generation of Theravada Buddhism in America.* Chicago: University of Chicago Press, 2004.

Chan, Sucheng. *Survivors: Cambodian Refugees in the United States.* Champaign: University of Illinois Press, 2004.

Faderman, Lillian, with Ghia Xiong. *I Begin My Life All Over: The Hmong and the American Immigrant Experience.* Boston: Beacon, 1998.

Perreira, Todd. "Sasana Sakon and the New Asian American: Intermarriage and Identity at a Thai Buddhist Temple in Silicon Valley." In Tony Carnes and Fenggang Yang, eds., *Asian American Religions,* pp. 313–37. New York: New York University Press, 2004.

United Kingdom

Wendy D. Roth

It will undoubtedly surprise many, migration scholars as well as casual observers, to discover that the British are still among the largest foreign-born populations in the United States. The enormous influx of British immigrants from the colonial period to the early 19th century is widely recognized, as are the ensuing cultural, political, and institutional debts owed to the United Kingdom. But this influence, and British migration more generally, has become characterized as a thing of the past. The topic of British migration is now left to historians, while contemporary migration studies emphasize the changing regional, racial, and cultural character of immigrants to the U.S.

In fact, according to the 2000 Census, the population born in the United Kingdom is the ninth largest of all foreign-born populations in the U.S. It falls just behind more commonly researched sending nations—Mexico, the Philippines, India, China, Vietnam, and Cuba—as well as Germany and Canada. If the presence of a large U.K.-born population is easy to overlook owing to the almost complete absence of contemporary scholarship on this group, that lack of scholarship is itself explained by two factors. First, the cultural, linguistic, religious, and ethnic characteristics the British share with the majority of Americans make their integration particularly swift and unproblematic. In this, they are aided by their mainly middle-class professional status. British migrants' high education and strong occupational prospects have necessitated few services to support their incorporation. Second, the changing nature of British migration has removed this population from the focus of many contemporary immigration studies. The majority of those born in the U.K. come to the U.S. not as immigrants with intentions to settle permanently but as temporary workers, students, and short-term transferees within a company. Although many temporary visitors later become permanent residents, their entry and presence in the U.S. is overlooked by those in search of more traditional settlement patterns.

The U.K.-Born Population Today

In 2000 there were 824,239 people living in the U.S. who were born in the United Kingdom, 2.5 percent of the total foreign-born population. Of these, 64 percent were born in England, 12 percent were born in Scotland, 1.4 percent in Wales, and 1.7 percent in Northern Ireland. The remaining 21 percent did not specify what part of the United Kingdom they were born in.

Moreover, the population of those born in the U.K. was growing at the end of the 20th century. Between 1980 and 2000, the overall U.K.-born population increased by about 11 percent (see Table 1). Yet during this period, the number from

Table 1   U.K. citizen nonimmigrants and U.K.-born immigrants admitted to the U.S., 1983–2004

Year	Students	Temporary workers	Exchange visitors	Fiancés	Intracompany transferees	Total non-immigrants	U.K.-born immigrants
1983	8,396	9,262	8,205	424	12,196	38,483	14,830
1984	7,180	10,187	9,920	416	12,307	40,073	13,949
1985	8,108	10,270	12,675	428	12,399	43,880	13,408
1986	8,176	10,716	16,375	424	12,725	48,416	13,657
1987	8,147	12,186	19,591	339	12,761	53,024	13,497
1988	9,544	13,745	22,982	360	12,189	58,820	13,228
1989	9,928	15,152	23,717	407	11,417	60,621	14,090
1990	9,306	16,918	22,807	486	11,713	61,230	15,928
1991	7,246	18,982	22,516	581	12,483	61,808	13,903
1992	5,329	19,481	22,993	508	13,335	61,646	19,973
1993	6,205	18,530	22,242	526	14,222	61,725	18,783
1994	9,636	20,641	25,559	441	17,405	73,682	16,326
1995	8,683	21,849	22,820	381	20,210	73,943	12,427
1996	10,224	25,198	24,575	422	24,872	85,291	13,624
1997							10,708
1998	13,719	38,770	24,006	657	38,960	116,112	9,018
1999	13,626	42,226	25,090	827	44,989	126,758	7,690
2000	15,076	46,381	26,287	960	55,917	144,621	13,385
2001	15,498	47,592	28,016	1,007	60,615	152,728	18,436
2002	16,502	46,959	24,334	1,058	55,315	144,168	16,181
2003	14,852	46,990	21,856	976	51,989	136,663	9,601
2004	15,341	48,236	21,301	1,082	53,397	139,357	14,915
Percent change, 1983–2004	+82.7	+420.8	+159.6	+155.2	+337.8	+262.1	+0.6

Source: U.S. Immigration and Naturalization Service, *Statistical Yearbooks,* 1983–2004 (Washington, D.C.: U.S. Dept. of Justice). Note that 1997 figures are not available.

England increased only slightly, while those from Scotland, Wales, and Northern Ireland actually declined. According to the 2000 Census, larger proportions of U.K. migrants born in Scotland (36.8 percent), Wales (32.0 percent), and Northern Ireland (35.7 percent) came to the U.S. before 1960 than those born in England (25.3 percent), while in the 1970s, 1980s, and 1990s, the proportion of U.K. migrants who came from England was typically higher than from other parts of the U.K. The growth in the English population is small, however, compared to the substantial growth in the proportion of migrants who say they are from the United Kingdom without specifying a country, which rose from 7.3 percent in 1980 to 20.7 percent in 2000. This group is more concentrated among recent migrants; while only 16.0 percent of them migrated to the U.S. before 1960, 36.1 percent arrived in the decade between 1990 and 2000, considerably more than any other U.K. group. Given their declining proportions, migrants from Scotland, Wales, and Northern Ireland may be more likely now to see the United Kingdom as a unified entity rather than a collection of distinct countries.

Why Do They Come?

The reasons for migration are sometimes not intuitive in the case of developed sending nations. From World War II through the mid-1980s, the United Kingdom experienced net losses in immigration (meaning that it lost more people than it gained). That this was so in the decades immediately after the end of the war, when economic growth, average living standards, and employment rates were at record highs in the U.K., speaks mainly to the even greater increases in standards of living in much of the rest of the developed world. By the 1960s and 1970s, rising British unemployment and economic recession gave further impetus to extant emigration flows.

But for those looking to improve their economic opportunities abroad, Britain's ties to the Commonwealth offered strong incentives for settlement. The British government at times actively encouraged such movement. In 1953, for example, the Commonwealth Relations Office created the Overseas Migration Board, which published information about economic opportunities in the Commonwealth and for a period offered subsidized passages of £10 per person to Commonwealth countries. In more recent years, the establishment of the European Union, with its reduction of residence restrictions, has offered additional settlement options for Britons seeking their economic fortunes abroad.

Still, despite the weightier entry regulations, the U.S. provides an attractive economic and educational draw for the British. The U.K. Office of National Statistics collects information on the flows of international migrants to and from the United Kingdom. Of those born in the U.K. who migrated to the U.S. from 1991 to 2000 (with an intention to stay for a year or more), the most common reasons given for migrating were work-related, stated by 39 percent of all migrants. Another common reason, stated by 36 percent of migrants, was to join or accompany a family member, presumably one who moved for work or study; 9.6 percent of U.K.-born migrants came to the U.S. for formal study.

According to U.S. immigration statistics, the British population that is admitted as immigrants each year comprises mainly those coming for work-related reasons (along with their spouses and children) and those who marry U.S. citizens. Thirty-nine percent of U.K.-born immigrants admitted to the U.S. in 2000 came under employment-based preferences, while 46 percent were the spouses of U.S. citizens. The most common class of admission for U.S. immigrants from all nations is the family-sponsored preference system, which allows relatives to bring over those lacking the employment skills to fit in other categories. Although 28 percent of all immigrants fell in this category in 2000, only 6 percent of British immigrants did. British immigrants thus lie outside the classic immigration story; they typically come to the U.S. not to join relatives already here in search of a new life but because they marry Americans or already have the advanced skills that American employers are looking for.

A community in flux? In considering the U.K.-born population in the U.S., however, we find that looking at immigrants is only half the picture—or, in this case, far less than half. According to the U.S. Department of Homeland Security, and formerly the INS, "immigrants" are persons lawfully admitted for permanent residence in the U.S. But the vast majority of migrants from the United Kingdom are admitted for temporary residence, under the category of "non-immigrants." This includes temporary workers and trainees, exchange visitors, employees transferred within a multinational corporation, students, and fiancé(e)s of U.S. citizens. In 2000, 144,621 British citizens meeting those descriptions were temporarily admitted, and they were accompanied by 31,552 family members. By contrast, only 13,385 U.K.-born legal immigrants were admitted.

Multinational corporations with offices in both the United Kingdom and the United States particularly contribute to Britons' living temporarily in the U.S. British businesses want to bring critical personnel to the U.S., and more citizens came to the U.S. as intracompany transferees in 2000 from Britain than from any other nation in the world. In fact, with 55,917 transferees, the U.K. contributed more than one third of all intracompany transferees from Europe and nearly one fifth of all worldwide transferees. The other major category of British non-immigrants is temporary workers and trainees (46,381). Only India sent more to the U.S. in 2000. U.K. citizens are also one of the largest groups to enter the U.S. on student visas—15,473 students and their families were admitted in 2000.

The number of British citizens who are admitted to the U.S. as non-immigrants has also been growing rapidly over time. As Table 1 shows, the total number of British non-immigrants admitted has increased more than three and a half times from

1983 to 2000, with the largest increases in the number of intracompany transferees and temporary workers. By contrast, the number of U.K.-born permanent immigrants admitted each year has remained fairly constant and at a much lower level.

That the large number of Britons staying temporarily in the U.S. for education, work, and training are not considered legal immigrants hides them from the view of many immigration scholars, even though most "non-immigrants" are captured in U.S. Census data. The presence of this large population of U.K.-born non-immigrants poses important questions for the meaning of transnationalism and cultural exchange. For many professional and highly educated Britons, a stint in the U.S. is a common part of an international program of training and education. The knowledge of U.S. society and culture among those who return to the U.K. may well influence the culture of their home country. Similarly, a large flow of temporary U.K. workers and students into the U.S. increases Americans' familiarity with contemporary British society. Yet studies of transnationalism frequently overlook the role of temporary migrants and workers, particularly those at the higher end of the socioeconomic spectrum.

Is the U.K.-born community in the U.S., then, constantly in flux as temporary migrants come and go, or do many of these non-immigrants eventually settle here? This is a difficult question to answer definitively, but statistical data from both the U.K. and the U.S. offer some indication of the general trends. The U.K. Office of National Statistics' international migration data report how many people born in the U.K. migrate to the U.S. and how many U.K.-born migrants to the U.S. arrive back in the U.K. with the intention to stay for a year or more—"return migrants," by its definition. Between 1991 and 2000, an estimated 104,600 people born in the U.K. migrated back from the U.S., while 153,800 migrated to the U.S.; the United Kingdom thus suffered a net loss of 49,200 Britons to the U.S. over this period. Most return migrants intend to stay in the U.K. on a relatively long-term basis, while more of those who migrate to the U.S. plan to stay for only a few years. Four fifths (79.9 percent) of British return migrants plan on remaining in the U.K. for more than four years, while only one third (31.7 percent) of migrants to the U.S. plan on staying here as long.

Although these data represent only the period from 1991 to 2000 and many British migrants to the U.S. may return to their native country after longer periods of time, U.S. immigration data confirm that a significant number of Britons who enter the U.S. as non-immigrants later adjust their status to become permanent residents. The INS Statistical Yearbook shows that in 2000, 9,379 people born in the U.K. adjusted their status from short-term non-immigrant to immigrant or permanent resident of the U.S. This represents 70 percent of all the U.K.-born immigrants legally admitted in 2000, and the proportions are comparably high (60 to 70 percent) for each year since 1996. In other words, most recent U.K. immigrants entered the U.S. first as temporary non-immigrants, only to decide later to stay longer.

The fact that British immigrants who become American citizens retain their British citizenship may encourage some migrants in this course by offering them additional flexibility, although as we shall see, declining naturalization rates of the U.K.-born suggest that it is unlikely to be a major factor. Most expatriates do return to the U.K., but a sizable portion of them find their way into a permanent life in the U.S.

The "Invisible Immigrants"

In their book *Legacies,* Alejandro Portes and Rubén Rumbaut write: "A well-estab-lished sociological principle holds that the more similar new minorities are in terms of physical appearance, class background, language, and religion to society's main-stream, the more favorable their reception and the more rapid their integration" (p. 47). Few immigrant groups have more in common with Americans than the British. Referring to earlier migration waves, Charlotte Erickson described the Brit-ish as "invisible immigrants," because they see themselves as deriving from the same ethnic and cultural origins, and sharing many of the same social institutions, as the majority of Americans. The invisibility of British immigrants remains true today.

British migrants arrive in the U.S. with few language barriers and are able to adapt easily to regional linguistic differences. According to the 2000 Census, 98.4 percent of the U.K.-born population over age five either speak English only or speak English very well. They also face few racial barriers to integration. In 2000, 90.4 percent of the U.K.-born population overall—and 98 percent of those from Scotland, Wales, and Northern Ireland—marked "white" as their only race. To this day, Britons' integration is further aided by the institutional similarities in law, gov-ernment, and religion that the societies share, the result of Britain's social and cul-tural influence in the early years of the United States' formation.

Migrants from the U.K. are a skilled population, with high levels of educational attainment and large proportions in professional and managerial occupations. Of the U.K.-born population aged 25 to 64 in 2000, 40.3 percent have a bachelor's de-gree or higher, while 54.1 percent have a high school degree. As for employment, 43.4 percent work in managerial or professional jobs and another 26.6 percent work in technical, sales, or administrative jobs. Accordingly, the British have among the highest incomes of all foreign-born populations in the U.S. There are differ-ences within the U.K.-born population, however; those who do not specify a coun-try of birth within the U.K. have the highest socioeconomic status, followed by those from Wales. The Scottish-born population has considerably lower socioeco-nomic status in educational attainment, occupation, and income than all other U.K.-born groups. Only 30.0 percent of Scots have a bachelor's degree or higher, compared with 50.3 percent of the Welsh and 51.3 percent of those stating only the United Kingdom. While 50.7 percent of those not specifying a country within the U.K. work in managerial or professional occupations, only 35.8 percent of Scots do so. Apparently, a "United Kingdom" identity is embraced more by the well-educated, professional classes. The relatively high economic status of the U.K.-born population overall helps them integrate easily into their new lives in the U.S. They have little trouble finding employment and are unlikely to surface on the radar of the social policy world.

The British community's cloak of invisibility is spread further by the geographic dispersion of its members. Although the British have flocked to particular states, especially California and Florida, where the sunny weather contrasts with what most knew at home, they have tended to spread throughout the country, with little geographic concentration in particular regions or cities. California had the greatest number of U.K.-born residents in 2000; nearly one fifth (18.4 percent) of all Britons in the U.S. lived in the Golden State. Yet California's largest geographical concentration, in the Los Angeles–Long Beach metropolitan area, incorporated only 6.1 percent of them. The second largest, the San Francisco–Oakland area, included only 3.6 percent. Britons tend to live outside of urban areas, further contributing to their residential diffusion; 82.9 percent of all Britons in the U.S. live outside of cities.

The ultimate sign of Britons' ease of integration is their rate of intermarriage with native-born Americans. Such intermarriage is extremely common among the British population in the U.S., even among the first generation, showing that Britons truly lack the cultural barriers to incorporation that many other immigrant groups face. Of all the U.S. households headed by a married couple involving at least one Briton in 2000, only 15.5 percent are marriages between two Britons; the vast majority—71.3 percent—involve a Briton marrying a native-born American. British women are slightly more likely than British men to marry Americans. By contrast, British women and men in the U.S. are equally likely to marry someone who is neither British nor American-born. Most of the intermarriages that are not with Americans are with other Europeans, Asians, Middle Easterners, or Canadians.

Of British intramarriages (those uniting two people born in the U.K.), most involve people marrying others from their own country within the U.K.; only 12.2 percent involve partners from two different U.K. countries. In the majority of marriages involving two Britons, both partners migrated to the U.S. in the same year (57.4 percent), suggesting that they married before moving to the U.S. In another 12 percent of British intramarriages, one partner migrated only a year or two after the other, increasing the odds that one partner later joined the other. Only in 30.6 percent of British intramarriages, or 4.8 percent of all marriages involving one British partner, did the partners migrate to the U.S. at sufficiently different times to suggest that they met in the U.S. It is therefore not the common pattern for the British to marry conationals they meet in this country. Other British migrants do not provide the main marriage pool because single Britons are granted unobstructed access to the much larger pool of native-born Americans.

Being and becoming citizens. A relatively large minority of the U.K.-born population in the U.S. are U.S. citizens born abroad to American parents. According to the U.S. Census, 17.7 percent of the U.K.-born population in the U.S. in 2000 were born to American parents. This is a diverse population, and their families are more similar to middle-class Americans in their socioeconomic status and geographic distribution than to other Britons in the U.S. Moreover, this group has been increasing; it grew from 10.0 percent of the U.K.-born population in the U.S. in 1980. With increased globalization and international business opportunities, Americans are also residing temporarily in Britain for work or study and giving birth to more children there before their families return to the U.S.

Of the U.K.-born who are not American citizens by birth, the proportion who become U.S. citizens has been declining. In 1980, 59.8 percent were naturalized citizens. By 1990 this proportion had fallen to 49.9 percent, and by 2000 it had dropped to 46.5 percent. The Welsh, Scottish, and Northern Irish are considerably more likely to naturalize than are the English or those who identify only with the United Kingdom. Yet these declines in naturalization rates over time have occurred across the board.

The 1990s saw an overall increase in the number of naturalization applications, a result of several factors, including new recognition of dual citizenship by several sending countries and concern over potential encroachments on the rights of immigrants that culminated in the 1996 welfare reforms. Yet British migrants' naturalization rates have been immune from such trends. Restriction of immigrants' eligibility for federal assistance provides little naturalization incentive for this population of relatively high earners, who could receive greater governmental assistance by returning to their country of origin.

De facto dual citizenship has also been a longtime reality for Britons in the U.S. The United Kingdom has formally embraced dual citizenship since 1949 and facilitated it in practice even earlier. In fact, so strong was the principle of "perpetual allegiance" to the crown that for many years Great Britain did not even recognize its subjects' capacity to give up their British citizenship. Now when British citizens naturalize abroad, they retain their U.K. nationality unless they specifically apply to renounce it. Those who become naturalized American citizens must pledge to abandon their previous citizenship, but in practice this oath has never been enforced, and in recent decades hostility to dual nationality has diminished. Britons who naturalize in the U.S. have effectively enjoyed the benefits of both passports for decades. It is nonetheless understandable that British naturalization rates should decline as the proportion of the U.K.-born who are temporary non-immigrants rises. Even if some British migrants eventually do marry or stay longer in the U.S., most see themselves as likely to return to their native land.

Ethnic Identities and Institutions

As a group of "invisible immigrants," able to assimilate easily to American society, the British are generally thought to shed their immigrant identities quickly. Charlotte Erickson noted that early immigrants from England often lost their group identity after the first generation. Yet if the children of British immigrants easily join the American mainstream, they and their descendants often willingly embrace British cultural identities on a symbolic level. Herbert Gans has described the growth of symbolic ethnicities among the third and later generations, who embrace the ethnic symbols of their forebears—their music, food, dance, and customs—often in isolation from the larger ethnic community and institutions. Such ethnic identities are optional, as Mary Waters explains, bringing color to an otherwise indistinguishable American identity with few of the social or economic consequences that ascribed racial identities bring with them.

A large number of societies, organizations, and clubs for people of British ancestry exist across the U.S. Among the most extensive national organizations with local chapters in many states or regions are the Daughters of the British Empire, the Caledonian Club and St. Andrew's Society, the Cornish American Heritage Society, Cornish Cousins, and the North American Manx Association, which celebrates the ethnic heritage of the Isle of Man. Numerous local societies not linked to national umbrellas devote themselves to practically every region of the United Kingdom. Some of these are primarily genealogical societies, offering historical information about immigrant settlements of earlier centuries. Others promote traditions, music, and food, sometimes sponsoring large conventions or meetings for hundreds of visitors interested in highland games, Celtic dance, or simply exploring British heritage. The membership requirements of these organizations vary; some welcome anyone with an interest in the culture, while others restrict membership to those who can trace their ancestry to the country within a specified number of generations. Most of these organizations welcome the U.K.-born, but their activities focus on native-born Americans of British descent who seek to connect with an ethnic origin that, without active pursuit, would have little role in their daily lives.

Americans of British descent far outnumber the U.K.-born in U.S. society, conferring a historical flavor to the majority of British cultural organizations. Yet many first-generation Britons have carved out ethnic institutions of their own, fostered by two important forces: the growing number of British "expatriates" and the uniting power of the Internet. These organizations take the form of many immigrant societies of previous generations—offering a chance for conationals to socialize, share memories of home, and help one another in business or with the legal and practical requirements of migration. The Internet simply adds a new twist to this old form, by effortlessly connecting people spread across large distances.

Some of these societies offer regular social gatherings and a taste of home for Britons in particular cities or regions. The Mayflower Club in Los Angeles, with over 2,000 members and a history of more than 40 years, offers pub nights, a cricket team, and Christmas pantomime. The Chicago Tafia Society, founded in 2000 by a Welsh man married to an American woman, is mainly composed of Welsh expatriates and offers advice on immigration issues, Welsh lessons, Welsh stalls at local Celtic festivals, and information on where to find Welsh and British food and entertainment products. The Florida Society of British Businesses promotes business dealings within the large British community in Florida. Its efforts are aided by the *Union Jack British Newspaper,* a monthly publication since 1982 which unites Britons in the U.S. with a readership of more than 200,000, approximately 80 percent of whom are British expatriates.

Internet sites for British expatriates offer virtual or real meeting places, bringing together Britons who were otherwise unconnected. An International Expat Brit Meetup allows Britons living abroad to meet locally, with the intent of strengthening the British expatriate community. Numerous websites provide chat groups and services for the community of Britons living in the U.S., including overseas shipping and calling plans, migration consultancies, satellite service to receive British television, and imported British goods. Websites even offer British dating services, perhaps foretelling a future decline in British intermarriage rates.

Those who have started such Internet sites and societies are self-described "expatriates." Most employ this term to signify a permanent resident who primarily identifies as a British person living abroad. For Britons, the word has its roots in the people of Anglo-Saxon stock who moved to British colonies or Commonwealth countries without ever intending to assimilate to their local cultures. Although it is unclear how an "expatriate" differs from an immigrant who does not assimilate, the word "immigrant" is rarely mentioned in this context. Yet these virtual ethnic communities are fostered not only by the increase of British migrants to the U.S. but by the growth of British expatriates throughout the world for business and study. Some websites target British expatriates not only in the U.S. but throughout Europe, Asia, and the former Commonwealth. Providing services to this growing community has become a booming industry, and the Internet is the key to reaching this geographically diverse community dominated by educated young professionals with the technological capacity to use it.

The transitory nature of a community in which a large proportion are only temporary migrants may contribute to the lack of a defined ethnic community. Yet in the case of Britons in the U.S., a community that would otherwise quickly lose its cultural identity through intermarriage and assimilation, the regular flow of British nationals helps to preserve expatriate identities, aided by technological advances that keep those identities alive by connecting dispersed Britons. Such identities may still not survive past the first generation, but they help British immigrants to become less invisible than they have previously been.

However, even if British ethnic communities and identities continue to grow, their visibility will be largely symbolic. The affinity the United Kingdom and United States have for one another, as well as the racial, linguistic, and cultural similarities of their citizens, remove any structural barriers to socioeconomic integration. An expatriate or immigrant identity may not be optional for first-generation British migrants, but it is an identity that is unlikely to affect their socioeconomic incorporation, a claim few other immigrant groups can make.

Bibliography

Erickson, Charlotte J. 1972. *Invisible Immigrants: The Adaptation of English and Scottish Immigrants in 19th Century America.* Leicester, Eng.: Leicester University Press.

———. 1980. "English." In Stephen Thernstrom, Ann Orlov, and Oscar Handlin, eds., *Harvard Encyclopedia of American Ethnic Groups,* pp. 319–36. Cambridge, Mass.: Belknap.

Gans, Herbert. 1979. "Symbolic Ethnicity: The Future of Ethnic Groups and Cultures in America." *Ethnic and Racial Studies* 2 (Jan.): 1–20.

Hansen, Randall, and Patrick Weil, eds. 2002. *Dual Nationality, Social Rights and Federal Citizenship in the U.S. and Europe.* New York: Berghahn.

Kershaw, Roger. 2002. *Emigrants and Expats: A Guide to Sources on UK Emigration and Residents Overseas.* Richmond, Eng.: Public Record Office.

Office for National Statistics. 2002. *International Migration: Migrants Entering or Leaving the United Kingdom and England and Wales, 2002.* Series MN, no.29. London: Her Majesty's Stationery Office.

O'Reilly, Karen. 2000. *The British on the Costa del Sol: Transnational Identities and Local Communities.* New York: Routledge.

Portes, Alejandro, and Rubén G. Rumbaut. 2001. *Legacies: The Story of the Immigrant Second Generation.* Berkeley: University of California Press.

Tranter, N. L. 1996. *British Population in the Twentieth Century.* New York: St. Martin's.

Virden, Jenel. 1996. *Good-bye, Piccadilly: British War Brides in America.* Chicago: University of Illinois Press.

Waters, Mary C. 1990. *Ethnic Options: Choosing Identities in America.* Berkeley: University of California Press.

Vietnam

Rubén G. Rumbaut

In the years following the end of the Vietnam War in 1975, 1.5 million refugees and immigrants from Vietnam, Laos, and Cambodia arrived in the United States. Together with their nearly half a million American-born children, by the year 2000 they already represented more than one out of every six Asian Americans, adding significantly not only to the size but to the diversity of the Asian-origin population in the U.S. But the story of their migration and incorporation differs fundamentally from that of other Asian Americans. Except for people of Japanese descent, the overwhelming majority of today's Asian Americans are foreign-born, reflecting the central role of contemporary immigration in the formation of these ethnic groups. But unlike the others, most of the Vietnamese (and the Laotians and Cambodians) have come as refugees rather than as immigrants. Unlike post-1965 immigrants from the Philippines, Korea, China, India, and elsewhere in Asia, whose large-scale immigration was influenced by the abolition of racist quotas in U.S. immigration law, the Vietnamese entered outside of regular immigration channels as part of the largest refugee resettlement program in U.S. history, peaking in 1980 and continuing since. As refugees from a country devastated by war, they experienced contexts of exit more traumatic than those of other recent newcomers, and they had no realistic prospects of returning to their homeland. Their reception also entailed an entry status that gave them access to a variety of public assistance programs to which other immigrants were not equally entitled. The American welfare state has shaped their incorporation far more than that of any other immigrant group in U.S. history, even as their exodus and resettlement were themselves complex, unintended consequences of U.S. foreign policies and of the American warfare state.

The Vietnamese do not have a history (often harsh) of several generations in America, as do the Chinese and Japanese, nor of a half-century of direct U.S. colonization, as do the Filipinos. At first they could not be resettled into coethnic communities established by earlier immigration, since these were essentially nonexistent before 1975; and in the resettlement process they were more likely to be dispersed throughout the country than other large immigrant groups. Unlike recent Asian immigrant flows, most notably those from India and Taiwan, which have been characterized by large proportions of highly educated professionals and managers, those from Vietnam included greater proportions of less-educated people from rural areas, with the notable exception of the first wave of South Vietnamese, evacuated in 1975. At the same time, the population from Vietnam comprises not only the majority ethnic Vietnamese but also national minorities such as the ethnic Chinese and the indigenous Montagnards from the Central Highlands. They range from members of the elite of the former U.S.-backed governments to the "boat people," and differ by social class, by "waves" or cohorts of arrival, and by gender and generation. Tens of thousands of Amerasians—children of Vietnamese mothers and American fathers who served in Vietnam during the war—were also resettled in the U.S. under a special law enacted in 1987 (the Amerasian Homecoming Act); stigmatized as *bui doi* (children of the "dust of life"), they form yet another distinct and poignant legacy of the war. All of these characteristics and contexts of exit and reception have shaped this group's adaptation to the American economy, polity, and society.

Historical Background

The Vietnamese refugees are a product of the longest war in modern history, the Vietnam War (1945–1975). An immensely complex conflict that still creates bitter controversy, the war was a tragedy of staggering proportions for Americans and Vietnamese alike. With the exception of the American Civil War, the Vietnam War was the most divisive event in U.S. history. In a 1995 national poll, two decades after the war's end, 72 percent of respondents called it "one of the worst moments in American history," while a mere 2 percent saw it as among the nation's "finest moments"; most (55 percent) said that the U.S. remained "deeply divided" over the war. The war also produced a huge refugee population for whom the U.S. assumed a historic responsibility. Not coincidentally, Vietnam represented at once the worst defeat of U.S. foreign policy in the cold war era and the leading example (with Cuba) of the functions of U.S. refugee policy: Vietnamese (and Cubans) admitted to the U.S. as political refugees served as potent symbols of the legitimacy of American power and global policy. The circumstances of the U.S. withdrawal from Vietnam and the dramatic fall of Saigon and its aftermath also gave moral and political justification for significantly expanded domestic refugee programs, providing cash and medical assistance and social services.

Yet if the war divided America, it devastated Vietnam. It is estimated that during the period of U.S. involvement after the defeat of the French at Dien Bien Phu in

1954, over 4 million Vietnamese soldiers and civilians on both sides were killed or wounded—nearly 10 percent of the total population. The amount of firepower used by the U.S. on Vietnam exceeded that used by the U.S. in all its previous wars combined, including both world wars. In South Vietnam alone, a third of the population was internally displaced during the war, and over half of the forest area and some 10 percent of the agricultural land were partially destroyed by aerial bombardment, tractor clearing, and chemical defoliation. The war shattered the region's economy and traditional society. A tragedy of epic proportions, the "war that nobody won" left Vietnam, Laos, and Cambodia among the poorest countries in the world.

After the war ended in 1975, well over 2 million refugees fled Vietnam, Laos, and Cambodia. As is true of refugee movements elsewhere, the first waves were disproportionately made up of elites who left because of ideological and political opposition to the new regimes, while later flows included masses of people of more modest backgrounds fleeing continuing regional conflicts and deteriorating economic conditions. Vietnamese professionals and former notables were greatly overrepresented among those who were evacuated to American bases in Guam and the Philippines under emergency conditions during the fall of Saigon; also overrepresented were Vietnamese Catholics (many of whom had fled from Hanoi to Saigon during the partition of Vietnam in 1954). In Vietnam, meanwhile, several hundred thousand people with ties to the former regimes were interned in "reeducation camps"; many years later, beginning in 1989, over 50,000 of these former political detainees were resettled in the U.S. under special legislation. But the exodus of the 1975 refugees was only the start of an extraordinary emigration.

An enormous increase of refugees beginning in late 1978 was triggered by the Vietnamese invasion of Cambodia, which quickly ended three years of Khmer Rouge rule, and the subsequent border war between Vietnam and China in early 1979, which accelerated the expulsion of the ethnic Chinese petite bourgeoisie from Vietnam. About 250,000 ethnic Chinese from North Vietnam moved across the border into China, and tens of thousands of Chinese and Vietnamese "boat people" attempted to cross the South China Sea packed in rickety crafts suitable only for river travel; many of them drowned or were assaulted by Thai pirates preying on their boats in the Gulf of Thailand. By spring 1979 nearly 60,000 boat people were arriving monthly in the countries of the region. These events led to an international resettlement crisis later that year, when those "first-asylum" countries (principally Thailand, Malaysia, and Indonesia) refused to accept more refugees into their already swollen camps and often pushed boat refugees back out to sea, where many perished (Malaysia alone pushed out some 40,000). In response, under agreements reached at the Geneva Conference in July 1979, Western countries began to absorb significant numbers of the refugee camp population in Southeast Asia.

Soon thereafter Congress passed the landmark Refugee Act of 1980, which institutionalized resettlement assistance for refugees, overseen by the newly created Office of Refugee Resettlement (ORR). The rate of Indochinese refugee resettlement in the U.S., which had slowed to a trickle after the 1975 evacuations, increased dramatically, doubling from about 81,000 in 1979 to 167,000 in 1980, then stabilizing at an annual rate of 40,000 to 50,000 after 1982. By 1992 over 1 million had already been resettled in the U.S., 750,000 were resettled in other Western countries (principally Canada, Australia, and France), and many others still languished in refugee camps from the Thai-Cambodian border to Hong Kong. Harsh "humane deterrence" policies and occasional attempts at forced repatriation sought to brake the flow of refugees to first-asylum countries, with limited success. After 1979 the number of boat refugee arrivals declined, but it did not drop below 20,000 annually until it abruptly came to a halt in 1992, exacting a horrific cost in human lives: at least 100,000 boat people, and perhaps twice that number, drowned in the South China Sea. Beginning in the 1980s, the Orderly Departure Program (ODP) allowed the controlled immigration of thousands of Vietnamese directly from Vietnam to the U.S., including two groups with a unique tie to the war: Amerasians and former reeducation camp internees. By 1992 over 300,000 Vietnamese had immigrated to the U.S. through the ODP, including 161,400 in the regular family reunification program, 81,500 Amerasians and their accompanying relatives, and 61,000 former political prisoners and their families. Both the Amerasian program and refugee processing for former political prisoners largely ended by 1995. Most of the ODP family reunification cases in the 1990s left Vietnam as regular immigrants, not as refugees, a pattern that has become more pronounced over time.

Indeed, the end of the cold war in 1989, the collapse of the former Soviet Union in 1991, and the end of the U.S. trade embargo against Vietnam in February 1994 were only the most remarkable events of a compressed period of extraordinarily rapid and fundamental changes in international relations that transformed the nature of refugee resettlement in the U.S. Meanwhile, a rapidly growing second generation of young Vietnamese Americans was emerging, rooted in communities throughout the U.S., speaking accentless English, and oriented not toward their Vietnamese past but to an American future.

Immigration and Population Growth

Among Asian Americans, the Vietnamese are one of the most recently formed ethnic groups. The first officially recorded Vietnamese immigration to the U.S. occurred in 1952, when eight immigrants were admitted as permanent residents. As late as 1969, the total from Vietnam amounted to little more than 3,000—including "war brides"—not counting university students from elite families, diplomats,

Table 1 Foreign-born population from Vietnam, Laos, and Cambodia and the main ethnic groups from Vietnam, by year of arrival, 2000

| | Vietnam-origin groups | | | | | | Cambodia and Laos (foreign-born) | | Total Indochinese (foreign-born) | |
| | Vietnamese | | Chinese-Vietnamese | | Other Vietnam-born[a] | | | | | |
Year of arrival	Number	Percentage	Number	Percentage	Number	Percentage	Number	Percentage	Number	Percentage
Pre-1965	2,588	0.3	b	b	1,112	2.1	b	b	5,446	0.4
1965–1969	3,825	0.5	b	b	1,022	1.9	b	b	6,704	0.5
1970–1974	18,603	2.3	2,703	1.6	5,285	10.0	3,842	1.0	30,433	2.1
1975	87,708	10.8	6,885	4.0	5,044	9.6	7,220	1.8	106,857	7.4
1976	4,483	0.6	1,546	0.9	b	b	8,391	2.1	15,143	1.1
1977	5,168	0.6	1,821	1.1	b	b	2,828	0.7	10,435	0.7
1978	13,276	1.6	5,668	3.3	b	b	8,994	2.2	28,916	2.0
1979	30,569	3.8	27,496	16.1	1,601	3.0	28,918	7.2	88,584	6.2
1980	48,209	5.9	25,634	15.0	2,568	4.9	52,509	13.0	128,920	9.0
1981	32,632	4.0	11,145	6.5	1,671	3.2	41,331	10.3	86,779	6.0
1982	27,589	3.4	5,876	3.4	1,025	1.9	20,179	5.0	54,669	3.8
1983	18,334	2.3	4,602	2.7	894	1.7	16,300	4.0	40,130	2.8
1984	20,597	2.5	5,632	3.3	1,274	2.4	21,586	5.4	49,089	3.4
1985	21,792	2.7	6,098	3.6	1,661	3.1	23,430	5.8	52,981	3.7
1986	19,349	2.4	5,627	3.3	1,228	2.3	18,914	4.7	45,118	3.1
1987	14,451	1.8	5,206	3.1	962	1.8	17,473	4.3	38,092	2.6
1988	14,925	1.8	5,258	3.1	949	1.8	17,281	4.3	38,413	2.7

Year									
1989	30,429	3.7	6,553	3.8	1,730	3.3	18,175	4.5	56,887	4.0
1990	54,215	6.7	7,471	4.4	2,431	4.6	15,156	3.8	79,273	5.5
1991	56,428	6.9	5,896	3.5	2,432	4.6	12,025	3.0	76,781	5.3
1992	62,825	7.7	5,699	3.3	3,029	5.7	9,712	2.4	81,265	5.6
1993	48,801	6.0	3,652	2.1	1,721	3.3	11,183	2.8	65,357	4.5
1994	43,021	5.3	2,616	1.5	2,448	4.6	9,761	2.4	57,846	4.0
1995	38,161	4.7	2,116	1.2	2,547	4.8	8,216	2.0	51,040	3.5
1996	21,041	2.6	2,248	1.3	1,437	2.7	7,191	1.8	31,917	2.2
1997	21,058	2.6	3,135	1.8	1,698	3.2	5,887	1.5	31,778	2.2
1998	23,665	2.9	3,789	2.2	2,118	4.0	4,791	1.2	34,363	2.4
1999	24,200	3.0	3,461	2.0	1,973	3.7	6,273	1.6	35,907	2.5
2000	6,160	0.8	1,072	0.6	557	1.1	2,872	0.7	10,661	0.7
Total	814,102	100.0	170,342	100.0	52,736	100.0	402,604	100.0	1,439,784	100.0

Source: U.S. Census Bureau, 2000 Census, author's own 5% Public Use Microdata Sample. Figures are weighted estimates from a sample, weighted data.

a. Persons born in Vietnam who are neither ethnic Vietnamese or Chinese-Vietnamese by self-reported ancestry. Most are presumed to be Amerasians, and they may also include other ethnic minorities from Vietnam (e.g., the Montagnards).

b. Too few cases for reliable estimates.

military trainees, and others who entered with non-immigrant visas in the 1960s in the wake of the rapid expansion of U.S. involvement in Vietnam. In the early 1970s the number of immigrants from Vietnam quintupled—again, not counting an unknown number of non-immigrants. When Saigon fell in April 1975, there may have been as many as 30,000 Vietnamese in the U.S.

About 130,000 refugees, nearly all from South Vietnam, were resettled in the U.S. in 1975. A small number arrived from 1976 to 1978, but a significant new inflow began in late 1978, in the context of the international refugee crisis. About 450,000 Indochinese refugees arrived en masse during 1979–1982 alone, peaking in 1980 (the record year in U.S. refugee resettlement history). Compared with the 1975 first wave, this second wave of refugees was much more heterogeneous: they included the boat people from Vietnam, the survivors of the Pol Pot period in Cambodia, the lowland Lao, and the highland Hmong, many of them coming from rural backgrounds, with little education, knowledge of English, or transferable occupational skills, and having endured prolonged stays in refugee camps overseas. What is more, the timing and context of their entry into the U.S. further complicated their reception: the peak year of their arrival (1980) coincided both with the crisis of tens of thousands of Mariel Cubans and Haitians arriving in Florida in small boats and with the highest domestic inflation rates in memory, followed in 1981–1982 by the worst recession since the Great Depression. The confluence of these events in turn contributed to an accompanying political climate of intensifying nativism, racism, xenophobia, and "compassion fatigue."

For the rest of the decade after 1982, Indochinese arrivals ranged between 40,000 and 50,000 annually; the rate increased to between 70,000 and 80,000 a year between 1990 and 1992 and has decreased ever since. Vietnamese refugee admissions, which totaled over 650,000 from 1975 to 1992, were supplemented by a substantial though little-noticed flow of over 170,000 non-refugee Vietnamese *immigrants* who arrived in the U.S. during the same period—including people coming to the U.S. from other countries and from Vietnam through the ODP, among them the young Amerasians and their accompanying relatives mentioned earlier. U.S. government agencies such as ORR and the INS collect these data by nationality, not ethnicity, so it is impossible to determine the proportion of ethnic Chinese or other minority groups among them. Official immigration statistics, moreover, do not account for mortality (which may be assumed to be low, since this is a young population) or emigration (which has been negligible), or for natural increase (which is high). The decennial census, despite its shortcomings, remains the best source of national data to gauge the size, growth, and composition of this population.

Table 1 presents data from the 5% Public Use Microdata Sample (PUMS) of the 2000 Census for the foreign-born population of Vietnamese, Cambodians, and Laotians by the year of their arrival in the U.S. (not by their admission to permanent residency, which may take place years after their arrival). The patterns of their arrival, from the pre-1975 period to the 1975 evacuations to the peak years of resettlement in 1979–1982 and again in the early 1990s, correspond closely to the history of their migration. Overall, about 20 percent arrived before 1980 (mostly between 1975 and 1979), 40 percent between 1980 and 1989, and 40 percent after 1990. As shown in Table 1, by the time of the April 2000 Census, that first generation totaled about 1,440,000 people, including more than 1 million from Vietnam and just over 400,000 from Laos and Cambodia. (These figures include people born in other countries, such as Thailand, where many refugee children who identified as Vietnamese, Cambodian, Lao, or Hmong were born before their resettlement in the U.S.) The totals from Vietnam are broken down into three main groups: the Vietnamese majority (814,102), the ethnic Chinese Vietnamese (170,342), and others (52,736). Note that the first two ethnic groups differ sharply in the timing of their exodus: for the Vietnamese the peak year was 1975, and almost 40 percent arrived between 1990 and 1994; for the ethnic Chinese, almost 40 percent arrived between 1979 and 1981. The last group consists of more than 50,000 people born in Vietnam who did not identify as Vietnamese or Chinese in the race, ancestry, or language questions of the census; most are presumed to be Amerasians or members of other ethnic minorities.

The figures in Table 1 do not include another 450,000 people born in the U.S. to Indochinese parents (including 263,000 of Vietnamese origin), a rapidly growing second generation that brought the total Indochinese population counted by the 2000 Census to nearly 1.9 million, including 1.3 million of Vietnamese ancestry. Detailed analysis of the census data, combining self-reported "race" with birthplace, ancestry, and language spoken in the home, makes it possible to delineate the ethnic diversity within national-origin groupings. Specifically, ethnic Chinese groups (both foreign-born and U.S.-born) accounted for almost 200,000 of the Vietnamese totals and 20,000 of the Cambodian and Laotian totals—a sizable population that might otherwise be lumped with those marking "Chinese" on the race question of the census and subtracted from the Indochinese totals. Here we will distinguish between the Vietnamese and the ethnic Chinese from Vietnam, as there are significant differences between them which are obscured in accounts that lump these groups together by national origin.

Patterns of Settlement

The 130,000 (mostly Vietnamese) refugees who arrived in the U.S. in 1975 were sent initially to four government reception centers—at Camp Pendleton, California; Fort Indiantown Gap, Pennsylvania; Fort Chaffee, Arkansas; and Eglin Air Force Base, Florida—where they were interviewed by voluntary agencies and matched with sponsors throughout the country, including individuals, church groups,

Table 2   Selected areas of Vietnamese and Chinese-Vietnamese settlement, 2000 (percentages)

| Places of residence | Main Indochinese groups (N = 1,891,638) | | | | | Total other Asian (8,762,856) | Total non-Asian (270,767,412) | Total U.S. population (281,421,906) |
	Vietnamese (1,058,956)	Chinese-Vietnamese (188,446)	Cambodian (214,069)	Lao (203,825)	Hmong (173,606)			
States								
California	39.6	58.3	41.0	35.2	38.4	35.2	11.1	12.0
Texas	12.3	6.2	4.5	5.9	0.8	4.7	7.5	7.4
Washington	4.2	3.4	8.0	4.6	1.3	3.0	2.0	2.1
Massachusetts	3.1	3.1	10.2	2.2	0.7	2.0	2.3	2.3
Pennsylvania	2.5	2.4	5.4	1.5	0.3	2.0	4.5	4.4
Minnesota	1.8	0.6	2.2	4.9	24.8	0.7	1.8	1.7
Wisconsin	0.3	0.2	0.7	2.3	18.2	0.5	1.9	1.9
Michigan	1.2	0.8	1.3	1.9	2.4	1.7	3.6	3.5
North Carolina	1.4	0.6	1.0	2.3	4.1	1.0	2.9	2.9
New York	1.9	4.2	1.8	2.0	0.5	11.8	6.6	6.7
New Jersey	1.3	1.3	0.6	0.7	0.2	5.4	2.9	3.0
Illinois	1.6	1.7	2.1	2.8	0.3	4.5	4.4	4.4
Hawai'i	0.7	1.4	0.4	1.1	0.1	6.3	0.2	0.4

Metropolitan corridors

Los Angeles–Orange–San Diego	23.7	33.4	24.2	9.1	2.3	18.6	6.3	6.8
San Francisco Bay Area	12.6	20.8	6.5	6.4	0.5	12.8	1.8	2.3
Sacramento–Fresno	2.6	3.3	9.5	17.0	34.1	2.5	1.5	1.6
Houston–Galveston	6.0	2.9	1.7	1.0	0.1	1.8	1.6	1.7
Dallas–Ft. Worth	4.0	2.3	2.2	3.3	0.2	1.6	1.8	1.8
Seattle-Tacoma-Olympia	3.6	3.1	7.1	3.6	1.1	2.4	1.1	1.2
Boston-Lowell-Providence	2.7	2.4	11.9	3.3	0.7	1.8	1.8	1.8
Philadelphia	1.7	2.2	4.9	1.3	0.1	1.5	1.8	1.8
Minneapolis–St. Paul	1.6	0.5	1.7	4.0	24.3	0.6	1.1	1.1
Milwaukee-Madison	0.2	0.1	0.5	1.3	7.5	0.3	0.7	0.7
Wassau–Green Bay	0.1	0.1	0.0	0.7	7.3	0.1	0.3	0.3
Washington, D.C.–Baltimore	4.2	2.7	2.5	1.7	0.1	3.9	2.5	2.6
Chicago-Gary	1.4	1.5	1.9	1.7	0.3	4.1	3.1	3.1
New York–New Jersey	1.7	4.2	1.6	0.9	0.4	15.1	5.9	6.1
All others	31.5	19.6	22.3	43.0	20.6	31.8	67.2	65.9

Source: U.S. Census Bureau, 2000 Census, author's own 5% Public Use Microdata Sample, weighted data.

and other organizations. U.S. refugee placement policy aimed to disperse the refugee population to all 50 states in order to minimize any negative impacts on receiving communities, and the 1975 Vietnamese refugees were more significantly dispersed than other immigrant or refugee populations. They were initially placed in 813 separate zip code areas in every state, including Alaska, with about two thirds settling in areas that had fewer than 500 refugees and only 8.5 percent settling in places with more than 3,000 refugees. Less than half were sent to the state of their choice. Despite this general pattern of dispersal—shaped by government policy, the availability of sponsorships, and the relative absence of family ties and previously established ethnic communities in the U.S.—areas of Indochinese concentration began to emerge, particularly in California, and to grow rapidly as a result of secondary migration from other states. By 1980, 45 percent of the 1975 arrivals lived in a state other than the one they had originally been sent to, and the refugee population in California had doubled from about 20 percent to 40 percent; there they were concentrated in contiguous Southern California metropolitan areas and in the Silicon Valley city of San Jose.

As the much larger waves of refugees began to arrive after 1979 and as their social networks became increasingly consolidated, government policies and programs continued to aim to disperse refugees without family ties away from high-impact areas, while most others were reunited with family members already residing in areas of high concentration. By the early 1980s about a third of arriving refugees already had close relatives in the U.S. who could serve as sponsors, and another third had more distant relatives, leaving only the remaining third without kinship ties subject to the dispersal policy. In addition, different localities of concentration emerged for the different ethnic groups. By 1990 the largest Vietnamese enclave in the U.S. had formed in Orange County, with its hub in the communities of Santa Ana and Westminster ("Little Saigon"), where the Nguyens outnumbered the Smiths two to one among Orange County home-buyers; followed by San Jose, where the Nguyens outnumbered the Joneses in the phone book fourteen columns to eight. By 2000 a fourth of all Vietnamese Americans were concentrated in the metropolitan corridor from Los Angeles to San Diego, and another sixth were in the San Francisco Bay Area.

Vietnamese Americans continue to reside in every state of the nation, but their patterns of settlement differ in significant ways from each other and from those of other Asian Americans as well as the rest of the U.S. population. While California was home for 12 percent of the total U.S. population of 281 million in 2000, as Table 2 shows, 40 percent of the Vietnamese and 58 percent of the Chinese Vietnamese had settled there. After California, the Vietnamese were most concentrated in Texas (12 percent), with sizable communities in Houston and Dallas (which began to be formed by the 1975 cohort, attracted by employment opportunities) and along the Gulf Coast (especially shrimp fishers). Remarkably, although the Filipino, Chinese, and Asian Indian populations in the U.S. are larger, the Vietnamese today are the largest group of Asian origin in Texas and in the neighboring states of Louisiana, Mississippi, Arkansas, Missouri, Iowa, Nebraska, Kansas, Colorado, and Oklahoma.

Patterns of settlement also vary significantly by ethnicity within major national-origin groups. Consider the Vietnamese and ethnic Chinese minority groups from Vietnam and their concentrations in key metropolitan areas in California. Fully 25 percent of the Chinese Vietnamese population in the U.S. resided in Los Angeles County in 2000, compared with less than 7 percent of the Vietnamese; only 1 percent of the Vietnamese were in San Francisco, compared to 7 percent of the Chinese Vietnamese; but over 12 percent of all Vietnamese in the country resided in Orange County, compared to 5 percent of the Chinese Vietnamese.

Social and Economic Characteristics

Tables 3 and 4 present a summary of demographic and socioeconomic characteristics from the 2000 Census, again comparing the main Vietnamese ethnic groups to each other and to the other Asian groups and the total U.S. population. These data further underscore the significant differences between the various Indochinese ethnic groups and other Asian Americans. All of the Indochinese groups are younger than other Asian Americans and the total U.S. population, reflecting in part their much higher levels of fertility. As shown in Table 3, the median age for the Vietnamese and Chinese-Vietnamese second generation was only 9 or 10 years, compared with 17 years for other Asian Americans (two thirds of whom are first-generation immigrants) and 35 years for the remaining 271 million non-Asian Americans (only 10 percent of whom are immigrants, now mainly from Latin America). These indicators point to the dynamics of new ethnic group formation through immigration and rapid natural increase, and underscore both the potential implications of the very young age structure of this population for future reproduction and the socioeconomic importance among the Indochinese of families with a high proportion of dependent children. The structure of these families is a key social context shaping their adaptation, including their efforts at collective pooling of economic resources amid constant tension over changing gender roles and intergenerational conflicts.

Perhaps the most significant indicator of immigrant acculturation to American life is the degree of proficiency in the English language. As the most recently arrived and least educated Asian Americans, the majority of the Vietnamese and Chinese Vietnamese 5 years and older did not yet speak English "very well" at the time of the 2000 Census, although those proportions have increased over time despite continuing immigration during the 1990s. While 66 percent of other Asian Americans—and 93 percent of all non-Asian Americans—spoke English only or very well, fewer than one in ten of the Vietnamese and Chinese Vietnamese spoke English only and only about one in three spoke it very well. Conversely, while only 14

Table 3 Nativity, citizenship, age, and English proficiency of Vietnamese and Chinese-Vietnamese groups, 2000

| | Main Indochinese groups (N = 1,891,638) | | | | | | | |
	Vietnamese (1,058,956)	Chinese-Vietnamese (188,446)	Cambodian (214,069)	Lao (203,825)	Hmong (173,606)	Total other Asian (8,762,856)	Total non-Asian (270,767,412)	Total U.S population (281,421,906)
Nativity and citizenship								
Percentage foreign-born[a]	76.9	90.4	72.4	74.3	55.4	67.7	10.0	12.3
Percentage U.S. citizen	67.5	75.3	63.0	62.2	61.9	65.6	94.5	93.4
Age								
Percentage children under 18 years old	27.0	12.7	33.1	29.7	55.0	23.1	25.7	25.6
Median age (foreign-born)	35.5	37.6	35.0	35.0	27.5	38.4	33.2	36.7
Median age (U.S.-born)	8.7	9.6	10.3	9.4	9.1	17.1	34.8	34.5
Percentage who speak English (persons 5 years or older)								
Only	7.3	5.5	8.4	8.1	4.5	24.9	84.5	82.1
Very well	30.6	29.4	36.3	37.5	37.2	40.7	8.6	9.8
Well	31.7	31.5	27.5	27.9	31.7	20.5	3.2	3.9
Not well	25.1	26.1	22.1	21.1	20.2	11.0	2.5	2.9
Not at all	5.3	7.5	5.6	5.4	6.4	2.9	1.2	1.3
Percentage fluent in English[b]								
Born in the U.S.	92.5	92.5	90.5	92.4	87.3	97.1	99.3	99.3
Foreign-born, age at arrival								
12 or younger	92.0	94.5	93.8	94.5	88.2	94.8	91.1	91.6
13 to 34	67.9	63.4	61.8	62.1	50.8	86.6	66.2	69.8
35 or older	30.3	25.4	27.5	30.7	18.7	56.8	51.4	51.5
Percentage linguistically isolated[c]	42.6	39.2	27.1	27.6	32.7	20.0	4.1	4.9

Source: U.S. Census Bureau, 2000 Census, author's own 5% Public Use Microdata Sample, weighted data.

a. "Foreign-born" here includes persons with a parent who was a U.S. citizen or born in island territories (e.g., Puerto Rico).

b. "Fluent in English" refers to persons who speak English only, or well or very well.

c. Refers to households in which no person aged 14 or older speaks English "very well."

Table 4   Educational, occupational, and economic status of Vietnamese and Chinese-Vietnamese groups, 2000 (percentages)

	Main Indochinese groups (N = 1,891,638)					Total other Asian	Total non-Asian	Total U.S. population
Number	Vietnamese (1,058,956)	Chinese-Vietnamese (188,446)	Cambodian (214,069)	Lao (203,825)	Hmong (173,606)	(8,762,856)	(270,767,412)	(281,421,906)
Educational attainment (persons 25 years or older)								
8th grade or less	15.3	23.9	35.5	33.2	49.3	8.1	7.4	7.5
9th to 12th grade	19.8	15.5	16.4	16.6	10.1	7.3	12.2	12.1
High school graduate, GED	19.7	16.7	19.0	24.1	16.4	15.7	29.1	28.6
Some college, AA degree	26.9	26.1	19.0	18.2	16.9	20.5	27.6	27.4
College graduate	13.9	14.7	7.8	6.3	6.0	28.9	15.1	15.5
Advanced degree	4.5	3.2	2.4	1.6	1.3	19.5	8.5	8.9
High-to-low education ratio[a]	0.52	0.45	0.20	0.16	0.12	3.12	1.21	1.24
Employment (persons 16 years or older)								
In labor force	62.4	65.5	55.8	61.0	53.3	63.7	63.9	63.9
Unemployed	5.8	5.1	8.5	7.4	9.3	5.1	5.8	5.7
Occupational attainment (of those employed)[b]								
Low-wage labor (SEI < 25)	47.7	40.3	49.9	57.1	55.0	24.4	32.7	32.5
High-status jobs (SEI > 50)	30.0	33.0	22.6	17.1	18.6	51.7	38.1	38.4
High-to-low status ratio[c]	0.63	0.82	0.45	0.30	0.34	2.12	1.16	1.18
Economic situation								
Family-household size (N)	4.29	4.41	5.12	4.96	7.61	3.64	3.22	3.24
Median household income	$52,962	$56,473	$40,264	$45,942	$35,026	$62,000	$48,403	$48,925
Mean annual family income	$62,124	$65,867	$48,382	$50,592	$41,384	$75,700	$59,744	$60,231
Per capita annual income	$14,465	$14,920	$9,441	$10,190	$5,440	$20,814	$18,564	$18,576
Below poverty line	17.9	16.1	30.8	22.3	40.3	13.9	15.7	15.7
Own (or owe) home	59.3	59.1	47.9	56.5	44.0	61.0	69.5	69.2

Source: U.S. Census Bureau, 2000 Census, author's own 5% Public Use Microdata Sample, weighted data.

a. High-to-low education ratio is the ratio of college graduates to high school dropouts in the population of persons 25 or older.

b. SEI = Duncan Socioeconomic Index. High-status occupations (professional, managerial, technical) have SEI scores above 50. Low-status jobs with SEI scores below 25 include laborers, operators, fabricators, and low-wage services. Not shown are mid-status white-collar and skilled blue-collar jobs with SEI scores between 25 and 50.

c. Ratio of high-status professionals (SEI > 50) to low-wage laborers (SEI < 25) in the employed population.

percent of other Asian Americans—and less than 4 percent of all non-Asian Americans—spoke English "not well" or not at all, the corresponding figures were above 30 percent for the Vietnamese and Chinese Vietnamese, and even higher percentages of their households were classified as "linguistically isolated" (defined as households in which no person 14 or older spoke English very well). However, this pattern of linguistic disadvantage is erased by the U.S.-born second generation, over 90 percent of whom were fluent in English in 2000. The measure of English fluency employed in the Table 3 data combines the percent who speak English only with the ability to speak it very well or well into a single index of fluency. That degree of fluency is in part a function of length of time in the U.S. but much more powerfully a function of age at arrival and level of education. As Table 3 shows, the younger the immigrant at the time of arrival, the greater the fluency in English: over 90 percent of those who arrived in the U.S. as children under 13 were fluent (the same as their U.S.-born coethnics), while less than a third of the Vietnamese and Chinese Vietnamese who arrived as adults 35 or older were fluent in English in 2000.

A profile of the educational, occupational, and economic status of these groups is sketched in Table 4. Stark differences in the educational attainment of adults 25 and older were apparent between the Indochinese and all other Asian American groups. While a remarkable 48 percent of other Asian American adults were college graduates and 20 percent also had postgraduate degrees—double the level of educational attainment for the total non-Asian U.S. population (24 percent and 9 percent, respectively)—the Indochinese groups were much less educated on average, particularly the non-Vietnamese, underscoring the rural origins and severe social class disadvantages of many refugees in these ethnic groups. Still, while almost 20 percent of the Vietnamese had college degrees, nearly 40 percent lacked high school degrees. A measure of educational achievement calculated in Table 4—the ratio of college graduates to high school dropouts in the population of adults 25 and older—makes clear the ethnic group differences among Asian and non-Asian Americans. The ratio for the U.S. as a whole was 1.24—more than double the ratio for the Vietnamese (0.52) and the Chinese Vietnamese (0.45), but well below the exceptionally high ratio of 3.12 for all other Asian Americans. The U.S.-born second generation among Indochinese groups is still too young to permit analyses of intergenerational social mobility, but longitudinal findings suggest remarkable progress in educational attainment by young Vietnamese and Chinese-Vietnamese Americans.

Relative to the overall U.S. population, the other Asian Americans as a whole also showed average rates of labor force participation (64 percent), lower unemployment (5.1 percent), and a greater proportion of high-status professional, managerial, and kindred workers among those employed (52 percent); but the profile for each of the Indochinese groups was precisely the opposite in each of these indicators. The Hmong, Cambodian, Lao, and Vietnamese—in that order—had lower labor force participation and higher unemployment rates, and those employed were much more likely to have low-status jobs as operators and laborers and in low-wage services. Approximately half were at the bottom of the occupational hierarchy, compared to a third for the U.S. workforce as a whole and less than a fourth of other Asian Americans (the Chinese Vietnamese were the sole exception in these respects). A single measure of occupational attainment calculated in Table 4—the ratio of persons employed in high-status occupations to those in low-status jobs—sums up the status differences among these groups, paralleling the data on education. The occupational status ratio for the U.S. as a whole was 1.18—well above the ratios for the Vietnamese (0.67) and Chinese Vietnamese (0.82), but well below the ratio of 2.12 for other Asian Americans.

Finally, Table 4 sketches a comparative portrait of the economic situation of these groups in 2000, which is affected not only by their level of human capital and entrepreneurship but also by the size and structure of their families and the number of dependent children. Family/household size was fairly high for the Vietnamese (4.29 persons) and Chinese Vietnamese (4.41), compared to the national average of 3.24 and of 3.64 for other Asian Americans, but it was even higher for the Hmong (7.61) and Cambodians (5.12). The U.S. median annual household income of $48,925 was significantly exceeded by the median income of other Asian American households ($62,000) and also by the Vietnamese ($52,962) and Chinese Vietnamese ($56,473). But the per capita annual incomes of the groups from Vietnam (under $15,000) were below the average of $18,576 for the overall population and $20,814 for other Asian Americans.

In consequence, poverty rates for the refugee groups (especially for the Cambodians and the Hmong) were higher than for the U.S. population, as reflected also in disparities in homeownership and welfare dependency (although the 2000 Census was taken before the five-year lifetime limits on public assistance imposed in 1996 began to take effect). Between 16 and 18 percent of the Vietnamese groups fell below the federal poverty line in 2000, as did 22 percent of the Lao, 31 percent of Cambodians, and 40 percent of the Hmong (the highest in the U.S.). By comparison, the poverty rate was 15.7 percent for all Americans in 2000 and 13.9 percent for all other Asian Americans. The figures for the Vietnamese groups reflect a significant decrease from 1990 levels, when 26 percent were in poverty, as had been 35 percent of the Lao, 43 percent of Cambodians, and 64 percent of the Hmong. The diversity of these socioeconomic profiles underlines the widely different social class and ethnic backgrounds, migration histories, age and family structures, and modes of incorporation of these immigrants and refugees.

From Adolescence to Adulthood: A Longitudinal View

The decennial census provides only a snapshot of population characteristics and tells us relatively little of the progress over time of particular cohorts, especially of the growing 1.5 and second generation now entering adulthood in the U.S. To fill this gap in knowledge, the Children of Immigrants Longitudinal Study (CILS) followed the progress of a large sample of youth representing many different nationalities in two main areas of immigrant settlement, Southern California and south Florida. The initial survey, conducted in 1992, interviewed 2,420 students enrolled in eighth and ninth grade in the San Diego city schools, of whom 362 were Vietnamese or Chinese Vietnamese (the study is among the few to focus specifically on the ethnic Chinese from Vietnam). They were reinterviewed in 1995, when most were 17 to 18 years old and in their last year of high school (or had dropped out of school), and again during 2001–2003, when they were in their mid-twenties (ages 23 to 27). Key findings from this decade-long panel study are summarized in Table 5, broken down for the major ethnic groups.

Overall, 56 percent were foreign-born (the 1.5 generation) and 44 percent were U.S.-born (second generation), but the Indochinese groups were overwhelmingly foreign-born (most were born in 1977 or 1978 but came to the U.S. after 1980). About three out of five Vietnamese fathers had less than a high school education, as did two out of three of the Chinese-Vietnamese fathers, and the level of educational attainment was lower still for the mothers. The percent of college graduates among the Indochinese parents was in the single digits (except for Vietnamese fathers, 16 percent of whom had college degrees, especially those who came in the 1975 first wave). While the Vietnamese parents were the most educated of the Indochinese groups, the Chinese Vietnamese were the most likely to live in intact families (83 percent) and least likely to live in stepfamilies (3 percent). Analyses of CILS data show that family structure has long-term effects on school attainment, independent of parental socioeconomic status.

Table 5 shows two objective measures of the respondents' educational progress between the end of junior high and the end of high school—national percentiles in standardized math and reading (Stanford) achievement tests administered in fall 1991 and high school GPA by the end of spring 1995. Already by eighth grade large ethnic differences were observable in math and reading achievement test scores. The Chinese Vietnamese collectively scored at the 65th percentile nationally on math, compared with the 59th percentile for the Vietnamese—both well above the national norm—but both scored well below the average in reading. Despite the language handicaps reflected by the reading scores, by the end of high school in 1995 the Chinese Vietnamese as a group had achieved a very high average GPA of 3.36, followed by the Vietnamese (2.94)—again both well above the school district mean (2.21).

By 2001–2003, when they were 24 years old on average, only 2.2 percent of the Chinese Vietnamese and 4.9 percent of the Vietnamese had failed to complete high school or obtain a GED. In fact, 58 percent of the Chinese Vietnamese had already graduated from four-year colleges (including 9 percent who were in graduate school or had earned an advanced degree), as had 37 percent of the Vietnamese (including

3 percent in graduate programs). The women outperformed the men, just as they had in GPAs in junior high and high school. For example, among the Vietnamese, the gender gap in college graduation rates was 46 to 29 percent in favor of women; and among the Chinese Vietnamese—the highest achievers in the sample—71 percent of women were already college grads by age 24 (including 13 percent who were in graduate school or already had earned an advanced degree), compared to 29 percent of the men. Moreover, substantial numbers of them were still enrolled in college full-time.

Only 58 percent of the Chinese Vietnamese and 46 percent of the Vietnamese were employed full-time in 2001–2003. By age 24, few Vietnamese and ethnic Chinese were married or cohabiting, and less than 10 percent had one or more children. Among those who were married, cohabiting, or engaged, the Vietnamese and Chinese Vietnamese were more likely to be in interracial and interethnic relationships; and unlike other groups in the study, Vietnamese and Chinese women were less likely to have had a child than Vietnamese and Chinese men.

Table 5 also looks at language preferences measured in 1992, 1995, and 2001–2003 and their patterns of change across the span of a decade. Although a primary non-English language was spoken in all of their homes, in 1992 about half of the Vietnamese teenagers and 45 percent of the Chinese Vietnamese preferred English to their parents' native language; by 1995 their preference for English had swelled to more than 70 percent; and by 2001–2003 the shift to English was virtually complete. Fewer than 3 percent of the Vietnamese and fewer than 9 percent of the Chinese Vietnamese could be classified as fluent bilinguals by age 24, confirming the rapid language switch to English among the 1.5 and second generations of these new Americans.

Three other dimensions of relevance to this portrayal of incorporation among young adults concern their religious, political, and transnational ties. Nearly half of the Vietnamese and Chinese Vietnamese were Buddhists, mainly of the Mahayana tradition (in contrast, three fourths of the Lao and Cambodians were Theravada Buddhists). Reflecting premigration differences, about one fourth of the Vietnamese were Catholics, compared with a mere 2 percent of the Chinese Vietnamese; and 24 percent of the Vietnamese adhered to no religion, compared to a much higher 44 percent of the Chinese Vietnamese. By 2001–2003, the overwhelming majority of the respondents were American citizens (by birth or naturalization), including almost 90 percent of the Vietnamese and Chinese Vietnamese. In terms of political party preferences, Democrats outnumbered Republicans by 30 to 11 percent among the Chinese Vietnamese, a gap that narrowed to 25 to 18 percent among the Vietnamese; but more than half were politically disinterested or alienated and indicated no political affiliation at all. Coming from families of political refugees, most had never returned to Vietnam to visit (and most of the rest had done so only once)—compared to more frequent trips home among other Asian

Table 5 Longitudinal patterns of achievement and acculturation among young adult children of immigrants, by ethnicity (percentages) (CILS San Diego Sample, N = 2,420)

Characteristics	Main Indochinese groups (N = 663)					Other Asian (941)	Latin American (816)	Total-sample (2,420)
	Vietnamese (295)	Chinese-Vietnamese (67)	Cambodian (94)	Lao (154)	Hmong (53)			
Nativity and age								
Foreign-born	83.4	91.0	97.9	98.7	94.3	45.1	40.8	56.1
Age at 1992 survey	14.3	14.3	14.5	14.6	14.1	14.1	14.2	14.2
Age at 2001–2003 survey	24.1	24.1	24.2	24.4	24.7	24.1	24.2	24.2
Father's education								
Less than high school	61.7	64.2	77.7	66.2	86.8	15.8	62.6	45.7
College graduate	15.6	9.0	4.3	10.4	1.9	30.7	8.9	18.0
Mother's education								
Less than high school	70.2	68.7	86.2	76.6	98.1	21.4	69.5	52.6
College graduate	9.5	3.0	4.3	3.9	0.0	36.6	6.0	17.9
Family structure, 1992								
Intact family	70.8	83.6	69.1	72.1	77.4	78.3	57.6	69.8
Stepfamily	4.1	3.0	6.4	8.4	3.8	8.9	15.1	10.0
Single parent, other	25.1	13.4	24.5	19.5	18.9	12.8	27.3	20.2
Achievement tests, 1991[a]								
Math (national percentage)	59.0	64.5	35.0	41.9	29.7	60.4	32.2	48.2
Reading (national percentage)	35.3	44.5	13.6	21.9	15.2	52.6	28.3	38.3
Academic GPA, 1995[b]	2.94	3.36	2.55	2.85	2.65	2.93	2.29	2.70

Main Indochinese groups (N = 663)

Characteristics	Vietnamese (295)	Chinese-Vietnamese (67)	Cambodian (94)	Lao (154)	Hmong (53)	Other Asian (941)	Latin American (816)	Total-sample (2,420)
Education by age 24								
Some high school	4.9	2.2	11.7	4.4	3.3	1.8	8.5	4.8
High school graduate	8.3	8.9	46.7	35.6	46.7	13.1	28.5	20.6
Some college	50.0	31.1	38.3	36.7	43.3	55.8	52.1	51.2
College graduate	34.0	48.9	1.7	23.3	6.7	24.6	8.5	20.0
Graduate school	2.8	8.9	1.7	0.0	0.0	4.8	2.2	3.4
Labor force status, age 24								
Employed full-time	45.8	57.8	69.2	58.9	90.0	52.5	64.5	57.5
Employed part-time	23.6	24.4	15.4	14.4	6.7	27.1	19.6	22.7
In school full-time	13.4	6.7	4.7	5.6	3.3	8.5	3.4	6.9
Family formation, age 24								
Married, cohabiting	13.9	11.1	27.7	28.9	40.0	20.4	39.1	26.4
One or more children	9.7	6.7	24.6	22.2	36.7	18.0	38.7	24.0
Interracial relationship	31.1	31.6	29.4	11.6	16.7	43.1	23.3	32.0
Interethnic relationship	50.0	84.2	34.3	45.5	27.8	51.7	38.3	45.8
Language acculturation								
Preferred English, 1992	52.9	44.8	66.0	51.9	64.2	86.5	47.1	64.5
Preferred English, 1995	71.8	75.8	85.2	74.1	58.0	94.1	73.8	82.0
Preferred English, 2002	99.3	100.0	100.0	94.4	93.3	99.5	93.7	97.4
Fluent bilingual, 2002	2.2	8.3	1.6	7.8	20.0	10.3	52.6	22.2
Religious affiliation, age 24								
Catholic	23.8	2.2	3.1	2.2	3.3	69.6	65.8	53.5

Table 5 Longitudinal patterns of achievement and acculturation among young adult children of immigrants, by ethnicity (percentages) (CILS San Diego Sample, $N = 2,420$) (continued)

	Main Indochinese groups ($N = 663$)							
Characteristics	Vietnamese	Chinese-Vietnamese	Cambodian	Lao	Hmong	Other Asian	Latin American	Total-sample
	(295)	(67)	(94)	(154)	(53)	(941)	(816)	(2,420)
Protestant	1.4	0.0	0.0	1.1	3.3	5.7	2.7	3.7
Buddhist	46.9	45.7	75.4	77.8	6.7	1.1	0.5	14.7
Other religion	4.2	8.7	6.2	6.7	43.3	8.2	14.6	10.3
No religion	23.8	43.5	15.4	12.2	43.3	15.4	16.4	17.8
Political participation, age 24								
Registered to vote	57.8	54.5	16.7	33.3	13.3	68.3	58.0	58.2
Democrat	25.0	29.8	22.6	24.4	7.7	28.2	41.4	31.3
Republican	18.2	11.3	9.7	11.1	3.8	18.7	8.4	13.8
Independent, other	2.3	1.4	14.5	1.1	7.7	2.0	2.6	2.7
None	54.5	57.4	53.2	63.3	80.8	51.1	47.7	52.2
Transnational ties, age 24								
Never visited country of origin	70.6	69.6	92.2	81.1	93.3	34.9	25.0	43.0
Never sent remittances	68.3	76.1	63.1	64.0	86.7	69.4	78.0	71.9
USA feels most like home	88.8	87.0	95.4	88.9	93.3	89.4	82.7	87.6

Source: Children of Immigrants Longitudinal Study (CILS), 1991–2003.

a. Standardized Stanford Achievement Test scores collected by the San Diego school system in fall 1991, when the students were in the 8th or 9th grade. The figures given are national percentiles.

b. Academic grade point average by the end of high school (or latest), 1995–1996, weighted for honors and AP courses.

(mostly Filipino) and Latin American (mostly Mexican) immigrant groups—and only a minority sent remittances, as seen in Table 5. Indeed, nearly 9 in 10 indicated that the U.S. felt most like home.

The data reviewed here encapsulate processes of rapid change, social mobility, and acculturation over a decade among these young adults of refugee origins. The future of these new Americans—a legacy of the nation's bitterest and most divisive war of the 20th century—may be as diverse as their pasts. Many outcomes are possible, and will be reached by multiple paths throughout their life course. In their diversity, they are writing yet another chapter in the history of the American population and society, and in the process they are becoming, quintessentially, Americans.

Bibliography

Caplan, Nathan, John K. Whitmore, and Marcella H. Choy. 1989. *The Boat People and Achievement in America: A Study of Family Life, Hard Work, and Cultural Values.* Ann Arbor: University of Michigan Press.

Freeman, James M. 1995. *Changing Identities: Vietnamese Americans, 1975–1995.* Boston: Allyn and Bacon.

Haines, David W., ed. 1989. *Refugees as Immigrants: Cambodians, Laotians, and Vietnamese in America.* Totowa, N.J.: Rowman & Littlefield.

Hein, Jeremy. 1995. *From Vietnam, Laos, and Cambodia: A Refugee Experience in the United States.* New York: Twayne.

Kibria, Nazli. 1993. *Family Tightrope: The Changing Lives of Vietnamese Americans.* Princeton, N.J.: Princeton University Press.

Portes, Alejandro, and Rubén G. Rumbaut. 2001. *Legacies: The Story of the Immigrant Second Generation.* Berkeley: University of California Press.

Rumbaut, Rubén G. 1989. "The Structure of Refuge: Southeast Asian Refugees in the United States." *International Review of Comparative Public Policy* 1: 97–129.

———. 1991. "Migration, Adaptation, and Mental Health." In Howard Adelman, ed., *Refugee Policy: Canada and the United States,* pp. 383–427. Toronto: York Lanes.

———. 1996. "A Legacy of War: Refugees from Vietnam, Laos, and Cambodia." In S. Pedraza and R. G. Rumbaut, eds., *Origins and Destinies: Immigration, Race, and Ethnicity in America,* pp. 315–33. Belmont, Calif.: Wadsworth.

Zhou, Min, and Carl L. Bankston III. 1998. *Growing Up American: How Vietnamese Children Adapt to Life in the United States.* New York: Russell Sage Foundation.

West Indies

Antigua, Bahamas, Barbados, Grenada, Guadeloupe, Guyana, Martinique, St. Kitts, Trinidad

Calvin B. Holder

Voluntary migration to the U.S. from the Caribbean began in the 19th century, primarily after the abolition of slavery in the U.S. in 1865; by the end of the 19th century several thousand immigrants from the English and French West Indies resided in Boston, New York City, and Miami. However, it was the 20th century that witnessed the full bloom of this movement. Between 1900 and the Great Depression, well over 150,000 migrated. Migration was halted by the restrictive Immigration Act of 1924 and the subsequent economic crisis but resumed after World War II, though it was quickly terminated with the passage of the conservative 1952 Immigration Act. The 1965 Immigration Act liberalized the nation's immigration policy, resulting in new movement, one that still continues today.

Generally the term "West Indian" identifies immigrants from the Anglophone Caribbean, including Anguilla, Antigua, Bahamas, Barbados, Belize, Bermuda, Cayman Islands, Dominica, Grenada, Guyana, Jamaica, St. Kitts, St. Lucia, Montserrat, Trinidad, St. Vincent, and the American and British Virgin Islands. The immigrants themselves use this appellation, and so do others. However, here we use census data to describe the demographic profile and specific experiences of immigrants from Antigua, Bahamas, Barbados, Guadeloupe, Grenada, Guyana, St. Kitts, Martinique, and Trinidad (Guadeloupe and Martinique are part of the Francophone Caribbean).

Why, given the long history of American hostility toward people of color, have hundreds of thousands of blacks and other people of color voluntarily emigrated to the U.S.? Economic factors have always been the major motivating factor. Simply put, the U.S., and particularly its northern states, has offered these immigrants opportunities for self-improvement and material advancement that their homelands have proved incapable of providing. Because of this, immigrants from the West Indies have generally put aside their concerns and reservations about American racism and flocked here when the opportunity has presented itself. And once in the U.S., they have held steadfast to the view that racism should not be accepted as a legitimate reason for the failure of people of color—foreign- or native-born—to succeed. This view is especially entrenched among the post-1965 immigrants, now that legal segregation has been dismantled. Poverty and, to a lesser extent, political instability and class and color prejudice in their homelands have also been instrumental "push" factors for immigration.

Origins and Destinations

The post-1965 immigration began on a modest scale in the late 1960s and grew swiftly from the 1970s through the 1990s. In 1969 there were 52,114 West Indians in the U.S.; by 1980 their number had reached 181,600, and a decade later 359,181. In 2000, 550,480 West Indians resided in the country. The pace of migration slowed perceptibly in the 1990s. Still, hundreds of thousands of West Indians have made the U.S. their home in the past four decades.

West Indian immigration is a multiracial, multiethnic movement, comprising, according to the 2000 Census, Afro West Indians, Asian West Indians (overwhelmingly Indo West Indians, but also some West Indians of Chinese descent), whites, persons of "two or more races," and persons of "some other race." As of 2000, Afro West Indians accounted for 64.1 percent of the immigrants, persons of "two or more races" 13.3 percent, Asian West Indians 11.9 percent, persons of "some other race" 7.7 percent, and whites 2.9 percent. West Indian societies have a long history of miscegenation, involving primarily whites, blacks, and Asians, and "persons of two or more races" is a manifestation of this. Of the 42,620 such people among West Indians, 81.7 percent came from Guyana and 14.7 percent from Trinidad and Tobago. By 2000, they are most likely people with ties to both the dominant Afro and Indo West Indian communities who choose to identify as "some other race."

Since 1965, most West Indians have migrated to states on the eastern seaboard, because of geographical proximity to their homelands, aviation linkages, and prior settlement patterns. The majority now reside in New York, Florida, Connecticut, Massachusetts, and New Jersey. Immigrants have also settled in the nation's capital. For example, of the 181,600 West Indians in the U.S. in 1980, 87.3 percent lived in the five states mentioned and Washington, D.C. They were concentrated in New York and Florida, which accounted for 62 percent and 8.5 percent, respectively, of the West Indians in the country. Two decades later, the distribution remains fundamentally unchanged. Even so, West Indians in increasing numbers have chosen Florida as their state of residence, primarily because of its tropical climate and proximity to the Caribbean. They have gravitated to cities in the southern and central areas of the state and primarily live in Miami, Fort Lauderdale, West Palm Beach, and Orlando. New York City remains the major destination of West Indian immigrants, as it has been over the past century. But whereas earlier West Indian immigrants went mainly to Harlem, since 1965 they have gone to New York's outer boroughs—the Bronx, Queens, and Brooklyn—and suburbs. Over the past two decades, West Indian communities have been established in the North Bronx; in Richmond Hill, Cambria Heights, Laurelton, and Rosedale in Queens; and in Elmont, Uniondale, Hempstead, and Baldwin on Long Island. Brooklyn, however, has become home for most West Indians in New York City. In the 1960s immigrants joined compatriots from the earlier migration in Bedford-Stuyvesant and Crown Heights, and in the ensuing decades they also settled in Flatbush, East Flatbush, Flatlands, and Canarsie.

The post-1965 movement, like the earlier migration, has been selective. The desperately poor, the illiterate, the chronically unemployed, those without drive and ambition, agricultural laborers, and domestics have not been a significant part of the movement. Usually they have lacked the resources—the money, knowledge, and connections to immigrants already in the U.S.—necessary to emigrate. American immigration policies and consular practices have often posed additional barriers. As a result, West Indian migration has been a movement of professional and semiprofessional individuals, skilled and semiskilled workers, clerks, and industrial workers—in short, of the best and brightest of Afro and Indo West Indians. The process of emigrating has also favored young and middle-aged people. For example, in 1980 the median age of West Indian immigrants was 32.7 years; by 2000, after the passage of restrictive immigration laws in the 1980s and 1990s, their median age was 40.6. West Indians have immigrated at the height of their productive powers, and their immigration is a classic example of a brain drain.

At present there are two kinds of West Indian communities in the U.S. The first has an Afro West Indian majority, small numbers of Indo West Indians, who are mainly Muslims and Christians, and indeterminate numbers of persons of "some other race" and "two or more races." This kind was the first to develop and is to be found in Fort Lauderdale, Miami, Boston, and above all New York City. The second, which did not fully materialize until the 1990s, comprises mainly Hindu and Muslim Indo West Indians and some multiracial people who are mostly of Indian-black descent and are sometimes referred to as "douglas." Its residents come mainly from Trinidad and Guyana. Richmond Hill in Queens is the best example of this kind of community; Ozone Park, which is adjacent to Richmond Hill, is becoming another.

Indo West Indians in Richmond Hill and elsewhere in the U.S. are the descendants of Indian indentured servants. After slavery was abolished in the Anglophone Caribbean in 1834, many former slaves abandoned the sugar plantations, so the British government brought in the Indian servants to compensate for the labor shortage. This migration ended in the early 1900s. Today Indo West Indians are the majority of Guyana's population and arguably the largest group in Trinidad and Tobago.

Interestingly, many immigrants who described themselves as belonging to "two or more races" or "some other race" do not reside in West Indian communities. This is also the case with the overwhelming majority of white West Indians. Both groups seem to have become part of the larger society in Florida, New York, and elsewhere.

Gender and Household Composition

Post-1965 West Indian immigration has been dominated by women. In 1990 women made up 54 percent of the West Indians in the U.S.; in 2000 they were 55.5 percent. Though men are just as eager to emigrate, U.S. immigration laws have favored women—for example, by permitting tens of thousands of women to immigrate specifically to work as domestics.

Marriage has been the norm for West Indians, as the 2000 Census shows. Of the 522,245 West Indians aged 15 and older, 29.5 percent had never married, 51.4 percent were married, 5.1 percent were separated, 4.6 percent were widowed, and 9.3 percent were divorced. Thus, by 2000, 70.5 percent were or had been married. Women made up 80 percent of the widowed and 65 percent of the divorced immigrants. The data on separated immigrants do not address gender, but in all probability most in this category were women as well.

Generally, Afro West Indians choose spouses from within their group. Endogamy is perhaps even more entrenched among Indo West Indians, notably among the Hindus, mainly for religious, cultural, and racial reasons. Even when West Indian Hindus choose spouses outside their Hindu community, they select Muslim, white, and Afro West Indians. Religious considerations have been arguably paramount in Muslim West Indians' choice of spouses. As a result, they have married other Muslims, most of whom are also from the West Indies.

According to the 2000 Census, the total number of West Indian households in the U.S. was 241,080; of these, 184,395, or 76.8 percent, were "family households (families)" and 56,685, or 23.5 percent, were "nonfamily households"—that is, a single person or unrelated individuals living together. "Married-couple households" accounted for 61.3 percent of the family households, and "female householders with no husband present" for 30.8 percent. Other kinds of family households accounted for 7.9 percent. Children under 18 years old were present in 57.3 percent of married-couple households and 55.6 percent of female-headed households.

Migration poses some difficulties for West Indian families. Many women, especially Afro West Indians, are employed as live-in domestics, spending five or six days a week in their employers' homes and away from their husbands and children. Some marriages fail because the husbands reside in the West Indies and are unable or unwilling to migrate. Some West Indian children have grown up apart from one or both parents, sometimes for extended periods of time. Many are reared by relatives in the West Indies while their parents live in the U.S., providing for their support. When children come to join parents, family relations have sometimes been fraught with anxiety, tension, and conflict, owing to the years of separation. Often these children consider their former caretaker in the West Indies to be their parent.

Increasingly, West Indian families have moved in two distinctly different social directions. Some families have fully embraced the values, attitudes, and mores of the larger society—in short, middle-class America—but other families have not. The former generally have more stable families, higher incomes and more property, less conflict with law enforcement authorities, and higher levels of education.

Educational Profile

By 2000, of the 448,835 West Indians 25 years and older, 8.8 percent left school before the ninth grade, 17.2 percent attended high school but did not graduate, 29.8 percent were high school graduates, 18.3 percent went to college but did not earn a degree, 8.2 percent and 11.5 percent possessed associate and baccalaureate degrees, respectively, and 6.2 percent held graduate and professional degrees. Additionally, 109,788 West Indians were enrolled in school: 26.6 percent were in high school and 51.5 percent in college or graduate school. Because West Indian immigration has been a selective movement, many of the immigrants attended high school in the West Indies, sometimes elite schools. Some graduated from the University of the West Indies and colleges and universities in Canada and the United Kingdom, but the vast majority graduated from American universities and colleges. The U.S. offered them the opportunity for higher education, and they pursued it with determination and focus, convinced that education is the foremost means of social mobility. Other evidence points to their successful pursuit of education. The sociologist Douglas Massey and recently the *New York Times* have shown that West Indians have had a noteworthy representation among black students in some of the nation's elite private and public colleges and universities.

Yet a look at public schools in some West Indian neighborhoods in New York City makes clear that the immigrants' educational record has not been without blemishes. For years these schools have been plagued by drug use, low scores on English and mathematics tests, high drop-out rates, disciplinary problems, and/or violence, often associated with gangs. With security staffs and X-ray machines to detect weapons, the schools have not created an environment conducive to learning and therefore have not regularly produced graduates who have gone on to the elite colleges and universities. In fact, their students have often ended up engaging in criminal activity.

Crime, Drugs, and Health Problems

In working-class West Indian communities, particularly in New York City, crime has been at times a problem. In these communities West Indians have been involved in the illegal numbers lottery for decades; it is alleged that earlier West Indian immigrants introduced the lottery to Harlem in the 1920s. Since the 1970s West Indians have participated in drug distribution; they have been especially active in the marijuana trade. At the height of the New York crack epidemic in the 1980s and early 1990s, West Indian criminals were brazen in conducting illicit drug activities and in perpetrating violence against each other and innocent black New Yorkers. Partly as a result, the West Indian prison population in New York State has grown significantly over the past two decades. Some of the inmates have returned to their communities afflicted with full-blown AIDS or the HIV virus and other diseases.

Several working-class West Indian communities, particularly in New York, are also grappling with a health crisis. In the past decade West Indian communities such as Crown Heights, Flatbush, and East Flatbush have experienced significant numbers of cancers of the reproductive organs, infant deaths, and HIV/AIDS. According to the Caribbean Women's Health Association, an organization that provides Caribbean immigrants with health services, high infant mortality, AIDS, and HIV-positive cases are a pressing health problem in these communities. Afro West Indians, more than Indo and white West Indians, have been adversely affected by the AIDS crisis. For well over a decade, some West Indian organizations and institutions have been addressing some of these health problems.

Religious and Social Organizations

Recent West Indian immigrants have built upon existing social institutions and organizations or have created new ones. Churches, mosques, and temples are prime examples. In Boston, New York, and Miami, West Indians have given new life to Episcopal, Methodist, and other Protestant churches that their predecessors either took over or created. Similarly, they have established new churches or come to dominate those that had been controlled by whites. In Brooklyn and the Bronx, Episcopal churches, with a few exceptions, have West Indian congregations; frequently they have West Indian ministers, some recruited directly from the West Indies. In Brooklyn and Queens, West Indians have built mosques, temples, and private schools at which many of their children are educated. Without the presence of the immigrants' children, many Catholic schools in black communities in New York City would have closed years ago. Moreover, West Indians have created a host of secular social organizations. Some, like alumni and ex-police associations, have direct ties to the West Indies, and several predate the recent migration; for example, the Combermere Alumni Association USA, Inc., which is made up of graduates of an elite high school in Barbados, was founded in 1948.

These religious institutions and social organizations play no small role in calibrating the tempo of life in West Indian communities in the U.S. Because so many

West Indians have either direct or indirect ties to them, they have helped develop and maintain the social cohesion of the immigrants' communities.

A discussion of West Indian social institutions and organizations would be incomplete without a brief look at the West Indian American Day Carnival Association (WIADCA) and the event it has resurrected and institutionalized: Carnival, West Indians' signature cultural and social event in the U.S. Founded in the 1930s in Manhattan, West Indian Carnival had become moribund by the 1960s, but WIADCA revived the festivity in Brooklyn and over the decades has made it one of the largest public social events in the country. Trinidadians, whose homeland has celebrated Carnival for over a century and holds the largest annual Carnival in the Anglophone Caribbean, have played the principal role in the creation of WIADCA and the general success of the event. WIADCA has inspired Trinidadians and other West Indians in Miami, Atlanta, Washington, D.C., Baltimore, Hartford, and Boston to have their own Carnivals. Each year these festivals bring together millions of West Indians, African Americans, and whites for what are essentially mammoth street parties.

Intergroup Relations

African Americans and Afro West Indians have had in the main quite cordial relations. (Generally, Indo West Indians do not have close contact with African Americans.) In New York, Washington, D.C., and Boston, and their suburbs, Afro West Indians and African Americans live in the same neighborhoods, often in the same apartment buildings. Afro West Indians attend historically black colleges and universities and have been welcomed by their African American peers. Together, the two groups have struggled daily to improve the economic and political plight of blacks. When in the late 1990s a young Haitian immigrant was sodomized and grievously injured by a New York City police officer, thousands of Afro West Indians and African Americans took to the streets to register their outrage. Afro West Indians and African Americans have often had similar musical tastes, especially among youth. Many African Americans and Afro West Indians have dated and married, and many couples have successfully reared families.

But African American relations with Afro West Indians have not been without stress and tension, and occasionally violence. Tensions are evident in the groups' negative stereotypes of each other, in interpersonal disputes, and in competition in the marketplace and politics. Illicit drug activities have often been the cause of violence, especially in Washington, D.C., Boston, and New York City. Nonetheless, it seems that negative relations between the two groups have been overemphasized at the expense of positive ones.

West Indians' relations with whites have also tended to be both positive and negative. In New York City, Boston, and to a lesser extent Washington, D.C., many middle- and upper-middle-class white families have entrusted the day-to-day up-bringing of their children to Afro West Indian women; some of these women have become virtual surrogate mothers of their white charges. In general, many Afro West Indian domestic workers have been close to their white employers. Outside of private household employment, relations between Afro West Indians and whites have frequently been examined through the prism of African American–white relations, with a common emphasis on white employers' preference for West Indians over African Americans. Although Afro West Indians and whites generally work productively together and sometimes develop genuine friendships, they seldom have close relations. Afro West Indians may be favored by whites on the job, but this has not immunized them from white racism, which they resent with the same intensity that African Americans do. Tensions between whites and Afro West Indians have been most pronounced in encounters involving white policemen and working-class young men in Boston and New York.

Relations between Indo West Indians and whites have not been burdened by the same history of slavery and racism as relations between African Americans and whites. Moreover, whites associate Indo West Indians with Indians from the subcontinent, who are viewed as a "model minority." As a consequence, whites are more favorably disposed to Indo West Indians than to African Americans or Afro West Indians. Not surprisingly, Indo West Indians have viewed whites favorably. These mutually positive attitudes have produced cordial relations between the two groups in New York City and elsewhere, although a sustained hostile reaction to the presence of Muslims in the U.S. could alter their present relationship.

Political Activity

Indo West Indians, who migrated recently, became politically active only in the past decade and thus far have had little impact on the political process. Afro West Indians have had notable political success, especially in New York City. There they first attained political prominence in the 1930s, as the black community shifted its allegiance from the Republican Party to the Democratic Party. In the next three decades they were power-brokers in black politics: West Indians were the first black Democratic district leader, the first black borough president of Manhattan, the first black leader of Tammany Hall, and the first black state senator from Brooklyn. Moreover, West Indians held other elective offices and led some of the most powerful black Democratic clubs. These men often decided who was elected to public office and controlled much of the patronage dispensed to the black community.

Post-1965 Afro West Indians have been active in politics. They have run for elective office and been engaged in grassroots politics in cities like New York, Boston, and Miami. However, their political achievements do not come close to matching those of their predecessors. Despite the significant political gains of the black community since the 1960s, no Afro West Indian of the recent migration has been elected to Congress; Mervyn Dymally, a Trinidadian, served in Congress in the 1980s, representing a district in California, but he arrived in the U.S. before 1965. Nor has an Afro West Indian been elected mayor of a major American city or to an important statewide office. Even election to a state legislature has mostly eluded Afro West Indian politicians. Their lack of success has been most glaring in Brooklyn, which has the largest Afro West Indian community in the U.S. For more than a decade West Indians have been the majority in Central Brooklyn, a community of several hundred thousands. However, Afro West Indian politicians have failed repeatedly in their efforts to represent Central Brooklyn in Congress and have succeeded only in sending several representatives to the city council. Admittedly, most often incumbency has worked against them; the incumbents have been whites and African Americans. Perhaps equally important, Afro West Indian politicians have been unable to garner enough support from fellow West Indians to win election.

There are several reasons for this uninspiring record. In the first place, Afro West Indians and Indo West Indians have not regarded political activism as a major priority. Moreover, even though many are citizens, they have not voted in significant numbers in city and state elections. And, unlike in the past, Afro West Indians have not controlled the powerful political clubs in black communities and consequently have not influenced the outcome of local elections there. Finally, politics has not in the main attracted talented, ambitious immigrants nearly as much as it did in earlier years. New West Indians have placed much greater emphasis on economic activities than on politics.

Occupational Concentration

Generally, West Indians have been employed in the private sector of the American economy. According to the 2000 Census, 78.6 percent of the 325,770 employed West Indians aged 16 years and older were private wage and salary workers, 16.5 percent were government workers, 4.7 percent were self-employed, and 0.2 percent were unpaid family workers. Why are West Indians so heavily concentrated in the private sector when the public sector has historically been more receptive to the presence of blacks? Affirmative action policies are one reason; another is that West Indians reside mainly in New York, Florida, and Massachusetts, where there are millions of private-sector jobs and the economy has been sound. Moreover, many West Indians do not meet that important criterion necessary to work for the federal and some state governments: citizenship.

By 2000, as the census shows, 28.7 percent of West Indian immigrants worked in managerial, professional, and related occupations, 22.7 percent in service occupations, and 28 percent in sales and office occupations. West Indians also found work in construction and transportation; here the percentages were 9.3 and 11.3, respectively. West Indians' representation in skilled, white-collar, and professional employment was significant; moreover, it constitutes a marked change from what prevailed in 1980. The unemployment rate was 7.3 percent for this group.

After 1980 West Indians increasingly entered skilled, white-collar, and professional occupations for several reasons. Tens of thousands of skilled immigrants have arrived since the late 1970s, coming directly from the West Indies and by way of Canada and the United Kingdom, where they had lived in many cases for decades. Many West Indians acquired technical and professional training in the U.S. At the same time, the private and public sectors of the economy, in part responding to affirmative action policies, accorded blacks much greater access to high-level employment. West Indians took advantage of these new opportunities.

West Indians have achieved greater economic progress in New York City than elsewhere in the country. Tens of thousands of West Indian lawyers, physicians, nurses and medical technicians, teachers, and middle-level managers have worked in the city since 1965. Even larger numbers have been employed in the skilled trades. A small class of entrepreneurs and business people has also developed. Their enterprises cater to West Indians, and to a lesser degree to African Americans and whites.

Afro West Indians have been well situated among black professionals in New York, constituting a significant percentage of physicians, nurses, technicians, lawyers, teachers, managers, and other business people. They have had an even greater presence among skilled blacks. With some exceptions, they have been the black mechanics, plumbers, electricians, carpenters, and masons. Most skilled Afro and Indo West Indians acquired their training in the West Indies, where they had unfettered access to the skilled trades. In New York City in particular, they have found an environment where they can use those skills. Afro West Indians have also owned the majority of legitimate black businesses.

As for Indo West Indians, increasing numbers have entered business, the professions, and the skilled trades. In their main community, Richmond Hill, they have been the majority of skilled artisans, professionals, and business people, and in Central Brooklyn they have been successful restaurateurs.

Increasingly, West Indians of Indian and African ancestry have begun to make their presence felt as entrepreneurs. Their businesses cater to all West Indians. Several in Brooklyn and Queens own prosperous restaurants and bakeries that offer an African- and Indian-influenced cuisine. West Indians have also prospered from illicit business activities. They have acquired capital from the numbers lottery and the sale of illicit drugs, and some have invested their gains in legitimate businesses both here and in the West Indies.

Household income provides further insight into West Indians' economic circumstances. The 2000 Census shows the median household income for West Indians at $40,168. This compares quite favorably with the median household income for the general population, $41,190. A noticeably different picture emerges, however, when West Indians' median family income is examined: it was $44,959, as compared with a median family income of $50,732 for the general population. The larger household income for West Indians is likely due to larger numbers of earners in their households. The census indicated that 12 percent of 184,395 West Indian families lived below the poverty line. Females headed 56.1 percent of these poor families. This gender profile is similar to what obtains among poor African American families.

Comparing Afro West Indians and African Americans

In writing about the activities of Afro West Indians, social scientists often compare them with African Americans. Given American racial history and the fact that West Indians are largely voluntary migrants, these comparisons are to be expected. Some scholars have maintained that Afro West Indians are more prosperous than their African American counterparts. Others have argued that there are no substantial differences between them. Interestingly, both groups of social scientists have been able to support their assertions with data. It seems important to note that when such comparisons are made, certain sociological and historical facts should be kept in mind—facts that are sometimes insufficiently emphasized or ignored.

First, whereas Afro West Indians are a comparatively small, select group of immigrants who are concentrated in some of the most prosperous cities in the country, African Americans are a large national group, dispersed throughout the country and heavily centered in some of the poorest states. Second, with their immigrant mentality, Afro West Indians have embraced American society's mainstream values regarding hard work, education, individual responsibility, and material progress and success. An "oppositional culture" that eschews much of this middle-class ethos has not become deeply situated in Afro West Indian life. Third, Afro West Indians, particularly those from middle- and upper-middle-class backgrounds, possess distinct psychological advantages that they have brought to the American marketplace. Reared in societies where people of color are the overwhelming majority, they have not been treated as though they were an intractable social problem, as African Americans have been regarded for generations. Until their arrival in the U.S., many immigrants were not aware of toxicity of the word "nigger" and had been spared the word's malevolent psychological effects. Thousands of Afro West Indians come from relatively privileged backgrounds, many belonging to their societies' elite. They attended the best high schools, the University of the West Indies, and British and Canadian universities and held senior positions in the civil service and business, and did so without having their intellect and their right to hold these positions questioned. In fact, these immigrants often successfully competed with whites in the classroom and elsewhere. They arrived in the U.S. confident in their abilities, secure in their personhood, and imbued with the sense of entitlement that comes with being a member of an elite.

Naturalization and Transnational Activity

The incidence of naturalization among West Indian immigrants has been relatively low, although it has increased dramatically in the past decade. For example, of the 359,181 West Indians in 1990, 35.7 percent were naturalized American citizens; a decade later, when their population reached 550,480, 53.4 percent were naturalized. Why the significant change? Some West Indians have been spurred into naturalizing because, like immigrants before, they have severed their emotional ties with the West Indies and have adopted the U.S. as their homeland. Others have naturalized to meet the criterion for employment or advancement in the marketplace or to be eligible for government benefits that are denied to noncitizens. Still others have become American citizens because they are the beneficiaries of dual citizenship.

Evidence suggests that Afro West Indians and Indo West Indians have different attitudes toward naturalization. Because racism is less problematic for Indo West Indians, they feel less visceral opposition to becoming American citizens. In contrast, Afro West Indians have been notoriously reluctant to become naturalized citizens. Many reject naturalization not only because they abhor racism and the negative images it has created of African Americans and blacks generally, but also because they believe that by retaining their original citizenship, they disassociate themselves from these dehumanizing images.

West Indians' close and continuing ties to their homelands have also shaped their assimilation into American society. Each year tens of thousands of immigrants, many of whom have been in the U.S. for decades, regularly travel to their homelands. They go there for Christmas, Carnival, and the independence celebrations of their native countries, to see their relatives, to reside in their homes during the winter months, and to conduct business. Some have professional practices and businesses in both the U.S. and the West Indies. Although these West Indians are often American citizens and permanent U.S. residents, they remain emotionally tied to their homelands.

Although the U.S. bestowed "whiteness" on the Irish and other immigrants who migrated in the 19th and early 20th centuries, making them part of the American mainstream, it has enabled West Indians to achieve social and economic mobility but has not fully accepted them, especially Afro West Indians. Afro West Indians have been acutely aware of this fact, which has had a decisive role in determining the degree to which they have fully embraced American society. Indeed, many of their American-born children have adopted their posture vis-à-vis the country of their birth: they identify themselves as West Indians, not as West Indian Americans or African Americans; and at the West Indian Carnival on Eastern Parkway in Brooklyn, they wave the flags of their parents' countries as though they were their own.

Bibliography

Foner, Nancy, ed. *Islands in the City: West Indian Migration to New York.* Berkeley: University of California Press, 2001.

Henke, Holger. *The West Indian-American.* Westport, Conn.: Greenwood, 2001.

Bryce-Laporte, Roy S., ed. *Sourcebook on the New Immigration: Implications for the United States and the International Community.* New Brunswick, N.J.: Transaction, 1980.

Bryce-Laporte, Roy S., and Delores Mortimer, eds. *Caribbean Immigration to the United States.* Washington, D.C.: Research Institute on Immigration and Ethnic Studies, Smithsonian Institution, 1983.

James, Winston. *Holding Aloft the Banner of Ethiopia: Caribbean Radicalism in Early Twentieth-Century America.* London: Verso, 1998.

Kasinitz, Phillip. *Caribbean New York: Black Immigrants and the Politics of Race.* Ithaca, N.Y.: Cornell University Press, 1992.

Massey, Douglas S. *The Source of the River: The Social Origins of Freshmen at America's Selective Colleges and Universities.* Princeton, N.J.: Princeton University Press, 2003.

Palmer, Ransford, ed. *In Search of a Better Life: Perspectives on Migration from the Caribbean.* New York: Praeger, 1990.

Reid, Ira De A. *The Negro Immigrant.* New York: Columbia University Press, 1939.

Sutton, Constance, and Elsa M. Chaney, eds. *Caribbean Life in New York City: Sociocultural Dimensions.* New York: Center for Migration Studies, 1987.

Vickerman, Milton. *Crosscurrents: West Indian Immigrants and Race.* New York: Oxford University Press, 1999.

Waters, Mary C. *Black Identities: West Indian Immigrant Dreams and American Realities.* Cambridge, Mass.: Harvard University Press, 1999.

Appendix

Immigration and Naturalization Legislation

Source (pp. 687–698): Extracts from the text of Appendix 1 of U.S. Immigration and Naturalization Service, *Statistical Yearbook of the Immigration and Naturalization Service, 1998.* Washington, D.C.: U.S. Government Printing Office, 2000.
Source (pp. 698–699): Summarizes laws as posted on the Library of Congress website (thomas.loc.gov).

ACT OF MARCH 26, 1790 (1 Statutes-at-Large 103)
The first federal activity in an area previously under the control of the individual states, this act established a uniform rule for naturalization by setting the residence requirement at two years.

ACT OF JANUARY 29, 1795 (1 Statutes-at-Large 414)
Repealed the 1790 act, raised the residence requirement to five years and required a declaration of intention to seek citizenship at least three years before naturalization.

NATURALIZATION ACT OF JUNE 18, 1798 (1 Statutes-at-Large 566)
a. Clerks of court must furnish information about each record of naturalization to the Secretary of State.
b. Registry of each alien residing in the United States at that time, as well as those arriving thereafter.
c. Raised the residence requirement for naturalization to fourteen years.

ALIENS ACT OF JUNE 25, 1798 (1 Statutes-at-Large 570)
Represented the first Federal law pertinent to immigration rather than naturalization.
a. Authorized the President to arrest and/or deport any alien whom he deemed dangerous to the United States.
b. Required the captain of any vessel to report the arrival of aliens on board such vessel to the Collector, or other chief officer, of the Customs of the Port. (This law expired two years after its enactment.)

NATURALIZATION ACT OF APRIL 14, 1802 (2 Statutes-at-Large 153)

a. Reduced the residence period for naturalization from fourteen to five years.

b. Established basic requirements for naturalization including good moral character, allegiance to the Constitution, a formal declaration of intention, and witnesses.

STEERAGE ACT OF MARCH 2, 1819 (3 Statutes-at-Large 488)

First significant Federal law relating to immigration.

a. Established the continuing reporting of immigration to the United States by requiring that passenger lists or manifests of all arriving vessels be delivered to the local Collector of Customs, copies transmitted to the Secretary of State, and the information reported to Congress.

b. Set specific sustenance rules for passengers of ships leaving U.S. ports for Europe.

c. Somewhat restricted the number of passengers on all vessels either coming to or leaving the United States.

ACT OF MAY 26, 1824 (4 Statutes-at-Large 36)

Facilitated the naturalization of certain aliens who had entered the United States as minors, by setting a two-year instead of a three-year interval between declaration of intention and admission to citizenship.

ACT OF FEBRUARY 22, 1847 (9 Statutes-at-Large 127)

"Passenger Acts" provided specific regulations to safeguard passengers on merchant vessels. Subsequently amended by the Act of March 2, 1847 expanding the allowance of passenger space.

PASSENGER ACT OF MARCH 3, 1855 (10 Statutes-at-Large 715)

a. Repealed the Passenger Acts (see the 1847 act) and combined their provisions in a codified form.

b. Reaffirmed the duty of the captain of any vessel to report the arrival of alien passengers.

c. Established separate reporting to the Secretary of State distinguishing permanent and temporary immigration.

ACT OF FEBRUARY 19, 1862 (12 Statutes-at-Large 340)

Prohibited the transportation of Chinese "coolies" on American vessels.

ACT OF JULY 4, 1864 (13 Statutes-at-Large 385)

First Congressional attempt to centralize control of immigration.

a. A Commissioner of Immigration was appointed by the President to serve under the authority of the Secretary of State.

b. Authorized immigrant labor contracts whereby would-be immigrants would pledge their wages to pay for transportation. On March 30, 1868, the Act of July 4, 1864 was repealed.

NATURALIZATION ACT OF JULY 14, 1870 (16 Statutes-at-Large 254)

a. Established a system of controls on the naturalization process and penalties or fraudulent practices.

b. Extended the naturalization laws to aliens of African nativity and to persons of African descent.

ACT OF MARCH 3, 1875 (Page Act) (18 Statutes-at-Large 477)
Established the policy of direct federal regulation of immigration by prohibiting for the
first time entry to undesirable immigrants.
a. Excluded criminals and prostitutes from admission.
b. Prohibited the bringing of any Oriental persons without their free and voluntary consent; declared the contracting to supply "coolie" labor a felony.
c. Entrusted the inspection of immigrants to collectors of the ports.

CHINESE EXCLUSION ACT OF MAY 6, 1882 (22 Statutes-at-Large 58)
a. Suspended immigration of Chinese laborers to the United States for ten years.
b. Permitted Chinese laborers already in the United States to remain in the country after a
temporary absence.
c. Provided for deportation of Chinese illegally in the United States.
d. Barred Chinese from naturalization.
e. Permitted the entry of Chinese students, teachers, merchants, or those "proceeding to the
United States . . . from curiosity."

IMMIGRATION ACT OF AUGUST 3, 1882 (22 Statutes-at-Large 214)
First general immigration law, established a system of central control of immigration
through State Boards under the Secretary of the Treasury.
a. Broadened restrictions on immigration by adding to the classes of inadmissible aliens, including persons likely to become a public charge.
b. Introduced a tax of 50 cents on each passenger brought to the United States.

ACT OF FEBRUARY 26, 1885 (23 Statutes-at-Large 332)
The first "Contract Labor Law," made it unlawful to import aliens into the United States
under contract for the performance of labor or services of any kind. Exceptions were for
aliens temporarily in the United States engaging other foreigners as secretaries, servants, or
domestics; actors, artists, lecturers, and domestic servants; and skilled aliens working in an
industry not yet established in the United States.

ACT OF OCTOBER 19, 1888 (25 Statutes-at-Large 566)
First measure since the Aliens act of 1798 to provide for expulsion of aliens—directed the
return within one year after entry of any immigrant who had landed in violation of the
contract labor law.

IMMIGRATION ACT OF MARCH 3, 1891 (26 Statutes-at-Large 1084)
The first comprehensive law for national control of immigration.
a. Established the Bureau of Immigration under the Treasury Department to administer all
immigration laws (except the Chinese Exclusion Act).
b. Further restricted immigration by adding to the inadmissible classes persons likely to become public charges, persons suffering from certain contagious disease, felons, persons convicted of other crimes or misdemeanors, polygamists, aliens assisted by others by payment
of passage, and forbade the encouragement of immigration by means of advertisement.
c. Allowed the Secretary of the Treasury to prescribe rules for inspection along the borders

of Canada, British Columbia, and Mexico so as not to obstruct or unnecessarily delay, impede, or annoy passengers in ordinary travel between these countries and the United States.
d. Directed the deportation of any alien who entered the United States unlawfully.

ACT OF MARCH 3, 1893 (27 Statutes-at-Large 570)
a. Added to the reporting requirements regarding alien arrivals to the United States such new information as occupation, marital status, ability to read or write, amount of money in possession, and facts regarding physical and mental health. This information was needed to determine admissibility according to the expanding list of grounds for exclusion.
b. Established boards of special inquiry to decide the admissibility of alien arrivals.

ACT OF APRIL 29, 1902 (32 Statutes-at-Large 176)
Extended the existing Chinese exclusion acts until such time as a new treaty with China was negotiated, and extended the application of the exclusion acts to insular territories of the United States, including the requirement of a certificate of residence, except in Hawai'i.

ACT OF FEBRUARY 14, 1903 (32 Statutes-at-Large 825)
Transferred the Bureau of Immigration to the newly-created Department of Commerce and Labor, and expanded the authority of the Commissioner-General of Immigration in the areas of rulemaking and enforcement of immigration laws.

IMMIGRATION ACT OF MARCH 3, 1903 (32 Statutes-at-Large 1213)
An extensive codification of existing immigration law.
a. Added to the list of inadmissible immigrants.
b. First measure to provide for the exclusion of aliens on the grounds of proscribed opinions by excluding "anarchists, or persons who believe in, or advocate, the overthrow by force or violence the government of the United States, or of all government, or of all forms of law, or the assassination of public officials."
c. Extended to three years after entry the period during which an alien who was inadmissible at the time of entry could be deported.
d. Provided for the deportation of aliens who became public charges within two years after entry from causes existing prior to their landing.
e. Reaffirmed the Contract Labor Law (see the 1885 act).

ACT OF APRIL 27, 1904 (33 Statutes-at-Large 428)
Reaffirmed and made permanent the Chinese exclusion laws. In addition, clarified the territories from which Chinese were to be excluded.

NATURALIZATION ACT OF JUNE 29, 1906 (34 Statutes-at-Large 596)
a. Combined the immigration and naturalization functions of the federal government, changing the Bureau of Immigration to the Bureau of Immigration and Naturalization.
b. Established fundamental procedural safeguards regarding naturalization, such as fixed fees and uniform naturalization forms.
c. Made knowledge of the English language a requirement for naturalization.

IMMIGRATION ACT OF FEBRUARY 20, 1907 (34 Statutes-at-Large 898)
A major codifying act that incorporated and consolidated earlier legislation:
a. Required aliens to declare intention of permanent or temporary stay in the United States and officially classified arriving aliens as immigrants and non-immigrants, respectively.

b. Increased the head tax to $4.00 (established by the Act of August 3, 1882, and raised subsequently).

c. Added to the excludable classes imbeciles, feeble-minded persons, persons with physical or mental defects which may affect their ability to earn a living, persons afflicted with tuberculosis, children unaccompanied by their parents, persons who admitted the commission of a crime involving moral turpitude, and women coming to the United States for immoral purposes.

d. Exempted from the provisions of the contract labor law professional actors, artists, singers, ministers, professors, and domestic servants.

e. Extended from two to three years after entry authority to deport an alien who had become a public charge from causes which existed before the alien's entry.

f. Authorized the President to refuse admission to certain persons when he was satisfied that their immigration was detrimental to labor conditions in the United States. This was aimed mainly at Japanese laborers.

g. Created a Joint Commission on Immigration to make an investigation of the immigration system in the United States. The findings of this Commission were the basis for the comprehensive Immigration Act of 1917.

h. Reaffirmed the requirement for manifesting of aliens arriving by water and added a like requirement with regard to departing aliens.

WHITE SLAVE ACT OF JUNE 25, 1910 (Mann Act) (36 Statutes-at-Large 825)
The Mann Act prohibited the importation or interstate transportation of women for immoral purposes.

ACT OF MARCH 4, 1913 (37 Statutes-at-Large 737)
Divided the Department of Commerce and Labor into separate departments and transferred the Bureau of Immigration and Naturalization to the Department of Labor. It further divided the Bureau of Immigration and Naturalization into a separate Bureau of Immigration and Bureau of Naturalization, each headed by its own Commissioner.

IMMIGRATION ACT OF FEBRUARY 5, 1917 (39 Statutes-at-Large 874)
Codified all previously enacted exclusion provisions. In addition:
a. Excluded illiterate aliens from entry.
b. Expanded the list of aliens excluded for mental health and other reasons.
c. Further restricted the immigration of Asian persons, creating the "barred zone" (known as the Asia-Pacific triangle), natives of which were declared inadmissible.
d. Considerably broadened the classes of aliens deportable from the United States and introduced the requirement of deportation without statute of limitation in certain more serious cases.

ACT OF MAY 22, 1918 (40 Statutes-at-Large 559)
"Entry and Departure Controls Act," authorized the President to control the departure and entry in times of war or national emergency of any alien whose presence was deemed contrary to public safety.

IMMIGRATION ACT OF MAY 19, 1921 (First Quota Act) (42 Statutes-at-Large 5)
The first quantitative immigration law.
a. Limited the number of aliens of any nationality entering the United States to three per-

cent of the foreign-born persons of that nationality who lived in the United States in 1910. Approximately 350,000 such aliens were permitted to enter each year as quota immigrants, mostly from northern and western Europe.

b. Exempted from this limitation aliens who had resided continuously for at least one year immediately preceding their application in one of the independent countries of the Western Hemisphere; nonimmigrant aliens such as government officials and their households, aliens in transit through the United States, and temporary visitors for business and pleasure; and aliens whose immigration is regulated by immigration treaty.

c. Actors, artists, lecturers, singers, nurses, ministers, professors, aliens belonging to any recognized learned profession, and aliens employed as domestic servants were placed on a nonquota basis.

ACT OF May 22, 1922 (Cable Act) (42 Statutes-at-Large 1021)
Provided for a procedure for the naturalization of alien adult females that was independent of their marital status.

IMMIGRATION ACT OF MAY 26, 1924 (Second Quota Act; Johnson-Reed Act) (43 Statutes-at-Large 153)
The first permanent limitation on immigration established the national-origins quota system. In conjunction with the Immigration Act of 1917, governed American immigration policy until 1952 (see the Immigration Act of 1952). It contained two quota provisions: 1. In effect until June 30, 1927—set the annual quota of any quota nationality at two percent of the number of foreign-born persons of such nationality resident in the continental United States in 1890 (total quota—164,667); 2. From July 1, 1927 (later postponed to July 1, 1929) to December 31, 1952—used the national-origins quota system: the annual quota for any country or nationality had the same relation to 150,000 as the number of inhabitants in the continental United States in 1920 having that national origin had to the total number of inhabitants in the continental United States in 1920.

a. Preference quota status was established for: unmarried children under 21; parents; spouses of U.S. citizens aged 21 and over; and for quota immigrants aged 21 and over who are skilled in agriculture, together with their wives and dependent children under age 16.

b. Nonquota status was accorded to: wives and unmarried children under 18 of U.S. citizens; natives of Western Hemisphere countries, with their families; non-immigrants; and certain others. Subsequent amendments eliminated certain elements of this law's inherent discrimination against women but comprehensive elimination was not achieved until 1952 (see the Immigration Act of 1952).

c. Established the "consular control system" of immigration by mandating that no alien may be permitted entrance to the United States without an unexpired immigration visa issued by an American consular officer abroad. Thus, the State Department and the Immigration and Naturalization Service shared control of immigration.

d. Introduced the provision that, as a rule, no alien ineligible to become a citizen shall be admitted to the United States as an immigrant. This was aimed primarily at Japanese aliens,

e. Imposed fines on transportation companies who landed aliens in violation of U.S. immigration laws.

f. Defined the term "immigrant" and designated all other alien entries into the United States as "non-immigrant" (temporary visitor). Established classes of admission for non-immigrant entries.

ACT OF APRIL 29, 1943 (57 Statutes-at-Large 70)
Provided for the importation of temporary agricultural laborers to the United States from North, South, and Central America to aid agriculture during World War II. This program was later extended through 1947, then served as the legal basis of the Mexican "*bracero* program," which lasted through 1964.

ACT OF DECEMBER 17, 1943 (57 Statutes-at-Large 600)
Amended the Alien Registration Act of 1940, adding to the classes eligible for naturalization Chinese persons or persons of Chinese descent. A quota of 105 per year was established (effectively repealing the Chinese exclusion laws—see the act of May 6, 1882).

ACT OF FEBRUARY 14, 1944 (58 Statutes-at-Large 11)
Provided for the importation of temporary workers from countries in the Western Hemisphere pursuant to agreements with such countries for employment in industries and services essential to the war efforts. Agreements were subsequently made with British Honduras, Jamaica, Barbados, and the British West Indies.

WAR BRIDES ACT OF DECEMBER 28, 1945 (59 Statutes-at-Large 659)
Waived visa requirements and provisions of immigration law excluding physical and mental defectives when they concerned members of the American armed forces who, during World War II, had married nationals of foreign countries.

G.I. FIANCÉES ACT OF JUNE 29, 1946 (60 Statutes-at-Large 339)
Facilitated the admission to the United States of fiancé(e)s of members of the American armed forces.

ACT OF JULY 2, 1946 (Luce-Celler Act) (60 Statutes-at-Large 416)
Amended the Immigration Act of 1917, granting the privilege of admission to the United States as quota immigrants and eligibility for naturalization races indigenous to India and persons of Filipino descent.

DISPLACED PERSONS ACT OF JUNE 25, 1948 (62 Statutes-at-Large 1009)
First expression of U.S. policy for admitting persons fleeing persecution. Permitted the admission of up to 205,000 displaced persons during the two-year period beginning July 1, 1948 (chargeable against future year's quotas). Aimed at reducing the problem created by the presence in Germany, Austria, and Italy of more than one million displaced persons.

INTERNAL SECURITY ACT OF SEPTEMBER 22, 1950 (64 Statutes-at-Large 987)
Amended various immigration laws with a view toward strengthening security screening in cases of aliens in the United States or applying for entry.

IMMIGRATION ACT OF JUNE 27, 1952 (McCarran-Walter Act) (66 Statutes-at-Large 163)
Brought into one comprehensive statute the multiple laws which, before its enactment,

governed immigration and naturalization in the United States, In general, perpetuated the immigration policies from earlier statutes with the following significant modifications:

a. Made all races eligible for naturalization, thus eliminating race as a bar to immigration.

b. Eliminated discrimination between sexes with respect to immigration.

c. Revised the national-origins quota system of the Immigration Act of 1924 by changing the national-origins quota formula: set the annual quota for an area at one-sixth of one percent of the number of inhabitants in the continental United States in 1920 whose ancestry or national origin was attributable to that area. All countries were allowed a minimum quota of 100, with a ceiling of 2,000 on most natives of countries in the Asia-Pacific triangle, which broadly encompassed the Asian countries.

d. Introduced a system of selected immigration by giving a quota preference to skilled aliens whose services are urgently needed in the United States and to relatives of U.S. citizens and aliens.

e. Placed a limit on the use of the governing country's quota by natives of colonies and dependent areas.

f. Provided an "escape clause" permitting the immigration of certain former voluntary members of proscribed organizations.

g. Broadened the grounds for exclusion and deportation of aliens.

h. Provided procedures for the adjustment of status of non-immigrant aliens to that of permanent resident aliens.

i. Modified and added significantly to the existing classes of non-immigrant admission.

j. Afforded greater procedural safeguards to aliens subject to deportation.

k. Introduced the alien address report system whereby all aliens in the United States (including most temporary visitors) were required annually to report their current address to the INS.

l. Established a central index of all aliens in the United States for use by security and enforcement agencies.

m. Repealed the ban on contract labor (see Act of March 30, 1868) but added other qualitative exclusions.

REFUGEE RELIEF ACT OF AUGUST 7, 1953 (67 Statutes-at-Large 400)
Authorized the issuance of special nonquota visas allowing 214,000 aliens to become permanent residents of the United States, in addition to those whose admission was authorized by the Immigration Act of 1952.

ACT OF SEPTEMBER 3, 1954 (68 Statutes-at-Large 1146)
Provided for the expatriation of persons convicted of engaging in a conspiracy to overthrow or levy war against the U.S. government.

REFUGEE-ESCAPEE ACT OF SEPTEMBER 11, 1957 (71 Statutes-at-Large 639)
a. Addressed the problem of quota oversubscription by removing the "mortgaging" of immigrant quotas imposed under the Displaced Persons Act of 1948 and other subsequent acts.

b. Provided for the granting of nonquota status to aliens qualifying under the first three preference groups on whose behalf petitions had been filed by a specified date.

c. Facilitated the admission into the United States of stepchildren, illegitimate children, and adopted children.

d. Conferred first preference status on spouse and children of first preference immigrants if following to join the immigrant.

e. Set an age limit of fourteen for the adoption of orphans to qualify for nonquota status and further defined which orphans were eligible under the act.

f. Gave the Attorney General authority to admit certain aliens formerly excludable from the United States.

ACT OF JULY 25, 1958 (72 Statutes-at-Large 419)

Granted admission for permanent residence to Hungarian parolees of at least two years' residence in the United States, on condition that the alien was admissible at time of entry and still admissible.

IMMIGRATION ACT: AMENDMENTS OF OCTOBER 3, 1965 (Hart-Celler Act) (79 Statutes-at-Large 911)

a. Abolished the national-origins quota system (see the Immigration Act of 1924 and the Immigration Act of 1952), eliminating national origin, race, or ancestry as a basis for immigration to the United States.

b. Established allocation of immigrant visas on a first come, first served basis, subject to a seven-category preference system for relatives of U.S. citizens and permanent resident aliens (for the reunification of families) and for persons with special occupational skills, abilities, or training (needed in the United States).

c. Established two categories of immigrants not subject to numerical restrictions.

d. Maintained the principle of numerical restriction, expanding limits to world coverage by limiting Eastern Hemisphere immigration to 170,000 and placing a ceiling on Western Hemisphere immigration (120,000) for the first time. However, neither the preference categories nor the 20,000 per-country limit were applied to the Western Hemisphere.

e. Introduced a prerequisite for the issuance of a visa of an affirmative finding by the Secretary of Labor that an alien seeking to enter as a worker will not replace a worker in the United States nor adversely affect the wages and working conditions of similarly employed individuals in the United States.

REFUGEE ACT OF MARCH 17, 1980 (94 Statutes-at-Large 102)

Provided the first permanent and systematic procedure for the admission and effective resettlement of refugees of special humanitarian concern to the United States:

a. Eliminated refugees as a category of the preference system.

b. Set the worldwide ceiling of immigration to the United States at 270,000, exclusive of refugees.

c. Established procedures for annual consultation with Congress on numbers and allocations of refugees to be admitted in each fiscal year, as well as procedures for responding to emergency refugee situations.

d. Defined the term "refugee" (to conform to the 1967 United Nations Protocol on Refugees) and made clear the distinction between refugee and asylee status.

e. Established a comprehensive program for domestic resettlement of refugees.

f. Provided for adjustment to permanent resident status of refugees who have been physically present in the United States for at least one year and of asylees one year after asylum is granted.

IMMIGRATION REFORM AND CONTROL ACT OF NOVEMBER 6, 1986 (IRCA)
(100 Statutes-at-Large 3359)
Comprehensive immigration legislation:
a. Authorized legalization (i.e., temporary and then permanent resident status) for aliens who had resided in the United States in an unlawful status since January 1, 1982 (entering illegally or as temporary visitors with authorized stay expiring before that date or with the government's knowledge of their unlawful status before that date) and are not excludable.
b. Created sanctions prohibiting employers from knowingly hiring, recruiting, or referring for a fee aliens not authorized to work in the United States.
c. Increased enforcement at U.S. borders.
d. Created a new classification of seasonal agricultural worker and provisions for the legalization of certain such workers.
e. Extended the registry date (i.e., the date from which an alien has resided illegally and continuously in the United States and thus qualifies for adjustment to permanent resident status) from June 30, 1948 to January 1, 1972.
f. Authorized adjustment to permanent resident status for Cubans and Haitians who entered the United States without inspection and had continuously resided in country since January 1, 1982.
g. Increased the numerical limitation for immigrants admitted under the preference system for dependent areas from 600 to 5,000 beginning in fiscal year 1988.
h. Created a new special immigrant category for certain retired employees of international organizations and their families and a new non-immigrant status for parents and children of such immigrants.
i. Created a non-immigrant Visa Waiver Pilot Program allowing certain aliens to visit the United States without applying for a non-immigrant visa.
j. Allocated 5,000 nonpreference visas in each of fiscal years 1987 and 1988 for aliens born in countries from which immigration was adversely affected by the 1965 act.

AMERASIAN HOMECOMING ACT OF DECEMBER 22, 1987 (101 Statutes-at-Large 1329)
An appropriations law providing for admission of children born in Vietnam between specified dates to Vietnamese mothers and American fathers, together with their immediate relatives. They are admitted as nonquota immigrants but receive refugee program benefits,

ACT OF SEPTEMBER 28, 1988 (United States-Canada Free-Trade Agreement Implementation Act) (102 Statutes-at-Large 1876)
a. Facilitated temporary entry on a reciprocal basis between the United States and Canada.
b. Established procedures for the temporary entry into the United States of Canadian citizen professional business persons to render services for remuneration.
c. No non-immigrant visa, prior petition, labor certification, or prior approval required, but appropriate documentation must be presented to the inspecting officer establishing Canadian citizenship and professional engagement in one of the occupations listed in the qualifying occupation schedule.

IMMIGRATION ACT OF NOVEMBER 29, 1990 (104 Statutes-at-Large 4978)
A major overhaul of immigration law:
a. Increased total immigration under an overall flexible cap of 675,000 immigrants beginning in fiscal year 1995, preceded by a 700,000 level during fiscal years 1992 through 1994. The 675,000 level to consist of: 480,000 family-sponsored; 140,000 employment-based; and 55,000 "diversity immigrants."
b. Revised all grounds for exclusion and deportation, significantly rewriting the political and ideological grounds. For example, repealed the bar against the admission of communists as non-immigrants and limited the exclusion of aliens on foreign policy grounds.
c. Authorized the Attorney General to grant temporary protected status to undocumented alien nationals of designated countries subject to armed conflict or natural disasters.
d. Revised and established new non-immigrant admission categories.
e. Revised and extended the Visa Waiver Pilot Program through fiscal year 1994.
f. Revised naturalization authority and requirements.
g. Revised enforcement activities.
h. Recodified the 32 grounds for exclusion into nine categories, including revising and repealing some of the grounds (especially health grounds).

NORTH AMERICAN FREE-TRADE AGREEMENT IMPLEMENTATION ACT OF DECEMBER 8, 1993 (107 Statutes-at-Large 2057)
Supersedes the United States-Canada Free-Trade Agreement Act of September 28, 1988.
a. Facilitated temporary entry on a reciprocal basis between the United States and Canada and Mexico.
b. Established procedures for the temporary entry into the United States of Canadian and Mexican citizen professional business persons to render services for remuneration.

ANTITERRORISM AND EFFECTIVE DEATH PENALTY ACT OF APRIL 24, 1996 (110 Statutes-at-Large 1214)
a. Expedited procedures for the removal of alien terrorists.
b. Established specific measures to exclude members and representatives of terrorist organizations.
c. Modified asylum procedures to improve identification and processing of alien terrorists.
d. Provided for criminal alien procedural improvements.

PERSONAL RESPONSIBILITY AND WORK OPPORTUNITY RECONCILIATION ACT OF AUGUST 22, 1996 (110 Statutes-At-Large 2105)
a. Established restrictions on the eligibility of legal immigrants for means-tested public assistance.
b. Broadened the restricitons on public benefits for illegal aliens and non-immigrants.

ILLEGAL IMMIGRATION REFORM AND IMMIGRANT RESPONSIBILITY ACT OF SEPTEMBER 30, 1996 (110 Statutes-at-Large 3009)
a. Established measures to control U.S. borders, protect legal workers through worksite enforcement, and remove criminal and other deportable aliens.
b. Placed added restrictions on benefits for aliens.
c. Miscellaneous.
1. Recodified existing INS regulations regarding asylum.

2. Provided that the Attorney General's parole authority may be exercised only on a case-by-case basis for urgent humanitarian reasons or significant public benefit.

3. Created new limits on the ability of F-I students to attend public schools without reimbursing those institutions.

4. Established new mandates for educational institutions to collect information on foreign students' status and nationality and provide it to INS.

5. Tightened restrictions regarding foreign physicians' ability to work in the United States.

6. Added new consular processing provisions and revised the Visa Waiver Program.

NICARAGUAN ADJUSTMENT AND CENTRAL AMERICAN RELIEF ACT (NACARA) OF NOVEMBER 19, 1997 (111 Statutes-at-Large 2193)

Pertains to certain Central American and other aliens who were long-term illegal residents in the United States when hardship relief rules were made more stringent by the Illegal Immigration Reform and Immigrant Responsibility Act (IIRIRA).

a. Allowed approximately 150,000 Nicaraguans and 5,000 Cubans adjustment to permanent resident status without having to make any hardship showing.

b. Allowed approximately 200,000 Salvadorans and 50,000 Guatemalans as well as certain aliens from the former Soviet Union to seek hardship relief under more lenient hardship rules than existed prior to IIRIRA amendments.

UNITING AND STRENGTHENING AMERICA BY PROVIDING APPROPRIATE TOOLS REQUIRED TO INTERCEPT AND OBSTRUCT TERRORISM ACT OF OCTOBER 26, 2001 (PATRIOT ACT) (115 Statutes-at-Large 272)

a. Authorized appropriations to: (1) triple the number of Border Patrol, Customs Service, and INS personnel (and support facilities) at points of entry and along the northern border; and (2) INS and Customs for related border monitoring technology and equipment.

b. Required the Attorney General and the Federal Bureau of Investigation (FBI) to provide the Department of State and INS with access to specified criminal history extracts in order to determine whether or not a visa or admissions applicant has a criminal history. Directs the FBI to provide periodic extract updates. Provides for confidentiality.

c. Directed the Attorney General and the Secretary of State to develop a technology standard to identify visa and admissions applicants, which shall be the basis for an electronic system of law enforcement and intelligence sharing system available to consular, law enforcement, intelligence, and Federal border inspection personnel.

d. Broadened the scope of aliens ineligible for admission or deportable due to terrorist activities. Provides for mandatory detention until removal from the United States (regardless of any relief from removal) of an alien certified by the Attorney General as a suspected terrorist or threat to national security. Requires release of such alien after seven days if removal proceedings have not commenced, or the alien has not been charged with a criminal offense. Authorizes detention for additional periods of up to six months of an alien not likely to be deported in the reasonably foreseeable future only if release will threaten U.S. national security or the safety of the community or any person. Limits judicial review to habeas corpus proceedings in the U.S. Supreme Court, the U.S. Court of Appeals for the District of Columbia, or any district court with jurisdiction to entertain a habeas corpus petition. Restricts to the U.S. Court of Appeals for the District of Columbia the right of appeal of any final order by a circuit or district judge.

HOMELAND SECURITY ACT OF NOVEMBER 25, 2002 (116 Statutes-at-Large 2135)

Transferred the functions of the Immigration and Naturalization Service (INS) of the Department of Justice to the Department of Homeland Security (DHS). The existence of the INS was ended. Within the Department of Homeland Security, the Directorate of Border and Transportation Security was assigned immigration enforcement functions, and the U.S. Citizenship and Immigration Services was given control of immigration service functions.

Acknowledgments

Carl L. Bankston III and Danielle Antoinette Hidalgo: Wendy Cadge and Todd LeRoy Perreira gave us useful suggestions and information.

Donna R. Gabaccia: I would like to acknowledge the research assistance of Connie Oxford at the University of Pittsburgh.

Herbert J. Gans: I would like to thank Richard Alba, Rogers Brubaker, Rubén Rumbaut, and Roger Waldinger.

Steven J. Gold and Mehdi Bozorgmehr (Middle East): Helen Marrow professionally and generously ran the census PUMS data on Middle Eastern immigrants, and Jen'nan Ghazal Read provided assistance with cross tabulation. Anny Bakalian commented extensively on earlier drafts of this article.

Steven J. Gold (Russia): I would like to thank Jerry Pankhurst, Mary Waters, Reed Ueda, Helen Marrow, and an anonymous reviewer for providing information and assistance for the preparation of this article.

Luis Eduardo Guarnizo: I would like to thank Krystyna von Henneberg for her comments on an earlier draft.

Marilyn Halter: I would like to acknowledge Violet M. Johnson, Professor of History, Agnes Scott College.

Calvin B. Holder: I would like to acknowledge Aubrey Bonnett, Roy Bryce-LaPorte, Aisha M. B. Holder, and Oshun D. K. Layne-Holder.

David López and Vanesa Estrada: We would like to thank Mary Waters for her patience and her very substantial editorial support.

Helen B. Marrow: I would like to thank Gay Seidman, Department of Sociology, University of Wisconsin-Madison, for patient and critical feedback and Steve Gold and Mehdi Bozorgmehr for help running data.

Cecilia Menjívar: I would like to thank the editors and the reviewers for their very useful comments and Helen Marrow for her prompt assistance and for making the process go smoothly.

Wendy D. Roth: I would like to thank the Office of National Statistics (UK), and especially Rhian Tyler, International Migration Supervisor.

Rubén G. Rumbaut: My one and main acknowledgment is to Helen Marrow.

Xiao-huang Yin: I would like to acknowledge the following scholars for their help with my essay on PRC immigrants: Roger Daniels, Lynn Dumenil, and Xiaojian Zhao.

Aristide R. Zolberg: I would like to express my general gratitude to friends and colleagues at the Migration Policy Institute, who constitute a model "think-tank" that generously provides basic resources to the entire research community. Closer to home, I would like to acknowledge two New School research and administrative assistants, Allison Clarkin and Myra Waterbury, without whom I would not have been able to produce this and other papers in the past half-dozen years; fortunately, they have now gone on to professional careers worthy of their talent.

The editors would like to thank Jennifer Snodgrass for instigating this project, and for her wise counsel, patience, and good advice along the way. We would also like to thank the advisory editors and all of the anonymous reviewers for their careful feedback and close readings of all of the entries. Liz Duvall and Elizabeth Gilbert of the Press provided excellent copyediting and help in the production process. We very much appreciate the expert programming and help with the census data provided by Cheri Minton of the Harvard Sociology Department. The terrific assistance of Dorothy Friendly, Suzanne Washington, Lauren Dye, and Jackie Piracini of the Harvard Sociology Department helped keep this project and many simultaneous others flowing smoothly and cheerfully. This work was greatly aided by a year of sabbatical leave for Mary Waters during 2005–06 at the Radcliffe Institute for Advanced Study, and by the intellectual stimulation of the immigration cluster at Radcliffe, which was funded by the Andrew W. Mellon Foundation. Finally, we would like to gratefully acknowledge with much love our wonderful families, who lived with this project for far too long: Ric, Katie, Harry, and Maggie Bayly; Peggy, Katya Andrea, and Alyona Ruth Ueda; Mike Redd, and Jim, Molly, and Owen Marrow.

Contributors

Richard Alba
Department of Sociology
The University at Albany, State University of New York

Carl L. Bankston III
Department of Sociology
Tulane University

Frank D. Bean
Sociology Department
University of California, Irvine

Mehdi Bozorgmehr
Middle East and Middle Eastern American Center
Graduate Center of the City University of New York

Albert M. Camarillo
Department of History
Stanford University

Catherine Ceniza Choy
Department of Ethnic Studies
University of California, Berkeley

Norma Stoltz Chinchilla
Departments of Sociology and Women's Studies
California State University, Long Beach

Diana L. Eck
Harvard Divinity School
Harvard University

Mary Patrice Erdmans
Department of Sociology
Central Connecticut State University

Marilyn Espitia
Center for Immigration Research
University of Houston

Vanesa Estrada
Department of Sociology
University of California, Los Angeles

Nancy Foner
Department of Sociology
Hunter College and Graduate Center of the City University of New York

Donna R. Gabaccia
Department of History and Director, Immigration History Research Center
University of Minnesota

Herbert J. Gans
Department of Sociology
Columbia University

Steven J. Gold
Department of Sociology
Michigan State University

Luis Eduardo Guarnizo
Department of Human and Community Development
University of California, Davis

David W. Haines
Department of Sociology and Anthropology
George Mason University

Marilyn Halter
Department of History
Boston University

Nora Hamilton
Department of Political Science
University of Southern California

Danielle Antoinette Hidalgo
Department of Sociology
Tulane University

Jennifer L. Hochschild
Departments of Government and African and African American Studies
Harvard University

Jennifer Holdaway
Migration Program
Social Science Research Council
New York, NY

Calvin B. Holder
Department of History
College of Staten Island, City University of New York

Simone Ispa-Landa
Department of Sociology
Harvard University

Michael Jones-Correa
Department of Government
Cornell University

Philip Kasinitz
Department of Sociology
Hunter College and Graduate Center of the City University of New York

Neeraj Kaushal
School of Social Work
Columbia University

Nazli Kibria
Department of Sociology
Boston University

Lisa Konczal
Department of Sociology and Criminology
Barry University

Abdi M. Kusow
Department of Sociology
Oakland University

Karen Ka-man Lee
State of the Art, Inc.
Washington, D.C.

Karen Isaksen Leonard
Departments of Anthropology and Asian American Studies
University of California, Irvine

Peggy Levitt
Department of Sociology
Wellesley College

John R. Logan
Department of Sociology
Brown University

David López
Department of Sociology
University of California, Los Angeles

B. Lindsay Lowell
Institute for the Study of International Migration
Georgetown University

Helen B. Marrow
Departments of Sociology and Social Policy
Harvard University

Cecilia Menjívar
Department of Sociology
Arizona State University

Pyong Gap Min
Department of Sociology
Queens College and Graduate Center of the City University of New York

Ewa Morawska
Department of Sociology
University of Essex

Victor Nee
Department of Sociology
Cornell University

Nana Oishi
Department of Sociology and Anthropology
International Christian University

Lisandro Pérez
Department of Sociology and Anthropology
Florida International University

Joel Perlmann
Levy Economics Institute
Bard College

Patricia R. Pessar
American Studies Program
Yale University

Cordelia W. Reimers
Department of Economics, Emeritus
Hunter College and Graduate Center of the City University of New York

David M. Reimers
Department of History, Emeritus
New York University

Wendy D. Roth
Department of Anthropology and Sociology
University of British Columbia

Rubén G. Rumbaut
Department of Sociology
University of California, Irvine

Cathy A. Small
Department of Anthropology
Northern Arizona University

Peter H. Schuck
Yale Law School
Yale University

Alex Stepick
Director, Immigration and Ethnicity Institute
Florida International University

Carola Suárez-Orozco
Department of Applied Psychology, Steinhardt School of Education and Co-Director,
Immigration Studies at New York University

Marcelo Suárez-Orozco
University Professor of Globalization and Education and Co-Director,
Immigration Studies at New York University

Reed Ueda
Department of History
Tufts University

Milton Vickerman
Department of Sociology
University of Virginia

Contributors

K. Viswanath
Department of Society, Human Development, and Health
Harvard School of Public Health
Harvard University

Roger Waldinger
Sociology Department
University of California, Los Angeles

Mary C. Waters
Department of Sociology
Harvard University

Xiao-huang Yin
American Studies Program
Occidental College

Aristide R. Zolberg
Department of Political Science and Committee on Historical Studies
New School for Social Research

Index